THE UNIVERSITY LIBRARY

NUMBER EIGHT
COLUMBIA UNIVERSITY STUDIES
IN LIBRARY SERVICE

The UNIVERSITY LIBRARY

THE ORGANIZATION, ADMINISTRATION, AND
FUNCTIONS OF ACADEMIC LIBRARIES

By LOUIS ROUND WILSON
and MAURICE F. TAUBER

Second Edition

COLUMBIA UNIVERSITY PRESS

NEW YORK AND LONDON

Library of Congress Catalog Card Number: 55-11184

Manufactured in the United States of America

Columbia University Studies in Library Service

PREFACE TO THE SECOND EDITION

UNIVERSITY librarianship in the last decade has been characterized by an effort to seek out fundamentals and principles of service. Close scrutiny is being given to the three prongs of service—books, personnel, and quarters—and re-evaluations of previously accepted patterns of work are becoming more common. University libraries have been subjected to criticism not only by librarians themselves but also by administrative officers, faculty members, and surveying bodies. This scrutiny is important for the future of the university library, which exists for the purpose of supporting instructional and research programs.

The present work retains the original form of presentation of the first edition in terms of chapter headings. However, except for certain sections dealing with background material and the more stabilized areas, each chapter has been substantially revised. Many of the charts and tables used in the first edition have been omitted from this edition. Some of these have been replaced by new charts or tables; others have been introduced for the first time. Bibliographical references have been brought up to date. Special mention should be made of the series of organization charts supplied by the University of California Library at Berkeley and of the extension service charts prepared by Clover M. Flanders, Chief Extension Librarian at the University of Michigan. Librarian Donald Coney and his staff at California have been particularly helpful in providing a basis for the systematic examination of the departmental structure of a complex university library system. Librarians Robert B. Downs of the University of Illinois, Herman H. Fussler of the University of Chicago, Richard H. Logsdon of Columbia University, and

Keyes D. Metcalf of Harvard University and their staffs likewise supplied special materials. The librarians of other universities, especially the members of the Association of Research Libraries, have been most cooperative in furnishing charts and data necessary for preparing the revision. The authors wish to take this opportunity of expressing their gratitude to all of them.

The authors acknowledge with thanks the aid given them by C. Donald Cook, John Rather, and Richard Schimmelpfeng, research associates in the School of Library Service, Columbia University, and Carlyle J. Frarey, of the School of Library Science, University of North Carolina, who helped in assembling bibliographical and other data. Miss Darthula Wilcox, Librarian of the School of Library Service, Columbia University, systematically acquired and routed materials useful to the authors. Miss Bertha M. Frick, Associate Professor, School of Library Service, Columbia University, kindly assisted in the proofreading.

LOUIS ROUND WILSON
MAURICE F. TAUBER

Chapel Hill, North Carolina and
New York, New York
July, 1955

PREFACE TO THE FIRST EDITION

THE INCREASE in university library resources since 1900 has been one of the most distinctive aspects of modern university development in the United States. In spite of this fact and of the corresponding increase in the extent and complexity of university library administrative procedures, there has been no systematic study of the principles and methods which characterize library organization and administration in the major universities of the United States or any formulation of generalizations concerning them.

The need for such a study has long been apparent. The present volume has been prepared to meet this need. Specifically, the purpose of the authors in the preparation of the volume has been to consider systematically the principles and methods of university library organization and administration and to formulate generalizations concerning them which may be useful to university librarians in the performance of their highly important task of aiding scholars in teaching and research. While this is a major purpose of the authors, it is also their hope that the study may prove of value to university administrators who are largely responsible for obtaining financial support of the library, to members of university faculties and learned societies who make extensive use of university library materials, and to students of library science who are preparing to cope with the problems of university library administration.

In the preparation of the volume the authors have received generous assistance from many university librarians and university administrators. They are especially indebted to Andrew Eaton, Raynard Swank, and Harold Tucker, who have served as research assistants in collecting statistical and bibliographical information, and to Mrs. Doris Flowers, who assisted in seeing the volume through the press. They are likewise indebted to Ralph A. Beals, Leon Carnovsky, Donald Coney, Carleton B. Joeckel, Guy R. Lyle, and John Dale Russell, who have read the manuscript in part or in whole and have been most generous in constructive suggestion and criticism.

L.R.W. AND M.F.T.

Chapel Hill, North Carolina,
and Chicago, Illinois
August, 1944

CONTENTS

Introduction   3

I.   The Functions of the University and Its Library   13

II.   Governmental and Administrative Relationships   28

III.   Financial Administration   71

IV.   Administrative Organization   114

V.   Departmental Organization: Acquisition and Preparation   161

VI.   Departmental Organization: Service   209

VII.   Personnel: Training and Selection of the Staff   253

VIII.   Personnel: Salaries and Staff Relations   296

IX.   Book Collections: Acquisition Policies and Procedures   346

X.   Book Collections: General Materials   365

XI.   Book Collections: Special Materials   394

XII.   The Teaching Function of the University Library   425

XIII.   Cooperation and Specialization   449

XIV.   Buildings and Equipment   481

XV.   Off-Campus Relations of the Librarian   526

XVI.   Public Relations: Evaluation through Records, Reports, and Surveys   552

XVII.   Problems in University Library Development   586

        Index   611

FIGURES

1. Organization Chart, Harvard University Library, 1953   130
2. Organization Chart, Montana State University   133
3. Organization Chart, University of Illinois Library and Library School, 1954   135
4. Organization Chart, University of Chicago Library, 1955   136
5. Organization Chart, Columbia University Libraries, 1944–48   137
6. Organization Chart, Columbia University Libraries, July 1, 1955   138
7. General Organization Chart, University of California (Berkeley) General Library, 1955   139
8. Organization Chart of a University Library—I   143
9. Organization Chart of a University Library—II   145
10. Organization Chart, Order Department, University of California (Berkeley) General Library, 1955   167
11. Organization Chart, Gifts and Exchange Department, University of California (Berkeley) General Library, 1955   171
12. Organization Chart, Catalog Department, University of California (Berkeley) General Library, 1955   178
13. Organization Chart, Catalog Department, Harvard College Library, 1955   184
14. Organization Chart, Photographic Service, University of California (Berkeley) General Library, 1955   199
15. Organization Chart, Loan Department, University of California (Berkeley) General Library, 1955   220

16. Organization Chart, Serials Department, University of California (Berkeley) General Library, 1955   234

17. Library Extension Service, University of Michigan General Library, July 1, 1952—June 30, 1953   239

18. Package Service Including Debate Material, Library Extension Service, University of Michigan General Library, July 1, 1952—June 30, 1953   241

TABLES

1. Statistics of College and University Libraries, 1940–41   84
2. Statistics of College and University Libraries, 1953–54   86
3. Statistics of Southern College and University Libraries, 1940–41   88
4. Statistics of Southern College and University Libraries, 1952–53   89
5. Circulation Statistics, 1952–53, Library Extension Service, University of Michigan General Library   243
6. Growth in Size of Staff in 25 University Libraries, 1940–54   259
7. Size of Staffs in 70 Large College and University Libraries in 1954   260
8. Size of Professional Staffs in 70 Large College and University Libraries in 1954   260
9. Salaries of Chief Librarians and Assistant Librarians in 57 College and University Libraries   300
10. Distribution of Librarians under Retirement Plans in 66 Universities   325
11. Growth of University Libraries, 1900–1954   347
12. Size of Map Collections in 16 University Libraries   405
13. Size of Photograph and Print Collections in 15 University Libraries   414
14. Methods and Devices Used in Surveying the Personnel of University Libraries   573
15. Methods and Devices Used in Surveying the Financial Support of University Libraries   575
16. Methods and Devices Used in Surveying the Resources of University Libraries   576

THE UNIVERSITY LIBRARY

INTRODUCTION

THE MODERN university in the United States, with its large faculty, its tremendous enrollment, and its extensive financial and physical resources, has assumed a position of commanding prominence among the universities of the world. Through the development and achievements of its universities in the fields of science and technology, of the humanities and the social sciences, and of the professions and in many branches of research, the United States has made one of its greatest contributions to the civilization of the Western world.

Although the present-day university had its beginning, in a number of instances, in the Colonial college or in the state institutions called "universities" that were established in several states between the Revolutionary War and the Civil War, it had its real beginning in the establishment of Johns Hopkins University in 1876. Since that date it has largely assumed its present organization, characteristics, and functions. Its growth since 1900 has been particularly rapid, and its organization and activities have become correspondingly diverse and complex.

Some of the evidences of this rapidity of growth and of the diversity and complexity of organization may easily be pointed out. In the autumn of 1900 Harvard University had the then largest enrollment of any American institution of higher learning. Its full-time students numbered 4,288.[1] In 1954 the University of

[1] Most of the figures and statistics used or quoted in this Introduction are taken from the following sources: *International Yearbook; School and Society; American Universities and Colleges*, ed. by Mary Irwin. 6th ed. (Washington, American Council on Education [1952]); *The World Almanac and Book of Facts for 1954; Americana Annual;* "Statistics of College and University Libraries" (Princeton University Library) (mimeographed); "Statistics of College and University Libraries," *College and Research Libraries,* January, 1954; *Doctoral Dissertations Accepted by American Universities, 1952–1953,* ed. by Arnold H. Trotier and Marian Harman (New York,

California had the largest full-time enrollment among the state universities—35,273 students at Berkeley and Los Angeles; and Columbia, a private institution, enrolled 11,999. The total enrollment of undergraduate and graduate students in public and private universities, colleges, and schools of technology increased from 115,271 in 1900 to 1,895,280 in 846 institutions in 1954; and the faculties engaged in teaching and research, totaling 14,908 in 1900, numbered 163,536 in 1954. The physical plants required to house such universities are likewise so extensive and complicated that a description of them cannot be attempted here. Frequently branches of a given university are located on several campuses in different sections of a city or state or even in other states. In 1954 New York University had to provide facilities for 39,401 full-time and part-time students at various locations in New York City. The University of Chicago maintains an astronomical observatory in Wisconsin and is associated with the University of Texas in staffing an observatory in Texas. Funds for endowment and research have likewise grown in the five decades. Johns Hopkins had an endowment fund of $2,428,000 in 1900; in 1953 the amount had grown to over $42,000,000. Harvard had $12,600,000—an amount which had increased almost eighteenfold by 1953.

The most significant growth, however, has been in the fields of professional education and of graduate study and research. The graduate school, the professional school in various fields, and institutes for highly specialized investigation in many subjects—all embraced within the university's organization—have developed on an extensive scale and absorb a large percentage of the total expenditures for university purposes. The record of growth in the number of graduate students and advanced degrees awarded has been particularly notable. In 1890, there were only 2,383 students enrolled in graduate schools. In 1920, the number had grown to 15,612; in 1940, to 106,119; in 1950, to over 237,000. In 1890, only 70 Master's degrees were granted; in 1920, the number had increased to 3,873;

H. W. Wilson, 1953). Readers are advised to consult the 1945 edition of *The University Library* for some 1940–41 comparative figures.

in 1940, to 26,731; and in 1950, 58,219. Doctorates awarded for the same period were 164 in 1890; 532 were awarded in 1920, in 1940, 3,088, and in 1954, 8,604.[2]

Information concerning expenditures for research is not easily acquired, because the largest investments for this purpose are made by industry and government. But the role of the university is impressive in that it is the principal trainer of investigators: of the $1,160,000,000 spent for research in 1947, at least $45,000,000 was spent by universities.[3] Business and industry spent $450,000,000; the federal government, $625,000,000; and other agencies, $40,000,-000. Of the sum spent by the government, $200,000,000 was spent in government laboratories, and $425,000,000 on contract with industrial and university laboratories. In 1949–50 institutions of higher education reported a total of $225,341,000 for research.[4] To insure the publication of the results of investigation, the university press has been highly developed in many universities, and through it many significant publications are made available to the scholarly world. Sixteen of these presses published from 15 to 108 volumes of a scholarly nature in 1951. In 1954, one regularly issued as many as 23 scholarly journals.

Funds for scholarships and fellowships have increased considerably during the period. A report by the U.S. Office of Education showed that in 1949–50, totals of 124,223 scholarships valued at $27,000,963 and 13,659 fellowships worth $9,266,966 were awarded by 1,198 institutions.[5] Even these figures do not represent

[2] Trotier and Harman, *op. cit.*, p. iii.

[3] *Science and Public Policy, Vol. 1: A Program for the Nation.* President's Scientific Research Board (Washington, U.S. Govt. Print. Off., 1947), p. 12.

[4] U.S. Office of Education. *Statistics of Higher Education, 1949–50* (Washington, U.S. Govt. Print. Off., 1952). Raymond H. Ewell of the National Science Foundation points out that funds for research and development in the United States have been growing at an approximately exponential rate for the past 35 years, and that the annual expenditure is now almost four billion dollars—as much as was spent for research during the entire period, 1776 through 1933; see Ewell, "The Role of Research in Economic Research," *Chemical and Engineering News,* XXXIII (1955), 2980–85.

[5] Theresa B. Wilkins, *Scholarships and Fellowships Available at Institutions of Higher Education.* U.S. Office of Education, Bulletin No. 16, 1951 (Washington, U.S. Govt. Print. Off., 1951).

the total funds that go into scholarships and fellowships annually. The several philanthropic foundations provide aid in individual and institutional research projects. In addition to the Carnegie Corporation of New York, the General Education Board, the Rockefeller Foundation, and the John Simon Guggenheim Memorial Foundation, the more specialized groups—the National Research Council, the Social Sciences Research Council, the American Council of Learned Societies, the Institute of International Education, and various federal agencies, such as the U.S. Public Health Service—award funds for special training or study. The Ford Foundation, set up in 1950, stimulated both individuals and institutions to propose projects for investigation. Established in 1950, the National Science Foundation awarded its first fellowships in 1952. A number of science fellowships were also granted by the Atomic Energy Commission in 1948. The entire governmental program of education of military personnel and veterans, of course, has been based on the subsidization of young men and women enrolled in colleges and universities.

The American university library has shared in this growth. In fact, the increase in its resources and in its services to scholars has been one of the most pronounced aspects of university development. In many instances these resources and services have furnished the basis for much of the instruction and research of the institution. The rapid rate of growth has made the problem of providing facilities for both library materials and students one of the most perplexing that confronts the university administrator and librarian. With the last five decades the holdings of many university libraries have generally increased at least fourfold; in some instances, tenfold or more. In 1900 Harvard was the only university library to have over 500,000 volumes. At that time Yale had only 360,500; the University of Illinois, 42,314; and the University of North Carolina, 31,000. By 1953 these four libraries cataloged 5,702,947; 4,215,841; 2,656,103; and 633,665 volumes, respectively. Nineteen libraries reported over 1,000,000 volumes, while twenty-one others had collections of 500,000 or more.

The tremendous expansion of resources has been accompanied by greatly increased demands for space and personnel for the selection, acquisition, and use of library materials. Buildings or rooms for special collections for undergraduates; general reading rooms for reference materials and periodicals; seminar rooms, cubicles, and studies for graduate students and faculty members; space for bibliographical apparatus and service for the reproduction and use of special types of material; quarters for the administrative and technical operations; and special libraries in departments, institutes, and professional schools have been provided on a scale commensurate with the university's total program of activities and carefully adjusted to its needs.

To complicate the problems of the library still further, new responsibilities have been placed upon it. These have arisen in various ways. First of all, the character of materials acquired by libraries has undergone remarkable change. Journals, government documents, near-print, newspapers, manuscripts, pamphlets, phonograph records, prints, maps, films, microreproductions, and other forms of material have to be secured on an unprecedented scale; and major collections of a highly specialized nature have to be acquired, housed, and serviced. Chinese collections at Harvard, Hispanic-American materials at Tulane, Western history at California, Near East objects and materials at the University of Chicago, collections of archives at Virginia, and the seemingly endless variety of materials available in recent years through microphotography and other forms of reproduction suggest the range and complexity of these materials and the problems to which their acquisition and use give rise.

Card distribution by the Library of Congress and other libraries; the publication of union lists of serials, manuscripts, newspapers, and catalogs of major world-famed libraries; the development of local, regional, and national union catalogs; the formation of groups to aid in library acquisition; the establishment of library schools upon university campuses and usually within university libraries; the development of cooperative undertakings in the fields of specialization, documentation, and bibliographical service; participation in international conferences and organizations that are concerned with the facilitation of cooperation between American and foreign libraries—all have placed new responsibilities upon university libraries which were all but unknown in 1900.

This, in brief, is the situation which confronts the university librarian today. The problems which naturally grow out of these conditions are those with which the librarian must deal. The principal difficulty which he experiences in attempting to deal with them is the lack of a systematic review of information concerning organizational and administrative procedures essential to their proper solution. Such information is, of course, available. Library literature contains many articles which deal with certain aspects of university library administration. Information is likewise available through correspondence and through conference and visitation. The establishment of the Association of Research Libraries in 1931 and the Association of College and Reference Libraries in 1938; the publication programs of *College and Research Libraries, American Archivist, American Documentation, Library Trends, Journal of Documentation, Journal of Cataloging and Classification*, and *Serial Slants;* such institutional publications as the *Harvard Library Bulletin* and the Library of Congress *Information Bulletin;* and the publication of the results of surveys of a number of university libraries, of regional and national bibliographical undertakings, and of conferences on cooperation and specialization have relieved the situation somewhat. There is, however, continued need for subjecting available information to systematic scrutiny so that a body of generalizations concerning it may be developed.

The purpose of the present volume grows out of this situation: it is to review the changes which have taken place in the university library in response to the demands made upon it by university growth; to consider systematically the principles and methods of university and library administration; and to formulate generalizations concerning the organization, administration, and functions of the university library to the end that it may serve its clientele more adequately and efficiently than it has in the past. It is also intended to aid the university administrator in understanding the role of the total administration of the university, to acquaint faculty members and members of learned societies with the problems which are involved in adequate service to them, and to make available to students in library science a body of principles and methods bearing upon the problems of university library administration.

It will be observed that, while much has been done in developing university librarianship, there is still a great deal to accomplish. Criticism of library practices, by both librarians and nonlibrarians, makes it necessary for administrators to reappraise constantly technical procedures and readers' services. Undoubtedly, there is danger that some librarians may become so engrossed in technicalities that they will lose sight of the purposes of their work. There is also the danger that some librarians, engaged in a day-by-day task of operating complex library systems, will neglect to realize fully the implications of the assumption that knowledge is indivisible and that the pattern of librarianship inevitably reflects the pattern of educational policy. Finally, librarians should not overlook the fact that in many of the larger aspects of university librarianship the problems are universal, rather than local, and require cooperative, rather than individual, planning and action.

The information upon which this study is based has been drawn from many sources. These include studies such as the *Survey* by the American Library Association (1926); *College and University Library Problems*, by Works (1927); *Circulation Work in College and University Libraries*, by Brown and Bousfield (1933); *Principles of College Library Administration*, by Randall and Goodrich (1936 and 1941); *The Administration of the College Library*, by Lyle and others (1944 and 1949); *College and University Libraries and Librarianship*, edited by Carlson (1946); the proceedings of the Cooperative Committee on Library Building Plans (issued annually since 1946); *Library Buildings for Library Service*, edited by Fussler (1947); *Planning the University Library Building*, by Burchard and others (1949); *Education for Librarianship*, edited by

Berelson (1949); *Bibliographic Organization*, edited by Shera and Egan (1950); *The Place of the Library in a University*, issued by Harvard (1950); *Changing Patterns of Scholarship and the Future of Research Libraries*, edited by Hirsch (1951); *The Library in College Instruction*, by Wilson and others (1951); *Scholar's Workshop*, by Brough (1953); *Librarians, Scholars, and Booksellers at Mid-Century*, edited by Butler (1953); *The Subject Analysis of Library Materials*, edited by Tauber (1953); *Technical Services in Libraries*, by Tauber and Associates (1954); *The Function of the Library in the Modern College*, edited by Fussler (1954); *Problems and Prospects of the Research Library*, edited by Williams (1955); and descriptive and administrative surveys of the libraries of the University of Chicago (1933), of seven western and northwestern state universities (1938), and the universities of Georgia (1939), Florida, Indiana, Mississippi, and Pennsylvania (1940), Columbia (1944), South Carolina (1946), Denver and Stanford (1947), Cornell (1948), Alabama Polytechnic Institute, Minnesota, New Hampshire, and Virginia Polytechnic Institute (1949), Texas A. and M. College (1950), Montana (1951), and Idaho and Notre Dame (1952). The report on the Harvard libraries by Metcalf was issued in 1955. Other publications and theses concerning all aspects of library cooperation, resources for research, cataloging and classification, coordinate indexing, documentation, serial publications, technical reports, new reference services, photographic methods, preservation of materials, punched-card applications, library buildings and storage devices, and other subjects, which have appeared in increasing numbers in the past ten years, have likewise been drawn upon extensively. Such information has also been supplemented by personal visits and correspondence. The volumes of the Commission on Financing Higher Education (1952–53), particularly the one entitled *Financing Higher Education in the United States*, by Millett (1952); *The Finance of Higher Education*, by Russell (revised edition, 1954), and similar publications involving university problems have provided useful discussion and data.

The libraries considered are university libraries. Although universities in the United States invariably include undergraduate students, the principal emphasis is placed upon the problems of the university in its effort to provide its major service—research—to the upper divisions and to the graduate and professional schools and the special institutes of the university. The problems of the junior and senior colleges of the university are considered only as they are involved in the larger program of the university library.

Since the 1945 edition, there have appeared, as already noted, an increasing number of studies concerning the university library. There are still major questions, however, which need the careful examination of both practitioners and students. In the Introduction to the July, 1952, issue of *Library Trends*, which is devoted to current trends in college and university libraries, Robert B. Downs selected eighteen questions at random from the many raised by the contributors. These questions were concerned with resources, organization, technical operations, library use, library education, cataloging and classification, principles of management, microphotography, evaluation of library buildings, and fitting regional libraries into a national pattern. These and other matters suggest the changing and dynamic character of the American university library. But they also represent a limitation, since without systematic studies of the problems, librarians will continue to base their judgment on subjective impressions and conclusions rather than on factual evidence.

Another serious limitation has been the lack of comparable data covering the same institutions for a fairly long continuous period. The data which appear in the statistical compilations of the American Library Association, the Association of College and Reference Libraries, and of the U.S. Office of Education frequently have been incomplete, or their nature has been modified from one date to another. This is particularly true of financial data—a difficulty which is increased by the fact that a number of universities do not permit the publication of certain types of information. The data which are used cover primarily the period up to 1952–1953. Thus, many of the issues which have developed as a result of World War II and the Korean War are involved in the discussion.

The authors are hopeful that these limitations will not adversely affect the usefulness of the volume. The development of graduate programs in the library schools, even though a large number of them have dropped the Master's thesis as a requirement, may possibly result in studies which will fill in gaps in present knowledge.

I

THE FUNCTIONS OF THE UNIVERSITY
AND ITS LIBRARY

SINCE this volume is intended to deal with the organization, administration, and functions of the university library, it is important that consideration be given to the functions of the university itself, and that the relation of the library to the university, from which the objectives and significance of the library stem, be clearly shown. It is also important that any confusion which may exist in the reader's mind concerning the terms "college" and "university" be removed at the outset.

THE FUNCTIONS OF
THE AMERICAN
UNIVERSITY

Prior to the American Revolution, institutions of higher learning in this country were known as "colleges." It was not until the constitution of the state of Massachusetts was adopted in 1780 that Harvard College was referred to as "the University at Cambridge." The College and Academy of Philadelphia became the University of Pennsylvania in 1791, while Brown University adopted its present name in 1804, after having been known as the College of Rhode Island for thirty-nine years. The term "university" was first used to designate an institution that incorporated an extensive group of courses into its instructional program and maintained one or more professional or technical schools. Although several of the early institutions assumed some of the characteristics of present-day universities as early as 1850, they did not adopt the name "university" until comparatively recently. Princeton University did not change its name from the College of New

Jersey until 1896. King's College, which became Columbia College in 1784, did not become Columbia University until 1896, and Queen's College (Rutgers College, 1825), did not become Rutgers University until 1924.

Various definitions of the term "university" have been formulated. For the purposes of this volume the definition given by Daugherty and Blauch is used. As defined by them, "a university in the United States is an educational institution comprising an undergraduate college of liberal arts and sciences, professional schools, and a graduate college or school which provides programs for study and research beyond the levels of the baccalaureate and first professional degrees." [1]

The term has been used frequently to describe institutions which do not comply with these conditions. Sometimes the name "university" is officially used by a small college by virtue of its charter. Other institutions, on the other hand, retain the title "institute," "school," "seminary," or "college," although they offer graduate studies and confer advanced degrees. Massachusetts Institute of Technology, Colorado School of Mines, Union Theological Seminary, Bryn Mawr College, and Iowa State College are examples. Library problems in institutions of this type are similar to those encountered in institutions officially designated as "universities."

Dartmouth College, with a library of over 700,000 volumes, represents another type of institution of direct interest to research workers. Although Dartmouth College gives the Master's degree in but a few fields and does not have a doctoral program, the Dartmouth Library, by virtue of its rich collections in special fields and its extensive facilities for study, is equipped to furnish services similar to those found in university libraries.

The functions of the privately and publicly supported universities have been discussed at length in educational literature by Learned, Flexner, Hutchins, Foerster, Hofstadter and Hardy, Hollis, Hook, and many others. In 1939, Butts [2] presented a full

---

[1] Daugherty and Blauch, "The American University," in *American Universities and Colleges*, p. 45. Part II of this volume lists 181 accredited "universities."
[2] *The College Charts Its Course.*

discussion of the different and conflicting viewpoints which appear in the controversies regarding the "true function" of the American college and university. Butts traced the introduction of courses of a practical or utilitarian nature to show that they are part of curricular evolution in academic institutions. The rise and expansion of land-grant colleges, state universities, state-aided universities, and municipal universities show the trend of institutions of higher learning toward a more practical or utilitarian slant. While many educators and institutions have endeavored to retain the traditions of classical education, universities in general, and state universities in particular, have not held firmly to these traditions. Education for democracy and for practical and professional purposes appears to be a definite part of most university programs.

The development of agriculture, industry, and the professions has not been the only force that has made itself felt in the university. The impact of World War II brought the university and the federal government closer together than ever before.[3] This relationship has definitely affected the programs of academic institutions, not only in the type of students attracted to their campuses, but also in their teaching methods and research services and in the emphasis they have placed upon international problems and world understanding.[4]

Both college and university curricula and research programs adjust to the needs and demands of the time. The functions of the university, despite changes which may occur periodically, appear to follow a consistent pattern. They may be described as (1) conservation of knowledge and ideas, (2) teaching, (3) research, (4) publication, (5) extension and service, and (6) interpretation. Each of

[3] Brown, "Recent Trends in Higher Education," in *American Universities and Colleges,* pp. 69–73; Axt, *The Federal Government and Financing Higher Education.*

[4] In 1944, Robert M. Hutchins expressed the view that "the particular doctrine that the purpose of the University is the pursuit of truth by freely determined teaching and research is true if it is understood." (*The Organization and Purpose of the University* [Chicago, 1944], p. 8). Hutchins observed that the university could not stand aloof in the moral, intellectual, and spiritual conflict now facing the world. To do so "is to doom the University to sterility. It is to renounce the task of intellectual leadership. It is to deny at a great crisis in history our responsibility to mankind." (*Ibid.,* p. 12).

these functions is not wholly discrete and may be dealt with from the point of view of both the university and the university library.

CONSERVATION OF KNOWLEDGE AND IDEAS. During the past five hundred years the university has been the chief conserver of knowledge and ideas accumulated by man in his struggle to conquer the physical world, to relate himself effectively to the society of his fellow men, and to develop his intellectual and spiritual capacities. Through laboratories, libraries, and museums, the university, in conjunction with other social institutions, has conserved the heritage of the past essential to the education of the individual and to the interchange of ideas. The processes of social change are interwoven in the facts, ideas, and inventions of man; and each new idea or invention grows out of accumulated and conserved knowledge.[5]

TEACHING. The university, however, is not merely a conserver of the past. Through its instructional staff the knowledge and ideas conserved by it are revitalized and put to use in the education of youth who are to be leaders in society and workers in the field of research. The preservation of the physical object called the "book," for example, may not be important in itself. What is important is for the university to transmit to the oncoming generations the ideas which the book contains. The determination of which youth shall be taught the more important ideas, what methods shall be used in the process of instruction, and who shall do the teaching may well be matters of opinion and debate. However that may be, teaching is an unescapable function of the university and is not restricted to the undergraduate junior college or liberal arts college level but extends to the graduate and professional levels as well.

RESEARCH. The most distinctive difference between the college and the university is found in the latter's emphasis upon research. Through the methods of research the student is given an opportunity for independent work, and the laboratories and libraries become indispensable aids in an activity which is directed at the expansion of man's fund of knowledge. Through the Master's essay

[5] The theme of the Bicentennial of Columbia University during 1954 was "Man's Right to Knowledge and the Free Use Thereof."

in a limited way, the doctoral dissertation generally,[6] and special investigations by faculty members and research workers, the university continuously attempts to gain for man a full comprehension of his social and physical universe. And while the university makes this direct contribution to the advancement of knowledge, it serves as the principal training ground for those who carry on investigation in government, industry, the sciences, and other fields. Of the estimated 100,000 individuals engaged in research, one third are associated with colleges and universities.

PUBLICATION. Not only does the university actively engage in research and train research personnel generally, but it offers to the scholarly world and the public at large the results of investigation through the medium of publication. Through the maintenance of a press, members of the university staff and other scholars are provided with an instrument by which reports on research in the various fields of knowledge may be disseminated.[7] In 1954, there were 37 presses which were members of the Association of American University Presses. Some 40 other institutions are either actively engaged in publication under their own imprints, or use press imprints on university or college publications offered for sale, or maintain print shops to handle their domestic needs, also using press imprints.[8]

The publication of the results of research has not been the sole contribution which the university press has made to scholarship. By providing an agency near at hand through which publication can be assured, it has stimulated scholars to undertake investigations. It has likewise been notably successful in effecting an extensive documentation of special subject fields or regions and in rounding out and giving a cumulative effect to the university's entire educational program.

EXTENSION AND SERVICE. During the year 1949–50 a total of $86,-

[6] Trotier and Harman, *Doctoral Dissertations Accepted by American Universities, 1952–1953*. The greatest value of the doctoral dissertation is involved in the task of defining a problem, examining and organizing a large body of materials, and presenting the results in writing. See J. H. Tufts, "The Graduate School," in *Higher Education in America*, (Boston, Ginn, 1930), p. 356.

[7] Kerr, *A Report on American University Presses*.   [8] *Ibid.*, pp. 43–45.

674,000 was spent for extension work by institutions of higher education.[9] Begun in the last quarter of the nineteenth century in the form of lecture series off campus, extension work has assumed large scale proportions in the United States, particularly in publicly supported universities. Through the combined function of extension and service, the university assumes a position of leadership in the effort to raise the cultural level of the whole community. The university may serve as the head of the entire educational system of the state and as a court of final authority on all educational matters within the range of its experts. Both private and public university personnel have participated actively in industrial, business, and governmental affairs. World War II and the Korean War accelerated this participation. University research facilities are often specifically utilized in the solution of community social problems, and service to the community is offered on the university campus through institutes and short courses. In addition, the university often goes beyond its immediate campus boundaries and, through such means as extension courses, correspondence courses, agricultural extension, radio talks, television programs, adult education programs, and research through experiment stations contributes actively to the furtherance of the education of individuals and society in general.

INTERPRETATION. The value of research is obviously limited unless its results are made available not only to other scholars but to the public generally. Consequently, the faculties and research staffs of universities constantly attempt to interpret the results of their investigation to society in various ways. No sharp line of demarcation, therefore, can be made between the functions of teaching, publication, and extension, on the one hand, and that of interpretation, on the other. All are involved in the dissemination of the new knowledge which the university discovers and contributes to the modification and refinement of present practice and to the development of future theory.

[9] Daugherty and Blauch, "The American University," p. 67. "This figure represented approximately 5 percent of all current expenditures of higher institutions for educational and general purposes, but in some institutions one-third or more of the expenditure was for extension."

ESSENTIALS OF · A UNIVERSITY · LIBRARY PROGRAM · Any discussion of the organization, administration, and functions of the university library should be related to the institution whose objectives it is intended to advance.[10] However, such a discussion cannot be maintained under the identical rubrics used above. In the following consideration of the essentials of a university library program, such a regrouping of ideas has been effected as seems best to insure a proper presentation of the library's role in the attainment of the university's objectives.

The essentials that are fundamental to successful operation of the library and the coordination of its program with the teaching and research program of the university may be presented under eight heads: (1) resources for instruction, research, and extension; (2) a competent library staff; (3) organization of materials for use; (4) adequate space and equipment; (5) integration of the library with administrative and educational policies; (6) integration of the library with community, state, regional, national, and international library resources; (7) adequate financial support; and (8) a workable policy of library government. They may be considered briefly in the above order at this point. Each will be expanded in detail in later chapters.

RESOURCES FOR INSTRUCTION, RESEARCH, AND EXTENSION. Adequate resources for carrying out the university's objectives in instruction, research, and extension implement the function of preserving the accumulating source materials necessary for scholarly pursuits. The specific objectives of the library are determined by the university and are stated explicitly or indirectly by the institution in its various catalogs and announcements and in other ways. Once they are determined, the library must provide the bibliographical apparatus, books, journals, newspapers, manuscripts, films, and other materials necessary to this attainment. The library's acquisitional policy should constantly be directed toward the support of the

[10] This is demonstrated in the several surveys which have been made of specific library systems, e.g., Wilson, Downs, and Tauber, *Report of a Survey of the Libraries of Cornell University for the Library Board of Cornell University, October 1947–February 1948.*

various phases of the work of the institution and should be extended to support programs in such additional subjects or fields as may be determined from time to time by the university.

Whenever a change is made in the curriculum, or a new course, a new staff member, or a new department, school, or institute is added, or an extensive new program of investigation is planned, these changes, additions, and plans almost inevitably involve the use of library materials, whether proper provision is made for them in the library budget or not. Far too frequently such provision is not made in the budget of the new undertaking or of the library, and the new undertaking suffers accordingly.

A COMPETENT LIBRARY STAFF. The second essential of a university library program is a staff competent through training in professional and subject fields and sufficient in number to organize and administer the resources of the library at an effective teaching or research level, as opposed to the stripped-down administrative or housekeeping level at which libraries are usually forced to operate. Inasmuch as the library is concerned with graduate study and research, the training and experience of the staff should be carefully scrutinized for this exacting work. This means that a positive relation should be maintained between the amounts which are spent for staff and materials in a well-organized, functionally efficient library. In the 1945 edition of this work, the approximate formula of 50–60 percent for personnel, 30–40 percent for books, periodicals, and binding, and 10 percent for supplies and other purposes was suggested. A more recent examination of the formula suggests that the percentage for personnel is probably closer to 65 or 70 percent. The formula under any case will vary from library to library, since the local conditions affect it directly. It is important, however, for the university and library administrations to be cognizant of proper distribution of the funds. When new funds are added for the purchase of library materials, increase of personnel may be necessary if the materials are to be properly organized and serviced.

A high order of service cannot be maintained unless the library staff, through extended training in subject as well as in technical fields, understands the objectives of the university and can assist the university in making its work richly fruitful. Such an understanding must grow out of the systematic study of the curricula of the university and out of a knowledge of the spirit and methods of research as well as of the general administrative and educational procedures of the university. This implies that the university librarian must understand fully the objectives of the university in order to direct the library in such a way as to secure its greatest educational effectiveness.

ORGANIZATION OF MATERIALS FOR USE. Organization of the resources of the library for efficient use by various groups of patrons is the third essential. For example, the books used by undergraduates in the college library of a university can be given simpler treatment than those needed by research workers. The proper interrelation of all kinds of library materials, of catalogs and classifications, and of the library's total services can be made to contribute to this effectiveness, just as the failure to include in a central catalog the holdings of major collections located on the campus can defeat the maximum service of the library to its clientele. Even though a library may possess a wealth of resources, extreme centralization or decentralization of materials and administration and the lack of proper organization of service desks, indexes, catalogs, and bibliographical apparatus may seriously limit the service which should be provided.[11] One of the most serious handicaps with which the users of a library may have to contend is the failure of the library to maintain an adequate catalog of all materials as they are received.

ADEQUATE SPACE AND EQUIPMENT. The fourth essential—adequate space and equipment for the expeditious use of materials—can scarcely be separated from the third essential, organization of materials. The planning of the modern university library building, like that of buildings for industrial, commercial, and other purposes, must be carefully conceived if the maximum of efficiency in library

[11] Cf. "Current Trends in Cataloging and Classification," *Library Trends*, **II** (1953), 171-355.

use is to be attained. Consequently, the responsibility for the arrangement of space in the interior of the building or buildings devoted to library use should be placed upon the librarian, and the resulting organization of space and installation of equipment should express a complete understanding of the best functional organization of library materials and facilities.[12] Adequate space for acquisition and preparation of materials; for reference, bibliographical, and other services; for graduate reading rooms, seminars, stack cubicles, and faculty studies; for departmental, divisional, and school libraries; for administrative offices, stacks, and photographic laboratories; for special needs of undergraduate students; for reserves, browsing rooms, special collections, and rare books—adequate space for these and all other library purposes should be so planned as to secure the most effective integration possible.

INTEGRATION OF THE LIBRARY WITH ADMINISTRATIVE AND EDUCATIONAL POLICIES. The fifth essential of satisfactory library service is the close integration of the library with the administrative and educational policies and practices of the university. The library is not an end in itself. Essential services and technical operations should be kept in the background and administered in such a way as to promote the attainment of the educational objectives of the institution. The major function of the library is to support the administrative and educational policies of the university of which it is a part. To perform this function properly, the library staff must understand the institution's policies and maintain intimate contact with its activities. The mere granting of faculty status to the librarian or certain institutional privileges to members of the library staff will not insure the maintenance of all contacts that are essential. Like the president, the librarian is a university officer who serves the entire institution; and he should be so placed in relation to other administrative and policy-forming officers and bodies as to be informed concerning the interests of the university which the library should foster. Cloak and dagger maneuvers [13] may serve to effect some of

[12] Reece, "Building Planning and Equipment," *Library Trends*, I (1952), 136–55.
[13] Milczewski, "Cloak and Dagger in University Library Administration," *College and Research Libraries*, XIII (1952), 117–21.

these contacts, but a positive program should prove fruitful on a more uniform basis. Thus, the librarian should be in a position to know of all modifications in the curriculum, since they are likely to affect the library. Matters of concern to the graduate faculty invariably have their counterpart in the library. The decision to establish a departmental library in a new building involves the provision of library equipment, personnel, catalog service, and the maintenance of other library relationships. The participation of the librarian in matters of this character is fundamental to coordinated, effective library administration.

INTEGRATION OF THE LIBRARY WITH COMMUNITY, STATE, REGIONAL, NATIONAL, AND INTERNATIONAL LIBRARY RESOURCES. The close integration of the library program with that of the university may apply not only to university interests upon the immediate campus but to library interests within the community, state, region, and country and, to a certain degree, to research and scholarly interests throughout the world. In the 1930's, impetus was given to a wider extension of various forms of cooperation by college and university libraries.[14] In the 1940's, there was further development of group action by American college, university, and research libraries. The Library of Congress worked closely with academic and other libraries during World War II to insure the acquisition of materials. The Farmington Plan, which began in 1948, has as its premise that major research collections should coordinate their efforts better than they have done in the past.[15] The Midwest Inter-Library Center is the crystallization of the idea that a group of sixteen libraries can work together in their effort to control common problems of building growth, acquisitions, and storage.[16] These developments have grown out of the realization by university administrators, faculties, librarians, and representatives of educational foundations and learned societies that bibliographical apparatus and library resources

[14] Lowell, *College and University Library Consolidations;* McAnally, "Recent Developments in Cooperation," *College and Research Libraries,* XII (1951), 123–32; Edwin E. Williams, "Some Questions on Three Cooperative Projects," *Library Trends,* I (1952), 156–65.

[15] Williams, *Farmington Plan Handbook.*

[16] *Midwest Inter-Library Center Newsletter,* No. 1, Oct. 1949, to date.

within given areas and the nation at large could be greatly increased if emphasis were placed upon cooperation in the acquisition and use of materials and the provision of bibliographical facilities, rather than upon rivalry and duplication. The extension of interlibrary loans, the introduction of microreproductions for research purposes, and the support of union catalogs and bibliographical centers further emphasize this point.

ADEQUATE LIBRARY SUPPORT. Adequate financial support is basic to the maintenance of any program of library development and service that is to be significantly effective. To supply the necessary funds for the acquisition of materials for study and research, for the staff to administer the resources, and for buildings to house the materials, is a responsibility of the university administration which is cognizant of the role played by the library in the academic program.[17] The appointment of qualified personnel should insure the wise expenditure of funds allotted for the administration of the library.

A WORKABLE POLICY OR PLAN OF LIBRARY GOVERNMENT. The final essential in an adequate library program is a library policy or plan of library government which will insure the effective, functional operation of the main library and all its special units. As has been made abundantly clear through recent university library surveys, this phase of university administration is constantly in need of specification and clarification. The flow of authority from the administration to the library, the responsibility for the preparation of the budget, the selection of library personnel, the administration of departmental and school libraries, and the formulation of a well-conceived, comprehensive, long-term program of library development for the university as a whole—these and like considerations that are basic to effective administration have frequently been left largely to chance. Whatever policy exists has been allowed to grow according to individual interests or has been determined on a basis other

17 See, for example, the "Interim Report of the Library Committee, Academic Senate, Northern Section," *University Bulletin* (A Weekly Bulletin for the Staff of the University of California), II (1954), 133–34. Signed by James D. Hart, Chairman of the Library Committee.

than that of sound administrative principles. In order that the unfavorable conditions which naturally follow from such a situation as this may be obviated, it is fundamental that a policy be evolved and followed which will result in a well-organized, expertly directed library administration.

To summarize, it may be observed that the university is concerned with (1) conservation of knowledge and ideas, (2) teaching, (3) research, (4) publication, (5) extension and service, and (6) interpretation. The well-administered university library directs its activities toward the fulfillment of these functions. By accumulating and organizing books, manuscripts, journals, and other materials the university library serves as an invaluable aid in the conservation of knowledge and ideas and as an active force in the teaching, research, and extension programs of the university. Through direct assistance to the members of the faculty and research staff and through the service of members of the library staff as instructional officers, the university library participates in the interpretative function of the university. Through its many bibliographical and other reference services the library aids individuals of the instructional and research staffs who are engaged in the preparation of materials for publication.

In subsequent chapters these essentials of the university library program will be considered in detail. The order of the chapters, however, will differ somewhat from the order of the essentials discussed above.

BIBLIOGRAPHY

American Council on Education. Committee on Institutional Research Policy. Sponsored Research Policy of Colleges and Universities. Washington, D.C. [c1954].

Axt, Richard G. The Federal Government and Financing Higher Education. Published for the Commission on Financing Higher Education. New York, Columbia University Press, 1952.

Branscomb, Harvie. Teaching with Books: A Study of College Libraries. Chicago, Association of American Colleges and the American Library Association, 1940.

Brough, Kenneth J. Scholar's Workshop: Evolving Conceptions of Library Service. Urbana, University of Illinois Press, 1953.

Brown, Francis J. "Recent Trends in Higher Education," in *American Universities and Colleges*, ed. by Mary Irwin, pp. 69–73.

Butts, R. Freeman. The College Charts Its Course: Historical Conceptions and Current Proposals. New York, McGraw-Hill, 1939.

"Current Trends in Cataloging and Classification," *Library Trends*, II (1953), 173–355.

Danton, J. Periam. "University Librarianship—Notes on Its Philosophy," *College and Research Libraries*, II (1941), 195–204.

Daugherty, Donald H., and Lloyd E. Blauch. "The American University," in *American Universities and Colleges*, ed. by Mary Irwin, pp. 45–68.

Downs, Robert B. "Are College and University Librarians Academic?" *College and Research Libraries*, XV (1954), 9–14.

Ellsworth, Ralph E. "Trends in Higher Education Affecting the College and University Library," *Library Trends*, I (1952), 8–19. Contains bibliographical references.

Flexner, Abraham. Universities: American, English, German. New York, Oxford University Press, 1930.

Foerster, Norman. The American State University: Its Relation to Democracy. Chapel Hill, University of North Carolina Press, 1937.

Hofstadter, Richard, and C. DeWitt Hardy. The Development and Scope of Higher Education in the United States. Published for the Commission on Financing Higher Education. New York, Columbia University Press, 1952.

Hollis, E. V. Toward Improving Ph.D. Programs. Washington, American Council on Education, 1945.

Hook, Sidney. Education for Modern Man. New York, Dial Press, 1946.

Hutchins, Robert M. The Higher Learning in America. New Haven, Yale University Press, 1936.

Irwin, Mary (ed.). American Universities and Colleges. 6th ed. Washington, American Council on Education, 1952.

Jones, Howard Mumford. "Opportunities and Support for College and University Libraries," *College and Research Libraries*, XIV (1953), 9–21.

Kerr, Chester. A Report on American University Presses. [Washington, D.C.] The Association of American University Presses, 1949.

Kuhlman, A. F. (ed). The Development of University Centers in the South: Papers Presented at the Dedication of the Joint University Libraries, December Fifth and Sixth, 1941. Nashville, Tenn., Peabody Press and Vanderbilt University Press, 1942.

Learned, William S. The Quality of the Educational Process in the

United States and Europe. New York, Carnegie Foundation for the Advancement of Teaching, 1927.

Lowell, Mildred H. College and University Library Consolidations. Eugene, Ore., Oregon State System of Higher Education, 1942.

McAnally, Arthur M. "Recent Developments in Cooperation," *College and Research Libraries,* XII (1951), 123–32.

Midwest Inter-Library Center Newsletter, No. 1, October 1949 to date.

Milzcewski, Marion. "Cloak and Dagger in University Library Administration," *College and Research Libraries,* XIII (1952), 117–21.

Moberly, Walter H. The Universities and Cultural Leadership. Oxford, Oxford University Press, 1951.

Reece, Ernest J. "Building Planning and Equipment," *Library Trends,* I (1952), 136–55.

Tewksbury, Donald G. The Founding of the American Colleges before the Civil War. New York, Teachers College, Columbia University, 1932.

Trotier, Arnold H., and Marian Harman. Doctoral Dissertations Accepted by American Universities, 1952–1953. New York, H. W. Wilson, 1953.

Williams, Edwin E. Farmington Plan Handbook. [Bloomington, Ind.] Association of Research Libraries, 1953.

Wilson, Louis R., Robert B. Downs, and Maurice F. Tauber. Report of a Survey of the Libraries of Cornell University for the Library Board of Cornell University, October 1947—February 1948. Ithaca, 1948.

See also background chapters of various surveys of university libraries, e.g., Florida, Georgia, Indiana, Montana, Notre Dame, South Carolina, etc. (see Bibliography in chapter xvi.)

II

GOVERNMENTAL AND

ADMINISTRATIVE RELATIONSHIPS

THE VARIOUS aspects of governmental and administrative relationships of the library fall into three categories: (1) those that have been formalized and expressed in constitutions, laws, charters, articles of incorporation, and judicial decisions; (2) those that have been codified and stated in the university's "constitution" or "statutes"; and (3) those that have not been specifically codified by the university but are generally applied in daily administrative practices and routines. The latter are the more extensive and account for a considerable part of the following discussion. In some instances some of them are formalized in interoffice directives. In the study of these three aspects of university library administration it may be said that clearly expressed codes of library policy or government such as fall into category 2 and are particularly essential to efficient library administration do not exist in many institutions. In most of the surveys of libraries, it has been found that they are the exception rather than the rule.

University libraries in the United States, even when they are parts of state systems of higher education, have generally been operated independently of one another. There is, of course, no direct control by the federal government over university libraries, except in the case of service institutions, such as the Air University, United States Air Force, Maxwell Air Force Base, Alabama. In recent years, however, as a result of greater concentration of governmental control in several of the states, libraries of state universities, in common with the libraries of state institutions as a whole, have been influenced by reorganization and consolidation of state institutions effected by state legislative enactment. This has been true in the case of the libraries of higher education in Oregon and, to a lesser degree, in North Carolina, where important consolidations and reallocations of functions of higher institutions have been brought about by legislation. In Georgia, legislative action placing budgetary control of state institutions in the hands of the governor, as well as power to change the membership of the governing board, resulted in direct control of several state institutions in 1941. The relation between the state legislative power and a state university or system of higher education which has prerogatives provided by the state constitution occasionally becomes a center of litigation.[1] "A popularly initiated statute" to place nonteaching employees of the state university and state colleges in Arizona under a state civil service system was declared invalid because it conflicted with the constitutional authority of the Board of Regents of the University and State Colleges to deal with its own personnel. These instances, however, have not modified to any considerable extent the fundamental difference between the management of libraries in universities in decentralized, as contrasted with centralized, governments. The libraries of the universities, both private and public, share in the freedom from centralized control enjoyed by the institutions of which they are parts.

LEGAL BASES OF UNIVERSITY ORGANIZATION In seeking a pattern of university library organization and administration in the United States, recourse must be had to the laws of the various states concerning the institutions which the libraries serve. Although variation in pattern is to be expected, since the forty-eight states have dealt with the establishment of institutions of higher education in diverse ways, general patterns in the legal structure are evident and may be noted.

PRIVATE UNIVERSITIES. In the United States the privately supported university is regarded by legal authority as a public charity.

[1] Chambers, *The Colleges and the Courts, 1946–50*, p. 5.

Its establishment as a legal entity is provided through a charter or through articles of incorporation; and the possible state reservation of the right to alter, amend, or annul the charter or articles of incorporation determines the degree of independence which may be enjoyed by the university. If no such reservation has been made, the private university is free, within the limits of its charter, to develop its policy and program of education as it wishes, for the charter in such instances has the force of a contract with the state and is not subject to interference by the state or federal governments. This relationship of the university to the state was definitely decided by the Supreme Court of the United States in the Dartmouth College case (1819). In this decision the court maintained that the charter of the college constituted a contract between the college and the state and that the institution was consequently not subject to legislation which would in effect nullify the charter. This decision exercised a profound influence upon private colleges and universities and caused the states to pass general laws of incorporation by means of which certain controls are reserved to the states. It goes without saying that as an organic part of the university the library is directly bound up with the legal standing of the institution with which it is associated.

Since the privately controlled university is considered a public charity, tax exemption, as applied to property, is usually granted it. The income which the university library receives from benefaction and endowment, therefore, is usually free from taxation.[2] Such immunities as limited liability for torts and damages are also usually granted to the university because of its standing as a public charity. Finally, the exercise of control over students in matters of discipline and regulation has usually been construed by state courts as a legitimate function of the university. These rights and privileges which are extended to the university as a whole naturally affect the library as well as other units.

[2] M. M. Chambers, "Higher Education and the Courts in 1940–41," *Educational Record*, XXIII (1942), 58–62. See also Chambers, *The Colleges and the Courts*, chap. xi. Chambers has issued four volumes on the colleges and the courts, covering the periods 1819–1936, 1936–40, 1941–45, and 1946–50.

Since higher education is largely a matter of state concern, state courts have been called upon to render decisions when universities are involved in litigation. This applies to private and public universities alike. Libraries are likely to be subject to the same kind of control as that maintained over universities. This is exemplified by the control specified for the director of libraries over all libraries in the state system of higher education in Oregon.[3]

PUBLIC UNIVERSITIES. The state as a political unit has developed its institutions of higher education and has provided taxation for their support and operation. Legally, state and municipal universities are considered administrative units of government. As such, unless there is a constitutional provision to the contrary, they are subject to the will and action of the legislature and council. In some states, such as California, Michigan, and Minnesota, the governing bodies of the state universities are constitutional corporations and, in varying degrees, are free from interference by the legislature.[4] In about half the states no constitutional provisions for state universities exist. In these cases the universities are creations of the state legislatures and, as such, are subject to the legislative will. Policies and programs of education are also limited and controlled by the legislatures through their power of appropriation of funds and control of budgets.

A state or municipal university in its capacity as a governmental unit enjoys exemption from taxation, is entitled to the right of eminent domain, and possesses certain immunities in the matter of torts and damage suits. It may be presumed that members of the li-

[3] "In effect, the unification of the Oregon libraries has differentiated more and more from the unification as originally set up by the Board. The evolution has been definitely toward a group of autonomous libraries with the director of libraries serving more in an advisory and coordinating capacity for all the library affairs of the system, rather than as the central administrative office specified by the Board in 1931." See Carlson, "History and Present Status of the Centralization of the Libraries of the Oregon State System of Higher Education," *College and Research Libraries,* XIV (1953), 414–17. A revision of the Code statement has relieved the director of direct administrative responsibility of the units.

[4] For a detailed discussion of the status of universities as independent agencies of the state government, see Brody, *The American State and Higher Education,* pp. 165–225. For the special constitutional status of the University of Michigan and court decisions concerning it, see University of Michigan, *The University of Michigan, An Encyclopedic Survey,* I, 116–39.

brary staff, like professors and instructors, are considered by the courts as employees under contract rather than as public officers. The degree of independence maintained by the state or municipal university depends upon the state legislature or the city council, which may, unless restrained by constitutional provision, determine the policy and educational program, as well as the organization and administration, of the university.

This legal relation of the university to the state or city affects the university library. The program of the university library may be curtailed sharply if the appropriation of the university as a whole is reduced, or it may be expanded if the appropriation is increased. Moreover, the libraries of state or municipal institutions of higher education can be legally forced to contract or extend their services and activities. Minnesota thus requires the state university library to collect and preserve government documents. North Carolina and other states require the university libraries, along with other agencies of the government, to follow certain budgetary procedures and to purchase equipment and supplies according to specified routines. In some states civil service regulations are applicable to the university library.

Generally, a state university, in addition to being an administrative unit, also has a corporate existence. As such, it may enter into contracts, hold property in its own right, and undertake business ventures. The governing body of the university—the university board, the board of trustees, the board of regents, or any group of this type—may be permitted to issue bonds or borrow money as a direct obligation against itself. In some states such action in the case of state institutions in prohibited by law. Repayment of funds secured through bond issues or loans must be pledged from future earnings from investments, proprietary enterprises, or from special funds. It should be apparent that this corporate status of public universities directly affects the libraries. For instance, it may be inferred that a new library building or an extension of an old structure could be financed through a bond issue or loans.

The governmental status of both private and public universities is not a static matter. Social and economic changes react upon the attitudes held by the public toward institutions of higher education. It is possible that these changes may result in modifications in the legal status of universities. For example, tax exemption may alter to the extent that legislatures will modify or remove the exemptions.[5] Obviously, any changes in the functions of universities, or the addition of new functions, affect the activities of libraries. Unless the university librarian is aware of the legal basis upon which his authority exists, unless he knows what special rights and privileges have been granted to the library and what its relations to the government are, it is likely that he will not administer his responsibility so fully or so effectively as he should. Since legal changes may be made which directly affect the financial basis of the library, knowledge of the present situation and of state laws should enable the librarian to scrutinize intelligently any legislation which might make the university library a more effective educational unit or might act as a barrier to the development of library services.

LEGAL BASES OF UNIVERSITY LIBRARY GOVERNMENT The legal bases of authority upon which the establishment and maintenance of the university rest have an important bearing upon the government of the university library, whether it is part of a state, municipal, or private institution. These legal bases consist of constitutional provisions, charters, articles of incorporation, and general and special laws, applicable to the university, as well as judicial interpretations of these instruments. In a few cases in which the university library is specifically mentioned in legislative enactment, legal provisions permit or direct the governing body of the institution to purchase such books and equipment and to appoint such officers as are judged essential for carrying on the work of the library. In the case of the University of Wisconsin, however, the state statutes specifically empower the regents to prescribe rules and regulations for the management of the library. Likewise, *The Laws and Regulations of the University of*

[5] Chambers, *The Colleges and the Courts, 1946–50*, chap. xi.

Minnesota directly refer to such matters as the bases of library support, the powers, status, and responsibilities of the university librarian, and the various activities of units of the library.

The nature of the policy which governs the internal organization and administration of the university library depends, in most cases, on the prescribed regulations, by-laws, and proceedings of the governing body of the university or of the faculty or senate or other university body to which the governing body has delegated authority for formulating such policy. This is true of both public and private institutions. However, in a number of instances universities have not formulated such policies; or the formal regulations and by-laws which have been adopted for the government of their libraries fail to include such important matters as the scope and objectives of the library, the functions and responsibilities of the librarian and members of the staff, and the organic relationships of the library to other units and officials of the institution. In recent surveys of university libraries it has been found that lack of clarity on such points as these is usually attended by a corresponding lack of efficiency and adequacy of library service.[6]

INTERNAL GOVERNMENTAL POLICY OF THE UNIVERSITY LIBRARY   Thus far, attention has been paid to the relation of the university and of the university library to the state and to the governing body of the institution. It may now be appropriate to examine the essentials of a sound internal governmental policy for the university library. These essentials may be found in the practices of university libraries which have carried on successful programs. These practices indicate that the characteristics of a successful policy are usually as follows:

1. It defines clearly the relations of the librarian to the adminis-

[6] See, for example, Wilson and Swank, *Report of a Survey of the Library of Stanford University for Stanford University, November 1946–March 1947*, chap. iii, "Government of the Library." See also the article by Grieder, "The Reorganization of the Stanford University Libraries," *College and Research Libraries*, XIII (1952), 246–52.

tration. Inasmuch as the librarian is an officer who is charged with the administration of a major unit of the university which maintains contact with all other units and serves all schools, colleges, departments, and interests and assists them in the attainment of their various educational objectives, he should be nominated by the president and should be directly responsible to him, as are other chief administrative and educational officers.[7]

2. It makes clear what constitutes the library resources of the university. These generally should include all books, periodicals, pamphlets, and other graphic materials obtained by the general library or by any other unit of the university through purchase, exchange, gift, or otherwise for university purposes.

[7] *University of Illinois Statutes*, March, 1936. Section 19, on the Library, reads as follows:

"a) The Library includes all such books, pamphlets, periodicals, maps, music scores, photographs, prints, manuscripts, and other materials as are commonly preserved in libraries, purchased or acquired in any manner by the University to aid students and investigators.

"b) The Library shall be in charge of the Director of the Library, who shall be responsible for its arrangement and care and for the organization of the library staff; in the purchase of books and similar material, he shall act in accordance with business methods approved by the Comptroller. He shall make to the President an annual report on the condition and needs of the Library and on the work of the staff. With the approval of the President, the Director of the Library may establish branch libraries within the University when in their opinion efficiency in cataloguing, ordering, and other matters of library administration, and the general welfare of a particular college, school or department will thereby be promoted, and when action has been taken, the Director may delegate appropriate powers to the assistants in charge of such branches.

"c) The Director shall be elected biennially by the Board of Trustees, on the nomination of the President of the University. On the occasion of each such election, the President shall have the advice of the Senate Library Committee, to which for this purpose he shall add two members of the Library staff.

"d) Members of the Library staff shall be appointed by the Board of Trustees on the recommendation of the Director of the Library as approved by the President, and may be given appropriate academic rank.

"e) A standing committee of the Senate on the Library shall apportion the library book funds, and shall advise with the Director in matters pertaining to the Library. The Director shall be *ex-officio* a member of the Committee."

It should be pointed out, however, that the regulation in section (c) concerning tenure of the librarian seems to place him at a disadvantage as compared with the professional group and that the assistance given the library committee in allocating book funds, as described in section (e), should be of an advisory, rather than of an administrative, character. In June, 1944, the university statutes were revised to include all professional library staff members among the academic staff. See R. B. Downs, "Academic Status for University Librarians," *College and Research Libraries*, VII (1946), 6–9.

3. It places the administration of these resources, wherever located and by whatever unit acquired, under the administration of the librarian. In actual practice, there are many exceptions to this principle, especially in the case of the libraries of certain schools and special services, such as schools of medicine and law and agricultural experiment stations. The fact that there are exceptions, however, may be attributed more to tradition than to any inherent defect in the generalization.

4. It sets forth the duties of the librarian. It holds him responsible for the selection of books and periodicals of a general character for the main library and for the maintenance of a well-organized procedure for the selection of technical and special materials desired by and purchased for the various schools, colleges, and departments of the university. It likewise holds him responsible for the selection and direction of the members of the library staff, for the expenditure of such funds as are earmarked by the university for library purposes, for the acquisition and processing of library materials for the university as a whole, for the maintenance of adequate catalogs for the general library and departmental libraries, for the preparation of the library budget and its submission to the president, for the submission of an annual report or other reports, and for the performance of such other duties as are commonly embraced within university library administration.

5. It provides for a library committee, council, or board to assist the librarian in the allocation of book funds and in the formulation of a broad, general policy of library development. This committee should be representative of the university; its members should be chosen for their interest in the development of the library resources of the whole university rather than of one particular part; and its functions should be informative and advisory rather than administrative and executive.[8]

[8] See McCarthy, "Advisory Committee or Administrative Board?" *Library Quarterly*, XXII (1952), 223–31. McCarthy raises the question of whether or not librarians have been basing their contentions in support of an informative and advisory committee on historical situations which created difficulties for them, rather than on the actual facts of the case. He introduces developments in business and government, citing Baker's *Directors and Their Functions*, pp. 131–32. Instead of being set up

6. It defines the relationship of the librarian and the library staff to the administrative and educational units of the university in order that the library may be informed concerning all the administrative and educational policies of the university and may participate appropriately in their formation and execution. It likewise indicates the professional status of the librarian and the library staff and their relation to provisions of tenure, sabbatical leave, retirement, insurance, and vacations made by the university for its administrative, instructional, and professional members.[9]

Such a statement of principles is intended not to confer upon the librarian unusual or dictatorial powers but rather to give him the kind of administrative status which is usually granted to other officers of the university. It rests squarely upon the assumption that the librarian and the library staff are competent to merit such responsibility and to serve the various university interests in a cooperative, efficient manner and that the activities of the library are sufficiently important to the university to require centralized, expert direction.

RELATION OF THE LIBRARIAN TO GROUPS AND INDIVIDUALS COMPRISING THE UNIVERSITY ADMINISTRATION
The inclusion in the statutes of a university of legislation embodying a sound governmental policy for a university library, such as has been described in the preceding section, implies that specific relationships exist between the librarian and various groups and individuals on the campus. This assumption is well supported, since an unusually large number of relationships center in the office of the librarian. The librarian, like the president, is an officer of the entire university

---

merely to inform and advise, boards of directors in business enterprises *decide, confirm, counsel,* and *review.* McCarthy applies these actions to library administration. He admits that there are dangers which may develop, but he stresses the importance of the librarian's responsibility to present such evidence that divided authority will not appear. One may contend, however, that the informative and advisory functions, broadly interpreted, might well include decision, confirmation, and review.

[9] Wilson, *et al., Report of a Survey of the University of Florida Library for the University of Florida, February–May, 1940,* pp. 17–19.

and is concerned with the implementation of the teaching and research program of the whole university, so far as that can be effected by the library. Consequently, he has relations with all members of the university. The following list represents the various university and non-university groups, agencies, and individuals with which the librarian and his staff may have administrative, business, instructional, research, or service relations:

Trustees	Students
President	Counseling office
Legislative senate or faculty	Business office
Administrative board	Comptroller
Council	Registrar
Library committees	Auditor
Deans	Purchasing agent
Heads of departments	Buildings and grounds
Faculty members	University press and publications
University committees	Bookstore
Departmental librarians	Rental library
Professional school librarians	General public
Research institutes or seminars	Faculty families
Extension service	Employees of university
Home study	Alumni
Library school	Friends' group
Other libraries in community	Visiting scholars and research
Union catalogs, storage libraries, and bibliographical and inter-library centers	workers

Since these relationships are possible and do exist in many of the larger universities, it is perhaps useful to discuss them more concretely in an effort to show what effects they may have upon either the objectives or the activities of the university library. The point which requires emphasis is that the university librarian must work in close cooperation with all these groups, agencies, and individuals and must know how to adjust the library nicely to their varying requirements if it is to render maximum service to the university. Each of the relationships will be considered in the order noted above; but not all of the groups, agencies, and individuals will be discussed in detail. The order of the agencies and individuals listed does not represent hierarchical significance.

TRUSTEES OR GOVERNING BODY. The board of trustees or governing body of a university represents the university as a legal entity and assumes responsibility for the conduct of the institution.[10] As an administrative body, it is primarily concerned with the formulation of the general policies of the university, with the control of the institution's finances, with the selection of its president and chief officers of administration, and with the approval of recommendations and the confirmation of actions of administrative officers. In order that educational policies may be formulated in accord with approved educational principles and carried out effectively, the board selects the president and other important officers and delegates to them the duties of actually administering the institution.

Seldom does the governing board directly select the university librarian. Generally, it appoints the librarian upon the recommendation of the president, to whom has been delegated the power of selection of the faculty and of many of the administrative officers. This does not mean that the relationship between the trustees and the librarian is not important. Since the trustees control the budget, it is desirable that all avenues for keeping the board intelligently informed concerning the activities and needs of the library be maintained. When a library committee of the board exists, the medium of communication is direct. Otherwise, information concerning the library is usually made available through the president. Thus, while there may be no direct relation between the librarian and the board of trustees, unless there is a library committee of the trustees, as at Brown and Duke universities, the governing body passes upon the annual budget, decides upon rules recommended to it for the use of the library, and considers any plans for buildings or material alterations. In no sense is it a wise policy for the trustees to interfere with the internal administration of the library.

PRESIDENT. The president or chancellor is the chief executive

[10] Beck, *Men Who Control Our Universities*. This volume deals not only with the powers and functions of university governing boards, but also with qualifications, occupations, major business offices, incomes, ages, and other data of board members. Material on boards is also found in Hofstadter and Hardy, *The Development and Scope of Higher Education in the United States*.

officer of the university and is responsible to the governing body for the conduct of the institution. The relationship between the librarian and the president is direct. Usually the president recommends the appointment of the librarian; and while he, like the governing body, does not concern himself immediately with the internal management of the university library, recommendations made by the librarian concerning appointments, promotions, and dismissals of members of the staff are reviewed by him and, if approved, are transmitted by him to the board of trustees. He is kept informed concerning book funds; means employed in integrating the library with instruction, research, and extension; building improvements; large expenditures for equipment; and new activities which call for modification of buildings or unusual expenditure of funds. The librarian prepares the library budget and submits it to the president, makes recommendations to him for appointments to the staff, and generally seeks confirmation by him of decisions which alter the prevailing policies of the library in relation to other units of the university. No major university policy involving the library should be made without the knowledge of the president or other interested officer. It is equally important that no major decision concerning other activities of the university which will involve the library, such as the establishment of new departmental libraries or the inauguration of a new school or extensive research programs, should be made without the knowledge of the librarian. Many instances of inefficient library administration may be attributed to the non-observance of this policy.

THE LEGISLATIVE SENATE OR FACULTY. The functions of the senate or faculty of a university differ from institution to institution. Usually the senate or faculty is the legislative body to which the governing board delegates the responsibility of formulating educational policies and administrative procedures essential to the effective carrying out of the educational program.

The composition of the senate or faculty likewise differs in different institutions. The faculty is usually the more inclusive. However, in many faculties the privilege of voting is limited to the members who have attained certain grades of academic rank. The senate is usually a smaller body than the faculty, and membership in it is more strictly limited or is based on some plan of representation.

The importance of membership by the librarian in the senate or faculty is obvious. The resources and services of the library affect every phase of the university's program. Such membership of the principal officer of the library is therefore necessary if he is to be fully informed concerning the general policies of the university and is to administer the library most efficiently. Through his understanding of the problems of teaching and research and his knowledge of the ways in which the library may promote the ends of scholarship, he is in a strategic position to render his greatest service. Membership in these bodies by other qualified members of the library staff is likewise desirable, since the library must serve all the diverse interests of the university.

ADMINISTRATIVE BOARD. Whereas the university senate is usually concerned with the formulation of educational policies, the administrative board devotes its attention to the administration or execution of them. The activities of the administrative board are usually subject to the veto of the senate. At the University of Chicago the old general administrative board which was abolished several years ago was composed of various administrative officers of the university. It could alter or reverse the action of any university faculty or university board in any matter chiefly administrative in character. The director of libraries was a member of the general administrative board. As a result of his membership, he was able to participate in the discussion of any administrative problem which had a bearing on the library and voted upon all measures, including those which had implications for the library. Such membership also insured the library's inclusion in the routing of information from the president's office to the administrative officers. With the reorganization of the ruling bodies at Chicago, no analogous organization replaced the administrative board.

The organization and functions of the administrative board vary in different institutions. The board described in the preceding paragraph is not to be confused with another type of administrative board to be found in some institutions. At Columbia University, for example, administrative boards of the summer session, the School of International Affairs, and of the Schools of Dramatic Arts and Painting and Sculpture are maintained. They control their own units in the same way that faculties have statutory power and limitations thereof. Administrative boards are subject to the control of the University Council whenever a proposal is made which involves a change in the educational policy of the university in respect to requirements of admission, program of studies, or the conditions of graduation.

In some institutions a council serves the same purpose as the administrative board. Usually the council's composition is similar to that of the administrative board, except that members of the instructional staff, as well as administrative officers, are included. The council is usually empowered to review activities of the faculties and to consider proposals intended to increase efficiency in the educational program.

Whatever types of administrative bodies may exist in the university, it is apparent that the librarian who wishes to make the library contribute effectively to the attainment of the university's educational and administrative policies should maintain intimate contacts with them. Measures affecting the library are often discussed at the meetings of these bodies. Consequently, it is of the greatest importance that the librarian participate directly in the discussions or that he be fully informed concerning them.

LIBRARY COMMITTEES OR BOARDS. In carrying out the responsibilities involved in the administration of a large university library the services of a library committee of the trustees, of the faculty, or of librarians have usually been found to be desirable. Whether or not these committees exist depends upon the type of organization and the complexity of the situation.[11]

---

[11] McCarthy, "Advisory Committee or Administrative Board," p. 224, considers the difference between the library committee and the administrative board. See also Kientzle, "The College Librarian and the College Library Committee," *Library Quarterly*, XXI (1951), 120–26.

Few trustee committees on the library are found in American universities. It is probably a mistake to encourage board committees on the library or other units of the university. It takes the board into executive fields. It should be apparent, however, that the interests of the trustees in the library is essential, provided it is restricted to the general development of the library. It does not make for good administration if such a committee exists and takes an active part in the internal organization and administration of the library. The relationship of such a committee, as of other committees or boards on the library, should be informative and advisory.

A faculty committee or board on the library is found in most universities. Normally, it has few powers, as it is intended to serve in an advisory, rather than in an administrative, capacity. In cooperation with the librarian it concerns itself particularly with (1) formulating a library policy in relation to the development of resources for instruction and research; (2) advising in the allocation of book funds to the library and the various departments and schools; (3) advising on the policy of reproducing unique materials; (4) collaborating on decisions regarding the allocation of library space needed by departments of instruction; and (5) developing a general program of library service for all the interests of the university.[12] Acting in this capacity, it helps to keep the librarian informed concerning the library needs of the instructional and research staffs, and at the same time it assists the librarian in interpreting the library to the university. It can be useful in supporting proposals for increased book funds and for the extension of library service.

No uniformity exists in the method of selecting or designating members of such a committee or determining their number. In practice, the president, the deans, the university committee on committees, the faculty as a whole, or departmental or administrative groups have been responsible for such selection. Successful

[12] Specific suggestions for library committee activity are usually designated in library surveys, e.g., Wilson and Swank, *Report of a Survey of the Library of Stanford University, November 1946–March 1947*, pp. 31–32.

practice indicates that the responsibility is one which should be assumed by the president, and representation on the committee should be carefully considered in order that the best interests of the entire university may be served. If any one criterion for selection is to be emphasized above others, it should be interest in the development of the resources and services of the library as a whole rather than interest limited exclusively to the special field in which the member happens to work. The librarian should be a regular or ex-officio member of the committee, should meet with it, and should be responsible for the preparation of its agenda. It is desirable also that the president or some representative from the executive office sit with the committee. Representation from schools or departments, as such, should conform to standards of acceptable committee performance. In a few institutions, such as Montana State University, representatives from the student body have membership on the library committee. This raises a question which can be answered only on the basis of a local situation. At Montana, the representation has worked effectively in obtaining for the students prompt recognition of specific problems.

In addition to committees on the library of the trustees and of the faculty, the library often has relationships with other types of committees the members of which consist of librarians. Four types of such committees have been noted in university libraries; these are (1) the library council of a unified system of libraries, (2) the committee of departmental and school librarians, (3) the librarians' committee within an individual library, and (4) the committee or committees of the library staff. Each of these committees ordinarily serves a different purpose. More and more institutions apparently are establishing committees of the library staff for the preliminary examination of problems, personnel or otherwise, which are later brought to the desk of the librarian.

DEANS, HEADS OF DEPARTMENTS, AND SPECIAL COMMITTEES OF THE FACULTY. The duties of the librarian inevitably bring him into administrative relationship with deans, department heads, and committees of the faculty charged with the administration of specific activities involving expenditures, personnel, and buildings for library use. These duties may usually be divided into two classes: (1) those that relate to the acquistion of materials, and (2) those that relate to the administration of the departmental or school library.

In controlling expenditures for library materials for school, departmental, and committee purposes the librarian keeps the heads of the various units informed concerning the amount of funds allocated and spent for acquisitions. Routines are also established by the library for receiving properly authorized suggestions for purchases from each unit. The book interests of a school, department, or special committee are usually best promoted by having a member or a committee of the unit serve as library representative. Contacts between the unit and the library can thus be maintained. Frequently it is found advisable for these contacts to be maintained by a staff member or committee of the unit rather than by the head. The appointment of a representative or committee is made by the administrative head of the unit, and the representative secures suggestions from colleagues concerning materials to be ordered and transmits them to the library. In instances in which a departmental or school librarian is immediately in charge of the collection, contact is maintained through him.

These routines are followed in carrying out the normal procedures involved in the library and in departments and schools. It is also important for the librarian to cooperate with the heads of the units or their representatives in meeting unusual demands for purchases or services. The value of the librarian to the university frequently evidences itself in the success with which he handles unusual situations of this character.

The employment and direction of the library personnel who are in charge of departmental libraries or are serving on special committees are subjects for consideration by both the librarian and the administrators of the various units. Sympathetic, intelligent collaboration at this point makes for efficient administration. This aspect of the librarian's relations to administrative officers is reserved for fuller discussion in chapter iv, which deals extensively with the subject of administration.

Problems relating to the administration of library rooms or buildings for departmental or school libraries or to the planning of such quarters involve close cooperation between the librarian and the department or school concerned. In institutions in which a general governmental policy for the library has been adopted, provision is usually made for the handling of matters of this character. Obviously, it is to the advantage of the institution to utilize the expert knowledge of the librarian in planning the equipment of reading rooms, stack installations, and such other equipment and installations as will contribute to the most efficient use of the library. It is equally obvious that the library requirements of the unit concerned should be clearly and fully set forth by the responsible head in order that its needs may be fully understood and properly met. In such instances close collaboration with the offices of the president, business manager, and possibly of the trustee or faculty committee in charge of buildings may also be desirable. Lack of collaboration of this character is responsible for much of the poor planning of present library installations serving departmental and school libraries.

THE FACULTY. Mention has already been made of the administrative relationships of the librarian with the faculty. Important as this aspect of his office is, it is not more important than his role as a colleague of the teaching and research staffs in increasing library resources for their work, in providing bibliographical facilities for their use, and in improving the quality of service to them. In his capacity as colleague there are four kinds of service which the librarian can render: (1) he can assist all members of the faculty in planning for the acquisition of materials to support their activities; (2) he can keep them informed concerning the reference and bibliographic services of the library and the use of materials; (3) with members of the library staff whose competence justifies it, he may participate in the conduct of courses in bibliography and source materials in special fields open to students beginning graduate study and engaged in advanced study and research; (4) he can cooperate with other librarians, with representatives of the faculties of other institutions, with foundations and learned societies, and with governmental agencies and research bodies in carrying out cooperative undertakings the object of which is to increase the service of libraries to scholars everywhere. The provision of all four types of service calls for a high degree of managerial ability and insight into the nature of scholarship and investigation.

UNIVERSITY COMMITTEES. A tendency in some universities is to place the supervision of research and instructional work upon various committees of the faculty. The formulation of educational policies and the determination of fields in which research is to be undertaken are matters with which faculty committees sometimes deal before they are approved by the university. The policies of the institution concerning publication and extension are similarly developed. The carrying into effect of all such policies or programs involves the resources and services of the library at some point. Consequently, the library should be fully informed concerning them.

Organizing the general courses in the college of a university, setting up a program of institutional cooperation between two or more libraries, planning a system of specialization in collecting, participating in an interlibrary or bibliographical center, developing a procedure for consolidating resources of several libraries, and checking a wide range of bibliographies for a library survey of holdings suggest various ways in which university committees may be called upon to work closely with librarians.

DEPARTMENTAL AND PROFESSIONAL SCHOOL LIBRARIES. Few questions concerning university libraries have been more extensively debated and less carefully studied than the desirability of the centralized administration of special libraries for departments and schools. This matter is considered in some detail in chapter iv, which deals with the organization and administration of the library in general. It is important, however, to discuss here the relation of the librarian to the departmental or school library in its effort to build up its collections and to facilitate the work of its specialists in instruction and research. The librarian has a function to perform whether the library concerned is under his direction or not.

The nature of this function is largely determined by the fact that the librarian administers an office which is supposed to serve all the interests of the university. He is the university's expert in the field of acquiring library materials and facilitating their use. He is supposed to understand the needs of scholars; and, as a student and colleague, it is assumed that he is interested in making available the entire resources of his office in promoting the library interests of the campus, whether they come under his direct control or not. Acting in this capacity, the librarian can render several types of service to the special libraries.

The first of these may be direct assistance in the acquisition of unusual sets or collections. Frequently information concerning collections in special fields comes to his attention but not to that of the special library. Or he may be aware of the fact that other departments of the main library are interested in the materials concerned and that a combination of funds can be effected for a joint purchase. Or the general library may have unrestricted funds which can be utilized for the acquisition of materials that cannot be purchased through the regular funds of the special library. The librarian may also find it possible to interest the administration or "friends of the library," either individually or collectively, in the acquisition of material that will give strength or distinction to the institution. It is in this field that some librarians have made their greatest contributions to the universities they have served. The presence of notable collections on many campuses may be attributed to the librarian's resourcefulness in this activity.

The second type of service that the librarian may render the special library is that of providing essential catalog facilities for the expeditious use of materials. Special libraries, if they are to be used satisfactorily, must be equipped with essential catalogs or other biographical keys. In many instances this service has not been provided, or it has been provided very inadequately. Again, it frequently happens that materials have been secured by special libraries for which there are no records in the main library. It should be noted that in many cases donors would not make substantial gifts of rare materials unless the library staff and facilities were ready to support the departmental or professional school library in taking proper care of valuable gifts. In situations of this nature the librarian can be of very great use in integrating the total library resources and services of the university.

A third service may be rendered the special libraries through the use of the facilities of the general library for reproducing materials photographically or securing them from other libraries. The development of microphotographic laboratories and the exchange of materials through interlibrary loans have contributed significantly to the extension of the service which the general library can make available to all the members of a university community. The materials secured in this way through the managerial activities of the general library have added greatly to the permanent collections of a number of special libraries, as well as to the effectiveness of the research of many individual faculty members.

RESEARCH INSTITUTES AND SEMINARS. The relations of the librarian to research institutes and seminars are not essentially different from those to departmental and school libraries. There is one difference, however, in that institutes are usually less firmly established than departments or schools. They may exist for a time and then be greatly modified, or they disappear entirely. They may be established for a definite purpose which is achieved within a given time. The managerial service of the library may well be employed by the institute in building up materials rapidly; and, if the work is of a temporary nature, in distributing the materials at the end of the period. An important consideration which should be kept in mind by the director of the institute is the amount of money required for library materials and library personnel in carrying on the investigation. The librarian might well supply information concerning these requirements. They are sometimes overlooked in estimating the total cost of the undertaking; and, if support is being secured from foundations or industry or the federal government, items for this purpose should be included at the outset. The importance of preliminary studies of bibliographies in the field should not be overlooked, since they constitute the first step in many types of investigation.

Seminars on a university-wide basis have some of the characteristics of the institute. They are generally smaller and the interests are more concentrated. They may have problems of a special nature which involve the library's resources and services.

EXTENSION SERVICE. The extension service of colleges and universities usually falls into the categories either of university or of agricultural extension.[13] Both types of service embrace a wide range of subjects and activities, many of which require library support if they are to be carried on effectively. The former is usually provided by state universities; the latter, by land-grant colleges. Some private universities have maintained university extension programs, but usually they are not as widely distributed as those of state-supported institutions.[14] The libraries of private universities seldom maintain extension service, though a number of them make loans to alumni and other groups.

University extension is normally provided through a regularly organized division of extension and is concerned with the conduct of formal courses and correspondence courses off the campus and with the assistance of individuals and groups through informal services of many kinds. Beneficiaries of such service have been teachers, members of clubs, alumni, and other individuals or groups engaged in studies of various kinds. The services include public lectures, radio talks, television programs, study outlines, package libraries, the loan of pictures, musical recordings, and professional literature. Many of the state universities work closely with state libraries in the development of extension programs.

Agricultural extension is provided through land-grant colleges

[13] See National University Extension Association, *University Extension in the United States*. The NUEA has at present 76 members. This volume contains a useful bibliography on extension work.

[14] Burrell, *A History of Adult Education at Columbia University*.

and is supported in part by federal funds. Its scope and importance were considerably expended by the passage of the Smith-Lever Act of 1914. A large staff of specialists in various forms of agricultural extension is engaged in directing the work on the campus and in the various agricultural counties of each state. In the counties the work of this staff is supplemented by that of county agents and home-demonstration agents. Until recently the use of print in support of educational work of the county workers has been limited almost entirely to farm- or home-demonstration bulletins. Greater use, however, is now being made of the resources of the library of the land-grant college and of local libraries.

Organized library extension service is in some instances administered directly by the university library, as at North Carolina; in others, it is administered by the university extension service, as at the University of Florida. In the former instance, the budget for the service is included in the library budget, and the staff has membership in the library staff. In the latter, the budget and staff are separate from those of the library. In state universities which include land-grant colleges, both university and agricultural extension services may be provided. Where this is true, the opportunity for service by the library is further extended. In all instances, whatever the administrative relationship of the library may be, the resources of the library are involved; and close cooperation between the extension divisions and the library are essential if the service of the university to its constituency is to be maintained at a high level. Furthermore, such service necessitates contacts not only within the university but with other libraries and state agencies, as well as with the individuals and agencies served. In Wisconsin, for example, there are six library agencies supported by the state which supply some form of library service. Since each agency specializes in certain kinds of materials, the group as a whole has worked out an arrangement by which a request for assistance received by one agency may be forwarded to another if the latter can give more satisfactory service.

HOME STUDY. Similar administrative relationships exist between the library and the university unit engaged in offering home-study or correspondence courses.[15] It is important for library officials to be apprised of the book needs for home-study courses so that appropriate steps may be taken to provide materials for students.

LIBRARY SCHOOL. Formal education for librarianship was begun in the United States in 1887. Prior to 1923 several of the most notable schools, such as the New York State Library School and the Library School of the New York Public Library (now combined in the School of Library Service of Columbia University), were not connected with degree-conferring institutions. Since that date all library schools not formerly associated with institutes, colleges, and universities have been transferred to such institutions or have been discontinued, and all new schools have been established on college and university campuses.

The relations of the library to the library school are, in many ways, similar to those which the library maintains with other departments and schools. But they differ in two important particulars. The library may provide physical quarters in the main library building for the housing of the school, and the librarian may serve as its directing head.

In the first instance the administration of the library and school may be separate. But the library may serve as the laboratory of the school, propose problems for research, assist in carrying out investigations, provide part-time or full-time employment for library school students, build up professional materials, bibliographical apparatus, and mechanical equipment of interest to both library and school, and, by maintaining an excellent *esprit de corps*, assist in developing within students a fine professional attitude. The library may likewise profit from the stimulation of association with library-school staff members engaged in the systematic consideration of library problems of libraries of all kinds and from participation in the work of library school students who are interested in the theory, as well as the practice, of librarianship.

[15] Burrell, *A History of Adult Education at Columbia University*, chap. iii, "Home-Study." Columbia discontinued its "Home-Study" program in 1937.

In the second instance these relations are extended by the addition of others. The librarian serves as director of the library and dean of the school, prepares and administers two budgets, supervises two staffs, and is able to effect such coordination between the library and the school as he may desire. At present, four of the older accredited library schools are administered by heads who also administer the libraries. Usually, a librarian-dean receives a higher salary than a librarian, he is a member of the teaching staff, and he is automatically placed in direct contact with the teaching staff by virtue of his membership in it.[16]

The problems to which the two types of organization give rise involve not only administrative but also educational relations.[17] Whether one arrangement or the other is to be followed should be determined in the light of the specific circumstances and needs of the institution concerned and of the principles which generally apply in the organization of instruction and research in other fields.

It can be pointed out, however, that the nature of the curriculum, the program of research, the number and quality of beginning and advanced students, and the qualifications of the faculty members are matters to which serious consideration should be given. The administration of a major university library is exacting in its demands, and it may leave little time for carefully considering educational theories and practices, for keeping up with the extensive literature relating to the various subject fields of librarianship, and particularly for suitably directing students engaged in advanced study and research.[18]

OTHER LIBRARIES IN THE COMMUNITY. One of the most interesting developments noted in librarianship during the past two decades has been the effort made by librarians to increase library resources intended for research through cooperation and specialization. This

[16] Although in most institutions in which the school is administered separately from the library, the librarian has academic status.

[17] For an extended discussion of the administrative advantages and disadvantages of joint direction of library and library school and of the educational implications of such direction, see Metcalf, *et al., The Program of Instruction in Library Schools,* pp. 109–11.

[18] Berelson (ed.), *Education for Librarianship.*

effort has been expressed in a number of ways; by combining the resources of a group of institutions in a community, by developing union catalogs, by preparing surveys of collections,[19] and by participating in bibliographical centers and storage libraries.

UNION CATALOGS, STORAGE LIBRARIES, AND BIBLIOGRAPHICAL AND INTERLIBRARY CENTERS. One of the principal means employed in cooperative enterprises has been union catalogs. University librarians have participated in their development; and in 1954, union catalogs at Atlanta, Cleveland, Nashville, and Seattle were housed in university library buildings.[20]

An allied movement has been the development of bibliographical centers. For many years a number of the major university libraries have not only maintained catalogs of their own collections but have assembled cards published by the Library of Congress and other scholarly libraries. These cards, brought together in a special catalog, have been used principally for the purposes of locating books not owned by the library and of supplying bibliographical and other information of use to the patrons of the library. Such card collections, when combined with extensive bibliographical apparatus and regional union catalogs, have proved valuable not only in locating materials but in supplying many kinds of information helpful to the development of library cooperation and specialization. Such undertakings have been described in library literature.[21]

Another activity in this area which should be noted is the storage library. This idea has been realized in the New England Deposit Library, a project which has been discussed at length by Doherty.[22]

[19] For example, see Downs, *The Resources of New York City Libraries.*

[20] One of the most recent surveys of various activities and problems of union catalogs is found in Sherwood and Campion, "Union Library Catalogue: Services, 1950. Quo Vadis?" *College and Research Libraries,* XIII (1952), 101–6+. An earlier publication which summarized basic problems is Downs (ed.), *Union Catalogs in the United States.*

[21] *Ibid.;* see also Bibliographical Planning Committee of Philadelphia. *Philadelphia Libraries,* "Regional Library Centers Today: A Symposium," *College and Research Libraries,* VIII (1947), 54–69; Esterquest, "Regional Library Centers, 1946–47," *College and Research Libraries,* IX (1948), 215–20.

[22] Doherty, "The New England Deposit Library: History and Development," *Library Quarterly,* XVIII (1948), 245–54; "The New England Deposit Library: Organization and Administration," *Library Quarterly,* XIX (1949), 1–18.

The theory of the storage library is to house books which are used less frequently in a central building so that economy in shelving may be achieved, and, at the same time, minimize duplication and spur specialization in collecting. Harvard has borne the initial cost in the project, but upkeep is shared by the participating libraries. While the storage library does relieve pressure on building space, Doherty observes that it has not eliminated duplication, and specialization is minimal.

A final development that warrants attention is the Midwest Inter-Library Center, established as a corporation in 1949 for the purpose of fostering cooperation in the Midwest. Its headquarters are on the University of Chicago campus, and at present sixteen libraries are participating members.[23] It represents one of the important developments in cooperation, and has been considered in relation to similar proposals in the Northeast, the West Coast, and Washington, D.C.

Participation in these activities has given the university librarian his greatest opportunity (sometimes not recognized or fully appreciated) not only for demonstrating his understanding of the instructional and research functions of the university but also for showing a like understanding of the essential unity of knowledge and the necessity of cooperation. The utilization of methods of reproducing materials through photography, sound recordings, and microreproduction has likewise extended his range of activities and increased his possibilities for distinguished service.

STUDENTS. The relation of the librarian to students seems, in most instances, indirect and remote. His contact with them is largely through others, particularly through those members of his staff responsible for the operation of the general information and circulation desks, special reading and reference rooms, and the special libraries of departments, divisions, schools, and institutes. There are, however, many ways in which his relation to students is ex-

[23] For detailed statements on the work of the Center, see its *Newsletter*, 1949+ and *Annual Reports*, 1950+. See also Esterquest, "Midwest Inter-Library Center: Acquisition Policy and Program, 1950–1953," *College and Research Libraries*, XV (1954), 47–49+.

pressed. One or two of these are administrative in nature. The librarian is responsible for the quiet, effective operation of all library services in order that student use of the library may be educationally profitable. He is charged also with the responsibility of seeing that certain students do not limit the use of the library for other students by the infringement of library rules.

The role of the librarian in the educational activities of the student may, however, be important, particularly if the librarian is thought of as serving the student directly and through his staff. The librarian or an appropriate staff member may acquaint the student with the library during orientation week. He may aid student advisers in extending the student's knowledge of the library through certain library services or types of publications. The reference librarian may perform a similar service. Formal courses in the use of books and libraries or assistance to students reading for honors or preparing term papers afford other opportunities. The organization and display of attractive exhibits may likewise stimulate student interest in different aspects of the work of the library.

Through special courses in bibliography and in introductory courses in graduate study offered generally by universities throughout the country, the librarian can contribute by acquainting the student with general catalogs, indexes, and handbooks which students in all departments will have occasion to use. The literature relating to special fields can be left to the specialists in the department. Participation in seminars at which source materials are discussed also gives the librarian the opportunity for establishing closer relationships with students.

The librarian can likewise be brought into effective relationship with the undergraduate student by promoting student use of leisure time in reading. Through the browsing room, the house library, the bookstore in the library, and informal readings by authors, and guidance by the instructional and library staff, opportunities are provided for extending the range of the students' contacts with books and to promote the library as a more effective educational and cultural instrument for the entire university.

One of the most important relations of the library to the student grows out of student employment in carrying on the work of the library. Through his activities in the library the student assistant sometimes discovers his interest in librarianship as a profession, and his training can be directed by the librarian to that end. Many librarians have begun their professional careers in this way.

COUNSELING OFFICE. Even though counseling offices existed before World War II and the Korean War, they have taken on heavier duties since the growth in enrollments in universities. Many personal and psychological problems have developed among students, and these sometimes are reflected in library situations. The librarian and members of his staff work closely with the counseling officers in an effort to help students with their problems. This relation requires a deep understanding on the part of the librarian of human difficulties, particularly in relation to effective educational work.

REGISTRAR. The librarian or appropriate members of his staff maintains relations with the registrar's office in connection with problems arising from library privileges and situations of discipline. It is frequently necessary to obtain approval for the use of the library by certain individuals, and information is ordinarily supplied by the registrar's office. The library should be informed of withdrawals of students or departures of faculty members. The office is also sometimes used to put pressure on students who are delinquent in returning books, or for refusal to pay fines. As a rule, librarians prefer to adjust situations of this kind without using the force of the registrar, who can withhold grades or even a diploma.

BUSINESS OFFICERS. Another major line of relationships which the librarian maintains with other members of the university community is that with the officers who are responsible for (1) the direction of the financial and business affairs of the university or (2) the administration of some special business activity. In many institutions some of the officers concerned with general financial administration are, like the librarian, responsible directly to the president. In others the comptroller and possibly other officers are directly responsible to the governing body but work in close co-operation with the president. Regardless of the type of organization and the titles of the officers, the administration of the library is related to these officers in a variety of ways. In state universities these activities may also involve state officers, particularly the director of the budget or the budget commission; but, if they do, it is usually through an officer of the university.

The three principal administrative relations which the librarian maintains with the business officers are: (1) the preparation and administration of the budget, (2) the acquisition of materials, and (3) the employment of personnel. These relations will now be considered briefly, but an extended consideration of the financial administration of the library will be found in chapter iii.

It is assumed that all university libraries operate on a budget which covers the estimated receipts and expenditures for library purposes. It was noted in the discussion of the librarian's relation to the president that the latter was, in most institutions, the chief budget officer. In some instances some other officer may perform this function. However, in the preparation of the library budget the librarian, after consultation with staff members, heads of departments, schools, and institutes, and the library committee of the faculty, submits the estimate of budget needs to the president for review. Information is supplied on all matters requiring special consideration, and the president includes the items for the library in the general budget submitted to the governing board. This consolidated budget may be presented by the president first to the finance committee of the governing body and then to the body as a whole. In institutions in which the comptroller is directly responsible to the governing body he may also be involved in the preparation of the budget. He or the finance committee of the governing body may be responsible for estimating income from endowment and other sources and seeing that the proposed expenditures do not exceed the estimated income.

In state and municipal universities the budgetary procedures may be handled somewhat differently, in that the estimates are usually prepared for a biennium. It should be noted, however, that although biennial estimates may be preferred by legislatures, the working budget will be annual. The data concerning the library are prepared as indicated above, but the consolidated budget prepared by the president and other responsible officers and approved by the governing body is reviewed and modified by the municipal or state budget officer. It may likewise be further modified by the appropriating body. Even after it is adopted, it may be subject to periodic review and further modified in accord with legislation governing it. The preparation and administration of the budget of the library consequently call for close cooperation between the librarian, on the one hand, and the president or other responsible officers, on the other.

Libraries in both private and public universities are frequently the beneficiaries of gifts and endowment to be employed in specific ways. The financial administration of such funds is usually left to the finance committee of the governing body or to the financial officer of the institution. It is also necessary in such instances for the purchasing agent and the librarian to have full information about such funds in order that they may be expended for the purposes intended and that the accounts may be kept properly. The importance of this relationship is indicated by the fact that all the book funds for the Harvard College Library (as differentiated from the University) come under this classification rather than under that of appropriations from the University.

When the budget is officially approved, the librarian can more or less pursue his own course of expenditure, subject only to the budgetary limitations and business procedures imposed. It is one of the duties of the business officer to see that these limitations are observed. He may have the added power of limiting expenditures during any given period. In many institutions, moreover, all proposed expenditures require at least the nominal approval of this officer, although this authority is often delegated to the librarian as far as book purchases are concerned. In some states the purchasing agent or auditor may refuse to authorize payments for materials unless there is strict compliance with detailed instructions.

The usual routine in most universities in the purchase of supplies and equipment is fairly simple. The librarian forwards such requisitions as are required to the business office or purchasing agent. The centralization of all purchasing occurs at this point. It is common, too, that estimates on contemplated purchase of major items be procured through the centralized office. Disbursements and payment of bills are also centralized.

The procedures which the librarian of a state university must follow in ordering books, materials, and supplies may differ considerably from those in a private institution. As a rule, they are more involved because expenditures are subject to the control of state budget officers, as well as that of the institution of which the library is a unit. The procedures also vary from state to state. In a study by Kelly and McNeely [24] in 1933 of state purchasing agency practice, three common patterns of control were found. Purchasing was centralized under (1) a single person's direction, or (2) that of a board, or (3) there might be no agency at all. Most states now have centralized purchasing. In many cases, however, the state university and a few other institutions are exempted by statute from its control.

These relationships call for close cooperation between the librarian and the business office. Particular care should be exercised by both officers to insure speed in ordering and delivering materials and in approving invoices for payment. Failure in these particulars leads to complaints by the faculty and students for whom materials are desired, and detracts greatly from efficient service. If the invoices are not paid promptly, the institution forfeits discounts usually allowed for prompt payment.

The employment of library personnel usually involves the president's office and that of the business manager. Appointments to both the professional and nonprofessional staffs are made upon the recommendation of the librarian. They may be considered by the

[24] *The State and Higher Education: Phases of Their Relationship.*

president only or by the president and the business manager. When appointments are made to the professional staff and recommendations concerning faculty status are involved, they are usually submitted to the president and, if approved, transmitted by him to the governing body. When appointment is made to the clerical staff, the recommendation may be submitted to the business officer. Questions of annuities, withholding of tax, social security, and insurance are handled directly with the business office.

The status of staff members, both professional and nonprofessional, involves matters with which both the president and business manager must deal and for which the university must develop specific regulations. The librarian should be fully informed concerning all these requirements and should cooperate with other officers in seeing that the library staff complies with them properly. At the same time, the librarian should insist that the status and remuneration of the staff, like that of the instructional staff, should be determined by means of a carefully devised personnel classification scheme based upon the training, competence, experience, and responsibilities of its members.[25] In the last decade more and more university libraries have followed the lead of public and government libraries in providing personnel classifications. There are some institutions, however, which still classify professional and scientific workers with nonprofessional and clerical staff.

One other relation between the librarian and the business office may be noted. The business office is usually the introducer of new mechanical devices for increasing the efficiency of clerical work. Many of the inventions are adaptable to library purposes. Librarians can learn of these if they keep in close touch with the business office. Sometimes they may share the use of such equipment as punched-card machines. Often the business office can help to explain and work out adaptations of equipment for library purposes.

The librarian, of course, may have direct contacts with equipment firms, usually prior to any consideration for purchase through

25 See American Library Association. Board on Personnel Administration, *Position Classification and Salary Administration in Libraries.*

the business office. Many librarians have worked out simplified forms and labor-saving devices through the assistance of specialists from firms concerned with management efficiency.

The librarian also maintains relations with another group of business officers or units of the general business office. These include: (1) the office of buildings and grounds, (2) the university press, (3) the bookstore, and (4) the rental library. Occasionally the library is involved also in a business relationship with a branch library of a public library.

BUILDINGS AND GROUNDS. The library, like other units of the university, is dependent upon the office of buildings and grounds for a number of services. The buildings and grounds department may be under the business office or may be independently responsible to the president. In most universities this office is responsible for (1) the operation of the university plant, (2) janitorial service, and (3) maintenance of university property. When extensive repairs or installations of equipment are required which call for special expenditures, they are likely to come under the jurisdiction of the president or business manager, even if they are carried out by this department. The librarian will find it desirable also to participate in the planning and in the supervision of the work.

Janitorial service is usually centralized under the buildings and grounds office. Work schedules of the janitors should be arranged jointly by the librarian and the department. Provision should be made for special services, such as book cleaning, floor waxing, packing and unpacking outgoing and incoming shipments (unless there is a library shipping department), moving books and equipment, and maintaining interlibrary deliveries of materials on the campus. Regular cleaning of the building, periodic decoration, prompt attention to lighting difficulties, adequate elevator operation, and other services, if properly rendered, contribute greatly to the efficiency of the administration of the library and should be given the consideration they deserve.

THE UNIVERSITY PRESS. The university press is an organization which has assumed increasing importance in American universities since 1900. Of the 35 presses which were members of the Association of American University Presses in 1949, Kerr found that 27 have had the status of a division or department of the university.[26] The remaining eight presses had separate corporate status. The presses may own their plants, or they may use commercial printers.

Whatever the organization under which they carry on this work, they are usually responsible for the publication of books, periodicals, university studies, and official catalogs and announcements of the university. If they own their plants, they may engage in printing stationery, forms, and other materials used by the university.

Obviously, these activities are of interest to the library. First of all, it is essential that the library receive copies of all publications of the university. Next, the library is usually charged with the maintenance of exchanges with other institutions. To carry on this activity successfully, it is important for it to have placed at its disposal sufficient copies of press publications to meet its needs. For these purposes the library should have a working arrangement with the press that would be fair to both, since both are engaged in the service of the university. If the library's exchange policy with respect to press publications is sound and carefully worked out—in other words, not an uncontrolled give-away policy—it does not matter whether funds involved in the transaction are placed on the library budget or the press budget. Probably a policy may be best worked out by a joint committee of library and press officials. Financial and bookkeeping curbs are needed if the library is indiscriminate in distribution. A special arrangement is also necessary when the press is separately incorporated.

If the library school is under the direction of the librarian and the official printing of the university is handled by the press, the publication of the school catalog and of any publications the school may issue will be handled by the press. The printing department of the press may also undertake certain services for the library, such as printing stationery, catalog cards, and forms used in library

[26] Kerr, *A Report on American University Presses*, p. 63. Chapter 3 deals with "Relations with the University."

routines. The library may cooperate with the press in the maintenance of a special collection on printing and the graphic arts; and the librarian, because of his knowledge of printing and publication, may serve as a member of the board of governors.

THE BOOKSTORE. The librarian's relations with the bookstore may involve both business transactions and cooperation in the stimulation of reading and book ownership. A number of university libraries have arrangements with the campus bookstores for the purchase of current books and supplies. It may be necessary to work out satisfactory discount agreements in cases of book purchases and to make certain that library orders will be given prompt attention.

The librarian may well justify his interest in reading by seeing that association with and ownership of books are made possible through the medium of an attractive bookstore. He may cooperate with the bookstore by participating in book talks and readings, by advising in the arrangement of exhibits of books and related library materials, and by sponsoring competition for the best student libraries.

THE RENTAL LIBRARY. Rental libraries make it possible for students to obtain books which are not subject to strict limitations of books placed on reserve or even of books loaned from the stacks for two weeks. Faculty members and faculty families also may make use of their services. The charges for the use of books are relatively low. The rental library is operated in various ways by different universities. It may be part of the university library, and associated with the reserve book room. In cases of this kind, reserve books may even circulate for a small charge. The ordinary rental books circulate for as long as the borrower wants them. The income may be used to pay for items added to the reserve or rental collection. The rental library may also be operated by the bookstore, and may have similar arrangements for the borrowing of books used in the curriculum. There are some rental libraries which specialize only in recent nonfiction and fiction titles. Used copies may be later sold to the library, or to students and faculty members. Finally, the rental library may be a part of a bookstore which is in the library building. At North Carolina, the rental library of the Bull's Head Shop, in the library, features general rather than curricular reading.

BRANCH LIBRARY OF THE PUBLIC LIBRARY. Infrequently the university library may house a branch of the public library. This is true in the case of the library of Columbia University. The University of Chattanooga shares a library building with the city public library. There are apparent advantages in such arrangements. On the credit side, the university gains for its clientele an additional book collection of considerable value, and it is saved from duplicating materials which otherwise it might have to obtain. On the other hand, the presence of a public library, unless it is immediately accessible from the street, as it is at Columbia, may interfere with the administration of the library. Special regulations regarding registration and use of the university library are usually necessary to avoid such interference. The service of the university in granting such space may be regarded as extension work, although the university does not provide the personnel for the library.

OTHER GROUPS. The relationships which the library maintains with administrative officers, the faculty, and financial and business officers have been considered in the preceding discussion. The library also maintains relations with a more heterogeneous group which is found in the university community. This usually includes: (1) the general public, (2) the families of faculty members and administrative officers, (3) employees of the university, (4) alumni, (5) members of the "friends-of-the-library" group, and (6) visiting librarians and scholars.

The library may serve the general public through its extension service or through a public library operated in the university library building. It may allow borrowing privileges to the residents of the immediate community. The library of Rutgers University, which is the state university of New Jersey, allows borrowing privileges to all residents of the state. Fees are sometimes charged to the general public for the use of the library. Free use of materials for reference purposes is generally permitted all persons who request such privileges. One of the conditions governing the distribution of public documents by the federal government to depository libraries is that they shall be available for reference purposes without cost. The extent to which a university library, particularly if it is a private institution, is justified in serving the public is contingent primarily upon its budget and the general policy of community service. If service to the public results in poorer service to faculty and students, it is obviously inadvisable to provide it.

Members of the families of faculty members and administrative officers and employees of the university are usually accorded the use of the library; and, in some institutions, the library extends special service to alumni, both in the university and at a distance. In its service to alumni the library may have the cooperation of the alumni office, as such service may constitute a part of a general program of the university in maintaining close relations with the alumni.

The "friends-of-the-library" movement has developed rather rapidly since 1910, and a number of such organizations are to be found connected with university libraries. They are interested primarily in building up the collections of the library, rather than in library use. They can be very helpful in providing unrestricted funds for library use, in acquiring special materials, and in making known the needs of the library to the public.

The privileges of the library are usually accorded visiting librarians and scholars. The responsibility for making arrangements for extending such privileges is generally placed upon the librarian, though in some universities, where there are many requests for the use of laboratories and other facilities, arrangements may be made by the departments immediately concerned. In recent years, some private universities have found it desirable to charge library fees for those who are not taking courses currently in the institutions.[27] There have been some protests from scholars at this innovation.

[27] See "Fees for Research Library Use by 'Outsiders': A Symposium," *College and Research Libraries*, XIII (1952), 295–302. Four statements by Wylie Sypher, Keyes D. Metcalf, Carl M. White, and Louis R. Wilson.

SUMMARY   Three major problems of the university library have been discussed in this chapter. They are: (1) the legal bases upon which the government of the university (and through it the library) rest; (2) the provisions which a sound governmental policy for the library should contain; and (3) the relations which the librarian must maintain with other officers and members of the university and university community in the successful administration of the library.

The successful administration of the library depends, in large measure, upon the clarity of the understanding which the university and the library have of these matters. The president of the university and the librarian alike must know what the essentials of a sound, well-conceived governmental policy for the library are. The president must place the librarian in such a position that it will be possible for the latter to adjust the services of the library effectively to the various interests of the university. University library administration frequently breaks down at this point. Finally, it is imperative that the librarian match the opportunities presented him with the understanding, imagination, and resourcefulness which the administration of a university library devoted to the furtherance of instruction and research requires. The library is an integral part—an indispensable part—of the university. It serves all the university interests. Consequently, whatever contributes to its efficient organization and administration contributes directly and greatly to the university's total achievement.

BIBLIOGRAPHY

American Library Association. Board on Personnel Administration. Personnel Organization and Procedure: A Manual Suggested for Use in College and University Libraries. Chicago, American Library Association, 1952.

American Library Association. Board on Personnel Administration. Position Classification and Salary Administration in Libraries. Chicago, American Library Association, 1951.

Baker, John C. Directors and Their Functions. Boston, Harvard University, Graduate School of Business Administration, 1945.

Beals, Ralph A. Aspects of Post-Collegiate Education. New York, American Association for Adult Education, 1935.

Beck, Hubert P. Men Who Control Our Universities: The Economic and Social Composition of Governing Boards of Thirty Leading American Universities. New York, King's Crown Press, 1947.

Berelson, Bernard (ed.). Education for Librarianship: Papers Presented at the Library Conference, University of Chicago, August 16–21, 1948. Chicago, American Library Association, 1949.

Bibliographical Planning Committee of Philadelphia. Philadelphia Libraries: A Survey of Facilities, Needs and Opportunities. Philadelphia, University of Pennsylvania, 1942.

Brody, Alexander. The American State and Higher Education: The Legal, Political, and Constitutional Relationships. Washington, American Council on Education, 1935.

Burrell, John A. A History of Adult Education at Columbia University: University Extension and the School of General Studies. New York, Columbia University Press, 1954.

Carlson, William H. The Development and Financial Support of Seven Western and Northwestern State University Libraries. Berkeley, University of California Press, 1938.

——— "History and Present Status of the Centralization of the Libraries of the Oregon State System of Higher Education," *College and Research Libraries,* XIV (1953), 414–17.

Chambers, M. M. The Colleges and the Courts, 1946–50; Judicial Decisions Regarding Higher Education in the United States. New York, Columbia University Press, 1952. There were three earlier volumes covering the period from 1819 to 1945.

——— "Higher Education and the Courts in 1940–41," *Educational Record,* XXIII (1942), 58–82.

Chicago, University of. Commission on the Future Policy of the University Libraries. Tentative Report, January, 1924. Chicago, University of Chicago Press, 1924.

Danton, J. Periam. Education for Librarianship: Criticisms, Dilemmas, and Proposals. New York, School of Library Service, Columbia University, 1946.

Doherty, Francis X. "The New England Deposit Library: History and Development," *Library Quarterly,* XVIII (1948), 245–54.

——— "New England Deposit Library: The Organization and Administration," *Library Quarterly,* XIX (1949), 1–18.

Downs, Robert B. "Academic Status for University Librarians: A New Approach," *College and Research Libraries,* XII (1946), 6–9+.

——— The Resources of New York City Libraries. Chicago, American Library Association, 1942.

Downs, Robert B. (ed.). Union Catalogs in the United States. Chicago, American Library Association, 1942.

Elliott, Edward C., *et al.* The Government of Higher Education. New York, American Book Co., 1935.

Esterquest, Ralph T. "Midwest Inter-Library Center: Acquisition Policy and Program, 1950–1953," *College and Research Libraries*, XV (1954), 47–49+.

Grieder, Elmer M. "The Reorganization of the Stanford University Libraries," *College and Research Libraries*, XIII (1952), 246–52.

Hofstadter, Richard, and C. DeWitt Hardy. The Development and Scope of Higher Education in the United States. Published for the Commission on Financing Higher Education. New York, Columbia University Press, 1952.

Kelly, Fred J., and J. H. McNeely. The State and Higher Education: Phases of Their Relationships. New York, Carnegie Foundation for the Advancement of Teaching, 1933.

Kerr, Chester. A Report on American University Presses. [Washington] American Association of University Presses, 1949.

Kientzle, Elizabeth. "The College Librarian and the Library Committee," *Library Quarterly*, XXI (1951), 120–26.

McCarthy, Stephen A. "Advisory Committee or Administrative Board?" *Library Quarterly*, XXII (1952), 223–31.

Metcalf, Keyes D., *et al.* The Program of Instruction in Library Schools. Urbana, University of Illinois Press, 1943.

Miller, Robert A. "Centralization versus Decentralization," *Bulletin of the American Library Association*, XXXIII (1939), 75–79.

National Education Association. Department of Higher Education. Current Issues in Higher Education. Washington, 1945.

National University Extension Association. University Extension in the United States. John R. Morton, director. [Birmingham] University of Alabama Press, 1953.

North Carolina. Commission on University Consolidation. Report. Raleigh, 1932.

Powell, Lawrence Clark. "Education for Academic Librarianship," in Bernard Berelson (ed.), *Education for Librarianship; Papers Presented at the Library Conference, University of Chicago, August 16–21, 1948*. Chicago, American Library Association, (1949), pp. 133–46. Other papers in this volume, particularly those by Louis R. Wilson and Bernard Berelson, are relevant to the problem of training the academic librarian.

Reece, Ernest J. The Task and Training of Librarians. New York, King's Crown Press, 1949.

Sherwood, Janice W., and Eleanor E. Campion, "Union Library Catalogues: Services, 1950. Quo Vadis?" *College and Research Libraries,* XII (1952), 101–6+.

Shores, Louis. Origins of the American College Library, 1638–1800. Nashville, Tenn., Peabody College for Teachers, 1934.

Wheeler, Joseph L. Progress and Problems in Education for Librarianship. New York, Carnegie Corporation of New York, 1946.

Wilson, Louis R., and R. C. Swank. Report of a Survey of the Library of Stanford University for Stanford University, November 1946–March 1947. Chicago, American Library Association, 1947.

Wilson, Louis R., *et al.* Report of a Survey of the University of Florida Library for the University of Florida, February–May, 1940. Chicago, American Library Association, 1940 (mimeographed).

Works, George A. College and University Library Problems. Chicago, American Library Association, 1927.

See also relevant chapters in surveys of libraries. (See Bibliography in chapter xvi).

III

FINANCIAL ADMINISTRATION

THE EFFECTIVE administration of the finances of a university library requires considerable skill on the part of the librarian, since budgets of several university libraries range from $500,000 to $1,000,000 or more annually and involve the employment of staffs of more than one hundred members, not including student assistants. The largest staff in 1954 numbered 358, with a payroll of $1,107,510. Another library, with a staff of 299, budgeted $1,433,031 for staff and student assistant salaries.[1] Although the library, unlike a business enterprise, is relieved of the necessity of making a profit, the librarian is expected to use efficiently the funds put at his disposal.[2] To do this he should be familiar with the methods which are employed in the administration of institutions of higher education.

[1] "Statistics for College and University Libraries, 1953–54." In addition to their expenditures for salaries, 30 libraries spent from $101,010 to $506,422 for books, periodicals, and binding in the same year. Seven libraries reported total operating expenditures of over $1,000,000.

[2] Millett, *Financing of Higher Education in the United States.* (The Staff Report of the Commission on Financing Higher Education), pp. 122–26. Millett's observations on the financing of libraries aroused some university administrators, as well as legislative bodies, as to the alleged failure of librarians to solve their problems economically. The effect of the statements in the Millett volume was to raise questions in the minds of some regarding the growing size of libraries, the rising costs of service, and competition among librarians. Millett observed: "Librarians rate the importance of their jobs and examine their salary scale in the light of the size of their book collections, the number of their employees, and their total expenditures. The librarian [sic] profession as such puts little emphasis on economy; the pressure comes from college presidents and deans when they make up the annual budget," p. 123. In his review of the Millett volume, Wyllis E. Wright calls attention to the failure to supply evidence for these generalizations, and points up some of the developments in modern librarianship which question the charges. See W. E. Wright, "Financing College Libraries," *College and Research Libraries,* XIV (1953), 342–44; Archie L. McNeal, "Financial Problems of University Libraries," *College and Research Libraries,* XV (1954), 407–10+; and Melvin J. Voigt, "Ratio of Professional to Clerical Staff," *College Research Libraries,* XVI (1955), 76–77.

Following the administrative principle of grouping homogeneous functions under a single authority, most universities have centralized business activities under a business manager. Functions ordinarily assigned to this office include financial accounting (involving budget control), collection of revenues, purchasing, payment of bills, selling, supervision of stores, financial reporting, assistance in budget formulation, plant supervision, supervision of supplementary business activities, financial relations with students, and endowment management. In varying degrees, the university library is involved in each of these. This chapter will describe four major aspects of financial administration of the university library: (1) business functions and relationships, (2) sources of income, (3) budgetary procedure, and (4) accounting and financial reporting.

BUSINESS FUNCTIONS   The library system of a university is seldom
AND RELATIONSHIPS   large enough to warrant the establishment
                       of a separate office to handle all its business
matters. In a few of the larger university libraries assistant directors have been assigned the responsibility of handling many of the business activities. These generally include payroll and accounting, supplies, building and equipment, telephone service, personnel, correspondence, and files. In several libraries, assistants to the director have charge of personnel. In the majority of libraries, however, business functions are not centralized. Instead, the activities are generally handled by the librarian, with the help of one or more assistant directors, office assistants, an executive secretary, and the head of the acquisitions department.

The business functions of every library involve relationships with the business office of the university. In state institutions the relationships may differ considerably from those in institutions which are privately supported. The differences appear principally in purchasing and accounting activities, but may also involve personnel in civil service situations.[3] Certain business functions, however, are performed in libraries of both private and public institutions. These

[3] See chap. ii.

are: (a) bookkeeping, (b) recording income, (c) purchasing, (d) paying bills, (e) obtaining discounts, (f) collecting fines, (g) receiving deposits, and (h) evaluating for insurance.

BOOKKEEPING   Two sets of books are usually kept for university library expenditures—one in the business office and the other in the librarian's office. Although the totals of the two records should agree, different classifications of data are included in each. Records kept by the library are broken down in considerable detail. It is important that they show expenditures by the general library and its subdivisions, by the various departments and other university organizations, and by all classifications or divisions set up in the budget. They should show, for example, the balance of the history department's book budget or how much the catalog department has spent on hourly service. In regard to book purchases, the kind of bookkeeping a library must undertake requires that each account be debited by the estimated cost of each order when the order is placed and that this charge must be revised when the invoices are received. Bookkeeping records have been successfully kept by the use of accounting machines at several university libraries. These machines are usually designed for large-scale operations, and in any plan to use them arrangements should be made to provide the library office with frequent statements.

The results of bookkeeping have a direct relationship to budget-making and supply the record of expenditure to use in making appropriations for the coming year. Whereas a budget is, in a sense, a norm by which to guide performance, bookkeeping is a means by which expenditure is controlled in accordance with the budgetary norms. The bookkeeping records of the business office are more concerned with totals which may be charged under a comparatively few budgetary classifications and with the prompt payment of bills.

RECORDING INCOME   The responsibility for collecting revenues for the whole institution is usually lodged in the business office of the university. Student fees which are earmarked for the library and income from library endowments and special funds are collected by the business office. Monetary gifts as grants-in-aid for the library are also received and disbursed through the business office. The library, however, usually collects fines and rental fees; and it may be charged with the responsibility of sanctioning other fees and payments for duplicates and library publications sold to other institutions. When the statutes of the institution permit, the library office may be held responsible for handling student and nonstudent deposits which are held to cover fines or possible loss of books. Sums collected in various parts of the library are accumulated in the library office.

PURCHASING   The usual routine for the purchase of books and supplies is fairly simple in the private university. The librarian prepares orders for materials in accord with routines established by the business office and sends them to the business office or purchasing agent. The orders are then checked and forwarded by the purchasing agent. Standardized materials, such as typewriters and carbon papers, are ordered by the business office on the basis of the annual estimates from the various units of the institution.

The system of purchasing for the state university may be more complex than that for the library of an endowed institution.[4] Depending upon state laws, the librarian may be required to follow one of four procedures. He may be required: (1) to purchase all supplies, including books and periodicals, through the state purchasing agent; (2) to order all materials and books through a central library order department; (3) to secure library books and supplies through the university purchasing agent; or (4) to buy all supplies independently. The third practice appears to be the prevalent practice. Even where this exists, however, some items may be

[4] See, for example, Tauber and Wilson, *Report of a Survey of the Library of Montana State University, January–May, 1951*, pp. 60–62; Orr and Carlson, *Report of a Survey of the Library of Texas A. and M. College, October, 1949, to February, 1950*, pp. 98–100.

purchased directly by the librarian. Purchasing through a central library department of a state is a rare procedure.[5] Although not recommended as an ideal procedure by purchasing experts, acquiring materials through a state purchasing agent is relatively frequent.[6] Few librarians are permitted to buy all supplies independently of the business office.

Variations, of course, exist in all of the above procedures except that of the central library order department of the state. The variations may concern the time and form of the requisitions, the number of copies of the requisition, the proper authorization, the routine for the itemization of supplies and materials, and the specifications of the dealer. Since the purchase of books and certain library materials requires specialized knowledge, the purchasing office generally welcomes the suggestion of names of qualified dealers. State statutes, however, may specify that the purchasing agent of the state or of the university must submit the list of materials to several dealers for bids. They may also require bids for materials costing more than a given amount (e.g., $100 or more) and forbid the purchase of materials from members of the governing body or officers of the library. In most institutions, in which purchasing is based upon quarterly, rather than annual, allotments of funds, exceptions may be made in the case of the library for the purchase of books and periodicals. The library may also be granted a contingent fund, held by the university purchasing agent for the

[5] Carlson, "History and Present Status of Centralization of the Libraries of the Oregon State System of Higher Education," pp. 414–417. Carlson points out that the original plan to purchase materials for all Oregon institutions in the system had to be modified, because the University of Oregon at Eugene had too extensive an order business. The Central Library office at Corvallis has continued to handle the complete order process for the College of Education Libraries. Centralized bookkeeping for these libraries also has been successful.

[6] Orr and Carlson, *Report of a Survey of the Library of Texas A. and M. College*, pp. 99–100. At Texas A. and M., "All serials, including periodicals, must be purchased through the State Board of Control on a contract basis. A contract is let for American and Canadian periodicals. Another contract is let for English periodicals, and still another one is let for domestic scientific and technical periodicals." The State Board of Control, at the time of the survey, insisted on asking for bids on such items, even though only one publisher might be involved and the subscription price was fixed.

purchase of books as needed.[7] In other cases the university may have separate or special funds which may be exempt from such regulation. It is evident that the librarian of a state institution which has to comply with the regulations of a central purchasing agency operating on a quarterly basis is more restricted in placing orders than is the librarian of a private institution in which there are no such requirements.

In some state and private institutions the library is given complete authority in purchasing books, periodicals, and continuations. Under this arrangement the order department of the library receives bids for periodicals, seeks discounts on books, makes out purchase orders, and places orders directly with dealers. The business office requires copies of orders for accounting purposes. Supplies and equipment are more frequently obtained through the university purchasing agent.

PAYMENT OF BILLS   University business offices usually specify that invoices be supplied in duplicate, triplicate, or quadruplicate, depending upon the number of officers needing a copy of each invoice. The library order department checks materials received against the requisition and invoice. A copy of the invoice is retained in the library for bookkeeping purposes, and the other copies go to the business office for distribution. Library vouchers approving payment, signed by the librarian, the order librarian, or the assistant in charge of orders, accompany the invoices. Payment of bills is made by the business office.[8]

For the payment of minor freight charges and small purchases

[7] Tauber and Wilson, *Report of a Survey of the Library of Montana State University*, p. 61. In 1949, the Montana State University Library "was given the authority to purchase small items (less than $1.00) from a postage fund established for the Library by the Controller. This postage fund which varies between $75.00 and $100.00 annually is requested in the Librarian's Annual Budget. The Acquisitions Librarian or his delegated authority requisitions portions of this from the Business Office in amounts of not less than $25.00. In requisitioning from this fund account is given of how the previous amount has been dispersed, i.e., so much for postage, so much for printed matter."

[8] Bennett, "Prompt Payment of Bookdealers' Invoices," *College and Research Libraries*, XIV (1953), 387-92+. This is a useful article in pointing out the factors involved and the problems which arise in the clearance of invoices in libraries.

needed in emergency, it is not unusual for the library to use funds from petty cash. Transportation and freight charges which involve relatively large sums are paid by the business office and charged against the appropriation of the library.

DISCOUNTS   Discounts on library purchases, always a matter of interest to librarians, are of two kinds: (1) discounts of a small percentage on the total amount of the invoice usually granted when invoices are paid promptly [9] and (2) discounts of a larger percentage on the prices of individual books included in the invoices. Since the small discount is not allowed unless payment is made within a given period, the librarian is obligated to check invoices promptly and turn them over to the business office for payment.

The second type of discount is that received from book dealers on books. College and university libraries generally do not receive discounts as large as those obtained by large public libraries. Frequently, public libraries advertise for bids from jobbers who supply current American books for a given period of time. A large public library, for example, may let its book contract to the lowest bidder for each calendar year. The bid is based on discounts later applicable to different book-trade categories, such as the usual trade books, textbooks, scientific and technical books, popular copyrights, and reprints. The successful bidder may also allow an additional discount on quantity orders, such as fifty copies or more, depending on the title.

Although many university libraries work with book and periodical budgets which are as large as or larger than those of public libraries, quantity buying is kept to a minimum, except for rental and reserve book collections. Moreover, the university library buys single copies of most items, as well as many foreign and out-of-print titles. These two factors—small quantity buying and the need

[9] In an early study, *Efficiency in College Management*, J. D. Russell found that many colleges failed to pay their bills promptly enough to earn discounts (p. 55). Bennett, "Prompt Payment of Bookdealers' Invoices," p. 388, points out some of the difficulties of business offices and state disbursing offices in making prompt payments, even though the libraries may clear invoices rapidly.

to use many agents—reduces the opportunity of the university library to demand the discounts that a large public library can obtain. While the latter may get up to 40 percent discount on some items, such as popular trade books, the usual discount for university libraries is about 25 percent. Scientific and technical books are normally discounted at about the same rate for all types of libraries, from 10 to 15 percent.

Some efforts at cooperative buying have been made by groups of libraries. University libraries have benefitted from such projects as the Library of Congress Cooperative Acquisitions Program and the Farmington Plan. The Documents Expediting Project has also made it possible for university libraries as a group to acquire materials at relatively lower rates than if they attempted individually to acquire the items involved. Bibliographical centers have endeavored to introduce cooperative purchasing programs, but these have not been uniformly successful. Purchasing for a state system of educational institutions, as in Oregon (with the exception of the University of Oregon), is another possible way of receiving larger discounts.

COLLECTING FINES   The assessment of fines in university libraries is a punitive procedure rather than a means of obtaining income. If the funds are collected by the library, they are regularly turned over to the business office. In a few institutions the fines are paid by the students at the business office. Another variation is the collection by the business office of a deposit specifically for library fines. This deposit, which varies from $1.00 to $10.00, is drawn against for fines incurred. It is obvious that the deposit system requires considerable clerical work in checking the fines incurred and in making refunds.

Whether or not the library is credited with or reimbursed for the fines collected varies among universities. In some institutions they are credited to the library account and are available for expenditure immediately. In others they are deposited in a general university fund and are administered in accord with the special regulations governing the use of such funds.

In recent years, some college and university librarians have experimented with circulation regulations which do not contain fine penalties. No detailed reports on the problems involved have yet appeared. There are also no definitive studies on fines systems in general. A thorough analysis of what the library pays in salaries, stationery, and postage to collect fines may be useful in pointing out the advantages or disadvantages of elaborate fine systems.

Variation exists also in the methods of assessing charges for lost books. In some libraries the borrower pays only the price of the book plus the fines which have accumulated. In others he is required to pay not only the cost of the book and the accumulated fines but also a charge to cover the expense of ordering and cataloging a new copy.

RECEIVING DEPOSITS   In many libraries fixed fees or deposits are required of users of the library who are not regular members of the university. These deposits are drawn against for the privilege of borrowing books and for fines and lost books. In urban universities, which frequently provide library service to residents of the community, deposits may represent a considerable sum and may require special handling by either the library or the business offices. Generally, deposits are returned to the patrons when they relinquish their library privileges, but in some institutions they are considered fees and are retained by the business office.

EVALUATING FOR INSURANCE   A library's collections generally increase annually in value. This is true not only of rare items, but of the bulk of book, periodical, pamphlet, and other groups of materials. Equipment, such as catalogs, also grows in value. Many libraries, particularly those of private universities, have sought to protect their holdings from fire and theft through insurance policies, which may or may not be part of general university plans.[10] At

[10] A suggestive general manual on insurance is that by Singer, *The Insurance of Libraries*. A particularly useful article is by Charles W. Mixer, "Insurance Evaluation of a University Library's Collections," *College and Research Libraries*, XIII (1952), 18–23+, which deals with the Columbia University Libraries procedures in insurance; also applicable in some ways is the article by Rogers, "Appraising a Research Collection," *College and Research Libraries*, XIII (1952), 24–29. Many state

Columbia, which works on a triennial reappraisal of its collections for fire insurance purposes, the formula for evaluation varies according to the type of books involved, e.g., general books, scientific books in general, engineering, chemistry and physics books, law books, medical books, medical periodicals, architectural books and fine arts books. Such items as incunabula, manuscripts, and other rare items are listed and appraised individually. The insurance evaluation on catalogs at Columbia is based on the cost of the cards plus the cost of personnel to duplicate them; it does not include the actual cost of cataloging. The presence of a microfilm copy of the card catalog has made it possible to pay minimal premiums on that record.

Although library insurance is usually handled by the business office and in many cases is part of a blanket insurance policy for the whole university, the librarian should have a clear understanding of the values of all materials and equipment so that adequate protection will be secured. In addition to the normal annual increase of the value of the collections, allowances should be made for depreciation of binding, duplicating, photographic, and other equipment.

SOURCES
OF INCOME
The problem of income for university libraries is a crucial one, since income is the basis for operation. University librarians, therefore, are constantly concerned with questions of finance, budget, size of staff, salaries, and book funds.[11] It is obvious that any discussion of the adequacy of a university library's income must take into consideration the financial condition of the entire institution.[12] For data on the income of the institution as a whole,

---

institutions do not undertake to insure their buildings or resources in the same way as private universities.

[11] See, for example, University of Missouri Library, "Budget Situation, 1953–1954." This statement shows the effects of budget reductions (34 percent) on the acquisitional program and library services.

[12] Millett, *Financing Higher Education in the United States,* is a general source of information on the financing of academic institutions. Two important analyses of university and research library financial problems are Hamlin, "The Financial and Economic Status of Research Libraries," *Library Quarterly,* XXIII (1953), 190–98, and McCarthy, "Financial Support of College and University Libraries." *Library Trends,* I (1952), 105–22.

the reports of the president, comptroller, or other business officer can be consulted. These reports, however, infrequently subdivide these data so as to indicate the sources of income for the library. In fact, it is even difficult for librarians to report such data.[13] In available published statistics, the same institutions have not reported consistently over a period of years, and only a small proportion of the nation's colleges and universities have been included.

University libraries, in varying degrees, receive their income from five principal sources: (1) funds allocated from the university budget; (2) endowment income; (3) gifts; (4) fees; and (5) miscellaneous sources, including fines, the sale of publications and duplicates, photographic work, the sale of catalog cards, charges for lending or rental services, and in some instances, government funds.

LIBRARIES IN ENDOWED UNIVERSITIES   Only a few of the larger private university libraries, such as those of Harvard, Yale, Princeton, and Columbia, receive substantial funds from endowments. The considerable growth of the Dartmouth College Library, which reaches the dimensions of a university collection, has been the direct result of a large endowment for the purchase of library materials. Yale, Harvard, and Princeton are among the few libraries able to draw on endowment funds which far exceed the funds granted to

[13] In the 1945 edition of this work, Table 2 (pp. 66–68), entitled "Library Income by Source in 10 Endowed Universities, 1931–40," and Table 5 (pp. 71–74), "Income by Source in 17 State University Libraries, 1930–40," contained serious gaps in the data. Tables 3 and 4 provided data on source of library income during 1938–39 and 1939–40 in 9 private universities. The variations in source of income from "allocation, endowment, gift, and other" were considerable at that time. The variations would probably be similar today if such compilations were made. In private universities, the percentages were approximately: allocations, 75; endowments, 12; gifts, 4; and others, 9. In state universities, the percentage for allocation was 98, and all others, 2. Hamlin, op. cit., p. 194, points out that "Endowment has always been an important item of income for private institutions of higher education. It provided 23.4 per cent of current income in 1939–40, but only 11.8 per cent eight years later."

Data on sources of income are given in "College and University Library Statistics," until 1943 published in the February issues of the Bulletin of the American Library Association, in College and Research Libraries, March issues, 1943 and 1944, and July issues, 1947 and 1948. Statistics, without sources of income, appear in College and Research Libraries, April issues, 1949 through 1951, and January issues, 1952 through 1955. The "Statistics of College and University Libraries," issued by the Princeton University Library, and "Statistics of Southern College and University Libraries," issued by Louisiana State University, do not contain a breakdown of sources of income.

many other institutions through university allocation. It should be pointed out in this connection that libraries are often restricted in their use of endowment funds. Frequently the funds are established with certain stipulations regarding the type of materials to be purchased or the subjects for which the funds are to be spent. The Bancroft fund at Columbia University, for example, which provides approximately $40,000 annually, is allocated to the purchase of materials in American history, broadly defined. Restrictions of this character may limit the effectiveness of the library in developing its resources and services systematically. Hamlin points out that libraries which depend largely or solely on endowment funds for current operations "face relatively lean years in the light of devaluation of the dollar and the low return on first-class investments." [14] Possibilities in obviating this decrease are changes in investments and increases in the principal of endowments. Tentative conclusions reached by McCarthy also suggest that "it is the libraries in the larger institutions or those in institutions with a long record of high level library support which have shown the greatest increases" in income, and that "A selected group of private institutions is spending appreciably more for library service than is a similar group of publicly controlled institutions." [15]

Tables 1 and 2 provide statistics for the group of university libraries which includes members of the Association of Research Libraries, showing growth from 1940–41 to 1953–54. Tables 3 and 4 give similar statistics for a group of southern institutions for 1940–41 to 1952–53.

STATE UNIVERSITY LIBRARIES   An examination of the income of state university libraries reveals that the appropriation income is the only source which appears to be fairly consistent and constant, even though, as Parker observed, there have been decreases when

[14] "Financial and Economic Status of Research Libraries," p. 193.

[15] "Administrative Organization and Financial Support of Land-Grant College and University Libraries," p. 117. See also Parker, "Libraries in an Inflationary Cycle," *College and Research Libraries*, XII (1951), 338–42+. Parker presents material on both library budgets and library salaries.

the total educational expenditures are compared.[16] An examination of Table 2 shows that in a number of libraries the amounts budgeted for books, periodicals, binding and rebinding for 1953–54 are less than the sums spent the preceding year. In most state university libraries, endowments are relatively infrequent and gifts constitute only a small part of the income. The emphasis on appropriations, therefore, is necessary. In surveys of various state university libraries, attention usually has been focused on the need for strong state support, even though recommendations propose the extension of gift and exchange programs. Whether or not this almost sole reliance on appropriations will continue in the future is difficult to say. Direct efforts are being made to promote the interest of alumni and private individuals and groups in the programs of state university libraries.[17] Although there has been an increase in the number of state-supported and city-supported institutions of higher education in recent years, "apparently state and municipal universities and colleges, and their libraries, will have to seek a larger share of income from fees and private gifts than was the case a few years ago." [18]

Both the private and the state university librarian must make a case for any appropriation. Justification for increased funds for materials, personnel, or facilities is an important part of the administrator's task. This task is lightened to the extent that the president and the faculty members are aware of the complex problems of the modern university library. The report of the Library Committee, Academic Senate, Northern Section, of the University of California,[19] was prepared for the purpose of providing some background information "on some reasons for the constantly increased

[16] *Op. cit.*, p. 339.

[17] An interesting brochure in this direction is University of North Carolina, The Friends of the Library, *Opportunities and Plans for the Present and Future of the University Library at Chapel Hill.*

[18] "Financial and Economic Status of Research Libraries," p. 192. See also H. K. Allen, in collaboration with R. G. Axt, *State Public Finance and State Institutions of Higher Education in the United States,* chap. iii.

[19] "Interim Report of the Library Committee, Academic Senate, Northern Section," *University Bulletin,* II (1954), 133–34.

TABLE 1: STATISTICS OF COLLEGE AND UNIVERSITY LIBRARIES, 1940-41

	(1)	(2)	(3)	(4)	(5)	(6)
Institution	Vols. in Library	Vols. Added	Spent for Books, Periodicals, Binding, Rebinding	Appropriation	Staff	Salaries
Brown [1]	592,566	16,098	$ 48,530.35	$ 54,179.82	54	$ 71,446.00
Calif., Berkeley [2]	1,124,858	45,616	112,937.57	102,300.00	86	149,441.94
Calif., Los Angeles	385,884	30,300	88,800.00	95,400.00	49	92,042.00
Chicago	1,330,152	29,367	123,990.24	140,332.87	100	164,508.43
Cincinnati [3]	511,974	20,437	36,391.97	56,111.24	39	54,634.02
Colorado [4]	457,935	34,502	35,559.14	28,639.03	23	37,280.00
Columbia [5]	1,845,611	51,959	200,885.45	178,542.85	292	457,767.00
Cornell	1,094,117	25,287	56,064.00	83,475.00	47	86,520.00
Duke	631,049	31,728	119,411.91	110,000.00	65	103,584.98
Harvard	4,265,792	106,186	277,442.93	—	175	251,915.28
Illinois [6]	1,262,046	44,371	133,724.68	137,500.00	138	244,124.00
Indiana	437,009	22,234	62,986.25	64,054.00	22	41,900.00
Iowa State College	313,715	17,515	51,104.32	51,000.00	37	51,929.03
Iowa University	492,819	20,602	45,915.99	45,000.00	53	77,325.70
Johns Hopkins	582,747	14,683	41,117.03	44,000.00	42	67,057.68
Joint Univ. Libs.	391,524	21,108	50,074.74	41,733.93	34	53,543.52
Kansas	331,108	11,520	38,664.00	24,090.00	20	30,875.00
Louisiana St. Univ. [7]	293,871	25,235	70,578.14	42,800.00	44	70,744.84
Mass. Inst. of Tech.	356,077	7,974	19,659.00	31,998.85	30	52,137.05
Michigan	1,134,052	36,780	138,060.00	140,260.00	147	266,223.00
Minnesota	1,183,562	54,108	108,396.16	110,375.00	102	148,535.00
Missouri	418,104	23,000	97,879.59	44,936.48	31	46,261.24
Nebraska	367,215	14,204	36,320.00	30,000.00	28	44,500.00
New York University	616,132	24,091	65,625.45	60,000.00	101	168,806.00
North Carolina [8]	403,051	17,864	40,865.75	25,500.00	35	54,392.66

	Col. 1	Col. 2	Col. 3	Col. 4	Col. 5	Col. 6
Northwestern	668,410	25,573	74,550.00	51,629.15	71	138,604.00
Ohio State Univ.	594,300	31,962	91,921.00	90,826.00	67	102,804.00
Pennsylvania	958,523	24,373	71,678.00	67,355.00	92½	116,076.00
Princeton	976,260	19,781	64,137.61	65,856.36	74	114,459.00
Rochester	376,660	16,476	63,257.00	66,491.00	45	84,268.91
Stanford	810,137	37,068	42,809.54	53,918.47	60	120,303.00
Texas	673,888	34,156	101,292.02	97,082.20	53	79,947.86
Virginia	359,811	21,276	60,643.21	44,290.00	55	79,377.04
Washington, St. Louis	481,137	14,915	29,750.00	29,750.00	34	50,000.00
Washington, Seattle	478,687	23,904	54,586.23	50,132.00	38	105,273.09
Wisconsin [10]	498,045	13,040	39,196.44	38,000.00	31	58,745.00
Yale [10]	3,074,817	106,119	179,835.00	151,521.00	196	330,513.00

[1] Column 1: all items 653,006. Column 2: all items 18,083, John Carter Brown Library figures: (1) 30,000; (2) 408; (3) $7,000; (4) 3,000; (5) 3; (6) $9,000.

[2] Columns 1, 2, and 3: rental and reserve collection not included. Column 3: includes $26,487.17 not in General Library budget but spent from other funds for "departmental books." Column 4: this amount is the General Library budget only. The amount allowed and actually expended for "departmental books" will not be known until the close of the fiscal year. All the figures do not include departments outside of Berkeley, nor do the last two columns include departmental librarians.

[3] A considerable sum of money was turned over to the Library last May against which a large volume of ordering was done so that on June 30 there were outstanding orders totaling $18,541.04, which are not included above as expenditures because not yet supplied nor paid for. An amount to cover these is added to the usual appropriation for this year, thus explaining the figures in column 4.

[4] Column 1: Documents Collection included for first time. Column 2: additions to Documents Collection included for first time.

[5] Includes separately administered libraries of Bard College, Barnard College, College of Pharmacy, New York School of Social Work, New York.

[6] Statistics include both Urbana and Chicago campuses. Column 5: a total of 138 professional and clerical people; of the professional group, 101 are full time and 11 are part time. In the clerical group, 19 work full time and 7 work part time.

[7] Columns 4, 5, and 6: General Library only.

[8] Column 3: includes income from special book funds totaling $7,754.91 and receipts from extraordinary sources, $7,510.84. Column 4: state appropriation.

[9] Column 3: exclusive of rebinding. Column 6: plus $9,005 for student assistants.

[10] These figures include school, college, departmental, and Sterling Memorial libraries.

TABLE 2: STATISTICS OF COLLEGE AND UNIVERSITY LIBRARIES, 1953-54

Institution	(1) Vols. in Library	(2) Vols. Added	(3) Spent for Books, Periodicals, Binding, Rebinding	(4) Available	(5) Staff	(6) Staff Salaries	(7) Student Salaries
1. Brown	807,902	18,056	$ 93,689	$ 89,800	55 9/38	$ 150,749	$ 16,055
2. Calif. Berkeley [1]	1,986,818	79,276	417,047	485,361	299.3	1,183,811	249,202
3. Calif. Los Angeles	1,051,677	63,799	389,734	398,535	165	643,329	180,972
4. Chicago	1,900,137	45,896	194,348	198,000	133	402,996	88,454
5. Cincinnati	672,989	14,808	66,142	76,330	47½	143,423	15,301
6. Colorado [2]	783,594	30,540	86,846	89,873	38	132,038	34,501
7. Columbia [3]	2,069,795	62,740	429,915	287,853	310.5	863,986	—
8. Cornell	1,674,735	64,775	240,705	252,740	169	516,354	53,957
9. Duke [4]	1,159,153	35,651	186,988	185,000	79½	234,187	31,659
10. Harvard	5,832,912	129,965	506,422	370,077	358	1,057,510	50,000
11. Illinois	2,789,863	133,760	436,000	400,000	242.75	842,919	92,742
12. Indiana	946,599	36,523	256,000	225,500	93½	326,895	46,817
13. Iowa State College	443,065	11,873	95,098	100,000	46½	151,688	21,393
14. Iowa University	826,838	30,216	154,227	156,500	78½	271,875	40,318
15. Johns Hopkins [5]	1,048,102	58,712	83,828	90,000	70½	184,433	13,175
16. Joint University Libs.	655,274	23,183	83,220	89,298	40½	121,347	30,965
17. Kansas [6]	601,192	60,416	202,237	192,000	64.5	204,312	45,346
18. Kentucky [7]	650,740	44,433	102,206	92,000	54	145,055	15,076
19. Louisiana State	625,813	34,683	188,190	179,170	77	252,333	25,520
20. Mass. Inst. Tech.	523,213	23,760	63,361	59,706	52	157,663	19,014
21. Michigan [8]	2,304,434	58,211	288,610	355,957	176	640,264	122,930
22. Minnesota	1,763,728	62,450	293,382	273,899	135	483,604	87,481
23. Missouri	708,679	20,116	105,356	105,000	41	125,213	18,036
24. Nebraska [9]	535,538	19,038	123,113	122,623	65	212,528	32,853
25. New York University [10]	1,017,226	31,291	125,585	102,470	145	436,071	—

	Column 1	Column 2	Column 3	Column 4	Column 5	Column 6	Column 7
26. North Carolina [11]	662,978	29,473	166,266	125,000	78½	256,939	42,731
27. Northwestern	1,146,163	42,996	197,295	175,000	98	289,410	60,155
28. Ohio State [12]	1,056,226	45,479	200,062	200,000	150	400,292	55,664
29. Pennsylvania	1,371,193	47,863	247,896	218,296	154 1/10	428,096	33,042
30. Princeton	1,275,703	34,018	151,685	143,303	113	308,085	13,750
31. Rochester	580,609	17,122	101,010	95,744	54	158,082	14,642
32. Stanford [13]	1,257,698	43,061	178,325	155,560	119	372,484	59,893
33. Texas	1,095,284	45,531	200,057	175,300	78⅚	260,343	82,154
34. Virginia	746,834	37,018	114,169	125,000	69	236,919	24,807
35. Washington, St. Louis [14]	577,690	14,812	98,745	116,893	55.67	141,291	27,965
36. Washington, Seattle	842,928	42,779	188,281	177,471	130	415,032	87,416
37. Wisconsin	947,896	38,310	210,946	209,500	106	433,414	66,435
38. Yale [15]	4,245,583	59,611	423,837	325,368	235.92	636,541	——

[1] All figures relate only to the library on Berkeley campus. Correction on last year's report: (1) 1,907,539; (2) 94,853.

[2] Column 1 includes government documents collection of 365,330 items. Does not include Denison Library of the School of Medicine in Denver.

[3] Columns 1 and 2 exclude Barnard, Teachers College, New York School of Social Work, School of Pharmacy. Column 5 excludes Director and Assistant Director. Column 6 includes students not segregated in record.

[4] Columns 1 and 2 use a combination of bibliographical and physical unit count.

[5] Column 2 includes the first report of collection of over 30,000 volumes received as gift several years ago.

[6] Column 1 is adjusted figure.

[7] Column 1 includes 18,086 unclassified physical volumes listed by authors only and not previously counted.

[8] Columns 1 and 2 use combination of bibliographical and physical count. Column 2 by recount, 697,949.

[9] Column 3 includes commercial binding account. Not included here are two full-time salaries in binding (see Column 6) and also binding supplies.

[10] Column 7 included in Column 6.

[11] Column 4 does not include anticipated income from trust funds, endowments and gifts. Column 7, not all students, but personnel paid on an hourly basis.

[12] Column 3 includes only $15,000 for outside binding. Has own bindery with major cost listed under salaries.

[13] Column 1 also has 1,837,025 volumes and pamphlets uncataloged but organized for use.

[14] Column 4 includes money available in special and endowed funds ($25,333), which does not appear in budget.

[15] Column 7, non-separable budget item. Payments are carried by University and not charged to Library.

TABLE 3*: STATISTICS OF SOUTHERN COLLEGE AND UNIVERSITY LIBRARIES, 1940-41

Institution	Volumes July 1, 1941	Volumes Added, 1940-41	Expended for Books, 1940-41	Appropriations for Books 1941-42	No. on Library Staff	Paid for Salaries, 1940-41	Paid for Student or Part-time Help, 1940-41	Total Expended for Library Services, 1940-41
Alabama University [1]	250,499	15,421	$39,196.21	—	22½	$37,129.92	$19,540.68	$56,670.60
Arkansas University	172,848	11,937	25,522.19	$25,370.00	17½	24,132.50	4,989.69	29,122.19
Baylor University [2]	87,844	3,857	10,736.49		6⅔	10,010.01	10,134.38	20,144.39
Emory University	191,136	14,330	21,332.91	22,350.00	21	30,257.65	2,175.00	32,432.65
Florida University [3]	226,384	12,796	20,952.00	23,000.00	16	31,214.00	12,514.00	43,728.00
Georgia School of Technology	52,865	5,914	18,117.60	12,000.00	6	8,749.88	393.30	9,143.18
Georgia University	146,772	7,793	51,530.00	29,000.00	33½	44,549.00	3,031.00	47,580.00
Kentucky University	302,889	22,701	18,684.18	19,300.00	21	34,875.00	7,928.40	42,803.40
Maryland University [4],[5]	151,715	9,773	28,611.91	27,600.00	19	29,163.06	2,723.95	31,887.01
Mississippi University	83,849	5,969	12,508.75		5 [6]	8,157.00 [11]	1,350.00	9,507.00
North Texas State Teachers College	111,453 [7]	9,353	19,179.12 [8]	16,000.00	13	22,625.29	11,642.13	34,267.42
Oklahoma University	227,853	10,612	22,000.00		15	24,098.00	10,453.55	34,551.55
Rice Institute	157,100	6,150	18,850.00	18,500.00	7		3,327.90	
South Carolina University	156,667	4,279	11,453.15 [9]	9,000.00	8	19,198.32	481.60	19,679.92
Southern Methodist University [7]	125,109	7,229	9,573.85	10,000.00	9	13,352.12	601.85	13,953.97
Tennessee University [10]	211,287	9,750	27,413.15 [11]	26,720.00	23	38,510.00 [12]	4,191.33	42,701.33
Texas A. & M. College	91,908	6,115	17,038.18	20,940.00	11 [13]	20,832.97	3,444.83	24,277.80
Texas Christian University	54,705	4,406	4,521.23	5,000.00	3	4,128.33	1,449.60	5,577.93
Texas University	673,888	34,156	97,858.83	92,776.00	52⅝	79,947.86	23,798.29	103,746.15
Virginia Polytechnic Institute	96,623	8,505	7,116.55		13	18,208.00 [14]	180.00	18,388.00 [14]
Washington & Lee University	124,142	4,137	6,258.00	6,500.00	8	11,890.00	662.00	12,552.00
West Virginia University	167,401	5,874	11,032.64	13,000.00	15	23,844.82	2,845.00	26,680.82

[1] All figures are for fiscal year ending September 30, 1941.

[2] Does not include Schools of Law, Medicine, Nursing, or Dentistry.

[3] Includes main, General Extension Division, P. K. Yonge School, Law, and Agricultural Experiment Station Libraries.

[4] Includes libraries of the Schools of Dentistry, Law, Medicine, and Pharmacy in Baltimore.

[5] Fiscal year October 1, 1940–September 30, 1941.

[6] Does not include medical librarian.

[7] August 31, 1941.

[8] Includes $2,780.99 from Carnegie Corporation.

[9] Does not include Law School Library; includes $2,673.59 from Carnegie Corporation.

[10] Includes Knoxville, Memphis, and Martin Divisions, and Agricultural Experiment Station.

[11] Includes funds not on library budget.

[12] Includes a half salary paid by Agricultural Experiment Station.

[13] Head Librarian is also full professor of English.

[14] Includes janitor.

* Adapted from Statistics of Southern College and University Libraries, 1940-41 (Baton Rouge: Louisiana State University,

TABLE 4 [*]: STATISTICS OF SOUTHERN COLLEGE AND UNIVERSITY LIBRARIES, 1952-53

Institution	Volumes in Library July 1, 1953	Total Library Expenditures 1952-53	Average Annual Expenditure for Books, Periodicals, and Binding, 1948-53	Expended for Books, Periodicals, and Binding, 1952-53	Paid for Salaries 1952-53 (Exclusive of Student Help)	Paid for Student Help 1952-53	NUMBER ON LIBRARY STAFF	
							Professional	Clerical and Sub-professional
Alabama University	438,857	$299,532.19 [1]	$115,791.43	$107,129.10	$152,223.06	$23,763.63	34	19
Arkansas University [2]	307,620	146,955.53	61,371.00	56,143.65	70,798.23	13,874.13	17½	8
Baylor University	192,123	134,426.00	36,077.00	41,726.00	45,780.00	19,197.00	10	3½
Emory University	393,997	220,505.00	85,245.00	81,063.00	120,412.00	13,350.00	21½	15
Florida State University	343,444	464,355.54	140,376.58	187,238.69	177,870.59	9,381.86	35	18
Florida University	528,013	578,282.00	157,345.00	220,818.00	286,332.00	56,673.00	42¼	51½
Georgia Institute of Technology	134,460 [3]	149,687.50	46,783.38	60,433.16	72,384.29	5,648.20	14	12
Georgia University	299,784	254,948.40	88,384.98	104,803.41	125,749.56	11,267.02	25	18
Kentucky University	588,221	278,747.72	94,734.79	108,319.55	144,457.61	13,034.17	26	27
Maryland University	273,830	257,686.10	72,318.52	98,436.84	128,802.42	20,751.77	24	16
Mississippi University	183,671	130,694.10	35,630.59	48,810.08	61,998.60	12,436.75	16	15
North Texas State College [4]	237,573	146,634.32	53,436.07	58,791.36	63,059.90	15,760.85	15¾	15
Oklahoma University	481,600	305,274.00	108,743.67	120,321.00	137,447.40	26,568.60	34½	—
Rice Institute	237,421	140,578.00	43,298.00	55,771.00	62,473.00	18,065.00	13½	29½
South Carolina University	285,047	154,659.25	45,861.39	51,767.49	85,548.77	13,716.77	12⅝	8
Southern Methodist University	348,624	191,716.67	65,974.31	71,674.08	99,352.47	14,922.01	23	21
Tennessee University	360,220	264,512.05	80,019.60	78,793.96	157,945.96	17,135.67	23	11½
Texas A. & M. College	241,436	184,144.95	73,210.43	79,528.06	91,743.14	6,372.29	22	36
Texas Christian University	217,520	82,976.23	24,056.16	29,027.96	47,198.76	3,724.70	12⅝	25
Virginia Polytechnic Institute	159,487	178,022.51	39,248.94	60,384.16	113,038.18	—	9	2
Washington & Lee University	153,635	32,710.25	9,747.31	11,554.13	19,410.14	800.00	17	23
West Virginia University [5]	270,888	234,643.27	69,079.50	62,386.50	118,372.88	30,152.41	3	3½
							22	30

[1] Excludes $102,697.00 capital outlay for air-conditioning.
[2] Excludes Medical School Library.
[3] Modified bibliographical count.
[4] For fiscal year ending August 31.

[5] Excludes Law Library.
[*] Adapted from Statistics for Southern College and University Libraries (Baton Rouge: Louisiana State University Library, 1953)

book budgets and to point out certain corollary effects upon the library structure." The report proceeds to relate the problem of rising budgets to (1) the rise in prices, (2) increased publication, (3) expansion of the University's research and teaching programs, and (4) the University's relative youth as a leading academic institution and its relative isolation from other great bibliographic centers.

LIBRARY FEES   An examination of the institutional exhibits in *American Universities and Colleges: 1952* [20] reveals that few of the major university libraries charge direct fees for library purposes. A number which had such charges in 1940 have dropped them. One large university under state control charges a combined laboratory and library fee of $30.00; a few institutions still have fees which range from $1.00 to $6.00 a semester or year. Although no effort was made to tabulate the number of institutions which listed "other" fees, it may be assumed that this term includes in some cases library, laboratory, and health fees. The institutions which still retain fees are those under state control. Endowed institutions generally charge a lump sum for tuition without itemization.

The tendency to do away with specific fees for library service conforms to the recommendation made in the *Survey of Land-Grant Colleges and Universities* in 1930 [21] and in 1932 by Reeves and his associates.[22] Since the library performs definite functions which are essential to the maintenance of the university, it should not depend upon special fees for support but should be supported, like other parts of the university, by appropriations from the institution's total income.

Charging fees for use of library facilities by individuals who are

[20] Irwin (ed.), *passim.*

[21] U.S. Office of Education. *Survey of Land-Grant Colleges and Universities,* I, 709–10. It was pointed out that the presence of fees for the library would create "grave danger in regarding library service as distinct from the educational and research fields and as service which must be a special charge."

[22] Reeves, *et al. The Liberal Arts College,* p. 620. It was urged that every college and university have "a single fee covering all the basic charges, with no extra fees for any academic purpose."

not part of the academic community, however, presents a different problem. The Harvard Library raised this question for consideration at the meetings of the Association of Research Libraries and the Association of College and Reference Libraries.[23] Harvard charges $5.00 to $10.00 annually for Harvard graduates and for other persons not connected with the university for the privilege of unlimited use of library books within the building and of withdrawing up to 50 books. A second $10.00 must be paid if more than 50 books are borrowed, but the time is then extended for a year. "Visiting scholars from outside the Boston metropolitan area continue to pay no fee, except that they are now regarded as local residents and charged $10.00 if they use the library for longer than three months or if they wish to take out books for home use." [24] Only transportation charges are made for interlibrary loans.

Since 1951, the Columbia University Libraries have had a library fee of $20.00 a semester for non-university users. This charge is made to alumni as well as to those who have had no connection with the university.[25]

A charge for library use is not made without protest. Sypher [26] has presented the point of view of the visiting scholar who is not interested in earning a degree. He writes: "In short, the current tendency to levy fees would seem to build tariff walls about the major research libraries and create a monopoly on research materials for those who are already affiliated with research. At the moment there are few enough inducements to enter either scholarship or teaching. One of these inducements has traditionally been freedom of access to books. A policy of fees could help close careers to talents, especially the younger talents." [27]

[23] Metcalf, "The Situation at Harvard," in "Fees for Research Library Use by 'Outsiders': A Symposium," *College and Research Libraries*, XIII (1952), 297-98.

[24] *Ibid.*, p. 297. Metcalf also notes that Harvard actually has had since 1878 a fee of $5.00 for those "who wished to use more of the Harvard College Library than its reading rooms and catalogues."

[25] White, "The Situation at Columbia," in "Fees for Research Library Use by 'Outsiders,' *College and Research Libraries*, XIII (1952), 299-301.

[26] Sypher, "Views on the Fee Policy," in "Fees for Research Library Use by 'Outsiders,' " *College and Research Libraries*, XIII (1952), 295-96.

[27] *Ibid.*, p. 296.

This problem of university library use is a very real one. There seems to be little doubt that students pursuing their studies though not officially registered for course work (those who may be working on a dissertation), alumni, and residents might pay some sort of fee. It is primarily with the visiting teachers and scholars that questions have been raised.[28] Through their libraries, universities can make a contribution to advancement of learning and scholarship in much the same way that they achieve other scholarly objectives through fellowships, grants-in-aid, and appropriations for research, publications, and other purposes.

Although some of the larger public libraries, such as the Detroit Public Library and the John Crerar Library in Chicago, have within the past few years set up programs of service for industry on the basis of fee payments, university libraries have not yet ventured into this field. Perhaps the development of the fee system such as now exists at Harvard and Columbia will stimulate use of university collections by researchers associated with industrial and business enterprises.

OTHER SOURCES OF INCOME   In addition to the income which the library may receive from allocations, endowments, gifts, and fees, it may also receive a portion of its funds from several other sources. A relatively small portion of income may, as has been pointed out, be derived from fines. The sale of publications may constitute another minor source. The sale of duplicates, particularly in those libraries which do not maintain extensive exchange programs, may also bring in substantial sums in the larger institutions. A few libraries seek by nominal charges to cover the cost of cards which are sent to other libraries. Usually photographic departments of libraries work on a nonprofit basis. Some effort is made to charge enough for the work to amortize the expensive equipment over a period of years. Generally, charges for various types of photographic work are slightly lower than those of commercial

[28] Wilson, "Should Research Libraries Impose Fees upon Visiting Scholars?" in "Fees for Research Library Use by 'Outsiders,'" *College and Research Libraries,* XIII (1952), 301–2.

photographers. Work, however, is restricted to that of the library, faculty members, students, and other members of the university. Similarly, the lending library service serves as a convenience to the university community, rather than as a means for obtaining income in excess of costs.

During World War II and since, libraries, as parts of the universities with which they are associated, have also been taken into consideration when governmental research contracts are arranged. Most research projects have library implications that make it necessary to earmark part of the funds for library purposes. Ordinarily, when separate funds are assigned from governmental contracts, strict accounting of expenditures is essential, since reports may need to be made to the government.

BUDGETARY PROCEDURE   THE UNIVERSITY BUDGET   A budget is a financial statement of the estimated revenues and expenditures of an institution for a definite period of time. It represents a logical, comprehensive, and forward-looking financial program for the coordination of the activities of the various functional divisions of the university. As a definite financial plan, as a forecast of the means for carrying the plan into effect, as a current guide, as a cost summary of operations, and as a historical record and basis for the formulation of future policy, it is an indispensable instrument in the hands of the university administrator.[29]

Certain facts concerning the university's budget procedure should be known to the librarian if he is to perform his responsibilities in this area satisfactorily. He should be aware of the time when the budget is closed for the fiscal year, when the preparation of the next year's budget must be begun, and when estimates for the fiscal year must be submitted. Since most universities operate on a fiscal year which dates from July 1 to June 30, work on the following year's budget generally is started in November or De-

[29] For a useful guide on budgets, see National Committee on the Preparation of a Manual on College and University Business Administration, *College and University Business Administration*, Vol. I, chap. iii, "Budgets and Budgetary Accounting."

cember. Actually, in a complex library situation, work on the following year's budget might well start on July 1. The tentative budget should be ready by January, and the final budget is usually approved by the governing board or legislature in March or April. In state-supported institutions the budget is usually for a two-year period, and has to be prepared considerably in advance of the session of the legislature.

Ordinarily, the budget can be considered from several points of view. Two of these may be emphasized here: (1) the total amount of revenue to be expended and (2) the distribution of funds within the total budget. Although the president of the university is in direct control of the preparation of the budget, the officers and departmental heads are responsible for preliminary estimates for their units. The financial officer usually furnishes the departmental heads with forms upon which to submit these estimates. The librarian's part in this procedure involves interrelating the library's functions with the rest of the educational program and coordinating library financial policies with those established by the president. After the budget is adopted, it may be necessary to revise it during the year if the university income is lower than was anticipated. The control of the budget is exercised through a system of records and reports in the business office and in the library.

Millett [30] has noted the fourfold interests of higher education as current operating income, endowment capital, physical plant needs, and scholarship funds. Of these income needs, the second and fourth are of greater concern to private institutions than to public institutions, "but both share a common interest in the adequacy of current operating income and of capital plant." The library, of course, is concerned with all of these factors in budget preparation. In recent years, university libraries have also sought funds for scholarships, in the form of assistantships and internships.

LIBRARY BUDGET   There are three ways in which the librarian can prepare budgetary estimates: (1) by comparison with past

[30] *Financing Higher Education in the United States,* p. 369.

expenditures, (2) by budgeting in accordance with the work program, and (3) by using arbitrary standards and norms.

COMPARISON. In preparing the budget the librarian is rarely faced with a situation for which there is absolutely no precedent. Unless it is a new institution, the university has had a library budget previously. Moreover, the librarian is generally aware of the relative value that has been placed on library service by the university, because past experience indicates this. Consequently, it is the function of the librarian to propose a budget which takes into consideration last year's expenditures, the appropriation for the current year, and the estimated expenditures for the next year. The proposed budget is based on the librarian's judgment of the adequacy of budgets of the previous and the current years. In order to emphasize inadequacies, comparisons of library support with the support of other departments in the university may be presented or comparisons may be made with other comparable university libraries. Comparisons of the latter type, however, should be primarily for information, since the administrative officers are not likely to be aware of library developments in other institutions.

THE WORK PROGRAM. When the budget is formulated on the basis of the library's needs in terms of service to be offered and work to be accomplished, the objectives of the individual university are taken into consideration. The librarian, in order to suggest an adequate program of library support, should be cognizant of any change in the educational program. Many modifications of the university programs involve library facilities and service and consequently affect the library budget.[31]

Budgetary estimates based upon the work program should cover fixed charges, modified fixed charges or service-station charges, and unit-cost estimates. Fixed charges include: maintenance of the li-

[31] See footnote 19. At the University of California at Berkeley, for example: "In the five years from 1946–47 to 1951–52 the number of professors, associate professors, assistant professors, instructors, and lecturers . . . increased by 50% from 823 to 1,233. A trend noticeable between 1950–51 and 1951–52 (the last year for which figures are available) is of particular importance to the library. During this year, while the number of lecturers and instructors decreased, the number of professors in the three ranks increased by 7%. This appears to portend an increasing emphasis on graduate instruction and research, with resultant demands for more books."

brarian's office, of rare book rooms and other special reading rooms, and of catalogs and other records; cost of reproducing cards and of such items as binding and rebinding, supplies, telephone, postage, freight and express, memberships, pensions, building maintenance, and insurance.

Modified fixed charges or service-station charges include the cost of maintaining essential desks. These charges may be modified if necessary, because some desks may be eliminated by reorganizational changes; hours of maintenance may be shortened or lengthened; the number of persons stationed at desks may vary according to pressure of work; or the introduction of new equipment, such as charging machines, may affect the total staff required.

Unit-cost estimates are concerned with the probable number of students and faculty members to be served, the extent of the research program, the size of the reserve and general circulation, the demands for bibliographical services, and the number of books and other materials which will probably be acquired, cataloged, and bound during the year. When these conditions are set forth quantitatively, it is then necessary to compute the cost in terms of personnel, equipment, and materials. Computation may be relatively easy if careful cost-accounting records are kept. If specific cost analyses are not available, approximations may be worked out for the individual library. Schemes of personnel classification and pay plans, such as those developed by the American Library Association,[32] and costs for certain operations, such as those in cataloging, acquisitions, or circulation, may be used.[33]

ARBITRARY STANDARDS. The progress of a profession is usually marked by the accumulation of an increasing number of generally

[32] American Library Association. Board on Personnel Administration. *Classification and Pay Plans for Libraries in Institutions of Higher Education;* also, its *Position Classification and Salary Administration in Libraries.*

[33] Early studies of cost accounting were made by Rider, "Library Cost Accounting," *Library Quarterly,* VI (1936), 331–81, and Miller, "Cost Accounting for Libraries: Acquisition and Cataloging," *Library Quarterly,* VII (1937), 511–36. Extensive bibliographies of recent efforts are included in Coney, "Management in College and University Libraries," *Library Trends,* I (1952), 83–94; and Felix Reichmann, "Costs of Cataloging," *Library Trends,* II (1953), 290–317.

accepted practices. As these practices are commonly approved, they are recognized as norms or standards and are regularly followed until more satisfactory methods are discovered. A measure of standardization thus characterizes normal development.

Various attempts have been made by library and educational associations and students of financial administration to set up standards for different aspects of university library work. Usually these attempts have been based upon the ratio of library expenditures to total institutional expenditures, expenditures for library purposes per student, expenditures per faculty member, or expenditures per library staff member. When summarized, these studies show considerable variation in the recommendations. The range of the percentage of the library budget to the entire college budget, for example, was from 4 to 12 percent. The surveyors of the Indiana University Library found that the median ratio of library expenditures to total university expenditure in 11 state universities for 1938–39 was 4.86.[34]

Any figures which are used to show how one university fares as compared to others must take into consideration local conditions. Such figures are always subject to this limitation, as well as to changing patterns of educational and research programs. The range of ratios of library expenditures to total institutional expenditures in 58 institutions in 1953–54 was 1.5 percent (Pennsylvania State) to 8.8 percent (University of California at Los Angeles).[35] The median for this group was 4 percent. In a study of 19 selected land-grant institutions in 1948, McCarthy found a range in the ratios from 1.14 to 9.3 percent, with a median of 2.31 percent.[36]

The library operating expenditures per student for 70 libraries

[34] Coney, *et al. Report of a Survey of the Indiana University Library for the Indiana University, February–July, 1940*, pp. 34–35. The 11 state universities were: Texas, Michigan, Washington, Illinois, Iowa, North Carolina, Louisiana, Oklahoma, Kansas, Indiana, and Nebraska.

[35] "College and University Library Statistics, 1953–54," *College and Research Libraries*, XVI (1955), 39.

[36] McCarthy, "Administrative Organization and Financial Support of Land-Grant College and University Libraries," *College and Research Libraries*, IX (1948), 329.

in 1953–54 ranged from a low of $13.11 to a high of $186.04, with a median of $47.15.[37] Some idea of the variety in the range of library expenditures per full-time faculty member may be gleaned from the following figures for five university libraries in different parts of the country: Alabama, $572; Cornell, $609; Iowa, $689; Texas, $800; and California (Berkeley), $967.[38]

It should be apparent that, because of the many variables which are involved and the variations in the needs of different institutions, no arbitrary standards will exactly fit a particular library. The nature of the curriculum, the status of the library's holdings, the amount and variety of research carried on, the number of personnel and the efficiency of the library organization, the physical layout of the library building or buildings, the availability of endowment and other funds, the nature of the library program—all have to be taken into consideration in determining what the budget of a given university library should be at a given time.

Undoubtedly such factors as the size of collections, the number of fields or departments the collections support, and the concentration of materials within those fields or departments determine to a large measure the institution's ability to carry on graduate study and research at the highest levels. Consequently, the relationship between the number of volumes in the library and the number of departments within a university considered adequate to grant the Ph.D. degree is important. It does not seem possible that a university can support programs leading to the doctorate in 25 to 30 departments with less than $200,000 annually for books, periodicals,

[37] "College and University Library Statistics," *College and Research Libraries,* XVI (1955), 39. McCarthy, "Financial Support of College and University Libraries," *Library Trends,* I (1952), 105–22, presents a number of tabular analyses of total library expenditures per student. For example, in Table 5 of this article, McCarthy develops expenditures for thirty selected universities on a per student basis for (a) books, periodicals, and binding, and (b) salaries. These are developed on "all resident" and "full-time" bases. Summary columns combine (a) and (b). For "all resident" students, McCarthy found a high of $132.02, a low of $10.80, and a median of $36.56. For "full-time" students, there was a high of $132.02, a low of $25.56, and a median of $49.86. (The median was an average of two medians.)

[38] Data derived from "College and University Library Statistics, 1952–53," *College and Research Libraries,* XV (1954), 68–69.

and other library materials.[39] McCarthy and Wilson and Milczewski also found that land-grant college libraries, even with growing programs in doctoral study and research, have not been supported as well as those of private institutions.

DISTRIBUTION OF BOOK FUNDS   The term "book funds" is conventionally defined to include funds for periodicals, continuations, and binding and rebinding, as well as for books. The funds for periodicals, continuations, and their binding, unlike those for books, are usually treated together as part of the general library budget instead of being allocated among the various academic departments of the university. University libraries have adopted this practice in order to decrease the number of broken sets. When the departments control their periodical and continuation subscriptions, cancellations due to changes in departmental personnel or to other causes frequently occur. When the university library controls these items, cancellation is practiced only in the case of publications which have seriously lessened in their importance to the educational program of the university.[40] This latter practice makes for a consistent policy and insures complete sets of journals. Similarly, the placement of all funds for binding purposes under the control of one person in one department of the library is likely to secure more uniform results than would be secured if the funds were scattered among the various units.

A number of university libraries with large book funds do not find it necessary to allocate funds to departments or schools. However, most libraries find it desirable to apportion funds among the various departments of the university. The responsibility for the distribution is often left in the hands of the librarian and the library

[39] See Wilson and Milczewski (eds.), *Libraries of the Southeast*, chap. v, "Libraries of Institutions of Higher Education," esp. pp. 164–70. It is difficult to determine the relationship statistically, but Table 59 lists 26 institutions, showing number of volumes, number of degrees, and number of subjects.

[40] See Brown, "Librarianship and the Sciences," in Louis Shores (ed.), *Challenges to Librarianship*, pp. 75–76. Brown points out the importance of retaining runs of scientific periodicals for research purposes, despite findings that earlier volumes were cited to a less extent than recent volumes.

committee. In order to provide for contingencies, a certain portion of the funds, which varies from library to library, is usually set aside to be spent under the direct supervision of the librarian. More and more libraries are being given increased funds for this purpose.

In those libraries which allocate funds to departments, annual reviews of the apportionments are necessary if the departmental representatives are to be kept satisfied with the way in which their collections are growing. One of the chief reasons that law and medical school library budgets are frequently entirely separate from the general university library budget has been the fear that the funds would in some way be limited by centralization.

If funds are allotted, it is important that flexibility be permitted. Rigid systems of allotments make it difficult for institutions to take advantage of special bargains which appear on the book market or to meet varying requirements of academic departments.

There have been a number of attempts to solve the problem of apportionment of book funds in an impartial and objective manner.[41] Such factors as registration, courses offered, faculty, graduate majors, nonquantitative elements affecting book needs (adequacy of department's present library collections), teaching methods, recent new faculty or courses, permanent value of material normally purchased, publication rate in each department's field, and frequency with which faculty members publish books and articles, and cost of material are weighted in an effort to assign funds on an objective basis.[42] The possibility of establishing a formula which

[41] Two of the efforts are described in articles by Ellsworth, "Some Aspects of the Problem of Allocating Book Funds among Departments in Universities," *Library Quarterly*, XII (1942), 487–88, and Coney, "An Experimental Index for Apportioning Departmental Book Funds for a University Library," *Library Quarterly*, XII (1942), 422–28. These experiments in isolating factors which should be considered in apportioning schemes were developed in connection with the problem at Colorado and Texas universities, respectively. A useful summary of the points involved in a plan of allocation is Vosper, "Allocation of the Book Budget: Experience at U.C.L.A.," *College and Research Libraries*, X (1949), 215–18+.

[42] Coney, *op. cit.*, pp. 424–26. Ellsworth introduced several other factors, such as credit-hour loads, relative use of library materials by different types of courses, number of Master's and doctoral studies. See also Ellsworth, "Summary of Current Practices of Colleges and Universities with Respect to the Management of Book Funds," *College and Research Libraries*, III (1942), 252–55.

could be used indiscriminately by university libraries appears remote, since local conditions are so important.

OTHER OPERATING EXPENSES   In addition to salaries and books, portions of the funds are used for various other purposes. These include supplies, such as catalog cards and stationery; communication, such as telephone and telegraph; printing; duplicating; travel; entertainment; organization memberships; express, freight and postage; and insurance. In 69 libraries in 1953–54, these expenditures ranged from $986.00 to $257,295.00, with a median of $16,998.00.[43]

ACCOUNTING
AND FINANCIAL
REPORTING

GENERAL CONSIDERATIONS   Most university libraries, with budgets running into hundreds of thousands of dollars, have found it necessary to adopt modern methods of accounting and financial reporting. This does not mean that the accounting methods need to be complex. The various bodies which collect information concerning university libraries, such as the Association of College and Reference Libraries, the United States Office of Education, and other accrediting agencies do not find it as difficult to obtain data as they once did.

Since the university librarian frequently finds it necessary to have library funds increased or reallocated and must present evidence in the form of statistics, it is important that he be able to make accessible to university officials more detailed accounting information concerning the library than is generally provided by the business office. In those institutions in which punched card procedures have been adopted, the business office has taken the responsibility of providing essential information.[44]

Financial statistics included in annual reports should be concise. Important expenditures should be itemized. If faculty members are shown that certain portions of the budget are necessary for bind-

[43] "College and University Library Statistics, 1953–54," *College and Research Libraries,* XVI (1955), 39.

[44] Parker, *Library Applications of Punched Cards,* chap. vii, "Financial Administration." Parker explains the use of IBM and Remington Rand equipment.

ing and periodicals, they can understand better why funds for books are limited.

Most librarians keep a permanent record of the cost of each purchased book. This information is commonly placed on the order card, although the accession record and the shelf list have sometimes been used for this record. The data are useful in making replacements, in adding copies, and in determining the value of materials for insurance purposes. Order cards are also used sometimes for a fund catalog if they are not filed as a permanent record. If a correlated order form is used, a separate slip may be designated for a fund file.

Librarians have also found it useful to separate different types of expenditures. Thus, separate records are kept for purchases of books and periodicals, for binding, and for continuations. Unless equipment and supplies are purchased through the university business office, they should be accounted for in the same way as books. It is also necessary to keep accurate records of expenditures for personnel.[45]

Many librarians do not retain duplicate bills in their files. They are often useful, at least for a brief period of time. When kept, they comprise a dealers' file, since the bills are filed alphabetically by dealer and then chronologically. In some instances this form of record is kept on cards arranged by dealer. The date, number of bill, amount, and date approved are provided on the card. This record may be made into a record of bills payable by adding the date approved when the bill is checked and sent to the business office.

It is often necessary for the librarian to get exact figures from the business office in the payment of foreign drafts. Rates of exchange vary and the figures need careful checking if payments are to be correct. The foreign book market is ordinarily an important source of materials for the university library.

More and more libraries are ordering books on multiple or correlated order forms, although in some cases it may be necessary to

[45] *Ibid*. Punched cards have been devised for control of payments to personnel.

use sheet order blanks. Some of the state university libraries are not able, in order to conform to state purchasing agency requirements, to use multiple 3 x 5 inch slips. Whatever the procedure, duplicates or triplicates, or more copies, are usually made, as the situation requires. Another record of outstanding orders is the original order file of cards furnished either by individual faculty members or by departmental representatives or made by members of the library staff.

Estimated totals of departmental commitments are usually kept in order to control the purchases. Because of such factors as discounts, costs of different editions, fluctuations in foreign currency, and cancellations, the amounts can be only approximate. But this record seems essential to prevent excess expenditures. Moreover, in university libraries where appropriations or income from endowments or special funds revert to the state, to the general fund of the university, or to the donor, it is necessary to spend such funds within certain periods in order to forestall possible reversion. A careful check of these funds will insure the spending of all available balances, as well as preventing unwise spending in a short period at the end of the year. Only a few libraries are able to retain funds for the next year if not spent during the fiscal period.

ACCOUNTING METHOD   The librarian (or any library officer responsible for a portion of the budget) should be able to know at all times, easily and conveniently, the relations between income, expenditures, and obligations incurred for the entire library budget, divided into as many accounts as are needed for control. Various schemes of accounting have been followed in libraries. These range from practically complete control by the library, involving notification of the comptroller or business office of actual purchases by clearance of invoices for payment, to relatively complete control by the business office, which, through the use of IBM or other punched-card equipment, is able to provide statements on encumbrances and expenditures.[46] It is important for the librarian, if

[46] Parker, *Library Applications of Punched Cards*, pp. 48–52.

punched-card arrangements are made, to be certain that the business office can produce records when needed.[47]

Unless it is possible, therefore, to set up an efficient relationship between the library and the business office through the use of punched-card equipment, experience indicates that a library might embody the following division of responsibility:

1. Detailed accounting for the library's book appropriations is made the responsibility of the library rather than of the university's accounting office, and the library has the responsibility for the accounting of encumbrances for outstanding orders.

2. The university accounting office limits its library book accounts to appropriations and invoices, leaving to the library the production of free balances (reflecting encumbrances), and supplies the library with monthly statements so that the library bookkeeper may keep his totals in line with official totals.

If this division is followed, the library must assume the duty of keeping a sound set of books on the library book accounts, since

[47] The following statement, dated March 19, 1954, from the director of a large state university library suggests the difficulties which may arise: "The auditor's department did not relish the idea [of taking over some 30–40 library accounts on IBM records], but its members have always been most cooperative and the decision was to eliminate our clerical assistant. It was not long before two serious problems arose. The statements of departmental balances were not coming through frequently enough for us to control our departmental funds. No matter how much we badgered the auditor's office, it was simply impossible for them to turn out the records frequently enough for us. It must be remembered that the I.B.M. record of a small amount of money involves just as much clerical and mechanical labor as if they were handling a million dollars. The second problem was that toward the end of the year when some departmental balances were used up and others were not, we had to put through formal budget transfers to revert each free balance to one general fund. This not only calls for a great deal of paper work but it also gives the impression of bad library budgeting when a great many official transfers have to be made.

"The following year and this year we have tried to eliminate this difficulty by asking the auditor's department to set up on the I.B.M. records only four or five major funds covering research, general fund, gift fund, etc. In addition, we asked them to keep the departmental accounts by hand and not to set them up in the regular auditor's procedure in order that we might eliminate the necessity of formal budget transfers at the end of the year. This they agreed to do, but we find that the manual records of departmental balances which they keep in their office are now frequently inaccurate and again they are late in coming through. I really do not know what the final decision will be or what the solution is, but it is quite obvious from our experience that our original arrangement of having a clerk in the Acquisitions Department to keep all book fund accounts worked better than anything else we have done here."

the free balance which reflects obligations for outstanding orders is the purchasing control figure. The university accounts would simply note the initial appropriation, changes made therein during the fiscal year, and invoices paid from this amount. These balances would be cash, rather than free, balances. The university accounting office would have no record in its own accounts of orders outstanding.[48]

The argument in favor of this division of responsibility for the book accounts lies in the special problem of maintaining accounts which involve the ordering of a very large number of separate items, in relation to the amount of money expended, and the delivery of the orders over a long period of time—often on several invoices per order. If the job of accounting for outstanding orders in the library accounts is separate from the university's general accounting procedure and is assigned to the library, this special situation can receive the specific attention of a staff member whose business is primarily to deal with this matter.

A standard posting machine should be carefully considered as a device for keeping all library accounts. While such machines are initially expensive, they are long-lived, economical of time, and have the important advantage of maintaining all ledgers on a current basis, showing a free balance at the end of each posting transaction.

CENTRALIZATION   In large libraries, several important values result from centralizing bookkeeping and assigning the accounting responsibility to the library. In the first place, such organization would enable the librarian to obtain full and detailed financial state-

---

[48] The following statement, dated March 18, 1954, from the associate librarian of a large private university describes this relationship: "We have no drawn up statement which describes our accounting procedures. I can say that our system gives us absolute control as to what is outstanding against the hundred funds which we use. When our order slips are written up in multiple copies, one copy goes to our bookkeeper who is able, day by day, to enter such items as outstanding. At the end of each month she therefore can show a cash balance for a fund, and then a deduction from that to cover outstanding items leaving the free balance, which is perfectly safe to use. We also draw up a monthly balance sheet which brings together the balances for all funds, shows total payments made for bills, as well as totals of outstanding orders."

ments at any time with a minimum of inconvenience. This is an important administrative consideration. By centralizing the book-keeping in one person's hands the library can afford to employ a competent professional bookkeeper and assure itself, and the university, of accuracy and professional competence in its financial records. Finally, by separating bookkeeping from the activities which originate the expenditures recorded in the accounts, a check is set up and important protection obtained. Such separation is customary in business practice. To the reasonable objection that the book-account ledgers should be maintained in the acquisition department for its convenience, it can be observed that weekly statements can be made by the bookkeeper to the head of that department—if not throughout the year, at least toward the close of the fiscal year. Furthermore, if a posting machine is used, the acquisitions department (or any person, for that matter) can obtain currently accurate information as to a free balance by telephoning the bookkeeper.

BOOKKEEPING RECORDS   The essential elements of a satisfactory method of bookkeeping for the library book accounts, requiring three records, can be summarized as follows: [49]

1. A ledger for each account showing for *income* the following items: (a) appropriation, (b) new income to the account—transfers from other accounts or additional appropriations, (c) transfers from the account, (d) credits (i.e., appropriation spent but returned for respending through a credit transaction); and for *expenditure* these items: (a) encumbrances, (b) clearance of encumbrances, (c) expenditures (or the posting of invoices); and, finally, the current *free balance*. It is obvious that not of all of these items will be shown for a given posting, since when a given order is first posted, the amount will be entered as an encumbrance, whereas the clearance of the encumbrance and the posting of the expenditure cannot occur until an invoice has been received. If a posting ma-

[49] Wilson, Metcalf, and Coney, *A Report on Certain Problems of the Libraries and School of Library Service of Columbia University*, chap. iv, "Accounting and Fiscal Records" (Coney).

chine is used, the current free balance will appear at the end of each transaction.

2. A duplicate order record consisting of a file of carbon copies of orders.

3. An invoice file.

Only order totals are encumbered on the ledger, the duplicate order sheet showing the itemization of the total. This duplicate order sheet must, consequently, be keyed to the entry on the ledger by date and dealer's name or by serial number or by some other such means.

The clearing of an encumbrance and the posting of expenditures from the invoices are by totals; that is, if an order for several items is delivered under several invoices, the items on each invoice should be cleared in terms of the total estimated cost of the invoiced items from the duplicate order, and the cost should be posted on the total of the invoice. The itemization of the invoice total is found in the invoice file.

By relying on copies of the invoices and orders, the labor of transferring items from the order to the ledger is eliminated and, with it, the consequent hazard of error in copying.

PUNCHED-CARD SYSTEMS   Reference has already been made to the possible application of punched-card equipment to the financial administration of the university library. Among a partial list of users of punched-card equipment, Parker refers to the universities of California, Florida, Missouri, and Texas.[50] Columbia has used IBM for many years. Various college, public, and governmental libraries have also introduced punched-card systems for financial record work. In the use of IBM and similar equipment, it is essential that tabulating cards be used for each transaction or group of

[50] Parker, *Library Applications of Punched Cards*, p. 70. See also Moffit, "Punched Cards Records in Acquisition Work," *College and Research Libraries*, VII (1946), 10–13; Blasingame, "Application of IBM in Libraries." Marginal punched cards for internal financial control have also been used; see Brown, "Use of Punched Cards in Acquisition Work: Experience at Illinois," *College and Research Libraries*, X (1949), 219–20+ and McGaw, *Marginal Punched Cards in College and University Libraries*.

data. The account, operation code or expenditure classification, and other items are also punched on these cards. As Parker has pointed out, information should be so arranged that the cards can be co-ordinated with cards used for other processes. He further observes: "Cards for appropriations, gifts, payrolls, book orders, subscription records, budget transfers, and repair bills, while separate accounts, will have to be tabulated together at times; and certain of these cards will have to be combined on occasion with nonaccounting cards, such as catalog statistics cards, loan record cards, etc. Coordination at the time a system is installed will eliminate confusion and permit more complete integration of the accounting process with other phases of record keeping." [51] Those librarians who have used punched-card systems have found, for the most part, that they have simplified operations. However, they still represent a relatively new device in financial administration. Since libraries use punched-card equipment usually in cooperation with business offices, coordination is essential if both parties are to be satisfied.

COST CONTROL   Earlier in this chapter reference was made to the study by Millett on *Financing Higher Education in the United States.*[52] One of his observations was critical of the growth of expenditures of academic libraries. While Millett did not carefully distinguish between the programs of college libraries and those of university libraries, and there are other questions which may be raised in regard to his generalizations, he did touch upon a situation which has concerned librarians as well as administrators of universities. What do libraries get for the hundreds of thousands of dollars they spend? Or, more exactly, what do the universities get? In a recent summary of problems in the management of college and

[51] *Op. cit.*, p. 49.
[52] See footnote 2. An important follow-up of the Millett statement is the volume edited by Williams, *Problems and Prospects of the Research Library*. This is a report of the Conference held at Monticello, Illinois, October 29–31, 1954, and sponsored by the Association of Research Libraries. Not only questions of finance, but also of programs and services, were discussed. The purpose of the Conference was to lay the groundwork for a proposed commission on financial problems of research libraries, which the Association of American Universities intends to sponsor.

university libraries, Coney [53] pointed out that "University libraries lack a comprehensive, comparative cost study of their operations in any way comparable to the one by Baldwin and Marcus for public libraries." This is still true, even though some university libraries have tried to study their own problems in local cost studies, and the Association of Research Libraries and other agencies have recognized the need for more basic data on costs. Cost control is designed to show the relation between the funds spent and the units produced by their expenditure. This is more than knowledge of total cost; it is information on what is done in each part of an organization. It is essential for efficient financial administration. The librarian owes it to his university to have available accurate and adequate data on the costs of such services as acquisitions, cataloging, binding, circulation, or reference, or a system of departmental libraries. Whether cost accounting, job analyses, and inventory evaluations are done by punched-card procedures or by other methods, it is important that the librarian have available such data as are necessary to justify his budget in every particular. With such justification, university presidents and other administrators who are interested in a library service which reinforces an effective instructional and research program will need no urging to provide an adequate income for the library system.[54]

BIBLIOGRAPHY

Allen, H. K., with the collaboration of R. G. Axt. State Public Finance and State Institutions of Higher Education in the United States. Published for the Commission on Financing Higher Education. New York, Columbia University Press, 1952.

American Library Association. Board on Personnel Administration. Classification and Pay Plans for Libraries of Institutions of Higher Education, 2d ed. Chicago, American Library Association, 1949. 3 vols.

[53] Donald Coney, "Management in College and University Libraries," p. 88. Coney referred to E. V. Baldwin and W. E. Marcus, *Library Costs and Budgets; A Study of Cost Accounting in Public Libraries.* (New York: R. R. Bowker, 1941). The Coney paper also contains a useful list of "References" on management problems.

[54] Paul Buck, "Looking Ahead," in Williams, *op. cit.,* 147–53.

——— Position Classification and Salary Administration in Libraries. Chicago, American Library Association, 1951.

Arnett, Trevor. College and University Finance. New York, General Education Board, 1922.

Bennett, Fleming. "Prompt Payment of Bookdealers' Invoices: An Approach to Standards," *College and Research Libraries*, XIV (1953), 387–92+.

Blasingame, Ralph U., Jr. "Application of International Business Machines in Libraries" (unpublished Master's thesis, Columbia University, 1950).

Brown, Charles H. "Librarianship and the Sciences," in Louis Shores (ed.), *Challenges to Librarianship* (Florida State University Studies, No. 12). Tallahassee, Florida State University, 1953.

Brown, George B. "Use of Punched Cards in Acquisition Work: Experience at Illinois," *College and Research Libraries*, X (1949), 219–20+.

California, University of. "Interim Report of the Library Committee, Academic Senate, Northern Section," in its *University Bulletin*, II (1954,), 133–34.

Carlson, William H. "History and Present Status of Centralization of the Libraries of the Oregon State System of Higher Education," *College and Research Libraries*, XIV (1953), 414–17.

"College and University Library Statistics," in *College and Research Libraries*. Since 1952 published in January issue; for earlier years, see indexes.

Coney, Donald. "An Experimental Index for Apportioning Department Book Funds in a University Library," *Library Quarterly*, XII (1942), 422–28.

——— "Management in College and University Libraries," *Library Trends*, I (1952), 83–94.

Coney, Donald, *et al.* Report of a Survey of the Indiana University Library for the Indiana University, February–July, 1940. Chicago, American Library Association, 1940.

Ellsworth, Ralph E. "Some Aspects of the Problem of Allocating Book Funds Among Departments of Universities," *Library Quarterly*, XII (1942), 486–94.

——— "Summary of Current Practices in Colleges and Universities with Respect to the Management of Book Funds," *College and Research Libraries*, III (1942), 252–55.

——— "Trends in University Expenditures for Library Resources and for Total Educational Purposes," *Library Quarterly*, XIV (1944), 1–8.

Hamlin, Arthur T. "Financial and Economic Status of Research Libraries," *Library Quarterly*, XXIII (1953), 190–98.

Irwin, Mary (ed.). American Universities and Colleges. 6th ed. Washington, American Council on Education, 1952.

Kipp, Laurence J. "Scientific Management in Research Libraries," *Library Trends*, II (1954), 390–400.

Lyle, Guy R. The Administration of the College Library. 2d ed., rev. New York, H. W. Wilson, 1949.

McCarthy, Stephen A. "Administrative Organization and Financial Support of Land-Grant College and University Libraries," *College and Research Libraries*, IX (1948), 327–31.

—— "Financial Support of College and University Libraries," *Library Trends*, I (1952), 105–22.

McGaw, Howard F. Marginal Punched Cards in College and University Libraries. Washington, Scarecrow Press, 1952.

McNeal, A. L. "Financial Problems of University Libraries," *College and Research Libraries*, XV (1954), 407–10.

Metcalf, Keyes D., "Financial Problems of University Libraries: A Proposal for a Conference," *Harvard Library Bulletin*, VIII (1954), 5–13.

—— "The Situation at Harvard," in "Fees for Research Library Use by 'Outsiders': A Symposium," *College and Research Libraries*, XIII (1952), 297–98.

Miller, R. A. "Cost Accounting in Libraries: Acquisition and Cataloging," *Library Quarterly*, XII (1937), 511–36.

Millett, John A. Financing Higher Education in the United States. Published for the Commission on Financing Higher Education. New York, Columbia University Press, 1952.

Missouri, University of, Library. "Budget Situation, 1953–54." Columbia, Mo., 1953 (mimeographed).

Mixer, Charles W. "Insurance Evaluation of a University Library's Collections," *College and Research Libraries*, XIII (1952), 18–23.

—— "New Insurance for Library Collections," *Library Journal*, LXXIX (1954), 1539–43.

Moffit, Alexander. "Punched Card Records in Serials Acquisitions," *College and Research Libraries*, VII (1946), 10–13.

Muller, Hans. "Management of College Library Book Budgets," *College and Research Libraries*, II (1941), 320–26.

National Committee on the Preparation of a Manual on College and University Business Administration. College and University Business Administration. Vol. 1. Washington, American Council on Education, 1952.

North Carolina, University of. Friends of the Library. Opportunities and Plans for the Present and Future of the University Library at Chapel Hill. Chapel Hill, 1953.

Orr, Robert W., and William H. Carlson. Report of a Survey of the

Library of Texas A. and M. College, October, 1949 to February, 1950. College Station, Texas, Texas A. and M. College, 1950.

Parker, Ralph H. "Libraries in an Inflationary Cycle," *College and Research Libraries*, XII (1951), 338–42.

—— Library Application of Punched Cards: A Description of Mechanical Systems. Chicago, American Library Association, 1952.

Reeves, F. W., *et al.* The Liberal Arts College. Chicago, University of Chicago Press, 1932.

Reichmann, Felix. "Costs of Cataloging," *Library Trends*, II (1953), 290–317.

Rider, Fremont. "Library Cost Accounting," *Library Quarterly*, VI (1936), 331–81.

Russell, John D. Efficiency in College Management. Bloomington, Ind., Bureau of Cooperative Research, Indiana University, 1931.

—— The Finance of Higher Education. 2d ed. Chicago, University of Chicago Press, 1954.

Scheps, Clarence. Accounting for Colleges and Universities. Baton Rouge, Louisiana State University Press, 1949.

Shaw, R. R. "Scientific Management in the Library," *Wilson Library Bulletin*, XXI (1947), 349–52.

—— The Use of Photography for Clerical Routines. Washington, American Council of Learned Societies, 1953.

Singer, Dorothea. The Insurance of Libraries. Chicago, American Library Association, 1946.

"Statistics of Southern College and University Libraries." Louisiana State University Library (mimeographed).

"Statistics for College and University Libraries." Princeton University Library (mimeographed).

Sypher, Wylie. "Views on the Fee Policy," in "Fees for Research Library Use by 'Outsiders': A Symposium," *College and Research Libraries*, XIII (1952), 295–96.

Tauber, Maurice F., and Eugene H. Wilson. Report of a Survey of the Library of Montana State University, January–May, 1951. Chicago, American Library Association, 1951.

Trent, Robert M. "Financial Records for College Libraries" (unpublished Master's thesis, Columbia University, 1939).

U.S. Office of Education. Survey of Land-Grant Colleges and Universities. Bull. No. 9 (1930). Washington, Government Printing Office, 1930.

Voigt, Melvin J. "Ratio of Professional to Clerical Staff," *College and Research Libraries*, XVI (1955), 76–77.

Vosper, Robert. "Allocation of the Book Budget: Experiences at U.C.L.A.," *College and Research Libraries*, X (1949), 215–18+.

Waples, Douglas, *et al.* The Evaluation of Higher Institutions. Vol. IV: The Library. Chicago, University of Chicago Press, 1936.

White, Carl M. "The Situation at Columbia," in "Fees for Research Library Use by 'Outsiders': A Symposium," *College and Research Libraries*, XIII (1949), 299–301.

Williams, Edwin E. (ed.). Problems and Prospects of the Research Library. Published for the Association of Research Libraries. New Brunswick, N.J., The Scarecrow Press, 1955.

Wilson, Louis R. "Should Research Libraries Impose Fees upon Visiting Scholars?" in "Fees for Research Library Use by 'Outsiders': A Symposium," *College and Research Libraries*, XIII (1952), 301–2.

Wilson, Louis R., and Marion A. Milczewski (eds.). Libraries of the Southeast: A Report of the Southeastern States Cooperative Library Survey, 1946–1947. Chapel Hill, Published for the Southeastern Library Association by the University of North Carolina Press, 1949.

Wilson, Louis R., Keyes D. Metcalf, and Donald Coney. A Report on Certain Problems of the Libraries and School of Library Service of Columbia University. New York, Columbia University Libraries, 1947.

See also chapters on "Finance" in library surveys. (See Bibliography in chapter xvi).

IV

ADMINISTRATIVE ORGANIZATION

VARIOUS governmental and financial aspects of the administration of the university library have been discussed in the
preceding chapters. It is now pertinent to consider those aspects of
administrative organization which help the library effectively perform its function in carrying out the educational and research program of the modern university. Within the library, administrative
and departmental organization, operational functions, book collections, personnel, buildings and equipment, records and reports,
and methods of measurement present many administrative and educational problems.

In this chapter, in developing the thesis of the need of sound
internal organization for the university library, the following topics
will be treated: (1) the theory of administrative organization; (2)
library administration; (3) officers of administration; (4) duties of
the officers; (5) lines of responsibility and authority; (6) organizational systems; and (7) departmental library systems. Functional
departmental organization will be discussed in chapters v and vi,
and the training and remuneration of administrative officers, in
chapters vii and viii. The application of certain principles of administration will be noted by reference to a selected number of
university library organizations as represented by charts, since
charts are useful devices for showing relationships. It should be
borne in mind, however, that they frequently fail to reveal fully
certain elements or factors of internal organization, which, in varying degrees, affect the efficiency of the library's operation.

THE THEORY OF   Administration as a field of study has been
ADMINISTRATIVE   well established in present-day education.
ORGANIZATION   Brought into prominence by Henri Fayol in
                          his *Industrial and General Administration* in
1916, the subject has been developed considerably since then. The
works of Gulick and Urwick [1] and others [2] have helped to build
up a generally accepted body of theory, particularly in the fields
of industry and business and public administration. This theory has
been applied not only in these fields but in practically every major
enterprise and institution. The science of administration has become
a force which the administrator, in whatever field, may study and
apply with profit.

The theory has been expressed in generalizations concerning the
elements of the administrative function and the principles which
are most commonly associated with it. It may constantly serve as
a frame of reference for the administrator in the performance of
his duties as a directing officer; and it should enable him to recognize clearly the distinction between administration, on the one
hand, and operation, on the other, a distinction which, if not made
—many administrators do not make it easily—leads to confusion
and lack of efficiency.[3]

These elements and principles have been so generally covered in
studies on scientific administration that it is unnecessary to give
them extended consideration here. It is desirable, however, to re-
state them and to indicate their relation to the organization and
administration of the university library.

ELEMENTS OF ADMINISTRATION   The function of administration
has frequently been broken down into the elements of planning,
organizing, staffing, directing, coordinating, reporting, and budgeting, as follows:

Planning has been described as outlining broadly what needs to

---

[1] Gulick and Urwick (eds.), *Papers on the Science of Administration.*

[2] In various aspects of the field, e.g., scientific management, office management,
business administration, public administration, personnel administration, etc.

[3] See Copeland, *The Executive at Work.*

be done and indicating the methods necessary to achieve determined purposes. Unless planning is made an essential part of the university administrative program, it is difficult to see how the librarian and his aides can either foresee or prepare for the future. Planning effectively requires a wide knowledge of the educational program of the university and a recognition of the philosophical and practical aspects of university librarianship.

The element of *organizing* relates to the establishment of a structure of authority which is carefully defined and coordinated for the attainment of specific objectives. Applied to the university library, it involves the instituting of precise relationships which facilitate management and operation. This element is clarified in detail in chapters v and vi, in which the technical and readers' departments of the university library, respectively, are discussed.

Staffing is concerned with personnel, dealing with employment, training, and the maintenance of favorable working conditions. A definite personnel policy for the university library is basic to a sound program of service. Unquestionably, personnel problems are among the most important in the library, and an able administrator devotes considerable attention to them.

Making decisions and incorporating them in specific and general orders are embodied in the element of *directing*. Library administrators, whether the chief librarian or his subordinates, are constantly called upon to issue orders which determine the current and future policies of service.

The element of *coordinating* is concerned with interrelating the various parts of an organization's work. In a library it may refer to the entire organization or to any one of its units. Unless the technical and readers' services of the library are fully coordinated, for example, operations may be introduced which are inconsistent with the objectives of the institution.

The administrator is obligated to keep his superiors informed of his organization's performance and needs. This is done by *reporting*. Through adequate records, research, and accumulation of data the librarian is able to reveal the condition of the library. This information also provides him with evidence for determining the efficiency of the enterprise for which he is held responsible.

In the preceding chapter considerable attention was given to the question of *budgeting*. This element of administration, as was pointed out, requires careful planning, accounting, and control. The administrator is obligated to study continuously the library needs of the university and to try to secure the funds necessary to support them. Scientific management is an essential basis for proper budgeting.

PRINCIPLES OF ADMINISTRATION   A "principle" may be defined as a settled rule for action. But a principle is something higher than a rule, since it forms the basis for the rule. If principles are ascertained by experience, as Fayol's were, they are more than a mere summing-up; they are generalizations grounded on carefully analyzed case studies.

Since Fayol defines the administrative function as being concerned only with the human portion of the undertaking, his administrative principles are also concerned with the human portion. None of the principles he sets forth is rigid; everything is a question of degree. The same principle is seldom used twice in the same way because of the many variables. There is no limit to the number of administrative principles, since any rule or device strengthening the human part of the organization takes it place among the principles only so long as it is worthy of this position. Any change in conditions may bring about a change in the rules. How to adapt the principles considered in the following paragraphs to the need is as important as the principles themselves and requires intelligence, experience, judgment, and a keen sense of values in human relationships.

DIVISION OF LABOR. Although an important administrative principle, division of labor is also the foundation of organization. Through it specialized skills are developed by which efficiency is increased. There are, however, certain limits beyond which division of labor should not go: (1) it should not set up a task requiring less than the full time of one person; (2) it should consider limitations of technology and custom at a given place and time; and (3) it must not be an unrealistic division of human effort.

If one person in a library ordered, cataloged, classified, prepared, shelved, and serviced the books, there would be no division of labor. In a very small library this might be necessary, but the confusion and inefficiency resulting from having all the assistants in a university library perform all these functions is obvious.

AUTHORITY AND RESPONSIBILITY. Authority is of two kinds: statutory (that belonging to a given position) and personal (which is a result of the possession of the qualities of leadership). Authority to give orders may be delegated by the head of a department to his first assistant. Possession of authority must also involve responsibility for actions. Once an executive has delegated authority for a certain activity, he no longer possesses that authority; but, if it is misused, he may recall it. In the case of responsibility, the executive continues to share it and is responsible to his chief for the work accomplished by his subordinate. In this manner the chief librarian is responsible for all that goes on in a library, no matter by whom the actual work is done.

DISCIPLINE. Discipline should not be thought of as something imposed by a strict taskmaster. It is respect for agreements whose object is obedience, diligence, energy, and outward marks of respect. It applies to men in the highest positions as well as to those in the lowest. The most effective ways of establishing and maintaining discipline are providing good leadership throughout the staff, settling disputes clearly and fairly, and enforcing penalties judiciously. The professional staff of a university library probably presents fewer serious disciplinary problems than do clerical workers and student assistants, but the principle applies to all.

UNITY OF COMMAND. One person should be responsible to, and receive orders from, only one superior. If the head of a combined technical services department in a university library should take it upon himself to give orders to an assistant in the serials division, which is under his general jurisdiction but under the direct supervision of the chief of the serials division, he would be violating this principle. Any orders he has to give should be transmitted to the workers through the divisional chiefs.

UNITY OF MANAGEMENT. Fayol expresses this as "one manager and one plan for all the operations which have the same objective in view." Unity of command is distinguished from unity of management in that the former depends on the staff's working properly together, while the latter is provided for by properly arranging the organization. The catalog department should have one manager and a plan of operation to facilitate getting books cataloged correctly and quickly.

SUBORDINATION OF INDIVIDUAL INTERESTS TO THE COMMON GOOD. This is an obvious principle as it stands. It may be visualized more concretely by considering the matter of time schedules in a university library. A reference assistant, for example, should not be permitted to enroll in a course which is scheduled for hours when he is most needed at the reference desk.

REMUNERATION. Salaries should be fair, and increases should reward successful effort in order to provide an incentive to the individual for professional growth and increased efficiency. Some idea of the fairness of the salaries of the university library staff may be obtained by comparing them with those of the teaching staff having equivalent educational achievements.

CENTRALIZATION. Centralization of administration may be used in varying degrees, depending on the situation. In a university library it would not be desirable to have the function of ordering books so decentralized that each department does its own searching, keeps its own records, and makes purchases independent of the other departments. In such an organization there would be expensive duplication of bibliographical tools, records, and probably books purchased. On the other hand, book selection might be highly decentralized, since the department heads presumably know more about their respective fields than a central order librarian would. A limited degree of decentralization of managerial functions makes for better operation and takes advantage of the special knowledge of lesser staff members.

THE HIERARCHY. The hierarchy is also known as the "scalar principle," since it involves a series of steps, rising according to the degree of authority at each level. Each level is subordinate to the one above it. The scale or hierarchy extends in an unbroken line from the chief executive to the lowest employee. This line serves as a means of communication; orders go down the line and information and appeals go up it. At each level there must be an official having authority over all others at that level; and at the top there is one person, the chief librarian in the case of the university library.

SPAN OF CONTROL. This term means the number of persons with whom an administrator must deal directly. An executive's span of control is limited because of limits of his own knowledge, time, and energy. It is impossible to state a "best" number to cover all situations. The number recommended by various authorities ranges from not less than three to not more than ten or twelve. Factors other than the executive himself which affect the span of control are the type of work (routine or complicated), homogeneity of work, and dispersion of work.

In the university library the chief of the catalog department can direct the work of a fairly large number of workers because of the essential similarity of their work and because they will ordinarily be all located in one place. The factors mentioned above, however, may make it necessary for the head cataloger to have several supervisory assistants who report to him. The chief librarian usually must deal with such diverse and scattered functions as technical services, reference, circulation, and departmental libraries. In order to make his load easier, he generally has assistant librarians and supervisors who relieve him of the need of dealing directly with the head of each unit.

DEPARTMENTATION. Departmentation is closely related to division of labor, the span of control, and the hierarchy. It is the grouping together of activities on the basis of homogeneity under the control of one administrative officer. The bases for forming departments are several; but the most important to the university library are function (cataloging, circulation, etc.), commodity (subject departmentation), geographical (departmental libraries), or persons served (undergraduate library).

LINE AND STAFF. Line is synonymous with authority and command; staff, with advice and counsel. The line forms the links in the chain of the scalar organization; the staff has no authority. Both line and staff begin with the chief executive and may be found at every level downward. Staff officers are always directly responsible to line officers, and they have no voice to command except through the line officers. It is only in very large organizations that the staff exists as a separate body; frequently one person may serve as both line and staff. This is exemplified in the university library when the chief librarian calls in a department head, because of his special equipment, to make a study of some projected scheme of reorganization. This device may be used to take advantage of the special knowledge of any employee without raising his status in the hierarchy.

ORDER. In the physical sense, "order" means the best arrangement for the most efficient operation. In a university library it would hardly seem efficient to receive books at one end of the building, catalog them at the other end, and have them return to the center of the building for preparation for the shelves. The arrangement should expedite activities and conserve the materials used.

In relation to employees, order concerns the placement of the right person in the job for which he is most suited. Ordinarily, a chief librarian would not put an expert cataloger at the circulation desk. The cataloger might do effective work at the circulation desk, but his training and experience would fit him most effectively in cataloging.

EQUITY. Equity means uniform treatment of the staff. It is the result of combining friendliness with justice on the part of an executive toward the staff. In its application it may mean that the pay of a reference librarian should not exceed that of a cataloger with equal education, experience, ability, and responsibility; nor should an executive give preferential treatment, not warranted by ability, to certain employees.

STABILITY OF STAFF. Rapid turnover of staff is both a cause and an indication of lack of success. It is conceivably better to have some positions in the library filled with mediocre persons who remain in them for a relatively long period than with excellent or troublesome ones who move on rapidly. There is always some instability and rightfully so, for without it unfit employees are permitted to retain their jobs and the more capable workers do not move on to greater responsibilities. So far as the organization permits it, opportunities for promotion should be available to competent staff.

INITIATIVE. Initiative of the employee should be aroused and encouraged within the limits of respect for authority and discipline. Permission to exercise initiative gives the employee satisfaction and supplements the drive of the manager. At least one large library gives citations to staff members who make suggestions which result in wider service or savings in manpower.

ESPRIT DE CORPS. Harmony and unity are a great source of strength and should be fostered and encouraged by the library administration. Equity, unity of command, initiative, and availability of managers do much to promote *esprit de corps*. The chief librarian should be available to the lowest ranked employee in certain situations unresolved at lower administrative levels.

LIBRARY ADMINISTRATION   The questions may now be asked: How extensively has this body of theory been recognized by librarians, and to what extent have the elements and principles of administration been consciously applied in the administration of libraries? To these questions there are several answers.

In a recent issue of *Library Trends*,[4] Ralph R. Shaw, former librarian at the United States Department of Agriculture and exponent for the introduction of scientific management in libraries, wrote "that there is a trend toward the application of scientific management in libraries—and indeed a rapid one. Such an issue

[4] "Scientific Management in Libraries," *Library Trends*, II (1954), 359–483.

would have been quite impossible twenty years ago, and even now some of the articles record directions of growth rather than achievements." The issue contains articles on scientific method and library administration, scientific management in public libraries, scientific management in research libraries, time and motion studies in libraries, standardization as a tool of scientific management, consequences of management surveys, the management engineer, standards of performance for hospital libraries, building design for library management, and scientific management in cataloging. Other issues of *Library Trends* contain papers which demonstrate the interest of librarians in the application of administrative theory to library problems.[5]

The literature of librarianship is reflecting more and more attention to the subject of administration and management.[6] In his general report of the Public Library Inquiry, Leigh [7] called attention to the problem from the point of view of library education. He observed that while librarians, like other professional groups, are not quick to accept changes suggested by outside specialists, it is "of great importance that the skills of management analysis and scientific personnel administration be assimilated within the general administration of libraries and professional training of librarians rather than occasionally presented as an intrusion of outsiders to measure work, to analyze and classify positions, or to establish salary grades." The implications of this statement for university librarianship are apparent. Leigh also pointed out that some of the library schools, in their newer programs, have attempted to provide courses which deal with the organization and the operating problems of different types of libraries. Workshops and institutes on library administration and management have fur-

[5] See, for example, Coney, "Management in College and University Libraries," *Library Trends*, I (1952), 83–94; see also other issues of *Library Trends*, which have dealt with special libraries, school libraries, public libraries, libraries of the United States government, cataloging and classification, library resources, personnel administration, public services in libraries, library associations, and current acquisitions.

[6] See, for example, the volumes of *College and Research Libraries*, and the citations in American Library Association, *Personnel Administration for Libraries*.

[7] Leigh, *Public Library in the United States*, p. 172.

ther aided in the program of developing the backgrounds of librarians in meeting administrative problems.

Librarians of state and municipal universities have had a longer history of working with officials who have been cognizant of the implications of scientific management than have librarians of private universities. Like librarians of public and governmental libraries—federal, state, and city—they have had to administer the financial operations of their libraries in accord with the financial procedures of the governmental unit. They also have to maintain other relations with the governmental unit which make it necessary for them to be acquainted with the general field of municipal and public administration. Although their consideration of the subject in the past has been more from the point of view of political science than of administration as such, in recent years there has been definite progress in the application of scientific management to the solution of internal problems in their libraries. The Library of Congress, the New York Public Library, the Brooklyn Public Library, and other public libraries have sought to introduce modern practices of personnel administration and scientific management. More consideration is being given to evaluation of different forms of library organization, job analysis, personnel administration, library cooperation, and adaptation of mechanical appliances of all kinds.

But much remains to be done in all of these areas. A random sampling of questions, selected by Downs,[8] in the July, 1952, issue of *Library Trends* reveals the need of evidence on major administrative matters. The critical observations of nonlibrarians on the extent of the support of the library in the educational and research framework of the university should be subjected to close study by heads of libraries who have not thought in terms of coordinated administrative organization, proper personnel programs, and efficient operations and procedures. Librarians, and particularly university librarians, should have first-hand acquaintance with management literature and orientation in the management field.[9]

[8] "Introduction," *Library Trends*, I (1952), 4.
[9] Coney, "Management in College and University Libraries," p. 91.

It will not always be easy to apply principles of administration to particular university libraries. Despite many likenesses, university libraries differ in many respects among themselves, and, consequently, present different patterns of organization. The history of the library, the structure of the building, the governmental relationships, the existing personnel, the financial support given by the administration, the variety of subjects offered by the university for which the library must furnish materials, and the type and nature of the work performed—one or several of these factors may account for the diversity of organization and the depth of application of management principles. In some instances in the past the librarian may have been chosen for his knowledge of a subject of research rather than for his skill in administration and, consequently, may have found it difficult to apply theoretical principles to practical problems when conditions called for such application.

No longer is the library to be left in a vacuum as a nonprofit-making unit of the university. Since universities themselves are seeking to employ administrators who make the most of the limited funds at their disposal, so libraries will have to be operated by individuals who are accountable for administrative efficiency. This does not mean that efficiency is the sole criterion of a successful librarian. As Coney succinctly notes: "It hardly seems necessary to add that management is only one of the aspects of librarianship, and that 'library work' and an appreciation of the uses of books are of even greater importance." [10]

OFFICERS OF ADMINISTRATION The success of the library in performing its appropriate function depends, in considerable measure, upon the nature of its administrative organization. As enrollments increase, new courses are offered, new schools are added, or other changes are made within the university which affect the library, corresponding changes must be made by the library to adjust itself to them.

It is clear from the preceding discussion that the actual administrative effectiveness of the library also depends upon the character,

[10] *Ibid.*

knowledge, and administrative skill of the librarian and the principal assistants who aid him in administrating the library. Consequently, these officers should be chosen on the basis of their known qualifications; the general sphere of their activities should be clearly defined; and they should be so placed in the general administrative organization of the university that they will be able to direct the library successfully.

TITLES OF ADMINISTRATIVE OFFICERS   The titles of chief administrative officers in the university library have not been uniform. Although in the majority of instances the head officer of the library is known as the "librarian" or "university librarian," more and more institutions, particularly in those in which departmental and school libraries are under one jurisdiction, refer to him as "director of libraries" or "director of the library." [11]

Other titles of administrative officers which appear frequently in listings [12] of library staff include the following: associate or assistant librarian (or director), with or without some qualification, for example, technical services or readers' services; assistant to the librarian; head of the acquisitions department, or order librarian; head of the catalog department, or catalog librarian; head of the reference department, or reference librarian; head of the circulation department, or circulation librarian; head of the periodicals (or serials) department, or periodicals (or serials) librarian; head of the photographic services department; supervisor (or librarian) of special collections; head of the bindery, or binding librarian; and supervisor of departmental libraries. There are many variations in these titles, as well as in other titles involving the names of curators, custodians, and superintendents. College librarian, extension librarian, reserve book librarian, map librarian, rare books librarian, and archivist are titles used to designate individuals who generally have some administrative functions. Departmental libraries may be

[11] McAnally, "Organization of College and University Libraries," *Library Trends,* I (1952), 23.

[12] See American Library Association. Board on Salaries, Staff, and Tenure, *Classification and Pay Plans for Libraries in Institutions of Higher Education.*

supervised by individuals who are designated by the subject field covered by the library, such as geology librarian, chemistry librarian, or education librarian. Or, in library systems having grouped libraries, the heads of the divisions may be titled humanities librarian, social sciences librarian, or science librarian (or natural sciences librarian and bio-medical sciences librarian). The possibilities appear endless. It might be desirable, if library terminology is to have meaning, that there be more uniformity in the designations of officers. In fact, standard nomenclature is a characteristic of a profession.

DUTIES OF THE LIBRARIAN (OR DIRECTOR)   While the duties of the librarian or director may differ from library to library in the attention that may be given to specific items, a listing of the varied activities of the chief officer reveals a pattern that is similar to the following:

1. To formulate and administer policies, rules, and regulations for the purpose of securing the most complete use of the library by students, faculty members, and other members of the university community

2. To participate in the formulation of the educational policies of the university

3. To participate in the activities of the university library committee as a member and as an officer (usually secretary, rather than chairman)

4. To maintain relationships with the president, deans, and other university officials

5. To bear responsibility to the president for the satisfactory government and administration of the library

6. To select a harmonious administrative, technical, and service staff and to recommend their employment to the president

7. To make recommendations to the president on all matters pertaining to the status, promotion, change in position, or dismissal of members of the library staff

8. To guide the development of the book collections of the uni-

versity libraries and to be responsible for all book collections of the university

9. To represent the university library to its users, the general public, and in educational and library groups

10. To make reports to the president or board of trustees and to library agencies

11. To assist in securing gifts for the library

12. To prepare and execute the annual budget for the operation of the library

13. To cooperate with librarians and scholars in making resources available for research.

DUTIES OF THE ASSISTANT LIBRARIAN (OR DIRECTOR)   1. To supervise the work of the library staff and prepare work schedules for them

2. To help conduct staff meetings

3. To act as chief adviser to the director in matters of administration

4. To formulate administrative and library policies and present them to the librarian for consideration

5. To direct the attention of faculty members to the coordination of the instructional and research programs of the university with the use of the library

6. To aid the director in the preparation of the budget

7. To make reports to the director regarding the work of the library

8. To supervise the technical and/or service departments

9. To cooperate with the heads of departments in the nomination of new staff members and to make suggestions to the director regarding the promotion, change of position, or other action concerning staff members

10. To act as principal administrative officer during the absence of the director and to represent him at designated meetings

11. To act as liaison officer between staff members and director

12. To be responsible for building problems and general equipment.

Like the librarian, the assistant librarian and departmental heads should be accessible to staff members for consultation. The major administrative officers are expected to be cognizant of developments in every aspect of university librarianship, even if they are not aware of all details. By participating actively in professional associations, the officers are enabled to come into contact with plans and programs which may have direct application to their own institution. While administrators are busy people, they have recognized an obligation to the professional development of librarianship. This has been demonstrated most effectively by the contributions that administrators have made to the literature of the field.[13]

Many of the duties of the departmental heads are similar to those of the librarian and assistant librarian, since they arise out of the elements and principles of administration—planning, staffing, etc.— but they differ as they apply to specific departments. The following list of duties, therefore, applies equally to the reference librarian, the head cataloger, or the order librarian. In the following two chapters the specific duties of major departmental heads will be considered.

DUTIES OF THE DEPARTMENTAL HEAD   1. To lay out and assign work for the departmental staff and see that they are effectively employed

2. To give directions and suggestions to the staff, aiding them in the solution of difficult problems and revising their work

3. To develop the procedures and routines of the department to meet the needs of the users of the library

4. To cooperate with the heads of other departments and to coordinate the work of the library

5. To prepare reports and memoranda for the assistant director, director, and other members of the staff or faculty

6. To make recommendations concerning appointments, promotions, salary adjustments, and other personnel matters.

[13] Wilson, "The Challenge of Library Literature to Education for Librarianship, 1923–1953," in Shores (ed.), *Challenges to Librarianship.*

FIGURE 1. ORGANIZATION CHART, HARVARD UNIVERSITY LIBRARY, 1953

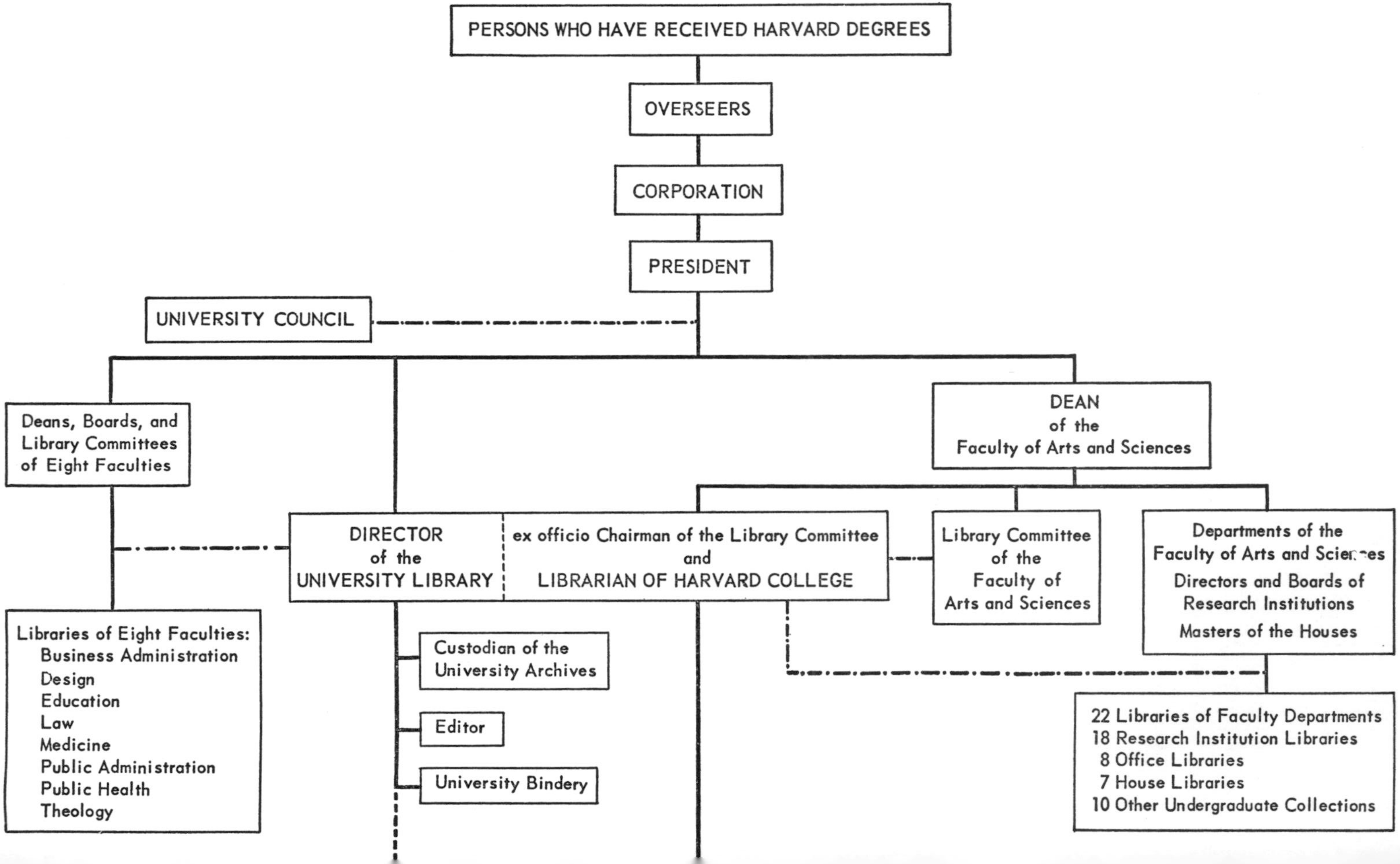

PERSONS WHO HAVE RECEIVED HARVARD DEGREES

OVERSEERS

CORPORATION

PRESIDENT

UNIVERSITY COUNCIL

DEAN of the Faculty of Arts and Sciences

Library Committee of the Faculty of Arts and Sciences

ex officio Chairman of the Library Committee and LIBRARIAN OF HARVARD COLLEGE

DIRECTOR of the UNIVERSITY LIBRARY

Custodian of the University Archives

Editor

University Bindery

Departments of the Faculty of Arts and Sciences
Directors and Boards of Research Institutions
Masters of the Houses

22 Libraries of Faculty Departments
18 Research Institution Libraries
8 Office Libraries
7 House Libraries
10 Other Undergraduate Collections

Deans, Boards, and Library Committees of Eight Faculties

Libraries of Eight Faculties:
Business Administration
Design
Education
Law
Medicine
Public Administration
Public Health
Theology

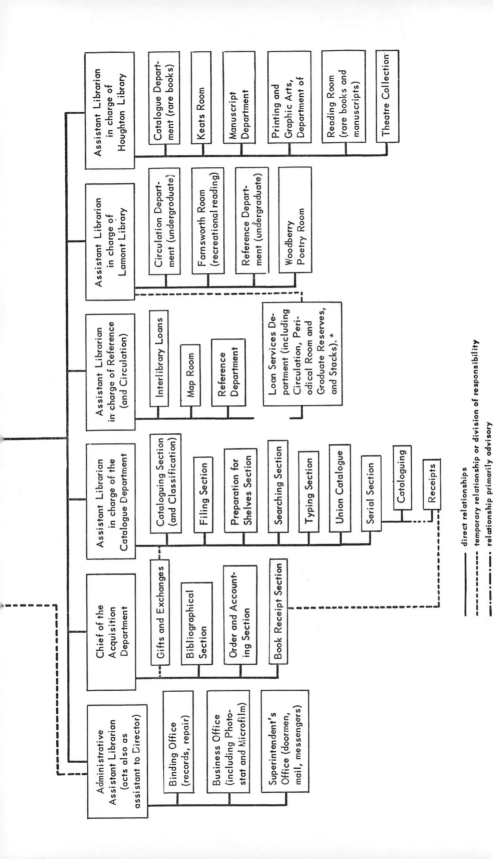

Administrative Assistant Librarian (acts also as assistant to Director)

Binding Office (records, repair)

Business Office (including Photostat and Microfilm)

Superintendent's Office (doormen, mail, messengers)

Chief of the Acquisition Department

Gifts and Exchanges

Bibliographical Section

Order and Accounting Section

Book Receipt Section

Assistant Librarian in charge of the Catalogue Department

Cataloguing Section (and Classification)

Filing Section

Preparation for Shelves Section

Searching Section

Typing Section

Union Catalogue

Serial Section

Cataloguing

Receipts

Assistant Librarian in charge of Reference (and Circulation)

Interlibrary Loans

Map Room

Reference Department

Loan Services Department (including Circulation, Periodical Room and Graduate Reserves, and Stacks). *

Assistant Librarian in charge of Lamont Library

Circulation Department (undergraduate)

Farnsworth Room (recreational reading)

Reference Department (undergraduate)

Woodberry Poetry Room

Assistant Librarian in charge of Houghton Library

Catalogue Department (rare books)

Keats Room

Manuscript Department

Printing and Graphic Arts, Department of

Reading Room (rare books and manuscripts)

Theatre Collection

—— direct relationships

- - - temporary relationship or division of responsibility

·-·-· relationship primarily advisory

* The Assistant Librarian in charge of Lamont temporarily directs the Loan Service Department in Widener.

7. To rate staff members on their efficiency
8. To see that essential records and statistics are kept.

LINES OF   The administrative organization of the uni-
RESPONSIBILITY   versity library is concerned with the relationship (1) of the librarian to the board of
trustees and to the president or other officers and (2) of the various
library officers to one another. It is also concerned with the way in
which lines of responsibility descend from the superior officer or
board to the librarian (or director) and other officers of the library.

RELATION OF THE LIBRARIAN TO THE PRESIDENT   In the large
majority of university library organizations the librarian is directly
responsible to the president. This follows the pattern at Harvard
University (Figure 1), which is typical of most universities. But
other lines of responsibility may be noted. For example, at Montana
State University, the librarian is immediately responsible to the
senior academic dean (Figure 2). In a few cases, where a chancellor
exists, the librarian may be responsible to the provost; in some
instances, the librarian may deal directly with the vice-president.

Experience has demonstrated that the most workable arrangement, from the point of view of the best interests of the library, is
the direct relationship of the librarian to the president; but institutional differences should be considered in any attempt to discuss the effectiveness of a particular organization. It should also
be pointed out that, although the line of authority may formally
extend from the librarian to some individual or board other than
the president, in practice the control is delegated to the latter.

ASSISTANT LIBRARIAN AND THE LIBRARIAN   Generally, the assistant
(or associate) librarian in the university library is responsible for
the active operation of the processes and services. As the first
officer under the librarian in the hierarchy, he supervises the work
of the subordinate officers and stands between the departmental
heads and the librarian. In a growing number of libraries, however,

FIGURE 2. ORGANIZATION CHART, MONTANA STATE UNIVERSITY

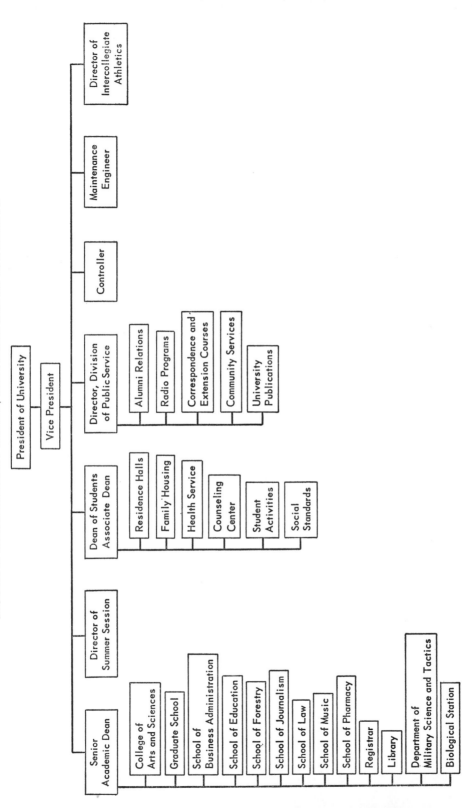

there has developed an organizational pattern which distributes administrative responsibility under the chief librarian to two or more assistant (or associate) librarians. An example of this type of organization is shown in Figure 3.

In his review of organizational patterns in university libraries, McAnally [14] observed that considerable experimentation has been going on in developing effective plans of organization. He writes: "At least three different forms of divisional organization were tried at Columbia, Harvard, Illinois, and other universities between 1941 and 1950." [15] Moreover, while some of the early efforts may have resulted from "insufficient understanding of the principles of administrative organization," local factors frequently play an important role. These factors involve personnel, physical conditions, and the general nature of the university library system.

In most of the changes in organizational pattern which resulted in the setting up of two or more assistant librarians, an effort was made to relieve the librarian of dealing directly with a score or more units. This is evident in the organization at Chicago (Figure 4). Columbia, which from 1944 until 1948 had three assistant directors (technical services, readers' services, and general administration) (Figure 5), in 1953 had only a single assistant librarian (Figure 6); although the head cataloger reports directly to the director, the binding and photographic services are supervised by the head of acquisitions. The three assistant librarians at the University of California at Berkeley (Figure 7) have primary responsibility for personnel, service, and finance, respectively. As may be seen from the chart, they also have specific assignments for certain areas of work.

A number of libraries have established in recent years "administrative" or "library" councils. At California this body is known as the "administrative conference." It consists of the librarian, who is chairman, and the three assistant librarians. Meetings are informal. As Figure 7 indicates, the conference deals with future plans, questions of policy, and problems which involve the whole or a

[14] "Organization of College and University Libraries." *Library Trends,* I (1952), 20–36.
[15] *Ibid.,* p. 22.

FIGURE 3. ORGANIZATION CHART, UNIVERSITY OF ILLINOIS LIBRARY
AND LIBRARY SCHOOL, 1954

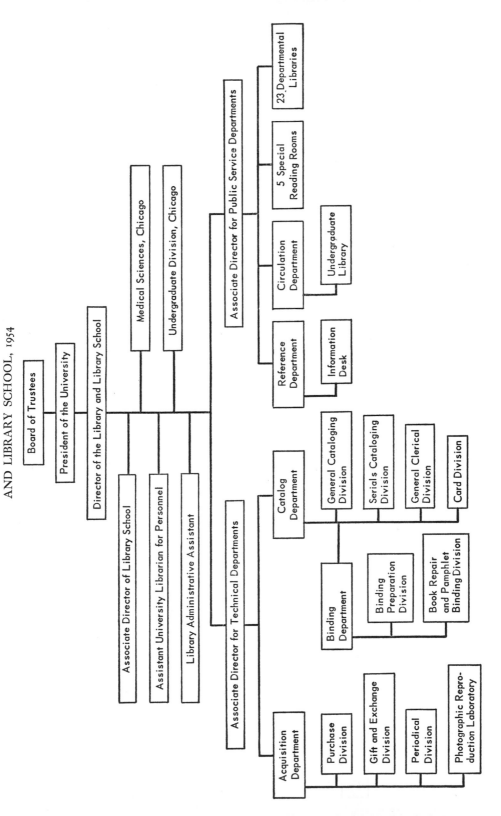

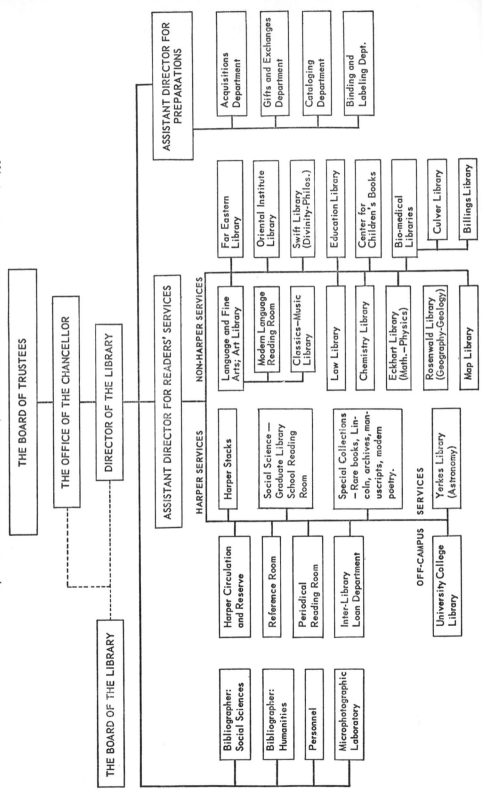

FIGURE 4. ORGANIZATION CHART, UNIVERSITY OF CHICAGO LIBRARY, 1955

THE BOARD OF TRUSTEES

THE OFFICE OF THE CHANCELLOR

DIRECTOR OF THE LIBRARY

THE BOARD OF THE LIBRARY

ASSISTANT DIRECTOR FOR PREPARATIONS

Acquisitions Department

Gifts and Exchanges Department

Cataloging Department

Binding and Labeling Dept.

ASSISTANT DIRECTOR FOR READERS' SERVICES

NON-HARPER SERVICES

Far Eastern Library

Oriental Institute Library

Swift Library (Divinity–Philos.)

Education Library

Center for Children's Books

Bio-medical Libraries

Culver Library

Billings Library

Language and Fine Arts; Art Library

Modern Language Reading Room

Classics–Music Library

Law Library

Chemistry Library

Eckhart Library (Math.–Physics)

Rosenwald Library (Geography-Geology)

Map Library

HARPER SERVICES

Harper Stacks

Social Science — Graduate Library School Reading Room

Special Collections – Rare books, Lincoln, archives, manuscripts, modern poetry.

SERVICES

Yerkes Library (Astronomy)

OFF-CAMPUS

University College Library

Harper Circulation and Reserve

Reference Room

Periodical Reading Room

Inter-Library Loan Department

Bibliographer: Social Sciences

Bibliographer: Humanities

Personnel

Microphotographic Laboratory

FIGURE 5. ORGANIZATION CHART, COLUMBIA UNIVERSITY LIBRARIES, 1944–48

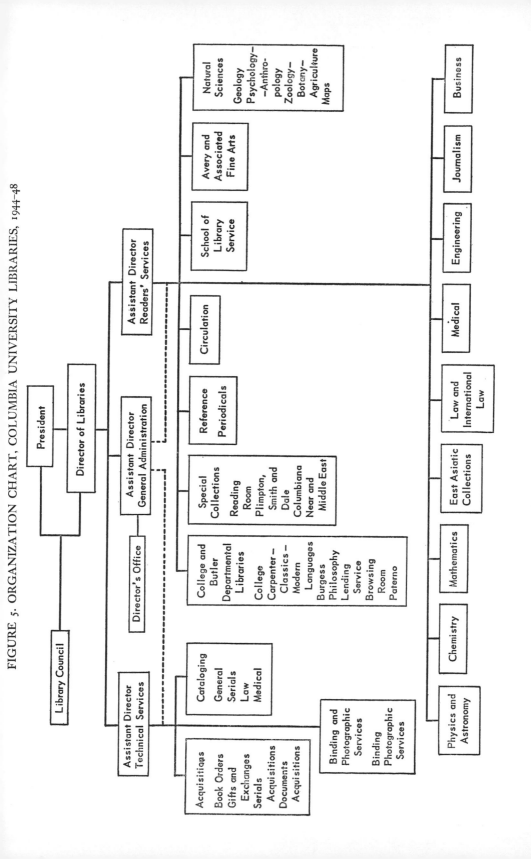

FIGURE 6. ORGANIZATION CHART, COLUMBIA UNIVERSITY LIBRARIES, JULY 1, 1955

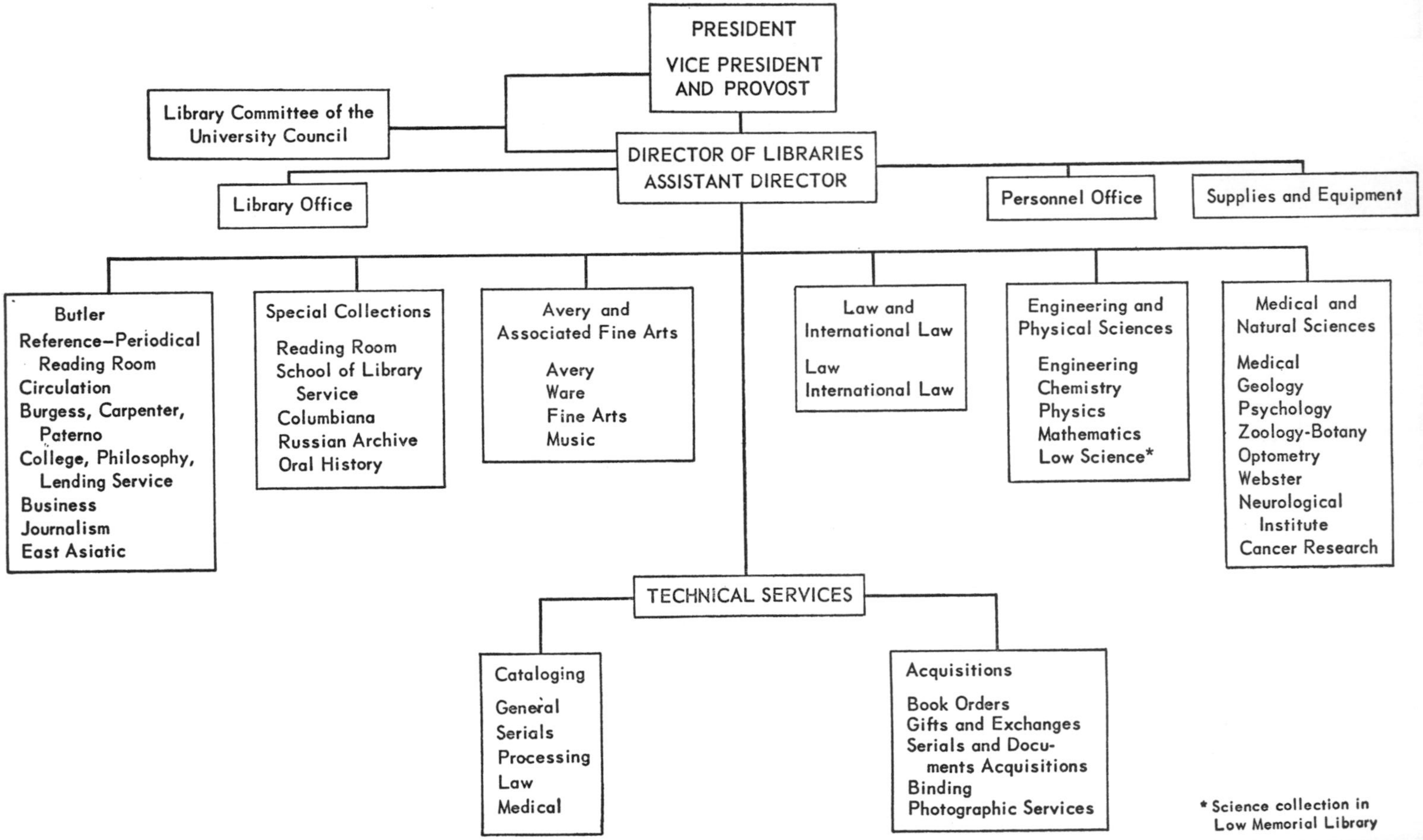

PRESIDENT
VICE PRESIDENT AND PROVOST

Library Committee of the University Council

DIRECTOR OF LIBRARIES
ASSISTANT DIRECTOR

Library Office

Personnel Office

Supplies and Equipment

Butler
Reference–Periodical Reading Room
Circulation
Burgess, Carpenter, Paterno
College, Philosophy, Lending Service
Business
Journalism
East Asiatic

Special Collections
Reading Room
School of Library Service
Columbiana
Russian Archive
Oral History

Avery and Associated Fine Arts
Avery
Ware
Fine Arts
Music

Law and International Law
Law
International Law

Engineering and Physical Sciences
Engineering
Chemistry
Physics
Mathematics
Low Science*

Medical and Natural Sciences
Medical
Geology
Psychology
Zoology-Botany
Optometry
Webster
Neurological Institute
Cancer Research

TECHNICAL SERVICES

Cataloging
General
Serials
Processing
Law
Medical

Acquisitions
Book Orders
Gifts and Exchanges
Serials and Documents Acquisitions
Binding
Photographic Services

* Science collection in Low Memorial Library

FIGURE 7. GENERAL ORGANIZATION CHART,
UNIVERSITY OF CALIFORNIA (BERKELEY)
GENERAL LIBRARY, 1955

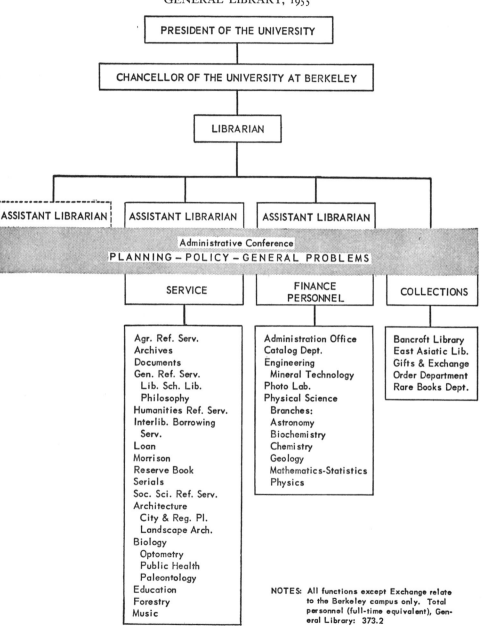

large section of the library organization. The conference also serves as a means of keeping each of the four administrative officers informed of the work in all areas.

DEPARTMENTAL HEADS AND THE ASSISTANT LIBRARIAN OR LIBRARIANS In efficiently administered libraries the departmental heads are given freedom to supervise their specific units of work, subject to the ordinary direction of the assistant librarian and the librarian. Departmental heads usually delegate specific operations to subordinate section heads when the quantity of work requires further subdivision.

One of the simplest ways in which the administrator of a large library can develop the effectiveness of his organization is by selecting qualified individuals and permitting them full control of certain areas of work. The delegation of authority to an individual who has been carefully selected because of his knowledge and competency will do much to develop responsibility and stimulate imagination. One of the glaring faults among some university librarians has been their unwillingness to permit the departmental head to experiment with new devices or introduce new practices which have been found effective in other libraries or in comparable undertakings. The librarian and the assistant librarian, by requiring records and reports from departmental heads, by insisting upon the use of up-to-date equipment and routines, and by encouraging studies of costs and use, can effectively influence the activities of subordinate officers.

ASSISTANT TO THE LIBRARIAN   In some libraries, there is an officer attached to the library office who is called "administrative assistant," "research officer," or "assistant to the librarian." Depending on the nature of the library organization, the duties of this staff member may vary considerably, involving at times personnel problems, building matters, financial questions, or special projects. The assistant librarians and the departmental heads may work closely with this officer on general problems affecting the library system as a whole.

ORGANIZATIONAL SYSTEMS The type of organizational system which exists in a university library, as has been pointed out, depends on many local factors. Even though a particular organization under which a library operates has been introduced to facilitate efficiency, it generally provides for these institutional differences. Some librarians, growing up under a certain type of organization, have come to believe that the type of organization has little or no effect upon the quality of service. Experiences of librarians have not only disproved this assumption but have indicated that changes in administrative organization may be of considerable importance from the standpoint of stepping up efficiency.

The form of administrative organization should be simple if efficiency is the goal. In the last decade, as may be seen from an examination of Tables 1–4, the growth of libraries in financial support and personnel has made it necessary in many cases for university librarians to think constantly in terms of the organizational pattern. The adding of a new service, or departmental library, or even a staff member usually requires the attention of the administrator to the library program as a whole. Since personnel are so important to the organization, each staff member should fit neatly into the system; otherwise, personnel difficulties may make it difficult to alter the administrative pattern. This fact has been made evident to surveyors of university libraries. Another factor which has a direct influence on the type of organization is the nature of the library building. Well-coordinated supervision is more difficult to achieve in a poorly planned building which separates homogeneous divisions and departments than in a well-planned structure.

The administrative organization of a university library system varies from complete centralization (at least, from the point of view of central control) to partial centralization.[16] The University of Illinois represents an example of complete centralization (Figure 3). There are a number of library systems which are partially centralized; that is, the central or main library and departmental libraries may be under the control of the chief librarian, but certain special collections and professional school libraries retain their autonomy. At Cornell, where there exist libraries which are part of the endowed schools as well as those associated with the state units, it is not easy to achieve centralization to the same extent as in an institution which is under a single authority.[17]

The difficulty in arriving at principles of administrative organization for an individual institution is obvious. It is important, however, for university administrators and librarians to be aware of organizational patterns which result in expensive and inadequate service so that necessary changes can be readily made.

The external administrative organization of the university library generally affects the internal organization. Centralization of acquisitional or cataloging policies, for example, depends primarily upon the authority given the director of the central library over all the book collections of the university. While the functional type of internal organization is prevalent in university libraries, there is an increasing number of cases where the divisional, or subject, arrangement appears.

FUNCTIONAL ARRANGEMENT   The functional type of arrangement usually provides for acquisitions, cataloging, circulation, reference, and periodicals (or serials) departments. Departments of business or finance and divisions of departmental libraries, professional school libraries, and special reading rooms and collections

[16] The wholly centralized system of libraries of state institutions, as originally established in Oregon, is a rarity in library organization. Some of the practical difficulties of operating such a system administratively are pointed out in Carlson, "History and Present Status of the Centralization of the Libraries of the Oregon State System of Higher Education," *College and Research Libraries*, XIV (1953), 414–17.

[17] Wilson, Downs, and Tauber, *Report of a Survey of the Libraries of Cornell University for the Library Board of Cornell University, October 1947—February 1948*, chap. v. See especially figures 1, 2, and 3.

FIGURE 8. ORGANIZATION CHART OF A UNIVERSITY LIBRARY—I

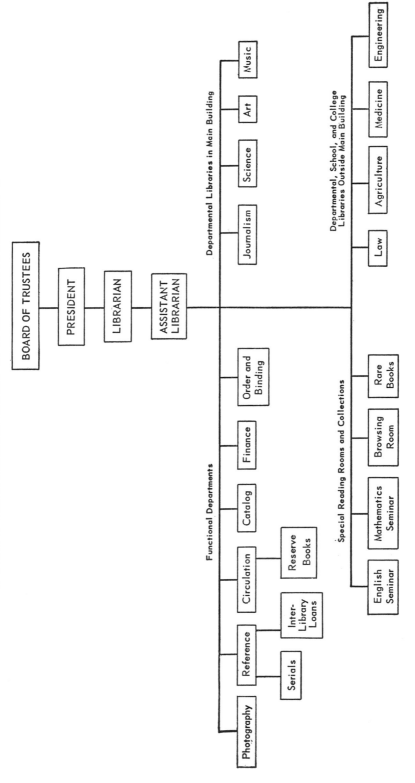

may also be present. An illustration of the functional type of arrangement is presented in Figure 8.

One of the principal criticisms of the functional arrangement, probably exaggerated in some cases, is the lack of close coordination between related activities, such as acquisitions and cataloging units.[18] Another criticism which has been made of this type of organization, particularly when it involves a large number of relatively important departmental and professional school libraries and special collections, is that the span of control is often too wide to permit efficient supervision by the major administrative officers. This may be especially true where the librarian works directly with the supervisory officers without the intermediary of an assistant librarian.

To offset the administrative difficulties of the common form of functional organization, a variation has been introduced. An illustration of this type of arrangement is presented in Figure 9. Under this form of arrangement, three individuals report to the librarian, five to the assistant librarian in charge of public services, and four to the assistant librarian in charge of technical services. The officer in charge of special collections and school libraries has a wide span of control, but direct supervision is usually limited to the special reading rooms and collections and the departmental libraries in the main building. At Columbia, for example, the Nicholas Murray Butler Librarian is in charge of all departmental collections in the central library. Divisional librarians, however, such as the bio-medical librarian and the physical sciences librarian, have charge of related groups of libraries (Figures 5 and 6).

Although there are economic aspects attached to multiplying the number of assistant librarians who have direct charge of related units, the advantages in some institutions have outweighed the apparent additional costs in administration. In the first place, the librarian, with a reduced span of control, is able to spend more time for planning, promoting faculty-library and student-library re-

[18] A discussion and bibliographical documentation of this question are included in Tauber and Associates, *Technical Services in Libraries*, chap. ii.

FIGURE 9. ORGANIZATION CHART OF A UNIVERSITY LIBRARY—II

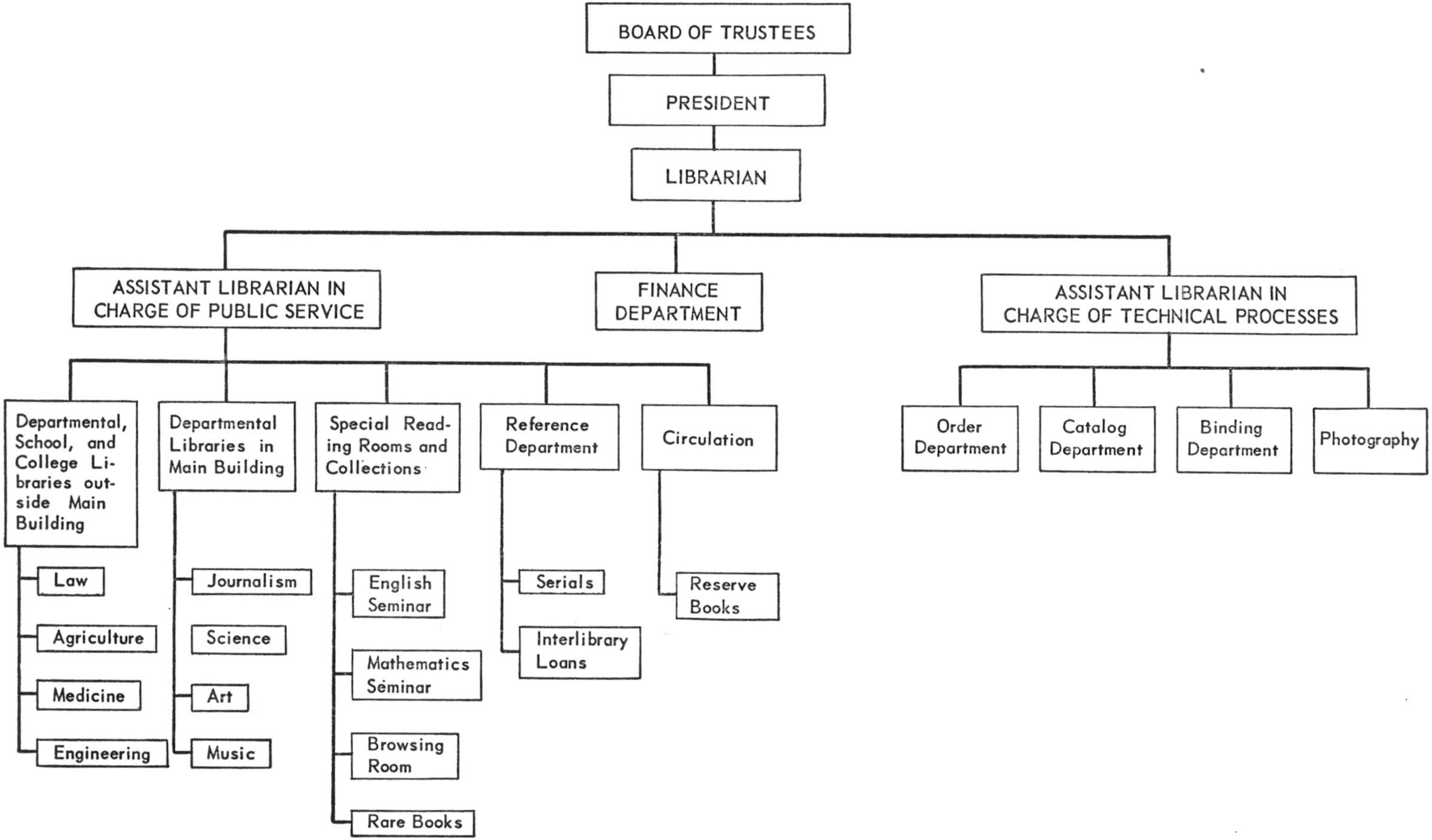

lationships, making contacts, and engaging in activities of a scholarly nature. In the second place, the concentration of coordinated activities, in either the technical or the service departments, emphasizes the relationships of certain tasks. It also provides, within certain limitations, for a fluid personnel. In the third place, the assistant librarians, with no immediate routine responsibilities, can devote time to policy matters and long-term projects. And, finally, examination of all operations and techniques in the technical and service departments may result in reduced costs.

As has been pointed out, however, it is difficult to assess the achievements of the divisional organization,[19] even though there is wide acceptance of it in recent years. Undoubtedly, some evaluation should be forthcoming in the future.

SUBJECT ARRANGEMENT   In the larger libraries, there has been a trend to reorganize the service departments. "The traditional organization by forms of materials, such as periodicals and maps, and by types of service, as reference and reserve, is giving way to organization by subject divisions." [20] This is not a new thing in libraries, as many public libraries, such as Cleveland, Los Angeles, Baltimore, Rochester, and Toledo, have been organized on the basis of subject divisions.[21] The Johns Hopkins University Library and the University of Chicago Libraries used subject departments as a basis for organization even before it was applied in public libraries. In the last fifteen years or so such institutions as Brown University, the University of Colorado, the University of Oregon, and the University of Nebraska, among others, have introduced subject divisions. These divisions generally are open-shelf study areas, with adjacent stack, and frequently with typewriter and conference rooms.[22] In many of the libraries, the major groupings

19 McAnally, "Organization of College and University Libraries," p. 25.
20 Swank, "The Educational Function of the University Library," *Library Trends*, I (1952), 41–42.
21 Maizell, "The Subject-Departmentalized Public Library," *College and Research Libraries*, XII (1951), 255–60.
22 Ellsworth, "The Significance of the Divisional Room Plan for University Li-

are humanities, social sciences, and science—usually for the upper-division and graduate students. An undergraduate reading room may also be provided. The work of the circulation department is reduced considerably, since it is concerned with subject areas not covered specifically by the divisions. Reference questions are directed to the divisional specialists. Usually, the divisional librarians have graduate degrees in one of the subjects in their respective units, as well as library training. They are therefore in a position to support actively the classroom program. Swank makes the following observation in this connection: "The educational significance of the subject-divisional plan derives from the association of library services with specific departments of the instructional program. The library divisions are given subject content and curricular motivation. Their efforts are focused on a definite clientele, with whose projects and problems the library staff can become familiar. The library's services are varied to satisfy the widely different needs of physical scientists, social scientists, and humanists. Definite parts of the library belong to them. Library staff members specialize in their divisional subjects, identify themselves with the faculties of instructional departments, and may in fact become active members of those faculties." [23]

Administratively, the type of arrangement provided by the divisional plan is ordinarily more expensive to operate than the traditional functional organization. Actually, for the smaller university library which is endeavoring to reduce or eliminate departmental libraries, the divisional plan may be more economical. The educational implications of the subject arrangement, however, are inescapable. When conditions are favorable to it, it is undoubtedly a system of internal arrangement that should be carefully considered in putting up a new building or remodeling an old one.

---

braries," *University of Colorado Studies,* Ser. A. (general) XXVI, No. 4 (1941), 33–39; Swank, "The Educational Function of the University Library," pp. 41–42; Lundy, "The Divisional Library at Nebraska," *Library Journal,* LXXX (1955), 1302–3.

[23] "The Educational Function of the University Library," p. 42.

DEPARTMENTAL
LIBRARY
SYSTEMS

Reference to figures on the preceding pages will reveal the existence of departmental libraries in the several organizations presented. At Illinois, for example, there are twenty-three departmental libraries, while Harvard has over fifty such collections. University librarians and educators have long discussed the administrative and educational problems which arise from housing book collections apart from the main library.[24] Although recent reports indicate that there is a tendency toward centralization, a movement which has been influenced by the erection of new buildings in some cases, and the need to economize, in others, there is still a strong belief, particularly on the part of faculty members, that separate facilities are important for educational programs. There is also no uniform pattern in the ways in which universities are handling their professional school departmental, seminar, and laboratory libraries. The purpose of this section is to present some of the organizational, administrative, and educational aspects of these various types of libraries and collections, to record available data relating to current practices, and to summarize tentative principles for future policy.

[24] An early report, which still contains much useful information on the question, is the University of Chicago, Commission on the Future Policy of the University Libraries, *Tentative Report, January, 1924;* see also Thompson, "The Historical Background of Departmental and Collegiate Libraries," *Library Quarterly,* XII (1942), 49–74; Hanson, "Central versus Departmental Libraries," *Library Quarterly,* XIII (1943), 132–35; McAnally, "Co-ordinating the Departmental Library System"; Brough, *Scholar's Workshop,* chap. v, "The Accessibility of the Collections." The arguments expressed by Miller in his comprehensive paper "Centralization versus Decentralization," *ALA Bulletin,* XXXIII (1939), 75–79, 134–35, are concerned with the factors of accessibility, cost, efficiency, adequacy, use of books, interrelation of subject fields, and educational significance. He concludes: "The cause of the central library is favored by the conclusions drawn from the arguments on cost, interrelationship, efficiency, and educational significance. The arguments on efficiency and educational significance, however, can be made to serve the decentralist provided the institution has a budget which will afford good service for both general and separate libraries and the maintenance of a general collection of books for the correlation of the library needs of the collegiate departments." The arguments raised by Miller are of value in deciding on the approach of individual institutions. This is made most clear by the examination of the chapters on organization and administration in many of the recent academic library surveys, e.g., Cornell, Stanford, Montana, Virginia Polytechnic Institute, etc.

DEPARTMENTAL AND PROFESSIONAL SCHOOL LIBRARIES   Since departmental and professional school libraries raise more complex problems than do special collections, they may be dealt with first. Although these types may be similar administratively, it may be well to define what is meant by each. Generally speaking, a departmental library (sometimes called a branch library) is a collection of books and other materials attached to a department of instruction which forms part of a college administration. The departmental libraries of Illinois and Texas fall within this definition, as do also the Chemistry Library, Fine Arts Library, and Music Library of Columbia University.

A professional school library (also called a "collegiate" or "college" library) in a university library system is a collection of books related to the work of the particular school or college and administered either separately by the school or college or as a part of the university library system. The Avery Architectural Library and the Library of the College of Physicians and Surgeons of Columbia University are examples of professional school libraries.

ORGANIZATION. The relationship of the departmental or professional school library to the central library varies from institution to institution. Professional school libraries, such as those for law, medicine, dentistry, pharmacy, engineering, and journalism, are more likely to be separated from the central library administration than are departmental libraries, such as those for history, philosophy, or chemistry.[25] Libraries for single academic departments occur in both college and university organizations, but professional school libraries generally appear only in universities. Seminar li-

[25] See Hausdorfer, "Professional School and Departmental Libraries Survey," pp. 6–8 (mimeographed). This summary by Hausdorfer considers the administrative organization, quarters and equipment, personnel, financial administration, preparatory processes, service to the clientele, and public relations of professional school and departmental libraries. See also the report by Works, *College and University Library Problems*, pp. 68–73. While these are relatively early studies, more recent comment in surveys (Cornell, Stanford, etc.) and in other studies, reveals that while some merging of libraries has developed, professional school libraries are still more likely to be independent of the main library than are departmental libraries.

braries, which, as Thompson [26] has pointed out, were in many instances the predecessors of departmental libraries, are not extensively developed today. Usually they are directly under central library control.

Factors which need to be considered in determining the extent of centralization which exists in a university library system include the line of responsibility of the departmental and professional school librarians, the extent to which income is derived from the general library budget, centralization of purchasing and technical services, appointment and control of personnel, and fluidity of the book collections.[27]

ADMINISTRATIVE AND EDUCATIONAL ASPECTS. One of the earliest and among the most complete statements on the question of departmental libraries was made by the University of Chicago Commission on the Future Policy of the University Libraries in its *Tentative Report* in 1924.[28] This was an unusual report, not only because it developed specific arguments for and against centralization, but because it was the product of a faculty committee which approached it from the points of view of building requirements and subject interrelationships. The arguments were considered in relation to two building plans, one a great central library, and the other the present library building with divisional libraries attached to it or constructed on other parts of the campus. The essential emphasis, obviously, is directed at the interrelationship of the subject areas. As specialization increases, there is also evidence that the separate disciplines are so interrelated that the segregation of

[26] "The Historical Background of Departmental and Collegiate Libraries," pp. 65–66.

[27] An example of how a complex departmental system may grow up in a university on a decentralized basis is found in Wilson, Downs, and Tauber, *Report of a Survey of the Libraries of Cornell University*, chap. v.

[28] This report is discussed in detail in the 1945 edition of *The University Library*. Many changes have occurred in the organization of the University of Chicago Library since that time. These have been developed along lines which have been influenced by such factors as the construction of the Midwest Inter-Library Center, merging of certain departmental libraries, etc. The *Tentative Report*, however, is a useful document to examine for the traditional arguments which are raised when the question of centralization *vs.* decentralization arises.

materials departmentally places many investigators at a disadvantage, unless there is expensive duplication. This has been clear in several of the library systems which have been surveyed in the last decade.

If a university had as much funds as it needed for library services, perhaps the ideal situation would provide a self-sufficient library for each department or school in need of special facilities. Metcalf, writing of the Harvard situation and the departmental problem, observes:

In spite of our conviction that we are overly decentralized here at Harvard, we believe in decentralization in a large, physically scattered university—'coordinated decentralization,' as we call it. The arguments for decentralization may be summarized as follows:
1. It places the books in convenient locations for those who make the greatest use of them.
2. It broadens the basis of support of the university library system.
3. It gives the various departments a direct interest in their libraries.
4. By breaking down the collections into units by subjects, special library methods can be introduced which give better service at no greater cost.
Some of the objections to decentralization are:
1. Decentralization often results in unnecessary duplication; the various libraries in the biological sciences at Harvard are a good example.
2. The policies of the departmental libraries may get out of line with those for the university library as a whole, in respect to staff organization, salaries, and book acquisition.
3. Departmental libraries offer a ready opportunity for overdevelopment through the interest and promotional ability of a particular librarian or head of a graduate school. Costs then get out of bounds, and subsequent reduction of expenses is difficult because of the bulk of material already at hand. Further, if such reduction is enforced, the collection rapidly deteriorates in relative importance, since gaps in acquisition of new material greatly reduce the value of the collection as a whole and much money previously spent is wasted.[29]

Thus Metcalf, writing in 1949, stresses the important arguments —from administrative and educational standpoints—that were dis-

[29] Metcalf, "Harvard Faces Its Library Problems," in *The Place of the Library in a University*, p. 47.

cussed in the Chicago *Tentative Report* of 1924. The twenty-five-year interval undoubtedly had made many university administrators and librarians conscious of the need to re-evaluate the departmental library situation on the basis of what a particular institution could afford.[30] This has been true at Cornell, Michigan, Nebraska, and Oklahoma.

One of the chief criticisms of the departmental library is emphasized by Metcalf. This is the independence of the branch unit. Harvard, which is still decentralized administratively, has not considered this a serious difficulty. Metcalf writes: "We believe there is no need here at Harvard for the Director of the University Library to administer the departmental libraries, particularly the larger ones, so long as he is able to intervene without embarrassment to anyone concerned when a major policy decision is to be made on staff salaries, staff organization, book selection, cataloguing, or public services. The Director of the University Library at Harvard should be primarily an advisory, planning, and co-ordinating officer." [31]

While this situation of general autonomy may be satisfactory at Harvard, it has not worked effectively without some uniform rules and regulations at other institutions. For example, the University of California at Los Angeles Library has used a "Branch Library Code" to institute a general pattern of operation for the departmental libraries.[32] Major topics listed in this code include administration; circulation of books; reference service and materials; location, duplication, and transfer of library materials; acquisition of books (statistics, gifts, exchanges, duplicates); cataloging; and binding. Undoubtedly a code of this sort should help to reduce the difficulties which may easily arise in a system of libraries dispersed on a large campus.

PRINCIPLES FOR FUTURE POLICY. The variety of local problems which exist on a university campus obviously makes it undesirable

[30] McAnally, "Co-ordinating the Departmental Library System," *Library Quarterly*, XXI (1951), 113–19.
[31] "Harvard Faces Its Library Problems," pp. 47–48.
[32] University of California at Los Angeles Library, "Branch Library Code."

to answer the problem of centralization categorically. The development of the divisional system of internal organization has had a definite influence in some universities of curtailing the growth of separate departmental libraries. This is especially true in institutions which have erected new buildings. Also, in many institutions in which departmental systems are strongly intrenched, more administrative organization has taken place.

The basic principles of organization and administration of the university library apply directly to departmental and professional school libraries. New departmental collections should be established and maintained outside the general library only upon the official approval of the president and the librarian. All books and other appropriate materials constitute the library. All expenditures for library materials and the arrangement for using them should be made under the direction of the university librarian. All libraries on the campus should be administrative parts of the general library. Duplication of materials already existing in the general library, while recognized as desirable in the interest of teaching, should be based on real need and should be practiced only with reasonable regard for the limitation of library funds. Control of the location of library materials rests with the librarian and should be determined by him in such ways as to serve the best interests of the respective users. Whenever economy and efficiency warrant them, the librarian should institute policies of centralization in technical services and other operations.

SPECIAL COLLECTIONS, LABORATORY COLLECTIONS, AND SEMINAR LIBRARIES As may be seen from the accompanying charts, in addition to formally organized departmental and professional school libraries there may be present, either in the general library building or in other buildings of the university, special collections, laboratory collections, and seminar libraries. A special collection may be described as "an assemblage of materials in some field of knowledge which includes at least some of the rarer and more unusual items and a greater proportion of other titles bearing upon the special

subject than would be included ordinarily in a library of the size." [33]
Generally, special collections present fewer administrative problems than do professional school or departmental libraries. Sometimes a special collection attains the proportions of a departmental or special library—and requires precise definitions of its relations to the librarian, financial administration, technical operations, and services to the public. The Hoover Library of War, Revolution, and Peace of Stanford University is an example of this type of special collection. The existence of a number of special collections within a library system may warrant the establishment of a department of special collections, and a number of universities maintain such a unit. Experience has demonstrated that special collections are effectively administered under such control, but the economy of a completely centralized service has not been studied.

Laboratory collections are less likely to grow to a size which warrants organizing them into separate libraries than are special collections. Usually, laboratory collections are considered to be parts of laboratory equipment, in the same sense as microscopes, beakers, and scales. So far as possible, they should duplicate holdings of the general library. These collections of books and other materials, which are used constantly by research workers and scholars, have been recognized by librarians as essential adjuncts of the laboratory or office. However, they present certain administrative problems which the librarian needs to consider if the collections are not to become personal assemblages of books which remain inaccessible to the university community. When these collections are under the control of the general library, they are centrally purchased, cataloged and bound, as well as kept within reasonable limits. The librarian should be given the responsibility of removing to the general collection those items which are no longer of immediate use to the laboratory workers. Moreover, he should be able to decide whether new or valuable acquisitions to the library should be placed in the laboratories or teachers' offices

[33] Randall and Goodrich, *Principles of College Library Administration*, p. 195. See also special collections listed under "Library" in institutional exhibits in *American Universities and Colleges.* 6th ed., American Council on Education, [1952].

or made more accessible in the general or departmental libraries.

Thompson has traced the German origin of seminar libraries in American universities.[34] They developed because faculty members found that they served their instructional and research needs more effectively than general libraries. Although in many cases they have been transformed into departmental libraries, they may still be found on some American university campuses. They differ from departmental libraries by their closer association with instruction. Seminar collections are frequently housed in classrooms, and are used by faculty members and students during class periods. In many cases they are accessible only to those individuals who have been granted keys to the rooms, usually under the authority of members of the teaching staff. Like materials in separately housed special and laboratory collections, books in seminar libraries are not so accessible generally as those in the central library or even in departmental libraries. The use of carrels and studies (either offices or designated areas) has also operated adversely against the maintenance of seminar collections. While seminar collections, like laboratory collections, may implement instruction, a precise administrative policy should define their status. The librarian should discourage the tendency of the teaching staff to regard seminar collections as their personal property. He should also reserve the right to remove materials when he deems it necessary for giving adequate service to the majority of readers.

THE COLLEGE LIBRARY   An important unit of the university library is the college library. While many of the administrative decisions are based on the policies of the university library, the college librarian of a university will frequently be faced with problems which are peculiar to his unit. Because of the emphasis that has been placed on research in the university library, in some institutions the undergraduate students have not fared too well in obtaining the services that they require. It is therefore not unusual that special

[34] "The Historical Background of Departmental and Collegiate Libraries," pp. 60–66.

quarters, sometimes within the same building (as at Columbia University) or in a separate building (Lamont Library at Harvard), have been provided. Coney,[35] writing of the Lamont Library as an adequate and direct solution to the undergraduate problem, observed that it would not be easy for the larger state universities to duplicate the Harvard structure. He estimated that it would require a minimum of four and a quarter million dollars to provide a library of the Lamont type for the University of California at Berkeley campus. He says further:

A Lamont Library can be realized on state university campuses only if administrators and librarians are skillful in presenting the library needs of the state's youth so persuasively that legislatures will see the light, for it is to state legislatures—and not to private wealth—that the state universities must turn for the provision of this library essential to undergraduate education. More important than this act of persuasion, however, is a decision which must be taken earlier, and by librarians and university administrators. I mean the decision that, important as it is to have libraries for books, it is also important to have libraries for people.[36]

Other librarians have been concerned with proper library service for undergraduates, and the University of Michigan has drawn up plans for a college library on the Ann Arbor campus. Consideration of the variety of questions and a description of the efforts to solve the general problem at Chicago, Rice Institute, Harvard, and Cincinnati are set forth in a recent series of articles.[37] The *Harvard Library Bulletin* has also run a series of articles on the history and development of library services in Harvard College, the growth of the collections, the extension of hours of service, the increase in borrowing privileges, and the rise of the reserved book, classroom, and laboratory collections.

[35] "The Future of Libraries in Academic Institutions," pp. 54–56.
[36] *Ibid.*, p. 55.
[37] "Library Service to Undergraduates: A Symposium," *College and Research Libraries*, XIV (1953), 266–75. An important work on all aspects of the college library is Fussler (ed.), *The Function of the Library in the Modern College.* The problem of library service to students in a college affiliated with a university is discussed in Tauber, *Barnard College Library: A Report on Facilities and Services.* Although Barnard College is affiliated with Columbia University and maintains a separate library, the fact that it is located on a university campus has had direct effects upon its acquisitional policy and other services.

SUMMARY   Considerable variation exists in the administrative organization of university libraries. As has been pointed out, no uniform terminology is used to describe the administrative officers of the university library. There has been progress, however, in the description of the duties of the librarian and other administrative officers. More and more libraries are introducing job analyses and personnel classifications as means for setting up career services. The application of accepted principles of administration and scientific management to solve library problems is a notable development of the last decade. Library surveys have helped in directing attention to the establishment of workable administrative organizations.

While functional administrative organization is still prevalent, especially in the smaller and medium-sized university libraries, there has been a movement to introduce the divisional arrangement. The time has come when a thorough study of the divisional arrangement should be made so that its administrative and educational values in libraries may be evaluated.

Departmental and professional school libraries have been developed to meet the needs of specialists in the various subject fields. Departmental libraries generally are necessary where the academic and research units of a university are spread over an extensive campus. So far as administration is concerned, experience has demonstrated that economical management and effective service are obtained when the librarian has control and supervision, even though these may be delegated to responsible personnel, over all the book resources of the university, whether they are in departmental libraries, professional school libraries, special collections, laboratories, offices, classrooms, or a college library.

BIBLIOGRAPHY

American Library Association. Board on Personnel Administration. Personnel Administration in Libraries: A Bibliographic Essay. Prepared by Ralph E. McCoy, assisted by a Subcommittee on Bibliography. Chicago, 1953.

American Library Association. Board on Salaries, Staff, and Tenure. Classification and Pay Plans for Libraries in Institutions of Higher Education. 2d ed. Vol. III—Universities. Chicago, 1947.

Blanchard, J. R. "Departmental Libraries in Divisional Plan University Libraries," *College and Research Libraries*, XIV (1953), 243–48.

Brough, Kenneth J. Scholar's Workshop. Urbana, University of Illinois Press, 1953.

California, University of (Los Angeles). Library. "Branch Library Code." Los Angeles, 1949 (mimeographed).

Carlson, William H. "History and Present Status of the Centralization of the Libraries of the Oregon State System of Higher Education," *College and Research Libraries*, XIV (1953), 414–17.

Chapman, John D., et al. "The Role of the Divisional Librarian," *College and Research Libraries*, XV (1954), 148–54.

Chicago, University of. Commission on the Future Policy of the University Libraries. Tentative Report, January, 1924. Chicago, University of Chicago Press, 1924.

Coney, Donald. "Management in College and University Libraries," *Library Trends*, I (1952), 83–94. This paper has a useful bibliography.

Copeland, Melvin T. The Executive at Work. Cambridge, Harvard University Press, 1951.

Ellsworth, Ralph E. "The Significance of the Divisional Room Plan for University Libraries," *University of Colorado Studies*, Ser. A (general), XXVI, No. 4 (1941), 33–39.

———— "Trends in Higher Education Affecting the College and University Library," *Library Trends*, I (1952), 8–19.

Fayol, Henri. General and Industrial Management. Trans. by Constance Storrs. London, Pitman, 1949.

Fussler, Herman H. "Readjustments by the Librarian," in Pierce Butler (ed.), *Librarians, Scholars, and Booksellers at Mid-Century*. Chicago, University of Chicago Press, 1953, 60–73. Also in *Library Quarterly*, XXIII (1953), 216–29.

Fussler, Herman H. (ed.). The Function of the Library in the Modern College: Papers Presented before the Nineteenth Annual Conference of the University of Chicago, June 14–18, 1954. Chicago, University of Chicago, Graduate Library School, 1954. Also published in *Library Quarterly*, October, 1954.

Gulick, Luther H., and L. Urwick (eds.). Papers on the Science of Administration. New York, Institute of Public Administration, Columbia University, 1937.

Hanson, J. C. M. "Central versus Departmental Libraries," *Library Quarterly*, XIII (1943), 132–35.

Harvard Library Bulletin (various issues, dealing with administrative problems).

Harvard University Library. The Place of the Library in a University:

A Conference Held at Harvard University, 30–31 March 1949. Cambridge, 1950.

Hausdorfer, Walter. Professional School and Departmental Libraries Survey. New York, Special Libraries Association, 1938 (mimeographed).

Henkle, H. H. "Principles and Practice of Administrative Organization in the University Library," College and Research Libraries, IV (1943), 277–84.

Hintz, Carl W. E. "Some Management Aspects of the University of Oregon Library's Subject Divisional Plan," The Call Number, XIV (1952), 4–5.

Howard, Paul. "Library Staff Manuals and a Theory of Library Management" (unpublished Master's paper, Graduate Library School, University of Chicago, 1939).

Irwin, Mary (ed.). American Universities and Colleges. 6th ed. Washington, D.C., American Council on Education, 1952.

Joeckel, Carleton B. (ed.). Current Issues in Library Administration: Papers Presented before the Library Institute at the University of Chicago, August 1–12, 1938. Chicago, University of Chicago Press, 1939.

Leigh, Robert D. The Public Library in the United States. New York, Columbia University Press, 1950.

"Library Service to Undergraduates: A Symposium," College and Research Libraries, XIV (1953), 266–75.

Logsdon, Richard H. "Changes in Organization at Columbia," College and Research Libraries, XV (1954), 158–60.

Lundy, Frank A. "The Divisional Library at Nebraska," Library Journal, LXXX (1955), 1302–3.

Lyle, Guy R. The Administration of the College Library. 2d ed. New York H. W. Wilson, 1949, Chap. III.

McAnally, Arthur M. "Co-ordinating the Department Library System," Library Quarterly, XXI (1951), 113–19.

——— "Organization of College and University Libraries," Library Trends, I (1952), 20–36.

Maizell, Robert E. "The Subject Departmentalized Public Library," College and Research Libraries, XII (1951), 255–60.

Metcalf, Keyes D. "Harvard Faces Its Library Problems," in The Place of the Library in a University: A Conference Held at Harvard University, 30–31 March 1949. Cambridge, Harvard University Library, 1950.

Miller, Robert A. "Centralization versus Decentralization," ALA Bulletin, XXXIII (1939), 75–79, 134–35.

Morrison, Percy D. "Variation of the Subject Divisional Plan at Oregon," College and Research Libraries, XIV (1953), 158–63.

Randall, William M., and F. L. D. Goodrich. Principles of College

Library Administration. 2d ed. Chicago, American Library Association and the University of Chicago Press, 1941.

Rautenstrauch, Walter. Principles of Modern Industrial Organization. New York, Pitman, 1943.

——— Economics of Industrial Management. New York, Funk and Wagnalls, 1949.

Rohlf, Robert A. "The Freshman-Sophomore Library at Minnesota," *College and Research Libraries*, XIV (1953), 164–66.

"Scientific Management in Libraries," *Library Trends*, II (1954), 359–483.

Shaw, Ralph R. "Management, Machines, and the Bibliographic Problems of the Twentieth Century," in J. H. Shera and M. E. Egan (eds.), *Bibliographic Organization*. Chicago, University of Chicago Press, 1951, pp. 200–25.

Swank, Raynard C. "The Educational Function of the University Library," *Library Trends*, I (1952), 37–48.

Tauber, Maurice F. Barnard College Library: A Report on Facilities and Services, Prepared at the Request of the Barnard College Administration. New York, 1954.

Tauber, Maurice F., and Associates. Technical Services in Libraries. New York, Columbia University Press, 1954.

Thompson, Lawrence S. "The Historical Background of Departmental and Collegiate Libraries," *Library Quarterly*, XII (1942), 49–74.

White, Carl M. "Assistant Directors in Columbia University Libraries," *College and Research Libraries*, XIII (1947), 360-67.

Wilson, Louis R. "The Challenge of Library Literature to Education for Librarianship, 1923–1953," in Louis Shores (ed.) *Challenges to Librarianship*. (Florida State University Studies, No. 12) Tallahassee, Florida State University, 1953, pp. 125–40.

Wilson, Louis R., Robert B. Downs, and Maurice F. Tauber. Report of a Survey of the Libraries of Cornell University for the Library Board of Cornell University, October 1947—February 1948. Ithaca, Cornell University, 1948.

Works, George A. College and University Problems: A Study of a Selected Group of Institutions Prepared for the Association of American Universities. Chicago, American Library Association, 1927.

V

DEPARTMENTAL ORGANIZATION:

ACQUISITION AND PREPARATION

THE DIVISION of university libraries into functional departments has not followed a uniform pattern. Tradition, personnel, physical arrangements, financial considerations, curriculums, types of collections, and the personalities and attitudes of administrative officers account for variations. In recent years there has been some experimentation with departmental organization, and it is likely that this will continue.[1] The large number of variables, however, render generalizations regarding a preferred departmental organization difficult, if not impossible.

In the majority of large university libraries, departmental organization revolves about the functional units. In the preceding chapter the divisional organization of departments was discussed. In this chapter attention will be directed toward the organization and operations of two major functional groupings of activities: (1) acquisitions; and (2) preparation, including cataloging, photographic reproduction, and binding. Illustrations will be drawn from the field in order to point out important distinctions and to suggest possible lines of effective organization, and reference will be made to the various organizational charts included in chapter iv.

ACQUISITIONS   The acquisition of library materials is obviously one of the most important activities of the university library. To acquire most effectively the books and other materials needed for the instructional and research purposes

[1] McAnally, "Organization of College and University Libraries," *Library Trends,* I (1952), 20–36; Wright, "Some Aspects of Technical Processes," *Library Trends,*

of the faculty and students in a university demands careful consideration of the factors of library organization, personnel, purchasing, finance, and records. The administrative officer of the acquisitions department, therefore, should not only have substantial knowledge of publishing, the book market, and other sources of materials, but he should be able to direct, supervise, and control an important business unit of the library. The variety and complexity of the materials acquired by the large university library make it essential for the administration to provide a sufficient number of order librarians who are trained in bibliography, languages, and business methods. The addition of new funds to the book budget of a library should always be examined in relation to the load on the acquisitions department.

In addition to the general duties of a departmental head which have been listed previously, the acquisitions librarian is responsible for the following specific duties:

1. To develop procedures to meet the needs of the library
2. To handle personally difficult or important correspondence or problems relating to the ordering of books, serials, documents, periodicals, maps, pamphlets, films, and other materials
3. To make recommendations to the faculty concerning book selection
4. To consult with heads of other departments and divisions concerning book orders
5. To notify the faculty of the nonexpenditure of book funds
6. To watch carefully auction, rare-book, and second-hand dealers' catalogs for opportunities to purchase items on desiderata lists
7. To have materials filmed or otherwise reproduced when they are out of print or otherwise unavailable in the original
8. To interview publishers' representatives, book dealers, collectors, and others who are interested in building up the university's book collections

I (1952), 73–82; Trotier, "Organization and Administration of Cataloging Processes," *Library Trends*, II (1953), 264–78; Tauber and Associates, *Technical Services in Libraries*.

9. To read and appraise books and other materials and make recommendations for their acquisition

10. To supervise the handling of all gifts and exchanges coming into the library.

ORDER
PROCEDURE [2]

The largest amount of book selection in college and university libraries originates with faculty members. Like the college library, the university library collects standard books of general reference, standard reference books useful for specific fields covered by the curriculum, and adequate supplies of general books, books for each curricular field, books concerning important fields not covered by the curriculum, books for leisure reading, and general and standard scholarly periodicals. But while efforts are made to limit the size of some college libraries, particularly those in liberal arts institutions with little or no research interests, the university library staff is normally faced with the responsibility of collecting various types of scholarly materials—research monographs, serials, pamphlets, documents, microreproductions of several kinds, prints, maps, music, recordings, manuscripts, archives, and reports. Materials come from all over the world, and personnel with linguistic ability are essential for prompt and economical handling of accessions.[3]

Book orders, originating with the faculty members, usually bear the approval of faculty library representatives or the administrative heads of instructional departments. In those few universities in which funds are ample to cover practically every request, orders may go direct to the librarian from the faculty member. Records which indicate expenditures of the instructional departments or schools are generally maintained in the library office.

[2] The financial aspects of order work are treated in chap. iii. Chap. ix is concerned with acquisition policies and procedures. Detailed consideration of acquisition work, involving university as well as other types of libraries, is included in Tauber and Associates, *Technical Services in Libraries*, chaps. iii–vii.

[3] The development of inter-library centers (such as the Midwest Inter-Library Center in Chicago) and such programs for specialization in collecting as the Farmington Plan (see Williams, *Farmington Plan Handbook*), already have had a direct effect upon the acquisition work of university libraries.

The order procedure of an effective acquisitions department is directed toward securing quick delivery of materials by dealers. In his cost study of acquisitional work and cataloging, Miller sketched the major activities involved in getting material into a library.[4] The following outline, based on Miller's list, suggests the principal purchasing operations in the acquisitions department:

ROUTINES INVOLVED IN ACQUISITIONAL WORK:

PURCHASES

1. Preparatory activities:
    a) Order card received
    b) Order card stamped
    c) Order card marked by department
    d) Order card placed in preliminary file
2. Checking:
    e) Unchecked order cards arranged
    f) Order cards checked against catalog
    g) Order cards checked against orders-out file, and gift and exchange file
    h) Order cards checked against ready-to-order file
3. Bibliographical preparation:
    i) Order cards prepared bibliographically (author, title, edition, etc.)
4. Ordering:
    j) Order cards filed in ready-to-order file
    k) Order cards sorted as to agent
    l) Order cards typed into order letters or on multiple-form order slips
    m) Order letters or slips revised and mailed
    n) Order cards stamped and filed (in libraries using multiple-form order slips, original order cards are attached to several forms for later use)

[4] "Cost Accounting for Libraries," p. 57. See also his "Cost of Technical Operations," in Randall (ed.), *The Acquisition and Cataloging of Books*, pp. 220–38; and Fleming and Moriarty, "Essentials in the Organization of Acquisitions Work in University Libraries." *College and Research Libraries*, I (1940), 229–34.

5. Receiving:
   o) Receipt of shipment and unpacking
   p) Checking in receipts
   q) Receipts and replacements counted
   r) Revision of items
   s) Order cards filed in orders-received file
   t) Invoices filed
   u) Items placed on truck for distribution
6. Shipping:
   v) Return of items unwanted for certain reasons.

ORGANIZATION. The actual organization of the acquisitions department depends upon a number of variable factors, such as quantity and complexity of materials received, personnel, and physical conditions. Some departments are organized on the basis of types of materials received (books and pamphlets, serials, documents, archives, etc.); while others are arranged by methods of acquisition (purchases, exchanges, and gifts).

In a library with a relatively small number of annual accessions all materials acquired may pass through a single office or the hands of a single individual, regardless of the method of acquisition. Libraries with large annual accessions are likely to be organized into subsections, on the basis of either form of materials or methods of acquisition. Many of the larger libraries are organized on the latter basis, although they may have one or more sections concerned with a special type of material, such as serials or documents. An example of the organization of an order department in a large library is shown in Figure 10.

In chapter iv the development of the technical services divisions in university libraries was considered. Some of the library surveys have recommended setting up such divisions, particularly if the acquisitions department had been using obsolete methods and its work was not integrated with that of the other units of the library.[5] Sometimes the acquisitions departments had been in charge

[5] Wilson, Downs, and Tauber, *Report of a Survey of the Libraries of Cornell University for the Library Board of Cornell University, October 1947—February 1948*, pp. 59–61.

of individuals who were profound bookmen but knew little or nothing about running an efficient enterprise. The local conditions of a university library should be the basis for the type of organization needed. The librarian perforce is obligated to introduce such organization as is consistent with administrative principles, particularly centralization and control.

PERSONNEL. The general and specific duties of the head of the acquisitions department place upon him many responsibilities for personnel.[6] So much routine is involved in the work of acquisition that the administrator should be cautious about overloading it with individuals who are qualified to do work at a high professional level. Clerical and business operations can be handled by subprofessional assistants. In some institutions, which have introduced technical services divisions, the placement of qualified professional assistants in the acquisitions department has permitted the integration of the order work with cataloging. This is particularly true in such work as establishing entries for the catalogs.[7]

PURCHASES

The routines for purchases in university libraries are fairly simple, although complications may occur in the purchase of foreign titles. The information on the order cards for regular book purchases is verified in trade bibliographies. In order to prevent unintentional duplication of titles, a check is made in the library's catalogs and the acquisitions department's files. Faculty members are notified if the book has already been received by the library and is either available or in process.

After checking, order cards are turned over to the departmental typist. The names of the funds to which the items are charged are

[6] See, for example, American Library Association, Board on Salaries, Tenure, and Staff, *Classification and Pay Plans for Libraries in Institutions of Higher Education*, pp. 65–72: see also Brown, "In-Service Training in Acquisition Work," *College and Research Libraries*, XII (1951), 29–32.

[7] Two studies have recently discussed the coordination of technical services: the Division of Cataloging and Classification of the ALA, through its Committee on Administration (Bella Shachtman, chairman), has made a study of policies and coordination in technical services, and Felix Reichmann of Cornell University has reported an investigation of the organization and services of acquisitions departments in a group of member institutions in the Association of Research Libraries. See Reichmann's "Management and Operation," *Library Trends*, III (1955), 462–70.

FIGURE 10. ORGANIZATION CHART, ORDER DEPARTMENT,

UNIVERSITY OF CALIFORNIA (BERKELEY) GENERAL LIBRARY, 1955

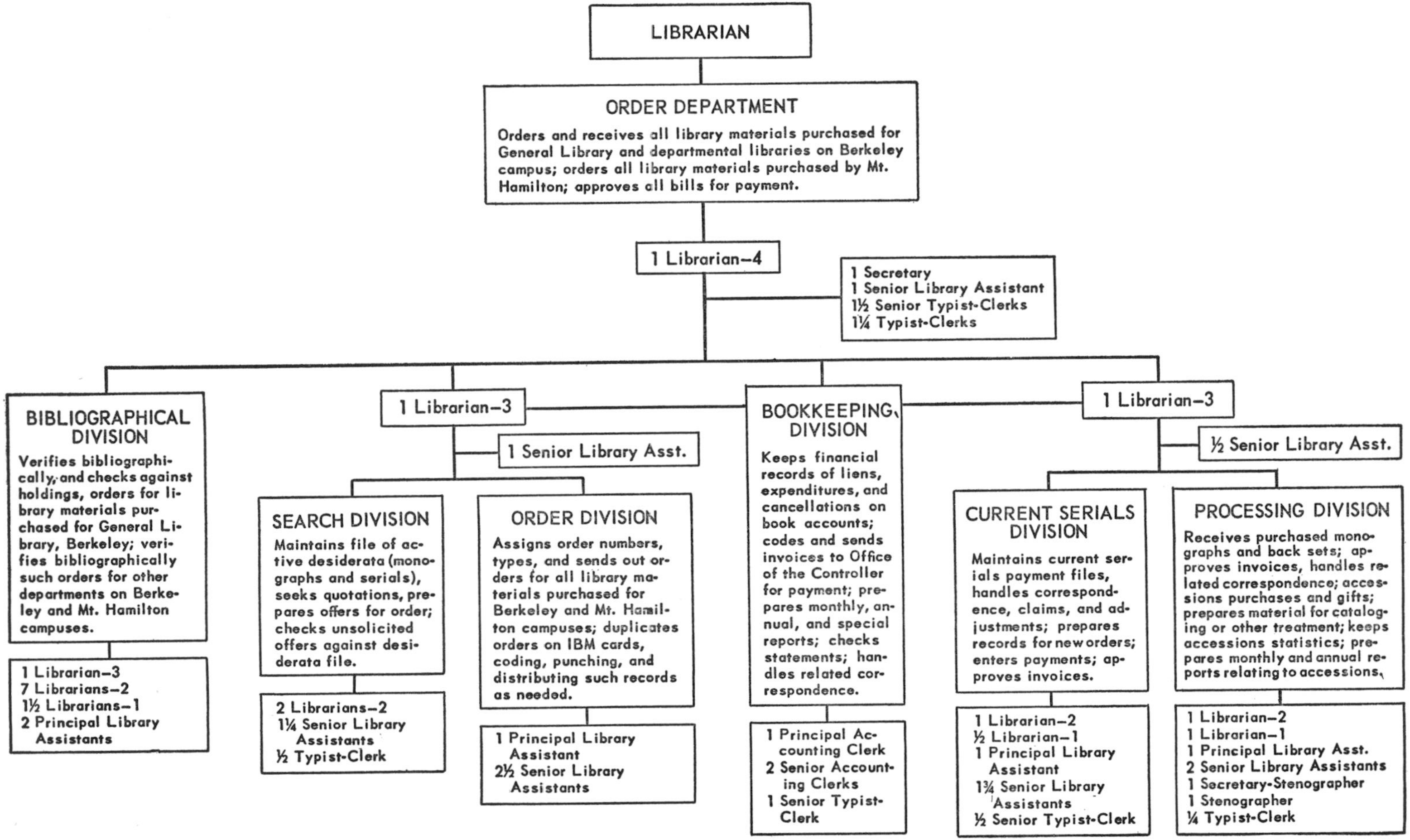

LIBRARIAN

ORDER DEPARTMENT

Orders and receives all library materials purchased for General Library and departmental libraries on Berkeley campus; orders all library materials purchased by Mt. Hamilton; approves all bills for payment.

1 Librarian—4

1 Secretary
1 Senior Library Assistant
1½ Senior Typist-Clerks
1¼ Typist-Clerks

1 Librarian—3

½ Senior Library Asst.

PROCESSING DIVISION

Receives purchased monographs and back sets; approves invoices, handles related correspondence; accessions purchases and gifts; prepares material for cataloging or other treatment; keeps accessions statistics; prepares monthly and annual reports relating to accessions,

1 Librarian—2
1 Librarian—1
1 Principal Library Asst.
2 Senior Library Assistants
1 Secretary-Stenographer
1 Stenographer
¼ Typist-Clerk

CURRENT SERIALS DIVISION

Maintains current serials payment files, handles correspondence, claims, and adjustments; prepares records for new orders; enters payments; approves invoices.

1 Librarian—2
½ Librarian—1
1 Principal Library Assistant
1¼ Senior Library Assistants
½ Senior Typist-Clerk

BOOKKEEPING DIVISION

Keeps financial records of liens, expenditures, and cancellations on book accounts; codes and sends invoices to Office of the Controller for payment; prepares monthly, annual, and special reports; checks statements; handles related correspondence.

1 Principal Accounting Clerk
2 Senior Accounting Clerks
1 Senior Typist-Clerk

1 Librarian—3

1 Senior Library Asst.

ORDER DIVISION

Assigns order numbers, types, and sends out orders for all library materials purchased for Berkeley and Mt. Hamilton campuses; duplicates orders on IBM cards; coding, punching, and distributing such records as needed.

1 Principal Library Assistant
2½ Senior Library Assistants

SEARCH DIVISION

Maintains file of active desiderata (monographs and serials), seeks quotations, prepares offers for order; checks unsolicited offers against desiderata file.

2 Librarians—2
1¼ Senior Library Assistants
½ Typist-Clerk

BIBLIOGRAPHICAL DIVISION

Verifies bibliographically and checks against holdings, orders for library materials purchased for General Library, Berkeley; verifies bibliographically such orders for other departments on Berkeley and Mt. Hamilton campuses.

1 Librarian—3
7 Librarians—2
1½ Librarians—1
2 Principal Library Assistants

noted, and the dealers' names are placed on the cards. Generally, a single dealer is maintained for current American titles, while one or more dealers are used to obtain English and other foreign publications. Dealers suggested by faculty members are sometimes used for unusual materials. Rare or out-of-print items located in second-hand or auction catalogs are ordered directly, sometimes by telegraph and cable, from the dealers offering the materials. In a number of instances it is necessary to order directly from the publisher. This is true particularly of titles published by organizations and learned societies.

Many libraries are now using multiple-form order slips (also called correlated order forms). Through the use of carbons, several records may be made at one typing. The forms, for example, may include a dealer's order slip, an order department record, a slip for the departmental library, a book-fund order record, an auditor's record, and a faculty information slip. Other slips which may be part of the form include a Library of Congress card order, a claim slip, a dealer's slip (to be returned with the ordered item), and a temporary catalog card. Since each slip places a responsibility on the department for its care and routing, caution is necessary in order to prevent the addition of little-used forms. A large university library, for example, eliminated the Library of Congress card order slip because it was found that it was used in less than half the orders prepared. A temporary catalog slip is a useful device, but it raises problems of filing and withdrawal. Prompt cataloging would make it unnecessary.

EXCHANGES AND GIFTS

While the bulk of the important acquisitions of the university library is likely to be obtained through direct purchase, accessions through gift and exchange have reached imposing totals in a number of institutions.[8] These two latter channels of acquisition must frequently be used to secure items which are not available in the regular book trade or are not for sale. Often, too, the library does

[8] Lane, "Exchange Work in College and University Libraries."

not have sufficient funds to purchase items which are desirable for instructional or research purposes.

Librarians who have paid considerable attention to the acquisition of materials through gift and exchange generally have found their efforts well rewarded. Since these materials have a vital place in the building up of a library's collections, they should be given a definite place in the administrative organization of the library. If the volume of business is sufficiently large, the two activities may be handled as separate units, but usually they are combined in a division of the acquisitions department. The organization of gifts and exchange work at the University of California at Berkeley is shown in Figure 11.

EXCHANGE   One of the decisions that the librarian has to make in regard to exchange work is whether or not it is to be pursued deliberately as a means for building up the collections. No extensive program is possible, of course, unless a library has available from the university press and other units of the institution a supply of materials suitable for exchange. Official publications, press publications (monographs, serials, and periodicals), dissertations, library publications, and other items have been used for exchange purposes. Duplicates also represent a source of materials useful for exchange.[9]

The library as a rule has no problem in obtaining official university and library publications, as well as dissertations, for exchange purposes. In relation to press publications, however, special arrangements usually have to be made. Both the library and the press have to maintain accounts. Usually, the press is required to operate without a deficit, so it must charge the library a reasonable rate for copies of publications wanted for exchange purposes. Undoubtedly, the indiscriminate distribution of exchange copies would reduce the possibility of sale to libraries. Favorable press-library relations would take into consideration the fact that both units are part of the

[9] *Ibid.* See also MacIver, "The Exchange of Publications as a Medium for the Development of the Book Collection," *Library Quarterly,* VIII (1938), 491–502.

same institution, and it is sometimes not possible to obtain certain research materials unless there is a body of exchange material available. Apparently, some of the state universities have been able to work out satisfactory relationships between the press and the library with greater ease than private institutions. In a few cases, the librarian, as a member of the publications committee of the university, has been able to assist with the development of the press program.

Another relationship with the press is worth brief mention. In order to develop foreign exchanges, a few presses have made arrangements for the library to take over stock remainders. Since this is done after the greater bulk of domestic sale has occurred, the plan provides the library with resources which are useful in procuring foreign research materials.

The duplicate collection is another source of materials used in exchange. Although individual library programs are common in the exchange of duplicates, a number of associations, such as the Association of College and Reference Libraries, the Medical Library Association, the American Association of Law Libraries, and the Special Libraries Association, have introduced effective institutional exchange relationships. The bibliographic and interlibrary centers have likewise participated in helping member institutions in their exchange problems with duplicate materials. UNESCO, on an international scale, has promoted exchange relationships between libraries in various countries, including the United States. Another program that has had foreign participation is the United States Book Exchange, an independent organization housed in the Library of Congress.[10]

GIFTS   Gifts furnish an important supply of materials in most university libraries. Many of the older universities owe their great strength to the gifts of individuals. Coney makes the following observation on gifts as related to the University of California:

The great libraries of the private eastern universities have in a very large measure grown up out of the benefactions of books or money

[10] These various projects are discussed in Tauber and Associates, *Technical Services in Libraries*, chap. vii.

FIGURE 11. ORGANIZATION CHART,
GIFTS AND EXCHANGE DEPARTMENT,
UNIVERSITY OF CALIFORNIA (BERKELEY)
GENERAL LIBRARY, 1955

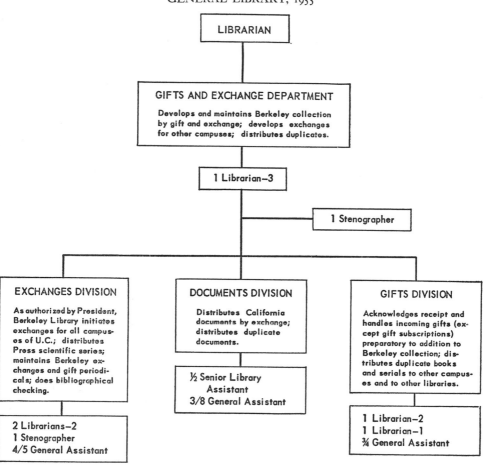

from alumni and friends. In the newer, less wealthy regions of the western part of the United States public funds, for the most part, have had to supply such scholarly libraries as there are. Yet there is an encouraging stream of gifts directed toward the libraries of the University of California. The University library at Berkeley has, for instance, enjoyed among others for many years income for general books from the Horace David endowment and the Michael Reese Library fund, the fine Horace W. Carpentier endowment for materials in Asiatic civilization, the Lois T. Howison fund for philosophy, and the various funds given by Mrs. Jane K. Sather for classics and history. These and other endowments and gifts of money and books have carried the library a long way toward its present eminence. While public funds may be expected to provide the innumerable bread-and-butter books required by the processes of teaching and scholarship, it is most appropriate that rare and special books come as the result of benefactions.[11]

Since gifts frequently raise administrative problems involving relations with donors, procedures of acceptance and publicity, and technical decisions, the librarian should keep close watch on the gift program of the library. In most universities, the librarian plans the gift program carefully, and seeks to interest friends-of-the-library groups, faculty members, students, alumni, individual collectors, and the community at large in the work of the library. While many gifts come in unsolicited, the gift unit of the library generally is on the watch for potential sources of gifts, such as educational, industrial, commercial, and governmental organizations and learned societies. The extent to which each of these sources may serve to build up the book collections of a library is discussed in detail in chapter ix.

MATERIALS. Gifts to the university library may be in the form of money or of books or other graphic materials. Gifts of money present several problems to the librarian. In the first place, the librarian himself may be instrumental in obtaining money for library purposes. Generally, he turns the money over to the business office, and the administration and the trustees and possibly other interested members of the university or friends group may make official ac-

[11] Coney, "The University Library: University and Society—VII," *California Monthly*, LXIII (1953), 3-4.

knowledgments. Usually, the librarian also acknowledges gifts of money. In the second place, the librarian will usually be charged with the expenditure of money. When definite stipulations are made for the use of the funds, the librarian must see that these are carried out to the letter, as living donors or their heirs are interested in what is done with endowments or money designated to be spent for specific purposes. Gifts of books, paintings, portraits, statuary, or museum pieces are often obtained by the librarian and acknowledged by him, the president, the trustees, or other officers.

GIFT POLICY. In 1952, Lewis C. Branscomb, director of the Ohio State University Libraries, studied the gift policies of twelve university libraries (California at Berkeley, Chicago, Cornell, Duke, Harvard, Illinois, Indiana, Iowa, Michigan, Missouri, Princeton, and Stanford). Only one of these libraries actually had a written statement of policy concerning gifts, and this was used for internal purposes. Several of the librarians writing to Branscomb indicated a belief that a written statement tends toward rigidity and in some cases might scare away prospective donors by what appeared to be inflexible policies. It was suggested that verbal conferences were more effective in clarifying particular situations with donors.

Although no written statements were available, the other eleven libraries had definite policies in respect to gifts. Most of the points raised are similar to those which have been followed in recent years by university libraries.

In the first place, the libraries generally refuse to accept gifts with strings attached to them, unless there are special circumstances. It was noted that any refusal of a gift should be weighed carefully, since possible future gifts may be sent elsewhere. Only outstanding gifts are considered for retention in a fixed location without dispersal of any sort. Space commitments are serious decisions, and a few libraries which make exceptions for such commitments suggest to the prospective donor that they be allowed to make changes in the future if administration and use of the collection so indicate. In a few institutions, the approval of the president and trustees is necessary in the acceptance of gifts with strings attached to them.

In the second place, gifts should be examined in relation to the instructional and research program of the institution on a long-range basis. Possible future developments of the educational program, as well as the current curriculum, need to be considered.

In the third place, any gift accepted with stipulations should be examined in connection with internal problems of shelving, housing, curatorship, special problems of cataloging and classification, and use. If a collection has a high monetary value or approximate completeness, it may justify separation, with special catalogs. If the collection consists of rare items, the librarian, as well as the donor, should be interested in limiting use. In regard to miscellaneous collections, an agreement with the donor should be reached as to such procedures as integrating, discarding, selling, or exchanging items.

In the fourth place, the future cost of maintenance requires consideration. A special collection may involve high maintenance costs if it is kept up to date. Not only space requirements and special attention are involved; will the library want to purchase items in the field of the special collection? If the gift is accompanied by endowment, this is not a serious problem. If diversion of the limited funds of the library becomes necessary, the gift may place a heavy load on the budget.

These considerations, therefore, make it necessary for the librarian to have a gift policy, even if it is unwritten. However, a written policy, subject to change, may be useful for internal administrative purposes, as well as having instructive value for new librarians.

It is a general practice of most university libraries to express willingness to design special bookplates, to issue brochures or lists of items, to provide publicity, and to arrange exhibits for gift materials. The use of appropriate plaques or other designations in the stacks has also been a satisfactory procedure for many donors.

PREPARATION
OF MATERIALS:
CATALOG
DEPARTMENT

The acquisitional processes form one of the three major technical aspects of library work. The preparational processes—classification, cataloging, and mechanical preparation—form the second major aspect. In recent years, considerable attention has been given to those activities which are designed to make materials easily available to users.[12] This has been an area of work in which administrators have been especially concerned because of the pressures which have been placed on budgets, as well as because of the increase in and complexity of the flow of materials into university libraries. Administrators and catalogers have raised a number of questions about the current practices in organizing materials, and efforts to simplify have been prominent in the last decade.

This chapter assumes that there will not be, at least for the immediate future, a general upheaval in present procedures.[13] There is considerable discussion of cataloging rules, however, and some changes are likely to occur in this area. It is also within the realm of possibility that an effort will be made to reduce the present size of catalogs of some university libraries.

The development of card catalogs received its greatest impetus in the 1880's but many libraries did not abandon the book catalog until the first decade of the twentieth century. There is little doubt that the initiation of card printing and distribution by the Library of Congress hastened the change from the printed book to the card catalog form. Because it contained many advantages over the inflexible book catalog, the card catalog was hailed as one of the greatest improvements in library technology. But these catalogs have grown in size and complexity, and university librarians have been

[12] Two works which discuss with some detail problems of classification and cataloging are the following: Tauber (ed.), *The Subject Analysis of Library Materials,* and "Current Trends in Cataloging and Classification." See also Tauber and Associates, *Technical Services in Libraries,* chaps. viii–xiv.

[13] Gull, "Substitutes for the Card Catalog," *Library Trends,* II (1953), 318–29. Gull, after reviewing the various substitutes that have been suggested for the card catalog, notes that there has not yet been revealed any technique which will become "available in the near future to replace the card catalog as a library's basic record" (p. 328).

considering what may be done with the multi-million card files which are being increased annually by 75,000 to 150,000 cards. It is the purpose of this chapter to discuss problems of cataloging and classification under the following heads: (1) the scope of work of the catalog and classification department of the university library, with special emphasis on the purpose and functions of the various types of catalogs prepared; (2) the physical arrangement and internal organization of the department; (3) administrative standards, codes, and measurements of efficiency; (4) some administrative problems, involving such matters as accessioning, inventory, assistance in the use of the catalog, classification and reclassification, handling of nonbook materials, special collections of departmental libraries, and costs of cataloging and utility of the card catalog and its future development.

SCOPE OF WORK   The catalog department prepares and maintains the records which reveal the holdings of the library. The major operations involved in this preparation of records consist of descriptive cataloging, subject cataloging, and classification. Since most catalog departments combine the cataloging and classifying operations, reference to the catalog department will hereafter imply inclusion of classification. The classification function itself is directed toward an orderly arrangement within subject groups of books on the shelves. Classification and subject cataloging represent efforts to show the contents of the library's holdings. Descriptive cataloging refers to the making of card entries which provide bibliographical information regarding titles of various kinds.

The catalog department ordinarily has the responsibility for cataloging and classifying books, periodicals, newspapers, and other serials, pamphlets, documents, manuscripts, films, recordings, music, and other items. The product of the department consists of necessary records for the public catalog, the official catalog, the shelf list, departmental library catalogs, and other special catalogs. The scope and wide range of operations of a large catalog department are depicted in Figure 12. As may be seen from this chart, the department also has the responsibility for maintaining a union catalog of cards received from various research libraries. Other libraries may cooperate in the preparation of cards for storage library or interlibrary centers. A few libraries still retain an LC card depository catalog.

Producing records, however, is not the only duty of the department. Such processes as accessioning, taking inventory, or issuing bulletins of new titles added to the library may be part of its work.

The purposes and functions of five catalogs that have been mentioned—the public, official, depository, and union catalogs, and the shelf list—may now be treated in more detail.

PUBLIC CATALOG. The public catalog is the principal tool produced by the catalog department, so far as the users of the library and the staff are concerned. In university libraries this is usually a dictionary catalog containing author, subject, title, reference, and guide cards, intended to enable the person consulting it to find either a definite work or a class of works and to choose different books or different editions of a work on the basis of information given on the catalog entry. It may be a catalog of materials in the main building only or a union catalog of materials in that unit and in branch or departmental libraries as well.

Although the dictionary catalog is predominant in American libraries, it should be pointed out that "dictionary" is used in a general sense, since there may be various sub-alphabets within the main alphabet, geographical and chronological arrangements, and other modifications. In recent years, some libraries using the dictionary catalog have endeavored to simplify its use through reducing the variations from strict alphabetical listing.

Not all university libraries maintain a dictionary catalog. Boston University, for example, has installed a classified catalog, arranged by the Library of Congress classification.[14] Although several scientific libraries provide classified catalogs, these are seldom found in academic libraries. More common is the divided catalog, which

[14] Herrick, "The Development of a Classified Catalog for a University Library," *College and Research Libraries*, XIV (1953), 418–24.

FIGURE 12. ORGANIZATION CHART, CATALOG DEPARTMENT,
UNIVERSITY OF CALIFORNIA (BERKELEY) GENERAL LIBRARY, 1955

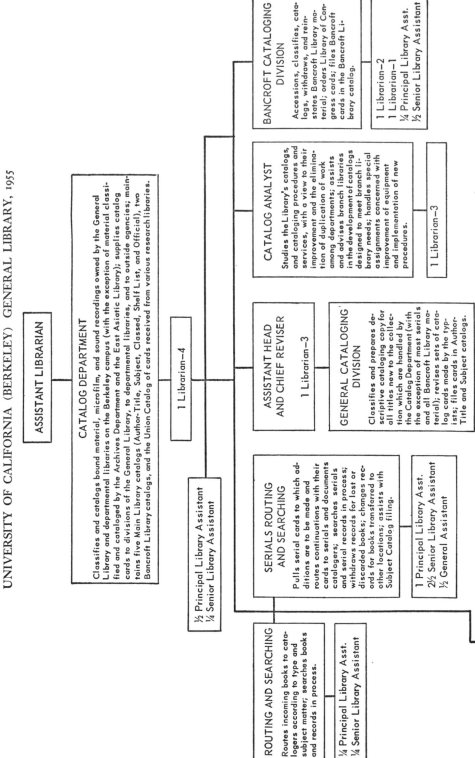

ASSISTANT CHIEF REVISER
1 Librarian—3

CATALOGING SECTION 5
Classifies and catalogs government documents (including those on microfilm); adds volumes records which already have been made; catalogs material owned by the Rare Books Department.

2 Librarians—2
¾ Librarian—1

FILING SECTION
Files cards in alphabetical catalogs (Author-Title and Subject); has charge of the filing manuals for these catalogs.

¼ Principal Library Assistant
½ Principal Library Assistant
½ Senior Library Asst.
¼ General Assistant

CATALOGING SECTION 4 [c]
Classifies and catalogs books in the fields of literature, agriculture, education, social sciences, political science, law, and library science, most books acquired by the Farmington Plan, microfilm and Microcards; on request of the Library of Congress, prepares descriptive cataloging copy from which the Library of Congress prints catalog cards.

4 Librarians—2
½ Principal Library Assistant
½ Senior Library Asst.

CATALOG MAINTENANCE ASSISTANCE
Changes books and records as directed by catalogers.

1 Senior Library Asst.

CATALOGING SECTION 1 [a]
Classifies and catalogs books in geography, history, philosophy, religion, music, art; classifies and catalogs music microfilm, sound recordings.

4 Librarians—2
¼ Librarian—1

CATALOGING SECTION 2
Classifies and catalogs Slavic language material in the Cyrillic alphabet.

1 Librarian—2

CATALOGING SECTION 3 [b]
Classifies and catalogs books in science and technology.

1 Librarian—2

PRELIMINARY CHECKING SECTION
Searches the Union Catalog for cards to be used in cataloging; compares headings with UC catalogs; pulls cards for adding of copies; makes author analytics.

¼ Principal Library Assistant
4 Senior Library Asst.
¼ General Assistant

LC CARD CATALOGING SECTION [a]
Catalogs most classes of books for which there are Library of Congress cards carrying call numbers; does descriptive cataloging and classification of UC theses; adds official decisions to classification schemes and cataloging codes; does record work required in keeping official lists of subject headings up to date and making current revisions in the Subject Catalog.

1½ Principal Library Assistant

SERIALS CATALOGING DIVISION
Adds volumes to catalog records; recatalogs serials when variations within sets make this necessary; catalogs and classifies most new serials; records additional copies on catalog cards which have been made by the General Cataloging Division; reinstates lost books when found.

1½ Librarians—2
1 Librarian—1
2 Principal Library Assistants

TYPING DIVISION
Types Xerox copy or sets of catalog cards from copy prepared by catalogers; types appropriate information on cards for various catalogs and outside agencies; takes charge of the Circulating Shelf List; files cards in catalogs arranged by call number (Official, Classed, and Shelf List); assists catalogers with processing of microfilm.

¾ Principal Library Assistant
6¼ Senior Library Assistants

UNION CATALOG DIVISION
Files Union Catalog cards; keeps Union Catalog records; revises call numbers in books, releases books to Loan Department.

½ Principal Library Assistant
1½ Senior Library Assistant
½ General Assistant

a Assistant Head serves as Head of this section.
b Catalog Analyst serves as Head of this section.
c Assistant Chief Reviser serves as Head of this section.

consists of an alphabetical-subject section and one which contains entries for authors, titles, editors, and other names.[15] Studies which have been made of the divided catalog indicate that it reduces complications in the use of the catalog by the university community. The catalog itself, however, is somewhat enlarged in size, since it is necessary to duplicate certain entries in both of its parts.

In recent years, the subject catalog, either as a separate unit or as part of a dictionary catalog, has been criticized sharply.[16] For some time, the primary criticisms were directed at the subject catalog as a principle. It was suggested that subject bibliographies and subject indexes would be more effective for users than the typical library subject catalog. Current questioning of the subject catalog has been concerned with making it a more efficient tool.[17] The Association of Research Libraries and the American Library Association Division of Cataloging and Classification have been directing attention at the possible standardization of subject headings for different types of libraries. The Library of Congress, which began issuing its subject catalog in 1952, has also been conscious of the need for increasing the value of subject analysis of textual materials.[18] Studies by Swank [19] and others emphasize the need of coordinating the subject catalog with subject bibliographies.

OFFICIAL CATALOG. Many of the larger university libraries maintain an official catalog, which is a card record kept in the catalog department for the use of staff members. It generally contains a main entry for every title in the library system, although it may include

[15] Thom, "The Divided Catalog in College and University Libraries," *College and Research Libraries,* X (1949), 236–41; see also Nyholm, "California Examines Its Divided Catalog," *College and Research Libraries,* IX (1948), 195–201, and Markley, "University of California Subject Catalog Inquiry: A Study of the Subject Catalog Based on Interviews with Users," *Journal of Cataloging and Classification,* VI (1950), 88–95.

[16] See Tauber (ed.), *The Subject Analysis of Library Materials.*

[17] Merritt, *Use of the Subject Catalog in the University of California Library.*

[18] Spalding, "Use of Catalog Entries at the Library of Congress," *Journal of Cataloging and Classification,* X (1950), 95–100.

[19] Swank, "The Organization of Library Materials for Research in English Literature" (unpublished Ph.D. dissertation, Graduate Library School, University of Chicago, 1944), and his "Subject Catalogs, Classifications, or Bibliographies?" *Library Quarterly,* XIV (1944), 316–32; Simonton, "Subject Catalogs vs. Bibliographies," in Tauber (ed.), *The Subject Analysis of Library Materials,* pp. 130–38.

various other entries as well. It may also be combined with other types of catalogs, such as union catalogs and authority files.

The official catalog has developed in libraries for either or both of two reasons: (1) it is a tool which makes it possible for catalogers and other staff members to search for entries without having congestion at the public catalog; and (2) it has developed as a result of the location of the catalog department in relation to the public catalog. The administrator should seriously consider the continuing expense in equipment and staff time before starting a catalog of this type. Physical conditions in the library, however, may make it an esssential record for efficient processing.

DEPOSITORY AND UNION CATALOGS. In 1942, when the Library of Congress issued its *Catalog of Books Represented by Library of Congress Printed Cards*, many university libraries abandoned the basic LC depository card catalog. A few libraries still maintain it, but many which have given it up supplement the printed catalog with temporary proof-sheet slips. Undoubtedly, the card depository, kept up to date, is a more satisfactory tool for quick searching, since only one source is involved. However, the expense of maintaining the card depository has apparently influenced librarians to retire it as an active record.

Some libraries which have given up the LC card depository have continued to maintain union catalogs of cards received from other libraries. Those having LC depositories sometimes interfile the cards with those sent by other institutions.

Little effort has been made to study the use of either depository or union catalogs. In 1946, however, Munson [20] reported on a study of the LC depository catalog at Columbia University. She found that predominant consultation of the depository was by the catalogers, who used the data on the cards for the preparation of entries for the university catalog. Apparently the findings were sufficient to convince the administration that the card catalog was not essential since the printed catalog was available.

[20] Munson, "Use of the Depository Catalog in a University Library," (unpublished M.S. thesis), abstract in *College and Research Libraries*, VIII (1947), 151–56.

SHELF LIST. The shelf list is found in practically every library. In some libraries, it is kept on slips or sheets. In the large library, such a record should be kept on cards for purposes of speeding up the work of the classifiers. It is most economically produced by making an extra card at the time other records are being prepared. By purchasing an extra Library of Congress card or by typing or otherwise reproducing an extra card for books for which there are no printed cards, a shelf list is built up simultaneously with the card catalog. In library systems with branch or departmental libraries the shelf list in the central library should be a union list, designating the location of materials in all units. More often than not the departmental or professional school library is furnished a shelf list for its particular collection.

The shelf list has many advantages from an administrative point of view. It may be utilized as a classified catalog to indicate the weaknesses or strength of the collections. If it is practical to allow users to consult the shelf list as a classified catalog, it could serve as a direct source of information on holdings in special fields. The shelf list is also used in inventory checks. Classifiers must refer to it constantly in order to incorporate new titles into the library collections on a consistent basis.

ORGANIZATION AND ADMINISTRATION   To produce catalogs carefully and efficiently, to classify books systematically, and to carry on the other functions which have been delegated to the catalog department, it is essential that the librarian and the head cataloger thoughtfully plan the unit with consideration of its internal arrangement and its physical arrangement.[21] Under the heading of internal organization, such topics as interdepartmental relations, personnel, division of work, and reference sources will be discussed. Physical arrangement will be considered in chapter xiv.

ORGANIZATION. Mention has already been made of the grouping of all library services into two major divisions, the technical services and the readers' services. In his study of technical services in libraries,

[21] Tauber and Associates, *Technical Services in Libraries*, chap. xiv.

Cohen [22] found that university libraries were prominent among the institutions which had introduced this type of organization. Various surveys of university libraries have also recommended this division as an effective administrative device for coordinating related operations. Under such an organization, cataloging and classification are placed in a single unit, supervised by a head cataloger.

The internal organization of the catalog department, however, will differ from library to library, depending on local problems. An example of a complex organization is shown in Figure 13, a chart of the catalog department of the Harvard College Library. In this organization there are six major divisions—the clerical group, the searchers, the public catalog, the union catalog, the serial division, and the catalogers. It will be observed that the catalogers are divided into three groups—subject and language catalogers, catalogers of slow-moving materials, and catalogers of fast-moving materials. An examination of the California organization, in Figure 12, which is a different type of chart, will show some similarities to the Harvard arrangement, with sections on routing and searching, serials routing and searching, serials cataloging, union catalog division, and catalogers in five groups—two groups organized by subject, a Slavic language cataloging unit, a documents cataloging unit, and an LC card cataloging section. In most libraries, a unit similar to the LC card cataloging section exists to prepare quickly materials which have already been cataloged by the national library.

These divisions of work suggest the nature of the work arrangements in the catalog department. There are four methods, other than those based on the difficulty of cataloging, whereby the work of the department may be organized.

First the work may be organized by process. This procedure disregards the subject and type of material. One group takes care of author or descriptive cataloging; another, of classifying; and still another, of subject cataloging. There are probably only a few libraries which are still organized in this way, as there is general

[22] Cohen, "The Technical Services Division in Libraries," *College and Research Libraries*, X (1949), 46–49.

FIGURE 13. ORGANIZATION CHART, CATALOG DEPARTMENT,
HARVARD COLLEGE LIBRARY, 1955

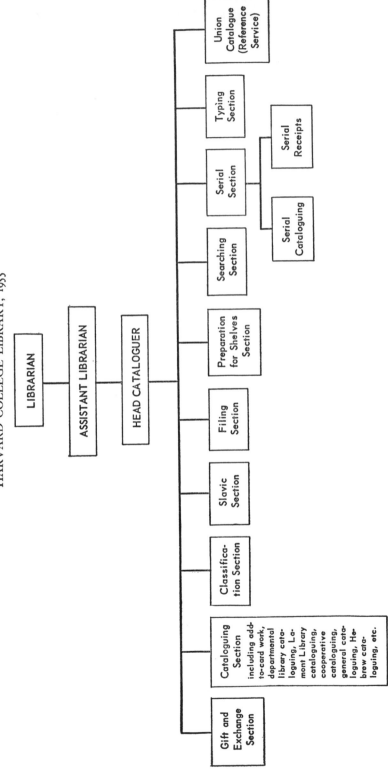

recognition that subject cataloging and classifying are similar operations.[23] A number of libraries, however, combine subject cataloging and classification in the hands of certain personnel, and maintain a descriptive cataloging staff. Probably the largest group of libraries are organized on the basis of cataloging personnel performing all tasks with most materials; exceptions may be on the basis of specialized and linguistic knowledge. For example, the documents catalogers at Columbia University establish the entry for cataloging but do no subject cataloging or classification. This is also true of some catalogers in other libraries who prepare entries for materials in the more difficult languages.

Second, the materials may be divided by subject or subject divisions. Both Harvard and California provide for this distinction. Whether it is geography or the social sciences, the cataloger establishes the entry, conducts bibliographical research, and assigns subject headings and classification numbers to all books within the subject or subject division for which he is responsible.

The third method is to divide the material by language. This may be a desirable procedure in a large university library which receives considerable materials in oriental languages and less commonly known European languages. A unit on Slavic language materials exists at both Harvard and California.

The fourth method of division is by form or type of material. A serials cataloging unit, for example, may be responsible for all work dealing with serials.

In many of the larger libraries, a combination of these methods is necessary in order to expedite the work. Coney [24] early pointed out the need for specialization in cataloging, particularly as size or quantity of work becomes a crucial factor.

The question of centralized *versus* decentralized cataloging and classification is linked with the problem of distribution of materials. Those who favor decentralization argue that the experts in the

[23] Morsch, "Scientific Management in Cataloging," *Library Trends*, II (1954), 476–77; Trotier, "Organization and Administration of Cataloging Processes," *Library Trends*, II (1953), 264–67.
[24] "The Administration of Technical Processes," p. 163.

special departments or schools are better acquainted with specialized subject-heading and classification problems than are catalogers in the central department.[25] As a matter of fact, many of the larger university library systems, which have professional school and departmental libraries of some scope, maintain separate cataloging units. Harvard, Cornell, Columbia, and other institutions contain such units, with varying degrees of administrative control from central catalog departments. Central administrative authority appears to be desirable, even though decentralized units are introduced for purposes of efficiency and consistent subject analysis.

PERSONNEL. As may be seen from the organization charts, the personnel of the catalog department consists of various levels of staff members: the head cataloger, the supervisors, the catalogers of several kinds, and the clerical staff. For a smoothly operating department, these individuals must have proper training and personal qualifications.

The head of the catalog department of the large university library is a key officer. He should possess a combination of scholarship, administrative ability, technical training, and experience. In addition to the general duties of the departmental head outlined in the preceding chapter, the head cataloger is specifically concerned with the following activities:

1. To lay out the cataloging and related work of the cataloging staff

2. To aid staff members in their difficult cataloging and classification problems

3. To develop the catalogs and cataloging operations to meet the needs of the general library, departmental libraries, and special collections

4. To see that necessary bibliographical tools, reference works, and mechanical equipment are available

5. To coordinate the routines of the catalog department with those of the acquisition, circulation, and other departments

[25] Swank, "Subject Cataloging in the Subject-Departmentalized Library," in Shera and Egan (eds.), *Bibliographic Organization*, pp. 187-99.

6. To cooperate with the faculty and departments in the placement of materials.

The importance of selecting an individual who can place cataloging
operations in their proper relation to other activities of the library
cannot be overestimated, since the librarian cannot assume direct
responsibility for the supervision of the department. Although the
librarian should be aware of the fundamental problems that exist in
cataloging and preparing books for use and be able to detect in-
efficiencies in either policy or operation, he must delegate authority
and responsibility to the head cataloger.

Many head catalogers work under considerable pressure, since
acquisitions frequently are so abundant that the staff cannot handle
them promptly. The head cataloger, who must plan, lay out, and
coordinate the work of his staff, should have a definite program
which relates the technical work to the aims, services, and policies
of the entire library organization. Cataloging and other technical
operations are useful only in so far as they support the readers'
services. The head cataloger is necessarily concerned with promptness of work, accuracy, and technical detail. Careful distribution of
work among professional and clerical staff is essential for economical
administration.[26]

More and more librarians are analyzing the operations of the
various departments so that work will not only be properly distributed, but so that appropriate simplifications will be introduced
and new equipment utilized.[27] The efficient head cataloger will not
only be amenable to change, but will search for possible ways of
improving operations.

REFERENCE AND BIBLIOGRAPHICAL APPARATUS. Most large catalog
departments maintain a collection of reference and bibliographical
works which are needed in the preparation of entries. When the
catalog department is located conveniently to the order and refer-

[26] See personnel specifications in American Library Association, Board on
Salaries, Staff, and Tenure. *Classification and Pay Plans for Libraries in Libraries
in Institutions of Higher Education: Volume III—Universities*, pp. 31-45.

[27] See "Management Improvements in Libraries," *College and Research Libraries*,
XV (1954), 188-204.

ence departments, this collection may be kept relatively small and expensive duplication will be minimized.

ADMINISTRATIVE STANDARDS   The work of the catalog department should be constantly evaluated as to operations and production. Efficient departments make use of manuals and codes for establishing uniformity in procedures. In addition, various devices are available for determining the relative efficiency of the department.

MANUALS AND CODES. The insistence upon uniformity and consistency in the work of the catalog department has made it desirable to organize general policies and specific routines into staff manuals and codes. The extent to which a library department should go into listing procedures depends largely upon the size and diversity of the system, the nature of the personnel, and the types and quantity of materials handled.[28]

In general, it may be said that the department should list the policies of the unit, as well as the routines for specific processes or groups of processes, such as accessioning, inventory, classification and cataloging variations from generally accepted classification schedules and catalog codes, and filing. Sometimes variations are written into published rules, such as those of the American Library Association and the Library of Congress. Sometimes, these are kept on cards.

In the catalog department, a manual should reduce to a minimum the need to repeat routine directions, facilitate the training of new assistants, and make available to the administrator and other staff members a statement of policy and procedure.

MEASUREMENT OF EFFICIENCY. From a quantitative standpoint, such items as cataloging arrears, promptness in processing materials, and success in obtaining simultaneous mechanical preparation of books and reproduction and filing of cards may be used to measure the efficiency of the catalog department. Qualitative measurements may be concerned with the degree of success users and staff mem-

[28] See, for example, the manuals of the University of Illinois, Montana State University, University of Nebraska, and Temple University. Many institutions have manuals which are not published.

bers meet in having the catalog answer their questions or with the success of the classification system in grouping books to the satisfaction of stack-users.

Centralization of cataloging may be considered as an indication of coordination, particularly if cataloging arrears of departmental libraries are kept at a minimum. Centralization, likewise, should result in a complete record of the holdings of the entire system of libraries of a university—a product which sometimes is not obtained by a decentralization of technical operations.

A number of libraries have been developing definite programs to eliminate arrears in cataloging.[29] While the libraries differ in their approach to the problem, the results indicate that a positive approach, involving organization of work, personnel, and method can be successful.

SOME ADMINISTRATIVE PROBLEMS   In addition to the production of catalogs, the catalog department may be faced with other responsibilities which merit brief treatment. These include: accessioning, inventory, assistance in the use of the catalog, reclassification, maintenance of the catalogs, cataloging of special collections and departmental libraries, and costs of cataloging.

ACCESSIONING. The practice of accessioning individual items varies considerably among libraries. This activity is often performed in the acquisition department or in a separate unit of the library. Many libraries have been abandoning the standard type of accession book and the use of serial accession numbers on individual volumes. In some libraries, accession information is kept on order cards or shelf-list entries; in others, invoices and multiple-form order slips represent the basic accession record. A number of libraries retain the accession numbering of items, without placing any information in accession books. It has been claimed that these numbers are useful in identifying particular titles, especially in circulation work.

There seems to be little question that accessioning can be time

[29] "Cataloging Arrearages," *Journal of Cataloging and Classification*, VII (1951), 89–109; Osborn, " 'Arrearages'—Ugly Word," *Library Journal*, LXXVI (1951), 1863–67.

consuming without any real advantage. The administrator should evaluate this practice in relation to actual service provided by the resultant record.

INVENTORY. While the major responsibility for inventory is usually given to the circulation department, the catalog personnel are involved. Inventories of the larger collections are arduous and some librarians have avoided them. Instead of complete inventories, continual reading of the shelves is performed by the circulation staff. Departmental librarians generally take an annual inventory.

The cataloging staff are called into the procedure because of the necessary decisions which have to be made concerning missing items. Inventories also reveal inconsistencies in entries or classification which require the attention of the catalogers.

ASSISTANCE IN USE OF THE CATALOG. A number of libraries have staff members who assist users in their consultation of the card catalog. Usually, these are attached to the reference staff, but in some cases, they are cataloging personnel. The catalog department generally is ready to assist the reference librarians in problems of catalog use, and in some libraries prepares visual aids and guides which help the patrons.

RECLASSIFICATION AND RECATALOGING. Any large-scale reclassification and recataloging program represents an important undertaking for a library. Since the early 1920's a number of university libraries have reclassified from various classification systems to that of the Library of Congress.[30]

Complete reclassification requires a careful study of methods and organization if the process is not to overwhelm the library staff and the users. Only in a small operation, with adequate staff, is it possible to reclassify and still carry on the current work of the catalog department. A special budget is essential if reclassification

[30] Tauber, "Reclassification and Recataloging of Materials in College and University Libraries" (unpublished Ph.D. dissertation, University of Chicago, 1941). Various articles taken from this study have been published in several journals. See Bentz and Cavender, "Reclassification and Recataloging," *Library Trends*, II (1953), 249–63. Among the libraries reclassifying in the last few years are Cornell, Iowa University, Miami, Mississippi, Tennessee, and Washington University (St. Louis).

is to be completed within a short period of time. Apparently those libraries which have reclassified to the Library of Congress system without modification have been able to perform the task rapidly. Recataloging should also take advantage of the available LC printed cards.

Some librarians have partially reclassified their collections. Partial reclassification involves many of the problems in the total operation, but usually can be handled with the normal staff.

MAINTENANCE OF THE CATALOGS. Libraries with large catalogs face many problems in editing and general upkeep. Osborn and Haskins [31] have singled out many of the difficulties of catalog maintenance. With the Harvard catalog as an example, they show the importance of a regular program if the catalog is to be an effective instrument. A budgetary allotment is necessary for systematic editing of the catalog, which, in the large library, may represent an investment of millions of dollars, if it is to serve users adequately. Most large libraries need one or more staff members who have responsibility for taking care of the current problems of the catalogs as well as planning for their future direction.

SPECIAL COLLECTIONS AND DEPARTMENTAL LIBRARIES. The maintenance of special collections within a library system presents problems for the catalog department administrator in the form of special catalogs, special types of cataloging, and, often, special systems of classification.[32] Some differences may be required for the special purposes of the collections, but the administrator should examine all variations in relation to the purposes of the library. There have been many cases where variations merely reflected the personal judgments of curators rather than a real need.

Similar problems arise in the handling of materials for departmental and professional school libraries. Particular heed should be given to special needs for collections in these libraries, but here too there should be caution against excessive variations which are not based on factual evidence.

[31] Osborn and Haskins, "Catalog Maintenance," *Library Trends*, II (1953), 279–89.
[32] Tauber and Associates, *Technical Services in Libraries*, chap. xv.

COSTS OF CATALOGING. Reichmann's study [33] shows the considerable attention that has been given to the problem of cataloging costs. Administrators of libraries justifiably have been concerned with the growing costs of cataloging, abetted by inflation, as reflected in salaries, and by the great size of many catalogs. Morsch aptly points out that cost studies can supply an important contribution within a given institution, but they should be made only after broader aspects of management are considered.[34] It is obviously impossible to compare the costs of one library with those of another without taking into consideration the many fine distinctions in the kind of cataloging done, the materials handled, the personnel available, and the administrative organization. Cataloging costs need to be considered in the light of the purposes of the library.

UTILITY AND FUTURE DEVELOPMENT. More and more administrators have become concerned about the utility of the card catalog. Frarey [35] has summarized the various studies that have been made of the use of the subject catalog. Since many of these studies deal with non-university users, the findings do not always apply. Frarey clearly shows, however, that all the necessary evidence for drastic change in the catalog structure is not yet at hand.

Most of the concern apparently has been for the subject portion of the catalog. Attention has been given to the author portion, too, and many of the simplifications introduced in the Library of Congress rules and in the practices of libraries have developed from a consciousness that excessive bibliographical detail is not essential for most users. At the present time, the Division of Cataloging and Classification of the American Library Association is sponsoring studies of the basic rules of author entry.

While the general assumption at the beginning of the discussion on cataloging in this section is that there is not likely to be an upheaval in present procedures or in the current nature of the card

[33] Reichmann, "Costs of Cataloging," *Library Trends*, II (1953), 290–317.
[34] Morsch, "Scientific Management in Cataloging," p. 473.
[35] Frarey, "Studies of Use of the Subject Catalog: Summary and Evaluation," in Tauber (ed.), *The Subject Analysis of Library Materials*, pp. 147–66.

catalog, there is considerable thought being expended on the future of the record. Osborn and Haskins [36] observe that many of the larger catalogs are increasing by a million cards every ten years. They suggest two cooperative measures: (1) studies in catalog maintenance, as well as new cataloging rules and practices, "can be made on the basis of common experience and judgment." And (2) book catalogs might be published as joint ventures. They write:

The dictionary catalog has served American libraries well for fifty years. The next fifty years may well tell a different story if timely and adequate steps are not taken. It would be courting disaster to go on into the second half of the twentieth century without fundamental re-thinking of the nature and function of the dictionary catalog. Multi-million card catalogs can be expected to double in size before the century ends. The difficulties will be far more than doubled if a large measure of control is not forthcoming.

BINDING
DEPARTMENT

The third major aspect of the technical services of the library is binding. This part of library service has become crucial in recent years, since prices of binding have increased to a greater extent proportionately than have the binding budgets of university libraries. Moreover, many foreign materials which were formerly imported in bound form are now being received in paper covers. Finally, as more periodicals are being issued for special fields, librarians are faced with the need of obtaining additional funds for binding. In many of the recent surveys of libraries, recommendations for increased binding funds, as well as for stipulated amounts for clearing arrears in binding, are included. In 62 libraries which reported on binding funds for 1953–54, only nine had sums of $40,000 or more; sixteen libraries had budgets of less than $10,000. The median for the group was $13,929.[37]

Pelham Barr, who, for a number of years before his death, was director of the Library Binding Institute, summarized many of

---

[36] *Op. cit.*, p. 288.
[37] "College and University Library Statistics, 1953–54 (Group I)," *College and Research Libraries*, XVI (1955), 39.

the pertinent questions which arise in the administration of a university library binding program.[38] An important part of his criticisms of university library practice was the failure on the part of librarians to organize the binding service systematically. Evidence from a number of library surveys has tended to bear him out in this observation. However, in recent years, with libraries growing in size and complexity, binding has occupied an important place in the library organization.[39]

In the remaining portion of this section, attention will be given to the organization of the binding service, the library bindery, commercial binders, repair work, and the handling of special materials.

ORGANIZATION OF BINDING SERVICE   In some of the university libraries which have an organized technical services division, binding is one of the units under the general supervision of the director of the division. In the larger libraries, the binding department may consist of a half-dozen or more staff members, with a professional librarian or an experienced binder as head.

The responsibilities of the binding librarian are many and varied. He must be able not only to plan and organize the work of the department, but he must develop procedures for his particular library. He is called upon to make decisions as to whether a specific volume should be bound (and the manner of binding), mended, repaired, or replaced (usually with consultation of service personnel). He should have a wide knowledge of publications and their peculiarities, so that proper sewing, cloths and buckrams, boards, and lettering will be applied to volumes needing binding. Obviously, in the university library which normally acquires many foreign titles, particularly serials, the need for linguistically adept personnel is important. In the binding department, the head and perhaps other staff members must be familiar with foreign languages in order to collate materials accurately.

[38] Barr, "Book Conservation and the University Library," *College and Research Libraries*, VII (1946), 214–19.
[39] Tauber and Associates, *Technical Services in Libraries*, chaps. xv–xvii.

Like other heads of departments, the binding librarian should set up procedures so that materials will move smoothly and promptly through all necessary operations to enable users to have ready access to materials. Proper scheduling of shipments to commercial binders is essential. Various records of the department, manuals of routines, and files of patterns for previously bound titles should be maintained. The binding librarian generally keeps statistics of the work of the department, and prepares reports and memoranda for the library administration. Relationships to the several departments and departmental libraries must be maintained by the binding librarian. In one university, for example, new staff members who prepare binding slips for material being sent to commercial binderies make scheduled visits to the binding department of the library so that they can better understand the binding process and see the final use of the instructions which they record on the binding slips. The binding librarian should strive to set standards for the entire library system, so that expensive variations will not be allowed to develop.

LIBRARY BINDERY   The question of whether or not the university library should maintain its own bindery cannot be categorically answered. Practically every large library has studied this question at some time. A few of the larger libraries, such as Minnesota, have binderies of their own. More libraries have quarters and equipment for pamphlet and small book binding.

The theoretical advantages which have been claimed for the university bindery in the library may be noted. It has been said that a bindery in the library permits personal supervision and the application of special methods to the needs and conditions of the institution. Moreover, it has been claimed that financial savings can be made in the institutions in which university binderies are operated. The most significant advantage is the fact that there is usually a greater degree of accessibility to the materials which are in the process of binding.

What do these advantages mean in practice? A library which has its own bindery may be in a position to experiment with less expensive types of binding. For example, the following statement is taken from a recent annual report of a university librarian:

The Binding Department has found, after experimentation, two ways to reinforce publications which previously either could not be preserved or could be preserved only at a cost which was considered too high in relation to their probable use. The first of these was the development of what is called "budget binding," a cheaper type of binding which was evolved by one of the binderies in consultation with the Head of our Binding Department and which gives adequate protection to certain categories of publications, such as annual reports of hospitals, that are of value but will never have heavy wear and tear. The second device was the successful use of plastic adhesives which enable the Department to repair and hold together volumes which have such narrow margins that they could not previously have been bound or rebound and hence would have had to be withdrawn from the collections.[40]

The question of financial savings on an over-all basis is not so easy to answer. Undoubtedly there is considerable saving in the binding of pamphlets, small books, and perhaps even some minor periodical volumes. In the rebinding of the usual run of books and periodicals, however, administrators of library binderies have been concerned about rising costs. In 1951, the University of Minnesota Library was seriously questioning the continuance of its bindery.[41] Attention was called to the inability of an individual library bindery to use mass production methods, such as is done in large commercial binderies. The library bindery was finding it more difficult to do the custom or specialized work at standard rates. Qualified personnel for binding is also scarce. Other library binderies have been faced with similar problems.

COMMERCIAL BINDERIES   Objections to the university library bindery are not based merely on monetary matters. The efforts of commercial binderies have been directed at making the binding problems of university libraries relatively simple. They are equipped to handle difficult binding jobs. They have also formulated standards by which the university librarian can estimate the quality of the

---

[40] Columbia University. *Report of the Director of Libraries for the Years 1949–1950 through 1952–1953*, p. 32.
[41] *University of Minnesota Library News*, May 28, 1951.

product. Much of the work in establishing standards for binding has been done by the Library Binding Institute, which has had close relations with the American Library Association through a Joint Committee. The Library Binding Institute has a membership of a group of binders who have been certified on the basis of their work and other criteria.[42] However, it should be observed that membership in the Institute should not be the sole basis for the selection of a commercial binder. If a binder is able to meet a library's specifications, is responsible and reliable, charges reasonable prices, provides insurance, and fulfills other professional and commercial obligations, he should be given consideration.

REPAIR WORK   Although a library may not provide for a full-scale bindery, it should be so equipped that its personnel can make minor repairs, and place small pamphlets in binders or folders. Some of the larger university libraries employ staff members who are expert craftsmen in binding, and these individuals have responsibility for the restoration of rarities.

The repair of a book is necessary when pages are loose or torn, when the back breaks at the joints, or when the super has been pulled away from the contents. Materials which are in great demand, such as reserve books, may be repaired without too great difficulty. It is important that some staff member have the knowledge and the responsibility for seeing that mending will not make it difficult or impossible for the binder to work with volumes which are wanted for the permanent collections. The circulation department personnel and the departmental librarians can help reduce the burden on the binding budget by singling out volumes which can be easily repaired within the library. Most of the large library supply houses sell materials and equipment for repair work.

SPECIAL MATERIALS   The conservation program of the university library is not confined to books. Periodicals and other serials, newspapers, pamphlets, leather-bound items, clippings, maps, music,

[42] Feipel and Browning, *Library Binding Manual.*

posters, and films present special problems of care.[43] The Association of Research Libraries has become interested in the preservation of different types of material, particularly those on wood pulp paper.[44] Various other agencies and libraries, such as the National Archives, the New York Public Library, and the Huntington Library have studied problems related to the preserving of archival and manuscript collections. The extent to which microreproductions in various forms can be used to replace deteriorating newspapers and journals is also being currently considered.[45] Undoubtedly, some of the problems of preservation will need to be solved through cooperative enterprises.

Many university libraries are making special provisions for the care of rare materials. The Clements Library at Michigan, the Houghton Library at Harvard, and the rare book rooms at Duke, North Carolina, Northwestern, Yale, and other libraries suggest the type of physical quarters which are needed for the adequate protection of these items. Undoubtedly, those libraries which have made efforts to maintain special collections properly have gained the interest of benevolent bibliophiles.

DEPARTMENT OF PHOTOGRAPHY Few university libraries have full-fledged departments of photography. Figure 14 shows the organization of the Photographic Service of the University of California at Berkeley. Some university libraries maintain photographic services on a limited basis. Many of the new library buildings, such as those of Georgia and Wisconsin, have provided photographic installations. A number of institutions, such as Harvard and Michigan, have utilized commercial firms for film work in the past.

---

[43] See Tauber, *Technical Services in Libraries*, chap. xvii. The "Notes" for this chapter contain suggestive references on the care of special materials. For current discussion, see "Special Materials and Services," *Library Trends*, IV (1955), 119–212.

[44] Kremer, "The Preservation of Wood Pulp Publications," *College and Research Libraries*, XV (1954), 205–9.

[45] "Proposed Statement of Principles to Guide Large Scale Acquisition and Preservation of Library Materials on Microfilm," *College and Research Libraries*, XIV (1953), 288–91+; "Microtext in the Management of Book Collections: A Symposium," *College and Research Libraries*, XIV (1953), 292–302.

FIGURE 14. ORGANIZATION CHART, PHOTOGRAPHIC SERVICE,
UNIVERSITY OF CALIFORNIA (BERKELEY) GENERAL LIBRARY, 1955

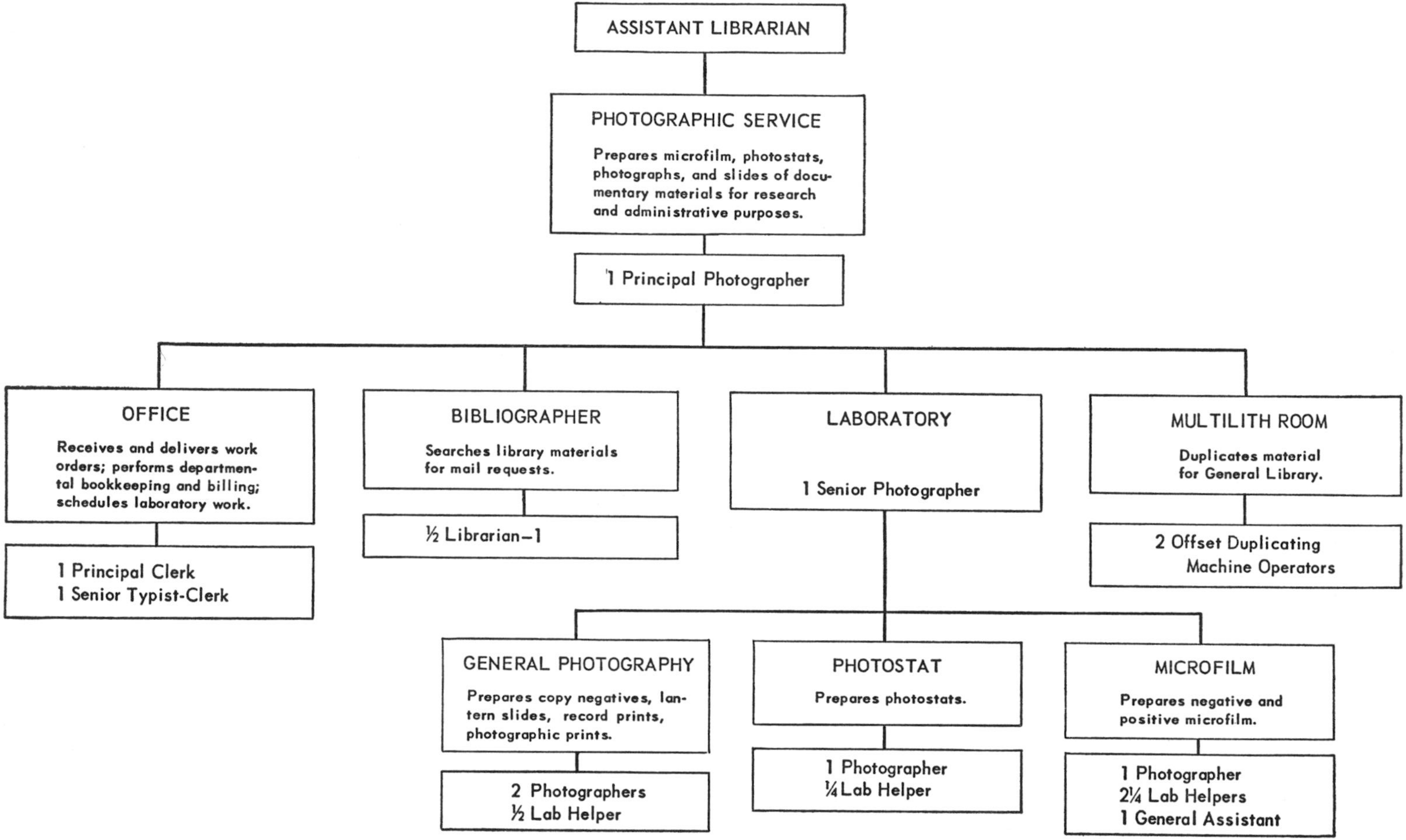

ASSISTANT LIBRARIAN
PHOTOGRAPHIC SERVICE
Prepares microfilm, photostats, photographs, and slides of documentary materials for research and administrative purposes.
1 Principal Photographer
OFFICE
Receives and delivers work orders; performs departmental bookkeeping and billing; schedules laboratory work.
1 Principal Clerk
1 Senior Typist-Clerk
BIBLIOGRAPHER
Searches library materials for mail requests.
½ Librarian–1
LABORATORY
1 Senior Photographer
MULTILITH ROOM
Duplicates material for General Library.
2 Offset Duplicating Machine Operators
GENERAL PHOTOGRAPHY
Prepares copy negatives, lantern slides, record prints, photographic prints.
2 Photographers
½ Lab Helper
PHOTOSTAT
Prepares photostats.
1 Photographer
¼ Lab Helper
MICROFILM
Prepares negative and positive microfilm.
1 Photographer
2¼ Lab Helpers
1 General Assistant

Fussler has described the work of the department of photography of a library.[46] According to such evidence as there is, experience has shown that when the institution operates the department, costs are usually lower, orders are filled more promptly, and administrative conflicts are absent. When the commercial laboratory which may be used by a library is off campus, special problems of control arise. First of all, librarians are not always willing to loan expensive or rare materials for use outside the building. Further, the separation from the library makes it difficult to check references, secure materials readily, determine immediately whether materials are suitable for photography, settle problems of copyright, estimate prices for the work, maintain high quality of work, and supervise the use to which a reproduction may be put.

Whether or not a separate department for photographic work should be set up depends largely upon the extent and type of work the library expects to do. If the photographic work of the library can be combined with similar work performed by other units of the university, the advantages of consolidation—reduced personnel, less work space and equipment, and lower costs of operation and administration—are gained. In those universities in which photographic units are already existent, such as in hospitals or scientific laboratories, the better procedure may well be for the library to establish its own department, especially if it intends to be concerned primarily with microphotographic reproduction. It is generally agreed that, whether or not the department is an independent unit or part of a larger photographic division, it should be practically self-supporting after the initial expense for equipment, with the possible exception of costs of administration in whole or in part.

The demand for high standards and quality in library microreproductive activity requires that the photographic technicians be reasonably well trained in both the technical phases of photography and the bibliographic aspects of library work. The head of the department of photography should not only be able to plan and organize the work of the unit, supervise the activities of other mem-

[46] *Photographic Reproduction for Libraries.*

bers of the staff, and maintain such business procedures as are needed; he must also be able to film books, manuscripts, periodicals, and other materials. He must have a detailed knowledge of processes and equipment, and should keep in touch with developments in a field which is changing rapidly. In some of the larger libraries, the services of the photographic department extend beyond the making of microreproductions. Photostats, prints, and lantern slides are usually among the other products of the department.[47]

As libraries establish photographic services, it is more than likely that trained personnel will be needed. Several of the library schools have provided special courses to acquaint librarians, administrators, and others with the many problems that are presented by development of photographic processes. *American Documentation*, the *Journal of Documentation*, and *College and Research Libraries* frequently contain articles and reports on experiments and innovations in photographic applications to librarianship.

RELATION TO OTHER DEPARTMENTS OF THE LIBRARY   The department of photography works closely with the other units of the library. The circulation department is concerned with checking records for interlibrary loans, the reference department with checking entries and information, and the rare-book and special collections departments with the loan and physical handling of items. The librarian must establish the policy in regard to the restriction of reproduction, to starting special filming projects, and to engaging in cooperative undertakings.

A strong relationship exists between the person in charge of interlibrary loans and the head of photographic work. The degree to which this relationship is definitely established will determine the smoothness with which materials may be loaned or borrowed for photographic purposes. According to Fussler, microphotography might well be the technique for servicing well-defined groups of materials:

[47] Two recent discussions of reproduction are Fussler, "Photographic Reproduction of Research Materials," *Library Trends*, II (1954), 532–44, and Tate, "Microreproduction and the Acquisitions Program," *Library Trends*, III (1955), 432–47.

1. All rare, fragile, or expensive items
2. All items where the expense of physical shipment will be greater than or equal to the cost of microfilm
3. All material in constant use in the lending library
4. Material from periodical or serial sets where loss would be serious, owing to the break in continuity
5. Items of a few pages, separately or in a large volume
6. Cases where the item is borrowed regularly or where the borrowing library wishes to have a permanent copy
7. Newspapers
8. Instances where the lender would prefer not to lend the original
9. Thesis and archival material, with certain restrictions.[48]

It is important to note that the lending of these various types of materials through the use of film carries further the interlibrary co-operation of libraries. Hitherto much of the material in the above list could not be borrowed through the regular interlibrary lending channels. In recent years, libraries have become somewhat more generous in the direct lending of materials which were formerly restricted.

Libraries vary in their practices of lending the films themselves. Positive copies of films are likely to be lent in much the same way as books. Some libraries, however, have been reluctant to lend master negatives, unless they are regarded as expendable.

If the department is a separate unit of the library, it should have charge of all routines concerned with orders and accounting. Orders should be taken directly from the public, so that no confusion as to the type of job, costs, and time promised will arise. While the department should collect charges for work, the actual depositing of funds may be done through the librarian's office.

The preparation of the film for the shelves so that it may be used by the patrons of the library is generally not a responsibility of the photography librarian. While he may inspect the film which comes into the library, the cataloging, classifying, and shelving of the

48 Fussler, "Microphotography and the Future of Inter-Library Loans," *Journal of Documentary Reproduction,* II (1939), 3–10.

material may go through the same processes as do books or other items acquired by the library.

The cataloging of film has been standardized for those libraries which follow Library of Congress rules.[49] An effort has been made to make cataloging of film relatively simple. Many libraries do not classify film, since the materials are not usually placed on the regular shelves and access is through the catalog. In these libraries, assignment of serial numbers apparently is sufficient. In a few instances, cards for film copies of books and other items have been placed in the shelf list so that the researcher may have a complete approach to all materials on a certain subject. This approach, of course, may also be taken care of through the placement of subject entries in the main catalog.

A university library which operates a photographic department will generally build up collections of both positive and negative films. The negatives are generally to be used, not in the reading machines, but as a reserve file for the duplication of film either for the particular library or for individuals and libraries in other institutions.[50]

Another problem in regard to film is that of storage. Precautions which the university librarian should take in the preservation of film are to provide a storage place free from dust and to maintain here a temperature of about 70°F. and a relative humidity of 50 percent. A number of the new library buildings have made special provisions for the care of film.

In the production of film, the librarian is also faced with responsibility for not violating copyrights. Fussler [51] has noted the three main categories of material which should be taken into account

[49] U.S. Library of Congress. Descriptive Cataloging Division. *Rules for Descriptive Cataloging in the Library of Congress.* [Sect.] 10. Facsimiles, Photocopies and Microfilms, pp. 97–100. A separate publication, *Rules for Descriptive Cataloging in the Library of Congress: Motion Pictures and Filmstrips,* was issued in a second preliminary edition in 1953. The Library of Congress started issuing cards for motion pictures and filmstrips in 1951.

[50] The *Union List of Microfilms,* issued by the Philadelphia Bibliographical Center and Union Library Catalogue in 1951, is a useful source of information concerning availability of film. The "Microfilm Clearing House," which appears in the Library of Congress *Information Bulletin* at irregular intervals, is another source of current projects.

[51] "Microphotography and the Future of Inter-Library Loans," *Journal of Documentary Reproduction,* II (1939), 3–10.

under the copyright law. These are: (1) published materials which are not copyrighted or on which the copyright has expired; (2) copyrighted materials or items on which copyrights have not expired, and (3) unpublished material. The first group, which includes many scholarly and scientific journals and some newspapers, may be reproduced without permission. The second group requires the written permission of the author or publisher. So far as the third group is concerned, the scholar should discover whether or not property rights are owned by the library.[52] As pointed out in the report of the Committee on the Use of Manuscripts by Visiting Scholars, established by the Association of Research Libraries, "freedom of access does not include the right to publish." [53] Photographic reproduction of large manuscript collections should be done under the sponsorship of another library, "and the reproduction should be sent to that library with the understanding that it will take the responsibility of supervising the use of the reproductions, permitting freedom of access but referring requests to publish to the original library." [54]

Photographic departments of libraries usually require individuals to sign a form which contains a statement to the effect that the patron assumes responsibility for violation of copyright. The librarian, of course, should be aware of all copyright involvements.

BIBLIOGRAPHY

American Library Association. Board on Salaries, Tenure, and Staff. Classification and Pay Plans for Libraries in Institutions of Higher Education. 2d ed. Vol. III: Universities. Chicago, American Library Association, 1947.

Barr, Pelham. "Book Conservation and the University Library," *College and Research Libraries*, VII (1946), 214-19.

Bentz, Dale M., and Thera P. Cavender. "Reclassification and Recataloging," *Library Trends*, II (1953), 249-63.

[52] Shaw, *Literary Property in the United States*, pp. 147-56.

[53] *College and Research Libraries*, XIII (1952), 59.

[54] *Ibid*. This report should be read in entirety, since it contains other material on the question of literary property.

Brown, George B. "In-Service Training in Acquisition Work," *College and Research Libraries*, XII (1951), 29–32.

"Cataloging Arrearages," *Journal of Cataloging and Classification*, VII (1951), 89–109.

Clark, Walter. "Document Reproduction by Photography in the United States," *Photographic Science and Technique*, Ser. II, Vol. I (1954), 31–37.

Cohen, Joseph L. "A General Consideration of the Technical Services Division in Libraries," in "The Technical Services Division in Libraries," *College and Research Libraries*, X (1949), 46–49.

"College and University Library Statistics, 1953–54 (Group I)," *College and Research Libraries*, XVI (1955), 39.

Columbia University. Report of the Director of Libraries for the Years 1949–50 through 1952–53. New York, 1954.

Coney, Donald. "The Administration of Technical Processes," in C. B. Joeckel (ed.), *Current Issues in Library Administration*, University of Chicago Press, 1939, pp. 163–80.

———— "The University Library: University and Society—VII," *California Monthly*, LXIII (1953), 3–4.

"Current Trends in Cataloging and Classification," *Library Trends*, II (1953), 173–355.

"Current Trends in College and University Libraries," *Library Trends*, I (1952), 3–165.

Downs, Robert B. Union Catalogs in the United States. Chicago, American Library Association, 1942.

Feipel, L. N., and E. W. Browning. Library Binding Manual. Prepared under the Direction of the Joint Committee of the ALA and the LBI. Chicago, American Library Association, 1951.

Fleming, Thomas P., and J. H. Moriarty. "Essentials in the Organization of Acquisitions Work in University Libraries," *College and Research Libraries*, I (1940), 229–34.

Frarey, Carlyle J. "Studies of Use of the Subject Catalog: Summary and Evaluation," in Tauber (ed.), *The Subject Analysis of Library Materials*, pp. 147–66.

Fussler, Herman H. "Microphotography and the Future of Inter-Library Loans," *Journal of Documentary Reproduction*, II (1939), 3–10.

———— Photographic Reproduction for Libraries: A Study of Administrative Problems. Chicago, University of Chicago Press, 1942.

———— "Photographic Reproduction of Research Materials," *Library Trends*, II (1954), 532–44.

Gull, C. D. "Substitutes for the Card Catalog," *Library Trends*, II (1953), 318–29.

Herrick, Mary D. "The Development of a Classified Catalog for a

University Library," *College and Research Libraries*, XIV (1953), 418–24.

International Federation for Documentation. Manual on Document Reproduction and Selection. The Hague, 1953. Sections A and B. Other parts to appear (looseleaf).

Kingery, Robert E. "A Management Engineering Look at Cataloging," *College and Research Libraries*, XIV (1953), 52–56.

—— "What Happens When the Management Engineers Leave?" *College and Research Libraries*, XV (1954), 202–4.

Kremer, Alvin W. "The Preservation of Wood Pulp Publications," *College and Research Libraries*, XV (1954), 205–9.

Lane, Alfred H. "Exchange Work in College and University Libraries" (unpublished Master's Essay, Columbia University, 1950).

Lubetzky, Seymour. Cataloging Rules and Principles: A Critique of the A.L.A. Rules for Entry and a Proposed Design for Their Revision. Washington, Processing Department, Library of Congress, 1953.

McAnally, Arthur M. "Organization of College and University Libraries," *Library Trends*, I (1952), 20–36.

MacIver, Ivander. "The Exchange of Publications as a Medium for the Development of the Book Collection," *Library Quarterly*, VII (1938), 491–502.

"Management Improvements in Libraries," *College and Research Libraries*, XV (1954), 188–204. Papers by Maurice F. Tauber, T. D. Morris, and Robert E. Kingery.

Markley, Anne Ethelyn. "University of California Subject Catalog Inquiry: A Study of the Subject Catalog Based on Interviews with Users," *Journal of Cataloging and Classification*, VI (1950), 88–95.

Merritt, Leroy C. Use of the Subject Catalog in the University of California Library. (University of California Publications in Librarianship, Vol. I, No. 1). Berkeley, University of California Press, 1951.

"Microtext in the Management of Book Collections: A Symposium," *College and Research Libraries*, XIV (1953), 292–302.

Miller, Robert A. "Cost Accounting for Libraries: A Technique for Determining the Labor Costs of Acquisition and Cataloging Work" (unpublished Ph.D. dissertation, Graduate Library School, University of Chicago, 1936).

Morris, T. D. "The Management Consultant in the Library," *College and Research Libraries*, XV (1954), 196–201.

Morsch, Lucile M. "Scientific Management in Cataloging," *Library Trends*, II (1954), 470–83.

Muller, Robert H. "Microfilming Services of Large University and Research Libraries in the United States," *College and Research Libraries,* XVI (1955), 261–66.

Munson, Frances L. "Use of the Depository Catalog in a University Library" (unpublished Master's Thesis, Columbia University, 1946); also published as abstract, *College and Research Libraries,* VIII (1947), 151–56.

Nyholm, Amy Wood. "California Examines Its Divided Catalog," *College and Research Libraries,* IX (1948), 195–201.

Osborn, Andrew D. " 'Arrearages'—Ugly Word," *Library Journal,* LXVI (1951), 1863–67.

Osborn, Andrew D., and Susan M. Haskins. "Catalog Maintenance," *Library Trends,* II (1953), 279–89.

"Proposed Statement of Principles to Guide Large Scale Acquisition and Preservation of Library Materials on Microfilm," *College and Research Libraries,* XIV (1953), 288–91+.

Randall, William M. (ed.). The Acquisition and Cataloging of Books: Papers Presented before the Library Institute at the University of Chicago, July 29 to August 9, 1940. Chicago, University of Chicago Press, 1940.

Reichmann, Felix. "Costs of Cataloging," *Library Trends,* II (1953), 290–317.

——— "Management and Operation," *Library Trends,* III (1955), 462–70.

Rider, Fremont. The Scholar and the Future of the Research Library. New York, Hadham Press, 1944.

"Scientific Management in Libraries," *Library Trends,* II (1954), 359–483.

Shachtman, Bella (ed.). "Technical Services: Policy, Organization, and Coordination," *Journal of Cataloging and Classification,* XI (1955), 59–114.

Shaw, Ralph R. Literary Property in the United States. Washington, Scarecrow Press, 1950.

Simonton, Wesley. "Subject Catalogs *vs.* Bibliographies," in Tauber (ed.), *The Subject Analysis of Library Materials,* pp. 130–38.

Spalding, C. Sumner. "Use of Catalog Entries at the Library of Congress," *Journal of Cataloging and Classification,* VI (1950), 95–100.

"Special Materials and Services," *Library Trends,* IV (1955), 119–212.

Swank, Raynard C. "The Organization of Library Materials for Research in English Literature," *Library Quarterly,* XV (1945), 49–74.

——— Report on Selected Problems of the Technical Departments of the University of Illinois Library. (University of Illinois Library School Occasional Papers, No. 42). Urbana, 1955.

——— "Subject Catalogs, Classifications, or Bibliographies? A Review of Critical Discussions, 1876–1942," *Library Quarterly*, XIV (1944), 316–32.

—— "Subject Cataloging in the Subject-Departmentalized Library," in J. H. Shera and M. E. Egan (eds.), *Bibliographic Organization*. Chicago, University of Chicago Press, 1951, pp. 187–99.

Tate, Vernon D. "Microreproduction and the Acquisitions Program," *Library Trends*, III (1955), 432–47.

Tauber, Maurice F. "Reclassification and Recataloging of Materials in College and University Libraries" (unpublished Ph.D. dissertation, University of Chicago, 1941).

Tauber, Maurice F. (ed.). The Subject Analysis of Library Materials. New York, School of Library Service, Columbia University, 1953.

Tauber, Maurice F., and Associates. Technical Services in Libraries. New York, Columbia University Press, 1954.

Thom, Ian W. "The Divided Catalog in College and University Libraries," *College and Research Libraries*, X (1949), 236–41.

Trotier, Arnold H. "Organization and Administration of Cataloging Processes," *Library Trends*, II (1953), 264–78.

U.S. Library of Congress. Descriptive Cataloging Division. Rules for Descriptive Cataloging in the Library of Congress. Washington, 1949.

—— Rules for Descriptive Cataloging in the Library of Congress: Motion Pictures and Filmstrips. 2d preliminary ed. Washington, 1953.

University of Minnesota Library News, May 28, 1951.

Williams, Edwin E. Farmington Plan Handbook. [Bloomington, Ind.] Association of Research Libraries, 1953.

Wilson, Louis R., Robert B. Downs, and Maurice F. Tauber. "Report of a Survey of the Libraries of Cornell University for the Library Board of Cornell University, October 1947—February 1948." Ithaca, Cornell University, 1948.

Wright, Wyllis E. "Some Aspects of Technical Processes," *Library Trends*, I (1952), 73–82.

See also chapters on technical services in the various surveys of libraries listed in Bibliography in chapter xvi.

VI

DEPARTMENTAL ORGANIZATION: SERVICE

THE PRINCIPAL object of the administrative officers and the staffs of the acquisitions and preparations departments of the university library is to enable the service personnel to meet the instructional and research needs of students and faculty members. This may be achieved in various ways. Service units found in university libraries include the general reference department, the circulation department, divisional libraries, departmental and professional school libraries and reading rooms, the reserve book room, the periodicals department, the serials department, the special collections department, and the extension department.

REFERENCE
SERVICE

The term "reference service" in libraries has not been defined with sufficient clarity to be universally accepted. Possibly it may be described by analyzing the activities performed by members of the reference department for the benefit of students, faculty members, and other clients of the library. For the reference librarians these activities or duties are of a twofold nature: (1) assistance to students and faculty members in becoming acquainted with the scope and character of libraries and publications, and (2) instruction of the clientele in the most effective methods of using library materials and facilities. If this dual function is to be performed effectively, the administrator should give careful attention to the organization of reference work; the place of the reference department within the service program of the library; the qualifications, responsibilities, and duties of the reference personnel; the apparatus of reference service; and the use of library materials.

ADMINISTRATIVE ORGANIZATION

In university libraries, reference service may be provided by (1) a central reference department in a general library building, (2) a central reference department plus several divisional libraries, or (3) decentralized departments either within the central building or in separate departmental libraries on or off campus. Actually, in most library systems of universities, departmental or professional school libraries exist. Despite the apparent increase in the number of libraries organized on a divisional basis, the predominant type of organization is still the central reference service aided by special reading rooms and departmental libraries.

The controversy of centralization *versus* decentralization was discussed to some extent in chapter iv. This controversy, obviously, extends to the reference service. Proponents of centralization have argued that a central reference department, equipped with a well-qualified personnel and an adequate collection of bibliographical and reference works, is in a more favorable position to offer reference service than is a system of divisional libraries or a scattered network of departmental libraries. Actually, the central reference department in the average university library is rarely equipped with the personnel or reference works to give the complete service claimed for it. For one thing, the reference materials of the subject fields contained in the departmental libraries are not conveniently available to the staff or clientele of the central reference department unless there is expensive and virtually complete duplication of items. Also, universities are unwilling to duplicate personnel having specialized knowledge of the various fields of literature both in the branch libraries and in the central reference department. Given the problem of placing a good chemistry librarian who has familiarity with chemical literature, the average administrator properly will place him in the chemistry library rather than in the central reference department.

The case for central reference service was noted in chapter iv. It was especially pointed out that it is more economical from the standpoint of building needs, equipment, book stock, administrative cost of operation, and total personnel; but it also gives the faculty members and students the opportunity to use, in one place, materials in fields which definitely overlap in subject matter.

On a theoretical basis, a strong argument can be made for subject divisions or departments. It may be said, at this point, that in larger libraries social sciences and humanities tend to remain in the central building, whereas the literature of science, technology, and the professions tends to be dispersed among the branch libraries. This may be the course of natural library development. It conforms to the assumption that materials in fields which definitely overlap in subject matter are best kept together, inasmuch as workers in the fields first mentioned generally use materials in adjacent fields, whereas workers in the sciences, technologies, and professions tend to restrict themselves pretty much to their own literature. However, even the latter group has begun to work in related areas.

Much of the pressure for departmental libraries comes from faculty members. To ascertain prevailing practices in American colleges and universities which might have a bearing upon decisions being made at North Dakota Agricultural College on the future status of the chemistry departmental library there, Broberg and Dunbar [1] sent questionnaires to 166 accredited chemistry departments in the United States. Of the blanks, 90 percent were returned by departmental chairmen or their representatives, since opinions of librarians were not sought. On the basis of the responses, the authors concluded that (1) practically all important chemistry departments maintain extensive, well-organized departmental libraries for chemistry; (2) there is a trend toward establishing more and better chemistry departmental libraries; (3) it is the concensus that a de-

[1] "Current Status of Departmental Libraries in Chemistry," *Journal of Chemical Education*, XXVIII (1951), 435–36.

partmental library is essential to an efficient, up-to-date department;
(4) good administration and supervision of the departmental library are essential; (5) departmental libraries should be available
to students under conditions comparable to those available in the
main library; and (6) departmental libraries in chemistry exhibit
greater convenience, saving of student and staff time, increased use
of journals and reference works, and better training of chemists and
research workers. Although chemistry was the subject involved
in this inquiry, the findings are applicable to other sciences. It also
should be pointed out that accrediting agencies for certain fields and
professions require institutions to maintain strong departmental
libraries or collections in their respective areas.

Divisional organization, of course, has a definite effect upon reference service, particularly if the organization is reflected in the
physical consolidation of resources in related subject areas—humanities, social sciences, and science and technology.[2] But the "division" concept applies to administrative control as well as to physical
organization.[3] For example, the Divisional Librarian in Science and
Technology at Nebraska supervises the Science Reading Room as
well as the departmental libraries in science and technology. Particularly through his close relationship to faculty members and through
his responsibility for book selection, the divisional librarian, according to those who have worked with divisional organization, is able
to build strong collections and a coordinated service program to
support the teaching and research carried on in the university.

GENERAL READERS' DEPARTMENT. The consolidation of all services
to the reader under one supervision has been effected in some large
university libraries (see Figures 3 and 7). In its most comprehensive
aspects and on a theoretical basis a coordinated readers' department
would include all units which serve the reader or circulate materials.

[2] Wilson and Lundy, *Report of a Survey of the Library of the University of
Notre Dame for the University of Notre Dame, November 1950–March 1952*, chap.
vi; Chapman, Hopp, and Vennix, "The Role of the Divisional Librarian," *College
and Research Libraries*, XV (1954), 148–54.

[3] Chapman, Hopp, and Vennix, *op. cit.*, p. 152; see also Blanchard, "Departmental
Libraries in Divisional Plan Libraries," *College and Research Libraries*, XIV (1953),
243–48.

Such a department would include an assistant librarian as head, with supervisory officers in charge of circulation, reference, special collections, and branch and departmental libraries. The circulation unit would include the loan desk, reserve book room, recreational reading room, stack control, information desk, rental library, dormitory libraries, and fraternity libraries. The reference unit would include the reference desk, interlibrary loan service, exhibits, and periodicals. The special-collections units would include documents, newspapers, pamphlet files, rare books, archives, and manuscripts. The branch or departmental libraries unit would include the botany, chemistry, education, law, medical, and other libraries of this type. On a less extensive basis, it would comprise only the reference and circulation units. In library systems in which there is considerable departmentation (that is, a series of special departments and departmental libraries), it should be apparent that unless some centralized supervision is provided the resulting service will lack unity. Since each special subject department and departmental library performs a reference function, the range and quality of service will depend upon the qualifications of the staff members responsible for integrating the reference collection and the resources of the library as a whole.[4]

The assistant librarian in charge of readers' services should be an able administrator, sensitive to the clients' problems in using a large research library. He will have responsibilities in supervising and developing the book collections, in promoting the improvement of the services to authorized users, and in serving as the line officer in the line or chain of authority between the director of libraries and the heads of the departments which make up the readers' services. To carry out these responsibilities on a high level, he should have extensive knowledge of modern library organization, procedure, and policy, particularly as they relate to the administration of a complex university library system having departmental and professional school and college libraries under the control of a central li-

[4] Wilson and Lundy, *op. cit.* The "divisional librarian" in the divisional type of organization has this responsibility.

brary. He should be able to work with faculty members and research workers, understand fully the problems of scholarship and research methodology, and possess a good knowledge of the objectives and procedures of higher education.

REFERENCE DEPARTMENT. Since the prevailing type of reference organization in the university library consists of the general reference department, supplemented by the services of special departments and departmental libraries, it may be considered in detail. Variations in this type of organization occur in relation to building conditions, the amount of departmentation, and the personnel available. The general reference service may be confined to the general reference collections in the main reading room; or, it may include direction of the periodical room and such special materials as documents, pamphlets, maps, and serials.

In many institutions, the central reference department integrates reference functions and methods throughout the library system, in the main building and in the departmental libraries. Its activities usually involve those of other departments, since reference work is directly related to book selection and the preparation and circulation of materials.

Except in the very largest organizations, the head of the reference department is likely to have fewer administrative duties than the heads of some of the other departments of the library, such as the circulation and catalog departments. His general administrative duties, however, are similar to those outlined in chapter iv.

The activities of the reference librarian have been discussed by Wyer, Hutchins, and others.[5] The operations may be conveniently grouped about the two major functions of the reference department —namely, (1) making resources available and (2) instruction. In the first category such operations as the following may be included: building up the reference collection; assisting in selecting materials

[5] Wyer, *Reference Work;* Hutchins, *Reference Work;* Butler (ed.), *The Reference Function of the Library;* American Library Association, Board on Salaries, Staff and Tenure. *Classification and Pay Plans for Libraries in Institutions of Higher Education—Vol. III, Universities,* pp. 81–98. See also Dunlap, "Services to Readers," *Library Trends,* I (1952), 49–57.

for the general collections; maintaining a clipping and pamphlet file; exhibiting materials for publicity or for public information; preparing new book lists and bibliographies; preserving university ephemera; compiling lists of faculty publications; providing materials through interlibrary loan service or photographic reproduction; reviewing books; indexing and abstracting materials; providing a translation service; cooperating with bibliographical centers and union catalogs; and amassing information regarding library resources of the region, nation, and foreign countries. In the second category the reference librarian is concerned with helping students and faculty members to use the catalog and reference tools, in providing information service to the users and the administration, in preparing special bibliographies, in supervising readers, and in teaching.

PERSONNEL. The special qualifications of the reference librarian and his staff should be determined largely by the functions which the department is to perform. Not only should the reference librarian possess the training and experience for departmental heads as outlined in chapter iv, but he should have a thorough knowledge of reference procedure. This calls for a wide knowledge of reference tools and other materials. He should be able to use efficiently card catalogs, bibliographies, book lists, indexes, dictionaries, encyclopedias, and abstracts. He should have a thorough knowledge of the aims of library service; he should understand the principles and procedure of library organization; and he should be able to integrate these effectively with the educational objectives and procedures of the university. Familiarity with foreign languages, extensive knowledge of foreign literatures, appreciation of the history of scholarship, an understanding of the methods and spirit of research, and knowledge of the educational and research program of the institution are likewise indispensable for the reference librarian. In addition, he should be able to bring his varied abilities to bear upon the solution of the problems of students and faculty members; and since his work is so closely related to that of students and faculty, he should possess teaching ability of a high order. This teaching differs somewhat from that of the classroom instructor. The reference ibrarian's teaching is confined largely to a person-to-person instructional relationship on an informal and limited, rather than on a formal and systematic, basis. Reference work developed from the activity of librarians to meet the specific needs of individual readers.[6] Dunlap has referred to the "assumption by the library of the responsibility to make any part of the collections readily available to any qualified user probably . . . [as] . . . the most revolutionary change in the development of American librarianship."[7] To meet the specific needs of individuals, the reference librarian has gone beyond the confines of his own library, and has sought information and materials wherever they may be.

RESEARCH AND THE REFERENCE LIBRARIAN. Since furthering research is a function of the university, the library, through its staff and resources, has an important role in the process. While service to undergraduates occupies an increasingly important place in the functions of the university, such service in many of the larger institutions is being segregated in either distinct parts of the main building or in separate buildings. Thus, the effort is made to remove the special needs of undergraduates from those engaged in research.

There has been a progressive interest in the role of the reference librarian in aiding research.[8] One has only to read the prefaces in many works of scholarship to realize the exceptional part played by reference librarians in aiding researchers to isolate the information and sources needed in their work. The tributes paid to reference librarians and other staff members are legion.

The reference librarian in the university or other large research library has a special problem in getting the right materials to the

[6] Rothstein, "The Development of the Concept of Reference Service in American Libraries, 1850–1900," *Library Quarterly*, XXIII (1953), 1–15; Kaplan, *The Growth of Reference Service in the United States from 1876 to 1893.*

[7] "Services to Readers," p. 54.

[8] Noé, "The University Library and Research," *Library Quarterly*, IV (1934), 300–305; Borden, "The Research Librarian Idea," *Library Journal*, LVIII (1933), 104–6; and "The College Librarian and Research," *Bulletin of the American Library Association*, XXIX (1935), 412–16; Hurt, "Staff Specialization: A Possible Substitute for Departmentalization," *Bulletin of the American Library Association*, XXIX (1935), 417–21; King, "Assistance to the Faculty in Library Research: Report from Cornell University," *College and Research Libraries*, IX (1948), 227–30.

scholar as easily as possible. But the scholar finds it necessary to use many libraries in his quest for sources and his gathering of source materials. Clinton L. Rossiter, author of *Seedtime of the Republic*,[9] winner of the 1953 Bancroft award, located his major sources in the Cornell University Library but also found materials in the Houghton Library and the main library of Harvard University, Boston University Library, Brown University Library, Yale University Library, and the library of the College of William and Mary. Sources were also consulted in the Essex Institute (Salem, Mass.), the Massachusetts Historical Society, the Connecticut Historical Society and the Connecticut State Library, the New York Public Library, the New York Society Library, the Historical Society of Pennsylvania, the American Philosophical Society, the Maryland Historical Society, the Maryland State Library, the Library of Congress, the Colonial Williamsburg Library, the Virginia State Library, the Charleston Society Library, and on the West Coast, in the Huntington Library, at San Marino, California.

Rossiter's journey down the eastern seaboard and west to the Huntington to visit the various libraries was more or less indicated by the nature of his study. Reference librarians are able to assist the scholar who has a clearly defined subject. Their backgrounds are ever expanding as a result of experience and working with materials. They do, however, have a procedure for acquiring specialized knowledge of the literature of a subject. The procedure involves securing a topical outline of the subject content of the field, briefly considering the principal encyclopedic works, examining all guides to the literature of the field, preparing a basic list of textbooks and treatises devoted to the entire field and examining selected titles, studying materials on the special aspects of the field, noting the sources of printed materials, familiarizing themselves with the periodical and serial literature, considering the pamphlet and ephemeral material, studying thoroughly the reference works, observing publications appearing in related fields, and learning the trends of re-

[9] Clinton L. Rossiter, *Seedtime of the Republic: The Origin of the American Tradition of Political Liberty* (New York, Harcourt, Brace, 1953). Preface.

search in the subject. In examining any item in the literature of the field, it has been suggested that critical evaluation be applied regarding the extent and nature of the field, its significance to the subject, and its possible use.

Dunlap [10] has pointed out that there has not been a comprehensive study of the use of university libraries by graduate students, even though studies have been made of dissertations prepared by Ph.D. students in the fields of English literature, American history, and certain other areas.[11] As Dunlap further notes, these studies are suggestive, rather than conclusive. Perhaps more information will be available after several studies, arising out of American Library Association and National Science Foundation sponsorship,[12] have been completed. Related to the studies of use, and implied in some of the studies which have already been made, is the factor of characteristics of the materials. Fussler [13] has sought to isolate the characteristics of the materials used by chemists and physicists. Such studies should help librarians to understand better the needs of researchers.[14] They have a definite relation to the problem of book selection and the building of research collections.

REFERENCE COLLECTIONS. Despite the existence of an intelligent and resourceful reference personnel, service on both an informational and research level will not be fruitful unless a well-selected and adequate collection of tools is assembled. Dictionaries, encyclopedias, compendiums, yearbooks, indexes, bibliographies, atlases,

---

[10] "Services to Readers," p. 51.

[11] Swank, "Organization of Library Materials for Research in English Literature," *Library Quarterly*, XV (1945), 49–74; McAnally, "Characteristics of Materials Used in Research in United States History"; Stevens, "Use of Library Materials in Doctoral Research: A Study of the Effect of Differences in Research Method."

[12] American Library Association, *Basic Study of Bibliographical Organization*. A study in progress on the methods of scientists in using libraries, by Ralph R. Shaw, is supported by National Science Foundation. A study on the use of materials by scientists was recently reported by Saul Herner, "How Scientists Seek and Obtain Information," *Industrial and Engineering Chemistry*, XL (1954), 228–36.

[13] Fussler, "Characteristics of Research Literature Used by Chemists and Physicists in the United States," *Library Quarterly*, XIX (1949), 19–35, 119–43.

[14] Although directed primarily at the undergraduate student, the effort of getting at student needs and problems has received additional impetus since World War II. See Maxfield, "Counselor Librarianship at U.I.C.," *College and Research Libraries*, XV (1954), 161–66+.

and similar materials constitute the basic types of materials which reference librarians use in their work.[15] The entire library collection, of course, is utilized by the reference librarian in his efforts to help the user. Furthermore, as has been indicated, the reference staff in the large library particularly is likely to seek materials in any library in which they may be located.

CIRCULATION   The circulation department is a major unit of
DEPARTMENT   the public service of the library. In the uni-
                   versity library the lending of materials to
readers is carried on by the central loan desk, the reserve department, the departmental libraries, the periodicals department, and other units of the system. In the traditional type of library, with a large central stack and few departmental and other desks, the greatest percentage of loans is made through the central circulation department. In the divisional type of library, the major points for circulation are the divisional libraries, with general circulation left to the central loan desk.

ADMINISTRATIVE ORGANIZATION

If the circulation department is a part of the general readers' department described in the preceding section, the head of the department is directly responsible to the chief of the larger unit. For example, the loan department of the University of California Library is under the supervision of an assistant librarian (Figure 15). Similarly, at the University of Illinois, the circulation department is under the supervision of the assistant director for public services (Figure 3). In most institutions, however, the head of the circulation department is likely to report directly to the librarian.

Just as in other departments of the library, centralization of authority is necessary if a uniform lending policy is to be established throughout the library system. Nothing seems to be more annoying to students and faculty members who use various departments and

[15] As described in Winchell, *Guide to Reference Books*, and Shores, *Basic Reference Books*, and the many subject bibliographies which are useful to researchers.

FIGURE 15. ORGANIZATION CHART, LOAN DEPARTMENT,
UNIVERSITY OF CALIFORNIA (BERKELEY) GENERAL LIBRARY, 1955

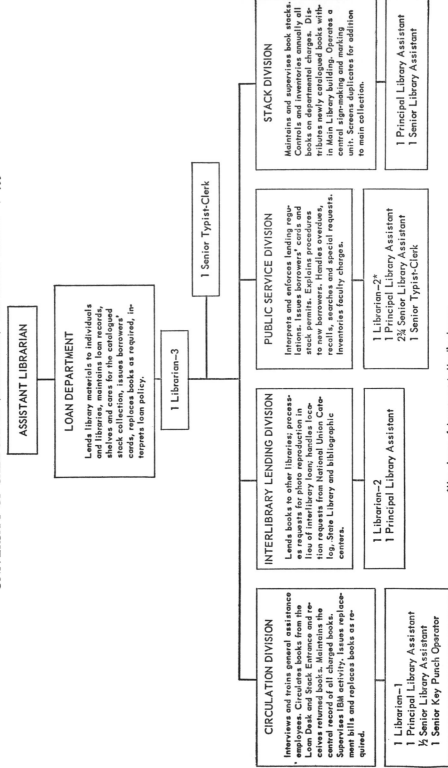

ASSISTANT LIBRARIAN

LOAN DEPARTMENT

Lends library materials to individuals and libraries, maintains loan records, shelves and cares for the catalogued stack collection, issues borrowers' cards, replaces books as required, interprets loan policy.

1 Librarian—3

1 Senior Typist-Clerk

CIRCULATION DIVISION

Interviews and trains general assistance employees. Circulates books from the Loan Desk and Stack Entrance and receives returned books. Maintains the central record of all charged books. Supervises IBM activity. Issues replacement bills and replaces books as required.

1 Librarian—1
1 Principal Library Assistant
½ Senior Library Assistant
1 Senior Key Punch Operator

INTERLIBRARY LENDING DIVISION

Lends books to other libraries; processes requests for photo reproduction in lieu of interlibrary loan; handles location requests from National Union Catalog, State Library and bibliographic centers.

1 Librarian—2
1 Principal Library Assistant

PUBLIC SERVICE DIVISION

Interprets and enforces lending regulations. Issues borrowers' cards and stack permits. Explains procedures to new borrowers. Handles overdues, recalls, searches and special requests. Inventories faculty charges.

1 Librarian—2*
1 Principal Library Assistant
2¾ Senior Library Assistant
1 Senior Typist-Clerk

STACK DIVISION

Maintains and supervises book stacks. Controls and inventories annually all books on departmental charges. Distributes newly catalogued books within Main Library building. Operates a central sign-making and marking unit. Screens duplicates for addition to main collection.

1 Principal Library Assistant
1 Senior Library Assistant

*Has charge of department in Head's absence.
NOTE: 30½ General Assistant Employees are assigned to the Department.

branches of a library than to find dissimilar hours of opening, borrowing privileges, lending periods, and fines. Sometimes, however, particularly in the interest of economy, service hours may have to vary. Whereas a main building or a very active branch library may be open continuously for approximately fourteen hours a day, many branches may necessarily close for meal hours or may eliminate evening hours. To open them would mean a waste of money. On the other hand, law and medical branches of the university library may be open several hours after the main library has closed. Hours of opening and loan periods should be adjusted to the need and demand for reading space and materials and should be as flexible as possible. Borrowing privileges and fines should, of course, be uniform throughout the different units.

Local conditions affect the type or number of units controlled by the circulation department. While interlibrary lending may be the responsibility of one circulation department, in another library it may be handled by the reference librarian. The work may even be distributed between the two units.

FUNCTIONS OF THE CIRCULATION DEPARTMENT

The primary function of the circulation department is to get materials to the reader expeditiously. In America quick service is the rule. Foreigners visiting American libraries are frequently astonished by the fact that a reader may be presented with a volume two or three minutes after he handed the call slip to the attendant at the circulation desk. Because of the many tasks that require prompt and efficient performance, librarians may consider such activity as speedy circulation to be the major objective of the loan department rather than a means for achieving the main purpose of the university library, namely, the promotion of the instructional and research program of the university. There is also the danger that certain aspects of the library service will be overlooked or neglected because of the failure to outline specific programs or procedures. Instances of this sort, particularly in connection with record keeping in university libraries, will be discussed later in this section.

In addition to quick delivery of materials, the loan assistants may give help and instruction in the use of the card catalog and reference works, aid students in selecting books, and stimulate individual reading interests. When a university loan department has control over the reserve book room, rental library, browsing room, interlibrary loan, and similar activities, it is not difficult to conclude that various assistants in the unit will be concerned with some duties which are commonly allotted to the reference department. In the traditional type of library organization, the central circulation desk will be concerned with the delivery of materials to readers. The general practice in organizations of this type is to refer the user to the reference department on questions which involve search.

In the divisional type of library, however, the staff members are likely to work as a team, and the professional librarians perform the tasks of reference specialists. In one university library,[16] the staff of the central loan desk, which handles book charges from the main stack area only, spends much time in instructing patrons in the use of the public catalog and in giving general directional service. The circulation department is also the center for many decisions on general policies pertaining to all reading rooms.

ROUTINES. As may be seen from Figure 15 the work of the loan department may include such activities as lending library materials to individuals and libraries, maintaining loan records, shelving and caring for the cataloged stack collection, issuing borrowers' cards, replacing books as required, and interpreting loan policy. At California, these activities are performed through four major divisions: Circulation, Interlibrary Lending, Public Service, and Stack. The detailed routines differ from library to library, depending on the organization, but the essential activity is provision of the means for quick and efficient access to materials by the reader.[17]

PERSONNEL. The qualifications necessary for the chief circulation

[16] Marvin, "Circulation in the Divisional Library: The New Plan of Service," *College and Research Libraries*, XII (1951), 241–44+.

[17] For a discussion of various charging systems and routines see Geer, *Charging Systems.*

librarian are similar to those required of other departmental heads
In addition to knowledge of books, reference works, and library
organization, he should be acquainted with the special procedures,
problems, and modern equipment of circulation operations. He
should have the ability to direct interdepartmental work within the
central library and among other units of the library system.

Because the contacts of faculty members and students with the
library are largely confined to the circulation desk, it is important
that the professional, clerical, and student assistants recognize the
strategic importance of their positions. The circulation staff should
not only be able to get along well with people but should meet the
students and faculty members pleasantly. Such qualities as initiative, good judgment, tact, orderliness, accuracy, good memory,
adaptability, sense of humor, and patience are necessary in any
phase of librarianship; but they are particularly important in loan
work.[19]

DIVISION OF WORK. In many university libraries careful work
analyses have resulted in clear distinctions between the professional
and clerical operations in circulation work. In those libraries in
which the circulation desk serves also as a reference center, the need
for differentiation of responsibility is particularly important if the
readers are to be provided with high-level service. Such activities
as registering borrowers, charging and discharging books, slipping
books, arranging and filing cards, shelf work, counting and recording statistics, maintaining reserve records, and sending overdue notices are normally handled by the clerical staff. Major professional
responsibilities include deciding matters of policy, maintaining relations with the public, dealing with the faculty and other departmental heads, and supervising the staff.

EFFICIENCY OF SERVICE. Prompt delivery of materials to readers

[18] American Library Association, Board on Salaries, Staff and Tenure. *Classification and Pay Plans for Libraries in Institutions of Higher Education. Vol. III—
Universities*, pp. 46–58.
[19] Altick, "The Scholar's Paradise," *College and Research Libraries*, XV (1954),
375–82.

on request is the principal service required of the circulation department. A measure of efficiency used by surveyors of libraries is the proportion (in percentage) of deliveries and reports of locations (in other units of the library system or elsewhere) to the total number of requests.

Most libraries have a regular procedure for tracing items which are not found in their proper places on the shelves.[20] Good public relations require the circulation department staff to report to a reader an unsuccessful effort to locate a particular volume.

REGULATIONS. Policies concerning the use of books are normally decided by the librarian, frequently with the advice of the library committee. Most libraries permit books to circulate to students for two-week periods, although since the mid-1940s a number of institutions have introduced one month loans. Experiments with semester loans to students at a few institutions indicated that this was too long a period for most needs.

There are shorter loan periods for certain materials. Some current books of special interest circulate for three or seven days; reserve books circulate for a fixed period—for overnight, or, in some cases, for slightly longer periods; rare books generally are not permitted to leave the library. Faculty members and graduate students may be given special privileges as to the length of time they may retain books. Library staff members and university employees may have privileges which range from those granted to students to those given faculty members.

Faculty members generally have not been restricted in the number of books they may borrow, nor have they been subjected to the same two-week loan period provided for students. In many instances, there have been serious abuses by faculty members of the library lending privilege. While instructional staff should be assisted in their research projects, they should be cautioned about the tendency to stock their personal libraries or office shelves with borrowed books. Most libraries require faculty members to return

[20] Cf. "Time and Efficiency Study," *The Library at Iowa State*, VIII (1953), 40–42; DeVolder, "The Circulation Department: A Service Agency," *The Call Number*, XV (1954), 7.

books at the end of a semester or quarter, usually with the stipula-
tion that books which are still needed may be renewed.

FINES. In order to make the greatest number of books available
to the greatest number of students and faculty members at all times,
a system of fines is generally employed in libraries. A few libraries
in recent years have experimented with a no-fine system without
untoward results.

Fine systems vary in those libraries which have them. A certain
sum, ranging from two to five cents per day, may be charged for
the overdue stack book. Larger sums are charged for reserve books.
Fixed amounts may be charged after a fine has reached a figure
equal to the price of the book involved.

In large library systems, the control of materials for the use of
the majority involves close attention to overdues. Difficult cases
may require cooperation between the librarian and the dean, registrar, and bursar or comptroller. These officers are not appealed to
until the library has exhausted its own procedures. Delinquencies
that reach maturity during the progress of a semester or quarter
may be adjusted through the office of the dean. The office of the
registrar, however, may prove more effective; but it can act only
at the close of one term or the beginning of another. The registrar
may withhold grades, transcripts, certificates, or degrees from delinquent students. He may also refuse enrollment to such students
until they have settled their delinquencies. In some cases, delinquent accounts are turned over to the business office for collection.
These are entered on the students' accounts and collected with
other bills due the university.

OTHER CIRCULATION SERVICES

RESERVE BOOK ROOM. A common service offered primarily at the
undergraduate level, but involving also both the graduate and professional school libraries, is the reserve book service. Dunlap [21] has
observed that the "segregation of books to meet the demands of a
group of readers appears in its most unhappy form in the reserve

[21] "Services to Readers," p. 53.

book room." Whether the reserve book room has open or closed shelves, or a combination of these two practices, the purpose is to meet the needs of students who have been assigned specific readings.[22] Reserve book rooms have developed because of the pressure of a large number of users on a restricted body of material. Students, librarians, and faculty members alike have been critical of reserve book rooms, but the provision of the service is still common. Few libraries have followed the practice of renting books for supplementary reading, even though in the long run it may be less expensive to operate than the usual reserve room and probably more satisfactory to the readers.

Since it is likely that reserve book rooms are to be continued for some time, it is important that the librarian organize them so that they will serve the readers effectively. Close cooperation with faculty members is essential for smooth operation.

Among the conditions which support effective reserve book room service are: (1) having faculty members make certain that the titles they need are in the library collections, (2) urging the faculty members to inform the library staff early enough to insure rapid acquisition, if the items are not owned by the library, or quick assembly, if they are at the bindery or at some other point in the library system, (3) insisting that faculty members carefully discriminate in selecting titles for the reserve shelves,[23] (4) providing a sufficient number of duplicate copies of titles so that students will have equal opportunity to use materials during the period of assignment, and (5) organizing the volumes on the shelves so that they are easily available to the readers.

Certain books in which long assignments are made or which are recommended for optional reading are generally loaned for longer

[22] Lansberg, "Current Trends in the College Reserve Room," *College and Research Libraries*, XI (1950), 120–24+.

[23] Tauber and Wilson, *Report of a Survey of the Montana State University Library for the Montana State University, January–May, 1951*, p. 88. "A check of 560 books on various reserve lists for the Fall Quarter in 1950 shows that 276, or 49.3 per cent, were not used a single time. Some entire lists of reserved books were not used during the quarter." This is not an uncommon situation in reserve book rooms. See also "Use of Reserved Books in the University of Idaho Library," *The Bookmark*, VI (1953), 1–4.

periods than the usual overnight loan for reserved titles. Open-shelf reserves are, of course, preferable; but in an undergraduate room they are impractical unless there is close supervision of students at the exit.

In some university libraries, provision is made for divisional reading rooms for the use of graduate students and upperclassmen. In these graduate reading rooms most of the books are on open reserve. The criterion for open or closed reserves is the specific assignment within a limited time. An assignment might cover only certain pages in a book with time enough allowed for reading to permit the book to remain on open shelves. On the other hand, a whole book may have been assigned for reading within a semester, but so many students may have put off using it as to require it to be restricted toward the end of the semester.

Books in the reserve room may be arranged either by course number in the curriculum or by author and title of the book. Many professors prefer arrangement by course number because it enables them and their students to see all titles reserved for their courses at one time. However, many books may be recommended in a number of courses, and the same title may be needed by more than one class. The usual arrangement is by author of the book. An author list, usually on cards, is kept of all books on reserve. This author file may be supplemented by a sheet list of the books arranged by course number.

The number of assistants needed to administer the reserve book room depends on the number of students to be served and the number of books kept on closed reserve. For the undergraduate reserve room it is usually not considered necessary to place a trained librarian in charge, especially if the room is under the general supervision of a competent loan librarian. It is unwise, however, to leave an isolated reserve room in charge of clerical assistants unless the staff includes persons with mature judgment and considerable experience in the library system in which they work. Not only are there many administrative problems which require solution if a reserve book room is to be operated properly, but seasoned person-

nel are necessary for the handling of loan and disciplinary difficulties which sometimes arise. Divisional and graduate reading
rooms are usually supervised by trained librarians who are subject
specialists.

BOOK STACKS. Efficient operation of the book stacks is essential if
good service is to be provided. In many of the larger libraries a
superintendent of the stacks, or stackmaster, usually responsible to
the head of the circulation department, has a number of important
duties. These include obtaining books from the shelves for readers,
shelving returned books, arranging books on the shelves at regular
intervals, supervising the cleaning of books and shelves, participating in inventories, removing damaged books for the bindery, assisting readers, and generally maintaining discipline among users in
the stacks. In many instances, student assistants are used for some
of these tasks, especially those concerned with locating and arranging books.

The superintendent of the stacks should have administrative
competence, a keen sense of orderliness, and the ability to get along
well with faculty members, students, departmental heads, and other
staff members. With the development of more open stack collections and reading areas and the increase in the number of carrels
and desks, the supervision of stacks has become somewhat more
complicated than it was in the past.

RENTAL COLLECTIONS. Rental collections supplement the general
library book collection with books needed for class work and also
with general books for recreational reading. A few libraries maintain rental collections in connection with the reserve book room.
There have also been instances of rental collections operated by
the university bookstore.

BROWSING ROOMS AND DORMITORY AND FRATERNITY LIBRARIES.
Many university libraries, like college libraries, have provided
browsing rooms.[24] These rooms are primarily designed to assist in
developing students' interest in good reading, to provide an opportunity for students to examine and read titles in a well-selected

[24] See Lyle, *The Administration of the College Library*, chap. viii, "The Encouragement of Reading."

collection, and to foster the idea of personal book ownership. The most effective browsing rooms are usually supervised, and a readers' advisory service is made available to the students. Strategically placed near the circulation desk, the browsing room can be easily supervised. Moreover, such an arrangement makes materials easily accessible to passing students and faculty and presents an element of spontaneity that is often lacking in formal browsing rooms located in the less-used portions of the building.

Browsing rooms have been criticized by some as being an expensive secondary function which is not effective in attracting students. Some members of the instructional staff have been concerned with the nature of the volumes which have been selected for browsing rooms. A survey in 1948 [25] among forty-seven college and university libraries revealed that "93 per cent of the libraries having browsing rooms agreed that they were considered successful." Among the factors considered significant in making them effective are strong current book collections, informality characterized by liberal rules and general availability of materials, long hours of opening, and smoking privileges. Apparently, the most successful browsing rooms are coordinated in a general reading program in which both the library staff and the faculty participate wholeheartedly.

Dormitory and fraternity-house libraries are fairly common in universities.[26] Books housed in dormitory libraries are generally the property of the university, whereas the fraternity libraries are frequently owned by the organizations. In a number of institutions, dormitory and house libraries are supplied with books and equipment through the central libraries. If any supervision of these types of libraries is provided, generally it is student assistance. Books are sometimes charged not only to the dormitories and residence halls but also to individual students for a school term. The collections are usually of a popular nature, but in some cases the titles support

[25] Vahey, "A 1948 Survey of Browsing Rooms," *Catholic Library World*, XX (1949), 242–46.
[26] Allen, "Dormitory Library," *Library Journal*, LXXVI (1951), 920–23; Homes, "Case for Domitory Libraries," *Missouri Library Association Quarterly*, XI (1950), 27–30.

curricular work. Like those in browsing rooms, the collections in dormitory and fraternity libraries should be both current and vital; otherwise, interest in them will lag.

DOCUMENTS DEPARTMENT

The importance of government publications in university libraries is discussed in some detail in chapter xi, "Book Collections." Few university libraries maintain a separately organized documents department. In most cases, documents represent a form of material handled by the major departments—acquisitions, catalog, circulation, and reference—of the library. However, in several universities separate documents departments have been established in order to provide special service to users.[27]

The organization of documents departments varies. In one university library, for example, federal and other documents are shelved in a single room. Instead of the documents being cataloged, they are arranged and shelf-listed according to the issuing office. Access to the collections is made through printed catalogs, indexes and bibliographies.[28] This procedure has been found satisfactory and has made it possible to acquire and make available quickly and economically all documents received.

The proponents of the separate documents department claim that more effective service can be provided in this way because the librarian of the unit becomes thoroughly familiar with the contents of the collection and handles the materials in it as a specialist. The documents librarian usually has the responsibility for acquisition and reference use.[29] Cataloging and classification are generally left to the catalog department.

[27] Armstrong, "Documents Librarian Has Share in Many Library Services," *Library Journal*, LXXIV (1949), 1798–1800. Erlandson, "The Organization of Federal Government Publications in Depository Libraries," in Boyd, *United States Government Publications*, pp. 569–79.

[28] See "Federal Depository Libraries: A Symposium," *College and Research Libraries*, XII (1951), 37–47+; "Official Checklists and Indexes *versus* Cataloging of Government Publications: A Symposium," *College and Research Libraries*, XII (1951), 158–70.

[29] Tauber and Wilson, *Report of a Survey of the Montana State University Library*, p. 44. The Documents and Serials Department at Montana State University Library included the functions of acquisitions, cataloging, reference, and binding.

Even though there may be a central documents department, most departmental and professional school libraries will collect documents in their special fields. The existence of many special units, therefore, may leave an independent documents department with the handling of general material and the central record of acquisitions. The placement of documents in collections on the basis of subject appears logical if one considers the approach of research workers. The latter are not concerned with the form of the material; instead, they are interested in content. Divisional reading rooms built around correlated fields of interest might well contain the appropriate documents for the several units.[30]

PERIODICALS DEPARTMENT

Many university libraries maintain a periodicals department. However, the administration of periodicals is generally associated with the circulation or reference departments, even though a separate room is provided for housing current periodicals.

The separation of periodicals work from other services rests on the assumption that more effective service may be given in this way. The factors which warrant the establishment of such a unit are similar to those outlined in the preceding section for documents. In fact, in a few instances, there have been consolidations of periodicals and documents into a single department. This unit, known as the Periodicals and Documents Department, or by a designation such as the "Current Affairs Room," combines two groups of materials which are normally consulted by students in their search for up-to-date information.

The routines of periodicals librarians are well defined and may be listed as: (1) receiving, recording, and stamping periodicals acquired by the library, (2) distributing periodicals to the current reading room shelves or to departmental and professional school libraries, (3) claiming missing numbers and returning imperfect

[30] Wilson and Lundy, *Report of a Survey of the Library of the University of Notre Dame for the University of Notre Dame, November 1950—March 1952*, p. 65. See also Jackson, *The Administration of the Government Documents Collection*, ACRL Monograph No. 5.

numbers, (4) keeping necessary records and statistics, (5) developing periodical procedures, (6) checking exchange lists, (7) examining periodicals and rendering reference service in connection with them, (8) maintaining exhibits, and (9) preparing periodicals for binding.[31]

To insure effective service in periodicals work in a university library, the personnel in charge must know the role which learned journals play, as well as the best methods for their care and use. A thorough acquaintance with periodical indexes, abstracting services, bibliographical works and the competence to read titles in foreign languages are indispensable.

SERIALS DEPARTMENT

Many documents and all periodicals may be described as "serials." Other serials include society transactions, continuations, yearbooks, and similar materials. In university libraries these publications represent an important part of the collections. They require special administrative attention if they are to be acquired systematically, processed quickly and economically, and made available for reference use.

The arguments for a separate serials department are similar to those advanced for the separate documents or periodicals department. Centralization in a single department has been recommended on the grounds that (1) the work may be more efficiently performed where the records are kept, (2) trained serial workers would be available, (3) overdepartmentalization would be eliminated, (4) duplication of records would be eliminated, (5) duplication of materials would be minimized, and (6) service to readers would be generally improved. Thus, the selection, acquisition, cataloging, classification, binding, shelving, circulation, and reference work regarding serials would be concentrated in one department. These claims fit in with the general principle of administra-

[31] A useful source of information on the handling of periodicals and other serials is Osborn, *Serial Publications: Their Place and Treatment in Libraries. Serial Slants,* a quarterly issued by the Serials Round Table of the American Library Association, provides current information.

tion that, when a certain type of work becomes extensive enough to warrant the handling by specialists, it is advisable to isolate the work in a special unit.

The important problem is to determine when such specialization is necessary. The major question is whether an office of record should also be an agency of service. The administrator should be cautious in adopting any policy which necessitates the establishment of duplicate departments, such as acquisitions and catalog departments.

Since serials possess certain distinct peculiarities, it is not uncommon to find separate serials departments in university libraries, even though they may or may not have direct service responsibilities. As may be observed in Figure 16, the Serials Department in the University of California Library has functions which involve acquisitions, cataloging, circulation, and binding operations. Moreover, it is responsible for bibliographical work of the Newspaper Microfilm Project and with Cyrillic alphabet material.

A subscription to a serial usually represents a permanent charge against the budget in two ways: it becomes an annual item on the periodicals or serials fund, and, in most cases, entails a binding cost. Hence, the selection of serials may be a more serious matter than the selection of books. Selection may be concerned with first orders, renewals, and purchase of back volumes. Renewals are made more or less automatically, especially if there is no reduction in the budget. The temporary suspension of a serial subscription may later lead to difficulty in filling the gaps, and frequently may require the expenditure of more funds than if obtained when the materials were current. Back volumes are generally acquired as they appear on the market at acceptable prices. University libraries are generally more concerned with purchasing back volumes than are either public or college libraries.

Reference service of the serials department involves giving specific information on serials through consultation of trade bibliographies, directories, union lists, and similar tools; guiding readers to find facts that can be obtained in periodical articles; aiding in the

FIGURE 16. ORGANIZATION CHART, SERIALS DEPARTMENT,
UNIVERSITY OF CALIFORNIA (BERKELEY) GENERAL LIBRARY, 1955

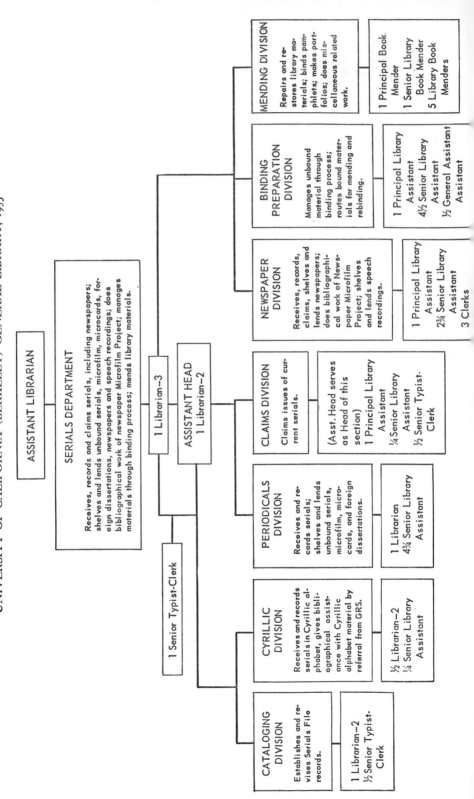

preparation of bibliographies; and providing assistance in the use of indexes and abstracts. These services are identical with those usually offered in the reference department of a university library. In libraries having both a general reference department and a serials department it is essential that there be close cooperation in the guidance of readers who need information on their projects, regardless of whether the information is in books, documents, or serials.

Although there have been in many university libraries rather rigid restrictions on the lending of periodicals and other serials for home use, a number of institutions have relaxed these regulations. A growing number of libraries allow bound volumes to go out of the buildings on loan, and short-term loans for current periodicals are not uncommon. In well-regulated programs of binding, efforts are made to have the materials available for the readers when they are needed. This requires careful scheduling on the part of the library and cooperation by the binders.

With the development of divisional reading rooms, with emphasis on the subject content rather than the form of the material, it would appear that serials departments are likely to be general in their function. While such a department as is described in Figure 16 naturally grows out of the complexity of large quantities of serials, it does not necessarily follow that it should also absorb the complete reference and circulating responsibilities concerning the materials. Local library conditions are important in any decision to set up a complete library service built around a form of material.

ARCHIVES AND MANUSCRIPTS

Many university libraries in recent years have been building up their archival and manuscript collections to the extent that special housing and curatorship are necessary. As in the case of documents, periodicals, and serials, the problem of separate care becomes important when the mass of materials becomes exceptionally varied and large. Usually the archives and manuscripts department is under the general supervision of the reference department, although in some instances it may be part of the special collections department.

The character of archival collections varies from library to library. The problem of collecting these materials is discussed in chapter xi. It is worth noting here, however, that certain definite responsibilities have been assigned archivists. While his general administrative duties are similar to those of other officers of the library, the archivist is also directly involved in obtaining and preparing materials appropriate for the university archives. He must be on the watch for possible gifts and exchanges. If the collections contain local and regional history materials as well as university archives, he will be active in reference work and the compilation of suitable bibliographical records.[32] Archivists are usually trained in historiography and have a strong aptitude for research and its methods.

Moreover, the handling of large and complex archival collections requires the skills and training of one experienced in record management. Mood and Carstensen,[33] who express gratitude for the efforts of professional librarians to collect and safeguard archives, call attention to the special background of the trained archivist. The question of whether or not the university archivist should be a member of the library staff is a controversial one. While the archivist at Harvard University is responsible to the librarian, this is not true in all institutions.

[32] Shipton, "The Harvard University Archives," *Harvard Library Bulletin*, I (1947), 101–8, and "The Collections of the Harvard University Archives," (1947), 176–84; Jennings, "Archival Collecting in American Universities and Colleges," *American Archivist*, XII (1949), 155–63; Browne, "A Plan of Organization for a University Archives," *American Archivist*, XII (1949), 355–58; Mood and Carstensen, "University Records and Their Relation to General University Administration," *College and Research Libraries*, XI (1950), 337–45; Butterfield, "Local History and University Archives in the University of Rochester Library," *College and Research Libraries*, XI (1950), 346–49; Fox, "The Development of the Regional History Collection at Cornell University," *College and Research Libraries*, XI (1950), 350–53; Wilson, "No Ivory Tower," *College and Research Libraries*, XIII (1952), 215–22.

[33] *Op. cit.*, pp. 343–45.

MAP ROOM

A number of the larger university libraries, in recent years, have developed their map collections to such an extent that they have become separate services. The Army Map Service perhaps has been an important factor in this development. During World War II, it was found that many American university libraries lacked adequate map collections to facilitate research work, although maps have always been acquired on a limited basis.

The map librarian, like other specialists in charge of a form material, generally has responsibilities which go beyond service to readers. He is the person who will need to initiate efforts to collect the maps which meet the particular needs of the institution.[34] The map librarian, in addition, will have the responsibility for proper care and organization of the maps, which obviously present problems different from those for books.[35]

Woods [36] has called attention to the variety of materials which may be included in a map collection. At the University of Illinois, for example, in 1952 there were in the collection about 145,000 maps, some 3,000 books and atlases, 18,500 aerial photographs, 850 pamphlets, and four globes. Other units of the University of Illinois also contained small collections of maps, atlases, and aerial photographs. At Yale [37] a collection of over 50,000 maps, sheet and roll, as well as charts, is available for research and teaching purposes. The map librarian usually should have a background in cartography and history if he is to help users to make the most effective use of the materials.

LIBRARY EXTENSION DEPARTMENT

Library extension service, like other informal services offered by universities, has generally been developed in response to public de-

[34] Espenshade, "Maps for the College Library," *College and Research Libraries*, VIII (1947), 132–37, and "A Guide to Map Sources for Building a College Map Library," *College and Research Libraries*, IX (1948), 45–53.
[35] Brandon, "The Map Room," *Columbia Library World*, V (1951), 1–3.
[36] *A Guide to the Map Collection in the University of Illinois Library*.
[37] Yale University Library. *Staff Manual*, pp. 23–24.

mand. Faced with the inadequacy of library service in extensive rural areas, a few institutions of higher learning have realized for more than forty years that many citizens would have little access to printed materials unless they were furnished them directly. This need, combined with the demand for library materials required in their general extension programs, has led these institutions to provide some form of library extension service. As a result, these universities are supplying large quantities of printed materials to numerous individuals and groups.

Library services have followed, generally, the development of university extension work itself, beginning with furnishing materials for formal credit and noncredit courses on the subjects offered on the campus and gradually expanding to furnish materials for informal educational services. At present these include programs which involve: lectures; forums; radio broadcasts and television programs; institutes; contests; publications; advisory assistance to groups; vocational guidance; promotion of study programs; assistance in community organization; informal, advisory, and demonstration services in public health; community recreation; child welfare; dramatics; music; art; and visual education. It is obvious that the university library or some agency for the distribution of printed materials is a vital link in such activities. While private institutions have joined in such activities, extension of informal education has been primarily the function of the tax-supported state institution.

OPERATING EXPENSES   In state institutions the greater portion of the funds for library extension comes from the general appropriation for the university and is allocated to the library extension division. In private institutions the grants may come from the general budget, or in some cases from special funds. To offset a part of the operating expense, funds may also be secured through sales of study outlines, from fees for the loan of books or package libraries, and from charges for transportation.

FIGURE 17. LIBRARY EXTENSION SERVICE
UNIVERSITY OF MICHIGAN GENERAL LIBRARY
July 1, 1952–June 30, 1953

LEGEND

○ CHILDREN S BOOKS

⚲ SCHOOL VISITS

+ EXHIBITS

⊸ EXTENSION COLLECTION
 BOOKS

● BIBLIOGRAPHIES & ALUMNI
 READING LISTS

Prepared by Clover M. Flanders, Chief Extension Librarian
at the University of Michigan

In addition to the services provided in Michigan, alumni reading lists were sent to the following states: Alabama, Connecticut, Florida, Georgia, Indiana, Maine, Massachusetts, Minnesota, Mississippi, New Jersey, New York, Ohio, Pennsylvania, Texas, Virginia, Wisconsin, Washington, D.C.

AREA SERVED   Library extension service provided by state institutions is generally limited to the state in which the university is located. This is not strictly held to, however. Figures 17 and 18 show the distribution of the library extension service and the package service of the Library Extension Service of the General Library of the University of Michigan for the period July 1, 1952 to June 30, 1953. In addition to the service to Michigan readers, alumni reading lists were sent to individuals in sixteen states and Washington, D.C.

Private institutions are restricted only by the funds available for extension service. By means of the interlibrary loan, often indistinguishable from the library extension service, any university library, public or private, can and does cross state lines with its extension services. Reading lists and study outlines are frequently sold to individuals and groups outside the state.

ORGANIZATION OF EXTENSION SERVICE   The organization of extension service varies from university to university. Usually the extension division is responsible for it. In this case, a special bureau or department of the division usually, but not always, performs the work. Such units as a department of debating and public discussion, or a bureau of general information, or a communications center, may be responsible for extension service. In some universities the work is divided among two or more bureaus. In others, generally those in which the service is not highly developed, no special bureau or department has been set up for it. In a very few institutions, a division of the state library agency located at the university operates the service. One of the common types of service provided by such agencies is the package loan library, which lends pamphlet and other materials to borrowers throughout the state. The extension division supervised by the university library, as at Michigan and a number of other institutions, has a wider program.

FACILITIES AND RESOURCES FOR LIBRARY EXTENSION   The library extension division usually possesses a special collection which includes many different kinds of materials, such as package libraries,

FIGURE 18. PACKAGE SERVICE INCLUDING DEBATE MATERIAL
LIBRARY EXTENSION SERVICE
UNIVERSITY OF MICHIGAN GENERAL LIBRARY
July 1, 1952–June 30, 1953

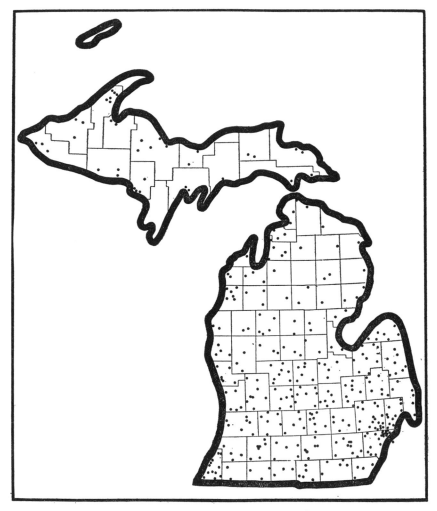

Prepared by Clover M. Flanders, Chief Extension Librarian
at the University of Michigan

plays, pamphlets, documents, motion pictures, maps, photographs, slides, prints, phonograph records, study outlines, readings, recitations, posters, and charts. Sometimes it has the privilege of drawing on the whole university library for materials. Generally, campus needs take precedence over off-campus requests, and only those materials that are not in demand for course work on the campus may be sent out on extension loans. When courses are given off-campus, however, the demands of the users are seriously considered. At the University of Maryland, for example, a bookmobile serves students who take courses in centers off the campus.[38] The bookmobile, operating under the university library, has a collection of about 1,500 volumes related to the courses offered. Audio-visual aids, including a motion picture projector and wall maps, are also furnished off-campus students of the university.

Table 5 shows the nature of the work of the Extension Division of the University of Michigan General Library. As may be observed, there is a variety of services offered, including a general package service, preparation of alumni reading lists, distribution of children's books, work with schools, exhibit work, distribution of special lists, and circulation of books from the extension collection.

SERVICES OF LIBRARY EXTENSION DEPARTMENT: BOOKS FOR COURSES
The provision of books for courses conducted off campus is one of the primary functions of the library extension division. Whether it is by bookmobile or through the setting up of branch libraries at off-campus centers, the university has the obligation to provide proper materials to students who are taking courses under the auspices of the institution. If necessary, titles should be duplicated to handle the needs of the off-campus students.

PACKAGE LIBRARIES. The package library is one of the most common devices used for library extension service. Usually, it consists of a collection of material on a subject of current interest to individuals or groups, and is made up of clippings, pamphlets, docu-

[38] Hayes, "University of Maryland Inaugurates Library Service to Off-Campus Students," *Between Librarians*, XX (1953), 20.

TABLE 5: CIRCULATION STATISTICS, 1952–53, LIBRARY EXTENSION
SERVICE, UNIVERSITY OF MICHIGAN GENERAL LIBRARY *

		Number of Requests	Units of Service (packages and sets of books)	Number of Items (pamphlets, lists, circ. books)
General Package Service		990	1,929	17,259
Service to Michigan High School Forensic Association				
Debate material		166	166	5,001
Second semester material		247	247	988
(catalogs listing readings, declamations, etc.)				
Alumni reading lists		140		209
Children's books (Edith Thomas Book Project)		152		
Sets circulated				
No. of sets sent to schools direct	246			
Sets sent to county commissioners of schools	94			
Sets used for exhibits	56			
Sets sent as permanent gifts				
Central Michigan Children's Clinic (Traverse City)	2			
Worn books still usable sent to University of Michigan Fresh Air Camp	6			
Total sets sent	404		404	
Books Circulated				
Books circulated to schools	10,692			
Books used in 46 exhibits	1,512			
Books sent as permanent gifts	225			
Total	12,429			12,429
Special Lists Distributed				
Books for Boys and Girls Selected from the Notable Publications of July 1952–53				850
A Selected List of Recent Children's Books (Christmas List)				350
A List of Books for Easy Reading				125
1952–1953 Debate Bibliography on the Atlantic Union				275
Parent Education List				240
Michigan Materials—A Classified List of Free and Inexpensive Pamphlet Material				140
A List of Selected References on Michigan				90
Housing the Aging				225
Totals		1,695	2,746	38,181
Extension Collection Books				2,853
Grand Total				41,034

* Source: Library Extension Division, University of Michigan General Library.

ments, and other ephemeral materials. Social, political, and economic problems, international affairs, literature, and art are popular topics. Some library extension divisions are willing to make up libraries on almost any subject requested; other divisions limit their services to specific fields. In addition to general package libraries, a few institutions supply collections on special subjects, such as medicine, engineering, and industry.

READING COURSES AND LISTS. The provision of reading courses and lists is regarded as a type of informal instruction which goes beyond the mere provision of printed materials. The reading course is a short introductory presentation of a specific field with suggestions for further study. Some extension divisions rely on published courses of reading, while others work with faculty members and prepare their own. These reading courses are either loaned or sold. In some institutions they have been organized into more or less formal courses with reports of reading sent into the university, certificates being issued on completion.

Provision of reading lists is another form of extension service. Such lists vary from complete bibliographies to short lists on current topics. By collecting large numbers of printed lists and supplementing them by preparation of lists on subjects not covered, the library can meet any demand for guides to reading.

STUDY OUTLINES. Study outlines are quite similar to the reading courses but differ in that they are prepared for use by groups in studying economic and social problems or cultural subjects. They suggest aspects of the subject that should be studied in detail and they recommend printed materials to help in the preparation of articles on the various phases of the subject. Some institutions prepare and publish such outlines for the use of clubs and local societies.

DRAMA AND RELATED MATERIALS. Plays, readings, recitations, orations, pageants, operettas, and information concerning staging, costuming, lighting, and makeup are frequently made available to teachers and directors of dramatics through library extension service. Some libraries also maintain extensive collections of plays which are loaned for reading or for performance.

INFORMATION AND REFERENCE SERVICE. Some university library extension agencies provide reference and information service for persons who have limited library service or who are entirely without such service. The resources and facilities of the library are placed at the service of residents in such areas. In some instances the response made to a request for information may be answered through a reference to a publication that can be found in a local library. Other requests may involve extensive investigation and the sending of several publications. Several libraries provide reference service in special fields, particularly if the libraries are part of state universities or land-grant colleges. As Van Male [39] pointed out, however, university libraries as a group have not done much in serving the general public.

RADIO AND TELEVISION. Universities and their libraries have long utilized radio as a medium for presenting information, particularly as it concerns authors and books, and cultural programs to the general public.[40] With the coming of television, a new medium has been opened up to the library.[41] The nature of the television programs in which libraries are directly involved is limited primarily to a discussion of books. However, libraries have also furnished photographs and other information needed by members of television staffs. Undoubtedly, as television outlets are used for educational purposes, the university library, along with other resources for instruction, should have an important role to play.

DEBATING MATERIALS. Much of the material mentioned under the heading of package libraries contains printed materials useful for high-school and other debating teams. Michigan and other libraries, however, make up special collections on subjects used by debaters.

ALUMNI. A responsibility which many university libraries have assumed is service to alumni. This service appears in various forms:

[39] "University Library Service and the General Public," *College and Research Libraries*, VII (1946), 306–10+.

[40] Kirkpatrick, "The Library on the Air: University of Utah," *College and Research Libraries*, VIII (1947), 36–37; Van Male, "The Library on the Air: University of South Carolina," *College and Research Libraries*, VIII (1947), 37–38; Orr, "Radio Programs for Land-Grant College and University Libraries," *College and Research Libraries*, VIII (1947), 234–38.

[41] Orr, "Television and the Library at Iowa State," *College and Research Libraries*, XIII (1952), 314–18.

(1) full use of the library—either entirely free, upon payment of a fee, or upon a returnable deposit; (2) distribution of reading lists, compiled either by members of the library staff or members of the instructional staff; (3) direct loan service, at the transportation expense of the alumnus; (4) loan service to alumni through interlibrary loans to public or other libraries; and (5) rental library service, ranging from three to five cents per day, exclusive of the time necessary for the transportation of the books.

The relationships to alumni are important, and more so if the university is interested in building up the library through their help. In recent years, there has been a notable growth in friends-of-the-library groups. Predominant among the friends in many of these groups are alumni, who, appreciating the services of the university, are willing to help it expand its program. Setting up barriers through fee regulations or similar restrictions may hinder the development of a smooth public relations program with an important source of assistance—the alumni. Administrative officers and librarians may well ponder the results of any action which suggests that graduates of a university are not to be given any special consideration in the use of library facilities and resources.

SERVICES TO OTHER LIBRARIES. Universities in areas in which general library service is poorly developed are frequently called upon to aid local libraries by sending books for the use of local readers. While such service may be handled by the interloan department of the university library, it is usually taken care of by the library extension division.

COORDINATION OF EXTENSION SERVICES   It is apparent from the foregoing discussion that university library extension service has reached many groups of people. It is also apparent that this service has not been closely coordinated with other local, university, or state-wide libraries or related services.[42] Although some strides have been made in the last decade, there is still much to be done if ex-

[42] Van Male, "The State as Librarian," *Library Quarterly*, XIV (1944), 36–46; Wilson and Milczewski (eds.) *Libraries of the Southeast*, pp. 208–9; Leigh, *The Public Library in the United States*, pp. 70–71.

tension service is to do the job that it might well perform in the United States. Since no single agency can supply all the library service of a locality or state, it is essential for the various agencies to cooperate if the needs of the communities are to be met. The university libraries, public and private, have a vital stake in this service to the general public. Whether it is to the tax-paying citizenry, who are concerned with both state institutions and tax-exempt private educational institutions, or to the specific groups of alumni, who are called upon for support, the university library, through its function of assisting in the efforts to advance the boundaries of knowledge, has a real opportunity of participating in national progress.

BIBLIOGRAPHY

Allen, F. L. "Dormitory Library," *Library Journal*, LXXVI (1951), 920–23.

Altick, Richard D. The Scholar Adventurers. New York, Macmillan, 1950.

———— "The Scholar's Paradise," *College and Research Libraries*, XV (1954), 375–82.

American Library Association. Basic Study of Bibliographical Organization. Chicago, 1952.

American Library Association. Board on Salaries, Staff, and Tenure. Classification and Pay Plans for Libraries in Institutions of Higher Education—Vol. III, Universities. Chicago, American Library Association, 1947.

Armstrong, Mary. "Documents Librarian Has Share in Many Library Services," *Library Journal*, LXXIV (1949), 1798–99.

Beals, Ralph A., and Leon Brody. The Literature of Adult Education. New York, American Association for Adult Education, 1941. See also Education Index for current citations.

Blanchard, J. R. "Departmental Libraries in Divisional Plan University Libraries," *College and Research Libraries*, XIV (1953), 243–48.

Borden, A. K. "The College Librarian and Research," *Bulletin of the American Library Association*, XXIV (1935), 412–16.

———— "The Research Librarian Idea," *Library Journal*, LVIII (1933), 104–6.

Bousfield, Humphrey G. "The Circulation Department: Organization and Personnel," *College and Research Libraries*, VI (1944), 45–50.

———— "Circulation Systems," *Library Trends*, III (1954), 164–76.

Boyd, Anne M. United States Government Publications. 3d ed. Rev. by Rae Elizabeth Rips. New York, H. W. Wilson, 1949.

Brandon, Edward L. "The Map Room," *Columbia Library World*, V (1951), 1–8.

Branscomb, Harvie. Teaching with Books: A Study of College Libraries. Chicago, Association of American Colleges and American Library Association, 1940.

Broberg, J. W., and R. E. Dunbar. "Current Status of Departmental Libraries in Chemistry," *Journal of Chemical Education*, XXVIII (1951), 435–36.

Brough, Kenneth J. Scholar's Workshop. Urbana, University of Illinois Press, 1952.

Brown, Charles H., and H. G. Bousfield. Circulation Work in College and University Libraries. Chicago, American Library Association, 1933.

Browne, Henry J. "A Plan of Organization for a University Archives," *American Archivist*, XII (1949), 355–58.

Butler, Pierce (ed.). The Reference Function of the Library. Chicago, University of Chicago Press, 1943.

Butterfield, Margaret. "Local History and University Archives in the University of Rochester Library," *College and Research Libraries*, XI (1950), 346–49.

California, University of (Los Angeles). Library. Statement of the Basic Policy on Branch and Departmental Libraries. Los Angeles, 1947.

Chapman, J. D., R. H. Hopp, and A. J. Vennix. "The Role of the Divisional Librarian," *College and Research Libraries*, XV (1954), 148–54.

Cole, Dorothy E. "Some Characteristics of Reference Work," *College and Research Libraries*, VII (1946), 45–51.

College and University Postwar Planning Committee of the American Library Association and the Association of College and Reference Libraries. College and University Libraries and Librarianship. (Planning for Libraries, No. 6) Chicago, American Library Association, 1946.

DeVolder, Arthur L. "The Circulation Department: A Service Agency, *The Call Number* (University of Oregon Library Staff Association), XV (1954), 7.

Downs, Robert B. (ed.). Union Catalogs in the United States. Chicago, American Library Association, 1942.

Dunlap, Leslie W. "Services to Readers," *Library Trends*, I (1952), 49–57.

Erlandson, Ruth M. "The Organization of Federal Government Publications in Depository Libraries," in Boyd, *United States Government Publications*, pp. 569–79.

Espenshade, Edward B., Jr. "A Guide to Map Sources for Building a College Map Library," *College and Research Libraries*, IX (1948), 45–53.

——— "Maps for the College Library," *College and Research Libraries*, VIII (1947), 132–37.

"Federal Depository Libraries: A Symposium," *College and Research Libraries*, XII (1951), 37–47+.

Fleming, Thomas P. "The Organization of Work with Public Documents in University Libraries," in American Library Association Committee on Public Documents, *Public Documents*. Chicago, American Library Association, 1935, pp. 101–27.

Fox, Edith M. "The Development of the Regional History Collection at Cornell University," *College and Research Libraries*, XI (1950), 350–53.

Fussler, Herman H. "Characteristics of Research Literature Used by Chemists and Physicists in the United States," *Library Quarterly* XIX (1949), 19–35, 119–43.

Gable, J. H. Manual of Serials Work. Chicago, American Library Association, 1937.

Geer, Helen T. Charging Systems. Chicago, American Library Association, 1955.

Hamlin, Arthur T. "On Understanding the Reader as Well as the Book," *Bulletin of the Louisiana Library Association*, XIII (1950), 65–69.

Hayes, Isabella M. "University of Maryland Inaugurates Library Service to Off-Campus Students," *Between Librarians*, XX (1953), 8.

Herner, Saul. "How Scientists Seek and Obtain Information," *Industrial and Engineering Chemistry*, XL (1954), 228–36.

Homes, Nellie M. "Case for Dormitory Libraries," *Missouri Library Association Quarterly*, XI (1950), 27–30.

Hurt, Peyton. "Staff Specialization: A Possible Substitute for Departmentalization," *Bulletin of the American Library Association*, XXIX (1935), 417–21.

Hutchins, Margaret. Introduction to Reference Work. Chicago, American Library Association, 1944.

Jackson, Ellen. The Administration of the Government Documents Collection. (ACRL Monograph No. 5) Chicago, Association of College and Reference Libraries, 1953.

——— A Manual for the Administration of the Federal Documents Collection in Libraries. Chicago, American Library Association, 1955.

Jennings, John M. "Archival Activity in American Universities and Colleges," *American Archivist*, XII (1949), 155–63.

Jesse, W. H., and E. E. Goehring. "University Library Charging Systems, *College and Research Libraries*, VI (1944), 51–53+.

Johnson, B. Lamar. Vitalizing a College Library. Chicago, American Library Association, 1939.

Kaplan, Louis. The Growth of Reference Service in the United States from 1876 to 1893. (ACRL Monograph No. 2) Chicago, Association of College and Reference Libraries, 1952.

King, H. H. "Assistance to the Faculty in Library Research: Report from Cornell University," *College and Research Libraries*, IX (1948), 227–30.

Kirkpatrick, H. L. "The Library on the Air: University of Utah," *College and Research Libraries*, VIII (1947), 36–37.

Lansberg, William R. "Current Trends in the College Reserve Room," *College and Research Libraries*, XI (1950), 120–24+.

Leigh, Robert D. The Public Library in the United States. New York, Columbia University Press, 1950.

Lundy, Frank A. "Reference *vs.* Catalog: a Basic Dilemma," *Library Journal*, LXXX (1955), 19–22.

Lyle, Guy R. The Administration of the College Library. 2d ed. rev. New York, H. W. Wilson, 1949.

McAnally, Arthur D. "Characteristics of Materials Used in Research in United States History" (unpublished Ph.D. dissertation, University of Chicago, 1951).

——— "Coordinating the Departmental Library System," *Library Quarterly*, XXI (1951), 113–19.

Maizell, Robert E. "The Subject-Departmentalized Public Library," *College and Research Libraries*, XII (1951), 255–60.

Marvin, Patricia. "Circulation in the Divisional Library: The New Plan of Service," *College and Research Libraries*, XII (1951), 241–44+.

Maxfield, David K. "Counselor Librarianship at U.I.C.," *College and Research Libraries*, XV (1954), 161–66+.

Miller, Marvin A. "Loan Clientele of State University and Land-Grant College Libraries," *College and Research Libraries*, VI (1944), 38–47.

Mood, Fulmer, and Vernon Carstensen. "University Records and Their Relation to General University Administration," *College and Research Libraries*, XI (1950), 337–45.

National University Extension Association. University Extension in the United States. Birmingham, University of Alabama Press, 1953.

Noé, A. C. "The University Library and Research," *Library Quarterly*, IV (1934), 300–305.

Orr, Robert W. "Radio Programs for Land-Grant College and University Libraries," *College and Research Libraries*, VIII (1947), 234–38.

———— "Television and the Library at Iowa State," *College and Research Libraries*, XIII (1952), 314–18.

Osborn, Andrew D. Serial Publications: Their Place and Treatment in Libraries. Chicago, American Library Association, 1955.

Rothman, F. B., and Sidney Ditzion. "Prevailing Practices in Handling Serials," *College and Research Libraries*, I (1940), 165–69.

Rothstein, Samuel. "Development of the Concept of Reference Service in American Libraries, 1850–1900," *Library Quarterly*, XXIII (1953), 1–15.

———— The Development of Reference Services through Academic Traditions, Public Library Practice, and Special Librarianship (ACRL Monographs No. 14) Chicago, American Library Association, 1955.

Shaw, Ralph R. "Internal Informational Aids to Research," in George P. Bush and Lowell H. Hattery (eds.) *Scientific Research: Its Administration and Organization*. Washington, D.C., The American University Press, 1950, pp. 115–21.

Shera, Jesse H., and Margaret E. Egan (eds.). Bibliographic Organization; Papers Presented before the Fifteenth Annual Conference of the Graduate Library School, July 24–29, 1950. Chicago, University of Chicago Press, 1951.

Shipton, Clifford K. "The Collections of the Harvard University Archives," *Harvard Library Bulletin*, I (1947), 176–84.

———— "The Harvard University Archives: Goal and Function," *Harvard Library Bulletin*, I (1947), 101–108.

Shores, Louis. Basic Reference Books. 3d ed. Chicago, American Library Association, 1954.

Stevens, Rolland E. "Use of Library Materials in Doctoral Research: A Study of the Effect of Differences in Research Method" (unpublished Ph.D. dissertation, University of Illinois, 1951).

Swank, Raynard C. "Organization of Library Materials for Research in English Literature," *Library Quarterly*, XV (1945), 49–74.

Tauber, Maurice F. (ed.). The Subject Analysis of Library Materials. New York, School of Library Service, Columbia University, 1953.

Tauber, Maurice F., and Associates. Technical Services in Libraries. New York, Columbia University Press, 1954, chapters xviii–xx, Circulation Operations.

Tauber, Maurice F., and Eugene H. Wilson. Report of a Survey of the Montana State University Library for the Montana State University, January–May, 1951. Chicago, American Library Association, 1951.

"Time and Efficiency Study," *The Library at Iowa State*, VIII (1953), 40–42.

Toal, E. B. "University Library Extension Service" (unpublished Master's thesis, University of Michigan, 1950).

"Use of Reserved Books in the University of Idaho Library," *The Bookmark*, VI (1953), 1–6.

Vahey, Mary Ricarda, Sister. "A 1948 Survey of Browsing Rooms," *Catholic Library World*, XX (1949), 242–46.

Van Male, John. The Library on the Air: University of South Carolina," *College and Research Libraries*, VIII (1947), 37–38.

—— "The State as Librarian," *Library Quarterly*, XIV (1944), 36–46.

—— "University Library Service and the General Public," *College and Research Libraries*, VII (1946), 306–10+.

Wilson, Dwight H. "No Ivory Tower: The Administration of a College or University Archives," *College and Research Libraries*, XIII (1952), 215–22.

Wilson, Louis R. "The Service of Libraries in Promoting Scholarship and Research," *Library Quarterly*, III (1933), 127–45.

Wilson, Louis R., and F. A. Lundy. Report of a Survey of the Library of the University of Notre Dame for the University of Notre Dame, November 1950–March 1951. Chicago, American Library Association, 1952.

Wilson, Louis R., and Marion Milczewski (eds.). Libraries of the Southeast. Chapel Hill, Published for the Southeastern Library Association by the University of North Carolina Press, 1949.

Winchell, Constance M. Guide to Reference Books. 7th ed. Chicago, American Library Association, 1951. Supplement, 1954.

Wolf, M. A. "Library Extension Services of the Colleges and Universities of the United States: A Bibliographical Survey" (unpublished Master's thesis, Western Reserve University, 1951).

Woods, Bill M. A Guide to the Map Collection in the University of Illinois Library (Occasional Papers, No. 31). Urbana, University of Illinois Library School, 1952.

Wyer, James I. Reference Work: A Textbook for Students of Library Work and Librarians. Chicago, American Library Association, 1930.

Yale University Library. Staff Manual. New Haven, 1949.

See also chapters on Readers' Services in various library surveys listed in Bibliography in chapter xvi.

VII

PERSONNEL: TRAINING AND
SELECTION OF THE STAFF

WHILE a university library is an organization which promotes educational and scholarly pursuits, it is at the same time a human organization in which the hopes and aspirations of individual staff members seek expression. Since this is true, the library administrator has two functions to perform: (1) he has to acquire and organize books, periodicals, and other materials and see that they are made easily available to students, faculty members, and other members of the university clientele, and (2) he must maintain an administrative organization in which a sufficient number of appropriately qualified workers may serve the clientele effectively and at the same time attain a maximum of professional development and satisfaction.

Much progress has been made in personnel administration in the last decade.[1] As Van Horne observed in regard to the practices of twenty-five or thirty years ago: "Little defense could be offered for the highly individual, frequently temperamental and quixotic handling of personnel matters a generation ago. Libraries as small units in local government or as parts of larger institutions, often enjoying independent or semi-independent status, frequently fell deplorably short of satisfactory standards of personnel practice." [2] Van Horne further pointed out that despite the fact that many libraries are still in this stage, there are significant trends in the

[1] "Current Trends in Personnel Administration," *Library Trends,* III (1954), 3–94.
[2] *Ibid.,* p. 3.

development of policies and practices which are essential for effective personnel programs.[3]

University library staffs are generally not so large as groups of workers in business, industry, or government, or even in large public libraries. Yet problems of personnel management in university libraries are many and complex. With the growing recognition that university librarianship requires trained individuals, the past tendency of administrative boards and officers to appoint unqualified persons to library posts is fast diminishing. Greater attention is being given to employee-administrator relations. There are planned programs for the recruitment, orientation, and development of the professional staff, and some of the larger university libraries have established personnel officers. Supervision and morale are primary concerns of administrators. Position classification, pay plans, retirement programs, and other considerations have become important parts of library management. It is the purpose of this chapter and the next to consider some of these matters under eight headings: (1) the nature and size of the staff, (2) training, (3) selection of staff members, (4) the measurement of staff effectiveness, (5) salaries, (6) hours of service, (7) professional development of staff members, and (8) staff relations. Topics 1–4 are discussed in this chapter and topics 5–8 in chapter viii.

NATURE AND   TYPES OF WORKERS   The history of uni-
SIZE OF   versity libraries reveals considerable change
THE STAFF   in the nature of library staffs, as well as a
                                      progressive growth in their size. In order to
meet the demands made upon the university library by increased book collections, by greater numbers of students and faculty members, and by additional services, the employment of large and varied staffs, many of whose members are specialists in limited fields of librarianship and scholarship, has been required.

The list of officers and the organization charts of university li-

[3] Cf. Kaiser, "Personnel: the Key to Administration," in Joeckel (ed.), *Current Issues in Library Administration,* pp. 279–300; Martin (ed.), *Personnel Administration in Libraries.*

braries included in the preceding chapters suggest the different types of workers usually employed in the operation of the university library. They further suggest that the organization is very complex and that staff members may be classified in various ways.[4]

In European libraries the members of the university library staff, together with members of the staffs of national and other major scholarly libraries, have usually been classified in three groups: (1) the scientific or superior service, (2) the middle service, and (3) the lower service.[5] Head librarians, experts in charge of major departments, and subject specialists constitute the first group; the main group of professional workers constitute the second; and clerical workers and other nonprofessional workers, the third. Specific types of training are prescribed for the three services.

In the United States, usually two categories have been indicated in classifying university library personnel: (1) professional workers; and (2) nonprofessional or clerical, and others. The American scheme, when reduced to graphic form, may be represented as follows:

General Classification	*First Expansion*	*Second Expansion*
Professional	Professional	Professional
	Administrative	Librarian
		Assistant librarian
		Personnel officer
		Departmental heads
		Special librarians
	Technical	Technical
		Order librarian
		Catalog librarian
		Binding librarian
		Photography librarian
	Research	Research
		Reference librarian
		Bibliographer
		Periodical librarian
		Special librarian
	Instructional	Instructional
		Reference librarian
		Circulation librarian
		Reserve book librarian
		Divisional librarian
		Special librarian

[4] Timmerman, "Position Classification and Pay Plans," *Library Trends*, III (1954), 67–79.

[5] Danton, *Education for Librarianship*, pp. 24–28.

General Classification	*First Expansion*	*Second Expansion*

Nonprofessional, or clerical and other	Clerical	Clerical
		  Bookkeeper
		  Secretaries
		  Typists
		  Filers

	Other	Other Routine workers (students, etc.) in all departments, janitors, and cleaners

There is a close relation between the systems of "ranking" of workers in libraries and the type of work they perform. In a few library systems, such as those of the University of California and Columbia University, schemes of grading are used to distinguish classes of personnel. The California and Columbia systems, which typify schemes in a state university and in a private university, respectively, are as follows:

UNIVERSITY OF CALIFORNIA
RANKING SYSTEM OF LIBRARY STAFF [6]

Professional

1. Chief librarian
2. Associate librarian; assistant librarian
3. Principal librarian; division heads
4. Department heads; supervising librarians
5. Branch librarians
6. Senior librarians ⎱
   Junior librarians ⎰ 4 grades

Nonprofessional

1. Administrative assistants
2. Stenographers; bookkeepers; senior office assistants
3. Typists and clerks; junior office assistants
4. Library aids, desk attendants, messengers
5. Pages and student assistants
6. Bindery assistants

COLUMBIA UNIVERSITY
RANKING SYSTEM OF LIBRARY STAFF [7]

Professional-Administrative

PA6. Administrative (law librarian, medical librarian, architecture librarian)
PA5. Librarian (head of acquisition department, head of cataloging department)
PA4. Associate librarian (department or professional school; assistant reference librarian; head of photographic services; head of binding department)
PA3. Librarian (assistant catalog librarian, assistant librarian in department, reference librarian (International Law)
PA2. Senior assistant (in department, e.g., senior cataloger); also some assistant librarians
PA1. Professional assistants (junior level)

Clerical-Fiscal [8]

CF5. Chief order clerk, chief bill clerk, chief desk assistant, photographer,

[6] See "Salaries in University and Four-Year College Libraries," *News Notes of California Libraries*, XLIX (1954), 296–99.

[7] Information from Charles W. Mixer, November, 1954. Several changes in classification, including discontinuance of PA1 and CF1, were made July 1, 1955.

[8] "General Assistant" class for part-time, hourly wage assistants, included here.

personnel clerk, supply-equipment clerk

CF4. Searcher (acquisitions), chief clerk, card clerk, senior binding assistant, senior desk assistant, secretary

CF3. Senior order clerk, shelflister, proofreader, cataloging assistant, binding assistant, serials clerk, clerk-typist, photographic assistant

CF2. Junior assistant (typist, clerk)

CF1. Page

Precise systems of classifications of professional and clerical workers are devised as bases for personnel procedures and provide a consistent pattern for action on matters involving appointments, promotions, salary scales, vacations, sabbatical leaves, and other privileges. When directly related to types of work, these distinctions are not always discrete. Two decades ago, it was not unusual to find that activities which have been classified professional in one library are regarded as nonprofessional or clerical in another.[9] Some effort at standardization has been attempted.[10] Undoubtedly, as university library staffs have grown larger and more complex, position classification has become basic in library personnel practice. Simply stated, a classification plan "is a grouping of positions into classes on the basis of their comparability in terms of work performed, the degree of responsibility of the work, and the experience and training requirements imposed by the duties of the position." [11] A classification plan includes (1) class descriptions comprised of (a) a clear analysis of each class, and of its special characteristics, (b) a listing of the duties of positions in each class, (c) types of knowledge and proficiency of staff members who are

[9] Akers, "Relation between Theory and Practice of Cataloging with Special Reference to Courses in Cataloging in Library School." Since this study was made, important strides have been made in many libraries in segregating clerical operations to be handled by nonprofessional assistants. This is evident in many of the larger cataloging departments.

[10] American Library Association. Board on Personnel Administration. *Descriptive List of Professional and Nonprofessional Duties in Libraries.*

[11] Pope, "Classification of Positions," in Martin (ed.), *Personnel Administration in Libraries,* p. 32.

required to do the work, and (d) the kind of experience and education needed for effective performance; (2) a system of titles for all classes of positions; and (3) records showing the allocation of positions to classes, as is made evident by assignments of individual staff members.[12]

A poor classification can do considerable harm to the library management. Evidences of poor classification include low morale among staff members, usually the result of inequities in rank or salary, assignment of position titles on the basis of individuals rather than jobs, faulty placement of new personnel, too great variation between pay in library positions as compared to other occupational fields, and the failure of the class descriptions to provide a basis for standards of work and evaluation of performance.

Problems included in making a classification survey, in outlining the role of the administrator and staff members, and in maintaining a position-classification plan with proper pay scales are discussed in some detail by Pope.[13] As position classifications assume a significant place in library management, more emphasis appears to be given to the difficulty and responsibility of work performed. This condition suggests the necessity for those in library education to work closely with practitioners in the organization of professional training programs for future librarians.[14]

SIZE OF STAFF   Table 6 shows the growth in the size of staffs of 25 university libraries from 1940 to 1954. The question of how large the university staff should be can be answered, of course, only in terms of the specific institution involved. Surveys have endeavored to isolate the work performed and to establish positions on the basis of the needs of the library. Size of staff apparently bears a definite relation to the number of volumes added annually, the number and types of students and faculty members served, the teaching and research programs of the university, the number of departmental libraries operated, the number of service desks maintained, and the nature of the internal organization of the library.

[12] *Ibid.*, p. 34.   [13] "Classification of Positions," pp. 40–49.
[14] Shaffer, "Personnel and the Library School," *Library Trends*, III (1954), 13–21.

The evidence indicates that all of these factors are involved in determining the size of university library staffs. The financial condition and the interest of the university administration in the library are basic factors involved in the provision of adequate and qualified staff members.

TABLE 6 *: GROWTH IN SIZE OF STAFF IN 25 UNIVERSITY
LIBRARIES, 1940–54

| | NO. OF STAFF MEMBERS | | | PERCENTAGE |
INSTITUTION	1940	1954 [a]	INCREASE	OF INCREASE
Brown	54	58	4	7
California (Berkeley)	80	299	219	274
Chicago	101	133 [b]	32	32
Columbia	283	316	33	12
Cornell	45	169	124	276
Harvard	169	358	189	112
Illinois	126	243	117	93
Indiana	22	94	72	327
Iowa	53	79	26	49
Johns Hopkins	41	71 [b]	30	73
Kansas	21	65	44	210
Michigan	138	154	16	12
Minnesota	126	135	9	7
Missouri	29	41	12	41
Nebraska	30	65	35	117
North Carolina	33	82	49	148
Northwestern	74	98	24	32
Ohio State	67	150	83	124
Oregon	24	55	31	129
Pennsylvania	89	154	65	73
Princeton	69	113	44	64
Stanford	58	119 [b]	61	105
Texas	53	79	26	49
Washington (Seattle)	38	117	79	208
Yale	163	236	73	45

* Data from "Statistics of College and University Libraries," Princeton University Library, covering period 1939–40 (mimeographed); "College and University Library Statistics, 1953–54," College and Research Libraries, XVI (1955), 41. See also Table 13, The University Library, 1945 edition, for indications of growth from 1925 to 1940.

[a] Figures have been rounded off to full-time persons, if staff members work more than half-time.

[b] Source: "Statistics of College and University Libraries," Princeton University Library, covering period 1953–54.

An examination of the sizes of staffs in 70 large college and university libraries reveals that 21 percent of the libraries have less than 40 staff members, 73 percent have less than 80. Table 7 shows a distribution of the libraries by size of staff.

TABLE 7 *: SIZE OF STAFFS IN 70 LARGE COLLEGE AND
UNIVERSITY LIBRARIES IN 1954

Size of Staff (Persons)	No. of Libraries	Percentage
341–60	1	1.4
321–40	0	0.0
301–20	1	1.4
281–300	1	1.4
261–80	0	0.0
241–60	1	1.4
221–40	1	1.4
201–20	0	0.0
181–200	0	0.0
161–80	2	2.8
141–60	3	4.3
121–40	2	2.8
101–20	3	4.3
81–100	4	5.7
61–80	11	15.7
41–60	25	35.7
21–40	10	14.2
1–20	5	7.1

* Data from "College and University Library Salary Statistics, 1953–54 (as of
September 1, 1954) (Group I)," *College and Research Libraries*, XVI (1955), 41.

When the staffs of these same libraries are broken down into
professional and nonprofessional workers, it is found that 72 percent of the libraries have less than 40 professionals and 30 percent
less than 20 (Table 8). In these 70 libraries the range in the size of

TABLE 8 *: SIZE OF PROFESSIONAL STAFFS IN 70 LARGE COLLEGE
AND UNIVERSITY LIBRARIES IN 1954

Size of Staff (Persons)	No. of Libraries
101–200 or more	5
81–100	4
61–80	1
41–60	9
21–40	30
1–20	21

* Data adapted from *College and Research Libraries*, XVI (1955), 41.

the total staffs is from 12 to 358 persons. The range of professional
workers is from 6 to 137, and the median size total staff is 55. Variations in the proportion of staff members classified as professional
as against those designated as nonprofessional reflect differences in

the library programs. Moreover, it is important to consider the hours of student assistance when estimating the total professional and nonprofessional staffs.[15] Voigt[16] has tabulated ratios of 2 to 1 of nonprofessional to professional staff in the majority of 32 university libraries when student help is included in the calculation. For the period 1953–54, the following hours of student assistance were furnished: California (Berkeley), 191,567; Harvard, 60,000; Wisconsin, 83,044; Minnesota, 89,143; and Vermont, 8,962. For 64 libraries, the median number of hours of student assistance was 30,690.[17]

So many factors condition the composition of a staff that it would be presumptuous to suggest that the personnel organization of a particular library is not well balanced. The library administrator with a sense of economic library management will make every effort to see that nonprofessional operations are not performed by professional personnel. On the other hand, considerable harm may be done in a library's service by manning professional posts with clerical assistants.

TRAINING OF THE STAFF   The effective administration of a university library calls for the steady application of experience and training to complex academic and technical problems. It likewise demands the pursuit of definite lines of action which conform to the needs of the university community and which are capable of being followed continuously or readily readjusted as conditions require. Because administrative

[15] American Library Association, Board on Salaries, Tenure and Staff. *Classification and Pay Plans for Libraries in Institutions of Higher Education—Vol. III. Universities*, pp. xxi–xxv. Directions are given for working out the service of the library in relation to professional and nonprofessional staff needs. A comparison of the percentages in the 1945 edition of *The University Library* with those which may be derived from the statistics in *College and Research Libraries*, XV (1954), 71, will show fluctuations which develop from local conditions of growth, new buildings, changes in service, and other factors.

[16] Voigt, "Ratio of Professional to Clerical Staff," *College and Research Libraries*, XVI (1955), 76–77. See also McNeal, "Financial Problems of University Libraries," *College and Research Libraries*, XV (1954), 407–10+.

[17] The data on which the discussion in this paragraph is based were taken from *College and Research Libraries*, XV (1955), 41.

decisions may be expected to have consequences long after the individuals who have made them have passed on, it is the responsibility of the president of a university to select a librarian who possesses a thorough knowledge not only of methods and purposes but also of the subject matter of instruction and research and of the techniques of librarianship broadly conceived.

In considering the essentials in a training program for the prospective university librarian, three important factors should be taken into account: (1) the nature and complexity of the position for which the university librarian is to be trained; (2) the character and extent of the demands which the university administration may make upon the university librarian and the library staff; and (3) the appropriate preparation of the librarian and the library staff for the effective discharge of their duties. In chapter iv the complexity of the administrative organization of the university library was outlined. Earlier, the growth of university libraries and the continued development of the universities themselves were pointed out. It was noted that the growth in student enrollments, physical plants, curricular offerings, and research has directly affected and expanded, intensively and extensively, the program of the university library. At this point, therefore, attention will be given to the third factor, namely, the preparation of the chief librarian and other members of the library staff.

Education for librarianship in the United States follows a fairly well-defined pattern. This pattern embraces three types of training: (1) undergraduate or preprofessional, leading to a Bachelor's degree; (2) professional, based usually upon graduation from a college or university and leading in most library schools to a Master's degree in library science; and (3) advanced professional, leading to the doctorate.

THE CHIEF LIBRARIAN   Training for the chief librarian of a university obviously should be extensive and specialized. The doctorate in librarianship is increasingly demanded, the reasons for which should be apparent to presidents and faculty members who are cognizant of the complexities of modern university library administration. The nature of the different stages of this training may now be indicated.

BASIC TRAINING. Unlike some of the other professions, such as law and medicine, librarianship has never insisted on prescribed preprofessional education. Only in recent years have library educators been thinking of guiding with somewhat more sureness the college training of prospective librarians. With the cooperation of practicing university librarians, who are important in the process of recruitment for the profession, this guidance, if properly organized, should help to develop a strengthened personnel.[18]

Fundamentally, the preprofessional training should consist of a broad general education. Through connected, well-ordered courses in the humanities, the social sciences, the biological sciences, and the physical sciences, the prospective university librarian should be introduced to the various subjects within these broad fields. During the first two years of college, in which this acquaintance is gained, he should also lay the foundation for specialization in the junior and senior years. The completion of this program usually leads to the Bachelor's degree. The value of such training would be enhanced if it included courses in ancient and modern languages, the elements and principles of administration and statistics, and the educational objectives and administrative practices of universities. Courses in the use of reference materials and libraries and part-time assistantships in actual library services would contribute to a final desired element in such training. Many of the most able librarians gained their interest in a library career, as well as a useful background, in nonprofessional posts while students.

THE FIRST-YEAR PROFESSIONAL TRAINING. The major objectives of the first year of professional training of the prospective university librarian should be (1) to give him a broad overview of librarianship, (2) to acquaint him with the principles and theories underlying the major subjects in the library field and the literature

[18] The question of basic training has been widely discussed in the literature. A listing of the more important items is included in the Bibliography of this chapter.

relating to them, (3) to give him command of library operations and techniques, and (4) to make clear to him the role which the university library plays in the attainment of the university's objectives. Such professional training is provided for by 35 library schools in the colleges, universities, and institutions accredited by the Board of Education for Librarianship of the American Library Association.

Before the close of the 1940's, library schools offered the Bachelor's degree for such a program. At the present time, with only one exception, the Master's degree is given. In some institutions, the period of residence has been extended, so that the student may have to spend a school year and a summer covering the essential course work. The length of time has not been standardized, but it has become increasingly clear that in order to complete the course content a period beyond the two-semester or three-quarter program is necessary. A few schools have endeavored to meet this requirement by scheduling orientation programs prior to the beginning of the professional program. Others have introduced a series of courses which are available to undergraduates in their senior year. The question of the provision of undergraduate minors in librarianship in a university has received considerable attention recently,[19] but it may be observed that academic librarianship, which is based on a broad educational background, requires a strong subject background.[20] Decreasing the number of academic courses taken in undergraduate programs may be the answer for some type of library positions, but it does not help to meet the criticisms which have been made of university library personnel.[21]

About half of the accredited library schools provide courses directed at the special problems of college and university libraries. In some instances, these are advanced courses which are taken by students who have had experience in the field, or who have selected academic librarianship as a career.

[19] Asheim (ed.) *The Core of Education for Librarianship.*
[20] Reece, *The Task and Training of Librarians,* chap. iv.
[21] "The University Librarian as Bookman and Administrator: A Symposium," *College and Research Libraries,* XV (1954), 313–31.

In connection with the discussion of the Master's program i.. library schools, mention should be made of the provisions that some schools have made for graduates of the former first-year course.[22] Other schools are studying their programs in order to meet the requests of earlier graduates for additional work.[23]

ADVANCED TRAINING. With the advent of the Master's degree for the first professional program, the character of advanced training has changed since 1948. Under the former two-year program for the Master's degree, the student became acquainted with the methods and spirit of graduate study in library science and related fields. He extended his knowledge of library science, strengthened his background in the special field of university librarianship, and was required to prepare a report or thesis in his field of specialization. As Berelson observed: "The transmission of certain professional knowledge and techniques is *one* reason for advanced training in librarianship, just as it is *the* reason for the beginning professional course."[24] Berelson also pointed out that other reasons for the development of advanced training were the need for a critical approach to problems and the growing awareness of professionalism.

Obviously, the burden has been on the library schools to provide in the new Master's program material of a genuine graduate nature. Requiring students to take additional courses, without introducing the factors of graduate study, will not help in producing librarians who are able to cope with the major problems facing the profession.

At the present time, five schools offer programs beyond the Master's degree—California, Chicago, Columbia, Illinois, and Michigan. California has announced programs leading to either the Doc-

[22] For example, University of Michigan, *Library Science* [Announcement of Courses] 1953–54. [Ann Arbor, 1953], p. 8. "Graduates of Type I and Type II library schools who have completed a full year's postbaccalaureate course in library science may fulfill requirements for the degree of Master of Arts in Library Science with the completion of twenty-four hours of approved courses in the Graduate School, at least twelve of which must be in library science. Courses numbered above 230 are recommended for such students."

[23] Morton, "The Admission to Master's Degree Programs of Applicants with Previous Professional and Advanced Graduate Study: A Summary of Policies," in Association of American Library Schools, *Newsletter*, VI (1954), 6–13.

[24] "Advanced Study and Research in Librarianship," in Berelson (ed.), *Education for Librarianship*, p. 211. See references cited by Berelson on p. 208.

tor of Philosophy or Doctor of Library Science degree. The advanced program at Columbia leads to the D.L.S. degree. Work toward the Ph.D. degree at Columbia is provided through the programs administered by the Faculties of Political Science, Philosophy, and Pure Sciences. Librarianship may be taken as a minor in this program. Chicago, Illinois and Michigan offer Ph.D. programs. Since the curricula of the five schools vary, it may be worth while examining their general programs.[25]

The D.L.S. program at California is intended primarily for those interested in the technical and administrative aspects of librarianship; the program for the Ph.D. degree is designed for those interested in teaching and research and in problems of a broadly historical and theoretical nature. The fields at present contemplated for the Ph.D. are: bibliography, history of libraries, history of books and printing, and the library as a social institution; those for the D.L.S. are: public libraries and college and university libraries. Graduate courses in all of these areas are offered.

Columbia University's School of Library Service has, in its revision of its curriculum, given up courses labeled "College and University Libraries," and "University Library Administration." A series of advanced level courses, in addition to seminars in book arts, foundations of librarianship, bibliographical research, communication research, library resources, organization of materials, and library administration, are available for the student interested in studying beyond the Master's degree. The degree of Doctor of Library Science, conferred on the completion of not less than sixty-six session hours of graduate and professional courses beyond the Bachelor's undergraduate, nonprofessional degree, and of other requirements, is designed for those who wish to prepare for positions of leadership in the profession.

Both Illinois and Michigan, which offer programs that are

[25] University of California Office of Public Information. [News Release] November 26, 1954; University of Chicago, *Announcements: The Graduate Library School for the Sessions of 1953–54 and 1954–55* (Chicago, 1953); Columbia University, *Announcement of the School of Library Service for . . . 1954–1955* (New York, 1954); University of Illinois Library School, *Announcement, 1953–1954* (Urbana, 1953); University of Michigan, *op. cit.*

tailored to the needs of those wishing to specialize in university librarianship, provide advanced courses and seminars in college and university library problems. In these institutions, as well as at California, Chicago, and Columbia, scholarships, fellowships, and part-time or full-time research or library assistantships are available for students of unusual ability. Thus, through courses designed to acquaint the student with the principles of administration in general and with the objectives of universities; through instruction in the literature and methods of investigation applicable to the subject; through service in the library school as assistant in research or instruction; and through training received in other fields which bears upon his work and broadens and deepens his understanding— by these the student of university librarianship can and does secure the same kind of graduate training that graduate students in other subjects receive—training that gives not only competence in the technical and functional operation of the library but, more important, an understanding of the nature and objectives of universities and of the role which libraries have played and are now playing in the development and the enrichment of scholarship.

Many of the schools which now offer the Master's degree for the program that follows the college or university Bachelor's degree are attracting students who have received Master's or Doctor's degrees in subject fields. This is a desirable program for those interested in careers in university libraries. Many of the libraries which are set up on a divisional scheme are seeking individuals who have strong subject backgrounds. Reference librarians, specialists in the catalog department, and departmental librarians are usually individuals who have advanced training in special subject disciplines.

A reference to the training of university librarians in European countries may be pertinent at this point. According to Briet,[26] training in France and Germany has not changed much since World

[26] Briet, *Enquiry concerning the Professional Education of Librarians and Documentalists;* see also Carnovsky, "Education for Librarianship Abroad," in Berelson (ed.), *Education for Librarianship,* pp. 68–83, and discussion by Thompson, pp. 83–89.

War II. In France, university librarians are appointed by the Ministry of Education and are usually required to be graduates of the École des Chartes, a division of the Sorbonne, founded in 1821 and devoted to the study of language and literature, paleography, bibliography, the history of manuscripts, diplomatics, books, libraries, archives, and related subjects. Rigid oral and written examinations are required, and a thesis on a subject in the field is presented.

Thorough training for university librarians has been required in Germany as far back as the 1890's. In accord with a decree in 1928, candidates for the higher positions in university libraries in Prussia were required to possess a Doctor's degree, pass an examination in a chosen subject field, complete a two-year course in librarianship, and pass a state examination in that field. The written examination consisted of an extended essay on a problem in librarianship, and the oral examination covered the following areas: Greek, Latin, and German paleography, particularly of the late Middle Ages; history of printing, particularly of its origins; history of literature and bibliography; and organization of libraries and library economy in general.[27] In Prussia, courses in librarianship have been provided by the University of Berlin and the Prussian State Library. Thompson [28] has called attention to recent statements by Georg Leyh and Albert Predeek on education for librarianship, in which pleas are made for the training of scholarly librarians. Thompson observes: "It is a rather curious situation that the Germans have theorized so extensively concerning education for academic librarianship and yet have never managed to set up a school or faculty similar to our library schools in colleges and universities." Predeek is concerned with "auxiliary disciplines" in his system, and Leyh also stresses aspects of librarianship generally taught in other departments.[29]

In England, "the British Library Association controls the preparation of librarians to a greater extent than does the American Library Association, even through its Board of Education for Librarian-

[27] Carnovsky, "Education for Librarianship Abroad," pp. 74–75.
[28] Thompson, "Preparation and Status of Librarians," *Library Trends*, I (1952), 98–99.
[29] Leyh, "The Education of the Librarian," *College and Research Libraries*, xv (1954), 140–47.

ship." [30] Carnovsky has described the steps taken by those wishing to receive professional recognition through the attainment of the designation F.L.A.—Fellow of the Library Association. Formal library training is provided at the University of London School of Librarianship, established in 1919, and by seven new library schools at technical colleges. It is not essential, however, to attend formal classes, if students can pass the examinations. Many members of the staffs of the libraries at Oxford, Cambridge, and other universities have been recruited from graduates of those institutions who have combined theoretical and practical studies in librarianship with their university studies, thereby extending the time normally spent in obtaining university degrees.

Carnovsky has observed that the "library training programs of Britain, France, and Germany provide the framework into which may be fitted, with variations, the programs of practically all other countries where library training has been instituted." [31] Considerable interest in library training has existed in Norway for many years. Training on the job, under supervision, has been followed. A large number of Norwegian librarians, particularly those in scholarly and technical libraries, have received their training in the United States. Belgium and Switzerland maintain systems of examinations and provide formal training on a limited basis in several institutions. Spain and Italy have been influenced by the French program, although the Vatican School has maintained a program directed toward providing personnel for the scholarly library. In Czechoslovakia, courses designed to prepare for scientific or scholarly libraries are provided at Charles University (Prague), while the Moscow Institute of Library Economy is a primary base for the training of librarians in Russia. Much of the development in library training in Latin American countries began in the 1940's.[32] In these countries, American influence has been considerable. This has also been true of the programs developed for Japan.

[30] Carnovsky, "Education for Librarianship Abroad," p. 67.
[31] Ibid., p. 78.
[32] Gropp, "Education for Librarians in the Americas," Library Quarterly, XVIII (1948), 108–17.

NONLIBRARIAN APPOINTEES. Occasionally, although not as frequently now as in the past, nonlibrarians are appointed to university and research librarianships. This procedure is important because it raises the question of whether librarianship is a profession, requiring extended training and experience in research, or a technical craft that may be easily learned on the job by a scholar from such fields as literature, history, and economics, or by a professional administrator or educator. It also makes clear certain fallacies concerning the nature of university librarianship upon which such appointments are made.

Most university administrators and boards have gone beyond Flexner,[33] who considered librarianship as purely technical; the University of Chicago Commission on the Future Policy of the University Libraries,[34] which concluded that only a faculty member could understand library problems as related to research; and Wriston,[35] who emphasized personal qualities as the most important qualification of the librarian. In going beyond these observers, who, it should be mentioned, made their comments fifteen or more years ago, university administrators and boards have recognized the essential characteristics of librarianship as a profession. They have recognized that librarianship (1) involves essentially intellectual operations, accompanied by large individual responsibility; (2) is learned by nature, and its members constantly study and apply the results of experimentation and research to all phases of library activity; (3) is definitely practical; (4) possesses a technique capable of communication through a highly specialized educational discipline; (5) is a brotherhood which engenders group consciousness, expressed in a professional organization; and (6) is concerned with the achievement of major social goals.[36]

The statements by Flexner and others may have had some point many years ago, particularly so since a large number of untrained

---

[33] *Universities: American, English, German*, Part I.

[34] *Tentative Report, January, 1924*, p. 147.

[35] "College and University Libraries," in E. M. Danton (ed.), *The Library of Tomorrow*, p. 147.

[36] Flexner, "Is Social Work a Profession?" *Proceedings of the National Conference of Charities and Corrections, 1915*, pp. 576–90.

persons were in charge of libraries. Today, university librarianship, instead of being concerned with mere technical operations, is a many-sided, far-ranging subject. A librarian possessing tact, imagination, and resourcefulness may achieve scholarly distinction in dealing with the problems in this field as well as in other fields of learning. The education of the librarian is designed to give him not only a scholarly command of his field but a knowledge of the functional organization and administration of the materials and personnel under his control, a knowledge with which the scholar or specialist trained in another field is wholly unacquainted. Although a scholar may be profound in one field, this carries no guaranty of particular competence in another field; and, in fact, it is also conceivable that a too narrow subject specialization may lead to a parochial, rather than a universal, point of view.

In truth, the effective university librarian of today is a combination of the technician, researcher, and administrator.[37] Because it is vital that the university librarian have an appreciation of research and an understanding of research needs, it does not follow that he cannot acquire them in the study of some aspect of librarianship or that this is all he must have. Provision for such study in librarianship is available today, and the field is as favorable to such study as many of the fields of humanistic and scientific interest. When one argues for the individual with library training, he does not urge the exclusion of training in research; he simply insists that training in both librarianship and research are indispensable and neither one by itself is enough. It might even be said that in the light of the changes which are taking place in student selection in library schools, and considering the nature of the training which is now available, the prospective librarian should possess an enthusiasm for research and the capacity to carry it on himself—and all this without sacrificing an interest in, and the ability to look after, the administrative and technical services of the university library.

[37] Cf. "Essentials in the Training of University Librarians," *College and Research Libraries*, I (1939), 13–38. Papers were presented by Louis R. Wilson, Sydney B. Mitchell, C. C. Williamson, and Robert J. Kerner, with comments by Nathan Van Patten and Carl M. White. See also Wilson, "What Type Research Librarian?" in *Changing Patterns of Scholarship and the Future of Research Libraries*.

Some observers have called attention to contributions made to librarianship by individuals without formal library training. As a matter of fact, such contributions were made long before the days of systematic training, and analogies may be found in the contributions of men in other professions before formal training programs for them were introduced. In librarianship, most of the successes were achieved when the administration of a major university library was very much simpler than it is at present—or than it will be in the future—and before systematic training for such positions had been provided through universities. Recent surveys of university libraries have indicated that fundamental and costly errors were due to the lack of professional knowledge by nonprofessional scholars and library committees that have not been aware of significant changes in library administration and professional practice. Administrative boards and officers who are aware of the manifold complexities of university library operation will not make the mistake that some of their colleagues have made in the past in appointing nonprofessionals. In some cases, the results have been almost disastrous.

The contributions to scholarship of Justin Winsor and John Shaw Billings (both notable librarians who had not been trained formally as librarians but who were students of bibliography before they became librarians) were made in large measure through their direct interest in those aspects of scholarship which were dependent upon library organization and use for their successful development. These librarians studied the problems of librarianship and contributed to library literature and thought in order that they might thereby promote and enrich scholarship generally.

The ultimate success, therefore, of appointments of nonlibrarians to important headships of university and other scholarly libraries should be determined by the contributions which the appointees make to the extension and enrichment of learning through their libraries rather than through continued teaching or publication in their fields of specialization. The American scholar has at hand today library resources for study and research many of which have been made possible not so much by his own activities as by the skill and the sustained, organized effort of university and research librarians in general.

These observations, however, should not close the door to entrance into university librarianship for persons of ability and scholarship in other fields. A scholarly director chosen from the faculty or an able administrator recruited from other fields may sometimes administer a complex, scholarly library with considerable skill. The probabilities that he can do this successfully, however, are attended by considerable risk unless several precautions are taken. He should be recruited young enough to make new adjustments easily. It should be demonstrated that his energy, tact, scholarship, and imagination will concern themselves with the major considerations of librarianship rather than with the narrow aspects of his former specialization. And, before he begins to make important decisions concerning the administration of the library, he should acquire an understanding of the principles upon which successful functional administration is based. Thus equipped, and provided he brings his entire abilities to bear upon his work as a librarian, he may be able to conceive of the library as a major functional unit of the university.

ASSOCIATE AND ASSISTANT LIBRARIANS AND DEPARTMENTAL HEADS
Associate and assistant librarians, and departmental heads, like the head librarian, are required to undergo a rigorous period of training—undergraduate, professional, and scholarly—if they are to qualify themselves for the complex administrative duties of operating a library. In recent years, much more attention has been paid to the training of these individuals than was true in the past. In fact, it has become common practice for universities to appoint to headships individuals who have served as associate or assistant librarians in other institutions. The availability of such persons undoubtedly has also had some deterrent effect upon the appointing of unqualified candidates.

Since associate and assistant directors are likely to be the head librarians of the future, training for the higher positions should become a part of the total program of professional education.[38] Among the methods whereby librarians with adequate experience and knowledge may be produced are the following: (1) delegating more administrative responsibility and authority to associates, (2) bringing more members of the staff into the determination of library policies, (3) developing more levels of administrative responsibility, (4) making wider use of an assistant or associate librarian as a general manager, (5) drawing a careful distinction between professional and clerical service, and (6) increasing the use of such administrative devices as assistants to the librarian. Experience is of little importance unless it is closely bound up with other important factors of personnel management, namely, recruitment and education.

If a criterion of a profession is its ability to prepare individuals who can carry on and develop the field, then it seems that a function of the university library is the training of potential administrators. The chief librarian, therefore, has the obligation of selecting individuals for his staff who are capable of filling important vacancies as they appear. This should include the head librarianship, as well as assistantships and departmental headships. Only through a clear-cut in-service training program can this be accomplished.[39]

SPECIAL AND DEPARTMENTAL LIBRARIANS   One of the most pressing personnel problems exists in the recruitment and training of special and departmental librarians for university library systems. Many large universities maintain business, industrial relations, engineering, agriculture, medical, dental, pharmacy, law, journalism, forestry, and music schools which require the services of librarians who are trained in the subject fields as well as in library practice.

[38] McDiarmid, "The Place of Experience in Developing College and University Librarians," *Library Quarterly*, XII (1942), 614-21.
[39] Powell, "Education for Academic Librarianship," in Berelson (ed.), *op. cit.*, pp. 135-36.

Moreover, many of the large departments of universities, such as chemistry, physics, geology, zoology, mathematics, architecture, and fine arts, may require the assistance of special librarians to handle collections and research demands in the respective subject fields. With the growth of divisional libraries, there has also been an emphasis on the recruitment of individuals trained in broad subject areas, such as the social sciences, humanities, biological sciences, natural sciences, and technology.

The important question that has been posed frequently has revolved about the kind of training which is best for the librarians of special collections or of departmental libraries. Is subject knowledge more important than a firm grasp of technical librarianship? Is the first-year professional curriculum sufficient to make it possible that a graduate can carry out the objectives and guide the technical operations of a special or a departmental library?

Unquestionably, subject specialization is wholly desirable, if not essential. It is expected that the effective librarian, working in a particular subject area, will continue to build up a strong background in the field. One cannot say that subject training is more or less important than library training; both are necessary for the proper operation of a library. Shera, writing on this question, observed that he "has seen too many examples of special libraries ruined by the inept practices of a subject specialist, turned amateur librarian, to be convinced that subject knowledge is the *sine qua non* of special librarianship." [40]

The implication, of course, is that library schools will need to provide programs which will assist in the training of subject specialists to take over special and departmental librarianships.[41] Although library schools have made efforts in this direction in the past, the emergence of new and more complex problems in industrial, technological, and scientific research, in universities as well as in private institutions and governmental agencies, requires a recon-

[40] Shera, "Education for Librarianship," pp. 129–30.
[41] *Ibid.*, pp. 11–17; see also Brown, "Librarianship and the Sciences," in Shores (ed.), *Challenges to Librarianship*, pp. 80–83.

sideration of library school curriculums so that able personnel will be attracted to the professional positions of special librarians.[42]

It appears that the time is past when individuals with only subject training can operate with efficiency a library serving a special clientele. While a subject specialist will have certain advantages, he will learn his library operations the hard way. Within reason, library school programs should assist by matching their offerings with the needs of the field. The library schools will need to arrange for closer relations with the other professional schools and subject departments on the campus. Professors in the sciences and other subject fields could help in recruiting potential librarians in special fields by recommending to students the possibility of librarianship as a profession. The relationship between the library schools and other units of the university could also be strengthened in terms of teaching personnel, since one of the real difficulties in training young librarians in special fields is providing teaching staff with strong backgrounds in science and technology. It has been much easier to supply individuals with majors in the social sciences and the humanities.

One other method of training should be noted here. This is through a system of internships.[43] In fact, the Medical Library Association has recognized this as an appropriate approach, and has worked with library schools in the preparation of individuals who could later take over positions as medical librarians. These individuals are always those who have had library experience and a background in the subject. In her summary of the problem of internship, Stallmann points out clearly that the success of a program will require the cooperation of libraries. Some librarians have observed the beneficial results of intern programs and have done well in re-

[42] In addition to the Shera and Brown articles cited, there are other items of interest on this subject. See Downs, "Preparation of Specialists for University Libraries," *Special Libraries*, XXXVII (1946), 209–13; Henkle, "Education for Special Librarianship," in Berelson (ed.), *Education for Librarianship*, 170–82; Waters, "Special Library Education," *Library Trends*, I (1952), 244–55; "Education for Special Librarianship," *Library Quarterly*, XXIV (1954), 1–20. The last item contains suggested programs for librarians in the following fields: finance, law, science and technology, medicine, music, theater, and journalism.

[43] Stallmann, *Library Internships*. See also Downs, *op. cit.*

cruiting able assistants. A work-study program requires the student to spend a longer time developing his experience and background, but in the long run both the individual and the library are the gainers. At the same time, the profession as a whole is strengthened.

As Brown and others have pointed out, the personnel of special and departmental libraries, who work closely with researchers, will accomplish most when they come to their positions with good linguistic backgrounds and have a precise knowledge of indexing, abstracting, publishing, and other matters associated with the general field of documentation.

OTHER MEMBERS OF THE PROFESSIONAL STAFF   Mention has been made earlier of the efforts in university libraries to differentiate between professional and clerical duties. The development of personnel classifications, based on job analyses, has resulted in both educational and administrative benefits. Strict adherence to a personnel classification in libraries should relieve the professionally trained staff members from tasks which do not involve the exercise of judgment dependent upon the mastery of principles and practices of library science but which are definitely routine in nature and can be satisfactorily performed by intelligent clerical assistants.

Professional members of the staff—acquisition assistants, catalogers, reference assistants, circulation assistants, bibliographers, branch and departmental assistants, and others—are better equipped for their work if they take the special courses in university library administration offered in a number of the library schools. These courses are usually supplementary to the other courses on general library administration which are required of students. For those professional assistants who have planned careers which involve administration, it is clear that acquaintance with such matters as the organization and administration of colleges and universities—particularly such aspects as curriculums, research programs, personnel administration, financial methods, and business techniques—is prerequisite to an effective program of training.

It is from the group of professional assistants that departmental heads and other administrative officers are chosen. For this reason, they should be carefully selected and given a chance to grow in the library system. Whether it is a cataloger who aspires to become head of the catalog department, or a reference assistant who is interested in supervising the reference department, the chief librarian and the departmental heads are in a position by directed guidance to help the young librarian to strengthen his background. Given responsibility, the opportunity to work on projects, and the chance to supervise in the absence of other officers, the promising librarian will see in university librarianship a worth-while career.

SUBPROFESSIONAL AND CLERICAL ASSISTANTS   Directly aiding the professional staff in carrying on library operations are subprofessional assistants, who, while not performing work on an administrative or theoretical level, are responsible for important routine processes which are peculiar to library work and require some knowledge of library practice. In some libraries, such workers are classified as clerical personnel. Training-class instruction or a brief elementary course in library work is generally considered sufficient technical background for the subprofessional assistants. In recent years, many of these assistants have been recruited from colleges where they have taken non-accredited courses in library methods. Since a basic college education is required usually of subprofessional assistants, these individuals may, by taking part-time and summer courses in library schools, eventually qualify for professional posts. In fact, many of the important university librarians occupied subprofessional posts in their early careers.

The tasks which are allotted to the subprofessional assistants vary from library to library, but they adhere consistently to a pattern. Typical tasks include bibliographical checking and searching in the order and reference departments, preliminary cataloging and filing in the catalog department, periodical checking in the periodical department, checking faculty reserves in the circulation department, and preparing work in the binding and photography departments.

The training of clerical and subprofessional workers has been given little attention.[44] With the increasing concern for the segregation of professional from nonprofessional duties, a recognition of the need to train nonprofessional assistants has taken a positive turn. McDiarmid has suggested that library schools take the initiative for "preparing people qualified to undertake clerical operations in libraries." [45] He further notes that education at the junior college level, on a two-year program, would be a proper procedure for the training of library technicians who are classified as nonprofessional assistants.

A large body of the total personnel of a university library consists of clerical workers. These are individuals who perform, under immediate supervision, processes which may require experience, speed, accuracy, and clerical ability of a high order, but who are not called upon to make decisions and who are not required to have knowledge of the theoretical or scientific aspects of library work.[46] A high-school education is generally required of the clerical assistant, as well as a course in business college. In fact, in many of the larger cities, recruiting for clerical positions in libraries is done through business colleges. Ordinarily, local residents are employed, as contrasted to national coverage in the recruitment of professional assistants.

The use of clerical assistants in university libraries varies considerably. They are used for routine searching and checking tasks, typing, filing, charging and discharging books, and similar activities. The object in using clerical assistants is to relieve the professional

[44] McDiarmid, "Training of Clerical and Subprofessional Workers," in Berelson (ed.), *Education for Librarianship*, pp. 232–48; "Discussion," by Alice Lohrer, pp. 248–53.

[45] *Ibid.*, p. 237.

[46] American Library Association, Board on Salaries, Staff and Tenure. *Classification and Pay Plans for Institutions of Higher Education. Vol. III—Universities*, p. xvi. "Positions in the library's *clerical service* are similar to clerical positions in the business and other offices of the institution. To hold a position in this service the incumbent is not required to have had prior library education or experience." Typical positions described are junior library clerk, junior binding clerk, junior catalog library clerk, junior circulation library clerk, junior order library clerk, and junior reference library clerk. See also American Library Association, Board on Personnel Administration. *Descriptive List of Professional and Nonprofessional Duties in Libraries.*

staff members so that they can concentrate upon major problems of reading, scholarship, and research. As Weber [47] has noted: "The principle of distinctions between tasks is generally unquestioned today. The problem has been one of putting these principles into practice." Moreover, it is important for the professional staff to take the attitude that the clerical assistants are contributing directly to the library service. They, like the professional assistants, are concerned about status and growth. Unless a carefully worked out program is maintained for the clerical staff, there will be instability, low production, and dissatisfaction. A low morale in the clerical staff can do untold damage to the library service as a whole. Libraries have strong competition from business and industry in the recruitment of clerical personnel, and they must regard the subprofessional staff as an integral part of the library program.[48]

STUDENT ASSISTANTS   Earlier in the chapter reference was made to the hours for student assistance which were expended by university libraries. The policy of helping students to carry on their educational programs by giving them work on the campus usually applies to the library as well as to other units of the institution. Indeed, students are more likely to benefit educationally from working experience in the library than from many other tasks at which they may be employed. Routine tasks in practically every department of the library are frequently performed by student assistants with satisfactory results. Close supervision of such assistants by professional or subprofessional members of the staff is generally necessary, as is true in the case of other clerical workers.

Although a considerable portion of the budget for salaries may be expended on student assistants, it is not unusual to find administrative laxity in the selection, training, and supervision of this grade of workers. Student assistants, no less than other members of the

[47] Weber, "The Clerical Staff," *Library Trends*, III (1954), 54.
[48] Two useful publications of interest to university librarians are Dickason, *Personnel Administration on the Campus*, and Albright, *A Study of Personnel Practices for College and University Office and Clerical Workers*.

staff, should be subject to administrative demands for efficient performance.

If an effective group of student assistants is to be assembled, it is essential that selection be made solely on the basis of merit rather than upon the pecuniary needs of students or the intervention of personal friends among administrative officials or faculty members. A number of libraries have used tests in selecting student assistants, as well as other clerical workers, and it has been found to be a profitable approach.

Since a high turnover exists among student assistants, it is important that their training be carefully organized so as to limit the instructional period. Staff manuals have been employed successfully for this purpose. Greater efficiency has been the result of employing few persons for longer periods than from that of giving a large number of students only a few hours of work each week. To recruit from freshman and sophomore classes when vacancies occur has also been an effective way of building up a strong corps of student assistants for service over a reasonably long period of time.

Several principles of supervision of student and other clerical assistants may be noted: (1) to require close cooperation between supervisors and the students assigned to them, (2) to urge supervisors to interpret for students the importance of their work in a larger enterprise, (3) to impress upon the students that a high standard of work is expected, (4) to require the supervisor to formulate clearly what the specific objectives of his department are, in order that students may be properly guided.

The responsibility for encouraging young student assistants to consider university librarianship as a career has been assumed by some administrators. Recruitment from among student assistants has been a profitable procedure for the profession. In those institutions in which library schools exist, student assistants may be selected from the enrollees, and permanent appointments of capable persons to the staff may follow upon their graduation from the library school.

SELECTION   CHIEF LIBRARIAN   The appointment of
OF STAFF   the chief librarian is one of the most im-
MEMBERS   portant administrative decisions the presi-
                   dent of a university has to make. What are
the qualities that a university president seeks in a librarian? If one
considers the variety of backgrounds of individuals who have been
appointed to university librarianships in the past decade, it is sometimes difficult to isolate the qualities. The criteria, professional and
personal, vary with the particular situation, but essentially they
follow a pattern. For most positions, a doctorate in either librarianship or a subject discipline has been required. Knowledge of library
operations and techniques, of the principles of and practices in library administrative organization, of books and other library materials on all levels and in many languages, of the objectives and
procedures of higher education, and of the methods of research are
essential. The amount and quality of training and experience are
usually taken into consideration.

In addition to professional qualifications, there are other important factors. These include age, philosophy of life, recommendations with respect to competence, the nature and quality of scholarly publications, and activities in professional organizations. Ability
to write and speak, and to meet individuals of all kinds cordially
and effectively is regarded as a primary requirement. Since the librarian is a key person on the university faculty, he should be able
to participate in general university matters and campus affairs.

If the president is library-minded, he will use every resource in
obtaining information concerning possible candidates for the position of university librarian. If the librarian is retiring, and an associate or assistant librarian has been groomed for the position, there
is no problem. On the basis of what actually has happened in the
past, however, this does not occur very frequently.

In many of the recent appointments, all-university faculty committees have been assigned the task of making recommendations
to the president. The difficulty about an all-university committee
is that usually none of the members knows librarians through per-

sonal acquaintance and observation at professional meetings and through professional publications. Deans, as a rule, do not scout for librarians as they do for professors. Presidents have not called on members of the library staff because it does not have the equivalent of full and associate professors who are usually available in the standard academic department or professional school. Consequently, selection by either the administration or the faculty has been difficult to make.

Reference may be made to a recent appointment at a midwestern university. Practically the entire country was canvassed by the faculty committee in charge of making a recommendation for a librarian. Among other items asked of candidates was that they outline a program of library service for the particular institution. At the time the screened candidates appeared for interviews, they were probed by the committee on points that members thought were important for the future of the library program.

Possible candidates for a particular librarianship are generally supplied by writing to the American Library Association, library schools, prominent librarians, and officers of educational foundations and national academies and learned societies. Frequently, the president or his representative may attend library conferences or visit institutions for the purpose of meeting prospects.

Once the candidate is selected on the basis of the criteria mentioned above, he should be invited to the institution for an interview, at the university's expense. If he makes a favorable impression on the president, the deans, the library committee, and other interested members of the university, negotiations are instituted regarding terms suitable to both the prospect and the university. If the terms are acceptable, the president sends the name of the candidate to the governing board or other authorizing body of the university for approval.

OTHER MEMBERS OF THE STAFF: INSTITUTIONS WITH LIBRARY SCHOOLS. In an institution that has a library school, there has been some selection of staff members for the library from those who have been trained in the school. There is some advantage in this procedure, since the librarian has easy access to the educational and experience record of those under consideration. Moreover, personal interviews are relatively simple to arrange.

There are other advantages in being able to select personnel who have been trained in the library school on the campus. The student has had an opportunity to acquire knowledge of the library during his work as a student. This knowledge can be applied without any loss if the student is placed in the library after graduation. The library, if its salary schedule is satisfactory, also may be able to attract the best members of the graduating class. On the other hand, there is danger of inbreeding. The acceptance of too many members from a particular school may result in the loss of stimulation which may be obtained by recruiting staff members from different schools. As a matter of fact, in recent years, supply has not been able to meet the demand, and librarians turn to any source that can provide satisfactory staff members.

INSTITUTIONS WITHOUT LIBRARY SCHOOLS. For institutions without library schools, the usual procedure in selecting staff members is through correspondence. Departmental heads and other administrative officers work closely with the head librarian in this situation, and may even do some of the correspondence in locating possible candidates for positions. Where there is a central personnel officer, all correspondence regarding staff is channeled through him. In the smaller library, the librarian usually retains full responsibility for the appointing of professional staff members, and the assistant librarian may be given the responsibility for selecting subprofessional and clerical workers. Student-assistants are sometimes selected by department heads.

Personal knowledge of individuals who might fill certain positions acceptably is frequently possessed by the librarian and the department heads. Such information is useful, and should be recorded in a systematic file showing the qualifications of the individuals concerned. Information of this character should be kept up to date.

Closely related to this type of record is the central file of applications that have been received in the past. This file should be of use in those cases in which the information of the officers of the library is incomplete and does not cover the particular position in question. Information furnished by this file is probably of less value than that mentioned above, but it should be reviewed to avoid missing any promising applicants.

There is no central agency for the employment of librarians, since the American Library Association abandoned its placement service in June, 1948. The Special Libraries Association and other library organizations maintain placement services for their memberships. The Association of College and Reference Libraries, a division of the American Library Association, does not maintain a systematic registry, but it helps in the listing of possible candidates for positions through its secretariat in Chicago.

The primary source of personnel is the library school. Some librarians keep in close touch with various library schools in the search for suitable personnel to fill vacancies which occur annually. Libraries under civil service, such as some state university and municipal university libraries, may have to work through their civil service agencies in the recruitment of personnel. In a few instances, university placement offices are used to obtain staff members, particularly those on a nonprofessional level.

In recent years, many librarians have followed systematic procedures in their inquiries concerning possible candidates for positions. They have reduced each position or class of position to a written statement, listing the title, characteristics, classification grade (if there is one), requirements, and other data, such as salary (with range), tenure, academic rank (if any), hours of service, sick leave, vacation allowance, study privileges, and other leave and retirement provisions. Reference to living costs in a particular part of the country is also useful information to the candidate.

The records of the individuals about whom information is received are examined to determine which are the best prospects for the vacancy. Direct contact with the individuals who have survived this screening should then be made. Such contact is necessarily carried on by correspondence unless the individuals under consideration are in the vicinity or unless interviews can be arranged on the campus, at library conferences, or elsewhere. If a full statement is sent at the beginning of negotiations, the necessity for considerable correspondence may be obviated.

Interviews are preferable for all appointments. For positions in which personality plays an important part—the higher administrative positions, from departmental first assistant upward—they are essential. Interviews may take several forms. The use of oral tests is infrequent in university libraries, although they have been used with some success in public libraries and in industry. A simple procedure usually followed is an informal talk between the librarian and the prospect. It may be more formalized if the librarian has a list of specific items on which he desires information. To make the rating more rounded by increasing the number of subjective opinions, the number of interviewers should be increased to three or four individuals. If the interview is not formalized to this extent, it is usually desirable to obtain the opinion of at least one other person, since the person employed must work with others in the library. The prospect should be interviewed at least by the departmental head under whom he will work, in addition to the librarian. If possible, he should also meet some of the other departmental heads. If it is a departmental head who is being selected, other departmental heads in the library should be permitted to take part in the interviewing.

INSTITUTIONS WITH CIVIL SERVICE. Selection of personnel in institutions under civil service is quite different from that in institutions that are not required to conform to civil service laws and rules. At present there are only a few university libraries affected by state civil service. Merit systems exist in other institutions, but they are regulated by the universities themselves.

Downs, in a recent article, is extremely critical of civil service. He writes:

I am convinced that civil service is an almost unmitigated curse when applied to university library staffs. All too frequently, it is used for the protection of the mediocre and inefficient, and reduces ambition and initiative. The library is handicapped in finding the best qualified persons for positions, because of restrictive residence and other special requirements, and examinations. The acute shortage of professional librarians which has prevailed for the past decade or more, and is likely to continue some years into the future, means that innumerable job opportunities are open to good people who do not have to submit to civil service examinations. This fact handicaps the library operating under civil service in attracting the strongest candidates. Another fault inherent in a civil service organization is the transfer of many vital elements of control of the library staff from the library administration to civil service officers. Such aspects as salary scales, vacations, holidays, sick leaves, leaves of absence, hours of work, retirement, and working conditions in general, are likely to be dictated by civil service regulations, and the librarian has little or no voice in these matters. Perhaps the most important consideration of all is that, in the academic atmosphere, professional librarians feel stigmatized by being classified as civil service workers, for ordinarily they alone among all university employees primarily engaged in academic activities are so designated.[49]

Downs's consideration of civil service is related to his strong views on academic status, a subject which is discussed in the following chapter. However, he is not the only librarian who has been critical of civil service. Kaiser, in his review of civil service in libraries, comments: "After working under civil service well over twenty-five of his total years as a library administrator, the present writer is still of the opinion that civil service as a system of public personnel administration control too seldom aids, as it could, and too often handicaps public libraries in obtaining and managing their own personnel to the best interests of the libraries' basic service functions." [50] Dunbar, however, in checking the conditions of government service against the seven major criteria for employer-employee relations, found that "the net result is a solid plus." [51] These criteria are concerned with the principle of equal

[49] "Are College and University Librarians Academic?" *College and Research Libraries*, XV (1954), 13.

[50] Kaiser, "Civil Service and Libraries," *Library Trends*, III (1954), 89. This article has an excellent bibliography on civil service.

[51] Dunbar, "Status of Personnel," *Library Trends*, II (1953), 81.

work for equal pay, favorable pay scales when compared with outside agencies, satisfactory tenure conditions, possible advancement, good working conditions, safeguarding of health, and provision of a retirement system. Bryan [52] also did not find great opposition to civil service in her study of the public librarian. She did point out, however, that librarians are definitely concerned with the application of the principles and practices of modern personnel management, regardless of whether it is done by personnel experts within or outside the library system.[53]

One can only speculate as to whether or not more university libraries will be placed under civil service in the future. Civil service authorities can do much to remove some of the difficulties of the program. Residence restrictions should be flexible, and the employer should be given some leeway in the selection of appointees from the candidates. It is also necessary that civil service officials comprehend library problems in order that positions may be accurately classified and that the examinations given may be fair and relate to the position involved.

PROBATIONARY PERIOD. The probationary period is a generally accepted device used in personnel administration. No system of selecting personnel yet devised is perfect. An error in selection may be made by the librarian, or personal or other factors that were not evident in the selective process may make themselves evident under actual working conditions. The probationary period gives the library an opportunity to correct mistakes made in selection and to rid itself of persons who have demonstrated that they cannot become satisfactory employees.

The probationary period lasts from six months to two years, one year being the usual period. If it is part of a library personnel program, it should be a positive device. During the period, the person supervising the probationer should discuss with him periodically, probably every three months, his strong and weak points and suggest ways to improve himself in the position. If quarterly service rating reports are made, the discussions may take place when they

---

[52] *The Public Librarian*, pp. 167–82.   [53] *Ibid.*, p. 181.

are drawn up for submission to the librarian. Some libraries give a new employee an opportunity in another position under a different supervisor if he does not perform satisfactorily in his first assignment. If there is grave doubt about the possibility of the new employee developing into a permanent staff member, the library is not obligated to keep him throughout the probationary period. In such cases, the probationer usually is given a month's notice if he is a professional, and two weeks' notice if he is a nonprofessional. A notice of severance of relations with the library should not be given without previous warning to that effect.[54]

MEASUREMENT OF STAFF EFFECTIVENESS Concern for the staff does not stop with selection. Although the greatest care may be taken in the selection of administrative assistants, departmental heads, and other members of the staff, their value to the library organization is made evident only by their performance under actual working conditions. In order to obtain the greatest quantity of work and highest quality of service, university librarians have been interested in the application of business and public administration efficiency-measuring methods to their work. The devices employed for measuring personnel effectiveness in other fields are: (1) production records, (2) periodic tests, and (3) rating devices.

PRODUCTION RECORDS The production record consists of a tabulation of the amount of work accomplished by an individual staff member. When used to measure the effectiveness of library workers, production records have certain definite limitations. Obviously, this sort of measurement applies primarily to library work in which tangible items may be recorded, such as items cataloged. Even in this instance, the relative difficulty of the work must be taken into account before any attempt is made to compare the effectiveness of one worker with that of another. Production records are most val-

[54] American Library Association, Board on Personnel Administration, *Personnel Organization and Procedure*, pp. 12–13.

uable as a means of measuring the work of employees when they are restricted to routine, repetitive types of work, such as filing, typing, mimeographing, and stencilling. It should be borne in mind that even in applying the production record as a means of measurement to routine tasks the quality of work is as important a factor as the quantity of production. Moreover, personality factors which cannot be measured in routine activities should be taken into consideration.

PERIODIC TESTS   Tests of efficiency, which are also used as part of a service-rating scheme for the measuring of routine and repetitive tasks performed by clerical workers, are subject to similar limitations. Such a test measures the productiveness of the employee only at given intervals, while the production record is based on an average covering a long period of time. Of the two, the production record is more accurate because it is employed under ordinary, rather than artificial, test conditions.

Some public libraries use examinations for promotional purposes. These, of course, are somewhat different from the periodic tests which are used to measure quantity and quality of specific types of work.

RATING SYSTEMS   Rating schemes have come to be considered the most accurate means for measuring the effectiveness of employees, whether in the library or elsewhere. Rating plans vary greatly in the degree of their informality and complexity. Whether formalized or not, some kind of procedure for the rating of employees is found in all libraries.

INFORMAL RATING SYSTEMS. The simplest and most informal kind of rating procedure found in libraries is based on the personal opinion of the administrator. A more advanced type is that in which the administrator consults frequently with the employee's immediate supervisor in order to gain an adequate knowledge of the character of the individual's work. A third informal form of rating involves the holding of occasional meetings of several administrative officers, at which the work and abilities of various members of the staff are discussed and informally appraised.

Informal rating schemes are ineffective since they lack definiteness of form, terminology, and time of application. In fact, it is possible that such ratings may take place only when promotions or dismissals are under consideration and the formulation of quick opinions is required.

FORMAL RATING SYSTEMS. The library personnel questionnaire is a somewhat more formalized rating device. It suggests the characteristics or qualities to be observed, but it does not give a final rating of the individual. A variant of the questionnaire form provides adjectives or phrases to each question asked and the adjective or phrase applicable to the individual is to be checked.

There is a growing use of the graphic or linear rating scale in librarianship.[55] It is one of the most formalized schemes and is used for interview purposes as well as for rating. The scale consists of traits or activities to be rated which are factors deemed necessary for success in the position; also descriptive adjectives or phrases indicating varying degrees of the activity or trait, ranging from high to low. The merit rating form used at Louisiana, described by Harrington and Lyle,[56] includes such factors as ability to follow instructions, accuracy, cooperativeness, initiative, job knowledge, judgment, loyalty, organization of work, professional spirit, quantity of work done, reading habits, and relationships with people. The form suggested by the American Library Association Board on Personnel Administration contains thirty-three factors grouped under major categories of performance, personal qualities, professional qualities, and administrative ability. Both of these forms have ratings which range from excellent or superior to poor or unsatisfactory.

There are other rating systems which may be applied to per-

[55] American Library Association, Board on Personnel Administration, *Personnel Organization and Procedure,* pp. 53–57, "Appendix IV, Personnel Service Rating Report"; Harrington and Lyle, "Recruiting and Developing a Library Staff," *College and Research Libraries,* VIII (1947), 427–35.

[56] *Ibid.,* p. 433.

sonnel administration in the university library. These are summarized in a report recently issued by the American Library Association.[57]

Important difficulties exist in the application of rating schemes, as: raters frequently judge from a personal, rather than a library point of view; rating sometimes becomes a mechanical, rather than a skilful, procedure; the terminology used in rating forms is interpreted differently by different raters; and raters are not aware of the several tendencies which color their judgments, such as placing too great emphasis on a single personality trait. These difficulties may be minimized to a certain degree by giving careful explanations to supervisors and by training them in the use of the rating system. Used cautiously, ratings may serve as an important administrative tool. It should be realized that they are not conclusive in themselves but are useful in presenting evidence concerning personnel.

BIBLIOGRAPHY

Akers, Susan G. "Relation between Theory and Practice of Cataloging with Special Reference to Courses in Cataloging in Library Schools" (unpublished Ph.D. dissertation, Graduate Library School University of Chicago, 1932).

Albright, Wilbur D. A Study of Personnel Practices for College and University Office and Clerical Workers. Champaign, Ill., College and University Personnel Association, 1954.

American Library Association. Board on Personnel Administration. Descriptive List of Professional and Nonprofessional Duties in Libraries. Chicago, 1948 (mimeographed).

———— Personnel Administration for Libraries: A Bibliographic Essay. Prepared by Ralph E. McCoy, assisted by a Subcommittee on Bibliography. Chicago, 1953.

———— Personnel Organization and Procedure: A Manual for Use in College and University Libraries. Chicago, 1952.

American Library Association. Board on Salaries, Tenure, and Staff. Classification and Pay Plans for Libraries in Institutions of Higher Education, Vol. III—Universities. Chicago, 1947.

[57] American Library Association, Board on Personnel Administration, *Personnel Administration for Libraries*, pp. 52–54. This report is a comprehensive bibliographical review of problems discussed in this and the next chapter.

Asheim, Lester (ed.). The Core of Education for Librarianship: A Report of a Workshop Held under the Auspices of the Graduate Library School of the University of Chicago, August 10–15, 1953. Chicago, American Library Association, 1954.

Berelson, Bernard (ed.). Education for Librarianship: Papers Presented at the Library Conference, University of Chicago, August 16–21, 1948. Chicago, American Library Association, 1949.

Briet, Suzanne. Enquiry concerning the Professional Education of Librarians and Documentalists. Paris, UNESCO, 1951.

Brown, Charles H. "Librarianship and the Sciences," in Louis Shores (ed.), *Challenges to Librarianship*, pp. 69–91.

Bryan, Alice I. The Public Librarian. New York, Columbia University Press, 1952.

Carnovsky, Leon. "Education for Librarianship Abroad," in Berelson (ed.), *Education for Librarianship*, pp. 66–83.

—— "Preparation for the Librarian's Profession," *Library Quarterly*, XII (1942), 404–11.

Chicago, University of. Commission on the Future Policy of the University. Tentative Report, January, 1924. Chicago, University of Chicago Press, 1924.

"Current Trends in Personnal Administration," *Library Trends*, III (1954), 3–94.

Danton, J. Periam. Education for Librarianship: Criticisms, Dilemmas, and Proposals. New York, Columbia University, School of Library Service, 1946.

Dickason, Donald E. Personnel Administration on the Campus. Champaign, Ill., College and University Personnel Association, 1954.

—— "Sleeves or Zigzag Lines: Salary Determination through Fair Evaluation," *College and Research Libraries*, VII (1946), 237–42.

Downs, Robert B. "Are College and University Librarians Academic?" *College and Research Libraries*, XV (1954), 9–14.

—— "Preparation of Specialists for University Libraries," *Special Libraries*, XXXVII (1946), 209–13.

Dunbar, Ralph M. "Status of Personnel," *Library Trends*, II (1953), 63–83.

"Education for Special Librarianship," *Library Quarterly*, XXIV (1954), 1–20.

Ellsworth, Ralph E. "The Training of Divisional Reading Room Librarians," *College and Research Libraries*, VI (1944), 4–7.

Flexner, Abraham. "Is Social Work a Profession?" *Proceedings of the National Conference of Charities and Correction, 1915*, pp. 576–90.

—— Universities: American, English, German. New York, Oxford University Press, 1930.

Gropp, Arthur E. "Education for Librarianship in the Americas," *Library Quarterly*, XVIII (1948), 108–17.

Harrington, Roseanne H., and Guy R. Lyle. "Recruiting and Developing a Library Staff," *College and Research Libraries,* VIII (1947), 427–35.

Henkle, Herman H. "Education for Special Librarianship," in Berelson (ed.), *Education for Librarianship,* pp. 170–82.

Hurt, Peyton. "Staff Specialization: A Possible Substitute for Departmentalization," *Bulletin of the American Library Association,* XXIX (1935), 417–21.

Joeckel, C. B. (ed.). Current Issues in Library Administration. Chicago, University of Chicago Press, 1946.

Kaiser, John B. "Civil Service and Libraries," *Library Trends,* III (1954), 80–94.

—— "Personnel: The Key to Administration," in C. B. Joeckel (ed.), *Current Issues in Library Administration,* pp. 279–300.

Kerner, Robert J. "Essentials in the Training of University Librarians," *College and Research Libraries,* I (1939), 33–34.

Kraus, J. W. "The Qualifications of University Librarians, 1948 and 1933," *College and Research Libraries,* XI (1950), 17–21.

Leyh, Georg. "The Education of the Librarian," *College and Research Libraries,* XV (1954), 140–47.

Lyle, Guy R. The Administration of the College Library. 2d ed. New York, H. W. Wilson Co., 1949, chap. ix, "Personnel," and chap. x, "Student Assistants."

McDiarmid, E. W. "The Place of Experience in Developing College and University Librarians," *Library Quarterly,* XII (1942), 614–21.

—— "Training of Clerical and Subprofessional Workers," in Berelson (ed.), *Education for Librarianship,* pp. 232–48.

McNeal, Archie L. "Financial Problems of University Libraries," *College and Research Libraries,* XV (1954), 407–10+.

Martin, Lowell (ed.). Personnel Administration in Libraries; Papers Presented before the Library Institute at the University of Chicago, August 27—September 1, 1945. Chicago, University of Chicago Press, 1946.

Metcalf, K. D., J. D. Russell, and A. D. Osborn. The Program of Instruction in Library Schools. Urbana, University of Illinois Press, 1943.

Morton, Florrinell F. "The Admission to Master's Degree Programs of Applicants with Previous Professional and Advanced Graduate Study: A Summary of Policies," Association of American Library Schools, *Newsletter,* VI (1954), 6–13.

Mosher, William E., J. D. Kingsley, and O. G. Stahl. Public Personnel Administration. 3d ed. New York, Harper, 1950.

Pope, Herman G. "Classification of Positions," in Martin (ed.), *Personnel Administration in Libraries,* pp. 32–49.

Powell, Lawrence C. "Education for Academic Librarianship," in Berelson (ed.), *Education for Librarianship*, pp. 133–46.

Reece, Ernest J. The Task and Training of Librarians. New York, King's Crown Press, 1949.

"Salaries in University and Four-Year College Libraries," *News Notes of California Libraries*, XLIX (1954), 296–99.

Shaffer, Kenneth R. "Personnel and the Library School," *Library Trends*, III (1954), 13–21.

Shera, Jesse H. "Education for Librarianship—An Integrated Approach." A Paper Presented at the Case-Reserve Conference on "Developments in Information Searching for Industry, November 17, 1953" (mimeographed); also published in *ALA Bulletin*, XLVIII (1954), 129–30.

Shores, Louis (ed.). Challenges to Librarianship. (Florida State University Studies, No. 12). Tallahassee, Florida State University, 1953.

Stallmann, Esther L. Library Internships: History, Purpose, and a Proposal. (University of Illinois Library School Occasional Papers, No. 37). Urbana, 1954.

Thompson, Lawrence S. "Preparation and Status of Librarians," *Library Trends*, I (1952), 95–104.

Timmerman, Hazel. "Position Classification and Pay Plans," *Library Trends*, III (1954), 67–79.

"University Librarian as Bookman and Administrator, The: A Symposium," *College and Research Libraries*, XV (1954), 313–31.

Voigt, Melvin J. "Ratio of Professional to Clerical Staff," *College and Research Libraries*, XVI (1955), 76–77.

Waters, Edward N. "Special Library Education," *Library Trends*, I (1952), 244–55.

Weber, Dorothy. "The Clerical Staff," *Library Trends*, III (1954), 52–58.

Wheeler, Joseph L. Progress and Problems in Education for Librarianship. New York, Carnegie Corporation of New York, 1946.

Wilson, Louis R. "What Type Research Librarian?" in *Changing Patterns of Scholarship and the Future of Research Libraries, a Symposium in Celebration of the 200th Anniversary of the Establishment of the University of Pennsylvania Library*. Philadelphia, University of Pennsylvania Press, 1951, pp. 112–33.

Winger, Howard W. "A Personnel Program for Student Assistants in University Libraries" (unpublished Master's thesis, University of Illinois, 1948).

Wriston, Henry M. "College and University Libraries," in Emily Danton (ed.), *The Library of Tomorrow*. Chicago, American Library Association, 1939, pp. 142–51.

VIII

PERSONNEL: SALARIES
AND STAFF RELATIONS

AS observed in earlier chapters, more attention is being given to personnel in libraries than was true a decade ago. With the development of personnel classifications for library staffs, the subject of the financial status of the chief librarian and other members of the staff is beginning to be clarified. Unquestionably, more university administrators have come to realize that there is a direct relationship between size of salaries and quality of library staff and service.

STAFF
SALARIES

Available data on salaries are not easy to obtain. This is particularly true of the salaries for the chief librarian and the assistant and associate librarians.[1] Although the Association of College and Reference Libraries has been making a systematic effort to provide complete annual statistics of salaries and other activities of college and university libraries, a number of important institutions are still not included. Sometimes, this has been due to failure of the university librarians to cooperate in supplying such information. In other cases, a number of universities consider information concerning salaries confidential and do not permit its publication. A few university librarians are reluctant to furnish salary data, even

[1] "College and University Library Salary Statistics, 1953–54 (As of September 1, 1954) (Group I)," *College and Research Libraries*, XVI (1955), 40–41. Of 70 libraries listed, data for 53 are given in respect to librarians' salaries; for 42, in respect to the minimum salaries of assistant or associate librarians and/or division heads, and for 21, in respect to maximum salaries for these staff members.

though there may be no official institutional restriction on so doing, because they do not wish to become involved in extensive explanations concerning their incomes or those of their staff when dual responsibilities are involved. In addition, advances or changes have been so frequent in recent years that it is difficult to know what they are at present.

The importance of adequate financial rewards in university library administration cannot be overestimated. Although university librarianship may prove attractive to many persons on account of its special characteristics, most individuals with ability will appraise the financial rewards of university library work in comparison with those of other professions. If salaries are relatively low, it may be expected that able young men and women who otherwise would become librarians will find their way into other types of work.[2]

In order to attract individuals who, by native ability, background, and training, are able to develop into effective chief librarians, assistant librarians, and professional assistants, it must be shown that university librarianship is many sided and affords an opportunity for challenging, creative work; that it presents many opportunities for administrative and scholarly activity; and that ability is rewarded with promotion, extension of responsibility, and ample financial compensation. Librarianship must be recognized as a responsible calling which requires a highly competent staff if effective results are to be achieved. University administrators who recognize the importance of the work involved in effective librarianship know that adequate remuneration must be provided not only for the head librarian but for the staff as well. Too often, only the librarian proves to be relatively well paid when the training and responsibilities of staff members are compared with those of other professional members of the university personnel. It is encouraging to observe that a number of able librarians have refused to accept

[2] Muller, "Tangible Rewards," *Library Journal*, LXXIX (1954), 410–14. Muller reports on a questionnaire on prevailing wage scales in 56 medium-sized university and college libraries. The article includes some interesting comparisons of hourly wages received by librarians and persons engaged in other types of work.

appointments to head libraries without a definite program to raise the salary level of the other members of the staff. These individuals realize that personnel is "the key to administration."

That the subject of the classification or status of the librarian and the staff has not received the careful consideration and clarification it merits may be difficult to demonstrate, but it is none the less true.[3] An examination of the different practices of universities will quickly reveal evidence in support of this point. In the case of the president of the university, of deans, and of members of the instructional staff, the responsibilities of the various positions, the certainty of tenure and financial reward, and the opportunities which service in the positions afford for study and for research, for teaching in the same institution during summer or in other institutions for additional compensation, or for rest and travel are usually definitely specified through institutional statutes or other regulations. Furthermore, they apply impersonally to all members of the group.

In the case of the librarian and the library staff, classification and such specification are frequently lacking and have to be determined on an individual basis or on the basis of a clerical or noninstructional or professional classification, which may completely fail to match the training, professional skill, and educational efficiency of these to whom it is applied.

The successful administration of a university library presupposes the possession by the librarian of extensive general and professional education, understanding of the nature and purposes of teaching and research, and experience in integrating the services of the library in the educational program of the university. It involves the direction of a comparatively large staff and the expenditure of an appreciable portion of the university's total budget. The development of well-conceived policies of acquisition and service and the selection and direction of a staff competent to operate the library

[3] *Cf.* Lundy, "Faculty Rank of Professional Librarians," *College and Research Libraries*, XII (1951), 11–19, 109–22; Downs, "Are College and University Librarians Academic?" *College and Research Libraries*, XV (1954), 9–14.

effectively in accord with those policies make extensive demands upon the ability, energy, and time of the librarian. The services of the library have to be maintained throughout the entire year rather than through the two academic semesters or three quarters.

In these respects the responsibilities of the librarian are comparable to those of deans or heads of major departments. In fact, they may be even more exacting because of their variety and complexity. Consequently, they should be taken into consideration when salaries, conditions of status and tenure, and opportunities for study, for the development of policies, and for other activity or rest are determined. Recognition of the abilities, training, experience, and responsibilities of the staff likewise should be carefully considered, and a classification corresponding to its professional and educational competence established. Clarification of these matters would eliminate the uncertainty which generally prevails concerning what constitutes the proper rewards and status of university librarians and would contribute to the improvement of university administration in general. In this connection, the examples of the University of Illinois [4] and the establishment by the federal government of a revised classification of positions might be studied with profit.[5]

CHIEF LIBRARIAN. The salaries received by chief university librarians in 53 institutions included in the statistics of the Association of College and Reference Libraries for 1953–54 ranged from $6,000 to $14,700.[6] The median for the group was $8,800 (Table 9). Salary data were not given for such institutions as Alabama, Columbia, Cornell, Denver, Harvard, Indiana, Joint University Libraries, Kentucky, Mississippi State, New Mexico, New York University, Princeton, Rochester, and Yale. Among other libraries not included in the statistics are Chicago, Duke, Johns Hopkins, Massachusetts, North Dakota, South Dakota, and Stanford.

[4] University of Illinois Library, *Staff Manual*, pp. 9–13.

[5] "The Classification Act of 1949," *United States Statutes at Large*, Vol. 63, Pt. 1, p. 954. A discussion of the relation of the Classification Act to government librarians is presented in Dunbar, "Status of Personnel," *Library Trends*, II (1953), 63–83, especially p. 64.

[6] "College and University Library Statistics, 1953–54," *College and Research Libraries*, XVI (1955), 40.

TABLE 9*: SALARIES OF CHIEF LIBRARIANS AND ASSISTANT LIBRARIANS IN 57 COLLEGE AND UNIVERSITY LIBRARIES

LIBRARIES	CHIEF LIBRARIAN	ASSISTANT OR ASSOCIATE LIBRARIAN Minimum	Maximum
Arizona	$ 7,250	$ 5,300	...
Brooklyn	9,700	...	...
Brown	7,000	...	...
California (Berkeley)	14,700	7,008	$ 9,384
California (Los Angeles)	12,600	6,360	8,112
Catholic Univ. of America	6,000	4,200	...
Cincinnati	8,136	...	...
City College (New York)	9,950	6,530	7,618
Colorado	8,800	6,300	...
Cornell	...	5,371	9,500
Florida	9,000	6,700	...
Florida State	9,000	5,460	7,200
Fordham	6,500	4,700	...
Georgia	8,100	5,800	...
Hawaii	9,120	5,400	6,400
Illinois	14,000	6,800	9,400
Iowa	10,700	7,500	...
Iowa State	9,800	7,200	...
Kansas	9,600	5,400	6,700
Louisiana State	7,000	6,070	8,000
Maine	6,400	...	...
Maryland	6,950	...	...
Miami (Florida)	9,000	...	...
Michigan	...	10,000	11,000
Michigan State	10,000	5,900	...
Minnesota	10,750	7,400	8,700
Mississippi	6,200	...	...
Missouri	7,800	4,700	...
Nebraska	8,500	5,900	6,000
New Hampshire	6,000	5,200	...
North Carolina	10,000	5,094	6,093
Northwestern	10,500	6,300	...
Ohio State	10,032	7,224	7,632
Oklahoma	...	6,000	6,300
Oregon	10,000	...	...
Oregon State	10,000	...	...
Pennsylvania	...	6,200	7,000
Pennsylvania State	8,400	6,408	6,408
Purdue	12,000	6,000	7,000
Rice	8,000	4,800	...
Rutgers	10,860	6,534	7,854
Saint Louis	12,000	5,400	...
South Carolina	6,500	...	...
Southern Methodist	6,636	...	...
Syracuse	7,900	4,380	...
Temple	7,000	4,500	...
Tennessee	8,500	6,000	...
Texas	9,620	6,720	...

LIBRARIES	CHIEF LIBRARIAN	ASSISTANT OR ASSOCIATE LIBRARIAN	
		Minimum	*Maximum*
Utah	$ 7,800	$ 6,400	. . .
Vermont	7,500	4,600	$ 4,700
Virginia	8,040	. . .	. . .
Washington (St. Louis)	7,600	. . .	. . .
Washington (Seattle)	11,004	. . .	. . .
Washington State	10,000	8,900	. . .
Wayne	11,700	. . .	. . .
West Virginia	6,750	5,020	. . .
Wisconsin	8,750	8,410	8,660

* Data from "College and University Library Salary Statistics, 1953–54," *College and Research Libraries*, XVI (1955), 40.

In comparison with the statistics gathered for the first edition of *The University Library*,[7] it may be observed that a larger number of libraries have provided salary information concerning chief librarians. The increase in the salaries over the 1941 figures reveals the effort to keep pace with rising costs of living and inflation. In the 29 libraries considered in the earlier edition, the median for the group was $4,807, as compared to the present $8,800. Seventeen of the librarians received less than $5,000 in 1941. While only one librarian was earning over $10,000 in 1941, there are seventeen reported in the figures now available. Many of the group not reporting data and those not listed in the tables earn salaries of $10,000 or more. Factors which appear to influence differentials between salaries of chief librarians include size of the institution, size of the library, and location.

ASSISTANT OR ASSOCIATE LIBRARIANS. As may be seen from Table 9, data for salaries for assistant or associate librarians are not complete in regard to maximums. Where figures do not appear in the minimum columns, this, according to the compiler, means that no personnel are assigned. In one case, statistics were not furnished. The lowest figure as a minimum salary for a full-time assistant or associate librarian is $4,200; the highest, $10,000. For the 42 libraries for which there are statistics, the median minimum salary is $6,035. For the 21 libraries for which figures are given, the median maximum salary is $7,618. The highest maximum salary is $11,000.

[7] Wilson and Tauber, *The University Library*, first edition, p. 264, Table 18. The figures are for 1941.

An equitable range between the salary of the librarian and the assistant librarian may be best determined by considering the responsibilities of each officer. When compared to the difference between salaries in 1941 and the present, it may be generally observed that current salaries for assistant or associate librarians approach those of the chief officers to a greater degree than formerly. This is as it should be. If the difference between the salaries is too great it is likely that mediocre individuals will be placed in the assistant librarianships. Further, the lower the salary of the assistant librarian, the lower ordinarily will be the salaries of departmental heads and professional assistants.

ADMINISTRATIVE OFFICE ASSISTANT. An individual of considerable importance in some university libraries is the administrative office assistant, also known as the executive secretary, the secretary to the librarian, or the assistant to the librarian. The work of this person may involve the handling of minor personnel problems, checking budget expenditures, referring building or equipment needs to the proper authorities, and acting as intermediary in certain matters between the librarian and members of the staff. The salary for the administrative office assistant will vary with the importance of his activities and responsibilities. In some cases, it may equal that of a departmental head.

In libraries which have introduced the system of having several assistant or associate librarians, many of the duties of the administrative office assistant are assigned to them. In these instances, the librarian usually operates with a general office secretary.

DEPARTMENTAL HEADS. The importance of the departmental head in the university library has been pointed out. In large systems, departmental headships constitute key positions and, as such, should be filled by individuals who have both administrative and technical backgrounds. Since these positions require relatively extensive academic training and experience, it is necessary, if qualified persons are to be obtained, to pay salaries commensurate with the training and responsibility involved. The minimum and maximum ranges of salaries for departmental heads in 65 libraries in large college and university libraries in 1953–54 were: [8]

	Minimum	Maximum *
High	$6,100	$9,935
Median	4,296	5,220
Low	2,520	3,800

* 63 libraries.

PROFESSIONAL ASSISTANTS. The professional assistants form the backbone of the university library. They handle the bulk of the professional work under the direction of superior administrative officers. Salaries of professional assistants vary with educational background, experience, type of work performed, and ability. Because of the wide variations paid by university libraries to professional assistants, it is not possible to generalize concerning salary. The minimum and maximum ranges of salaries for professional assistants in 70 large college and university libraries in 1953–54 were: [9]

	Minimum	Maximum
High	$4,530	$9,500
Median	3,200	4,470
Low	1,800	3,000

The American Library Association recommended in 1952 a range of $3,294–$3,774 for junior professional librarians. In 1952–53, the federal government provided a minimum professional salary of $3,410 for beginning professional positions (GS-5). In 1955, Strout [10] reported on the salaries at placement of 1954 graduates of library schools. In 35 schools, the professional librarian received for his first position an annual salary between $3,650 and $3,700. This is an increase of about $600 over salaries reported in 1951. Of 1,233 graduates included in the tabular data presented by Strout, 336

[8] College and Research Libraries, XVI (1955), 40.
[9] Ibid., p. 41.
[10] Strout, "Shortages Continue—Salaries Improve," Library Journal, LXXX (1955), 1452–57. See also Muller, "Tangible Rewards."

went into college and university work; of 1,370 graduates in 1952, 386 went to college and university libraries. Strout also observed that "Greatest student interest seems centered on the college and university field (for type of library), and on public services (for type of library work), both of these being far ahead of other fields of interest as reported by the schools. This, despite the fact that several reports identify college and university librarianship as a less active field and one where salaries tend to be weak by comparison with other fields." [11]

SUBPROFESSIONAL AND CLERICAL ASSISTANTS. The salaries paid to subprofessional and clerical assistants also vary greatly because of the same factors that affect salaries of professional workers and because the various types of work are done by different individuals. For example, a clerical worker doing routine typing would receive a lower salary than the secretary to the librarian. Prevailing local rates for clerical work often determine what the university library will pay for such services, because the clerical worker, as contrasted with the professional worker, is usually drawn from the university community or the region rather than from the nation at large. The rates are also definitely affected by the prevailing rates for such services in other departments of the university. The minimum and maximum ranges of salaries for nonprofessional assistants in 70 large college and university libraries for 1953–54 were: [12]

	Minimum	Maximum
High	$3,043	$6,300
Median	1,968	3,247
Low	1,200	2,196

STUDENT SERVICE. Since student service is ordinarily part-time work, it is paid on an hourly basis. The rates vary considerably from library to library, and depend upon the location and the prevailing rates for student service in the institution. Information indicates that these rates range from $0.60 to $1.25 per hour, depending upon the kind of work performed and the skill and experience of the students.

[11] *Ibid.*, p. 1456.   [12] *College and Research Libraries,* XVI (1955), 41.

HOURS OF
SERVICE
Most university libraries provide service throughout the week for their users. A study of recent library manuals and catalogs of universities reveal that the median is about 85 hours per week. A typical program is from 8 A.M. to 10 P.M., on weekdays, 8 A.M. to 5 P.M. on Saturdays, and 2 P.M. to 6 P.M. on Sundays—a total of 83 hours. At Princeton, the library building is open a total of 102 hours weekly, although services are not provided at all desks during the late evening hours.[13] (In 1870 the librarian at Princeton or his deputy was required to be in regular attendance twice each week for one hour for delivering books to students, who were allowed to borrow one book at a time.)

The long day that is usually provided for requires large and qualified staffs to handle the increased clienteles in university libraries. Reserve book rooms are generally open all hours that the library is open. Departmental and special collections, because of the budget restrictions and as a result of studies of use, are sometimes not open in the evenings or on week-ends. Librarians, as well as administrative officers, need to examine each situation as a separate problem, and provide service accordingly. On many campuses, despite the fact that the main library may close at 10 P.M., law and medical departmental libraries may provide service until midnight. In every case, however, the library should have one or more professional staff members on duty every hour that the library is open.

HOURS OF WORK. In a recent study, Muller [14] found that the modal practice in 49 libraries was the 40-hour week. The finding is not different from that of a study made in 1940. However, Muller found only one library which had a 44-hour week. The tendency definitely has been to shorten the work week in university libraries, even though the evidence still suggests that the 38 or 39-hour week, or the 7-hour day, is general in libraries.[15] A few libraries have

[13] Princeton University Library. *Handbook, 1953–1954,* inside cover.

[14] "Work Week, Vacations, and Salaries in Medium-Sized Universities and Colleges," *College and Research Libraries,* XV (1954), 84–86.

[15] American Library Association, Board on Personnel Administration. *Personnel Administration for Libraries,* p. 23. A 38-hour working week is suggested.

introduced alternate Saturday work for staffs, reducing the amount of work by three hours weekly. Fewer still have made it possible for acquisition and cataloging staffs to arrange the work week so that every Saturday is a nonworking day.

Understaffed libraries which attempt to offer high standards of service usually find it necessary to demand longer working weeks of their members. This not only makes the work more exacting, but the staff members are deprived of the opportunity of study or of developing themselves in other ways. Muller has shown that when the salary is reduced to an hourly basis, the length of the working week, as well as other factors such as holidays, sick leaves, etc., becomes a crucial item in determining the real income of the staff member.[16]

Hours of service for individual staff members should be considered in relation to hours of opening of the library. Undoubtedly, the longer working week leads some library administrators to use nonprofessional assistance to a greater extent than would be required with the shorter working week. The longer working week also has a direct effect upon the scheduling of individual members of the staff who are responsible for the manning of service desks, as well as upon the assignments of administrative officers.

SUNDAY HOURS. Many of the large university libraries are open for at least a few hours on Sunday afternoons and evenings. In one university library, the circulation desk gives service on Sunday from 2 P.M. to 10 P.M., while the reserve desk is open from 2 P.M. to midnight. Generally, the opening of libraries on Sundays has been the result of the pressure of students living on the campus. In order to keep operating expenses at a minimum, a few institutions open only a part of the building on Sundays. Unless a building is planned so that portions may be satisfactorily closed to users, partial opening may not be practicable. If the students really make use of the library on Sunday, costs of operation, including janitorial and other expenses, should be accepted as part of the normal administrative charges.

[16] "Work Week, Vacations, and Salaries. . . .", p. 86, Table III.

SUMMER AND HOLIDAY HOURS. During the summer sessions, hours of opening are reduced in some institutions. This is related to the shorter working hours of the personnel. Some libraries reduce the working week by four to six hours weekly for each staff member on these curtailed schedules, which usually involve shorter evening hours and Sunday closings.

University libraries are usually closed on important national holidays. Considerable variation, however, occurs in regard to holidays, the variations depending upon the religious affiliation, location, and other characteristics of the institutions. In libraries which remain open on general holidays, staff members who are required to work are usually granted equivalent time off at a later date.

OTHER CONDITIONS OF WORK. Staff members are usually allotted one hour for meals, time not included in the work week. These are ordinarily taken on a schedule, and administrators generally insist that staff members take the full hour. Most libraries permit short periods of relaxation, from 10 to 15 minutes, once or twice a day.

PROFESSIONAL
DEVELOPMENT
OF THE STAFF
It is a generally accepted assumption that the members of the university library staff should continue to develop themselves professionally. One of the acknowledged criteria of a profession is the existence of a group consciousness which centers about homogeneous purposes and activities. This consciousness is made tangible by professional organizations. Within the library itself there is the need for the development of attitudes which will contribute to professional homogeneity.

Primarily it is the responsibility of the librarian to encourage the professional development of staff members. If the librarian has a professional outlook himself, it is likely that his assistants and subordinates will also have a similar attitude toward librarianship. The whole tenor of the library must be conducive to this attitude or staff members are likely to relax their interests in professional responsibility. The head librarian should clarify and reveal to his staff the fundamental criteria of excellence in university library service. Moreover, he should, as the superior officer, provide an organization which basically is regarded as a professional unit by faculty and students. This requires him to be concerned with such factors as ethics, the avoidance of nepotism, morale, fair remuneration, and internal administrative relationships. Professional activity is hindered when friction arising from unethical practices, the appointment of relatives to the staff, low morale, and an unfair salary schedule is permitted to exist among the personnel. No greater obstacle to the development and maintenance of a professional attitude exists than the burdening of professional workers with clerical activities and of clerical workers with professional responsibilities which they cannot effectively perform.

One of the best methods of fostering professional attitudes is the participation of staff members in professional associations. It may be generally observed that those university libraries in which a large proportion of staff members are officers or active participants in library and other associations, write papers for journals, and participate in scholarly projects are ranked high as professional organizations by librarians and educators alike. The attitude of some university librarians that they live in a world alone, unaffected by the developments in libraries through the work of their colleagues, is unrealistic and based on rationalization. Members of the faculties of universities are almost to a man members of their particular societies and associations, and it is expected that librarians will support and participate in the work of their special organizations.

Since the staff is an essential part of the university library, it falls upon the university and library administrations to provide a plan for orienting new personnel and for improving the efficiency of the whole staff.[17] By providing a program of in-service training, by permitting attendance at meetings of library and other scholarly groups, by granting staff members the opportunity of taking courses, by promoting individuals when their work and advanced

[17] American Library Association, Board on Personnel Administration. *Personnel Administration for Libraries*, pp. 46–64.

training indicate that such recognition should be made, by allowing leaves of absence for special study or travel, by selecting staff members for participation in the teaching program for extra pay, and by establishing fellowships for persons who have displayed exceptional ability, the university builds a program that should result in an efficient and scholarly library personnel. Such matters as retirement and insurance must also be carefully considered if an effective staff is to be assembled and maintained.

IN-SERVICE TRAINING   In the last decade, more and more university librarians have established in-service training programs for both their professional and nonprofessional personnel, following the pace set by public librarians.[18] In-service training may be defined as

management's process of aiding employees to gain effectiveness in their present and future work assignments by providing, planning, and organizing a program of systematic instruction and practice on the job in order (1) to point out to the employee the way to apply the body of knowledge gained in pre-entry education and training to the concrete duties of a specific job, and (2) to develop appropriate habits of thought and action, skills, and knowledge essential to effective performance.[19]

In-service training thus becomes a deliberate function of management rather than one reserved to the individual. The program may be designed for orienting or inducting the new staff member, for increasing the efficiency of present staff members, and for preparing certain members of the staff for promotion.

INDUCTING AND TRAINING NEW PERSONNEL. Although professional staff members are expected to have a basic knowledge of library objectives, operations, and techniques, each library has a certain number of individual aims and procedures. In order that new staff members may be inducted with a minimum loss of time, certain devices have been successfully employed. These include the distribution of manuals, handbooks, and similar materials, holding

[18] Tucker, "In-Service Training in Large Public Libraries"; St. John, "Selection, Orientation, and Development of the Professional Staff," *Library Trends,* III (1954), 32–38; Bryan, *The Public Librarian,* chap. x.
[19] Tucker, *op. cit.,* p. 21.

personal conferences between new staff members and their superior officers, providing introductory lectures and inspection tours, offering induction courses, and giving preliminary full-time instruction to new members before they begin work.

TRAINING TO INCREASE EFFICIENCY. All training is intended to increase efficiency of staff members. Yet there are certain procedures which, if followed, would systematically develop the personnel. These include providing professional literature, instituting planned reading courses, encouraging meetings of special groups, sponsoring group discussions and conferences, urging the attendance of staff members at institutes, setting up an experience program whereby members of one department are given a chance to work in or to visit extensively in other departments,[20] assigning special studies of library problems to staff members, offering intermittent or occasional professional courses, participating in cooperative programs with educational organizations and learned societies, and requiring attendance at educational institutions.[21]

TRAINING FOR PROMOTION. Most university libraries have not been systematic in their promotional programs. Every staff member should have the opportunity to advance according to his capacity and ability. Employee morale is based on a fair system of promotions. In general, higher positions should be filled from current staff whenever possible. In order to accomplish this, provision should be made for staff members to understudy for higher positions. Opportunity, however, should be extended to the staff as widely as possible, and all qualified members of the staff should be allowed to apply for a particular position. When the library has kept adequate records and rating sheets on the individual staff members, these should prove helpful in making decisions concern-

[20] A review of the practice of the Library of Congress in regard to interns is given in Goodrum, "L.C. Trains Recruits," *Library Journal*, LXXVII (1952), 393–96.

[21] A few libraries have a special fund which is used to grant financial help to assistants who wish to further their education. *Cf.* Yale University Library. *Staff Manual*, p. 32. Internship programs of several of the large public libraries involve salaries which are sufficently large to permit the student to pay tuition toward a degree. While these involve pre-professional staff members, the programs have been successful in building up the strength of the personnel. St. John, "Selection, Orientation, and Development of the Professional Staff," p. 36.

ing promotions. Experts in the field of personnel have suggested that the opinions of the immediate supervisors are, in most cases, more valuable than those of higher executives in the situations which arise in regard to promotions.[22]

Mention should be made of the "three-position" plan of training for promotion, whereby a staff member trains a subordinate and is in turn trained by his superior. Many libraries have found this a valuable method for the development of departmental heads and senior assistants. Individuals who are selected for promotion may also be required to take additional courses in library school, or, if they are in nonprofessional positions, to attend library school over a prescribed period of time. Some libraries, in addition to providing for the understudy program, also plan job experiences for promising candidates for promotion, or require them to complete a series of special studies on which they either pass an examination or write a report. Most librarians will keep a special file of likely prospects for promotion within a library system.

The advantages of a systematic program of in-service training are clear cut.[23] Not only will it insure continuity of the objectives, policies, and services of a particular library, it will also help materially in stimulating morale and reducing turnover among the more capable members of the staff. Detailed consideration may now be given to some of the more important points raised in this section.

ATTENDANCE AT LIBRARY MEETINGS   Most university libraries provide some funds in their budgets for travel expenses of individual members of the staff.[24] As pointed out in a survey of 78 libraries, these funds are frequently so limited that payment of travel expenses (or partial expenses) to only a few staff members is possible. However, there has been a distinct effort on the part of administra-

[22] Mosher, Kingsley, and Stahl, *Public Personnel Administration*, pp. 179–80.
[23] *Cf.* Stewart, "Library In-Service Training," *Library Journal*, LXXII (1947), 16–18+; 146–48; 200–203.
[24] Pope and Thompson, "Travel Funds for University Library Staffs," *College and Research Libraries*, XI (1950), 22–27.

tors to obtain free time for those professional staff members who wish to attend library conferences. Pope and Thompson suggest that exceptional nonprofessional assistants might, when funds permit, be encouraged to attend such meetings as a recruiting device. In all cases, the administrator of the library is faced with the problem of making certain that services will not be impaired as a result of the absence of staff members who are attending meetings.

There seems to be no question that emphasis on broad professional activities by all members of the staff should be pressed by the administrator. In a few notable cases, where funds have been short, the librarian has remained on duty and allowed other staff members to attend meetings, particularly if the latter were officers or were participating in programs. Distribution of limited funds, so that partial payment of expenses is provided for several staff members, is another way of encouraging large attendance at meetings.

Several differences appear in the regulations governing travel allotments by state and private institutions. Some states allow only the administrative officer to travel outside of the state; others do not permit the use of state funds for conference expenses.

In some private universities travel funds are not distributed to individual departments. The librarian, along with other personnel, has to justify expenses for himself or for members of the staff for attendance at meetings. Ordinarily, however, free time for attendance is permitted.

In the preceding discussion, it is assumed that attendance at library conferences, institutes, workshops, and special meetings is desirable. Participating actively in committee work or on programs, listening to discussions and papers on current problems, exchanging views with colleagues engaged in similar activities, meeting librarians, recruiting staff members, examining new equipment and books which are on display—these are some of the advantages of such attendance. In many ways, the library and the university may be the beneficiary of a more responsible staff with relatively little investment.

OPPORTUNITIES FOR ADVANCED STUDY It is not unusual to find alert members of university library staffs who wish to increase their academic and professional knowledge by taking advanced courses either at the institutions with which they are associated or elsewhere. Many universities have recognized the value of such training and have made it possible for staff members to take courses frequently at reduced fees. The practices vary considerably among the public and private universities in this respect.[25] Few institutions exempt library staff members from the payment of all fees. Some institutions, situated in areas where it is difficult to recruit personnel, make special allowances for librarians in the payment of fees for advanced work. A number of institutions allow librarians to audit courses without payment of fees.

In general, it may be summarized that librarians are allowed to take courses which they believe might benefit them. Many librarians have obtained masters' and doctoral degrees in librarianship and in other subject fields while members of library staffs. In a few instances, there are restrictions as to which courses librarians may take, especially if they appear unrelated to their work.

PROMOTIONS Some attention has been given earlier to in-service training for promotion, as well as to the selection of the librarian and professional and other assistants. One of the major problems faced by university administrators is that of raising the assistant or associate librarian to the chief librarianship. An analysis of library appointments in recent years indicates rather clearly that only in exceptional cases does either the assistant librarian or another member of the staff succeed the retiring incumbent. Although the assistant librarian or a divisional head may be intrusted with the ad-

[25] Cf. "Opportunities for Advanced Study," *Pacific Northwest Library Association Quarterly*, V (1941), 94–95. Although the chart worked out for this survey is somewhat out of date, examination of staff manuals of a number of institutions reveals that the pattern has changed but little. Cf. University of Illinois Library, *Staff Manual*, p. 10. "Full-time professional library staff members may register for courses in the University, and may, at the discretion of the Director, be granted time for such class attendance not to exceed three hours per week. Full-time or part-time staff appointees enrolled in the graduate program of the University shall be exempt from fees, provided the income received for nine months' service does not exceed $2400."

ministration of a library during prolonged absences of the librarian, when the time comes for actual appointment to the chief office he is usually passed over in favor of an outside individual. Generally, the reason for this action on the part of the university lies in the desire to secure a new viewpoint in the library. In other cases, the assistant librarians with ability to operate the library for an occasional period may not be competent to take over complete control. A third reason, and one which has become increasingly important, is the desirability of securing a librarian with advanced training in modern university librarianship.

The university librarian himself is faced with a similar problem when he needs to fill the assistant librarianship or a divisional or departmental headship. Is the divisional librarian or the departmental head the logical person to be selected for the associate or assistant librarianship? If so, which person? Unless an actual library situation is considered, such questions are academic. It is not unusual to find that a new librarian will bring with him a new assistant librarian. In many libraries, however, there are individuals who by experience and training are capable of filling the assistantship. When one of these individuals is as fully equipped as any outside candidate, it would be a sound principle of personnel management to promote him to the position of assistant librarian.

In the selection of a departmental head for the assistant librarianship every endeavor should be made to consider all employees in the organization who may possess the necessary qualifications for the position. Such factors as age, past and present educational achievements, previous experience, connection with the library, professional activities, and the opinion of the librarian enter into the choice of an assistant. Sometimes the librarian may have a committee of the staff to make recommendations which are given consideration in the final selection. Unless an objective viewpoint is maintained, individuals who lack necessary qualities for administrative work may be placed in positions they cannot handle effectively. But librarians are as greatly interested in advancement in their profession as are other workers, and they are entitled to consideration before outsiders are brought in to fill important positions.

Are senior assistants to be considered in selecting a departmental head? In this case, as in the selection of a librarian or an assistant librarian, professional policy calls for a careful consideration of the members of the department. Level of performance, service ratings, promise of future growth, and educational, technical, and personal qualifications are criteria on which promotions should be based. Seniority should not be the principal criterion used in determining fitness for promotion. Long service, without increased efficiency and interest, is usually a reason for passing over a person. If no individual in the department is capable of filling the position as effectively as or better than the retiring individual, then the proper procedure is to select a candidate from the outside. Although non-administrative staff members are to be encouraged to look forward to advancement, the librarian will make promotional adjustments only in so far as they will aid him to administer the library efficiently. In the long run, such a promotional policy should encourage the younger members of the staff to develop their talents for administrative positions. The librarian himself, by judiciously selecting junior members of the staff, can create an organization which will provide capable individuals when the occasion requires it.

TRANSFER OF PERSONNEL. Often it is necessary in large libraries to transfer a staff member from one position to another. In most cases, these changes do not involve a change in salary, which occurs in promotions. A reference assistant is assigned to the catalog department, or vice versa. A cataloger may become an assistant in a departmental library. The possibilities are numerous. Transfers are made when necessary—to take care of increased loads at certain points in the library system, to remove a faulty assignment, personality problems, change of interest in a staff member, or the physical condition of the employee. It may be a positive method for stimulating the interest of the personnel. In some libraries with small staffs, interchange of personnel in the various departments may be useful not only in maintaining morale but may also be a device for economical administration.

Care is essential in the transfer of any individual who is shifted for personality difficulties. Solutions to such problems are seldom found in this step, unless the maladjusted individual is placed in a position where situations for personnel friction are eliminated.

TURNOVER OF PERSONNEL. Turnover of staff is one of the best means of evaluating the personnel policy of a library. If turnover is excessive, it may mean that individuals are anxious to leave the service of the library for certain reasons. It is usually costly to the library, since training becomes overly expensive, and it has a deadening effect upon the staff morale. On the other hand, if there is little or no turnover, the library personnel picture may take on a dull hue. This does not necessarily mean that individuals should not think in terms of a career in a particular library system. Some university libraries have done a remarkable job in training leaders for other library systems.

Industry and business have been much concerned with turnover of staff, primarily because of the financial burden it causes. Libraries have been concerned with it for this reason, as well as for the effect upon the services. There are many causes for turnover, and they differ from staff member to staff member who notifies the librarian that he is leaving. Hoage,[26] who studied turnover in two university libraries, found that if personal reasons such as marriage or wishing to be with a husband were discounted, the major reasons for resignations were economic, such as better opportunities elsewhere, limited chance to grow in a library system, lack of responsibility and challenge, dissatisfaction with status, and low salaries. "Working relations" also represented an important reason for departure.

DEMOTIONS AND DISMISSALS. Demotions in university library service are relatively infrequent. The general practice has been to withhold promotion and salary increases of ineffective individuals. In

[26] "Resignations in Two University Libraries," *College and Research Libraries*, XI (1950), 28–32+.

rarer instances, some staff members, after previous warnings and having been given opportunities to improve their performance, are demoted to a lower grade, with less compensation. Occasionally, it has been necessary for the librarian to remove a staff member in an administrative position because of inefficiency. Such individuals probably should be eliminated from the organization, but circumstances may prevent such action. McDiarmid, writing of tenure in this connection, observed:

Some institutions have tenure cases which have been brewing for many years. I like to call them inherited mistakes of administration. Under good personnel administration they would have been settled long ago, but one supervisor has passed the hot potato on to a second and the second on to a third. I have heard librarians mention people on their staff who should have been discharged ten years ago, when the action would have been fair and just to both parties. Is it fair and just to discharge them now? [27]

When the presence of an ineffective individual in an administrative post affects the smooth functioning of the library and it is impossible to dismiss him, a procedure sometimes employed has been to bring in an outside officer and place him in a superior position to the offending person. Another procedure, but of doubtful value, is to shift the individual to an inferior position in another department. A final procedure is to combine two departments, reducing the rank of the inefficient head. Any such situation is a delicate one and should be handled diplomatically by the librarian if later cooperation is to be expected. For those who have not become intrenched because of tenure reasons, careful scrutiny of service ratings and other records should make it possible for the librarian to reach a decision before situations arise which are similar to those described by McDiarmid.

Dismissal is a serious act, and the librarian should be sure of his evidence before attempting to discharge a staff member on permanent appointment.[28] In cases of financial exigency or the discon-

[27] McDiarmid, "A University Library Personnel Program," in Martin (ed.), *Personnel Administration in Libraries*, p. 81.

[28] American Library Association, Board on Personnel Administration. *Personnel Organization and Procedure*, pp. 21–22, also "Appendix II: Tenure in Libraries," pp.

tinuance of an activity, every effort should be made to relocate the individuals within the library system or to help them find positions elsewhere.

VACATIONS   In most university libraries, professional staff members are granted 26 days of vacation, exclusive of Sundays. Some stipulate one month or 31 days, and if a legal holiday falls within the period, it is extra. Vacation periods for nonprofessional staff members range from two to three weeks, depending on whether or not the individuals are under civil service and subject to the vacation allowances for clerical workers for the entire university.

The utilization of vacations as a means of developing the staffs of university libraries requires systematic attention by the university administration as well as by the librarian or the personnel officer of the library. The management and particularly the planning of a large, complicated library calls for the same kind of opportunity for observation, study, and reflection that is provided for heads of academic departments and schools. Three months may well be allotted at times if the librarian is to fill the role of an effective participator in the formulation of important administrative policies of the university and if he is to help advance librarianship generally. Similarly, when professional members of the staff have made plans for using the vacation period for further equipping themselves for the newer teaching aspects of librarianship, some consideration should be given to the possibility of lengthening the normal vacation period if no inconvenience is caused other members of the staff or if the service of the library is not adversely affected. Most university libraries must be prepared to render full service in all departments during the summer months, as summer sessions are the rule rather than the exception.

As an administrative officer, the chief librarian may well consider carefully the ways in which staff members spend their vacation periods. He should be able to decide whether or not an individual

41–50. This publication suggests steps that should be taken in difficult personnel cases.

is physically strong enough to spend his vacation studying formal courses rather than using the time to recuperate from the nervous strain that may result from a year's work. The duties and responsibilities of administrative officers, as well as the pressure of work upon the subordinate members of the staff, generally require periods of rest as aids to health and efficiency.

Most vacation periods are scheduled for summer months. In large libraries with staffs of forty or more individuals, it is necessary to begin vacation periods early in the year if the program of work is to be maintained at an even pace. Careful attention should be paid to the extent of service demanded by summer-school faculties and students, the amount of materials acquired during the summer months, and other demands upon the library. Rotation of vacation periods among staff members has been followed in some libraries. This procedure makes it possible for each staff member to be on duty during peak loads at least in alternate years.

PARTICIPATION IN TEACHING PROGRAM   The participation of library staff members in the teaching program is primarily associated with either library-school courses or instruction in library use. In a few institutions, however, librarians and other members of the staff participate in the teaching program in fields related to librarianship or in purely subject fields. Law librarians in several of the large universities have given courses in legal literature or other legal subjects. Reference librarians frequently give courses in the English department.

If it is part of the librarian's duty to conduct courses on the basis of his subject background, arrangements should be made for the continuous operation of the library while he is engaged in his class work. The policy of the university in regard to librarianship should determine whether or not teaching is considered an activity beyond the essential requirements of the librarian. Since modern university librarianship requires full-time application, it is clear that any additional teaching duties which the librarian or other staff members perform should be done at extra remuneration or that the time for preparation and for meeting classes be properly adjusted. Close collaboration of the librarian with the deans should result in the use of staff members who are qualified by background and training to teach in regular courses, evening courses, or summer and extension courses. The values to be derived from the use of the library staff for teaching should help considerably in integrating the library with the instructional and research programs of the university. Librarians engaged in teaching are usually given professorial ranking and enjoy the privileges associated with academic status.

ACADEMIC STATUS   No groups of librarians have been more concerned with professional recognition than those attached to universities and colleges.[29] They have argued that their close association with students and faculty members in furthering the educational and research program is sufficient basis for including them in the ranks of the teaching staff or other professional or scientific classification and assuring them of rewards and benefits in keeping with their services. Probably more important is the librarians' contention that their academic training is generally comparable to that of members of the instructional staff to whom faculty ranking, sabbatical leave, permanent tenure, long vacations, retirement and annuity benefits, and inclusion in the general academic activities and ceremonials are automatically given. They object to a classification which differentiates them adversely in these important particulars.

Both Maloy and McMillen found that faculty status for librarians

[29] Two early studies made of professional status of librarians were by Maloy, "Faculty Status of College Librarians," *ALA Bulletin,* XXXIII (1939), 232–33+, and McMillen, "Academic Status of Library Staff Members of Large Universities," *College and Research Libraries,* I (1940), 138–40. Recent statements and studies include Downs, "Academic Status for University Librarians—a New Approach," *College and Research Libraries,* VII (1946), 6–9+; Harrington and Lyle, "Recruiting and Developing a Library Staff," *College and Research Libraries,* VIII (1947), 427–35; Kirkpatrick, "Another Approach to Staff Status," *College and Research Libraries,* VIII (1947), 218–20; Spain, "Faculty Status of Librarians in Colleges and Universities in the South," pp. 45–53; Lundy, "Faculty Ranks of Professional Librarians"; Thompson, "Preparation and Status of Librarians," *Library Trends,* I (1952), 99–101; Muller, "Faculty Rank for Library Staff Members in Medium-Sized Universities and Colleges," *American Association of University Professors Bulletin,* XXXIX (1953), 421–31; Downs, "Are College and University Librarians Academic?" *College and Research Libraries,* XV (1954), 9–14.

did not have general recognition in the institutions they studied. They found that faculty status was ordinarily given to the head librarian and the chief assistants but not to the subordinate professional staff members.

In 14 of 35 institutions surveyed by Lundy, the library professional staff were identified with the teaching and research staff; in 8, the library staff were given faculty rank with varying reservations and limitations; in 7, the librarians indicated an interest in securing academic rank; and in the remaining group, "the assignment of academic rank was not regarded as the most convenient or suitable means of securing the recognition to which the majority of professionally trained librarians in the academic community would appear to be entitled at the present time." [30]

Much of the difficulty in the solution of the question of status has revolved about the question of salary. As Thompson has noted: "One fact is still abundantly and painfully obvious: in most academic institutions the salaries of librarians of all ranks are still distinctly lower than salaries for corresponding ranks in the teaching faculty. A survey conducted in 1950 by a special committee of the University of Kentucky chapter of the American Association of University Professors revealed that in only one of fifteen comparable institutions were library salaries higher for ranks corresponding to associate professor, assistant professor and instructor." [31] Spain[32] found that although library staffs were reported to receive salaries similar to those of faculty members in 55 out of 100 cases, frequently the librarians' salaries were in the lowest brackets of comparable ranks. Muller [33] has demonstrated that if professional assistants are compared to instructors, and library departmental heads with assistant professors, the salaries of the librarians on a twelve-month basis tend to be lower than the nine-month salaries of teachers of comparable rank.

[30] Lundy, "Faculty Rank of Professional Librarians," p. 122.
[31] "Preparation and Status of Librarians," p. 99.
[32] "Faculty and Status of Librarians in Colleges and Universities in the South," pp. 45–53.
[33] "Faculty Rank for Library Staff Members in Medium-Sized Universities and Colleges," pp. 430–31.

The objections of administrative officers and faculties of universities toward giving faculty rank to librarians have included both financial and other reasons. With the establishment of retirement systems in all state institutions, and general coverage in private institutions, the financial reason is no longer a valid one. The objections relating to the academic preparation, to the fact that library staffs are predominately women, and to the absence of formal teaching responsibilities on the part of librarians are not always as easy to answer, even though librarians have insisted that their professional duties are instructional in nature.

Although a number of institutions, such as Louisiana and Illinois, have introduced faculty rank for librarians, the issue is by no means a settled one. As Lundy and Downs have pointed out, there are a number of librarians who do not themselves consider faculty rank the answer to the question of status of librarians. The main argument suggests that the character of the training and the criteria for advancement for librarians are quite different from those of teachers. Library work as a whole is not considered to be the same as instructional work. In time, perhaps a satisfactory solution to the question will be found. In the meantime, it may be observed that the tendency for the last decade has been to extend faculty academic status to the professional library staff members who, by virtue of their educational background and responsibility, warrant such recognition. There appears to be no question about giving faculty rank to any member of the library staff who engages in formal class work as part of his duties.

LEAVES OF ABSENCE FOR STUDY OR PROJECTS. The decision as to whether or not staff members may be permitted to spend a semester or a year in study or to work on a project is usually made by the librarian, with the approval of the administration. As a professional procedure, the granting of such permission to capable individuals is a desirable one. In recent years, a number of staff members, as well as head librarians, have been included among the Fulbright scholars. In all cases, it is necessary to arrange for a capable substitute so that the service of the library will not suffer.

The possibility of losing staff members to other libraries after they have taken advantage of leaves of absence for study, especially those involving scholarships and fellowships, has been recognized as a risk of the arrangement. In the long run, the profession has gained by this advanced study, as additional leaders are developed. In those instances in which the members return to their positions, the libraries benefit by the extra training the individuals have received and the institutions have been provided with stronger staffs. Definite agreements should be made in regard to responsibility for returning, as well as for possible promotion, retirement payments, and other matters affecting the staff member's future.

The release of staff members to serve on survey teams and as consultants on library building or other projects is fairly common. Administrative officers have recognized that librarians, in ways similar to those followed by the professorial staff, can make contributions to other institutions, private industry, and agencies of the government. Many surveys of libraries have been made by librarians who have been granted the necessary time by their presidents.

SABBATICAL LEAVES. The university administration that is cognizant of the responsibilities of the librarian in education and research will provide the opportunity for him to spend a year in study, travel, observation, or work on a special project. Librarianship is a rapidly changing profession. If a librarian is to keep apace with the advance in education and research, he should have time to extend his knowledge of his own or related fields.

Usually, sabbatical leaves are granted only to head librarians. In some of the state universities, where sabbatical leaves are not granted, special arrangements may have to be made in order that the librarian may take a year off for special study. In some of the private institutions, sabbatical leaves may be granted to those staff members who have faculty ranking.

FELLOWSHIPS. Talented members of the library staff in a few institutions have been provided grants-in-aid or fellowships to attend library schools or graduate schools for additional training.

Unfortunately, since funds have been limited for this purpose, this has been done on a relatively minor scale. The benefits which are derived from such a procedure are similar to those gained from the policy of granting leaves of absence. The recipients of the awards, however, are generally required to return to their positions for a stipulated period.

RETIREMENT. Pension plans and retirement systems are of special interest to university librarians, just as they are to other employees in education, business, or government. In a review of the available information as reported in the literature up to 1950, Bitting [34] disclosed a variety of annuity and retirement practices. In state universities where retirement and pension systems apply to all employees, librarians are included in the schemes. Librarians are not always included in separate annuity systems for academic employees. Bitting further observed that "the larger college and university libraries have better coverage by retirement systems than do the smaller institutions." [35]

Few of the studies listed by Bitting are confined solely to university librarians. Stieg,[36] however, tabulated his findings on the basis of type of institution. Table 10 shows the plans in 44 public and 22 private universities. On the basis of information supplied by the group of 403 institutions which replied to the questionnaire distributed by the ALA Committee on Annuities, Pensions, and Life Insurance, Stieg observed that "the professional staff is eligible to participate in the retirement plans of about three-fourths of the institutions which have them for the faculty. Plans covering librarians are probably available in a little less than one-half of all the four-year institutions of higher education in the United States." [37]

Nonprofessional assistants have less opportunity to participate

[34] Bitting, "A Survey of Libraries and Librarians under Pension Plans," in American Library Association, Committee on Annuities, Pensions, and Life Insurance, *Retirement for Librarians*, p. 24.
[35] *Ibid.*, p. 34.
[36] "Retirement Plans for College and University Librarians," *College and Research Libraries*, XI (1950), 10–16.
[37] *Ibid.*, p. 16.

in pension plans than do professional librarians. Evidence of this appears in the figures shown in Table 10.

TABLE 10 *: DISTRIBUTION OF LIBRARIANS UNDER RETIREMENT
PLANS IN 66 UNIVERSITIES

	PUBLIC		PRIVATE	
	Number	Percent	Number	Percent
Institutions replying	44		22	
Faculty status for librarians	14	32	10	25
Administrative officer status for librarians, but not faculty	6	14	3	13
No retirement plan for faculty	2	5	3	14
Retirement plan for faculty				
State plan	20	47	0	0
T.I.A.A. plan	14	33	10	63
Other plan	9	20	6	37
Professional library staff included in faculty retirement plan	32	73	15	69
Clerical staff included in faculty retirement plan	25	57	8	36
Chief librarians only included	5	11	3	14
Separate plan for professional staff	5	11	1	5
Separate plan for clerical staff	10	23	2	9
Compulsory participation institutions with retirement plan	31	72	8	50
Voluntary participation—institutions with retirement plan	7	16	5	31

* Source: Stieg, "Retirement Plans for College and University Librarians," p. 11.

The lack of provision for retirement of university library workers, particularly in older and larger institutions, has a direct effect upon the type of service rendered. Trustees of universities have not always recognized this fact. The economic objectives of a retirement system are the elimination of inefficient individuals, the attraction of a high type of personnel, and the maintenance of consistently high morale objectives, which if attained result in advantage to the institution which provides the system. The social objective—provision against insecurity because of old age or disability—seems to be as necessary in the case of librarians as it does in that of any other class of workers.

Probably the soundest system of retirement requires contributions from both the employees and the university. The noncontributory plan, under which the university pays all the cost, is objected to because it has the characteristics of a charity and because, in times of financial difficulties, the university may discontinue or reduce the benefits.

The ALA Retirement Plan is designed for librarians in general. In 1954 about 1,400 librarians were active participants in it, and the number has been decreasing annually. Since most of the participants in this plan are not under a joint-contributory arrangement, the pensions will in these cases not be adequate to meet the needs of the retired librarians. The addition of Social Security coverage to include librarians helps to some degree.

PERSONAL INSURANCE. In those institutions in which pension and retirement plans are in effect, the employees are generally protected for disability and their dependents receive benefits in case of death. A large number of universities which may or may not have retirement plans for employees having academic rank provide plans of group insurance for both academic and nonacademic workers. Such plans usually terminate upon the withdrawal of the individual from the university service. Librarians of administrative rank who do not have academic rank are generally permitted to take out group insurance up to $5,000 if their salaries are $3,000 or more annually. Other library employees may participate in the plan in proportion to the salary received, the length of service rendered, and age.

Many institutions also provide opportunity for both professional and clerical staffs to participate in hospital and medical insurance plans. These plans are generally arranged through negotiations with commercial insurance agencies.

STAFF
RELATIONS
Success in staff coordination and cooperation is often influenced by the personal attitudes of individual staff members. In business and industry much attention has been given to such matters as working conditions and employee efficiency, manager-employee relations, employee dissatisfaction, and the social organization of employees. In recent years, increasing attention has also been given to the problems of librarians both as workers and as individuals.

Librarians, like other workers, have strengths and failings—ambitions, prejudices, and special interests—and are subject to the emotional, mental, and physical disturbances which beset all mankind. The chief librarian and other administrative officers should consciously strive to adjust personnel difficulties whenever they have a direct bearing upon the work of the library. This calls for a keen understanding of human relationships.

The following means and methods of developing inter-employee relationships are not offered as panaceas to insure smooth interaction of library services, but they have been employed successfully in developing morale in a number of institutions. They will be of considerable value if the basic personnel organization of the library is not well developed. On the other hand, if a policy of cooperation and coordination is firmly established and each member of the staff is encouraged to regard himself and his work as vital to the whole organization, much will have been done to insure efficient interaction as well as personal happiness. In this section consideration will be given to (1) staff ethics, (2) physical conditions and staff rooms, (3) staff recreation, (4) health of the staff, (5) staff associations, (6) staff meetings, (7) committees, (8) staff publications, (9) staff manuals, and (10) democracy in staff organization.

STAFF ETHICS [38]   The development of a professional consciousness is generally accompanied by a codification of ideal practices and relationships which, if followed, should improve the standards of the group and act as a deterrent upon those who may be guided by selfish motives. Despite weaknesses stemming from human frailty, ethical codes have had some influence in furthering such aims in medicine, law, engineering, education, and other professions. The possible applications to librarianship are clear.

Not only do individuals who enter librarianship assume an obligation to support ethical standards of behavior in relation to society and the governing body under whose authority they work, but

[38] Some of the points made in this section have been adapted from the Code of Ethics drawn up by a Committee of the American Library Association and published in the *ALA Bulletin*, XXXIII (1939), 128–30.

they are also obligated to maintain such standards in relation to the library constituency (faculty and students in the case of the university library), to their fellow-workers, and to the library profession generally. These ethical relationships may be divided more simply into those which are external, involving society and the governing authority, and those which are internal, involving interactions within the library.

ETHICAL RELATIONS TO SOCIETY AND THE GOVERNING AUTHORITY. Since the state university is part of a governmental unit, its employees are subject to state laws. To demonstrate how the state laws affect the library and its workers, even though indirectly, the relevant sections of the North Carolina Statutes [39] may be cited.

While specific references in the Statutes to personal manipulations in office for private profit on the part of trustees of public institutions are few, enough is included to make it clear that these officers are liable to penalties for using their positions for personal aggrandizement.

The portion of the Statutes dealing with "Misconduct in Public Office," for example, provides: (1) that a director of a public trust who contracts for his own benefit or makes a contract with another is guilty of a misdemeanor; [40] that a board member, director, manager, trustee, or employee of any educational, charitable, eleemosynary, or penal institution who receives any pecuniary benefit or gift for furnishing the institution any kind of supplies is subject to removal, guilty of a misdemeanor, and liable to fine and imprisonment at the direction of the court; [41] and (3) that "if any county board of education or school committee shall buy school supplies in which any member has a pecuniary interest, or if any school officers or teachers shall receive any gift, emolument, reward or promise of reward for influence in recommending or procuring the use of any school supplies for the schools for which they are connected, such person shall be removed from his position

[39] *The General Statutes of North Carolina . . .* [1943]. Ed. by A. H. Michie [and others].
[40] *Ibid.,* §14-234.   [41] *Ibid.,* §14-236.

in the public service and shall, upon conviction, be deemed guilty of a misdemeanor." [42] The part concerned with "Officers of State Institutions" states that "the directors, stewards, and superintendents of the state institutions shall not trade directly or indirectly with or among themselves, or with any concern in which they are interested, for any supplies needed by any such institutions." [43]

In the awarding of offices, restrictions are also imposed. Any person bargaining, buying or selling an office is guilty of a misdemeanor and is subject to removal and to imprisonment and fine at the discretion of the court.[44] The portion devoted to "Offices and Public Officers" provides that "all bargains, bonds and assurances made or given for the purchase or sale of any office whatsoever, the sale of which is contrary to law, shall be void," [45] and that any official or employee exacting a part of the salary of a subordinate is guilty of a misdemeanor and subject to removal.[46] Evidence of efforts to prevent any improper influence of board members also appears in the provisions that no board member of a state institution may be elected to any office under his board after the expiration of his membership in the board [47] and that "no person shall be appointed to any place or position in any of the state institutions under the supervision of the state board who is related by blood or marriage to any member of the state board or to any of the principal officers, superintendents, or wardens of state institutions." [48]

Although the last citation is strictly applicable only to institutions under the North Carolina State Board of Charities and Public Welfare, it raises the question of nepotism, which is equally important to libraries and schools. While favoritism to relatives is not so strong a force in a democratic society as it might be in a less impersonal one, it does exist and has been recognized by specific measures. A direct application to the university library is found in the following statement of the University of California "Staff Manual":

[42] *Ibid.*, §14-237.   [43] *Ibid.*, §143-113.   [44] *Ibid.*, §14-238.
[45] *Ibid.*, §128-3.   [46] *Ibid.*, §128-4.   [47] *Ibid.*, §143-11.
[48] *Ibid.*, §108-9.

Near relatives shall not be employed in the same department or division unless authorized by the President of the University. This includes: parents and children; husbands and wives; brothers and sisters; brothers-in-law and sisters-in-law; uncles; aunts; nieces and nephews.[49]

The establishment of laws against bargaining in materials or offices has as its objective the protection of public funds and institutions from exploitation by individuals and from the intrusion of considerations other than usefulness and economy in supplies and equipment and merit in personnel. Provisions against nepotism, in libraries as well as in other institutions, are designed to secure the individual independence of staff members and to prevent the development of conditions in which personal or family loyalties can interfere with the unhampered use of professional judgment. The legal or regulatory provisions made to this end are simply means by which action can be taken against officers violating these rules.

While legal statutes are not incorporated into institutional rulings of private institutions, they indirectly apply. Ethical standards in regard to purchasing and employment must be maintained in private as well as in public institutions. The library personnel must maintain strict business relationships with all agents and dealers who supply materials. Employment should be based on the qualifications of the individuals involved. Unless employment of relatives is permitted by the institution, nepotism must be scrupulously avoided.

ETHICAL RELATIONS WITHIN THE LIBRARY. The university library is not an entity in itself but a part of the institution with which it is associated. As such, the book collections and the organization and administration of the library should be carefully planned to provide the most efficient and the fullest service to students and faculty. This obligation places a responsibility of loyalty upon each member of the staff, from the chief librarian to the student assistant.

The attitudes which comprise loyalty in librarianship are not different from those demanded in other professions. Placing the interest of the institution before that of one's self is essential. Con-

[49] University of California, Library, *Staff Manual*, p. 18. See also University of California, *Personnel Rules for Nonacademic Employees*. Rule 7.1. Also includes "first cousins."

structive criticism of library policies and services, or of superior officers or other members of the staff, should be made through channels established by the library and available to all staff members. The provision of such channels is essential to the maintenance of effective organization.

The administrator can do much to eliminate personal friction by furnishing information regarding the library to staff members. Facts concerning the vital interests of the library should be made known to the staff. In some libraries the practice of not divulging information which concerns the staff as a group has resulted in creating misunderstanding and lowering confidence and morale in general. There is nothing so disturbing to the morale of staff members as to learn of important developments in their library from someone who is not a part of the library personnel.

Since the members of the staff are the representatives and interpreters of the library to students and faculty members, individual contacts are important. All persons entitled to use the library, therefore, should be given impartial and courteous treatment. Those staff members who are in direct contact with the constituency of the library are in a strategic position to create cordial relationships between patron and library.

Each department bears a definite relation to the whole service of the library. This fact requires each departmental head to review the work of his unit in relation to that of every other department and not attempt to impress upon others the indispensability of his own activities. Only in this way can understanding of and mutual responsibility for the library's service be developed.

The relations between subordinates of a department and its head should be in harmony. Opportunity for making suggestions on the part of assistants should not only be granted but should definitely be provided for by the head. New ideas are rare, and stifling the imagination of the young assistant may result in creating attitudes and behavior patterns which will limit the service of the library. Adjustment of differences between members of the department should be made by the head of the department. Assistants who

feel that they have been unfairly treated should discuss their grievances with the departmental head before appealing to the assistant
librarian or librarian. The assistants themselves should be willing
to accept criticisms by the head without personal resentment and
without the need of heated discussions with their fellow-workers.

An impersonal relationship between the student, clerical, or nonprofessional workers and the professional staff should be maintained. Assistants should be promoted on the basis of merit rather
than because of personal friendships. Granting personal favors
which affect the service of the library or staff morale should be
avoided. Adherence to the administrative principle "unity of command," which requires that a subordinate shall be responsible to
one officer only, is essential to the maintenance of harmonious relations. Although such practices as these are not new and are common
to business, industry, and the professions, they are not given the
consideration they deserve in some library systems.

The development of a profession requires the participation of its
members in those activities which generate a consciousness of
service. A profession is a brotherhood. The activities of a profession
are so definite and absorbing in interest, so rich in duties and responsibilities, that they completely engage their adherents. Thus,
group consciousness, expressed in an organization of the professional
group for its mutual improvement and the improvement of the
public service, develops from common interests and problems.
Criticism of professional organizations as not accomplishing certain ends should be accompanied by the willingness to do something positive in bettering the organizations. The librarian who
thinks he can work in a vacuum has not really developed a professional sense.

To acquire the group consciousness that is characteristic of professions, membership in library, educational, scientific, and other
cultural organizations and active participation in conferences,
meetings, and on committees are necessary. The place that librarianship will take among other professions that are interested in improving and developing social life and culture depends largely

upon the efforts of librarians to integrate their work with that of other humanistic and scientific agencies.

The university librarian can help materially in the furtherance of the ideals of librarianship by encouraging only those individuals who through ability and personality can contribute to the development of the profession. This requires honesty in the librarian's recommendations of persons who wish to enter library school or who apply for positions. Personal animosities should not enter into recommendations, particularly when it is often not possible for the victims of the blackballing to defend themselves. Within the library the librarian should be concerned with the maintenance of adequate salary schedules, proper working conditions, and inter-employee relations. Criticism of other librarians or of practices of other libraries should be avoided unless they are made to fulfill a professional end.

PHYSICAL CONDITIONS AND STAFF ROOMS   Industry and business have gone a long way in making working conditions attractive and comfortable for workers. Poor physical conditions make it difficult if not impossible for some libraries to recruit able workers. Such conditions are frequently related to discontent and a high turn-over, and consequently, higher operating expenses. In the long run, the institution does not save anything by inertia in providing a modern, safe, attractive, and efficient building. Well-lighted and spacious work rooms, adequate heating and ventilation (even air-conditioning in sections of the country which require it), sound-proofing, and up-to-date furniture and equipment go a long way in helping to secure and hold a satisfied staff.[50]

The presence of well-appointed staff rooms in the library building contributes greatly to the satisfaction of the library staff. Care taken in providing for the welfare of the staff through a staff room is profitable not only in conserving the strength of the personnel but also in building morale. The fact that the discomfort of library workers affects adversely the amount or quality of work is gen-

[50] Fussler (ed.), *Library Buildings for Library Service.*

erally recognized in the provision of staff rooms in new library buildings. Such space has also been provided in many older buildings through the conversion of quarters which had been designed for other purposes.

Used for personal needs and group occasions, the staff room can serve as a center for staff development. To the individual, it is a place to relax during the lunch hour or between working hours. To the staff as a whole, it may serve as a meeting place for teas, parties, and discussions of common problems.

STAFF RECREATION   One of the practices that is characteristic of many American university libraries in improving staff relationships is the afternoon tea. Practically all librarians permit such attendance, provided there is no disruption of the work of service departments. The use of working time for teas has been considered justifiable because of the beneficial effects of a brief rest period. It is important, however, that departmental heads do not permit the teas to develop into uncontrolled social gatherings. Staff rooms are usually equipped with kitchens and supplies for such activities. Staff members are generally allowed ten to fifteen minutes of free time for this purpose.

Another method for developing social relationships between staff members is the occasional dance, party, or picnic. Like the tea, these gatherings can serve to break down artificial personal barriers and promote a group consciousness that may be effective in building up a high level of service.

HEALTH OF THE STAFF   Mental health and personal poise of staff members are essential if satisfactory service is to be given students and faculty members. Staff members who are handicapped by ill health or physical disability constantly require medical attention and special leaves of absence. Their requests for irregular dispensations, beyond the usual sick-leave provisions, often work to the disadvantage of the more capable and responsible staff members. Frequently it is difficult to dismiss such individuals, and they are shifted from department to department in order to find a place in which they can work with the least inconvenience to patrons and fellow-workers.

In some of the larger libraries considerable attention has been given to this problem. New appointees to the staff are examined with reference to their state of health and physical fitness. Plans for the conservation of the health of employees during their working periods are instituted as a method of reducing loss of time from illness and of lessening the library's liability for benefits to employees provided under insurance or retirement programs. The establishment of rest rooms in the library building and the provision of medical service through the university hospital or clinic afford concrete evidence of the university's interest in this problem.

STAFF ORGANIZATIONS   To keep in pace with the progress of organization of workers in all fields, university librarians have given some consideration to the question of unions and staff associations. Except in some public and special libraries, staff members have not been concerned to any extent with unions. In a few instances members of university library staffs have joined local units of teachers unions which are affiliated with the American Teachers Union. As Phelps has pointed out, it is relatively easy to explain the limited success of trade unions among library staff members.[51] Most library employees work for public institutions, and the remainder for nonprofit public service institutions. Ninety percent of the librarians are women. As professional white-collar workers, widely dispersed in small groups throughout the country in most cases, library workers do not represent a group of employees who would attract union organizers. There have been, however, sporadic efforts, particularly in the large cities, on the part of unions to interest staff members of university libraries, particularly nonprofessional assistants, in joining various units of unions. But as Phelps further observes, "It is clear that neither the temperament

[51] Orme W. Phelps, "Organizations of Employees," in Martin (ed.), *Personnel Administration in Libraries*, pp. 94–113.

nor the surroundings of the library staff lend themselves to typical hard-hitting American business unionism, with its class-conflict basis and its anti-employer methodology." [52]

A number of librarians, particularly those in institutions which have given them academic status, are members of the American Association of University Professors. The association has a special committee on academic freedom and tenure, and investigates cases of alleged unjustified dismissals of associates. During its history the association has censured university and college administrations for not observing the generally recognized principles of academic freedom and tenure. The association maintains an employment service, and has made a number of studies relating to salaries and conditions of work.

The movement toward organization in university libraries, instead of following the line of unionization, has taken the form of staff associations. Such associations exist in several of the larger university libraries. Usually they have been started by members of the staff as a social or professional group, and they have been useful instruments for carrying out group action. In some cases the librarian has suggested the organization of staff members.

National recognition of staff associations and groups affiliated with unions is evident in the formation of the Staff Organizations Round Table of the American Library Association in 1939. In a study of staff associations in 1939, it was found that such groups existed in nine institutions.[53] Since that time a number of other university libraries have established staff associations. The Round Table of the American Library Association has published (since June, 1938), *SORT*, which records the activities of the various groups which are members.

Although the chief administrative officers of the library may not be members of a staff association, they are usually consulted in any action which concerns problems of internal administration. The

[52] *Ibid.*, pp. 106–7.
[53] Lodge, "Staff Associations in University Libraries," *California Library Association Bulletin*, II (1940), 135–37.

association as a group (or representatives of the group as such) is not permitted to communicate with the trustees, president, or faculty library committee concerning questions which should be proposed by the chief administrative officers of the library.

SOCIAL ACTIVITY. As social organizations, staff associations apparently have been largely successful in their purposes of orienting new staff members and providing social entertainment for a group of individuals who, in the main, have homogeneous interests. They have shown interest in programs and projects which are motivated by the desire to increase the efficiency of the library through a satisfied staff. Many programs have sought to combine social activities with informative papers and addresses.

PROFESSIONAL ACTIVITY. The activities of staff associations on a professional level have been concerned with staff status, staff morale, and library problems.

In some libraries, the chief librarian has worked closely with staff associations on matters relating to faculty rank, tenure, salary increases, promotions, sabbatical leaves, retirement allowances, attendance at conferences and meetings, leaves of absence for study, sick leave, and participation in academic functions and on university committees. Usually the staff associations, through committees, work up the materials for presentation to the university library administration, which, in turn, presents them to the university officials. The alert university librarian has found the staff association a useful ally in promoting interest in the development of a positive personnel program.

Staff associations have been successful also in improving staff morale. In a number of instances, they have sought and succeeded in securing the privilege of attending faculty functions, of using the faculty club, and of participating in academic functions. Within the staff itself, more evidence of coordinated activity has been achieved. Grievances among the staff members have been eliminated, disciplinary cases have been settled to the satisfaction of the group, staff schedules have been worked out with regard to personal problems, and interdepartmental cooperation has been strengthened.

The accomplishments of staff associations include: compiling orientation and staff manuals, establishing rental libraries, improving rest rooms, setting up browsing rooms, organizing professional libraries, issuing library handbooks and other publications, studying physical conditions so that new furnishings or equipment may be obtained, and participating in personnel classification plans.

In several institutions staff associations have taken up such tasks as acquainting new faculty members and students with the various services of the libraries, considering ways and means of improving departmental relations, suggesting new devices for improving services, and advising the librarian on building and other matters. Obviously, all of these activities should help to integrate the library in the instructional program of the university.

Since it is interested in the total service of the library, the staff association can promote departmental coordination. Interdepartmental relations may be clarified when they are considered at open staff meetings. Staff associations have also been instrumental in improving service by arranging for the interchange of staff members and by sponsoring trips of staff members to other libraries. Many of their activities have been directed toward stimulating the growth and development of the personnel.

Funds collected by staff associations, either as dues or for other purposes, have been used for maintaining staff quarters, purchasing books and periodicals for staff use, promoting social gatherings, establishing loan funds for study, sending staff members to library conferences, and paying honorariums for speakers at programs.

In those libraries in which no staff association exists, group action occurs through informal luncheons, monthly or annual meetings, committees for various activities, teas and parties, professional discussion groups, library clubs, and staff news sheets. Each of these activities has been profitably used to foster coordination and cooperation among the staff members and to maintain or develop a professional spirit.

STAFF MEETINGS   To clarify situations which involve interdepartmental relations or to inform the personnel of important library problems, staff meetings are usually called by the librarian. These meetings may involve the entire staff, the professional staff only, divisional and departmental librarians, or professional school librarians. In the larger libraries, a supervisors' council may meet regularly. In addition, meetings within a particular department may occasionally be held when special problems arise.

Meetings of the entire staff in large libraries present difficulties in matters of attendance and are seldom held. In smaller libraries, periodic meetings of the whole staff may be possible. In order to include the whole staff, some librarians call meetings before or after library hours, or during periods when the university is not in session—the week before the institution opens in the fall or during intervals between quarters or semesters.

Agenda for meetings should be carefully prepared, so that the time devoted to them will be spent profitably. The staff meeting provides an excellent opportunity for exchanging views on pressing problems of procedures, services, and personnel matters, as well as for introducing new plans or changes in organization. Prior information to the participants usually insures lively discussion. Reports on matters discussed in restricted meetings should be made to the entire staff as soon as possible after the meetings.

In some instances, staff meetings are attended by members of the university administration and faculty members. Frequently, these individuals participate in the program, particularly if the program has been designed to integrate the work of the library in some way in the instructional and research activities of the institution.

Many librarians have found it desirable to include nonprofessional staff members at certain meetings. These members of the staff have a responsible part in the efficiency of the library service, and their participation can promote their interest.

COMMITTEES   Four types of committees are found in university libraries: (1) the library council of a system of libraries, (2) the committee of librarians of departmental and school libraries, (3) the librarians' committee within an individual library, and (4) the committee of committees of the library staff. The activities of these committees differ from one another in a relative sense.

The term "library council" is sometimes used in the same sense as "library committee" within an individual library. However, a "library council" may describe a group of librarians who represent their individual libraries within a university or state system. The library council in this sense can be a coordinating agency for all the libraries of the system, which are sometimes located at different points on a particular campus and sometimes in various parts of a single community or a state.

The purpose of such councils is to plan for the library system as a whole, to formulate constructive policies, and to introduce co-operative measures so far as possible. Cooperation begins at home, and in the library council there is an active agency for screening projects and problems so that a university administration or a state government will be given as full a return on its investment in libraries as is possible.

A second type of committee includes librarians representing the various departmental and school libraries of a single university. The librarians of the units meet with the director of libraries at stated times—usually about twice a month—to discuss such matters of library policy as are common to the whole system. The importance of the meetings increases as the independence of the units in such matters as budgets, selection of personnel, and internal administration decreases. University library systems with a number of departmental and professional school libraries may well consider the possibilities of a committee of this type, since through its meetings steps may be taken to promote effective cooperative undertakings in all services.

The third type of committee is composed of the departmental and divisional heads of a library. Although the university librarian retains full control of the administration of the library, important powers may be delegated to this committee. The committee may, for example, have a strong voice in decisions concerning promotions. In some libraries, such committees deal with problems relating to the distribution of clerical help, disciplinary cases, rules and regulations of the libraries, staff activities, installation of new equipment, and techniques for the expansion or improvement of service.

The fourth type of committee of librarians has arisen out of the development of staff associations or the director's decision to place some of the responsibilities of running the library in the hands of a few individuals. In the first case the staff association may appoint various committees (social, departmental relations, personnel, etc.), which may confer with the librarian regarding their sphere of operation. The existence of administrative committees, whether they are part of the staff association or appointed by the librarian, does not mean that the head has relieved himself of ultimate responsibility for decisions.

STAFF PUBLICATIONS The staff publication has enjoyed a good deal of popularity in recent years and may be extremely useful in library personnel management. Its purposes are: (1) to express common interests and to supplement personal contacts; (2) to inform staff members of the professional and personal activities of members of the staff; (3) to relate the activities of departments or of departmental and professional school libraries to those of the system as a whole; (4) to record happenings in the scholarly world which are relevant to university librarianship. Like other methods of increasing cooperation and coordination in a complex organization, the bulletin should be used to focus the activities of the staff on integrated policies. Staff meetings and memoranda should be correlated with the bulletin.

Many staff publications are issued by library staff associations. In addition to a discussion of library activities, they include book reviews, articles on library problems, descriptions of collections, and miscellaneous bibliographical items. In some instances, they also contain lists of recent acquisitions.

Members of the staff may also serve as editors of publications issued as organs of friends groups. These publications have been increasing recently in libraries, and they serve an important function in developing public relations.

STAFF MANUALS   Staff manuals [54] are common administrative devices in libraries. These manuals usually provide a description of the library in action. They serve as a statement of details of policies and procedures, assign responsibilities, present a clear interpretation of the functions of the library to employees scattered in various departments, and promote uniform understanding and practice. They are also useful in instructing the university administration and the faculties in the facilities and services of the library.

Both staff bulletins and staff manuals should be edited carefully and presented in attractive format. Staff manuals serve an especially useful purpose in providing students of librarianship with basic information concerning library programs, and copies should be sent to library schools if they are reproduced for outside distribution.

DEMOCRACY IN STAFF ORGANIZATION   In the preceding sections of this chapter attention has been directed to a series of means by which the librarian may develop among his staff an understanding of common problems and instill in them a feeling of being a vital part of the library organization. There is a strong correlation between forceful administration and democracy in staff organization.

Although adherence to the administrative principle of centralized control in the hands of the chief is recognized as a necessity for effective management, participation of as many members of the staff as possible in the organizational activities leads to an *esprit de corps* that is generally reflected in a high grade of service. Not only through participation in book-selection activities and the preparation of annual or special reports, but through such means as cooperating in surveys, consulting on new appointments to the staff,

[54] Wilson and Tauber, "Staff Manuals in College and University Libraries," *College and Research Libraries*, II (1941), 126–35. See also Lyle, *The Administration of the College Library*, pp. 296–98.

making suggestions for improvements in service, and working on responsible committees or on projects, the whole library staff may establish an effective, democratic organization.

BIBLIOGRAPHY

American Library Association. Board of Personnel Administration. Personnel Administration for Libraries: A Bibliographic Essay. Prepared by Ralph E. McCoy, assisted by a Subcommittee on Bibliography. Chicago, 1953. Includes comprehensive bibliographies on all aspects of personnel.
———— Personnel Organization and Procedure: A Manual Suggested for College and University Libraries. Chicago, 1952.
American Library Association. Committee on Annuities, Pensions, and Life Insurance. Retirement for Librarians. Ed. by Herbert Goldhor. Chicago, 1951.
Berelson, Bernard (ed.). Education for Librarianship: Papers Presented at the Library Conference, University of Chicago, August 16–21, 1948. Chicago, American Library Association, 1949.
Boots, Rose. "Preparation of a Staff Manual," *Special Libraries*, XLIII (1952), 265–67.
Bryan, Alice I. The Public Librarian. New York, Columbia University Press, 1952.
Bryant, Douglas W., and Boynton S. Kaiser. "A University Library Position, Classification, and Compensation Plan," *Library Quarterly*, XVII (1947), 1–17.
California, University of. Personnel Rules for Non-academic Employees. Berkeley, 1947.
California, University of, Library. Staff Manual. Comp. by Committee of the Staff Association of the Library. Berkeley, University of California Library, 1938 (typewritten).
"Classification Act of 1949," *United States Statutes at Large*, Vol. 63, Pt. 1. Washington, U.S. Government Printing Office, 1950.
"College and University Library Salary Statistics, 1953–54 (as of September 1, 1954), (Group I)," *College and Research Libraries*, XVI (1955), 40–41.
"Current Trends in Personnel Administration," *Library Trends*, III (1954), 3–94.
Danton, J. Periam. "Our Libraries—the Trend Toward Democracy," *Library Quarterly*, IV (1934), 16–27.
Downs, Robert B. "Academic Status for University Librarians—a New Approach," *College and Research Libraries*, VII (1946), 6–9+.

———— "Are College and University Librarians Academic?" *College and Research Libraries*, XV (1937), 9–14.

Dunbar, Ralph M. "Status of Personnel," *Library Trends*, II (1953), 63–83.

Fay, Lucy E. "The Staff Manual for the College Library," *Bulletin of the American Library Association*, XXXI (1937), 464–68.

Fussler, Herman H. (ed.). Library Buildings for Library Service; Papers Presented before the Library Institute at the University of Chicago, August 5–10, 1946. Chicago, American Library Association, 1947.

General Statutes of North Carolina, The . . . 1943. Ed. by A. H. Michie [and others]. Charlottesville, Va., Michie Co., 1943–53.

Goodrum, Charles A. "L.C. Trains Recruits," *Library Journal*, LXXVII (1952), 393–96.

Harrington, Roseanne H., and Guy R. Lyle. "Recruiting and Developing a Library Staff," *College and Research Libraries*, VIII (1947), 427–35.

Herbert, Clara W. Personnel Administration in Public Libraries. Chicago, American Library Association, 1939.

Hoage, Annette. "Resignations in Two University Libraries," *College and Research Libraries*, XI (1950), 28–32.

Howard, Paul. "Library Staff Manuals and a Theory of Library Management" (unpublished Master's paper, Graduate Library School, University of Chicago, 1939).

Hutchins, Margaret. "Staff Manuals," *Library Journal*, LVII (1932), 1039–42.

Illinois, University of, Library. Staff Manual. Ed. by the Staff Manual Committee of the Librarians' Association of the University of Illinois Library. 2d ed. Urbana, 1948.

Kirkpatrick, Leonard H. "Another Approach to Staff Status," *College and Research Libraries*, VIII (1947), 218–20.

Kraus, Joe W. "The Qualifications of University Librarians, 1948 and 1933," *College and Research Libraries*, XI (1950), 17–21.

Lodge, Ardis. "Staff Associations in University Libraries," *California Library Association Bulletin*, II (1940), 135–37.

Lundy, Frank A. "Faculty Rank of Professional Librarians," *College and Research Libraries*, XII (1951), 11–19, 109–22.

Lyle, Guy R. The Administration of the College Library. 2d ed., rev. New York, H. W. Wilson, 1949.

McDiarmid, E. W., and John McDiarmid. The Administration of the American Public Library. Chicago, American Library Association and the University of Illinois Press, 1943.

McMillen, James A. "Academic Status of Library Staff Members of Large Universities," *College and Research Libraries*, I (1940), 138–40.

Maloy, Miriam C. "Faculty Status of College Librarians," *ALA Bulletin*, XXXIII (1939), 232–33+.

Martin, Lowell (ed.). Personnel Administration in Libraries; Papers Presented before the Library Institute at the University of Chicago, August 27–September 1, 1945. Chicago, University of Chicago Press, 1946.

Mosher, William E., J. D. Kingsley, and O. G. Stahl. Public Personnel Administration. 3d ed. New York, Harper, 1950.

Muller, Robert H. "Faculty Rank for Library Staff Members in Medium-sized Universities and Colleges," American Association of University Professors Bulletin, XXIX (1953), 421–31.

—— "Tangible Rewards," Library Journal, LXXIX (1954), 410–14.

—— "Work Week, Vacations, and Salaries in Medium-sized Universities and Colleges," College and Research Libraries, XV (1954), 84–86.

"Opportunities for Advanced Study: A Survey," Pacific Northwest Library Association Quarterly, V (1941), 94–95.

Pope, Mary F., and L. S. Thompson. "Travel Funds for University Library Staffs," College and Research Libraries, XI (1950), 22–27.

Princeton University Library. Handbook 1953–1954. Princeton, 1953.

St. John, Francis R. "Selection, Orientation, and Development of the Professional Staff," Library Trends, III (1954), 32–38.

SORT, Bulletin of the Staff Organizations Round Table, American Library Association. Irregular. June 1938–date.

Spain, Frances L. "Faculty Status of Librarians in Colleges and Universities in the South," in Southeastern Library Association, Papers and Proceedings: 13th Biennial Conference, Louisville, Ky., October 20–23, 1948, pp. 45–53.

Stewart, Nathaniel. "Library In-Service Training," Library Journal, LXXII (1947), 16–18+, 146–48, 200–203.

Stieg, Lewis F. "Retirement Plans for College and University Librarians," College and Research Libraries, XI (1950), 10–16.

Strout, Donald E. "Shortages Continue—Salaries Improve," Library Journal, XLXXX (1955), 1452–57.

Thompson, L. S. "Preparation and Status of Librarians," Library Trends, I (1952), 95–104.

Tucker, Harold W. "In-Service Training in Large Public Libraries" (unpublished Master's paper, Graduate Library School, University of Chicago, 1941).

Wilson, Louis R. and M. F. Tauber. "Staff Manuals in College and University Libraries," College and Research Libraries, II (1941), 126–35.

—— The University Library. Chicago, University of Chicago Press, 1945.

Yale University Library. Staff Manual. New Haven, 1952.

IX

BOOK COLLECTIONS: ACQUISITION
POLICIES AND PROCEDURES

UNIVERSITY librarians in the United States have long recognized their responsibility for gathering and making available
to scholars materials for study and research.[1] In recent years they
have been increasingly concerned with the growth in the size and
complexity of collections, as well as the concomitant problems of
supplying materials to support individual university courses, and
the number and character of journals and special types of materials
required for research by the various departments and schools. Important, too, is the consideration given to specialization in collecting
as a part of cooperative enterprises.

As stated in the Introduction, the rapidity of the growth of university libraries since 1900 has been one of their most notable characteristics. In 1900, no library had as many as a million volumes,
the largest library being Harvard with 575,000 volumes. In 1954,
there were 19 libraries with over a million volumes and 8 others with
more than 700,000 volumes.[2] Table 11 shows the number of volumes in a group of university libraries in 1900 and their increase
from that date to 1954.

Book collections, however, are measured not only in terms of
numbers. Despite the fact that qualified personnel and adequate

[1] Useful reviews of some of the problems relating to collections and the scholar
are the series of papers on "Availability of Library Research Materials," *Library
Trends*, II (1954), 487–586, and the papers on "Scholars, Librarians, and Booksellers
at Mid-Century," *Library Quarterly*, XXIII (1953), 153–266.

[2] "College and University Library Statistics (Group I)," *College and Research
Libraries*, XVI (1955), 38. Libraries with over a million volumes not included in
the statistics are Chicago, Duke, Michigan, and Stanford.

buildings are essential for efficient library service, their values are limited if books and other materials are not carefully selected. Consequently, book selection and book collecting are major activities of the librarian and his staff and of the administration and the faculties of the institution as well, and their integration with the instructional and research programs of the university is one of the

TABLE 11: GROWTH OF UNIVERSITY LIBRARIES, 1900–1954

	NUMBER OF VOLUMES			
INSTITUTION	1900–1901 [a]	1920–21 [b]	1940–41 [c]	1953–54 [d]
Brown	115,000	269,150	592,566	817,514
California (Berkeley)	88,000	413,824	1,124,858	1,986,818
Chicago	331,068	623,423	1,330,152	1,883,621 [f]
Columbia	311,000	797,106	1,845,611	2,069,795
Cornell	249,634	655,086	1,094,117	1,674,735
Harvard	575,000	2,101,200	4,265,792	5,833,116
Illinois	55,000	456,503	1,262,046	2,789,863
Indiana	35,000	141,658	437,009	946,599
Kansas	35,237	144,239	331,108	601,192
Minnesota	75,000	367,250	1,183,562	1,763,728
Missouri	36,000	177,320	418,104	708,679
Nebraska	52,000	153,925	367,215	535,538
North Carolina	35,000	108,405 [e]	403,051	662,978
Northwestern	45,764	201,734	668,410	1,146,163
Ohio State	36,000	223,063	594,300	1,056,226
Pennsylvania	200,000	509,796	958,523	1,371,193
Princeton	156,256	469,506	976,260	1,275,703
Texas	35,000	205,097	673,888	1,095,284
Virginia	50,775	120,000 [e]	359,811	746,834
Washington (Seattle)	12,520	104,776	478,687	842,928
Wisconsin	70,000	287,800	498,045	947,896
Yale	310,000	1,471,028	3,074,817	4,245,583

[a] Figures from U.S. Commissioner of Education. *Report . . . for the year 1900–1901* (2 vols. Washington, Government Printing Office, 1902), II, 1688–1707.
[b] Figures from "Statistics of University Libraries, 1920–21."
[c] Figures from "Statistics of University Libraries, 1940–41."
[d] Figures from *College and Research Libraries*, XVI (1955), 38.
[e] Figures from "Statistics of University Libraries, 1921–22."
[f] *American Library Directory*. 20th ed. (New York, Bowker, 1954).

librarian's greatest responsibilities. In this chapter, therefore, the general characteristics of a planned, systematic policy of acquisition and procedures for building up certain kinds of collections will be considered. In the two following chapters, which are also concerned with book collections, different types of materials will be considered. Chapter x will be devoted to the consideration of the more general types of materials, such as books, periodicals, documents, and newspapers; chapter xi, to the more specialized items, such as dissertations, manuscripts, archives, maps, music, and audiovisual and other materials.

ELEMENTS OF A   The development of an acquisition program
LIBRARY ACQUISITION   that will insure the development of a collec-
PROGRAM   tion of materials adequate to meet the de-
                       mands which the university makes upon it
depends basically upon the objectives of the university. Specific functions of the university, described in chapter i, include conservation of knowledge, instruction, research, publication, extension, and service. Of these functions, the three which most concern the university library are conservation, instruction, and research. These, in large measure, are basic in determining what kind of policy a given university library will follow in building up its collections. The size and nature of present holdings, the nature of the curriculum, the methods of teaching, the nature and extent of the research program, the number and kinds of students, the size and diversity of the faculty, and the physical organization of the library (centralized or decentralized) are matters that inevitably enter into consideration in formulating an acquisition policy. In general, they will determine the uses to which books and other materials will be put, and the kinds and amounts of materials acquired for instruction and research will depend largely upon the relative emphasis which the university places upon these and other aspects of its educational program.

Fussler [3] has observed that all libraries have acquisition policies. "A library's acquisition policy may represent anything . . . from the purely fortuitous to the most rigorous selection, but these practices in themselves constitute a policy of sorts. The extent to which a library fails to recognize the kinds of policies which it is following may possibly be a measure of the potential inadequacies of its

[3] Fussler, "Acquisition Policy," *College and Research Libraries*, XIV (1953), 363-67.

collection over a long period of time." [4] Undoubtedly, policies are likely to be most streamlined and precise in those institutions in which budgets are severely limited, which is a common condition in university libraries. But even in the cases of the few fortunate libraries which have sufficient funds to meet practically all requests for materials from members of the university faculty and library staff, a policy has to be followed to insure the most satisfactory results.

Since a unified, definite program of book buying is so essential to the effective development of the library, there are certain matters which the program should make clear. It should show: (1) who has the responsibility for seeing that a policy is set up and regularly carried out; (2) who should have final authority for directing and controlling the distribution of book funds; (3) what materials should be acquired; and (4) who should participate in the selection. It should leave no doubt in the minds of any members of the university concerning these particulars.

RESPONSIBILITY FOR ACQUISITION POLICY   In the public library, tradition has centered the responsibility for book selection in the hands of the librarian, since it has been assumed that he is better acquainted than his trustees and his public with books, the book trade, acquisitional techniques and relative values, and the library's aims in terms of the reading needs of his community. In the large public library the librarian commonly divides the responsibility for selecting books in specific fields of publication among the staff members who have academic backgrounds in special subjects. In the very large public library, such as the New York Public Library, specialists in the literature of specific subjects may be added to the acquisitions department staff as professional book selectors in order to insure the systematic development of particular divisions of the library's collections.

In a university library a different procedure is usually followed. The librarian is held responsible for seeing that a well-coordinated,

[4] *Ibid.*, p. 363.

systematic plan of selection is established and maintained; but responsibility for the actual selection of materials is generally divided between him and the library staff, on the one hand, and the faculty, on the other. The library committee or board also shares part of the responsibility. This part of the responsibility rests primarily with the participation of the committee in determining the general policies of acquisition and in allocating funds for the acquisition of books, periodicals, and other materials. As indicated in chapter ii, the librarian is usually charged with the responsibility of preparing the budget; and, where the library committee shares in the responsibility for allocating the book funds, its part is generally of an advisory, rather than an administrative, nature. Members of the faculty are usually charged with the responsibility for selecting materials in support of courses and programs of research, whereas the librarian and library staff are held responsible for selecting general reference books and bibliographical apparatus, noncurricular books, periodicals, and other material intended for general and recreational reading.[5]

This constitutes the first step in setting up the program. The next steps include: (1) the appointment by each department or other university unit of a committee to stimulate and supervise the selection of materials required by the department; (2) the periodic notification of the departmental committee concerning the annual allotment of funds and the status of the departmental fund from month to month; (3) the routing of information to the departmental committees and members of the faculty concerning materials which may be of interest to them; and (4) the designation of some member of the library staff (preferably of the acquisitions department) from whom information can be secured at any time concerning the status of funds and orders outstanding. The departmental committees are appointed by the departments. The member of the acquisitions department is designated by the librarian.

[5] A provocative series of papers relating to the collections and services of the research library is *Changing Patterns of Scholarship and the Future of Research: A Symposium in Celebration of the 200th Anniversary of the Establishment of the University of Pennsylvania Library.*

A mimeographed list of accessions issued regularly may also be found useful in keeping the instructional staff informed concerning new acquisitions. This list may also be supplemented, in the case of rush orders, by special notices sent direct to the faculty member for whom the material is intended.

These constitute the major, indispensable features of the library acquisition program usually authorized by the university. Once they have been determined, the policy can be put into operation by the librarian and should be steadfastly maintained. Certain observations, however, may well be made concerning such a policy.

In the first place, it is obvious that this formula will not fit every university and that the policy may vary in some particulars from institution to institution.

In the second place, a satisfactory formula for allocating book funds has not been developed. In fact, in some instances where the funds are large enough to meet the usual needs of all departments or individuals, there may be no specific allocation whatever. In some instances the funds may be left largely under the control of the librarian. However, where funds are limited, as they usually are, a definite allotment affords the department or unit a specific basis upon which to plan for its acquisitions. A division of the departmental allocation for books, periodicals, documents, films, and other types of material can be made which will insure a well-planned, long-term scheme of acquisition. The resources of the departments may be further increased if the librarian sets up an item in the general budget of the library which may be drawn upon, through special application, by a department for unusual and expensive materials.

In the third place—and most important—the assumption that the faculty is more competent than the library staff to select materials for the support of instruction and research may well be examined. Granting that faculty members may be more familiar with subject fields than are library staff members, it does not follow that the faculty can or will devote sufficient time to this activity to insure the systematic development of a collection that will be adequate to meet the demands made upon it. It is altogether possible that a library staff which includes members who are expert librarians as well as experts in special subject fields, whose task it is to review current publications and secondhand catalogs as a part of their regular duties, will be more successful than the faculty members, whose time, with few exceptions, is occupied in other ways.[6] A few university libraries have appointed staff bibliographers to select materials in special fields.

The major observation to be made concerning the program outlined above is not that responsibility is to be borne entirely by either the library or the faculty but that the program is to be well conceived and well coordinated and that all members of the university who are essential to its successful functioning participate in carrying it out.[7] Even in the selection of materials which fall into the category of cultural or recreational reading, for which librarians have usually assumed responsibility, the collaboration of the instructional staff may prove very valuable. The development of good habits of reading and study by students is a matter in which faculty members are as much interested as are members of the library staff, even though materials acquired for these purposes are not required for the support of any specific course.

The book-selection program of the university library is not confined to the librarian, the faculty, members of staff, special bibliographers, and departmental and professional school librarians. Friends-of-the-library groups, various other societies and organizations, and the student body also participate in an effectively planned program.

[6] Waples and Lasswell, *National Libraries and Foreign Scholarship*, pp. 69–82 (especially Fig. 18, p. 71). The authors point out that a library such as the New York Public Library, with a corps of subject specialists, was much more successful in selecting materials in the fields of economics, government, law, and sociology than several large university libraries. A list of 500 selected titles (books and periodicals) was used to check against. Budgets, of course, play an important part in the extensiveness of a library's coverage in a particular field.

[7] Fussler, "Acquisition Policy," pp. 366–67. Fussler emphasizes the role of the faculty member, especially in helping the librarian outline a policy which involves the "different areas and levels in the book collection of a single university."

FRIENDS OF THE UNIVERSITY LIBRARY   University libraries have always had benefactors.[8] Some of the great collections of American libraries have been developed through the donations of individuals, who have given either materials or endowments. Private philanthropic sources still continue to be a most fruitful source for special collections and rare items.[9]

In many university libraries there now exist formally organized groups called "friends," "associates," "library guild," or "book club members." These organizations represent a consolidation of the efforts of past donors and other individuals interested in building up the collections or equipment of specific academic libraries. The assumption underlying this movement has been that a formal organization not only channels the stream of gifts to the library but also enables the stream to widen to the extent of embracing others of a philanthropic bent.

The organizations of these groups have been both formal and informal. Whatever their nature, however, their purposes have been similar: to get individuals to donate books from private libraries, to solicit duplicate copies or unused books from alumni and other individuals, to interest collectors and others who may be willing to leave their libraries as memorials, and to stimulate alumni and friends to aid the library through gifts or money.[10] Despite these obvious purposes of friends groups, librarians like to believe that the organizations are more than mere devices to secure financial benefits for the libraries. They have assumed that the existence of these groups is a definite recognition, on the part of scholars and the general public, of the functions of the library in the field of higher education and as an enterprise for the cultural enrichment of the community. Programs held at the meetings of the groups are usually planned with the end in view of emphasizing the scholarly

[8] Shores, *Origins of the American College Library, 1638–1800.*

[9] See section on "Collections" in "News from the Field," in various issues of *College and Research Libraries.*

[10] McDiarmid, "Friends and Libraries," *Princeton University Library Chronicle,* X (1949), 173–79.

functions of the university library. Many of the groups issue publications which include articles on collections, rare volumes, bibliographical problems, and bibliophilic personalities.

Active, continuous planning is essential if these friends groups
are to do more than provide opportunities for book-minded people
to meet together for a social evening. Such groups as those which
exist at Brown, North Carolina, Princeton, and Yale report accessions of importance each year. Not only books, periodicals, and
funds, but also manuscripts, prints, etchings, newspapers, and other
library materials have been acquired through the activity of friends
groups. At Brown, the friends have added constantly to the book
collections of the library. At the University of North Carolina, the
friends group provided the new rare book rooms with furniture,
cases, rugs, paintings, panelling, and other materials, as well as
books.[11] At Princeton, special collections as well as equipment have
been obtained through the friends. The Associates at Yale have
done much to enrich the resources of the Library. One of the recent
issues of *The Call Number*, a publication of the Staff Association
of the University of Oregon Library, was devoted to the history
and activities of "The Association of Patrons and Friends." [12] Attention is given to the individuals who have helped to make the
group a successful one, materials received are described, mention
is made of the relations of the university group to the community,
and membership rules are explained.

SOCIETIES AND ORGANIZATIONS   In addition to friends groups,
various other societies and organizations, either independent of the
university or affiliated with it, may assist in developing the library
collections. Arrangements are sometimes made with libraries of
special groups to turn over to the university library materials which
they do not wish to keep but which are worth preserving in research collections.

[11] North Carolina, University of. *Friends of the Library.*
[12] "The Association of Patrons and Friends of the University of Oregon Library,"
The Call Number, XIII (1952), 3–18.

STUDENT BODY   Suggestions, by individual students, of materials to be purchased by the library are generally given consideration by the librarian. Student book clubs, however, are likely to purchase materials of their own choosing for the library unless the librarian has carefully outlined the needs of the book collection. If the librarian wishes to foster student-library relationships, he may encourage the participation of students in suggesting titles for purchase and in developing student and fraternity book clubs.

Graduate students requiring special materials for limited research studies, such as doctoral dissertations, occasionally assemble original or microreproduced items which they later turn over to the library. In some cases, the library will purchase such items if they appear to have potential further use.

TECHNICAL   OLDER MATERIALS   Only in rare instances
PROCEDURES IN   is the administrator of a university library
BOOK COLLECTING   called upon to start from the beginning in
                    building up a book collection as a whole.
However, in libraries in which the total collections are comparatively small or in libraries in which a collection must be built up in a subject area not previously developed by the library, such a situation is approximated. If such a situation does arise, the extent to which the librarian carefully analyzes the problem will determine the quality of the materials he assembles and the satisfaction with which they meet the demands of instruction and research.

The steps to be taken in developing a fundamental collection in a particular subject field follow a rather definite pattern. Librarians who are faced with the task of providing the materials essential for supporting a new course or curriculum or are called upon to assemble collections for graduate or research programs generally follow this pattern, including such steps as are needed for the particular levels of work.

Several assumptions should be made before the steps in the plan are described. In this description, the term "book selector" is used to mean the equivalent of the subject specialist, who is either a member of the faculty or of the library staff and who has been referred to earlier. It may be assumed that the book selector has made a general survey of the region where the collection is to be assembled and understands that such cooperative services as interlibrary lending and microphotography are available. He has even included them in his planning. It may also be assumed that the book selector has made a careful survey of the institution for which he is planning; that is, he has a detailed comprehension of all phases of the institution's activities which are related to the collection he is to assemble. This implies a sound knowledge of the institutional aims in general and of the departmental aims in particular. For the department, he has investigated the nature of the course offerings, the types of research performed and planned, the number and kinds of students, and the number and kinds of faculty members. Moreover, he has obtained a detailed estimate of the kinds and quantities of funds available for building the collection. Only when he has reviewed these various facts can he proceed intelligently to select the books and other materials for the special collection.

The primary element in building up any collection is a preliminary survey of the materials which the library already possesses. This initial step must be taken regardless of the size of the collection. First of all, the book selector must discover what basic books and other materials are already held by the library. Basic books are those which are cited as primary sources in contemporary general works. In this category are included the best-known editions of works of authors and the best sources of criticism of their texts and works. Experience has indicated that the first step may be accomplished by checking the collection against the bibliographies of good standard histories of the particular subject being considered.[13] The checking provides a basis for evaluating the strength of the

[13] For example, in a preliminary survey of the holdings in Italian literature of the Library of Congress, Jerrold Orne divided the field into twenty-five periods and checked the library's holdings for each period against a bibliography of basic or essential books. See *Annual Report of the Librarian of Congress for the Fiscal Year Ended June 30, 1940*, pp. 7–10.

library's collections, and serves as a guide for the compilation of a list of desiderata.

The next step involves a broader view of the problem. In checking holdings against the lists, basic texts and primary books of criticism are indicated. For a number of libraries, items selected in this manner may be sufficient. In the library of the large university, in which there is likely to be considerable advanced instruction and research in the particular subject, they may serve merely as a starting point. In that case the list of desirable items must be enlarged. It should be apparent, for reasons of cost and availability, that the building of a large collection must be a long-term project. Its growth must be coordinated with the program of instruction and research within the institution, so far as this is feasible. As courses are announced or anticipated, plans should be made for securing the materials essential to support them. This may involve further searching in subject bibliographies, check lists, and other sources of information concerning appropriate materials. The task becomes more difficult as the depth of specialization increases, and it is here that the subject specialist in the field can be most helpful. Collaboration with faculty subject specialists should be included in this procedure.[14]

Although extensive bibliographies may be checked for purposes of studying the collections of a library, they are seldom of value as buying guides, for they are usually neither selective nor annotated. The background and ingenuity of the book selector thus are thoroughly tested. Working from every source of critical information possible, he should prepare a careful bibliography of the author or topic he is considering.[15] Period histories, annotated bibliographies

[14] Brough, *Scholar's Workshop*, chapter iv, "The Nature and Extent of Collections." This discussion provides background material on the development of collections, particularly from the point of view of depth and completeness. See also Raney, *University of Chicago Survey, Vol. VII: The University Libraries*, p. 4. Raney describes the checking of some 400 bibliographies by faculty members to discover holdings and to note desiderata.

[15] See, for example, the section on "Lacunae Noted by the Faculty," in Wilson and Swank, *Report of a Survey of the Library of Stanford University for Stanford University, November 1946—March 1947*, pp. 159-68. Wilson and Swank point up several problems which exist in the development of collections for the large university library.

in critical works, and references in critical editions of the author's works will need to be checked. Bibliographies concerning the author as given in journals, encyclopedias, biographies, and elsewhere will need to be compared. When the book selector has checked every available source of critical bibliography that he can isolate, he is then in a position to discriminate in order to prepare a list of desiderata of all items published up to that particular point in his work. In addition, it is necessary for the selector to include the apparatus necessary for the study of the subject. Periodicals, society publications, and, for some subjects, manuscripts and other materials, are needed, as well as books.[16]

At this stage a word of caution should be introduced. Since the courses and research problems of the moment tend to assume disproportionate importance in the book-selection program of the university library, it is likely that pressure may be exerted to spend excessively on a single subject. If a plan of book selection is carried out in detail, however, excesses of this sort can be checked immediately. Ideally, perhaps, every item needed for course work or research should be available, but a logical book-selection plan will not permit the needs of a few to interfere with a long-term policy to serve a large number. This does not mean that the interests of a single faculty member will be disregarded. But these interests should be related to the library program as a whole, and the availability of resources elsewhere.

Fortified with a knowledge of regional resources, the book selector should be able to compromise with the faculty in the matter of the purchase of expensive materials. When academic groups are shown that other libraries in the area possess materials which can be made available through interlibrary lending or reproduction, they may be less insistent upon certain expensive purchases. Other informal or formal cooperative agreements, discussed in greater

---

[16] See Bibliographical Planning Committee of Philadelphia, *A Faculty Survey of the University of Pennsylvania Libraries*, for an example of the nature of various types of materials which might be included; David, "On the Survey of a Research Library by Scholars," *College and Research Libraries*, XV (1954), 290–91, 308. This is an explanation of the steps taken in the Pennsylvania survey.

detail in chapter xiii, may frequently be more effective than the outright purchase of every item required for an instructional or research program.[17]

Once it has been decided which materials are wanted, the various processes of acquisition—purchase, gift, and exchange—require attention. These processes are discussed in chapter v.[18] It may be pointed out here that considerable ingenuity is necessary in acquiring older materials. Desiderata lists should be specific. Agents in the United States and in foreign countries should be carefully selected. Faculty members and library personnel, especially when they visit foreign countries, should be recruited for collecting purposes whenever practicable. Exchange relations should be established with educational institutions, industrial organizations, societies, libraries, and other agencies. An active gift program is essential.[19]

CURRENT MATERIALS   Thus far the discussion of the problem of assembling a fundamental book collection seems to indicate that all the books on a particular subject have been written and that selection can be made without considering the possibility of change. A planned policy of book selection, however, requires considerable attention to current publications. This involves a constant scrutiny of American and foreign reviewing periodicals. The book selector has the responsibility of providing all the periodicals needed for the collection and should pay particular attention to those publications which contain the better book reviews. Preferences of faculty members may simplify the choice somewhat, and within a small field the working list of titles is limited enough to be well known. Ulrich's *Periodicals Directory* is a useful guide for subject lists of periodicals.

In addition to the general and special book-reviewing periodicals,

---

[17] Raney, *University of Chicago Survey*, pp. 6–7.

[18] Tauber and Associates, *Technical Services in Libraries*, chaps. iv–vii; see also Welch, "Publications Exchange," *Library Trends*, III (1955), 423–31.

[19] Thompson, "Of Bibliological Mendicancy," *College and Research Libraries*, XIV (1953), 373–78.

the book selector should maintain contact with publishers and book dealers in the particular fields in order to receive their announcements and catalogs of new publications and special sales. This source may be troublesome to keep up with, but it also may be extremely productive. The examining of catalogs requires a methodical approach which involves the use of faculty cooperation at every point where it is available. The librarian or the book selector, however, should be the final authority if the general plan in building up the collections is to be consistently followed.

RELATION TO OTHER FIELDS   Any plan for building up a collection in a particular subject should include supplementary materials in closely related fields. Depending upon the work of the institution, the place of supplementary materials in the plan may be large, moderate, or small. Work in one branch of the sciences may make it necessary to have basic materials in other related sciences. Work in foreign literatures may require the acquisition of strong collections of linguistic materials, including grammars, dictionaries, encyclopedias, and histories of the languages. While the book selector for the field of the Romance languages may not have the responsibility for the choosing of books in the field of history, he should consider it his duty to encourage buying or otherwise acquiring whatever volumes of history he considers to be most useful to students in his field. While practice may vary somewhat in different institutions, the book selector will frequently find that many of the titles recommended by him are already in the library or are receiving consideration for purchase. Generally, a few books are sufficient, and cooperation of this character from other subject specialists, bibliographers, or faculty members is not difficult to obtain.

BUILDING LIBRARIES THROUGH *en bloc* ACQUISITION   A further device which has long been employed in building up collections of the kind considered above is that of purchasing collections *en bloc* which have been built up over a period of years by a scholar or book collector. Such collections were frequently available for purchase after World War I, and many of them found their way into libraries in the United States. They account, in part, for the rapid growth of some university libraries, to which reference has been made. Such collections usually include books, periodicals, bibliographies, and supplementary source materials. In some cases, they duplicate some of the materials already acquired by the library, but the disadvantages of duplication may be far outweighed by the positive advantages of securing a body of materials at one time which may have taken the lifetime of a specialist to assemble. The Furness Memorial Library of Shakespeariana at the University of Pennsylvania, described in *A Faculty Survey of the University of Pennsylvania Libraries*, affords an idea of the richness and value which might be added to a library through the acquisition of such collections.

Less frequently, there are collections which may be acquired from other libraries. The University of Kansas, for example, instituted a program in 1953 of acquiring large blocks of books out of scope in the John Crerar Library in Chicago. In 1954, about 10,000 volumes in political science, primarily materials dealing with comparative governments, and in sociology were selected for transfer to Lawrence. In addition, Kansas acquired *en bloc* Crerar's distinguished Gerritsen collection on the intellectual and social history of women. Numbering over 4,000 titles, this collection was the subject of a printed bibliography, A. H. Gerritsen's *La Femme et le féminisme*, printed in Paris in 1900. Crerar had held the collection since 1904.[20]

SUMMARY   This chapter serves as an introduction to a sequence of three chapters devoted to the problems of book collecting. In view of the great importance of maintaining a sound program of book acquisition, it makes clear the responsibility of the various members of the university community for setting up the program,

[20] *College and Research Libraries*, XV (1954), 448. On this same page is a statement concerning the acquisition by the University of Kentucky Library of the Chauncey H. Griffith collection of typography, including several thousand manuscripts, designs, and fugitive printed items of significance for typographical history.

providing for the selection of different types of materials, and seeing that the objectives of the university, especially those relating to the conservation of knowledge, instruction, and research, are furthered through the materials which are secured. The program that will prove best will involve all members of the university community, including faculty, library staff, students, and special organizations of alumni and friends.

The chapter also suggests procedures to be followed in building up materials in a special field. Five steps are suggested which may be summarized as follows: (1) a survey of the field, including the region, the university, the department, and the collection; (2) a basic selection, including texts, and major critical works; (3) an expanded selection, according to a definite plan based upon authors, periods, or subjects and coordinated with the immediate needs of the institution; (4) a selection of periodicals, publications of learned societies, biographies, and other supplementary and related materials, depending largely upon the use made of them in the institution and the place they have in relation to the plan of book selection; and (5) the purchase, or otherwise acquiring *en bloc*, of collections built up by scholars, book collectors, or libraries which contain various types of materials relating to the subject. Whether the field to be built up is Romance languages or sociology, ancient history or geology, the steps which have been outlined are applicable. Resourcefulness on the part of the book selector appears to be the key to the situation. While the responsibility for an effective book-collecting program may rest upon his shoulders, he can, through various ways and means, obtain the cooperation of those individuals on the campus who are, by background and experience, able to contribute immeasurably to the program.

BIBLIOGRAPHY

Allen, F. P. "Friends of the Library Organizations," *College and Research Libraries*, V (1944), 347–50.
American Library Association. Friends of the College and University Library Groups. Chicago, 1948 (mimeographed).

"Availability of Library Research Materials," *Library Trends*, II (1954), 487–580.

Bibliographical Planning Committee of Philadelphia. A Faculty Survey of the University of Pennsylvania Libraries. Philadelphia, University of Pennsylvania Press, 1942.

Brough, Kenneth J. Scholar's Workshop. Urbana, University of Illinois Press, 1953.

Changing Patterns of Scholarship and the Future of Research: A Symposium in Celebration of the 200th Anniversary of the Establishment of the University of Pennsylvania Library. [Ed. by Rudolf Hirsch] Philadelphia, University of Pennsylvania Press, 1951.

Clemons, Harry. History of the University of Virginia Library. Charlottesville, University of Virginia, 1954.

——— Survey of Research Materials in Virginia Libraries. Charlottesville, Alderman Library, 1941.

College and Research Libraries (Various issues, see "News of the Field" section).

"College and University Library Statistics (Group I)," *College and Research Libraries*, XVI (1955), 38–41.

Danton, J. Periam. "The Selection of Books for College Libraries: An Examination of Certain Factors Which Affect Excellence of Selection," *Library Quarterly*, V (1935), 419–56.

David, Charles W. "On the Survey of a Research Library by Scholars," *College and Research Libraries*, XV (1954), 290–91+.

Davidson, P. G., and A. F. Kuhlman (eds.). The Development of Library Resources and Graduate Work in the Cooperative University Centers in the South. Nashville, Joint University Libraries, 1944.

Downs, Robert B. Resources of American Libraries. Chicago, American Library Association, 1952.

Downs, Robert B. (ed.). The Resources of New York City Libraries: A Survey of Facilities for Advanced Study and Research. Chicago, American Library Association, 1942.

Fox, M. A. "Friends of the Library Groups in Colleges and Universities," *College and Research Libraries*, XII (1951), 353–54.

Fussler, Herman H. "Acquisition Policy: A Symposium; The Larger University Library," *College and Research Libraries*, XIV (1953), 363–67.

Lewis, Wilmarth S. Collector's Progress. New York, Knopf, 1951.

Library of Congress. Annual Report of the Librarian . . . for the Fiscal Year Ended June 20, 1940. Washington, Government Printing Office, 1941.

Library Quarterly (Various articles appearing in various issues on "Notable Materials Added to North American Libraries.")

McDiarmid, E. W. "Friends and Libraries," *Princeton University Library Chronicle*, X (1949), 173–79.

North Carolina, University of. Friends of the Library. Opportunities and Plans for the Present and Future of the University Library at Chapel Hill. Chapel Hill, 1953.

Pargellis, Stanley. "Book Supply and the Book Market," *Library Quarterly*, XXIII (1953), 199–204.

Powell, Lawrence C. "Book Collectors and California Libraries," *California Library Bulletin*, XI (1950),163–64.

——"From a Private Collection to Public Institution: the William Andrews Clark Memorial Library," *Library Quarterly*, XX (1950), 101–8.

Randall, William M. (ed.). The Acquisition and Cataloging of Books: Papers Presented before the Library Institute at the University of Chicago, July 29 to August 9, 1940. Chicago, University of Chicago Press, 1940.

Raney, M. L. University of Chicago Survey. Vol. VII: The University Libraries. Chicago, University of Chicago Press, 1933.

Shores, Louis. Origins of the American College Library, 1638–1800. Nashville, Tenn., George Peabody College, 1934.

"Special Materials and Services," *Library Trends*, III (1955), 119–212.

Tauber, Maurice F. and Associates. Technical Services in Libraries. New York, Columbia University Press, 1954.

Thompson, Lawrence S. "Of Bibliological Mendicancy," *College and Research Libraries*, XIV (1953), 373–78.

Waples, Douglas, and H. D. Lasswell. National Libraries and Foreign Scholarship. Chicago, University of Chicago Press, 1936.

Welch, Helen M. "Publications Exchange," *Library Trends*, III (1955), 423–31.

Wilson, Louis R. (ed.). The Practice of Book Selection: Papers Presented before the Library Institute at the University of Chicago, July 31 and August 13, 1939. Chicago, University of Chicago Press, 1940.

Wilson, Louis R., and R. C. Swank. Report of a Survey of the Library of Stanford University for Stanford University, November 1946—March 1947. Chicago, American Library Association, 1947.

See also chapters on "Holdings" or "Collections" in various surveys. (See Bibliography in chapter xvi).

X

BOOK COLLECTIONS:

GENERAL MATERIALS

THE RESEARCH function of the university has frequently been emphasized in earlier chapters of this study. It assumes special importance in its application to the book collections of the university library. Like the college library, the university library is generally concerned with acquiring the standard books of general reference, standard reference books useful in specific fields covered by the curriculum, important books not specific to any one curricular field, adequate collections for each curricular field, essential books concerning fields not covered by the curriculum, a stock of books appropriate for leisure reading, and subscriptions to a selected number of general and specific periodicals. But the program of the university library goes beyond these requirements, both quantitatively and qualitatively. While the college library may be concerned with the immediate use of a particular item, the university library, implementing the research function of the institution, takes a much longer view in considering a title for acquisition. Moreover, the university library has not been too much concerned with the problem of restricting the total collections in the way a college library must, although recently there has been a growing reaction against sheer size.[1] Finally, the university library must satisfy demands for materials which are neither books in the generally accepted sense nor periodicals—materials such as serials, documents,

[1] Metcalf, "Harvard Faces Its Library Problems," in *The Place of the Library in a University; A Conference Held at Harvard University, 30–31 March 1949*, pp. 44–45.

dissertations, newspapers, manuscripts, maps, fugitive materials of many kinds, music, archives, films, micro-reproductions, and museum objects. In this chapter, consideration will be given to the collection of general materials, including books, periodicals, serials, government publications, and newspapers.

BOOKS   Books form one of the major items in university library holdings. Beginning with incunabula and coming down to the most recently published titles, the book collections of large university libraries usually include from several hundred thousand to one or more million volumes, many of which fall into special categories, in accord with the acquisition policy of the library.

REFERENCE COLLECTION. The kinds of works which constitute the reference collection of the university library have been discussed at length in library literature.[2] These books—encyclopedias, dictionaries, bibliographies, atlases, concordances, indexes, abstracts, etc.—are generally consulted for specific information and fill an important place in university library book collections. Standard treatises and important outlines of subject fields which generally are not read through for recreation or course work are likewise considered for inclusion in the reference collection. It is true that reference books contain materials which are useful for other purposes than supplying bits of information and that any book in the collection may serve a reference purpose. Some libraries have recognized this fact, and books which are shelved in the reference room are frequently permitted to circulate outside the library.

The departmentalized systems of university libraries usually require considerable duplication of reference books, not only in the catalog, periodical, and other functional departments within the central library but also in the branch, departmental, and professional school libraries. In a large library system reference works may be

[2] Winchell, *Guide to Reference Books;* Shores, *Basic Reference Sources;* L. N. Malclès, *Les sources du travail bibliographique;* see also lists of "Selected Reference Books" appearing in the January and July issues of *College and Research Libraries,* prepared by Constance M. Winchell.

duplicated excessively unless care is taken by the librarian or by members of the acquisition and catalog departments.

CURRICULAR COLLECTIONS. Despite the emphasis upon research, the university library is confronted with the problem of providing materials which are used in connection with undergraduate and graduate courses offered in the institution. The type of material which is included in this category may best be illustrated by examining titles which appear in two recent lists.[3] Universities, like colleges, differ in the acquisition of such materials in relation to their curriculums. In both colleges and universities, there is a constant need for careful selection of titles to support the educational program.[4] The librarian should be observant of the effectiveness of the library in providing a sufficient number of titles to keep students and faculty members abreast of their subjects. Limited funds make it necessary for faculty members who request books for required, optional, or collateral reading to consider each purchase in relation to the specific course, the curriculum, and the book collection as a whole. This is particularly true of duplicates which are purchased for required readings.

GENERAL BOOK COLLECTION. Apart from the reference and curricular materials which are needed in the university library, modern library practice, particularly as it relates to undergraduates, requires the provision of materials which satisfy the general reading function of the library. Most university libraries provide such materials as a matter of course. Standard fiction and non-fiction are usually acquired through systematic checking of current book lists and review journals. This is particularly true of American and English publications. Faculty members are generally consulted in the acquisition of other foreign titles. Bennett has reviewed problems which arise in acquiring current books.[5]

RESEARCH COLLECTIONS. While the college library emphasizes in

[3] For example, Harvard University Library (Lamont Library), *Catalogue of the Lamont Library, Harvard College,* and Bertalan, *Books for Junior Colleges.* There are several older lists, such as those by Charles B. Shaw and Foster E. Mohrhardt, which are also available.

[4] Wilson, Lowell, and Reed, *Library in College Instruction.*

[5] "The Current Bookmarket," *Library Trends,* III (1955), 376–84.

its acquisition program the selection of materials which fulfill reference and curricular functions, the university library centers its
attention upon the provision of research materials. Books are necessary, but periodicals and other serial publications, manuscript and
archival materials, documents of all kinds, films, and other types of
materials form the resources for investigation of scientific and humanistic problems. These materials, representing miles of shelving
in the large university libraries, are the backbone sources of research.
Whether they are acquired directly for a library's collection, or
through the Farmington Plan, or in cooperation with an interlibrary
center, they represent "the instruments of scholarship," which, as
Zechariah Chafee, Jr., when writing of the professional school library, observed:

> may include hundreds and thousands of books within the scope of
> professional knowledge—they are not read often, but you never know
> when something will be needed. . . . One of the very best cases in my
> field of law is found only in the diary of Narcissus Luttrell, which is
> really a collection of seventeenth-century Kiplinger newsletters. Horace
> Binney of Philadelphia established the great Stephen Girard Trust in
> the Supreme Court largely by using a book of Irish decisions which was
> in the Harvard Law School Library.[6]

Where to stop in the collecting of resources on the level beyond
the college grades is a question which currently concerns all university librarians. The growth of libraries continues at a great pace,
and necessary shelving and building space are limited in many institutions. The potential use of such items as Luttrell's diary or a book
of Irish court decisions, to say nothing of the thousands of titles in
languages which have little or no demand by readers, has been an
assumption held by librarians and supported by faculty members. If
the university is to be the center for recruiting undergraduates for
research work, for serving as a focal point in preliminary training

---

[6] Zechariah Chafee, Jr., "The Library and the Professional School," in *The Place
of the Library in a University*, p. 22. For a discussion of the usefulness of runs of
periodicals in a research library, see Charles H. Brown, "Librarianship and the Sciences," in Shores (ed.), *Challenges to Librarianship*, pp. 69–91. A general discussion
of scientific and technical publications is Jenkins, "The Acquisition of Scientific and
Technological Material," *Library Trends*, III (1955), 414–22.

in research, and for originating research problems and distributing research findings, its library should be equipped to implement the program. Insufficient resources of a graphic nature, dealing with the more specific aspects of the physical sciences, the biological sciences, the humanities, and the social sciences, can seriously hinder an effective research program. Indeed, one could hardly call it a "program" if no plans have been made for the systematic collection and preservation of research materials. Just how extensive and exhaustive the collections in the several subject fields should be depends entirely upon the university's research programs and its intentions for the future. Undoubtedly, however, the future will bring more effective cooperation among university libraries than now exists.[7]

RARE MATERIALS. Closely allied with the question of collecting research materials is the problem of acquiring rare books and other such items. What are the place and the responsibility of the university librarian in collecting and housing rarities? On the first point, Jackson makes the following observation:

This generation has witnessed a phenomenal growth of rare book collections in American university libraries. In the past such libraries have usually had a reserved section which contained a miscellany, including some real rarities, inferno books, and many other items which are neither rare nor important, but merely fragile or difficult to administer either because of their size or material, or because they really were not books at all but curiosities. Now, in most of the larger university libraries special departments have been established for the preservation and administration of rare books, and the relative growth in size and expense of these departments has frequently been greater than that of the libraries of which they are a part.[8]

Although some university libraries do not maintain a program of acquisition of rare materials because of budgetary limitations, there is a definite interest on the part of most institutions in collecting such items as incunabula, first editions of American authors, first

[7] "Availability of Research Materials," *Library Trends*, II (1954), 487–580.

[8] Jackson, "The Importance of Rare Books and Manuscripts in a University Library," in *The Place of the Library in a University*, p. 26. See also Wing and Vosper, "The Antiquarian Bookmarket and the Acquisition of Rare Books," *Library Trends*, III (1955), 385–92.

editions in various subject fields, local history, manuscripts, letters, examples from local printing presses, old newspapers and periodicals, broadsides, notices, programs, old maps, gift books, annuals, association copies, examples of fine binding, illumination, and typography, and copies of private press items.[9] Frequently a university library becomes a collector of rare items because it has been made the beneficiary of a private collection. If the collection has not been endowed, the library may be faced with the need of setting up an item in the budget for its maintenance and development.

Librarians and research workers who have been instrumental in the development of rich rare book collections are unanimous in their estimate of the need for such materials to support research. Particularly in the humanities is there a uniform high appraisal of their value, as Jackson has noted. "The sciences of epigraphy and palaeography, the newer procedures of bibliography, the patient assembling of data in history and biography, textual criticism— these are the time-proved methods and processes of humanistic scholarship, and scholarship will not remain sound unless training in such disciplines is widespread." [10] Access to rare materials is necessary in instructing young students to differentiate the real from the counterfeit. By handling rare books the student can learn to distinguish between a first edition, a first revised edition, the last edition published during an author's lifetime, the first effort at a critical edition, a modern popular edition, and the latest critical edition.[11] Such investigation is said to engender a discriminatory perspective in the average or exceptional student and is of value to those individuals who are interested in becoming bibliographers and librarians, students of literary development, or specialists in the graphic arts. "Because of their historical significance, their intrinsic value, their beauty, and sentimental associations, rare books, when intelligently grouped, have power to excite the imagination and

[9] Powell, "Rare Book Code," *College and Research Libraries*, X (1949), 307–8; Jackson, "The Importance of Rare Books and Manuscripts in the University Library," pp. 27–37.

[10] *Op. cit.*, p. 27.

[11] Adams, *The Whys and Wherefores of the William M. Clements Library.*

stimulate the intellectual curiosity of the student." [12] Rare books are highly useful as a means of publicizing the library, of brightening it with exhibitions, and of developing the interest of students, alumni, and friends.

As in all collecting, there should be a purpose behind building up rare book collections.[13] The materials in such collections should be related in some way to the functions of the university, whether it is teaching, public service, or research. The library should not try to approximate the activities of the professional book collector or bibliophile who assembles curiosa, first editions, autographs, association copies, or manuscripts because of the market value or the mere desire to possess unique materials. A rare book or manuscript as an object of art, of course, has a proper place in the instructional program of an academic institution.[14]

Such analyses as have been made of the uses of rare book collections reveal a pattern which involves both academic and nonacademic clientele.[15] The names of teaching and research staff, of students of all classes, of members of various crafts and professions who are concerned with historical materials in their special fields, and of many others engaged in serious, scholarly enterprises may be found in the registers of rare book rooms. If the use of one of these rooms is compared with that of an active, current departmental library, it would show up sadly in terms of numbers of visitors. But the use of such materials is not to be measured solely in terms of physical handling for the purpose of extracting bits of information. When discussing the meager use of the Van Antwerp copy of the first folio of Shakespeare in the Henry Elkins Widener Collection at Harvard, Jackson remarked: "But it has been frequently exhibited,

[12] Powell, "The Function of Rare Books," *College and Research Libraries*, I (1939), 101. Powell has frequently written on the value of knowledge of books on the part of academic librarians.

[13] Powell, "Rare Books in the University Library, *College and Research Libraries*, X (1949), 295–99.

[14] Wyllie, "Rare Books in the University Library: The Need," *College and Research Libraries*, X (1949), 291–94.

[15] Allen, "Who Reads Treasure Room Books?" *Harvard Library Notes*, III (1938), pp. 180–83; Young, "Uses of Rare Books and Manuscripts," *Yale University Library Gazette*, XVI (1941), 25–38.

and doubtless numbers of people have been moved by the sight of a copy of the book which alone has preserved twenty of Shakespeare's plays. In this way the volume has earned its board and keep many times over." [16]

Most libraries are not as fortunate as Harvard and Michigan in being able to provide separate buildings for housing their rare book collections. In the smaller libraries, usually a grilled section of the stacks is set aside, or a modest room is made available, for special materials. Many of the larger libraries have extensive space within their buildings for rare books. Among them are Brown, Chicago, Columbia, Duke, North Carolina, Oregon, Pennsylvania, Princeton, Texas, Virginia, and Yale. Practically all new buildings provide special accommodations for the housing of rarities.[17]

PERIODICALS   A "periodical" is a publication with a distinctive title intended to appear in successive (usually unbound) numbers or parts at stated or regular intervals and, as a rule, for an indefinite time. Since "periodical" refers to a *form* of material, it is found that reference collections, curricular and general reading collections, research collections, and rare-book collections, as well as some of the collections which will be discussed later, usually contain periodical items. For 66 libraries which provided information in 1953,[18] the median number of periodical titles received was 3,106; the range was from 914 (Rhode Island) to 21,025 (University of California, Berkeley). Eleven libraries received 7,000 or more titles. Several large libraries which have extensive periodical lists did not report information.

Libraries receive both general and special periodicals. Such general titles as *Harper's*, *Time*, and scores of similar ones are usually subscribed to by university libraries. These are not only useful for current information, but they serve to fulfill the general cultural

[16] "The Importance of Rare Books and Manuscripts in a University Library," p. 34.
[17] For a discussion of the housing of rare books, see chap. xiv, "Buildings and Equipment."
[18] "College and University Library Statistics, 1952–53 (Group I)," *College and Research Libraries*, XV (1954), 68.

reading function of the library. In numerous instances they afford materials which may be used by students for brief reports, term papers, and special problems.

The special periodicals form the backbone of the university library collection. Thousands of titles are available, and new ones appear annually.[19] They are the indispensable source materials for research workers in all fields, particularly in science and technology.

To which of the specialized periodicals a library should subscribe depends largely upon the instructional and research program of the university. When the program is fully understood, selection of necessary periodicals should follow a pattern similar to that for the selection of books. Generally, the selection of periodicals in restricted subject fields is left largely to faculty members. The decision to subscribe to a periodical involves a continuing budgetary item, as well as annual binding costs and housing. Because of the importance of this decision, it is not unusual to find that, although libraries maintain separate budgets for periodicals, the initial expense of a periodical, often for a three-year period, is borne by the department ordering the title. At the end of the period the item is placed on the regular university library periodical budget. For those periodicals which fall into no specific field, the charges are carried by the general fund of the library.

Since periodicals are essential in the support of research, special care has been taken to determine the comparative usefulness of individual titles in a number of subject fields. Gross and Gross [20]

[19] See lists of "New Periodicals" appearing in the April and October issues of *College and Research Libraries*, prepared 1940–46 by Carolyn F. Ulrich, and since 1947 by Edna Mae Brown. A useful source of information concerning older periodicals is *Ulrich's Periodicals Directory: A Classified Guide to a Selected List of Current Periodicals, Foreign and Domestic*. The *Union List of Serials* contains many titles usually acquired by university libraries. A comprehensive bibliography, classified by subject, of periodical and serial problems in libraries is Reiman's "Selected Bibliography of Articles Related to Serials, 1936–1952," *Serial Slants*, IV (1953), 49–94. *Serial Slants* is a publication of the ALA Serials Round Table, and contains practical papers and other information of direct use to those working with periodicals and other serials.

[20] "College Libraries and Chemical Education," *Science*, LXVI (1927), 385–89. By checking a volume of the *Journal of the American Chemical Society* it was found that 3,633 references were made to 247 journals. It was apparent that the majority of the citations were concentrated in 28 journals. Similar studies have been made

developed a technique for evaluating chemical periodicals in 1927. The idea behind this method of evaluation is that the periodicals most often referred to are the most important. The actual use of articles by scholars, according to the analysis, makes it possible to single out the most significant journals. It is obvious that numerous exceptions might affect the validity of the method.[21]

In addition to reference counting, other approaches to the evaluation of periodicals have included direct examination of titles by subject specialists, the extent to which titles are included in indexes and abstracting services, the holdings of a group of libraries, the pooled judgments of experts, and observations on the use of materials. Finally, there has been some measurement of periodical collections by examining the holdings of a particular library of titles on special lists of periodicals.

All of these approaches have limitations. The librarian and his staff should work closely with experts on the faculty to insure constant reviews of periodical receipts which are necessary for instruction and research. Periodicals change in their importance and require reappraisals.

SERIALS   Periodicals, discussed in the preceding section, form one division of serial literature. A "serial" is generally defined as a publication which is issued at regular or irregular intervals, with some scheme of consecutive numbering, and is intended to be continued indefinitely. Thus, both periodicals and continuations come under this definition. Continuations include annuals, reports, yearbooks, memoirs, journals, transactions, proceedings, house organs, college and university catalogs, and similar publications. Many government publications are issued as serials. If domestic and foreign serials are considered, a total of well over

---

for aviation, biochemistry, child guidance, dentistry, education, electrical engineering, endocrinology of sex, geology, mathematics, medicine, physiology, physics and radio, and other subjects.

[21] Cf. Brodman, "Choosing Physiology Journals," *Bulletin of the Medical Library Association*, XXXII (1944), 479–83. Brodman points out some of the limitations of the method. "Individuals using the method . . . should be aware of the small dependence which can scientifically be placed on its results" (p. 83).

100,000 thousand titles are available for libraries.[22] The larger university libraries contain thousands of bound volumes of serial literature.

Librarians are faced with difficult problems in distributing the funds for serials (which are relatively expensive) so that the educational and research functions of the university will be most effectively served. Surveyors have frequently found that the serials programs of university libraries have been weak in acquisitions, organization, and servicing. A basically sound program for serials requires a systematic linking of the materials with the course work and research policy of the institution.

The sheer number of serial publications and their importance in research emphasize the importance of selection. Efforts should always be made to eliminate titles which are not necessary to the institution's program, and where possible arrangements could be made for cooperative acquisition with other libraries of the region.[23] Checking of union lists provide a basis for selection, particularly when such checking is done by experts who are acquainted with the needs of the university and with the holdings of near-by libraries. Attention to new serials is also necessary. This often requires searching in out-of-the-way places, since serials, with the exception of new periodicals and some annuals, receive little publicity in the regular trade publications.[24]

Procedures for selecting serial publications are similar to those for selecting other materials. Comparison of basic and standard lists

[22] *Union List of Serials in Libraries of the United States and Canada,* ed. by Winifred Gregory. The *Union List of Serials* has been one of the main sources of information for librarians. Two editions of this work, which includes serials in libraries in the United States and Canada, have appeared. A decision has been made not to publish a third edition, nor additional supplements. Since January, 1953, the Library of Congress has issued *New Serial Titles,* a monthly publication, with self-cumulating annuals. Like *Serial Titles Newly Received,* its predecessor, *New Serial Titles* is prepared by punched-card methods. A comprehensive treatment of serials is Osborn's *Serial Publications: Their Place and Treatment in Libraries.*

[23] For example, Stern, "Texas Librarians Have a Union List of Serials for T.L.A.'s District V," *Serial Slants,* IV (1953), 43–48. There have been issued a number of union lists of holdings in serials in various parts of the United States.

[24] Osborn, "The Future of the *Union List of Serials,*" *College and Research Libraries,* XV (1954), 26–28. Suggestions for obtaining serials are included in Orr, "A Few Aspects of Acquiring Serials," *Library Trends,* III (1955), 393-402.

with the holdings of the library is a primary procedure. Little has been done, however, in preparing selective lists of serials besides those for periodicals. The aid of faculty members as subject specialists is also a procedure which fortifies the selective process.

ORGANIZATION AND ADMINISTRATION. Serials present special problems in acquisition, housing, handling, and servicing. They present a heavy drain on the library budget. As bulky items, they quickly absorb the stack space of the library. They occasion extra difficulties in cataloging and organizing for use. They present problems in service through indexes and abstracts.

As a result of these special problems, a few university libraries have established separate serials divisions which are responsible for all the technical and readers' services concerning them. The advantages of an independent serials division evidently include specialized services to readers, as well as centralized control over the technical operations which are so important in the handling and organizing for use of thousands of serials on all subjects and in many languages. Although no study has been made of relative costs, undoubtedly the separate division with responsibilities to the clientele is an expensive adjunct in the library organization. Reference librarians as a group do not make distinctions between materials on the basis of form; they are interested in contents, and will use a serial, book, pamphlet, or map to aid the user with his specific problem. While there appears to be much that may be said for special handling of serials as they are received by the library, the case for special reference service with serials has not been generally accepted. Divisional and departmental libraries, however, furnish such service.

GOVERNMENT   University libraries have been avid collectors
PUBLICATIONS   of government publications—federal, state,
                      county, local, and foreign. United Nations
publications are also acquired. As sources of information on a multitude of social, scientific, and technological problems, documents issued by the various governmental agencies represent an important body of literature in the university library. They are used

constantly by undergraduate and graduate students, and by members of the faculty.

However, they present serious problems of record, care, and housing. Many librarians have found it desirable to institute carefully planned programs of acquiring government publications, in much the same way that they have set up policies in collecting periodicals and other materials. In this area of collecting, cooperation has an important role to play,[25] even though efforts in this direction have been relatively few.

FEDERAL DOCUMENTS   Most libraries, both university and non-university, possess some documents issued by the various agencies of. the United States government.[26] The depository system established by law provides for the sending of one free copy of government publications to those libraries designated as depositories. In addition to the depositories designated for Congressional districts and the several states, a "special provision of the law stipulates that all state libraries and the libraries of land-grant colleges and universities shall be Federal depositories." [27] At the present time there are 556 depositories, although none of them receives all publications of the government. The Superintendent of Documents sends items to libraries as they are selected from a *Classified List of United States Government Publications*.[28] The Documents Expediting Project is a plan to aid libraries in acquiring elusive items.

[25] Esterquest, "Midwest Inter-Library Center," *College and Research Libraries,* XV (1954), 47–49+. "A Summary of the Acquisitions," p. 49, lists, among other publications, both foreign and domestic government publications. A recent summary of problems in procuring documents is Wilcox, "The Acquisition of Government Publications," *Library Trends,* III (1955), 403–13.

[26] A useful publication relating to government documents is Temple, *Federal Services to Libraries.* Pages xv–xx of this work contain a set of "Bibliographical Notes" which provide a guide to various titles which discuss different aspects of federal publications. See also Merritt, *The United States Government as Publisher,* which contains a discussion of document distribution and of the depository system.

[27] Temple, *Federal Services to Libraries,* pp. 64–65. See also "Problems of Document Bibliography and Distribution: A Symposium," *College and Research Libraries,* XV (1954), 33–46.

[28] The Division of Documents does not issue a catalog of all publications for sale. The bi-weekly, *Selected United States Government Publications,* lists selected titles. The *Monthly Catalog of U.S. Government Publications* is a comprehensive and

In addition to the depository system, a number of federal agencies have established their own arrangements for distributing publications to libraries. The Bureau of the Census, for example, distributes copies of its reports to an additional 162 institutions designated as census libraries. The Public Health Service sends its publications to about 150 libraries. The Atomic Energy Commission maintains a list of 42 libraries to which it distributes scientific and technical reports. It also sends to the depository libraries *Nuclear Science Abstracts*, a semi-monthly journal, as well as catalog cards for its reports. Other agencies of the government have made arrangements for the distribution of their publications and reports on a geographical basis.

Libraries are sometimes able to obtain single copies of noncurrent publications free from agencies, members of Congress, or the Superintendent of Documents. The general procedure for securing missing items, extra copies, or titles not on the depository distribution is to purchase them from the Superintendent of Documents. Orders are made on deposited sums, or directly with coupons previously bought from the Documents Office.

TECHNICAL REPORTS. One of the developments of World War II has been the issuance from governmental agencies and research organizations of great numbers of technical reports.[29] It is estimated that about 75,000 unpublished technical reports are issued annually in the United States by research projects supported by the federal government. Thousands of other reports are also produced by private agencies not on contract with the government. How to acquire, organize, record, and service them represent important questions to those working with research personnel.

current listing of all publications received and cataloged by the Superintendent of Documents during the month preceding the date of issue. Periodicals and statistical statements are included only twice a year in an appendix to the February and August issues. A depository library which elected to receive everything available would receive more than 16,000 individual pieces annually.

[29] Fry, *Library Organization and Management of Technical Reports Literature;* Fry, "An Introduction to Security-Classified Libraries for Universities," *College and Research Libraries,* XIII (1952), 227–31. Fry provides a comprehensive bibliography. See also Fry and Kortendick (eds.), *The Production and Use of Technical Reports.*

As Fry has pointed out, a number of universities "now operate through their defense-related research projects large, organized collections of classified and unclassified reports. Although such projects are under university contract, they tend to become separate organizations for operational purposes, with separate library service distinct from the university library system." [30] Because of the security element involved in the handling of classified materials, special controls are necessary. University libraries which have no clearance for security-classified publications are able to secure items as they are declassified. The Office of Technical Services, through its *U.S. Government Research Reports*, provides information about such publications. Declassified titles may be purchased.[31]

ORGANIZATION FOR USE. Practices in libraries vary considerably in the organization of documents for use.[32] Regularly printed documents, particularly those which appear in series, are generally analyzed in governmentally issued indexes and hence are not usually cataloged as fully as ordinary books and periodicals. The inadequate indexing of much near-print material, however, has made it necessary to catalog them more extensively than ordinary documents. A number of institutions have arranged their documents by the Superintendent of Documents classification system; others have run the documents into the book collections on the basis of subject, using the Dewey Decimal, Library of Congress, or some other classification. Libraries which have set up separate documents rooms or divisions ordinarily depend on the classification and indexes to retrieve materials. In those libraries which catalog documents, Library of Congress printed cards are used extensively.

[30] Fry, "An Introduction to Security-Classified Libraries for Universities," p. 230.

[31] Jackson, "Acquisitions: Sources and Techniques," *American Documentation*, III (1952), 94-100; also "How to Obtain Research and Development Reports from the Government," *Special Libraries*, XLIV (1953), 101-8.

[32] "Federal Depository Libraries: A Symposium," *College and Research Libraries*, XII (1951), 37-47+; "Official Checklists and Indexes *versus* Cataloging of Government Publications," *College and Research Libraries*, XII (1951), 158-70; Ward, "Processing Government Documents," *College and Research Libraries*, XII (1951), 48-51; Boyd and Rips, *United States Government Publications*; Jackson, *The Administration of the Government Documents Collection*; Jackson, *A Manual for the Administration of the Federal Documents Collection in Libraries*; Markley, *Library Records for Government Publications*.

STATE DOCUMENTS   Information concerning state publications was recently prepared by Hardin in a table of "Checklists of State Publications Currently Issued." [33] Another source of information, but not a comprehensive one, is the *Monthly Checklist of State Publications* issued by the Library of Congress. Hardin makes the following observation concerning the limitations of present sources of information relating to state publications:

Facing the state checklist situation squarely one is aware of the incomplete coverage of states and of the unequal value of the lists issued due to scant bibliographical detail. Cumulation of issues and indexes are infrequent. There are sometimes gaps in the historical coverage of a state. . . . Many of the present lists are issued in such impermanent form that there is no definite assurance of their continuance over a long period.[34]

Usually the state library of a particular state is designated as the depository for state publications. A few states, such as California and Louisiana, have set up depositories in other states. Libraries which are not depositories must make individual arrangements with the specific department of a state to secure its documents. State university libraries generally have been able to procure available documents of their own states. Other university libraries sometimes arrange to exchange materials for state documents through the state library.

The literature of librarianship contains many suggestions for improved distribution of state documents. The National Association of State Libraries, the Public Documents Committee of the American Library Association, and various state library associations have been interested in setting up regional document centers. While state libraries have been designated as depositories for state documents, they have not always organized their collections for easy use. For this reason, and in order to make the materials more available for research purposes, university libraries have been vitally concerned about the problem of systematic collecting of state publications. Cooperation among state libraries, state historical society libraries,

[33] "United States State Publications," *College and Research Libraries*, XII (1951), 160–63. Information concerning 19 states is provided.
[34] *Ibid.*, p. 163.

large public libraries, and university libraries has developed to some extent toward a solution of the problem. The university librarian, with the aid of other librarians, needs to work closely with legislative groups to insure proper distribution of a state's publications.

As in the case of federal publications, state document collections are sometimes cataloged and classified as books and placed in their proper places in the stacks. In other cases, special classifications have been devised for keeping them as separate collections. Since the indexing of these materials has been incomplete, they present special problems of control.[35]

COUNTY DOCUMENTS   Many of the problems which exist in regard to the procurement and handling of state documents exist with county documents. The development of research interest in rural activities, regionalism, and the relation of county governments to local and state governments has made it necessary for university libraries to acquire county publications. Reports by county auditors, assessors, recorders of deeds, courts, sheriffs' offices, mine inspectors, county park commissions, lunacy commissions, welfare relief commissioners, boards of education, finance, and health, and superintendents of the poor, as well as many manuals, directories, courses of study, proceedings, and tax lists, are examples of county publications which have value to students and research workers concerned with problems in the fields of political science, history, economics, education, law and sociology.

County publications are even more elusive than state documents. Usually they are issued in processed form and in limited editions. Unless the acquisition personnel are especially alert, the materials are not always available when needed. There is no current bibliography of county publications,[36] although some of them are listed in the *Bulletin of the Public Affairs Information Service*.

Undoubtedly, because of the scarcity and the likelihood of mini-

[35] The American Library Association has published a number of "state author-heading lists" which are useful in helping to organize state publications.

[36] Hodgson, *The Official Publications of American Counties.* So far as county archival materials are concerned, useful guides are provided through the publications of the Historical Records Survey.

mal use of county documents, cooperative acquisition should be a desirable approach. This step again involves close relations of the university library with public, state, and state historical libraries. The use of various microreproductive techniques in providing copies of materials for university libraries with active research programs has also been applied in some instances.

MUNICIPAL DOCUMENTS   Elusiveness and irregularity in publication characterize municipal documents also. Most smaller communities issue annual reports which cover the various municipal administrative activities. Larger cities are likely to issue a series of reports, each devoted to a separate department. Thus, there will be reports on the courts; the police, fire, education, engineering, and street-cleaning departments; housing, public parks and recreation, public libraries, and airports divisions; or other units of activity. Often only a single copy or a few mimeographed copies of departmental reports are made. Consequently, libraries are not always able to obtain reports in sequence for students and research workers who wish to examine the work of a department over a continuous period of time. Frequent changes in governmental personnel also affect adversely the contents and the continuity of municipal reports.

Allied to municipal documents are the publications of civic leagues, better government associations, and chambers of commerce. Bureaus of municipal research issue reports and monographs which are useful to the sociologist or political scientist. Information relating to municipalities is also included in uniform reports issued by some states and in the reports of the U.S. Bureau of the Census.

There is no comprehensive bibliography of municipal documents. Municipal reference libraries in Chicago, Los Angeles, Milwaukee, and New York issue lists which include major documents. The *Bulletin of the Public Affairs Information Service*, previously noted in connection with county documents, also includes entries of municipal publications.

It is apparent that a university library will need to work out a careful plan of acquiring municipal documents which are directly related to the research program of the institution. Like other documents, they are relatively expensive to organize and service. Cooperation in collecting and reproducing unpublished sources by photographic techniques is also essential in developing these resources for research.

FOREIGN DOCUMENTS   Foreign documents represent a considerable body of materials in large university libraries.[37] Since these materials are essential for advanced studies and special research projects in so many fields of world affairs, university librarians have been conscious of the difficulties of acquiring them systematically. Sources of information regarding foreign documents have not been uniform. As Cabeen has noted: "The bibliographical sources available for consultation when one undertakes to acquire the publications of foreign governments are far more numerous and varied in form than the official checklists and catalogs which can be found to implement collections." [38] There are many periodicals which have to be examined regularly and systematically for notices of important foreign government documents. National trade bibliographies of twelve countries contain listings of official documents. Cabeen also suggests the checking of "accessions lists and lists of books cataloged issued by libraries attached to government offices and private institutions which are concerned with international affairs in their many ramifications." [39]

British documents are included in various lists issued by the Stationery Office.[40] Daily, monthly, and consolidated lists offer American libraries a type of coverage that is not provided by

[37] Some 30,000 titles are included in the *List of the Serial Publications of Foreign Governments, 1815-1931*, ed. by Winifred Gregory. See also Winchell, *Guide to Reference Books*, pp. 109-10.

[38] "Foreign Government Publications," *College and Research Libraries*, XII (1951), 163-66. This article contains a useful section on "Bibliographical Aids." See also Conover, *Current National Bibliographies*, which includes latest information on sources of information concerning government publications of 67 countries.

[39] *Ibid.*, p. 163.

[40] Cox, "H.M.S.O. Publications," *ASLIB Proceedings*, I (1949), 251-56. The *British National Bibliography*, which began in 1951, lists government publications.

most other countries. The current bibliographies of French government documents are the fortnightly *Bibliographie sélective des publications officielles françaises* (a joint publication of the Comité de Coordination pour la Documentation des Sciences Sociales and the Commission Interministerielle de Documentation et Diffusion) and *Supplément F* of *Bibliographie de la France* both beginning with sections devoted to "Lois et traités" and "Assemblées constitutionnelles." [41]

Official bibliographies are issued also by Canada, Egypt, India, Ireland, the Netherlands, Sweden, and Switzerland. Such publications as the *Annual Catalog of Australian Publications*, issued by the Australian Commonwealth National Library, and *Bibliographie de Belgique*, issued by the Bibliothèque Royale of Belgium, are examples of library accessions lists useful to the acquisition librarian. The various *Guide[s] to the Official Publications of the Other American Republics*, issued by the Library of Congress, are of considerable aid in working with documents from Latin America. Separate listings are provided for the Caribbean, as well as for Central and South American countries.

Although information about documents may be available, it is not always easy to acquire the documents themselves. Despite the bibliographic coverage of publications in Britain, American libraries in the past have found certain obstacles placed before them in their acquisition programs.[42]

Systematic distribution of documents to American libraries by foreign countries has been lacking up to the present time. Federal and state institutions have been able to obtain some materials through exchange programs. University libraries have had to secure foreign documents in much the same way that they procure other materials. The major sources have been direct relations with governmental printers and administrative bureaus, established booksellers, who may serve as agents or correspondents; traveling professors and li-

[41] Roberts and Wojewodski, "French Parliamentary Documents," *College and Research Libraries*, XIV (1953), 255–58+. This paper describes many of the details of various French government publications. It also contains bibliographical footnotes.
[42] Ready, "The Acquisition Problem Concerning British Government Documents in the United States," *College and Research Libraries*, XV (1954), 411+.

brarians, who may purchase designated items, check for desiderata, and establish connections; and interested persons living in foreign countries, such as friends of the librarians, alumni, and diplomatic personnel. UNESCO, by acquainting personnel of governmental libraries in various countries of the world with the problem of document acquisition, has helped to foster the development of national bibliographies which include government publications.

Undoubtedly, cooperative acquisition has an important role to play in document collecting by university libraries. The formulation of cooperative policies, like those of Tulane University, Duke University, and the University of North Carolina in collecting Latin American documents, should be made on local, regional, state, and national levels. The University of Texas Library, coordinating its collecting policy with curricular needs, specializes in the acquisition of Mexican documents.[43] The Library of Congress, through its generous assistance to other libraries in the United States, has helped in distributing duplicate foreign documents to university libraries. Among the items prominent in the list of materials collected by the Midwest Inter-Library Center have been foreign government gazettes and parliamentary papers.[44]

UNITED NATIONS AND SPECIALIZED AGENCY DOCUMENTS   University libraries were among the most assiduous collectors of League of Nations publications. With the establishment of the United Nations, they have developed acquisition programs to obtain its extensive series of documents as well as those of the many specialized agencies.[45] The *United Nations Documents Index* is a general source of information concerning documents issued by the UN, as well as

[43] Ker, *Mexican Government Publications.*

[44] Esterquest, "Midwest Inter-Library Center," *College and Research Libraries,* XV (1954), 47-49+.

[45] Carroll, "League of Nations Documents and Publications Comparable with or Continued in United Nations Publications," *College and Research Libraries,* XIII (1952), 44-52+; Cassidy, "United Nations Documents in the Medium-Sized University—Nuisance or Necessity?" *College and Research Libraries,* XIII (1952), 107-10; Moor and Chamberlain, *How to Use United Nations Documents;* Cabeen and Cook, "Organization of Serials and Documents," *Library Trends,* II (1953), 199-216; United Nations, Department of Public Information, *Indexes and Bibliographies Published by the United Nations;* MacBride, "A Subject Approach to United Nations Documents," *College and Research Libraries,* XV (1954), 42-46.

those of the agencies which are sent to the United Nations. University libraries are among the thirty-three depository libraries which have been established by the United Nations in cooperation with the American Library Association. Nondepository libraries obtain documents through designated sales agents. Many mimeographed documents containing primary source material for research workers, which are sent to the depository libraries, are not offered for sale.

The publication program of the United Nations and the specialized agencies has been so prolific libraries have had to establish special operations for handling the materials. While the Library of Congress has issued printed cards for many major documents, it has not attempted to catalog the bulk of the titles. In many cases, libraries have organized the materials into separate collections. In order to make maximum use of the materials, however, it appears essential to have a precise binding and index policy.[46]

NEWSPAPERS   The newspaper collection forms a basic part of the university library's research materials. Valuable though it is, its administration has created a number of perplexing problems for librarians. Newspapers are expensive to acquire. They represent special problems in housing, binding, and preservation. The Association of Research Libraries has recognized these facts and recently has been giving particular attention to newspapers.[47]

Some idea of the problems raised by the newspaper in university libraries is provided by a brief examination of the extent of collecting. In 1953, the University of Illinois reported receiving 624 newspapers regularly.[48] Twenty-two of the 68 libraries which furnished data received 100 or more newspaper titles. The median for the

---

[46] Signor, "United Nations *versus* League of Nations Documentation," *Special Libraries*, XLIII (1952), 62–64; see also items in Note 45.

[47] "Minutes of the Association of Research Libraries, January 31, 1954, Madison, Wisconsin," p. 54. A special Committee on Cooperative Access to Newspapers and other Serials has been considering the possibility of "initiating a national pool of current foreign newspapers in microfilm form to be available by loan to subscribing institutions." A study of foreign newspaper coverage is part of the plan.

[48] *College and Research Libraries*, XV (1954), 68.

entire group was 54. To house these volumes, miles of special-type shelving in university library stacks are required.

NEWSPAPERS AS RESEARCH MATERIALS   The modern use of newspapers as primary sources is well known. They are particularly important in certain lines of reference work. As Winchell has observed: "Current issues are helpful on questions of the day, events, policies, opinion, politics, personalities, and many others. Back volumes serve the same purpose for the contemporary history of an earlier period and often record details of a situation local in its application that are not found in general reference works." [49]

Not only historians, but sociologists, political scientists, philologists, journalists, advertisers, economists, educators, and others, have used newspapers for research purposes. Newspapers vary greatly in their coverage, accuracy, and objectivity. They change frequently in policy as they change in ownership. Differences among newspapers affect the acquisition policies of libraries, for they must select and preserve from among the vast number of newspapers published throughout the world only those which are likely to be valuable as research materials. Newspaper collections should be representative, but they should include at least the best and most important papers from each region or country represented. Selection is an important element in a program of newspaper acquisition, and unless it is purposefully and intelligently planned, the newspaper collection cannot be of maximum use to scholars.[50]

Although domestic newspapers give university librarians enough trouble, foreign newspapers provide additional problems. Irregular deliveries, non-availability of duplicates for damaged or lost copies, and difficulties in obtaining information concerning titles increase the amount of time that is spent on collecting foreign newspapers.[51]

[49] Winchell, *Guide to Reference Books*, p. 100.

[50] Harlow, "Conservation of Newspaper Resources," *California Library Bulletin*, IX (1948), 89–91; X (1948), 19–21. In these two articles Harlow, primarily concerned with the problem of newspapers in California libraries, provides a useful summary of factors involved in a newspaper acquisition program.

[51] Kipp, "Microfilming Foreign Newspapers," *Harvard Library Bulletin*, II (1948), 410–12.

The changing nature of foreign newspapers is another factor that requires constant attention in so far as acquisition policy is concerned.

COOPERATIVE COLLECTING AND MICROFILMING   For a number of years, it has been evident that university libraries would not be able to continue individualistic programs in the acquiring of newspapers. In order to eliminate or minimize duplication within a region, agreements in collecting have been established. Thus Duke University and the University of North Carolina have been collecting in specified areas—Duke, acquiring materials from various regions of the United States and from foreign countries, and North Carolina, emphasizing the collecting of North Carolina newspapers. The Virginia State Library and the University of Virginia collect and preserve Virginia newspapers on an assigned basis. The California State Library and the University of California have worked out a program of cooperative collecting.

The American Library Association, as well as the Association of Research Libraries, has also been concerned about the problem of newspapers in libraries. One of the first projects of the ALA Committee on Cooperative Microfilm Projects was the preservation of American newspapers.[52] New possibilities in acquiring and preserving newspapers have been opened up through the improvement of microfilming techniques. Not only do microfilm copies eliminate the problem of deteriorating newspapers, but scattered files are brought together, accessibility is increased, and pressure on storage space remarkably decreased.[53] Library patrons have found microfilm copies of newspapers easy to handle. University libraries

[52] Eaton, "Toward a State-wide Newspaper Microfilming Project," *College and Research Libraries,* XIV (1953), 26–34. The author discusses a number of microfilming projects of newspapers.
[53] Harlow, "Conservation of Newspaper Resources"; Kipp, "Microfilming Foreign Newspapers"; Hamilton, "Microfilming of Newspapers," *Canadian Library Association Bulletin,* VIII (1951), 91–94; Shoemaker, "Remarks on Microcards and Microfilm for Newspapers," *American Documentation,* I (1950), 207–8; Schwegmann (comp.), *Newspapers on Microfilm.*

undoubtedly will further exploit the microfilm technique for newspaper preservation in the future.[54]

BIBLIOGRAPHY

Adams, Randolph G. The Whys and Wherefores of the William L. Clements Library: A Brief Essay on Book Collecting as a Fine Art. 2d ed. Ann Arbor, University of Michigan Press, 1930.

Allen, H. B. "Who Reads Treasure Room Books?" *Harvard Library Notes*, (May 1938), 180–83.

American Newspapers, 1821–1936: A Union List of Files Available in the United States and Canada. Ed. by Winifred Gregory, under the auspices of the Bibliographical Society of America. New York, H. W. Wilson, 1937.

"Availability of Research Materials," *Library Trends*, II (1954), 487–580.

Barnes, E. B. "The University Library—Services or Resources?" *Library Quarterly*, XXII (1952), 177–79.

Bennett, Fleming. "The Current Bookmarket," *Library Trends*, III (1955), 376–84.

Bertalan, Frank J. Books for Junior Colleges. Chicago, American Library Association, 1954.

Boyd, Anne M. United States Government Publications. 3d ed. Rev. by Rae Elizabeth Rips. New York, H. W. Wilson, 1952.

Brodman, Estelle. "Choosing Physiology Journals," *Bulletin of the Medical Library Association*, XXXII (1944), 479–83.

Brough, Kenneth J. Scholar's Workshop. Urbana, University of Illinois Press, 1953.

Cabeen, Violet A. "Foreign Government Publications," *College and Research Libraries*, XII (1951), 163–66. Contains a section of "Bibliographical Aids."

Cabeen, Violet A., and C. D. Cook. "Organization of Serials and Documents," *Library Trends*, II (1953), 199–216. Contains a lengthy bibliography including items on the acquisition of serials and documents.

Carroll, Marie J. "League of Nations Documents and Publications Comparable with or Continued in United Nations Publications," *College and Research Libraries*, XIII (1952), 44–52+.

Cassidy, Thomas R. "United Nations Documents in the Medium-sized

---

[54] Fussler, "Photographic Reproduction of Research Materials," *Library Trends*, II (1954), 532–44; Esterquest, "Midwest Inter-Library Center," pp. 49, 89.

University—Nuisance or Necessity?" *College and Research Libraries,* XIII (1952), 107–10.

Conover, Helen (comp.). Current National Bibliographies. Washington, D.C., Library of Congress, 1955.

Downs, Robert B. American Library Resources: A Bibliographical Guide. Chicago, American Library Association, 1951.

Eaton, Andrew J. "Toward a State-Wide Newspaper Microfilming Project," *College and Research Libraries,* XIV (1953), 26–34.

Esterquest, Ralph T. "Midwest Inter-Library Center: Acquisition Policy and Program," *College and Research Libraries,* XV (1954), 47-49+.

Fall, John. "Problems of American Libraries in Acquiring Foreign Publications," *Library Quarterly,* XXIV (1954), 101–13.

"Federal Depository Libraries: A Symposium," *College and Research Libraries,* XII (1951), 37–47+.

Fry, Bernard M. "An Introduction to Security-Classified Libraries for Universities," *College and Research Libraries,* XIII (1952), 227–31.

—————— Library Organization and Management of Technical Reports Literature. Washington, Catholic University of America Press, 1953. (Catholic University of America Studies in Library Science, No. 1)

Fry, Bernard M., and James J. Kortendick (eds.). The Production and Use of Technical Reports. Washington, D.C., Catholic University of America Press, 1955.

Fussler, Herman H. "Photographic Reproduction of Research Materials," *Library Trends,* II (1954), 532–44.

Gross, P. L. K., and E. M. Gross. "College Libraries and Chemical Education," *Science,* LXVI (1927), 385–89.

Hamilton, R. M. "Microfilming of Newspapers," *Canadian Library Association Bulletin,* VIII (1951), 91–94.

Hardin, Ruth. "United States State Publications," *College and Research Libraries,* XII (1951), 160–63.

Harlow, Neal. "Conservation of Newspaper Resources," *California Library Bulletin,* IX (1948), 89–91; X (1948), 19–21.

Harvard University. The Place of the Library in a University: A Conference Held at Harvard University, 30–31 March 1949. Cambridge, Harvard University Library, 1950.

Harvard University Library (Lamont Library). Catalogue of the Lamont Library, Harvard College, prepared by Philip B. McNiff and Members of the Library Staff. Cambridge, Harvard University Press, 1953.

Hodgson, J. G. "The Official Publications of American Counties: A Union List, with an Introduction on the Collecting of County Publications." Fort Collins, Colo., 1937.

Jackson, E. B. "Acquisitions: Sources and Techniques," *American Documentation*, III (1952), 94–100.

—— "How to Obtain Research and Development Reports from the Government," *Special Libraries*, XLIV (1953), 101–8.

Jackson, Ellen P. The Administration of the Government Documents Collection. (ACRL Monograph No. 5). Chicago, Association of College and Reference Libraries, 1953.

—— A Manual for the Administration of the Federal Documents Collection in Libraries. Chicago, American Library Association, 1955.

Jenkins, Frances B. "The Acquisition of Scientific and Technological Material," *Library Trends*, III (1955), 414–22.

Ker, Annita M. Mexican Government Publications: A Guide to the More Important Publications of the National Government of Mexico, 1821–1936. Washington, U.S. Government Printing Office, 1940.

Kipp, Lawrence. "Microfilming Foreign Newspapers," *Harvard Library Bulletin*, II (1948), 410–12.

List of Serial Publications of Foreign Governments, 1815–1931, ed. by Winifred Gregory. New York, H. W. Wilson, 1932.

MacBride, James H. "A Subject Approach to United Nations Documents," *College and Research Libraries*, XV (1954), 42–46.

Malclès, L. N. Les sources du travail bibliographique. 2 vols. (Vol. 3 in preparation). New York, Stechert-Hafner, 1953.

Markley, Anne Ethelyn. Library Records for Government Publications. Berkeley and Los Angeles, University of California Press, 1951.

Merritt, LeRoy C. The United States Government as Publisher. Chicago, University of Chicago Press, 1943.

Miller, Robert A. Purchasing of Books and Journals in Europe. (Occasional Paper, No. 36) Urbana, University of Illinois Library School, 1953 (mimeographed).

Moor, Carol C., and Waldo Chamberlain. How to Use United Nations Documents. New York, New York University Press, 1952.

New Serial Titles. Washington, Library of Congress, 1953–

"Official Checklists and Indexes *versus* Cataloging of Government Publications," *College and Research Libraries*, XII (1951), 158–70.

Orr, Robert W. "A Few Aspects of Acquiring Serials," *Library Trends*, III (1955), 393–402.

Osborn, Andrew D. "The Future of the Union List of Serials," *College and Research Libraries*, XV (1954), 26–28+.

—— Serial Publications: Their Place and Treatment in Libraries. Chicago, American Library Association, 1955.

Pargellis, Stanley. "Book Supply and the Book Market," *Library Quarterly*, XXIII (1953), 199–204.

Powell, L. C. "Rare Book Code," *College and Research Libraries*, X (1949), 307–8.

Ready, W. B. "The Acquisition Problem concerning British Government Documents in the United States," *College and Research Libraries*, XV (1954), 411+.

Reiman, Frederick M. "A Selected Bibliography of Articles Related to Serials, 1936–1952," *Serial Slants*, IV (1953), 49–94.

Roberts, A. D., and F. P. Wojewodski. "French Parliamentary Documents," *College and Research Libraries*, XIV (1953), 255–58+.

Schwegmann, George A., Jr. Newspapers on Microfilm. 2d ed. Washington, Library of Congress, 1953.

Shoemaker, R. J. "Remarks on Microcards and Microfilm for Newspapers," *American Documentation*, I (1950), 207–8.

Shores, Louis. Basic Reference Sources. Chicago, American Library Association, 1954.

Shores, Louis (ed.). Challenges to Librarianship. Tallahassee, Florida State University, 1953.

Signor, Nelle. "United Nations *versus* League of Nations Documentation," *Special Libraries*, XLIII (1952), 62–64+.

Stern, Sylvia O. "Texas Librarians Have a Union List of Serials for T.L.A.'s District V," *Serial Slants*, IV (1953), 43–48.

Temple, Phillips. Federal Services to Libraries. Chicago, American Library Association, 1954.

Ulrich's Periodicals Directory: A Classified Guide to a Selected List of Current Periodicals, Foreign and Domestic. 7th ed. By Eileen C. Graves. New York, Bowker, 1953.

Union List of Serials in Libraries of the United States and Canada, ed. by Winifred Gregory. 2d ed. New York: H. W. Wilson, 1943.

United Nations Department of Public Information. Indexes and Bibliographies Published by the United Nations. New York, United Nations, 1953.

Ward, Pauline. "Processing Government Documents," *College and Research Libraries*, XII (1951), 48–51.

Wilcox, Jerome K. "The Acquisition of Government Publications," *Library Trends*, III (1955), 403–13.

Wilson, Louis R., Mildred H. Lowell, and Sarah R. Reed. The Library in College Instruction: A Syllabus on the Improvement of College Instruction through Library Use. New York, H. W. Wilson, 1951.

Winchell, Constance M. Guide to Reference Books. 7th ed. Chicago: American Library Association, 1952; Supplement, 1954.

Wing, Donald S., and Robert Vosper. "The Antiquarian Bookmarket and the Acquisition of Rare Books," *Library Trends*, III (1955), 385–92.

Wyllie, John C. "Rare Books in the University Library: The Need," *College and Research Libraries*, X (1949), 291–99.

Young, K. "Uses of Rare Books and Manuscripts," *Yale University Library Gazette*, XVI (1941), 25.

Useful information on the collecting activities of specific libraries is provided in the series of articles entitled "Notable Materials Added to North American Libraries," which have appeared in the *Library Quarterly*. See also various library surveys, especially chapters on "Holdings" or "Collections."

XI

BOOK COLLECTIONS:

SPECIAL MATERIALS

IN ADDITION to the more general materials which university libraries acquire, there are many special types. The problems involved in procuring and organizing these materials are complex and require the constant attention of administrators and specialists on the staff if they are to be systematically acquired and made easily accessible to users. Since World War II the acquisition of special materials has greatly accelerated.[1]

DISSERTATIONS AND THESES — University libraries have been among the principal collectors of dissertations and theses. Doctoral dissertations, both foreign and American, especially represent a category of research material which has been sought after by students and faculty members working in narrow fields of investigation. Theses, usually prepared by students working for the Master's degree, generally do not receive the attention given to doctoral dissertations, but a number of them are published and many are obtained by libraries in microreproduction. Master's theses are among the items which have become generally available through microfilm and microcard. A university library, of course, collects copies of all dissertations and theses prepared in the departments of the institution of which it is a part.

DOCTORAL DISSERTATIONS. Since 1934, the Association of Research Libraries has sponsored the publication of a bibliography of all

[1] "Current Acquisitions Trends in American Libraries," *Library Trends*, III (1955), 333–470. The October, 1955, issue of *Library Trends* is devoted to "Special Materials and Services."

doctoral dissertations accepted by American universities.[2] Requirements for the publication of the dissertation as a separate monograph, either as an original book or in reprint form, have been lessened considerably in recent years. Of the 105 institutions in the United States which in 1951 granted the doctorate, 37 required publication of the dissertation in whole or in part (in some cases publication in a technical or scholarly journal is permitted). Microfilm copies of the typescript of the dissertation as a substitute for printing are acceptable in 20 institutions. Forty-three universities, including some of those which stipulate printing in fuller form, require publication of abstracts of doctoral dissertations.[3] Typescript copies are usually deposited in the university library. Those libraries which provide microfilm service usually are able to reproduce copies for sale to other institutions.

American university libraries have depended to some extent on dissertations for use in exchange programs.[4] Until World War II, the volume of foreign dissertations exceeded that from American institutions. In 1938, there were more than 9,000 dissertations from German universities.[5] In 1950, there were 7,594 dissertations, but of these only 346 were printed. While 1,091 took some form of typescript in reproduction, 6,157 remained in typewritten form.[6] Although the microfilming of dissertations in Europe is less centralized than it is in the United States (where considerable use is made of University Microfilms), copies are usually secured on a value-for-value, rather than on a piece-for-piece basis.

[2] *Doctoral Dissertations Accepted by American Universities.* The Catalog Division of the Library of Congress prepared a *List of American Doctoral Dissertations* for the period 1912–1938. Since 1938, University Microfilms, at Ann Arbor, Michigan, has issued *Microfilm Abstracts* (beginning with vol. 12, no. 1, 1952, changed format and title to *Dissertation Abstracts*). The dissertations included in this work are available in complete form on microfilm. In 1952, the United States Department of State issued *Abstracts of Completed Dissertations for the Year 1950–1951*. This work is concerned with dissertations in the social sciences on foreign areas; other issues are planned for the future.

[3] Figures in this paragraph taken from Mary Irwin (ed.) *American Colleges and Universities*, p. 60.

[4] Lane, "Exchange Work in College and University Libraries." See also Kleberg, "Report of the Sub-committee on the Exchange of University Publications," 121–23.

[5] *Jahresverzeichnis der deutschen Hochschulschriften, 1938.*

[6] *Ibid., 1950*, p. vii.

Winchell [7] has provided information concerning the bibliographical listing of dissertations prepared in Austria, Belgium, Canada, France, Germany, Great Britain, the Netherlands, Scandinavia, South Africa, Spain, and Switzerland. At the present time, the main sources of European dissertations are Belgium, Denmark, France, Norway, and Sweden.

In Europe, too, there is an increasing trend toward printed abstracts of dissertations in place of complete publications. It appears likely that photographic reproduction of original studies will play an increasingly important role in the area of such materials as dissertations, particularly if research workers are interested in copies of complete studies, rather than journal articles or abstracts. As Fussler has noted:

The direct distribution to libraries and investigators of data and research findings, in certain microtext formats, may reduce the costs of publishing, speed up the distribution of research information, extend the possibilities in the diffusion of knowledge in highly specialized areas, and may simplify certain problems of use and bibliographic organization.[8]

MASTERS' ESSAYS. While the Master's essay was formerly a general requirement of all universities, today a large number of institutions permit the substitution of "problem" or "project" courses. In 1950, a total of 58,219 Master's degrees were awarded.[9] The majority of the universities still require the writing of a Master's thesis. Except for the few Master's theses which are published in journals or as separates, there is no special problem of acquisition, as copies are generally restricted to the libraries of the institutions in which the degrees are granted. Thesis collections, however, do present problems of handling and service.

ADMINISTRATION AND ORGANIZATION. Practices vary considerably in university libraries in so far as the handling of dissertations and theses is concerned. Some institutions organize them into separate

---

[7] *Guide to Reference Books*, pp. 112–15; *Supplement, 1950–1952*, p. 20.

[8] "Photographic Reproduction of Research Materials," *Library Trends*, II (1954), 542.

[9] Irwin (ed.), *American Colleges and Universities*, pp. 52–53.

collections, arranged chronologically by the issuing university. Other libraries handle them in much the same way as books, particularly if they are doctoral dissertations. They are bound, cataloged, and classified along with other materials on the subjects involved. The Library of Congress has helped in this direction by supplying printed cards for many of the titles. Another example of cooperation in this respect is supplied by the practice of the New York State Medical Society Library, which receives medical dissertations, catalogs them, and furnishes cards to other libraries.

Although suggestions have been made in the past for cooperation in acquiring, maintaining, cataloging, and classifying collections of dissertations, especially those issued by foreign universities, little has been done in this connection.[10] The problem has been of interest to the Midwest Inter-Library Center, however, and Esterquest[11] reported that among the materials being acquired by the Center is the current output of theses of all universities in France.

The handling of dissertations and theses of a particular university by its library may be somewhat different from that provided for materials from other institutions. Some libraries maintain separate card catalogs, often with subject entries included.[12] In a number of instances, university libraries have issued printed bibliographies containing author and subject indexes which provide an adequate guide to the collection of dissertations.[13] Such bibliographies are not only useful to the institution itself, but provide a valuable source of information to researchers in other universities.[14]

[10] Faison, "Care of German Dissertations," *Bulletin of the American Library Association*, XXX (1936), 572–73.

[11] "Midwest Inter-Library Center: Acquisition Policy and Program, 1950–1953," *College and Research Libraries*, XV (1954), 89.

[12] Dean, "Subject Cataloging of Theses and Dissertations," *Journal of Cataloging and Classification*, VIII (1952), 24–26.

[13] Horn, "University Archivist and the Thesis Problem," *American Archivist*, XV (1952), 321–31.

[14] Palfrey and Coleman, *Guide to Bibliographies of Theses, United States and Canada;* Rosenberg, "Bibliographies of Theses in America," *Bulletin of Bibliography*, XVIII (1945), 181–82, 201–3.

MANUSCRIPTS   Manuscripts and archives, as primary
AND ARCHIVES   sources, provide the materials that are so
                      necessary for basic studies, whether these are
dissertations or other investigations. In another part of this section,
manuscripts which are contained in archival collections—governmental, educational, business, etc.—are considered separately. Attention is given here to those nonarchival manuscript materials, such
as Latin, Greek, and Hebrew manuscripts, which are primarily
valuable to researchers in art, biography, history, literature, paleography, philology, and religion; and such items as recent letters,
diaries, and similar papers of American and foreign origin. Into this
category fall a Dante manuscript, a letter of George Washington,
a manuscript poem of Shelley or Emerson, a psalter of the eleventh
century, or papers of Boswell.

University libraries attract the letters and papers of authors, military figures, statesmen, and other persons. While the Library of
Congress, the New York Public Library, the Newberry Library,
the Huntington Library, and other notable, large non-university
libraries are the recipients each year of valuable manuscript collections, the large university libraries increasingly have become the
repositories of such material.[15]

A number of university libraries have endeavored to prepare
guides to their manuscript collections.[16] California, Chicago,
Columbia, Cornell, Harvard, Pennsylvania, and Princeton, among
other institutions, have issued bibliographical contributions or
calendars of manuscripts.

Much attention has been given in recent years to the general
problem of acquiring, preserving, and using manuscript materials.
Both the American Historical Association and the Association of
Research Libraries have sought to formulate a policy which would

[15] Jones, "Opportunities and Support for College and University Libraries," *College and Research Libraries*, XIV (1953), 9–21; see also articles on "Notable Materials Added to American Libraries," in various issues of *Library Quarterly*. Later
title expanded to "North American Libraries."

[16] For example, see listings in Downs, *American Library Resources*, pp. 34–36. See
also Kennedy, *A Concise Bibliography for Students of English; Systematically Arranged*, pp. 28–33.

be helpful in making materials available readily to qualified scholars.[17] Since this is a problem of growing importance, it may be well to indicate the nature of the policy as set forth by the ARL. The following statement is taken from a committee report issued in 1952:

It is the duty of every librarian to encourage the proper use and publication of manuscripts under his care. It is his responsibility to make them (or photographic reproductions of them) easily available to qualified investigators, and to take such steps as are necessary to insure their physical safety and to preserve them in as nearly a pristine condition as possible for the use of scholars now and in the future. He should be alive to opportunities to acquire manuscripts, remembering, however, that selfish competition between libraries may encourage the owner to have a fanciful idea as to the monetary value of his manuscripts and thus defeat the common cause of preservation for use, as is the case when an integral collection is broken up at sale and scattered to the four winds. The cause of scholarship is best served by the librarian building on strength in his own institution, and directing to their proper home manuscripts which would fit into or supplement strong collections in other institutions. The librarian should make every effort to discourage restrictions on the use of manuscripts, such as are sometimes requested by former owners, and in any case require a terminal date for restrictions, and wherever possible he should acquire publication rights along with physical restrictions.[18]

The *ad hoc* committee on manuscripts set up by the American Historical Association was assigned to study the arrangement and use of large collections acquired since 1900.[19] The committee recognized that there would be many exceptions to any general policy, since each group of manuscripts may present a separate case. While consideration should be given to the scholar, there should be proper respect for the limitations of time, money, and personnel of most manuscript repositories. This report, as well as the one by the ARL

[17] Altick, "The Scholar's Paradise," *College and Research Libraries*, XV (1954), 375–82. Altick, among other criticisms of library practices, calls attention to the "practice of withholding certain materials, principally manuscripts, from the use of everyone but some privileged person who has successfully asserted his right to a monopoly."
[18] "Report of the Committee on the Use of Manuscripts by Visiting Scholars," *College and Research Libraries*, XIII (1952), 58–59.
[19] "Report of the Ad Hoc Committee on Manuscripts . . ." *American Archivist*, XIV (1951), 229–40.

which is based on it, contains recommendations concerning arrangement, guides, acquisition policies, physical protection of manuscripts, qualifications of users, restrictions on the use of content of manuscripts, facilitation of the use of collections, and protection of the researcher.[20]

ORGANIZATION FOR USE. As a rule, manuscript collections are preserved in rare book departments or archives rooms of university libraries. Depending upon such factors as the stipulations of the donors, the size of the manuscript collections, and the uses made of them, organization and cataloging may take a variety of forms. For example, at Harvard College Library, the early manuscripts are divided into three groups: (1) in a general series classified by language—as Latin, Greek, etc.; (2) in special collections grouped by subjects, such as Dante, folklore, or Harvard University sections; and (3) in special collections named after the original owners or donors, such as the Fearing and the Henry E. Widener collections. The large American history collections are not cataloged. Guides and calendars are provided, and the collections are administered by special staffs, the heads of which hold doctorates in history, with library and archival training. Suggestions for organizing materials have been provided by the practices of the National Archives and effective state archival programs.[21]

Usually, the early manuscripts are cataloged fully. Classification is less rigid for manuscripts than for books, and the materials are commonly arranged in chronological sequences or by some system which fits the local situation. The notation used for marking manuscripts should be fairly simple, since the purpose of cataloging is to facilitate locating manuscripts and returning them to their proper places.[22]

[20] Wilson and Dalton, "Restriction on the Use of Research Materials," *Library Trends*, II (1954), 545–53.

[21] At the present time, the Library of Congress is developing a set of rules for the cataloging of manuscripts. It is expected that it will be made available to the profession shortly.

[22] Bond, "Cataloguing of Manuscripts in the Houghton Library," *Harvard Library Bulletin*, IV (1950), 392–96; Russell and Roberts, "Processing Procedures in the Manuscripts Department of the Duke University Library," *American Archivist*, XII (1949), 369–80.

ARCHIVAL COLLECTIONS. Many of the above comments apply also to the materials in libraries which are called archives. "Archives" are usually differentiated from "manuscripts" in that the former are generally concerned with coordinated or undistributed collections of records of governmental agencies, societies, churches, universities, business firms, and other societies and institutions.[23] Within this definition, the term "manuscripts" is used to refer to one or more unrelated documents, historical or modern. While manuscripts may be given separate treatment in cataloging, archival collections are likely to be cataloged by collection.

Many universities have extensive archival collections, reaching into the hundreds of thousands or millions of pieces. Their acquisition places an unusual responsibility upon the librarian for special care and organization. The National Archives, the Society of American Archivists, and the American Historical Association have been concerned with special problems of interest to historical, university, and other research libraries. *The American Archivist* particularly contains many articles describing the handling of archival collections.

Suggestive criteria for collecting archives and unofficial manuscript materials include the following: (1) the materials should relate to a well-defined geographical or cultural area; (2) they should reflect the social, economic, political, scientific, and spiritual interests of the region; (3) they should have some relation to the programs of instruction and research of the university; and (4) they should possess an interest for scholars and authors outside the area. Some of the university libraries, such as that of the University of Virginia, have established such criteria. Virginia has assembled large regional collections which include manuscripts, letters, tax books, council minutes, war records, church papers, telegraphic dispatches, personal account books, plantation records, medical records, weather observations, family histories, business and industrial records, and personal diaries and travelogues. Writers and researchers in all fields

[23] Hensel, "Treatment of Nonbook Materials," *Library Trends,* II (1953), 187–98. Contains an extensive bibliography.

have found such materials indispensable in preparing scholarly works.

The collecting and care of archival materials are costly operations. For this reason, it is important that state university and private university libraries work closely with state historical societies in outlining a cooperative program of acquisition. With microreproduction available, it is not difficult for researchers to obtain copies of materials they need.

UNIVERSITY ARCHIVAL COLLECTIONS. The university library generally contains a collection of materials concerning the educational and administrative policy of the university, as well as publications by and about administrative officers, faculty members, students, alumni, and others connected with the institution. Administrative records usually consist of original manuscripts and documents from the various parts of the university. Minutes, papers, correspondence, committee records, and departmental records comprise a major portion of the collection.[24] Another primary division of the material consists of those items which relate to the university's activities. These include histories or descriptions of the institution as a whole or of any of its units, catalogs and registers, photographs of and commentaries on student life and undergraduate societies, programs, biographical materials of all kinds, alumni records, student newspapers and magazines, and other publications. Faculty publications and student dissertations and theses may also be included in the collection. Practically complete coverage has been obtained in those libraries which have used systematic procedures in requesting items for the archives. A number of libraries have stimulated faculty members and others to send materials by issuing at regular intervals bibliographies of the publications.

Large local archival collections require special systems of arrangement and cataloging. Harvard, Rochester, and New York universi-

[24] Wilson, "No Ivory Tower," *College and Research Libraries*, XIII (1952), 215-22. Wilson not only discusses the problems in organizing a collection of archives for an educational institution, but suggests an "Archives Charter or Plan of Organization"; see also Mood and Carstensen, "University Records and Their Relation to General University Administration," *College and Research Libraries*, XI (1950), 337-45.

ties, among others, have special classifications for the handling of this material.

INCUNABULA For students of art, printing, and related subjects, incunabula are source materials of the first order. American university libraries have been gradually adding to their collections of incunabula.[25] Among the libraries which have collections of 100 or more volumes are Harvard, Brown, North Carolina, Yale, Illinois, Cornell, Michigan, Columbia, Princeton, Pennsylvania, Chicago, and Virginia.

Except for the major university libraries which have endowed funds for the purchase of incunabula, most libraries obtain such materials through the benefactions of collectors or donors. Their administration presents comparatively few problems other than those of caring for their use and protecting their contents and bindings. Bibliographical description and cataloging of incunabula have received special attention.[26]

MAPS The use of maps for research purposes has become increasingly important in recent years. World War II especially impressed upon libraries the need to have available maps of all kinds to meet the demands of students, faculty members, and special research workers. At Illinois, for example, the Map Room serves not only university personnel, but also the members of the state surveys which are located on the campus.

Formerly, the collecting of maps in most libraries was almost completely restricted to those of a geographical nature. The University of Chicago Library, however, very early began to collect maps dealing with military, geological, metereological, commercial, physical, political, social, historical, agricultural, and numerous other subjects. But other libraries have only recently begun to organize

[25] Rider, "Holdings of Incunabula in American University Libraries," *Library Quarterly*, IX (1939), 273–84; also his "Incunabula in American Libraries," *Library Quarterly*, X (1940), 361–65. Locations of specific titles may be found in Stillwell (ed.), *Incunabula in American Libraries*.

[26] Bühler and others, *Standards of Bibliographical Description*; Dunkin, *How to Catalog a Rare Book*.

their map collections systematically. The Map Room at Illinois was formally opened in 1944.

The importance of a policy in acquiring and organizing maps is suggested by the following statement of Wilson and Swank:

Attention is called at this point to the urgent need, expressed by a number of faculty members, of an organized map collection and service in the Main Library. At present few maps are being acquired and none are being cataloged. Existing collections are scattered among the rare book, reference, and document rooms and the Hopkins Transportation Library. The maps now being distributed by the Army Map Service are being deposited in the Hoover Library where they are not conveniently accessible to many students. Other maps are, of course, located in other libraries on the campus, for example, the Geology Library. It is recommended that a map room be established for the care and servicing of all maps in the Main Library and that central indexes or descriptions of all map collections on the campus be kept in that room. The cost of developing, equipping, and staffing such a room would be considerable, but the returns would more than justify the expenditure.[27]

Although used constantly by students, faculty members, research workers, and librarians for quick reference purposes, maps are also used extensively for gathering and presenting data in theses and dissertations by students and in special reports and studies by faculty members. Like manuscripts and other nonbook materials, collections of maps require special handling and care if they are to be made easily available to users. In addition to keeping the university map collection active and modern, the librarian should be concerned with the problems of care, involving storage and equipment, and with problems of description, involving cataloging and arrangement.

ACQUISITION OF MAPS. How far the university library should go in the establishment of map collections depends upon the amount of use the materials will have in the instructional and research programs of the institution. Departments in the University of Chicago, for example, have used maps constantly. As a result of the extensive use, a separate map library was started in 1929. The library on the first floor of Rosenwald Hall has cases now housing 169,462 pieces,

[27] Wilson and Swank, *Report of a Survey of the Library of Stanford University for Stanford University*, p. 99.

including aerial photographs but not including weather maps. In 1941, California (Berkeley) reported 19,073 maps, but by 1954 the collection had grown to 103,359 (Table 12).

TABLE 12 *: SIZE OF MAP COLLECTIONS IN
16 UNIVERSITY LIBRARIES

Libraries	No. of Maps	Libraries	No. of Maps
Chicago	169,462 [a]	Iowa	49,594 [d]
Illinois	165,000	Washington (St. Louis)	36,922
California	103,592	Colorado	34,133
Virginia	90,695	Princeton	29,876
Wisconsin	90,000 [b]	Cincinnati	29,052
North Carolina	53,182	Brown	26,911
Columbia	51,000 [c]	Missouri	17,443
Kansas	50,000	Duke	16,553

* Data supplied by librarians, November, 1954.
[a] Includes aerial photographs.
[b] Also owns 40,000 aerial photographs.
[c] Also owns 600 historical maps in Special Collections.
[d] Excludes geological maps.

Maps, because of their method of publication, present special problems in acquisition to librarians.[28] There is no single source of information about maps, and acquisition is further complicated by the peculiar relationships of printers, publishers, and issuing agencies. Foreign maps especially are difficult to obtain. Many university libraries have acquired the map collections distributed by the Army Map Service, and in a number of instances these have been organized.

Authorities on map collections have emphasized the importance of a policy of selection. The policy generally covers the area to be covered, the types of maps to be collected, and the time period to be included. Starting from scratch, it is difficult for some institutions to acquire copies of old maps except through prints and microfilm and color photography. In many institutions the older maps probably will not be essential.

Among the sources for the selection of maps and atlases [29] are

[28] Espenshade, "No One Source for Acquiring Maps," *Library Journal*, LXXV (1950), 431–43; Yonge, "Map Procurement in the Special Library," *Special Libraries*, XLIV (1953), 173–74; DeWald, "Map Procurement in Government Agencies," *Special Libraries*, XLIV (1953), 175–77.

[29] Winchell, *Guide to Reference Books*, pp. 470–74. Winchell, in addition to listing the important bibliographies and reference books, outlines the essential points that should be considered in the acquisition of atlases.

the following: (1) publishers' catalogs, including those of the various agencies of the federal government, and those of foreign and domestic commercial map publishers, (2) foreign and domestic maps issued by geographical, geological, historical, and archaelogical societies, (3) the *Catalog of Copyright Entries* for maps, published by the Copyright Office of the Library of Congress, and (4) miscellaneous sources, such as parts of books and serials, reports of proceedings of professional groups, exhibits, bibliographical compilations of other map libraries, and maps issued by commercial, industrial, and technical services.[30]

STORAGE AND EQUIPMENT. Increasing attention has been given in recent years to the proper care of maps. Whitmarsh [31] has described the physical apparatus necessary for the efficient handling of maps. Although shallow drawers in special map cabinets have been used traditionally for the storage of maps, some libraries have used vertical files for this purpose. It is important for maps to remain flat if preservation and ease of handling are desired. In addition to the equipment for storing maps, provisions should also be made to facilitate their use by the arrangement of tables where students and research workers can consult, draft, and trace them. Facilities for the reproduction of materials might also be provided. Foreign language and special subject dictionaries, and an atlas reference collection are useful to individuals examining maps. A workroom for the staff is essential. Repair and mounting of maps [32] may be done in this room, unless such work is delegated to the university bindery.

ARRANGEMENT AND RECORDS. Libraries vary in their practices in cataloging and classifying maps. Some libraries follow the suggestions which have been set down by Boggs and Lewis,[33] while others do not try to do more than arrange them on a geographical basis. Boggs and Lewis have specified the following objectives in organizing a map collection:

[30] Yonge, "Map Procurement in the Special Library," *Special Libraries*, XLIV (1953), 173–74.
[31] "Maps and Photographs," in Fussler (ed.), *Library Buildings for Library Service*, pp. 78–80.
[32] LeGear, *Maps: Their Care, Repair and Preservation.*
[33] *The Cataloging and Classification of Maps and Atlases.*

1. *Classification:* (*a*) to provide for each map a definite position in the map files in relation to every other map; and (*b*) to bring together in the files, as closely as possible, those maps which consultants will most frequently have occasion to use in association with one another.
2. *Cataloging:* (*a*) to record that information which is pertinent, including that information which is peculiar to maps (e.g., scale and map projection), and (*b*) to make map catalog cards as nearly uniform as possible with printed Library of Congress book catalogs—in size, order of information, and typographical appearance.
3. *Subject cataloging* (*a*) to develop a system or body of headings relating to both the subject matters and the areas covered by the card, and (*b*) to make them similar to headings already used in library card catalogs for books and periodicals.

Since the principle of entry suggested by Boggs and Lewis differs from that of the Library of Congress, some libraries have preferred to use Library of Congress printed cards for its map cataloging. Brown [34] has discussed the problems which arise in the handling of old maps.

MUSIC

Music collections in university libraries range from a few to several thousand items. Librarians in universities which have departments or schools of music may be required to assemble and handle relatively large collections of such materials as orchestral scores, original manuscript scores, ballad operas, piano and vocal scores, choral cantatas, sheet music, song music, liturgies, oratorios, folk songs, and folk dances. Such works, in addition to national series or sets of complete works of American and foreign composers, are necessary for serious study and research in musicology.

Many of the larger collections in university libraries have been built up through the generosity of donors, usually alumni, faculty members, or friends. The rich music collections of Harvard have been acquired largely through gifts. In a few institutions, such as Harvard and Rochester, special endowment funds have been provided for the specific purchase of music materials. Several institutions with active music schools, however, are required to allot a

[34] *Notes on the Care and Cataloguing of Old Maps.*

portion of their budgets for the purchase of music. The interest not only of the music faculty but of members of other university departments is essential if an effective collection is to be assembled. For example, at the University of Pennsylvania, the interest of the University Museum and the faculty of the department of anthropology has fostered the development of an unusual and large collection of primitive music and music of ancient civilizations—both extremely useful in the study of musical forms and the culture of underdeveloped early peoples.

The methods of cataloging, classifying, and handling musical materials have been fairly well standardized. The Music Library Association has worked out codes of practice which are followed closely by libraries having substantial collections. Large music rooms, such as the one at Colorado which combines the functions of storage and of providing a place for musical functions, are not often found in university libraries. Very often music materials are housed in the departments or schools of music. At Rochester the Sibley Music Library has a building of its own to house its extensive music collections as well as materials relating to the theater and the dance. Effective service to users apparently calls for a close proximity of the music collections to the various music reference tools, such as dictionaries, encyclopedias, bibliographies and catalogs, and biographies of musicians.

Musical recordings are also being collected extensively by libraries. Brown, California, Columbia, Harvard, Illinois, and Rochester are among the institutions which have 10,000 or more of these recordings. A large number of other libraries contain 5,000 or more items.

Since scores, recordings, and other items of music are relatively expensive and need special attention in both organization and preservation, libraries should maintain strict acquisition policies in regard to them. Recordings particularly require adequate quarters and listening facilities if students and faculty members are to use them satisfactorily. A useful source of information about all aspects of music is the quarterly Music Library Association *Notes*.

FUGITIVE
MATERIALS
Into most university libraries come items which do not fall within those categories which have been described in the preceding sections. These items, often referred to as "fugitive materials," because they are not always easy to obtain and because they present unusual problems of care, organization, and administration, may be roughly divided into four groups: (1) printed items in unusual form, (2) archival and near-print materials, (3) nonprinted materials, and (4) museum pieces.

PRINTED MATERIALS IN UNUSUAL FORM

Most larger libraries and many smaller libraries collect materials which do not conform to the shape of the common book or periodical. The newspaper and the map, of course, have characteristics common to fugitive materials; yet they differ in other aspects peculiar to such items. Generally included in the category of "fugitive materials" are such holdings as broadsides, brochures, charts, clippings, dodgers, folders, leaflets, looseleaf services, pamphlets, playbills, posters, preprints and reprints, programs, tracts, trade catalogs, and various reports. The problem of technical reports was discussed in chapter x.

Egan and Keck [35] have called attention to the ephemeral character of some of the fugitive materials. They point out that such materials are most important to the research worker as they appear. "If the world of scholarship is to exert any influence in the midst of rapid changes," they write, "it must be provided with the very latest relevant data." The Industrial Relations Center Library of the University of Chicago is an example of an effort to segregate the acquisition and handling of such materials. The recognition of the usefulness of some of these types of publications for immediate use is not widespread in universities. The Chicago development represents an activity similar to that of special libraries of industry, business, science, and technology.

[35] Egan and Keck, "Fugitive Materials," in Fussler (ed.), *Library Buildings for Library Service*, pp. 73–74.

BROADSIDES. Large collections of broadsides are relatively rare in university libraries. The Harvard collection of early American broadsides is one of the best known in the United States. Brown University Library also has a relatively large collection. Libraries of historical and antiquarian societies have made a specialty of collecting these items, many of which have become documents of significant historical value. In modern times, governments, political organizations, and labor unions have used the broadside technique to advance their programs. Broadsides issued in relation to World War II have been collected by libraries building up their holdings of special materials on the war.

CHARTS. Printed charts of unusual size present the librarian with problems of handling. Charts of business, industrial, governmental, and educational organizations frequently are useful in research. Usually, such materials are acquired and stored in departmental libraries, since they frequently serve specific purposes.

BROCHURES, DODGERS, FOLDERS, AND LEAFLETS. The enormous flood of small printed items, issued in the forms of brochures, dodgers, folders, and leaflets, not only presents problems of care and organization but places a responsibility upon the librarian to select materials which are of permanent value. Ephemeral materials falling into these categories are normally kept on file in departmental libraries for current use. Such materials, unless they are of an unusual nature, are seldom cataloged. Like broadsides, they are often propaganda. They should not be discarded for this reason, however, since they may be items which can in the future serve students interested in historical and social research. Large university libraries may contain a million or more of these items, stored in vertical files and usually organized by subject. In some instances, they are bound into volumes. It is obvious that a rigorous selection policy is necessary if the staff is not to be overwhelmed by sheer quantity.

CLIPPINGS. Maintained commonly by the reference department and departmental libraries, clipping files often yield information that is unavailable elsewhere in the collections. Material in general clipping files has been found to be particularly useful to under-graduate students who are preparing papers for course work. Very often such material represents the most recent information on certain subjects. Special clipping files, such as those relating to a specific locality, person, or subject, generally require systematic scanning of newspapers, periodicals, and other publications to insure com-pleteness. Art, business, education, and journalism libraries have placed considerable value upon such files. In the journalism library, these files are primary tools for study and research purposes.

The sources for material for clipping files are duplicate news-papers, often ordered for clipping purposes, duplicate periodicals, and, to a lesser extent, discarded bulletins, pamphlets, and books. Clippings are often gathered into a single system of vertical files with other small fugitive materials, such as folders, leaflets, preprints, reprints, and pamphlets.

In some of the larger clipping collections, elaborate systems of accessioning and processing are maintained. Generally, however, such material is not accessioned, cataloged, or classified but, rather, is assembled in folders and grouped alphabetically by subjects. If cards are placed in the public catalog, it has been found effective to adopt the same system of subject headings used for books. In a few instances, most often in relation to local materials, clippings are mounted into bound volumes. This is an expensive practice which is not reasonable for the ordinary clipping file.

PAMPHLETS. In many cases, pamphlets present no special problem to the librarian, since they are treated as unbound books and handled in the same way after decisions are made to catalog and bind. A large amount of worth-while material, including reports of research studies, are issued in pamphlet form. Pamphlets issued by standard book publishers, societies, and educational institutions are commonly secured through the ordinary book channels. Many libraries have their gift and exchange divisions check such publications as the *Bulletin of the Public Affairs Information Service*, the *Vertical File Service Catalog, Publishers' Weekly*, and other publications for material of this type. Many pamphlets are distributed free by authors and publishers. No bibliography of American and foreign publications attempts to list all available pamphlets.

The handling of pamphlets in university libraries has taken various forms: (1) cataloging and classifying as separate items—methods which are too expensive for many libraries; (2) binding pamphlets on similar subjects together in volumes and cataloging and classifying them under broad subjects—a practice which is satisfactory if careful attention is given to the sizes of the pamphlets and the type of paper of each item included; (3) placing in folders in vertical files under broad or specific subject headings, along with other fugitive materials; and (4) placing on shelves in pamphlet boxes arranged by broad subject groupings and subarranged alphabetically by author. Some libraries may wish to use two or more of these practices depending on the types of pamphlets. Economical administration which permits rapid location and accessibility should be the criterion.

PLAYBILLS AND PROGRAMS. Some university libraries have relatively large collections of playbills and theater programs which are used for research purposes by students and faculty working in the fields of literature and the drama. These are generally arranged by subject entries in vertical files. Similar treatment is given programs and catalogs of various kinds of exhibitions.

POSTERS. Few university libraries have made a practice of collecting posters. In a number of institutions such materials have been acquired as gifts from collectors. The Hoover War Library, Stanford University, probably has the largest war-poster collection in the country. The use of such materials in sociological, psychological, and historical studies has encouraged a number of university librarians to collect them. Posters require special housing in flat cases similar to those used for preserving maps.

PREPRINTS AND REPRINTS. Sections of books and articles in periodicals which have been preprinted or reprinted accumulate rapidly in university libraries, particularly in departmental libraries specializing in narrow subject fields. Departmental librarians in scientific and technical fields generally make a practice of writing for reprints, and the materials form an important part of the collection. Faculty members frequently direct reprints to these departmental libraries as they receive them from their colleagues in other institutions or research organizations. Authors often send such items to the libraries. Particularly important are reprints which represent dissertations and special research studies. Frequently, such reprints are used for exchange purposes.

Systematic procedures for caring for reprints are necessary if they are to be easily made available to the clientele. Generally, reprints are treated as pamphlets and placed in vertical files. A common procedure of university libraries is to bind, catalog, and classify reprints which cover subjects which are likely to be used heavily, particularly if the library does not subscribe for the publications in which the originals appeared.

One type of reprint collected by some university libraries is that of publications by personnel connected with the institution. These are sometimes placed in university local collections. Systematic collecting of such items is usually necessary if complete coverage is sought. This is generally done by informing the faculty members of the policy of the library in preserving such items, and setting up a routing operation.

NONPRINTED MATERIALS

Since the university library emphasizes research, it is expected that it should direct special attention toward acquiring nonprinted materials which are often rare and even unique. These materials are of three types: (1) graphic, (2) photographic, and (3) auditory.

A. GRAPHIC MATERIALS   In the conduct of special studies and investigations, faculty members and graduate students often assemble data which have not yet reached the stage of publication. Data sheets, tabulation sheets, filled-in questionnaires, graphs, drawings, blueprints, and charts comprise this type of material, which may be consulted by scholars checking on work or seeking fuller explanations of phenomena. Special cabinets, vertical files, and similar equipment are necessary for the satisfactory care of these materials.

B. PHOTOGRAPHIC MATERIALS   Such nonprinted materials as photographs, pictures, prints, slides, Photostats, microfilms, Microprints, microcards, Microlex, motion pictures, and newsreels have also been acquired in increasing numbers by university libraries. More and more, writers and research workers have come to rely upon these resources for data concerning literary matters, biographical records, or social or historical conditions.

PHOTOGRAPHS, PRINTS, AND PICTURES. The use of photographs, prints, and pictures by scholars and students has developed greatly in recent years, as an examination of journals and books will quickly reveal. In science and technology particularly the use of pictorial materials for illustrative purposes has become relatively heavy. University libraries, therefore, have collected these materials for the use of their clienteles. Some idea of the size of a group of collections in this area is given in Table 13.

TABLE 13 *: SIZE OF PHOTOGRAPH AND PRINT COLLECTIONS IN
15 UNIVERSITY LIBRARIES

Libraries	No. of Photographs	Libraries	No. of Photographs
Yale	375,000	Rochester	10,957
Virginia	61,357	Pennsylvania	8,461
Princeton	53,025 [a]	Stanford	7,144
Illinois	35,000	California (Los Angeles)	7,121
Washington (St. Louis)	24,688	Kansas	4,350
North Carolina	19,090	Duke	3,200
California (Berkeley)	16,529 [b]	Columbia	1,575
Brown	13,916		

* Data from librarians, November–December, 1954. Includes photographs, prints, and in some cases, pictures. A number of librarians indicated that their libraries had large collections, but were not counted.
[a] Excludes Graphics Arts Collection.
[b] Processed items only. Estimated total for Bancroft Library is about three times as large.

A number of the libraries have developed special art collections of photographs, prints, and pictures. Like pamphlets, they are secured at little or no cost to the library. Discarded books, magazines, newspapers, catalogs, and circulars, as well as standard art publications, supply materials for the collections. Travel bureaus, publishing houses, governmental bureaus, chambers of commerce, tourist agencies, educational institutions, industrial and business organizations, and motion picture studios are also sources which have been tapped by libraries for pictorial materials.

The use of such materials is not restricted to research. The value of pictorial items for the general reader was early recognized. Many libraries have adopted a liberal policy in regard to the use and circulation of the materials. Some college libraries have framed collections of pictures and paintings which are permitted to circulate. In order to protect them during use and circulation, however, libraries have had to introduce a careful policy of preparing them for handling.[36]

Allied to the photograph collection is the postal card collection, which may grow to extensive proportions in some libraries. At Kentucky, for example, the postal card collection contains 58,738 pieces, of which 3,588 relate to Kentucky. These materials are obtainable from art dealers, museums, and civic organizations. Usually they are stored along with photographs and other pictures in flat cases or vertical files.

MICROFILMS, MICROPRINTS, AND MICROCARDS. Microreproductions have become standard materials in most research libraries.[37] Microfilms (including film strips); Microprints; microcards; Microlex (law materials in microprint form); microfiches (microfilm in sheet form) of materials in books, periodicals, newspapers, documents, pamphlets, manuscripts, archival materials, and other items are among the microreproductions acquired by university libraries. A survey in 1952 [38] provides in tabular form data concerning the

[36] Ireland, *The Picture File in School, College, and Public Libraries;* Whitmarsh, "Maps and Photographs."

[37] Tauber and Associates, *Technical Services in Libraries*, pp. 388–402, and bibliography, pp. 459–62; see also Tate, "Microreproduction and the Acquisitions Program," *Library Trends*, III (1955), 432–47.

[38] Harkins, Dimock, and Hanson, "Microfilm in University Libraries: A Report," *College and Research Libraries*, XIV (1953), 307–16.

holdings of microfilm in 76 college and university libraries. At the time of the survey, the libraries reported having 164,571 reels. Thirty-three of the libraries owned less than 1,000 reels each, 20 had from 1,000 to 1,999, and 23 reported 2,000 or more. Among libraries reporting 5,000 or more reels in 1954 [39] were California (Berkeley), California (Los Angeles), Chicago, Columbia, Duke, Illinois, Iowa, Kentucky, Louisiana, Michigan, Minnesota, North Carolina, Princeton, and Wisconsin (including the Wisconsin Historical Society collection).

Microfilms owned by the libraries cover practically all fields of knowledge, in many languages, and include items from the fifteenth to the twentieth century. One may obtain an idea of the variety of materials acquired by examining the *Union List of Microfilms*.[40] Undoubtedly, microfilms have established a place in library service, and as Fussler [41] has observed: "There are . . . certain items that in their original forms will probably tend to disappear or at least diminish in the future library. The most conspicuous and bulky are the newspapers. Microfilming of newspapers has been applied broadly and has, in general, proved successful."

The other forms of microreproduction, especially Microprint and microcard, also have a place in the research library. Various publishers are issuing microcards, and Microprint and Microlex represent processes which are likely to have a definite effect upon the materials collected by the university library.

SLIDES. As a teaching medium, slides have had considerable importance in many institutions. Lecturers and instructors have been able to employ them effectively in the biological and medical sciences, as well as in art, architecture, and archaeology. Slide collections may consist of various types—photographic specimens, sketches on etched glass or lumarith, or typed or ink-written Cellophane squares, made transparent by treatment with diethylphthalate.

[39] Data from questionnaire, November–December, 1954.
[40] Philadelphia Bibliographical Center and Union Library Catalogue. Committee on Microphotography. *Union List of Microfilms.* Also *Supplement* from 1949/52–
[41] "Photographic Reproduction," in Fussler (ed.), *Library Buildings for Library Service*, p. 85.

Slides are usually purchased by the library for a teaching department or come into the library through faculty members who have either made them or purchased them through departmental funds. In a number of instances, slides are retained as equipment of the instructional departments. With the centralization of visual materials, however, library slide collections are being extensively developed. In 1954 the slide collection at Pennsylvania totaled 54,188; at Illinois, over 30,000. There are many university libraries with collections of over 10,000 items.

Slides are often arranged in specially built files, containing drawers or trays that have individual slots which permit the slides to stand on their narrow ends. Other types of files are not so effective in preserving the slides from breakage. To facilitate the use of slides, broad subject arrangements have been employed. If slide collections are housed in the library, special provisions for use of projectors are necessary. At Florida State University, where audio-visual materials are centralized in the library school, special arrangements are made to service the items as they are needed by the instructional departments.

MOTION PICTURES AND NEWSREELS. Although the university library may have a photographic department and may have responsibility for making microreproductions and prints, it is not ordinarily a center for the storage of motion pictures and newsreels. Generally, the extension division and the teaching and visual education departments have assumed the task of acquiring and caring for films in their particular activities. Some university libraries, however, have taken the responsibility of storing and projecting films. Among them are Columbia, the Joint University Libraries, Virginia, and Washington University.

The sources of films are numerous, and educational, documentary, and recreational films are among the items which are available to libraries. Showings of rented films is a common occurrence, and new buildings frequently have included facilities for projection. Housing provisions which insure constancy of humidity and temperature for the preservation of the films are essential.

C. AUDITORY MATERIALS   The use of sound transcriptions in research and instruction has increased greatly in recent years. Such materials have been particularly useful in music, philology, anthropology, and history. With important historical addresses and messages being delivered over the radio, facilities for their reproduction have been extended. Some institutions have introduced programs of building up oral history collections. As with motion pictures, libraries as a group have not always had control of collections of phonorecords. Music departments have maintained control of musical recordings, and other departments have retained responsibility for non-musical items. Extension departments have also had the responsibility of distributing recordings. However, the libraries of Brown, California (Berkeley), Colorado, Columbia, Illinois, Louisiana, Michigan, North Carolina, Ohio State, Pennsylvania, Rochester, Stanford, Washington (St. Louis), and Yale report collections of 5,000 or more musical recordings.[42] The University of California Library in Berkeley has a collection of almost 2,000 nonmusical recordings.

MUSEUM OBJECTS

Many of the larger universities either possess museums or are affiliated with them. In a number of institutions, however, the library has taken the responsibility of collecting museum objects which may be used for research or instructional purposes. Paintings, statuary, cuneiform tablets, coins, models, and designs are some of the objects which have significance for the study of cultural institutions and social progress. Other materials, such as gavels, medals, scepters, masks, and machines are likely to find their way into university libraries for preservation. Whether or not the university library should attempt to collect such items should be a matter of policy, since museum collections require careful attention if they are to be made useful.

[42] Data from questionnaire, November–December, 1954.

BIBLIOGRAPHY

GENERAL

Angle, Paul. "Survey of Manuscript Collections, University of Chicago Libraries." Chicago, [1944] (mimeographed).

"Availability of Library Research Materials," *Library Trends*, II (1954), 487–586.

Bennett, Fleming. "Audio-Visual Service in Colleges and Universities in the United States," *College and Research Libraries*, XVI (1955), 11–19.

Book Collecting and Scholarship; Essays by Theodore C. Blegen, James Ford Bell, Stanley Pargellis, Colton Storm, and Louis B. Wright. Minneapolis, University of Minnesota Press, 1954.

"Current Acquisitions Trends in American Libraries," *Library Trends*, III (1955), 333–470.

Downs, Robert B. American Library Resources: A Bibliographical Guide. Chicago, American Library Association, 1951.

Downs, Robert B., John E. Van Male, and Carl W. E. Hintz. "Notable Materials Added to North American Libraries," series of articles appearing in *Library Quarterly* since 1940. See *Library Literature*.

Fussler, Herman H. Photographic Reproduction for Libraries. Chicago, University of Chicago Press, 1942.

Fussler, Herman H. (ed.). Library Buildings for Library Service: Papers Presented before the Library Institute of the University of Chicago, August 5–10, 1946. Chicago, American Library Association, 1947.

Harvard University Library. Research Services of the Harvard College Library. Cambridge, Mass., 1953.

Irwin, Mary (ed.). American Universities and Colleges. 6th ed. Washington, D.C., American Council on Education, 1952.

Rider, Fremont. The Scholar and the Future of the Research Library. New York, Hadham Press, 1944.

"Special Materials and Services," *Library Trends*, III (1955), 119–212.

Winchell, Constance M. Guide to Reference Books. 7th ed. Chicago, American Library Association, 1951. Supplement, 1950–52, 1954.

DISSERTATIONS

Dean, Helen E. "Subject Cataloging of Theses and Dissertations," *Journal of Cataloging and Classification*, VII (1952), 24–26.

Dissertation Abstracts, Vol. 1 to date. Ann Arbor, University Microfilms, 1938 to date (Vols. 1–11, 1938–51, issued with the title Microfilm Abstracts).

Doctoral Dissertations Accepted by American Universities, 1933/34–. Compiled for the Association of Research Libraries. New York, H. W. Wilson, 1934–.

Esterquest, Ralph T. "Midwest Inter-Library Center: Acquisition Policy and Program, 1950–53," *College and Research Libraries*, XV (1954), 47–49+.

Faison, Georgia H. "Care of German Dissertations," *Bulletin of the American Library Association*, XXX (1936), 572–73.

Horn, Andrew H. "University Archivist and the Thesis Problem," *American Archivist*, XV (1952), 321–31.

Jahresverzeichnis der deutschen Hochschulschriften, 1938. Berlin, 1938.

Kleberg, T. "Report of the Sub-Committee on the Exchange of University Publications," International Federation of Library Associations, *Publications*, XII (1947), 121–23.

Lane, Alfred. "Exchange Work in College and University Libraries" (unpublished Master's essay, Columbia University, 1950).

Palfrey, Thomas H., and Henry E. Coleman, Jr. Guide to Bibliographies of Theses, United States and Canada. 2d ed. Chicago, American Library Association, 1940.

Rosenberg, R. F. "Bibliographies of Theses in America," *Bulletin of Bibliography*, XVIII (1945), 18.

Tauber, Maurice F., and Associates. Technical Services in Libraries. New York, Columbia University Press, 1954.

U.S. Department of State. Abstracts of Completed Dissertations for the Year 1950–51. Washington, D.C., Government Printing Office, 1952.

U.S. Library of Congress. Catalog Division. List of American Doctoral Dissertations, for the Period 1912–1938. Washington, D.C., U.S. Government Printing Office, 1913–40.

MANUSCRIPTS AND ARCHIVES

Altick, Richard T. "The Scholar's Paradise," *College and Research Libraries*, XV (1954), 375–82.

Barrow, W. J. "An Evaluation of Document Restoration Processes," *American Documentation*, IV (1953), 50–54.

—— Procedures and Equipment Used in the Barrow Method of Restoring Manuscripts and Documents. Richmond, 1952.

Bond, W. H. "Cataloguing of Manuscripts in the Houghton Library," *Harvard Library Bulletin*, IV (1954), 392–96.

Hensel, Evelyn. "Treatment of Nonbook Materials," *Library Trends*, II (1953), 187–98.

Kennedy, Arthur G. A Concise Bibliography for Students of English, Systematically Arranged. 3d ed. Stanford, Stanford University Press, 1954.

Kremer, A. W. "The Preservation of Wood Pulp Publications," *College and Research Libraries*, XV (1950), 205–9.

Minogue, A. E. The Repair and Preservation of Records (Bulletin of the National Archives, No. 5). Washington, D.C., National Archives, 1943.

Mood, Fulmer, and Vernon Carstensen. "University Records and Their Relation to General University Administration," *College and Research Libraries*, XI (1950), 337–45.

"Report of the Ad Hoc Committee on Manuscripts Set up by the American Historical Association in December 1948," *American Archivist*, XIV (1951), 229–40.

"Report of the Committee on the Use of Manuscripts by Visiting Scholars, Set up by the Association of Research Libraries," *College and Research Libraries*, XIII (1952), 58–60.

Ricci, Seymour de, and J. W. Wilson (eds.). Census of Medieval and Renaissance Manuscripts in the United States and Canada. New York, H. W. Wilson, 1935–40.

Russell, M., and E. G. Roberts. "Processing Procedures of the Manuscripts Department of Duke University," *American Archivist*, XII (1949), 369–80.

Wilson, Dwight H. "No Ivory Tower: The Administration of a College or University Archives," *College and Research Libraries*, XI (1950), 337–45.

Wilson, Louis R., and Jack Dalton. "Restrictions Limiting the Use of Research Materials," *Library Trends*, II (1954), 545–53.

INCUNABULA

Bühler, Curt F., and others. Standards of Bibliographical Description. Philadelphia, University of Pennsylvania Press, 1949.

Dunkin, Paul A. How to Catalog a Rare Book. Chicago, American Library Association, 1951.

Rider, Fremont. "Holdings of Incunabula in American University Libraries," *Library Quarterly*, IX (1939), 273–84.

———— "Incunabula in American Libraries: A Supplement." *Library Quarterly*, X (1940), 361–65.

Stillwell, Margaret B. Incunabula in American Libraries. A Second Census of Fifteenth-Century Books Owned in the United States, Mexico, and Canada. New York, Bibliographical Society of America, 1940.

MAPS

Anderson, O. C. "No Best Method to Catalog Maps," *Library Journal*, LXXV (1950), 450–52.

Boggs, S. W., and Dorothy C. Lewis. Classification and Cataloging of Maps and Atlases. New York, Special Libraries Association, 1945.

Brown, Lloyd A. Notes on the Care and Cataloguing of Old Maps. Windham, Conn., Hawthorn House, 1940.

—— "Special Reference Problems in Map Collections," in Pierce Butler (ed.), *The Reference Function of the Library*. Chicago, University of Chicago Press, 1943, pp. 144–62.

DeWald, E. "Map Procurement in Government Agencies," *Special Libraries*, XLIV (1953), 175–77.

Espenshade, E. B. "Guide to Map Sources for Use in Building a College Map Library," *College and Research Libraries*, IX (1948), 45–53.

—— "Maps for the College Library," *College and Research Libraries*, VIII (1947), 132–37.

—— "No One Source for Acquiring Maps," *Library Journal*, VII (1950), 431–32.

LeGear, Clara E. Maps: Their Care, Repair and Preservation in Libraries. Washington, D.C., Library of Congress, 1949.

Riesner, M. "Acquisition of Map Material for a College Library" (unpublished Master's thesis, University of Michigan, 1948).

Spence, M. R. "Classifying, Cataloging, and Filing of Maps in College and University Libraries" (unpublished Master's thesis, Western Reserve University, 1951).

Webbert, C. A., and R. K. Waldron. "Map Service in the University Library," *Bookmark* (University of Idaho), V (1953), 102–3.

Whitmarsh, Agnes. "Maps and Photographs," in Herman H. Fussler (ed.), *Library Buildings for Library Service*. Chicago, American Library Association, 1947, pp. 78–80.

Wilson, Louis R., and Raynard C. Swank. Report of a Survey of the Library of Stanford University for Stanford University, November 1946—March 1947. Chicago, American Library Association, 1947.

Yonge, E. L. "Map Procurement in the Special Library," *Special Libraries*, XLIV (1953), 173–74.

MUSIC

Duckles, Vincent. "Problems of Music Library Equipment," Music Library Association *Notes*, XI (1954), 213–23.

Lyle, Guy R. The Administration of the College Library. 2d ed. New York, H. W. Wilson, 1949, pp. 406–12.

Music Library Association. Code for Cataloging Phonograph Records. [Washington, Music Library Association, 1942] (mimeographed).

Music Library Association *Notes* (quarterly). Contains articles, reviews, etc.

Shepard, Brooks. "Problems of Music Library Administration in the College or University Library," Music Library Association *Notes*, XI (1954), 359–65.

U.S. Library of Congress. Descriptive Cataloging Division. Rules for Descriptive Cataloging in the Library of Congress. Washington, D.C., 1949; Supplement, 1949–51. Washington, D.C., 1952, Phono-records, preliminary ed., Washington, D.C., 1953.

PHOTOGRAPHIC MATERIALS

American Association of Petroleum Geologists. Directory of Films and Slides of Possible Interest to Geologists. 2d ed. Tulsa, Okla., 1951.

Ballou, Hubbard. "Microcopying, Methods and Use," in M. P. Doss (ed.), *Information Processing Equipment.* New York, Reinhold, 1955, pp. 67–104.

Brown University Library. List of Latin American Imprints before 1800. Providence, R.I., 1952.

Canadian Library Association. Newspaper Microfilming Project: Catalogue. No. 1–   1948–   Ottawa, 1948–   .

Fussler, Herman H. "Photographic Reproduction of Research Materials," *Library Trends,* II (1954), 532–44.

Harkins, William G., Fred L. Dimock, and Mary E. Hanson. "Microfilm in University Libraries: A Report," *College and Research Libraries,* XIV (1953), 307–16.

Hawken, W. R. "New Methods of Photocopying," *Library Journal,* LXXIX (1954), 1115–22.

Ireland, Norma O. The Picture File in School, College and Public Libraries. rev. and enl. ed. Boston, Faxon, 1954.

The Microcard Bulletin. No. 1–   Sept., 1948–   Middletown, Conn., Microcard Foundation, 1948–   .

"Microfilm Clearing House Bulletin." No. 1–   March 19, 1951–   . Issued as an Appendix to the Library of Congress *Information Bulletin.*

Micro Photo, Inc., Cleveland. Newspapers on Microfilm. Cleveland, 1953.

Philadelphia Bibliographical Center and Union Library Catalogue. Committee on Microphotography. Union List of Microfilms. Ann Arbor, 1951. Also Supplement from 1949–52.

Tate, Vernon D. "Microreproduction and the Acquisitions Program," *Library Trends,* III (1955), 432–47.

Tauber, Maurice F., and Associates. Technical Services in Libraries. New York, Columbia University Press, 1954.

UNESCO Bulletin for Libraries. (Includes section on microfilm copies of out-of-print periodicals).

U.S. Library of Congress. A Guide to the Microfilm Collections of Early State Records. Washington, 1951.

———— General Reference and Bibliography Division. Microfilms and Microcards: Their Use in Research. Prepared by Blanche C. McCrum. Washington, 1950.

———— Union Catalog Division. Newspapers on Microfilm. By George A. Schwegmann, Jr. Washington, 1953.

U.S. National Archives. List of National Archives Microfilm Publications. 1953. Washington, 1953.

University Microfilms. Partial List of Microfilms of STC Books and a Cross Index by STC Number. Ann Arbor, Mich., 1937- .

FUGITIVE MATERIALS

Collison, R. L. Cataloguing, Arrangement, and Filing of Special Material in Special Libraries. London, Aslib, 1950.

Hensel, Evelyn M. "Treatment of Nonbook Materials," *Library Trends*, II (1953), 187–98.

Iiams, Thomas M. "Development of the Book Collections in the College Library: Special Collections, Rare Books and Gifts," *College and Research Libraries*, XII (1951), 361–64.

Jackson, W. A. "Importance of Rare Books and Manuscripts in a University Library," *Harvard Library Bulletin*, II (1949), 315–26.

Powell, L. C. "Policy and Administration," *College and Research Libraries*, X (1949), 295–99.

See also annual reports and staff manuals of libraries, and chapters on "Holdings" and "Collections" in surveys of libraries listed in chapter xvi.

XII

THE TEACHING FUNCTION
OF THE UNIVERSITY LIBRARY

IN THE preceding chapters those aspects of administration have been considered which are primarily concerned with the operations of the university library. In this chapter it is proposed to deal with certain aspects of administration which are intended to promote the effective use of the library by its patrons. Stated differently, it is proposed to consider the administration of the library at a teaching and research, as contrasted with a library-housekeeping level. On this level the library makes its maximum contribution to the university in the attainment of educational objectives.

The proposal presents a number of difficulties. The first and major obstacle is that there is no generally accepted idea of what is meant by "administering the library at a teaching and research level." A second difficulty is that there is no general agreement among university librarians and administrators that administration at such a level is desirable, although it is generally recognized that many students enter the university who have acquired very little experience in the use of library materials; that the catalogs, reference aids, and the resources of the university library are so extensive and complex as to make their use difficult by the uninitiated; and that significant graduate study and research are largely dependent upon knowledge of the literature and source materials in the field of specialization. A third difficulty is that, even if it is recognized as desirable to maintain the library at such a level, funds and means for implementing the proposal in the university program may be lacking, since the development of such a program obviously requires additional staff members with special training often not possessed by librarians. Furthermore, curriculums and programs of instruction and research have sometimes become so full and inflexible that there is little opportunity for introducing such innovations. Finally, the university may provide other agencies than the library through which it attempts to achieve some of the desired ends.

The major difficulty noted above may be obviated by defining the terms "housekeeping level" and "teaching and research levels." By "housekeeping level" is meant the employment of administrative procedures by which a minimum of service is provided for the various groups which comprise the university. The ordinary technical services of ordering, processing, and circulating books are maintained. But a minimum is done by the library staff during freshman week to familiarize new students with the library. Little attention is paid to educational guidance, remedial reading, or instruction in library use for beginning students. Little effort is made to stimulate student interest in reading. The loan desks are manned in the evening and on Sunday by student assistants and a minimum of professional staff members. Little or no organized instruction in library use is provided for undergraduate students, and little effort is made by the library to participate in the offering of courses intended to acquaint beginning graduate students in various fields with the bibliographical aids and special source materials in their fields. Reading rooms are not organized on divisional, graduate, undergraduate, or other special bases; and few subject experts who are also experts in the techniques of librarianship and bibliography are in charge of special collections or departments.

Administering the library at a teaching and research level means exactly the opposite of this. Such administration is based upon two assumptions: (1) that learning is promoted by means of various methods, including library use as well as the lecture, the discussion group, the laboratory exercise, and the field trip; and (2) that the library may be administered in such a way that it may make a maximum contribution to the learning process. In 1900 the railroad engine converted about 15 percent of the potential energy of coal into train-pulling power. The other 85 percent went up the smoke-stack or was lost through radiation or in some other way. Today the modern locomotive engine, as a result of careful studies and experimentation, translates a considerably higher percentage of the potential energy of fuel into actual traction power. The university library spends a considerable part of the total funds of the university. It acquires large collections of books, periodicals, and other materials used by students and scholars. It is housed in a relatively expensive university building and has departmental and school libraries in other buildings. All this equipment and personnel is intended to facilitate instruction and research and may contribute to them effectively when consciously utilized for this purpose. Administering the library at a teaching and research level involves the recognition of the idea that the library must play a positive, rather than a merely passive, role in university education. It emphasizes competence and specialization of staff and adequacy of facilities for close cooperation with the faculty and other agencies in achieving the educational goals of the university. It calls for programs of instruction in library use that are not casual or incidental but are so carefully planned and so well directed that a large proportion of students and faculty are aided in securing maximum assistance from the library. Such administration necessarily is correspondingly expensive and requires close cooperation with other members of the university. The educational benefits, however, should also be proportionately greater.

In organizing such programs libraries have kept certain well-defined groups in mind. Usually these have included (1) students at the lower and upper college or divisional levels, (2) graduate and professional students, and (3) members of the faculty. Libraries have also organized their services on a functional basis and have directed their efforts to some such ends as the following: (1) the orientation and counseling of the freshman or immature student concerning the location of library materials and general reference tools; (2) the stimulation of students' interest in reading; (3) the instruction of students, particularly those in the upper divisions, concerning the resources of the library for graduate and professional study; and (4) assistance to all members of the university who are engaged in advanced study and investigation.

ORIENTATION AND
COUNSELING
OF STUDENTS

The orientation and counseling of university students and the administration of tests to determine their reading rate and comprehension are usually placed in the hands of a group of officers and instructors who are specially trained in the handling of students' problems. Although certain members of a library staff may be competent to deal with personnel problems as related to library use, in most libraries there is no special organization for systematic examination and counseling of students. Perhaps the most outstanding effort in this connection has been exerted at the Chicago Undergraduate Division of the University of Illinois Library.[1] In this library, a Department of Library Instruction and Advisement, which replaced the Reference Department in 1951–52, answers reference questions, assists the faculty on research problems, cooperates with the English Department in providing instruction in the use of the library, and deals with the personal difficulties of students in their individual educational programs. Working closely with instructional and counseling services of other departments of the University, specially qualified Library Advisers seek to aid students in making the most of their college experience.

ORIENTATION. A number of librarians have seriously tried to solve the problem of acquainting new students with the functions of the library in education and research. They have endeavored to assist the members of the university community who are not familiar with the library to make effective use of its facilities. The methods employed have usually included: the preparation and distribution of guides or handbooks to the library, the arrangement of library exhibits, the publication of notices and articles concerning library resources or facilities in various university publications, the offering

---

[1] Maxfield, *Counselor Librarianship;* see also his "Counselor Librarianship at U.I.C.," *College and Research Libraries,* XV (1954), 161–66+.

of illustrated lectures concerning the library, the showing of motion pictures depicting library facilities and procedures, and the conduct of tours of the library.

Guides to the library vary from single mimeographed sheets to elaborately printed and illustrated handbooks.[2] Information concerning rules and regulations, location of rooms (often shown in maps and floor plans), library hours, and services and resources of the library and of neighboring libraries is included in such publications. Such information is supplemented by suggestions concerning the nature and use of the card catalog, the various periodical indexes, encyclopedias, dictionaries, atlases, and other reference works, including titles or directions on such subjects as how to study, how to take notes, and how to prepare bibliographies and manuscripts. Lyle,[3] writing of college library handbooks, indicated some of the points that should be considered in developing such tools: cover, text, arrangement, style, illustrations, diagrams, and typography. Some libraries on the university level have issued separate handbooks for undergraduates and for graduate students and faculty members.

In libraries in which materials are decentralized, the use of posters and signs are helpful in orienting the student in regard to the facilities available. Not only do such devices directly aid the student, but they reduce the number of questions to be answered by desk assistants concerning comparatively simple matters. Information concerning acquisitions, changes in library policy, the addition of new services, current exhibits, and public readings can usually be supplied through the cooperation of the student newspaper, monthly magazine, alumni bulletin, and other campus publications. Many university libraries now issue staff bulletins containing information about the libraries and lists of new books. These are circulated among faculty members, as well as among some students. Close relations are usually maintained with the public relations office of the university so that press releases on important acquisitions, collections,

[2] For a list of recent handbooks, see the heading "Handbooks" in *Library Literature, 1949–1951,* and the subsequent years.

[3] *The Administration of the College Library,* pp. 510–14.

exhibits, and activities will be distributed to the local and national newspapers.

Library tours and lectures on library use are frequently provided. If they are to be effective, they should be prepared carefully. This is especially true if they are scheduled when new students are being introduced to many activities and phases of university life during freshman week. Instruction in library use is more effective when it is not submerged in unrelated activities.

The orientation and direction of the student may be further facilitated by providing annotated book lists relating directly to their studies and by the preparation of displays and exhibits. The judicious use of book jackets and announcements of new books may serve to arouse the interest of students in materials which concern their course work.

Exhibits represent an effective device in developing student interest in the library and its activities. Exhibits have been used to publicize rare materials, stimulate reading, promote interest in specific subject fields, commemorate anniversaries and special occasions, relate books to specific courses, publicize gifts, encourage hobbies, foster the work of student organizations, and emphasize the research and other work of the faculty.[4] Each exhibit should have a specific objective. Skillful use of color contrasts, backgrounds, lighting and equipment should aid considerably in attracting the interests of students and other clientele. In some university libraries, the heads of the special collections departments have a primary responsibility for planning exhibits systematically for each year's program.

Since collaboration between the library and the faculty is essential to effective educational effort, it is necessary for the library staff and the faculty members to plan their programs cooperatively. Faculty members sometimes work with the staff in building collections of materials which concern educational, cultural, and vocational interests. These collections generally are made available in recreational reading rooms. Faculty counselors also meet with students to discuss individual reading programs.

[4] Reagan, "A Study of College Library Exhibit Policy and Practice."

Readers' advisory services have further contributed to the assistance rendered students. They have taken various forms, among which may be included assistance in the use of the card catalog, a highly developed consultant service,[5] special services to students engaged in writing papers and theses, and individual consultations. This service has been extended to include the assistance of students in the conduct of discussion programs or club meetings, in the development of forums, and in the promotion of interest in cultural reading—through browsing rooms, dormitory libraries, fraternity libraries, bookstores, reading prizes, book exhibits, and public readings.

VOCATIONAL COUNSELING. Special counselors and placement officers are usually charged with the responsibility of aiding students in the important problem of vocational adjustment. The university librarian however, can assist these officers by providing materials which relate to different occupations and professions. He can give specific advice to students who are interested in librarianship. Guidance shelves, including books on general vocational guidance and specific occupations and displays and exhibits relating to vocations, have often been used effectively in aiding students concerned with the problems of post-university careers.

OTHER ACTIVITIES. The relation of the librarian to dramatic associations, language clubs, science clubs, debating groups, writing clubs, the daily newspaper, and similar organizations on the campus is well established in university libraries. The possibilities of integrating the work of the library with these activities are considerable and can be promoted by various members of the university library staff. Student committees interested in the development of discipline and self-government among students frequently require library materials in carrying on their activities. They can also be of direct help to the librarian in matters relating to the use of books and the violation of library regulations.

[5] Teachers College Library at Columbia maintains a consultant service which includes informal work with individual students, preparation of materials of instruction, library lectures, special lectures on invitation of professors, special courses conducted by the Library Consultant staff, and project committee work.

The part which the library plays in acquainting students with books on methods of study and of taking notes and in inculcating moral and religious ideals among students may be indirect yet significant. The library may cooperate with student groups and religious directors and provide books which concern moral and religious issues. The library may likewise cooperate with the university organization charged with the care of student health.

ENCOURAGEMENT OF READING   One function which many university libraries have generally assumed has been the encouragement of reading among students. Acquiring the reading habit is perhaps one of the most worth-while effects of a college education. Since the library possesses many of the materials and facilities for developing the habit, the librarian is in a strategic position to cooperate with the faculty in stimulating reading and in fostering reading interests that will serve both practical and recreational purposes in the years after graduation.

The principal devices which librarians have used for this purpose are: (1) special reading courses; (2) open shelves; (3) browsing rooms; (4) rental collections; (5) dormitory, fraternity, and sorority libraries; (6) lower-level libraries; and (7) bookstores—each of which will be discussed below. Reading prizes, book exhibits, public readings, and promotion of personal libraries are other devices which have been used.

SPECIAL READING COURSES. The responsibility for stimulating student reading has generally been placed on the faculty. However, when the library supplements this activity by providing special reading courses, students are likely to benefit. This is particularly true if no systematic program of stimulation is carried on by the faculty or if browsing rooms and other facilities for encouraging reading are lacking. Librarians generally have a clear idea as to which of the faculty members are effective in successful encouragement of student reading.

OPEN SHELVES. In an effort to eliminate as many barriers as possible between students and books, a number of libraries are opening their stacks, or placing more materials on open shelves, for the use of their clientele.[6] Many of the new buildings have introduced free access to books. While it may be difficult in some of the older buildings to allow complete freedom of all users in a complex maze of stacks, it is more than likely that this practice of opening shelves of books to users will become more general in the future.

BROWSING ROOMS. Browsing rooms represent one effort to make books easily accessible to users. Books included in browsing rooms should have contemporary interest, should be nontechnical, should not be textbooks or reference books, and should be of interest to various groups of students. These recreational reading rooms are often memorials and bear the names of benefactors or individuals in whose memory they have been established. Unless a special fund is available for the purchase of new books for the browsing room, it may quickly deteriorate into a meeting, rather than a reading, room.

Browsing rooms should provide the type of surroundings which would attract students to come in and read for sheer personal pleasure. They should be located in an easily accessible part of the building. Frequently, they are placed near the main circulation desk so that supervision is readily available.

Criticisms of browsing rooms have been concerned with their undue expense in supplying materials to students who are readers anyway, and with the fact that not many students use them. Most librarians regard these criticisms as applying to browsing rooms which do not contain the proper materials, and with situations which have developed out of the failure of librarians to cooperate with faculty members in the extra-curricular reading of students.[7]

In addition to special browsing rooms, libraries have also attempted to provide reading materials for students through student unions.

[6] Hicks, "Open or Closed Shelves?" *College and Research Libraries*, XV (1954), 309–12.

[7] Vahey, "1948 Survey of Browsing Rooms," *Catholic Library World*, XX (1948), 242–46.

Collections in places where students gather informally may stimulate greater reading, perhaps, than those in elaborate browsing rooms.

RENTAL COLLECTIONS. The development of rental collections in libraries has been closely linked with limited book budgets or efforts of libraries to provide recreational reading materials at little cost. The use of such libraries in those institutions which maintain them has been of considerable value to students, faculty members, and staff members.

A number of libraries purchase new publications for the rental collection, and, after the initial demand for them has dwindled, they are either incorporated into the general stacks or sent to departmental libraries which can use them. Items not wanted for the permanent collections are usually sold to students or faculty members. Usually, the policy in selecting materials for the rental collection is to supplement other library services which are provided, rather than to set up an operation for the purpose of adding income. Frequently, titles are added which have little rental return, but they represent the type of material which is wanted for permanent acquisition. Estes [8] has described the purpose, problems, and procedures in a rental collection in a university library. Careful book selection on the basis of knowledge of the reading habits of the university community should result in the rental collection's paying its way.

University libraries which maintain rental collections usually restrict their clientele to personnel associated with the institution. This is to avoid any conflict with tax-paying commercial bookshops and rental libraries. It is desirable, from the point of view of the library purposes, that the commercial bookshops flourish and serve the reading public.

DORMITORY, FRATERNITY, AND SORORITY LIBRARIES. Through dormitory and residence-hall collections, university librarians have tried to stimulate the reading of students by making materials immediately

[8] "The Lending Service Library," *College and Research Libraries*, VII (1947), 256–59.

accessible.[9] Although the materials in these libraries are generally duplicates of titles in the general library, the total number of titles contained in them is frequently large. Sets of standard authors (fiction and nonfiction), books of current interest, periodicals, and, infrequently, reference books usually comprise the collections of dormitory libraries.

While residence-hall libraries contain collections which are useful to the undergraduates in their course work, there has been little effort to include titles required by the curriculum. In other words, there has been no attempt to substitute dormitory libraries for reserve book rooms or undergraduate libraries.

Policies governing the use of dormitory libraries vary from institution to institution. Practically all of them allow the circulation of books in students' rooms. Frequently students charge and discharge books themselves, or a student may be on hand to take care of administrative details.

On many campuses, fraternity and sorority houses have installed collections of books for the members. These collections, sometimes built up with the cooperation of the library staff, not only serve as recreational reading but in many cases contain items needed for course work.

LOWER-LEVEL LIBRARIES. A recent innovation in university libraries is the provision of special quarters for the freshman and sophomore classes.[10] The purpose of this action is to make it possible for the university library to provide a more direct service to undergraduates by bringing them closer to library materials they need immediately and making these materials conveniently available in an open-shelf reading area. At Minnesota it was found that the opening of a lower-level library reduced significantly the number of books placed on reserve by faculty members.

BOOKSTORES. In his evaluation of American librarianship Munthe [11]

[9] Allen, "Dormitory Library," *Library Journal*, LXXVI (1951), 920–23; Carnovsky, "The Dormitory Library," *Library Quarterly*, III (1933), 37–65.
[10] Rohlf, "The Freshman-Sophomore Library at Minnesota," *College and Research Libraries*, XIV (1953), 164–66.
[11] *American Librarianship from a European Angle*, pp. 9–15.

referred to the bookstores of northern Europe as "cultural institutions." In America the drug store, the rental library, the book clubs,
and the newsstand are among the chief commercial distributors of
reading materials. Paperback books have also assumed considerable
importance among the reading materials of Americans. In many instances, books distributed by these agencies, particularly the paper-
backs, are not of such a character as to stimulate intellectual curiosity
or to promote the development of personal libraries. The titles included in them are often of mediocre quality and ephemeral value,
and they are used primarily for recreational purposes. To meet the
needs of its college or university constituency and to serve both
faculty and students are the primary functions of the campus bookstore. Needs dictated by university classes may be expeditiously
met when close cooperation of the instructional staff and the bookstore exists. The university bookstore makes an effort to provide
promptly, accurately, and economically the books that are necessary
for the work of faculty and students. As an outlet for the university
press, the bookstore is likewise important. The local community
is friendly toward the publications of known authors, and their
works should be made readily available. Planographed and mimeographed textbooks and laboratory outlines usually have only a local
market, and the university bookstore is the logical distributor.

But the bookstore should be more than a supply depot for students. Studies show that immediate availability of good literature is
an important stimulus to reading. Attractive displays of worth-while
books can be suggestive, particularly if the books are permitted to
be inspected in surroundings conducive to leisurely and comfortable
reading. A well-arranged bookstore can be a place where scholars,
students, and books meet, where discerning literary judgments may
be developed, and where ownership of a personal collection is
encouraged.

In addition, the bookstore can play an important role in stimulating reading. In a number of instances, prizes have been offered
seniors for the best fundamental collection acquired throughout
college years. Stipulations usually prescribe that the collection in-

dicate discriminating judgment, that it contain works of general culture, and that the items included in it have value as a nucleus of a permanent personal library. The prizes frequently take the form of collections of selected books. Literary taste, the book-buying habit, and ownership are thus developed simultaneously.

Equally stimulating is the bookstore that functions as a meeting place of men of letters—a social meeting place where the commercial aspects of bookselling are minimized. The Bull's Head Bookshop of the University of North Carolina has served in this way. Although owned by the university bookstore, it is operated in the library under the direction of the library. Its stock embraces a liberal selection of recent books of educational and recreational value and literary merit which may be read, rented, or purchased. Interesting books of good quality are made available to students in an atmosphere conducive to browsing. Interest in books is also stimulated at frequent intervals through book talks and readings given by faculty members, visiting authors, and others and through informal social activities arranged by the members of the library staff and students of the library school.

All these activities which foster a love of good books and a desire for ownership are related to the program of the university library. If book ownership is fostered by bookstore activities, it should follow that students will need to place less reliance on the library for certain materials. Duplications can thus be decreased, and the funds released can be used for the acquisition of more scholarly works. Furthermore, there are many books of both educational and recreational value which the library cannot supply to readers, as they are not essential for either the instructional or the research program of the university. Such works may be made available through the bookstore. In this way the store complements library activities.

Mention has already been made of rental collections in university libraries. On some campuses, the bookstore has taken the responsibility of providing certain reserve materials on a rental basis. Fees are usually charged on a moderate basis to provide sufficient income to make the operation independent of any subsidy. This function of the bookstore is of inestimable value to the library. It not only saves the library money, which it can use in acquiring scholarly works, but it reduces the space which otherwise would be required for a reserve reading room.

COURSES Instruction in the use of libraries through
OF INSTRUCTION formal courses has long been recognized as
an effective means of increasing library use. The principal reasons why it is not provided have usually been lack of staff members and lack of opportunity to include additional courses in the curriculum. In general, such instruction, when provided, has been offered at three levels—undergraduate, graduate, and professional.

UNDERGRADUATE INSTRUCTION. In many institutions, library instruction has gone beyond the informal orientation or sight-seeing tour of the building. Variations of the informal approach are periods of library orientation during freshman week, or a visit to the library as part of a required freshman course, such as English. These approaches have many limitations, and are not considered effective in acquainting the students with their opportunities to work with library materials.[12]

Formal courses in the use of the library for which credit is given are offered undergraduates in a growing number of institutions. Such courses are usually offered in three forms: (1) complete courses for freshmen, which may be required;[13] (2) elective courses for freshmen or more advanced students;[14] and (3) abridged courses that are offered as a minor part of a course in some subject field.

[12] Jackson, "The Interpretation of Public Services," *Library Trends*, III (1954), 188–201.

[13] *Ibid.*, p. 189–90. Jackson summarizes the shortcomings of beginning students in college, as based on a study by Reed, "Do Colleges Need Reference Service?" *Library Quarterly*, XIII (1943), 232–40.

[14] Erickson, "Library Instruction in the Freshman Orientation Program," *College and Research Libraries*, X (1949), 445–48. Although a survey of teachers college libraries, this report on the practices in 61 libraries is suggestive of the trend to provide formal courses for students.

Whether required or elective, the courses in library instruction have followed a pattern. They include the mastery of information and working on problems which involve the parts of the book, encyclopedias, dictionaries, periodical indexes, indexes to collections, yearbooks, documents, pamphlet materials, reference books in special fields, the card catalog, classification of books on the shelves, facilities of special collections, and methods of constructing a bibliography. Most courses include a detailed tour of the library.[15] Frequently, standard textbooks or library manuals are used. These textbooks and manuals, in addition to lectures, tours, problems, and experience in applying theory to work in courses, have helped college students to build up the type of background that assists them in their educational program.[16] The observations of the librarians in the institutions in which instructional courses are provided indicate that beneficial results have been obtained, from the point of view of both the students and the library staff. Faculty members have generally supported such courses, and work cooperatively with the library staff. As Brough has noted, "Since individualized instruction is a costly method of imparting elementary instruction in common demand, librarians and other university officials have agreed on the importance of organized instruction in the use of the library." [17] Brough, however, ends on the dismal observation that "Librarians of the present day consider the provision of effective library instruction to be an unsolved problem." The problem is not an insolvable one if university administrations and librarians furnish the necessary personnel and wherewithal to do the job. Any investment in properly conceived courses should result in savings to the student as well as to the library.

GRADUATE LEVEL. The problem of familiarizing graduate students with the resources of the library and their effective use is dealt with in various ways in many universities. In a number of instances intro-

[15] Lyle, *The Administration of the College Library*, pp. 215-20.
[16] Wedemeyer, "Student Attitudes Toward Library Methods Courses in a University," *College and Research Libraries*, XV (1954), 285-89.
[17] *Scholar's Workshop*, p. 159.

ductory courses in methods of research and source materials are offered by the different departments of instruction. General courses in bibliographical method and historiography are common.

Some idea of the efforts of universities to assist in the program of developing students' skill in specific subject areas is afforded by the examination of seminars and other courses offered at various institutions. Among the schools and departments at Stanford [18] providing courses with emphasis on library resources are bacteriology, biology, business, chemistry, classical archaeology, engineering, English, geology, German, history, physics, and political science. Seminars in other fields undoubtedly offer courses which stress library resources. Similar listings have been made for other university libraries.[19]

Jackson [20] has commented on the limitations of such courses given in the subject areas by the departments. He calls attention to the emphasis that is likely to be given to a specific doctoral dissertation and to the duplication of general bibliographical information "in the offerings of the various departments, at least those in the humanities and social sciences." Teachers of such courses are also likely to be uncertain of bibliography outside of their specialties. Jackson suggested that a formal library course on an advanced level should be given upper division and graduate students.[21] The answer is probably a combination of specialized courses by faculty members who know the bibliography of their fields and a library course which would provide the students with information on such topics as bibliographic form, library catalogs, national and trade bibliographies, sources of data about current publications, bibliographies of bibliographies, indexes, abstracting services, union lists, union

[18] Wilson and Swank, *Report of a Survey of the Library of Stanford University*, p. 191.

[19] For example, Wilson, Downs, and Tauber, *Report of a Survey of the Libraries of Cornell University*, p. 174; Wilson and Lundy, *Report of a Survey of the Library of the University of Notre Dame*, p. 23.

[20] "The Interpretation of Public Services," p. 193–94. Jackson provides a bibliography of articles on the discussion of the problem of instruction.

[21] Although designed for the college library, the following volume provides a guide as to the content of a formal course: Wilson, Lowell, and Reed, *The Library in College Instruction*, esp. pp. 288–90.

catalogs, bibliographies of dissertations and research projects, resources and special services of the library, directories of library resources, and possibilities of obtaining materials from other libraries through interlibrary loan and photographic reproduction. Many of the manuals issued for faculty members and graduate students are designed to help them in orienting themselves to the resources, services, and facilities of particular libraries.[22]

PROFESSIONAL LEVEL. In much the same way as has been done for graduate students in the various disciplines in social sciences, humanities, and sciences, professional school libraries have introduced bibliographical and reference courses to aid their students. This is a relatively new development, but examples may be found of schools of agriculture, business, law, education, medicine, and engineering,[23] among others, working closely with their librarians in providing courses for professional students. Much of the impetus for courses of this type has come from the professionally trained librarians who are beginning to take over posts which were once filled by subject specialists.

INCREASING EFFECTIVE LIBRARY USE   The forms which efforts to increase effective library use may take include: (1) the organization of the library on functional and divisional bases; (2) the staffing of the library with experts; and (3) the provision of extensive bibliographical assistance through union catalogs and bibliographical resources.

FUNCTIONAL AND DIVISIONAL ORGANIZATION. The functional organization of the library referred to here relates to the organization of the facilities of the library for use by members of the university community. Such organization has been carefully developed in the last three decades. As a result, reserve reading rooms have been

[22] Jackson, *op. cit.*, pp. 196–99.
[23] Budington, "Teaching the Use of Engineering Libraries," *College and Research Libraries*, XII (1951), 268–72; see also Jackson, *op. cit.*, pp. 200–201, and Voigt, "Undergraduate Training in the Use of Printed Materials in Engineering and Science," *Journal of Engineering Education*, XLIII (1953), 519–23.

located and equipped physically according to certain pattern; the public catalog, the main delivery area, the reference and bibliographical apparatus have been organized in keeping with their functional relations to each other; divisional and graduate reading rooms have been placed near related materials in the stacks; and carrels, seminars, and studies have been arranged for the maximum use of materials under the most effective conditions. Departmental collections both within and outside of the central library have been developed in accordance with this principle. In those libraries with divisional organization, discussed in chapter iv, greater use of materials has been recorded, and the results of instruction and research are reported to have been considerably improved.

SERVICE THROUGH EXPERTS AND CONSULTANTS. Reference was made earlier in this chapter to the provision of a reader's advisory service in some libraries and to the staffing, at all hours, of various desks with professional librarians. In university libraries which maintain service at the teaching level, every effort is made to provide personnel who are equipped with proper subject and library training and experience in the handling of students' problems dealing with books and other materials.[24] The literature problem in the various disciplines, particularly in science and technology, has become so complex that expert counseling and guidance are essential if the scholar and the student are to succeed in the bibliographical conquest of their problems.

Special bibliographers in the acquisition departments of university libraries, faculty student-advisers, library service coordinators, and subject specialists have been recruited to assist in this program. Special bibliographers check catalogs issued by book dealers and generally help in the building of collections which are pertinent to the research program of the university. Faculty student-advisers work closely with the library in keeping syllabi up to date, in ad-

[24] Waterman, "Research and the Scholar," *Library Trends*, II (1954), 492–97; White, "Services to Scholars," *Library Trends*, III (1954), 148–63; Dunlap, "Services to Readers," *Library Trends*, I (1952), 49–57; Rothstein, *The Development of Reference Services through Academic Traditions, Public Library Practice, and Special Librarianship.*

vising the students concerning the various aspects of their courses, and counseling them on reading problems. Library coordinators relate the present or potential services of the public service units to the needs of clientele, especially undergraduates, solicit faculty advice in recommending new services and improving old ones, give instruction in library usage, and expedite the processing of materials needed for class use. Subject specialists in divisional or professional reading rooms keep abreast of the needs of the scholars and provide them with highly developed bibliographic services.[25] These specialists, who have a combination of subject and library training, are able to give expert aid on exploiting the collections, on preparing accurate bibliographies, and on using the various tools and services of the library. They have been especially useful in the development of the collections. They are aware of the applications of photographic services in libraries.[26]

BIBLIOGRAPHICAL APPARATUS. Union catalogs and other forms of bibliographical apparatus have further extended the use of university library resources for scholarly purposes. Interlibrary loans, the publication of various union lists, the services of bibliographical centers, and the National Union Catalog of the Library of Congress have been employed increasingly for this purpose, as well as the various techniques of microreproduction. The regional depository catalog, based upon the author cards of the Library of Congress and supplemented by cards from other major university and research libraries, has also come into fairly extensive use. In some libraries, these depository catalogs have been allowed to lapse with the issuance of the *Catalog of Books Represented by Library of Congress Printed Cards Issued to July 31, 1942*, and supplements. The Library of Congress has been of immeasurable assistance to the

[25] Gilman, "What the Scientist Expects of the Librarian," *College and Research Libraries*, VIII (1947), 329–32; Fleming, Brodman, and Robb, "A Continuous Bibliographic Service in University Libraries," *College and Research Libraries*, VIII (1947), 322–28; see also papers by Ralph W. McComb, Lois C. Bailey, and George S. Bonn, in Stallmann (ed.), *The Role of the Library in Collecting Information and Giving Service to the Student and Research Worker*, and papers in Shera and Egan (eds.), *Bibliographic Organization*.

[26] Tauber and Associates, *Technical Services in Libraries*, chap. xxi, "Photographic Services in Libraries."

scholarly world by its many other published catalogs and guides. National catalogs of other countries are also available to students and scholars who seek all material on subjects of their special interests.[27]

The descriptive survey of resources for research held by individual libraries or groups of libraries, the regional union catalog, the bibliographical center, and the interlibrary center have likewise been developed. This subject is treated in greater detail in chapter xiii, but it is important to mention it here, since it constitutes additional evidence of the means which university libraries have employed to increase, to the greatest extent possible, the use of library materials by students and scholars. The multiplication of depository catalogs, of union catalogs, and of collections of printed catalogs and subject bibliographies, for the location and description of materials, and the addition of expert bibliographers and subject specialists have aided in lifting the administration of the university library from a stripped-down, library-housekeeping level to a level of effective teaching and research. This accomplishment, where it has been effected, has constituted one of the most significant developments in American universities in the twentieth century.

This statement is not made with a sense of complacency. There is still much to be done. Examination of the problems and practices of bibliographical workers was the core of the proposal for a "Basic Study of Bibliographical Organization." [28] It was suggested that research workers would keep diaries and record their reading and sources of data. By showing in detail how they developed their special studies, it was anticipated that the librarian would have a body of information which would be of considerable value in determining the needs of users of the research library. Bibliographical

[27] Conover (comp.), *Current National Bibliographies.*
[28] *Basic Study of Bibliographical Organization;* see also Kathrine O. Murra, "History of Some Attempts to Organize Bibliography Internationally," in Shera and Egan (eds.), *Bibliographic Organization,* pp. 24–53. Murra includes an extensive bibliography. Another useful source of information on the problems of scholars and information is the April, 1954, issue of the *Library Quarterly;* see especially the papers by Maurice B. Visscher, Luther H. Evans, John Fall, and Robert W. Wadsworth.

control has no meaning except in terms of the user and his potential contribution to society.[29]

BIBLIOGRAPHY

Alexander, Carter, and Arvid J. Burke. How to Locate Educational Information and Data. 3d ed., rev. and enl. New York, Bureau of Publications, Teachers College, Columbia University, 1950.

Allen, Fern L. "Dormitory Library," Library Journal, LXXVI (1951), 920–23.

Basic Study of Bibliographical Organization. Chicago, American Library Association, 1952 (mimeographed).

Bibliographical Planning Committee of Philadelphia. A Faculty Survey of the University of Pennsylvania Libraries. Philadelphia, University of Pennsylvania Press, 1940.

Bishop, William W. "The Contribution of the Library to College Teaching," Association of American Colleges Bulletin, XIV (1928), 437–41.

Branscomb, Harvie. Teaching with Books: A Study of College Libraries. Chicago, Association of American Colleges and the American Library Association, 1940.

Brough, Kenneth J. Scholar's Workshop. Urbana, University of Illinois Press, 1953.

Budington, W. S. "Teaching the Use of Engineering Libraries," College and Research Libraries, XII (1951), 268–72.

California, University of, Library (Los Angeles). Rare Books and Research: Addresses Given at the Dedication of the Department of Special Collections, July 28, 1950. Los Angeles, University of California Library, 1951.

Carnovsky, Leon. "The Dormitory Library: An Experiment in Stimulating Reading," Library Quarterly, III (1933), 37–65.

Clapp, Verner W. "Indexing and Abstracting Services for Serial Literature," Library Trends, II (1954), 509–21.

Conover, Helen F. (comp.). Current National Bibliographies. Washington, D.C., Library of Congress, 1955.

Cross, T. P. Bibliographical Guide to English Studies. 9th ed. Chicago, University of Chicago Press, 1947.

Downs, Robert B. "Problems of Bibliographical Control," Library Trends, II (1954), 498–508.

[29] Downs, "Problems of Bibliographical Control," Library Trends, II (1954), 498–508; Clapp, "Indexing and Abstracting Services for Serial Literature," Library Trends, II (1954), 509–21; Ralph R. Shaw, "Mechanical and Electronic Aids for Bibliography," Library Trends, II (1954), 522–31.

Dunlap, Leslie W. "Services to Readers," *Library Trends*, I (1952), 49–57.

Ellsworth, Ralph E. "The Training of Divisional Reading Room Librarians," *College and Research Libraries*, VI (1944), 407.

Erickson, E. W. "Library Instruction in the Freshman Orientation Program," *College and Research Libraries*, X (1949), 445–48.

Estes, Rice. "The Lending Service Library," *College and Research Libraries*, VII (1946), 256–59.

Eurich, Alvin C. "Significance of Library Reading among College Students," *School and Society*, XXXVI (1932), 92–96.

Fleming, T. P., Estelle Brodman, and S. Robb. "A Continuous Bibliographic Service in University Libraries," *College and Research Libraries*, VIII (1947), 322–28.

Foreman, Clark. "Book Shops as a Cultural Asset," *Papers of the Southeastern Library Association*, VI (1930), 52–56.

Fussler, Herman H. "Some Problems in College Librarianship," *Library Quarterly*, XXIV (1954), 382–91.

Gilman, Henry. "What the Scientist Expects of the Librarian," *College and Research Libraries*, VIII (1947), 329–32.

Gwynn, Stanley E. "The Liberal Arts Function of the University Library," *Library Quarterly*, XXIV (1954), 311–21.

Hicks, Warren B. "Open or Closed Shelves?" *College and Research Libraries*, XV (1954), 309–12.

Hurt, Peyton. "The Need of College and University Instruction in the Use of the Library," *Library Quarterly*, IV (1934), 436–48.

Hutchins, Margaret. Introduction to Reference Work. Chicago, American Library Association, 1944.

Jackson, William V. "The Interpretation of Public Services," *Library Trends*, III (1954), 188–201.

King, Henry H. "Assistance to the Faculty in Library Research: Report from Cornell University," *College and Research Libraries*, IX (1948), 227–30.

Kuhlman, A. F. (ed.). The Development of University Centers in the South: Papers Presented at the Dedication of the Joint University Library, December Fifth and Sixth, 1941. Nashville, Tenn., Peabody Press and Vanderbilt University Press, 1942.

Lyle, Guy R. The Administration of the College Library. 2d ed., rev. New York, H. W. Wilson, 1949, chapters vii–viii.

McDiarmid, E. W. "Conditions Affecting the Use of the College Library," *Library Quarterly*, V (1935), 59–77.

Maxfield, David K. Counselor Librarianship: A New Departure (Occasional Papers, No. 38) Urbana, University of Illinois Library School, 1954.

—— "Counselor Librarianship at U.I.C.," *College and Research Libraries*, XV (1954), 161–66+.

Munthe, Wilhelm. American Librarianship from a European Angle. Chicago, American Library Association, 1939.

Murra, Kathrine O. "History of Some Attempts to Organize Bibliography Internationally," in Shera and Egan, *Bibliographic Organization*, pp. 24–53.

Reagan, Agnes. "A Study of College Library Exhibit Policy and Practice" (unpublished Master's thesis, University of Illinois Library School, 1943).

Reed, Lulu R. "Do Colleges Need Reference Service?" *Library Quarterly*, XIII (1943), 232–40.

Rohlf, Robert H. "The Freshman-Sophomore Library at Minnesota," *College and Research Libraries*, XIV (1953), 164–66.

Rothstein, Samuel. The Development of Reference Services through Academic Traditions, Public Library Practice, and Special Librarianship (ACRL Monograph No. 14) Chicago, Association of College and Reference Libraries, 1955.

Shaw, Ralph R. "Mechanical and Electronic Aids for Bibliography," *Library Trends*, II (1954), 522–31.

Shera, Jesse H. "The Role of the College Librarian—A Reappraisal," in *Library Instructional Integration on the College Level.* (ACRL Monograph No. 13) Chicago, Association of College and Reference Libraries, 1955, pp. 6–13. The monograph also contains other discussions on librarians.

Shera, Jesse H., and Margaret E. Egan (eds.). Bibliographic Organization; Papers Presented before the Fifteenth Annual Conference of the Graduate Library School, July 24–29, 1950. Chicago, University of Chicago Press, 1951.

Stallmann, Esther (ed.). The Role of the Library in Collecting Information and Giving Service to the Student and Research Worker: The Public Library, the College and University Library. Austin, Graduate School of Library Science of the University of Texas, 1954.

Tauber, Maurice F., and Associates. Technical Services in Libraries. New York, Columbia University Press, 1954, chap. xxi.

Vahey, Sister Mary Ricarda. "1948 Survey of Browsing Rooms," *Catholic Library World*, XX (1948), 242–46.

Voigt, Melvin J. "Undergraduate Training in the Use of Printed Materials in Engineering and Science," *Journal of Engineering Education*, XLIII (1953), 519–23.

Waterman, Alan T. "Research and the Scholar," *Library Trends*, II (1954), 492–97.

Wedemeyer, Josephine A. "Student Attitudes toward Library Methods Courses in a University," *College and Research Libraries*, XV (1954), 285–89.

White, Carl M. "Services to Scholars," *Library Trends*, III (1954), 148–63.

Wilson, Louis R. "The Library's Role in College Instruction," *College and Research Libraries*, V (1944), 126–33.

—— "Use of the Library in College Instruction," *Proceedings of the Institute for Administrative Officers of Higher Institutions*. Vol. XIII. "New Frontiers in Collegiate Education," pp. 103–13. Chicago, University of Chicago Press, 1941.

Wilson, Louis R., Robert B. Downs, and Maurice F. Tauber. Report of a Survey of the Libraries of Cornell University for the Library Board of Cornell University, October 1947—February 1948. Ithaca, Cornell University, 1948.

Wilson, Louis R., Mildred H. Lowell, and Sarah R. Reed. The Library in College Instruction. New York, H. W. Wilson, 1951.

Wilson, Louis R., and Frank A. Lundy. Report of a Survey of the Library of the University of Notre Dame for the University of Notre Dame, November 1950—March 1952. Chicago, American Library Association, 1952.

Wilson, Louis R., and Raynard C. Swank. Report of a Survey of the Library of Stanford University for Stanford University, November 1946—March 1947. Chicago, American Library Association, 1947.

Wriston, Henry M. "Objective Indices of Faculty Scholarship Obtainable through the Library," *Association of American Colleges Bulletin*, XVIII (1932), 176–85.

See also other surveys of libraries in Bibliography for chapter xvi, as well as "Handbooks" and "Staff Manuals" of particular libraries, listed in *Library Literature*.

XIII

COOPERATION AND SPECIALIZATION

Co-operation between universities in the United States of America is increasing rapidly in extent. More than forty co-operative programs involving colleges and universities are now in operation in this country. Some of these involve no more than two institutions. One of them involves as many as forty institutions of higher education.

All these co-operative programs are, of course, partial. That is to say, no university co-operates with another university in all activities and functions. Those of you who know universities will recognize this as an impossibility, since, to the best of my knowledge, there are no two universities in America which engage in exactly the same functions.[1]

COLWELL'S observation, made at the dedication of the Midwest Inter-Library Center on the University of Chicago campus on October 5, 1951, is important in the framework of a consideration of cooperation among libraries. American university and research librarians have long sought to increase cooperation among themselves. In fact, the development of the ways and means of various cooperative undertakings, imperfect though they may be, has been one of the most significant contributions that university libraries have made to scholarship in the United States. Such cooperation, however, should be appraised in the light of the limitations under which university libraries are forced to function.

The ways and means of library cooperation include: (1) interlibrary loan service; (2) cooperative and centralized cataloging; (3) multiplication of bibliographies, union lists, and surveys of library holdings; (4) development of the National Union Catalog at the Library of Congress, of regional and local union catalogs, and

[1] Colwell, "Inter-University Co-operation," *Library Quarterly*, XX (1952), 1.

of bibliographical centers; (5) specialization in collecting; (6) storage libraries and interlibrary centers; (7) cooperative photographic projects; and (8) international cooperation.

INTERLIBRARY LOAN PRACTICE — Lending of materials by one library to another for the use of a patron has long been a method of library cooperation. Advocated by Green [2] in the first issue of the *Library Journal* and by Richardson [3] in 1905, interlibrary lending has been accentuated by the development of devices for recording resources and by the provision of relatively low postal rates on books since 1938.[4] The increase in the amount of research and in the number of graduate students and faculty members in universities, as well as the growth in requests from public and special libraries, has added to extension of interlibrary lending.

PURPOSES OF INTERLIBRARY LOANS. The major purpose of interlibrary loans is to place every book, manuscript, archive, or other graphic record within the reach of persons who need them. Through union catalogs, union lists, and special bibliographies, materials are becoming more accessible than they ever were before; through interlibrary loans, and more recently, photographic reproduction, they are being made available.[5]

EXTENT OF INTERLIBRARY LENDING. Despite an increase in the use of microreproduction for obtaining copies of materials needed by

[2] "The Lending of Books to One Another by Libraries," *Library Journal*, I (1876), 15–16.

[3] Richardson, "The National Library Problem To-Day," *Library Journal*, XXX, No. 9 (1905), 3–9.

[4] Lucy, "Interlibrary Loans in a University Library," *College and Research Libraries*, XIII (1952), 344–49. Lucy compared costs of transportation and found that sending materials by first-class mail is cheaper than minimum express rate. (p. 349).

[5] See "General Interlibrary Loan Code, 1952," *College and Research Libraries*, XIII (1952), 350–58. The Code includes statements on definition of purpose, responsibility, conditions of loans, scope, expenses, placement of requests, information required on requests, photographic substitution, shipment of loans, duration of loan, insurance, renewal, recall, notification and acknowledgment, and violations. Information is also given on standard interlibrary loan shipping label specifications, the use of a standard interlibrary loan request form, standard abbreviations of sources of verification, bibliographic centers and selected union catalogs, and policy on interlibrary lending of microfilm.

users, interlibrary loan figures of most university libraries have continued to rise. For example, in a ten-month period, July 1, 1951, to April 30, 1952, Columbia University Libraries loaned 1,891 volumes to 419 libraries.[6] This may be compared to the 1938–39 statistics from the same library: 1,392 volumes to 247 libraries. The University of California Library at Los Angeles in 1953–54 reported an increase in interlibrary loan service of 4 percent.[7] The librarian noted:

The Biomedical Library alone showed a 30 per cent increase in volumes loaned to other libraries, mostly to hospital libraries in Southern California. The Music Library circulated orchestral scores to 81 organizations throughout the West. The success of bibliographical instruction to classes, also a responsibility of the Reference Department, resulted in an increase of faculty requests for more of this kind of service.[8]

Although there was a small decline in the interlibrary loans and borrowings in 1953–54 as against those of the previous year, at Cornell University Library the total titles sent were 3,602 (volumes, 3,916) and borrowed 2,200 titles (volumes, 2,341). Cornell, however, has been emphasizing the use of photostats and microfilms, and during the period 420 photostats and 160 microfilms were sent instead of the materials. Twenty-eight photostats and 57 microfilms were received.[9]

In a recent study by White [10] of the interlibrary loan service of twenty university libraries, he found that they made "59 per cent more loans to scholars through other libraries in 1952–53 than in 1947–48, and borrowed 22 per cent more during the same period." Although photocopying may have prevented a greater increase, such factors as enriched collections, gaps caused by the war, increased graduate study and post-doctoral research, new programs,

[6] Lucy, *op. cit.*, p. 345. In 1953–54, Columbia loaned 5,566 volumes to 728 institutions; it borrowed 968 volumes from 127 institutions. (Data from Reference Dept.)
[7] University of California Library (Los Angeles). "Report of the Librarian to the Chancellor for the Year 1953–54," p. 3.
[8] *Ibid.*
[9] Cornell University, "Report of the Director of the University Library, 1953–54," p. 13.
[10] "Services to Scholars," *Library Trends,* III (1954), 151.

and an expanding clientele are listed by White as keeping the curve on an upsweep. Programs of specialization in collecting, such as the Farmington Plan, by their very nature should also have some effect upon the growth in interlibrary lending.

Various studies which have been made of interlibrary lending transactions reveal the great dependence of the small library on the larger libraries. Some of the large university libraries, such as California, Chicago, Columbia, Cornell, Duke, Harvard, North Carolina, Pennsylvania, Princeton, Stanford, Texas, and Yale, are centers which naturally attract requests from smaller institutions. While loans may be concentrated in a particular region, such as the Midwest for the University of Chicago, or New England for Harvard, the larger libraries, along with the Library of Congress, the New York Public Library, and other large public libraries, are called upon to provide materials, or copies of materials, to users in all parts of the country.[11] The studies also reveal that the same centers must seek materials from other large institutions when their clients require titles not owned by the centers.

LIBRARIES BORROWED FROM. The interlibrary loans made by a university library are not limited to libraries of its own type. For example, books are borrowed from, as well as loaned to, college libraries, public libraries, and libraries of industrial organizations, schools, institutions of various kinds, business houses, and governmental units. With the development of union catalogs, many small libraries, including those of special organizations or private groups, have permitted more lending than in the past. There are, however, a number of private libraries which restrict lending rather severely.

MATERIALS. Any satisfactory system of interlibrary loans involves a strict definition of the types of materials that may be lent. For example, loans of the following materials are generally not made (except, perhaps, in the case of state university libraries which

[11] Schlundt, "Services Available from Large Libraries," *Special Libraries*, XLV (1954), 375–83. Includes a tabular presentation of resources, type and use, research service, translations, and photoduplication service. Interlibrary loan (with some restrictions as to materials) is permitted in all libraries listed. Columbia's policy, for example, is to lend to any library within the United States, Canada, or Mexico, and to other libraries in certain cases.

engage in extension programs): books which are easily available on the market at reasonable prices, reference works, books which are needed for instructional work, rare books, periodicals (particularly if they are current), fragile materials, manuscripts (except theses), music to be used in public performance, local history materials, unique copies of theses, and archival materials. Libraries which permit the borrowing of rare materials generally require proper insurance during transportation. In recent years, there has been a tendency on the part of more libraries to allow rare books to be circulated on interlibrary loan, if the situations under which the materials are to be used and the nature of the personnel using them are made clear.[12] More liberal ideas in interlibrary lending have evolved in regard to microfilm. Positive microfilm is usually loaned freely, but some restriction is placed on lending negative film, unless the lending library owns the original.

CLIENTELE. The functions of aiding research and meeting the book needs of the average reader suggest that the clientele of interlibrary loan service may comprise the entire student body, the faculty members and research members of the staff, administrative officers, library staff members, and other individuals or groups associated with the university.

The standard interlibrary loan request form, consisting of four parts (request, report, interim report, and notice of return) contains a space for the filling in of the name of the person, status, and department wanting the item. While some libraries will not lend items which are intended for undergraduate students, Melinat [13] found that an increasing number of libraries will permit such lending if the circumstances are described adequately.

Most borrowing is done for faculty members and graduate students. In a study conducted by Lucy [14] volumes were borrowed for

---

[12] Wright, "Interlibrary Loan—Smothered in Tradition," *College and Research Libraries,* XIII (1952), 332–36.

[13] "Interlibrary Loan Practice and the Interlibrary Loan Code," *College and Research Libraries,* XIII (1952), 342–44; and his "Interlibrary Lending," *Library Trends,* II (1954), 573–80. The latter article contains an extensive bibliography on interlibrary loans.

[14] "Interlibrary Loans in a University Library," p. 346.

45 faculty members, 23 lecturers and instructors, 120 Ph.D. candidates, 53 Master's candidates, and 32 other members of the university. Faculty members and graduate students are generally the greatest users of the interlibrary loan service.

ORGANIZATION. David [15] and Wright [16] have called attention to the need of making loans to individuals as easy as possible, at the same time cutting costs and speeding up the service. David observed that many of the loans now made through reference departments could be handled in a direct manner by the circulation departments of libraries, particularly if they were authorized by reciprocal interlibrary agreements.

In most libraries, however, the actual work of interlibrary lending is centralized in the reference department because the making of a loan sometimes requires checking by the borrowing library in order to make sure that the entry, title, and other items are bibliographically correct. Hodgson and Kidder [17] found that many careless errors were made in citations in interlibrary requests, although in only 8 percent of the cases were serious difficulties raised.

PROBLEMS INVOLVED. The General Interlibrary Code of 1952 [18] enumerates the various problems which arise in interlibrary loan service. Among these that warrant attention here are costs, recognition of responsibilities by borrowing libraries, and the need for cooperation in promoting smooth relationships between libraries engaged in the transactions.

A number of efforts have been made to determine the costs of interlibrary loans. In 1930, Hand [19] estimated the average cost of an interlibrary loan at the University of California at $1.59. The average cost of an interlibrary loan was calculated by Brown [20] in 1932 as

[15] David, "Remarks upon Interlibrary Loans: Mid-20th Century Style," *College and Research Libraries*, X (1949), 429–33.

[16] "Interlibrary Loan—Smothered in Tradition," *College and Research Libraries*, XIII (1952), 332–36.

[17] "Errors and Incomplete Entries in Interlibrary Loan Requests," *College and Research Libraries*, XIII (1952), 336–41.

[18] *Ibid.*

[19] "A Cost Survey in a University Library," *Library Journal*, LV (1930), 763–66.

[20] "Inter-Library Loans: an Unsolved Problem," *Library Journal*, LVII (1932), 887–89.

$3.56. In 1936 Rider [21] figured the labor costs of interlibrary lending as $1.11. The average cost of an interlibrary loan was estimated by David [22] in 1949 at Pennsylvania to be $7.00. Lucy [23] in 1952 calculated the cost for lending at $1.27; for borrowing at $2.70 ($2.08 net). As a result of these costs, which undoubtedly vary according to the efforts of the different libraries in executing requests, most libraries charge the users for all expenses in interlibrary loan service. Exceptions are most often made in the case of faculty members, who may be required to pay a fee or a portion of the charges. There seems to be no question that in the larger libraries, even in instances where charges are made, the fees do not pay for the entire service. The General Interlibrary Code of 1952 suggests that "payment of transportation costs both ways, including insurance, is to be met by the *borrowing library* except where agreements to the contrary exist." [24] Other conditions of costs are stipulated.[25]

Borrowing libraries are under the obligation to consider interlibrary loan service as a courtesy and a privilege, rather than a right. Since lending libraries must first consider their own clientele, borrowing libraries should restrict their requests to absolutely essential items. This does not mean that reasonable needs should not be considered, but discrimination is necessary. Small libraries should seek to supply their own clientele with essential materials without reliance on the larger research libraries. In the past, the large libraries have not been too much concerned with reciprocity in lending. The liberal attitude that is characteristic of research libraries, in providing service to scholars wherever they may be, has not changed even with the increase in interlibrary lending.[26]

As a group, libraries have come to recognize the need for systematic procedures in interlibrary loan service. Apparently, the

[21] "Library Cost Accounting," *Library Quarterly*, VI (1936), 331–81, esp. p. 359.
[22] "Remarks upon Interlibrary Loans," p. 431.
[23] "Interlibrary Loans in a University Library," pp. 348–49.
[24] *Op. cit.*, p. 351.
[25] A study of costs is being made by Hodgson. See his "A Preliminary Report on Interlibrary Loan Costs," *College and Research Libraries*, XIII (1952), 327–31.
[26] Wright, "Interlibrary Loan," pp. 335–36.

libraries which have introduced the standard interlibrary loan forms have found them satisfactory. All libraries, however, have not used them. Librarians engaged in interlibrary borrowing should provide all necessary information for the loans, should be cognizant of expense and promptness of transportation, should wrap and insure items properly, and should abide by the rules set by the lending library. These practices should minimize the hardships that are placed upon the research librarians who are willing to contribute to the free flow of materials from one library to another. Interlibrary loans can do much to foster scholarship, and, at the same time, be an integral part of the pattern of controlling the size of collections.

It is possible that the future may bring some important changes in interlibrary use of materials. Among the devices that have been singled out are the teletype, facsimile transmission, and such devices as Ultrafax and closed circuit television.[27] Communication between the Racine and the Milwaukee public libraries by teletype began in 1950. The Midwest Inter-Library Center joined the TWX teletype system in 1951. Libraries belonging to the Center are able to call the Center and each other, in addition to the Library of Congress and any other of the 29,000 teletype subscribers. By 1954, of the 16 members of the Center, 14 had teletype installations. "There has been a gradual increase in use during the year as libraries found that the teletype made it possible to give overnight service in the delivery of requested items." [28]

The development of facsimile transmission also offers new opportunities for libraries in obtaining materials needed by clientele.[29] Experiments in facsimile transmission between the Library of Congress and the National Institutes of Health Library suggest the possibilities of immediate transmission of exact, durable, and economical copies of material from library to library.

[27] Melinat, "Interlibrary Lending," p. 579.
[28] *Fifth Annual Report of the Midwest Inter-Library Corporation and the Midwest Inter-Library Center*, p. 12.
[29] Scott Adams, "Facsimile for Federal Libraries," *Special Libraries*, XLIV (1953), 169–72.

Shaw [30] has called attention to the possibilities of Ultrafax (capable of transmitting one million words per minute) for library applications. Similarly, closed circuit television has potential library use. The virtual disappearance of wrapping and mailing packages of material for interlibrary use is not an impossibility for the future.

COOPERATIVE AND   In 1851 Charles C. Jewett proposed an or-
CENTRALIZED   ganization of libraries in the United States
CATALOGING   with the Smithsonian Institution as a national center, which would engage in cooperative enterprises, including cooperative cataloging. The Smithsonian authorities declined to enter into the plan, however, and the idea gathered dust until 1876, when the American Library Association was organized. The development of standard cataloging rules and the adoption of the 3 x 5-inch card were principal achievements toward uniformity in practice during the nineteenth century.

In 1902 the first really centralized system of producing cards was started at the Library of Congress.[31] A cooperative agreement for acquiring card copy from other governmental departmental libraries was also put into effect. In 1902 there were 212 subscribers to the printed cards, returning a total of $3,785.19 to the United States Treasury. By 1955 the number of subscribers had grown to about 10,000 who purchased 23,450,243 cards. From the sale of cards and related publications over a million dollars was returned in 1954/55. The Library of Congress worked closely with the ALA Cooperative Cataloging Committee, established in 1926 with subsidies from the General Education Board.

Morsch [32] has reviewed the activities of cooperative and central-

[30] "Machines and the Bibliographical Problems of the Twentieth Century," in L. N. Ridenour, et al., Bibliography in an Age of Science, pp. 37–71; see also his "Mechanical and Electronic Aids for Bibliography," Library Trends, II (1954), 522–31.

[31] Walter, "Fifty Years Young: Library of Congress Cards," College and Research Libraries, XIII (1952), 305–8; the figures which follow are from Library of Congress Information Bulletin, XIV (Aug. 29, 1955), 1.

[32] "Cooperation and Centralization," Library Trends, II (1953), 342–55.

ized cataloging in the United States and in other countries. As she points out, the Library of Congress still "offers the most comprehensive service provided by any library or agency anywhere," although it does not cover all the needs of research libraries. The fact that it does not meet all the needs is only partially explained by the inability of the Library of Congress to catalog all of its acquisitions promptly. "The most urgent cataloging problem in the United States is that of finding a way by which the Library of Congress can increase its coverage, so that all or nearly all of the titles received in other American libraries will have been cataloged, and their printed cards made available, by the time the other libraries want them." [33]

A proposal by Ellsworth [34] in 1948 for the establishment of a Centralized Cataloging Service in the Library of Congress had as its objectives the elimination of duplicate cataloging effort in the country and the solution of difficulties arising from the shortage of cataloging personnel. Morsch has added the following objectives to these: to reduce the cost of cataloging, to increase the number of titles cataloged, to promote uniformity of cataloging and catalogs, and to raise the over-all level of the quality of cataloging.[35]

Cooperative cataloging is still considered essential if an effective job is to be done for university and other libraries by a centralized agency, such as the Library of Congress. The national library has coordinated the work done by other American libraries in its Cooperative Cataloging Section. Copy prepared by these libraries is printed and distributed by the Library of Congress. The cooperative cataloging statistics for 1953 show that the Library of Congress [36] prepared 8,746 "regular" and 4,020 motion picture titles for other libraries.

Morsch's conclusions favor supporting a centralized cataloging service "approximating complete and prompt coverage of books

[33] *Ibid.*, pp. 348–49.
[34] "Mr. Ellsworth's Report," Library of Congress *Information Bulletin,* Nov. 16–22, 1948. Appendix.
[35] *Op. cit.*, p. 350.
[36] U.S. Library of Congress. *Annual Report of the Librarian of Congress . . . 1953,* p. 131.

that are duplicated in several or many libraries." This service should be coordinated with a plan of cooperative cataloging which would take advantage of the work of individual catalog departments of libraries. Unusual linguistic, bibliographic, and subject materials could be handled by the central service. Undoubtedly, if such a central service were available and libraries took full advantage of its work, the catalog departments of the university libraries could accomplish more in keeping their records up to date and in making their catalogs more useful to the clientele. The Association of Research Libraries, composed primarily of university libraries, has through special committees shown an interest in developing practices which will help to relieve the pressure on individual catalog departments. While credit is given to the Library of Congress for its considerable efforts in providing cataloging service to libraries, Metcalf [37] observed that "we must continue the struggle to find better ways and means to carry on cooperative cataloging so as to hold down expenses in that field." Metcalf, after suggesting a comprehensive study of cooperative cataloging, as well as a review of the general cataloging situation in research libraries, further noted that jointly published catalogs in book form of older materials should be economical, convenient, and more useful for research than current card catalogs. Certainly, the end is not yet in sight in regard to the cataloging problem for the university library.

BIBLIOGRAPHIES AND UNION LISTS

University librarians have always emphasized the importance of compiling bibliographies. The activities of Gerould, Richardson, and others in this field are commented on in chapter xv. During recent years cooperative enterprises in the compilation of bibliographies and union lists have increased significantly. In the 1930's and 1940's federally aided projects aided materially in the production of bibliographic compilations. In the last decade the American Library Association, the Association of Research Libraries, the Association of College and

[37] "University Libraries Face the Future," *Library Quarterly*, XXII (1952), 10.

Reference Libraries, and the Special Libraries Association, sometimes working independently and sometimes jointly with other professional organizations and learned societies, have supported bibliographic projects.

Cooperative activity, in which university libraries have played a prominent role, has resulted in the publication of such lists as the following: *American Newspapers, 1821–1936: A Union List of Files Available in the United States and Canada*, edited by Winifred Gregory; *Census of Medieval and Renaissance Manuscripts in the United States and Canada*, edited by Seymour De Ricci; *International Congresses and Conferences, 1840–1937; Union List of Serials in Libraries of the United States and Canada*, edited by Winifred Gregory; and the *List of Serial Publications of Foreign Governments, 1815–1931*, also edited by Miss Gregory. University libraries contributed substantially to the editions and supplements of the *Union List of Serials*. The work done by individuals through federally supported projects was particularly notable in the compilation of union catalogs, and the preparation of many local lists of newspapers, municipal and state documents, and indexes to local historical collections. University libraries worked closely with the Historical Records Survey and the extensive American Imprints Inventory.[38]

Special bibliographies have also been prepared through the cooperation of university libraries. The *Bibliography of Research Studies in Education*, issued for many years by the U.S. Office of Education, received data directly from many university libraries. Similar efforts have resulted in the publication of *Doctoral Dissertations Accepted by American Universities*, which, since 1933–34, has been issued under the editorship of university librarians and the Association of Research Libraries. Many university librarians have assumed responsibility for issuing guides to theses and dissertations prepared at various institutions. The Association of Research Libraries also sponsored the publication of *A Catalog of Books Represented by Library of Congress Printed Cards Issued to July 31,*

[38] See Winchell, *Guide to Reference Books*, p. 23.

1942, and its *Supplement*, as well as *Newspapers on Microfilm: A Union Check List*, compiled under the direction of George A. Schwegmann, Jr. University libraries have contributed information essential for publishing the *Union List of Microfilms: A Basic List of Holdings in the United States and Canada*, and several supplements. Downs [39] and Winchell [40] have listed other union lists which have been compiled with the aid of university libraries.

Individual libraries have sponsored the publication of union lists. For example, the *Publications of Cook County, Illinois, Atlases in Chicago*, and *Newspapers in Libraries of Chicago: A Joint Checklist* were compilations of staff members of the University of Chicago Library.

Other publications of individual libraries have contributed to the growth of scholarship. Catalogs of the Vatican Library, the John Rylands Library, and the British Museum are examples of work done in Europe. Catalogs of the New York Public Library and the Library of Congress represent distinct contributions to scholarly activity. Similarly, university libraries have compiled and distributed catalogs and bibliographies of their holdings and special collections. Undoubtedly, much more in this area needs to be done, as Downs has pointed out:

In contrast to the libraries which have been so well covered bibliographically, we find a group of strong institutions that has been inactive in publishing, and which perforce does not show up to full advantage in the present compilation. Instances among universities are California, Chicago, Columbia, Illinois, Michigan (except Clements Library), Minnesota, Stanford (except Hoover Library), Northwestern, Indiana, Wisconsin, Ohio, and New York.[41]

Downs indicated that most of these institutions are state universities and have less funds than private institutions for publishing ventures, are more interested in building up general collections, and, with certain exceptions, have achieved status as major libraries only recently and are more concerned with collecting materials than with publicizing them. Nevertheless, bibliographies, hand-

---

[39] *American Library Resources*, pp. 21–26.   [40] *Op cit., passim.*
[41] *Op. cit.*, p. 2.

books, checklists, and surveys of resources are of immeasurable value to researchers who are concerned about the holdings of specific institutions.

UNION
CATALOGS AND
BIBLIOGRAPHICAL
CENTERS

In chapter ii mention was made of the relation of the university librarian to union catalogs and bibliographical centers. There it was pointed out that these union catalogs and centers were instrumental in providing services to university clientele, and, at the same time, placed certain responsibilities upon the university library administration. At this point attention will be given to the development and purposes, activities, and current problems of union catalogs and bibliographical centers.

DEVELOPMENT AND LOCATION   The development of union catalogs in the United States may be said to have started with the Union Catalog of the Library of Congress in 1901. To the basic set of Library of Congress printed cards were added author cards from the Boston Public Library, the New York Public Library, Harvard University Library, John Crerar Library, the University of Illinois Library, and several Washington libraries, increasing the card holdings of the national Union Catalog to 1,960,000 in 1927. A grant of $250,000 from John D. Rockefeller, Jr., in 1927 served as an impetus to the development of the Union Catalog. At present, it is the greatest tool of its kind. By 1954, it contained 12,831,122 cards, with contributions from more than 500 libraries.[42]

The distribution of depository catalogs by the Library of Congress marked another step in making available to scholars the resources of the national collections in Washington. Since the Library of Congress has been issuing printed book catalogs, however, some of these card depository catalogs, which were often combined with cards from other libraries, have been retired from active development.

[42] *American Library Directory*, p. 837. On pp. 837–38 of this volume is a list of 11 union catalogs and bibliographical centers, with information on size, number of libraries participating, and other matters.

In 1952, Sherwood and Campion [43] reported on the status and activity of five major union catalogs and bibliographical centers in the United States: the Union Catalog Division of the Library of Congress, the Union Library Catalogue of the Philadelphia Metropolitan Area, the Pacific Northwest Bibliographical Center at Seattle, the Bibliographical Center for Research at Denver, and the Union Catalog of the Western Reserve University Library in Cleveland. By 1954, the catalog at Philadelphia included card contributions from 171 libraries, and contained 4,500,000 cards. At Seattle, cards from 39 libraries plus L.C. depository cards totaled 3,907,912. Denver received cards from 35 libraries for its catalog of over 5,000,000 cards; Cleveland, from 47 libraries for its catalog of 2,521,386. [44]

There are many other union catalogs in the country, such as those maintained by state libraries in California, Nebraska, New Hampshire, Ohio, and Vermont. Others have been developed at Atlanta, Austin, Chapel Hill–Durham, and Nashville. Special union catalogs on art, medicine, and other subjects also exist.

ACTIVITIES   The primary purpose of the union catalog is to help locate specific items for readers. Among the other services which have been provided by union catalogs are checking bibliographies, compiling bibliographies, arranging for or even executing interlibrary loans, and checking lists of unlocated research items. Special services include supplying cataloging and classification data (Philadelphia assists industrial libraries in cataloging and classifying their collections), identifying publishing information, providing the National Union Catalog searching service for unfilled L.C. card orders and supplying photostatic copies of union catalog entries, and notifying clients of the location of new titles. Various publications have been issued by the union catalogs.

On a broad basis, union catalogs help to distribute the burden of interlibrary loans, to assist in the prevention of the unnecessary duplication of expensive or little-used materials, and to provide in-

[43] "Union Library Catalogue: Services, 1950. Quo Vadis?" *College and Research Libraries*, XIII (1952), 101–6, 110. Contains bibliographical footnotes.
[44] *American Library Directory*, pp. 837–38.

formation on gaps in the collections of the region covered. They have also assisted in exchange programs of libraries.

CURRENT PROBLEMS   Sherwood and Campion [45] summarize their survey of union catalogs and bibliographical centers with the following statement: "The very growth of these services within the four regions justifies their continuance and emphasizes the importance of their consideration in whatever local, regional or other library planning is undertaken." Libraries themselves must play a more aggressive role in the utilization of these catalogs for the needs of researchers and others. Undoubtedly, the biliographical centers built around union catalogs are in a position to offer greater and more varied services to all types of libraries if their potential values are to be exploited fully. Continued financial support, one of the constant problems of the centers, is essential if they are to develop their activities to meet the needs of libraries and industry.

The university library that houses a union catalog and a bibliographical center poses additional administrative problems for the librarian. This is particularly true if the responsibility for the catalog and the center is vested in the library administration. These problems involve providing space for the work, maintaining equipment, permitting the use of the university library bibliographical and reference tools for business which is frequently not of university origin, and collecting payments for the upkeep of the catalog. Generally, however, the actual operation of the catalog and center is placed in the hands of a special personnel.

Before leaving the question of regional union catalogs, mention should be made of the observation by some librarians that they are uneconomical, and that a properly completed National Union Catalog would make them unnecessary. At the present time, the National Union Catalog is able to locate in some library at least one copy of 79 percent of the titles it is requested to check. It is suggested further that such modern means of communication as telephone, teletype, telegraph, air mail, and perhaps facsimile trans-

[45] "Union Library Catalogue," p. 110.

mission would make a single, complete catalog a more profitable venture than a scattered system of regional catalogs. Whether or not a single national catalog could provide the types of services offered by the regional catalogs is conjectural. Up to the present, despite difficulties, the financial support given the regional centers is evidence of their effectiveness.[46]

SPECIALIZATION IN COLLECTING — One of the most important developments in university librarianship in recent years has been the change in attitude toward size of collections. Although there are more and more libraries accumulating a million or more volumes, there is a general recognition of the impossibility of each library acquiring all the materials from the presses of the world. University boards of trustees, presidents, executive officers, and faculty members, as well as members of learned societies and associations, have also become concerned with the need to control the size of libraries and to establish tangible lines of cooperation.

This new attitude is most evident in the willingness of university administrations, faculties, and library staffs to view the library situation in the United States as a total problem, and to support (at least theoretically) the principle of specialization in collecting— the concentration of collections in special subjects in particular institutions which already have strong collections from the standpoints of breadth and depth (Ph.D. and post-Ph.D. research), and which provide curriculums, faculty, and library specialists to work with the collections.

Although there is theoretical support of the idea of specialization, it is difficult to put into practice. Downs unquestionably isolated the primary problem when he noted: "I am convinced that no substantial economies can be achieved in university libraries, or, for that matter, any kind of libraries, unless the institutions of which they are a part are willing to reduce the scope of their activities.

[46] Downs, "Problems of Bibliographical Control," *Library Trends*, II (1954), 504-5.

As long as universities insist on carrying on instruction and research in virtually every subject under the sun, frequently in competition with one another, the libraries will be expected to support
these programs by providing materials and services." [47] In addition
to educational factors such as are implied in Downs's observation,
there are also administrative and library obstacles.

Among the administrative factors are financial instability in maintaining collections, the effects of gifts, distances between libraries,
restrictions on circulation and use of collections, legal problems,
and lack of facilities for the reproduction of materials. These problems are not insurmountable. A consistent budget for a library
program, however, is essential for support of a specialized acquisition policy. A more positive attitude toward rejection of irrelevant
gifts is necessary. Distances between libraries have been reduced
in importance by rapid communication, and by the possibility of
sending faculty members and qualified students to libraries with
specialized resources. Reciprocal use of collections must be a part
of the program. Legal difficulties apparently can be overcome by
carefully prepared agreements. Arrangements for systematic reproduction of materials appear to be increasing in number in the
libraries which have the research materials needed by scholars.

Library factors include such matters as fear of losing prestige,
changes in specialization, failure to maintain special collections,
and the need to remove artificial barriers which exist between different types of libraries. An entirely new attitude toward the idea of
prestige inherent in size or ownership of special materials is essential if progress in specialization in collecting is to be gained. So
long as educational institutions change curriculums, requiring
changes in library collecting, the road to systematic specialization
will be difficult. Institutional budgetary shifts may have a direct
effect upon a library's ability to maintain a special collection. Finally, all types of libraries should be part of the program if it is
to be effective.

[47] Downs, "A Realistic Look at Library Cooperation," in *Annual Meeting, 1954,*
Bibliographical Center for Research (Bulletin No. 11), pp. 7–8. See also Barcus and
Clapp, "Collecting in the National Interest," *Library Trends,* III (1955), 337–55.

The question of comprehensiveness *versus* selectivity is so bound up with the needs of individual institutions that no categorical statement is possible. Coney sums up the situation as follows:

The whole question of collection building is so colored by decisions of degree—there are so many variables—that we cannot pass a law nor map with a firm precise line the exact limits of our selective collections. The best we can do is to take a position and establish a focus.

I have proposed that we establish the focus of our collections by reflecting the needs of our present faculties. Implicit in this focus is a position we might well take: that we regard collections of books not as entities having shapes, sizes, and completenesses, of value in themselves, but rather as collections which are designed to satisfy as specific needs as we are able to determine.[48]

PROGRAMS OF SPECIALIZATION IN COLLECTING   Despite the difficulties in the way of attaining a high level of cooperative specialization in collecting, a number of informal and formal plans exist. For many years informal arrangements in collecting have existed in such localities as the following: Boston (Harvard University, Boston Public Library, and other libraries); Chicago (University of Chicago, John Crerar Library, Newberry Library, and other libraries); Florida (University of Florida and other libraries in the collecting of state newspapers); Iowa (collecting agreement between Iowa State College and the State University of Iowa); Louisiana (collecting newspapers, particularly in microfilm form); New York state (collecting in special fields by up-state academic libraries); New York City (Columbia University, New York Public Library, New York Academy of Medicine, Union Theological Seminary); North Carolina (Duke and North Carolina); North Central Area (Minnesota and Minnesota Historical Society); North Texas (academic libraries); Ohio (Kent State University and other academic libraries); Pacific Northwest (academic libraries); Providence (Brown University, Providence Athenaeum, Rhode Island Historical Society); Southeast (concentration of collections on the basis of curriculums); Virginia (University of Virginia and Vir-

[48] "Comments" on "Comprehensiveness *versus* Selectivity," in *Changing Patterns of Scholarship and the Future of Research Libraries*, pp. 88–89.

ginia State Library in newspaper collecting); and Wisconsin (University of Wisconsin and Wisconsin Historical Society). These are by no means all of the programs in the country, nor do they include all types of contractual arrangements, mergers, and complete consolidations which have been described by Lowell.[49] Neither do they include the types of deposit libraries and bibliographical centers which provide some basis for selectivity in acquisitions.

Perhaps the two outstanding efforts to place collecting on a more formal basis are the Library of Congress Cooperative Acquisitions Project [50] and the Farmington Plan.[51] The former was a plan to insure the placement of foreign publications in American libraries. The Library of Congress, working with the United States Department of State, assisted university and other libraries to obtain many publications which would have been difficult or impossible to acquire during World War II. Priorities were fixed on the basis of such factors, among others, as strength in existing collections, holdings in certain geographical areas, and current research programs. Although there was dissatisfaction with some of the materials received, particularly among the smaller libraries, the program suggested a pattern for the future.

Designed to obtain for American libraries copies of all books of research value published abroad, the Farmington Plan, evolved in 1948, is the present major plan to further specialization in collecting. It began with the publications of three western European countries, but it has expanded to include those of 99 countries. The 60 libraries which are participating have assumed responsibility for collecting in one or more specific subject fields or geographical areas. They have also agreed to list all acquisitions in the Union Catalog at the Library of Congress.

There have been criticisms of the Farmington Plan. Some librar-

[49] *College and University Library Consolidations.*

[50] Boyd, "A Landmark in the History of Library Cooperation in the United States," *College and Research Libraries,* VIII (1947), 101–9; Peiss, "Report from Europe," *College and Research Libraries,* VIII (1947), 113–19.

[51] Williams, *Farmington Plan Handbook.*

ians have observed that the Plan should be more selective. Others have suggested that it should go further, and that practically every publication issued abroad should be in some American library. At the present time, the Plan is not concerned with serial publications, newspapers, and government documents. The inclusion of such materials would unquestionably introduce complications in the Plan, but eventually attention probably will be given to coverage of all kinds of publications. In general, such studies as have been made of the results of the Plan suggest that it is doing an effective job.[52] To do the work that may be expected of this ambitious plan, the cooperation of administrative officers and faculty members of universities is as essential as that of the librarians.

STORAGE LIBRARIES AND INTERLIBRARY CENTERS   Administrative relationships involved in participating in storage libraries and bibliographical and interlibrary centers were noted in chapter ii. Storage libraries in the building program are discussed briefly in chapter xiv. It is the purpose of this section to consider in more detail the cooperative aspects of these ventures.

STORAGE LIBRARIES   Foreign libraries, such as the British Museum and the Bibliothèque nationale, and some public libraries in the United States, such as those of Cleveland, Newark, and Providence, have used individual storage libraries for some time. The New England Deposit Library, however, was designed for the purpose of housing little-used materials from a group of libraries. Erected and operated by Harvard University, the contributing libraries are

[52] Williams, op. cit.; David and Hirsch, "Importation of Foreign Monographs under the Early Influence of the Farmington Plan," College and Research Libraries, IX (1950), 101–5; Cook, "The Farmington Plan and the Select List of Unlocated Research Books," College and Research Libraries, XV (1954), 281–84+. The Williams volume contains an extensive bibliography on the Plan. The Farmington Plan Letter, issued irregularly, also contains information on the progress of the project. A general discussion of regional cooperation is presented in David and Hirsch, "Cooperation and Planning from the Regional Viewpoint," Library Trends, III (1955), 356–75.

from the Boston and Cambridge areas.[53] Ownership of materials sent for deposit is retained by the libraries.

Criticisms directed at the Deposit Library concern the policy of shelving each library's books in separate sections, with no effort to remove duplicates. Thus, there is considerable duplication, since the libraries tend to select the same titles for storage. It has been suggested that the duplicates be eliminated, and the remaining collections intershelved.

Cheaper shelving is the primary advantage of the present New England Deposit Library. Other advantages claimed for storage libraries in which groups of libraries cooperatively participate are: reduction and delay of the need of erecting new library buildings, elimination of costs for maintaining little-used books in active libraries, removal of unnecessary duplicates from an area, utilization of the benefits of cooperative cataloging, and participation in cooperative acquisition of expensive and seldom-used materials.

INTERLIBRARY CENTERS   The Midwest Inter-Library Center, which opened in 1951, includes libraries in eight states, from Ohio State University in the east to the University of Minnesota and the University of Kansas in the west. At the present time, 16 libraries—all university, except the John Crerar Library in Chicago—are members. Unlike the practice in the New England Deposit Library, the members give up individual ownership to materials deposited in the Center, which is located on the rim of the University of Chicago campus.[54] Either complete rights are relinquished, or it is agreed that the materials will remain in the Center as long as the organization exists. The Center discards duplicates rigorously.

The deposits received from the members for 1953–54 reveal the nature of the materials collected: miscellaneous serials and separates, domestic (federal, state, and local) and foreign documents,

[53] Metcalf, "The New England Deposit Library," *Library Quarterly*, XII (1942), 622–28; also his "The New England Deposit Library after Thirteen Years," *Harvard Library Bulletin*, VIII (1954), 312–22.

[54] A five-year summary of the Center appears in the *Fifth Annual Report of the Midwest Inter-Library Corporation and the Midwest Inter-Library Center, from July 1, 1953, to June 30, 1954.*

bookdealers' catalogs, dissertations, college catalogs, textbooks, house organs, medical serials and separates, patent specifications, alumni publications, railway guides, Japanese war crimes proceedings, fraternity publications, foreign radio broadcasts, trade and technical publications, annual statements of insurance companies, sport and game books, British press releases, wartime technical reports, Menger collection in philosophy, Braille periodicals, and newspapers.[55] Other materials received through gift include legal briefs and records, documents of all kinds, South American journals and newspapers, corporation reports, state railroad and warehouse commission reports, periodicals, and city directories.

The Center differs from bibliographical centers and deposit libraries in that it carries on an acquisition program of its own.[56] The program includes current newspapers on microfilms, current state documents, foreign documents, publications of university bureaus of research, insurance company reports, foreign dissertations, federal processed documents, foreign government information bulletins, house organs, college catalogs, and court briefs and records.

The Center also carries on a cataloging program and distributes cards to the member libraries. During the year 1953–54, a total of 9,408 master multiliths were prepared. Cards distributed to the member libraries as of June 30, 1954, totaled 489,295, including the cards sent to the Library of Congress.

Downs [57] has recently pointed out some tentative evaluations of the Center. The favorable points include saving considerable shelf space for the participants, making available more comprehensive groups of certain categories of materials, and developing a more intensive spirit of cooperation.

The weaknesses or liabilities noted by Downs include the following: eventually many of the publications on poor paper will de-

[55] *Ibid.*, p. 7.
[56] Ralph T. Esterquest, "Midwest Inter-Library Center," *College and Research Libraries*, XV (1954), 47–49+. See also the monthly *Newsletter* issued by the Center.
[57] "A Realistic Look at Library Cooperation," in *Annual Meeting, 1954*, Bibliographical Center for Research (Bulletin No. 11), pp. 9–12.

teriorate, so why not microfilm them now; the average cost of an interlibrary loan is uncomfortably high; the need to place more valuable materials in the Center (which undoubtedly will be resisted by faculty members of individual institutions); the fear that the acquisition program of the Center will become financially burdensome to the cooperating libraries; the inadequacy—when compared to that of a union catalog—and the cost of the teletype system; the possible need of special legislation in some states to clarify the question of ownership of materials; and the relatively high membership dues for those paying at the upper levels. As in most cooperative enterprises, the smaller libraries gain more from the Center than the larger universities. Perhaps it is too early to draw any final conclusions regarding the Midwest Inter-Library Center. It is the first operation on the scale that librarians have discussed for many years, and it probably should be given every chance to demonstrate its value.

In operation for about three years is the Hampshire Inter-Library Center, at South Hadley, Massachusetts. Four libraries—Mt. Holyoke, Smith, Amherst, and the University of Massachusetts—have pooled research collections in the Mt. Holyoke College Library. Duplicates are either sold or otherwise eliminated. The libraries have similar interests, are about the same size, and are within a few miles of each other. Recent indications suggest that the participants consider the program successful.

For a number of years librarians in the Northeastern states have been considering the establishment of a cooperative regional library.[58] The leaders in the discussions have been Columbia, Harvard, the New York Public Library and Yale, although the Library of Congress, Princeton, Pennsylvania, and Cornell have participated. There is great difference of opinion as to the nature of this proposed enterprise, with some favoring an organization similar to that of the Midwest Inter-Library Center and others inclined toward

[58] Metcalf, "A Proposal for the Northeastern Regional Library," *College and Research Libraries*, XI (1950), 238–44; White, "A New Mechanism in the Organization of Library Service in the Northeast," *College and Research Libraries*, XI (1950), 228–37.

inexpensive storage. The future may bring a resolution of such basic questions as objectives, location, control, and financing.

COOPERATIVE
PHOTOGRAPHIC
PROJECTS

Cooperative activity in photographic projects has been primarily concerned with microreproductions. Libraries have worked closely with commercial firms in this respect, and microfilms of periodicals and dissertations have been made available. University Microfilms, in Ann Arbor, has been active in this area. *Dissertation Abstracts* is a publication of this firm.

As noted earlier, microfilm has been used by libraries to reduce the need of sending original materials through interlibrary loan, to gain storage space through the elimination of bulky newspapers, and to procure materials which are not available in the original through loan or purchase. Since the close of World War II, interest in cooperative microphotography has increased.

Lacy [59] and Born [60] have pointed out the need for a national plan in regard to cooperative microfilming. Lacy called attention to such matters as commonly accepted technical standards, a clearing house for microfilming information, a planning committee, availability in terms of cost, and interlibrary loan. Both the Association of Research Libraries, working with the Library of Congress, and the American Library Association have been concerned with technical standards. The Library of Congress issues information on microfilming projects in its *Information Bulletin*. The Board on Resources of American Libraries of the American Library Association has been actively engaged in planning projects. Efforts are usually made to distribute the costs of extensive film undertakings. The new code for interlibrary loans suggests making easily available positive copies of films.

[59] "Microfilming as a Major Acquisition Tool," Library of Congress *Quarterly Journal of Current Acquisitions*, VI (1949), 8–17.
[60] "A National Plan for Extensive Microfilm Operations," *American Documentation*, I (1950), 66–75; also "Microfilming Abroad," *College and Research Libraries*, XI (1950), 250–58.

Born has directed attention to the need for an international network of microfilming centers. Some efforts have been made in this direction. The United Nations Educational, Scientific and Cultural Organization (UNESCO), for example, has sponsored a directory of world microfilm facilities.[61] UNESCO has also conducted a survey of microfilm use, which includes a directory of microfilm equipment and manufacturers.[62]

Fussler [63] has distinguished between the use of microfilm for specific purposes and the applications to meet potential needs of research workers. The latter projects include those which involve copying of materials at one institution and depositing them in another, and cooperatively reproducing materials with the purpose of placing copies in each of the cooperating institutions. For example, the Library of Congress has brought to the United States "for either its own use or on general cooperative projects microfilm copies of manuscripts and other important materials from Jerusalem, Mt. Sinai, Mexico City, the Japanese Foreign Office, a large number of British manuscript depositories, the National Library of Ireland, etc." [64]

The Library of Congress has also associated itself with the University of North Carolina in preparing microfilms of early state records of the American colonies.[65] A total of 1,701 rolls of microfilm have been made of statutory, constitutional, executive, administrative, judicial, and legislative records. The master negatives of the project are deposited in the Library of Congress. Positive copies of any or all of the reels of film can be purchased through the Photoduplication Service. Copies of the entire set are on deposit in the reading rooms of the Library of Congress and the University of North Carolina Library.

[61] International Federation for Documentation, *Directory of Microfilm and Photocopying Services;* also *Manual on Document Reproduction and Selection.* Part II of the *Manual* is to be issued later.

[62] *Enquête de l'Unesco sur l'emploi du microfilm, 1951: Unesco Survey of Microfilm Use, 1951.* (Paris: 1952). Reprint from *UNESCO Bulletin for Libraries,* VI (February–March, 1952), Nos. 2–3, and May–June, 1952, Nos. 5–6.

[63] "Photographic Reproduction of Research Materials," *Library Trends,* II (1954), 532–44 (esp. p. 535).

[64] *Ibid.*

[65] Jenkins (comp.), *A Guide to the Microfilm Collection of Early State Records.*

The Library of Congress has also worked with state historical groups in planning microfilm projects. It has been willing to allow groups of university libraries to acquire cooperatively microfilms of source materials in the Library.

Other cooperative activities include the work of the Philadelphia Bibliographical Center in issuing, with the cooperation of the libraries which contribute information, the *Union List of Microfilms;* the activities of various library groups, such as the Special Libraries Association, the American Documentation Institute, the Association of Research Libraries, the Association of College and Reference Libraries, and the Southeastern Library Association, in producing microfilms and other microreproductions for the general use of libraries; and the efforts of nonlibrary organizations, such as the American Historical Association, in conducting microfilm projects.

The end is not yet in sight as to the possibilities in photography and microreproductions for library use. Microprint, microcards, and Minicards offer opportunities for libraries in the future.[66] "The growing diversity of the processes should be a cause of satisfaction rather than alarm," writes Fussler, "for out of a diversity of processes and techniques a far more versatile tool is likely to be forged in the next ten to fifteen years directed toward the efficient service of scholarship and investigation." Library cooperation requires the attention of all librarians if it is to make progress in the next decade.

INTERNATIONAL
COOPERATION

Cooperating effectively on a campus, local, regional, state, and national level requires all the ingenuity that librarians possess. It may therefore be bewildering to nonlibrarians to learn that librarians are frequently engaged in problems of international cooperation. UNESCO especially has been conscious of the possibilities of achieving progress on common problems. The American Library Association, the United States Department of State, and other library and nonlibrary organizations have sought to improve the level of national bibliography, sources of scientific information,

[66] Fussler, "Photographic Reproduction of Research Materials," pp. 539–43; see also Tyler, Myers, and Kuipers, "The Application of the Kodak Minicard System to Problems of Documentation."

abstracting, indexing, publishing, cooperative cataloging, and training of personnel.

International conferences in Washington, such as the Inter-American Library Conference (1946) and the Assembly of Librarians of the Americas (1947), were designed to encourage library development in the Americas and to improve library relations among the various countries. The Princeton Conference on exchanges in 1946 sought to explore the bases of exchange programs among libraries of different countries. The Royal Society Scientific Information Conference in London in 1948, the International Conference on Science Abstracting in Paris in 1949, and the Conference of Medical Librarians in London in 1953 are others, among many, of the meetings of librarians to solve their problems on an international basis.[67] Librarians have long recognized the interdependence of knowledge and information.

BIBLIOGRAPHY

Adams, Scott. "Facsimile for Federal Libraries," *Special Libraries*, XLIV (1953), 169–72.

American Library Directory. 20th ed. New York, Bowker, 1954.

"Availability of Library Research Materials," *Library Trends*, II (1954), 487–580.

Barcus, Thomas R., and Verner W. Clapp. "Collecting in the National Interest," *Library Trends*, III (1955), 337–55.

Blegen, Theodore C. "The Scholar Looks at Inter-Library Co-operation," *Library Quarterly*, XXII (1952), 13–17.

Born, L. K. "Microfilming Abroad," *College and Research Libraries*, XI (1950), 250–58.

——— "A National Plan for Extensive Microfilm Operations," *American Documentation*, I (1950), 66–75.

Boyd, Julian P. "A Landmark in the History of Library Cooperation in the United States," *College and Research Libraries*, XIII (1947), 101–9.

Brown, Charles H. "Inter-Library Loans: An Unsolved Problem," *Library Journal*, LVII (1932), 887–89.

California, University of, Library (Los Angeles). Report of the Libraries to the Chancellor for the Year 1953–54. Los Angeles, 1954.

[67] Carnovsky (ed.), *International Aspects of Librarianship;* also appeared as April, 1954, issue of the *Library Quarterly*.

Carnovsky, Leon (ed.). International Aspects of Librarianship: Papers Presented before the Eighteenth Annual Conference of the Graduate Library School of the University of Chicago. Chicago, University of Chicago Press, 1954; also issued as April, 1954, issue of *Library Quarterly*.

Chandler, Harley. "Southeastern Research," *Library Journal*, LXXX (1955), 41–42.

Changing Patterns of Scholarship and the Future of Research Libraries: A Symposium in Celebration of the 200th Anniversary of the Establishment of the University of Pennsylvania Library. Philadelphia, University of Pennsylvania Press, 1951.

Colwell, Ernest C. "Inter-University Co-operation," *Library Quarterly*, XXII (1952), 1–4.

Cook, C. Donald. "The Farmington Plan and the *Select List of Unlocated Research Books*," *College and Research Libraries*, XV (1954), 281–84+.

Cornell University. Report of the Director of the University Library, 1953–54. Ithaca, N.Y., 1954.

David, Charles W. "Remarks upon Interlibrary Loans: Mid-20th Century Style," *College and Research Libraries*, X (1949), 429–33.

David, Charles W., and Rudolf Hirsch. "Cooperation and Planning from the Regional Viewpoint," *Library Trends*, III (1955), 356–75.

——— "Importation of Foreign Monographs under the Early Influence of the Farmington Plan," *College and Research Libraries*, IX (1950), 101–5.

Downs, Robert B. American Library Resources: A Bibliographical Guide. Chicago, American Library Association, 1951.

——— "Problems of Bibliographical Control," *Library Trends*, II (1954), 498–508.

——— "A Realistic Look at Library Cooperation," in *Annual Meeting, 1954*, Bibliographical Center for Research (Bulletin No. 11) Denver, 1954.

Downs, Robert B. (ed.). Union Catalogs in the United States. Chicago, American Library Association, 1942.

Dunkin, Paul. "Foundations in the Sky," *Library Quarterly*, XXIII (1953), 126–34.

Egan, Margaret E., and Jesse H. Shera. "Foundations of a Theory of Bibliography," *Library Quarterly*, XXII (1952), 125–37.

Ellsworth, Ralph E. "Mr. Ellsworth's Report," Library of Congress *Information Bulletin*, Nov. 16–22, 1948. Appendix.

——— "Tasks of the Immediate Future," *Library Quarterly*, XXII (1952), 18–20.

Esterquest, Ralph T. "Midwest Inter-Library Center: Acquisition Policy and Program, 1950–1953," *College and Research Libraries*, XV (1954), 47–49.

Evans, Luther H. "The Librarians' Agenda of Unfinished Business," *College and Research Libraries*, XII (1951), 309–13+.

Fussler, Herman H. "Photographic Reproduction of Research Materials," *Library Trends*, II (1954), 532–44.

"General Interlibrary Loan Code, 1952," *College and Research Libraries*, XIII (1952), 350–58. This issue of *College and Research Libraries* also contains "Interlibrary Loans: A Symposium," with articles by James G. Hodgson, Walter W. Wright, James G. Hodgson and Robert W. Kidder, Carl H. Melinat, and Mary L. Lucy.

Green, S. S. "The Lending of Books to One Another by Libraries," *Library Journal*, I (1876), 15–16.

Hand, Elinor. "A Cost Survey in a University Library," *Library Journal*, LV (1930), 763–66.

Hodgson, James G. "Preliminary Report on Interlibrary Loan Costs," *College and Research Libraries*, XIII (1952), 327–31.

Hodgson, James G., and Robert W. Kidder. "Errors and Incomplete Entries in Interlibrary Loan Requests," *College and Research Libraries*, XIII (1952), 336–41.

International Federation for Documentation. Directory of Microfilm and Photocopying Services. Preliminary ed. The Hague, 1950.

———— Manual on Document Reproduction and Selection (F.I.D. Publication No. 264) The Hague, 1953. Part I.

Jenkins, William S. (comp.) A Guide to the Microfilm Collection of Early State Records. Prepared by the Library of Congress in Association with the University of North Carolina. Ed. by Lillian A. Hamrick. Washington, D.C., Photoduplication Service, Library of Congress, 1950.

Lacy, Dan. "Microfilming as a Major Acquisition Tool: Policies, Plans, and Problems," Library of Congress *Quarterly Journal of Current Acquisitions*, VI (1949), 8–17.

Lowell, Mildred H. College and University Library Consolidations. Eugene, Oregon State System of Higher Education, 1942.

Lucy, Mary L. "Interlibrary Loans in a University Library," *College and Research Libraries*, XIII (1952), 344–49.

McAnally, Arthur M. "Recent Developments in Cooperation," *College and Research Libraries*, XII (1952), 123–32.

Melinat, Carl H. "The Administration of Interlibrary Loans in American Libraries" (Master's thesis, Syracuse University, 1949).

———— "Interlibrary Lending," *Library Trends*, II (1954), 573–80.

———— "Interlibrary Loan Practice and the Interlibrary Loan Code," *College and Research Libraries*, XIII (1952), 342–44.

Metcalf, Keyes D. "The New England Deposit Library," *Library Quarterly*, XII (1942), 622–28.

———— "The New England Deposit Library after Thirteen Years," *Harvard Library Bulletin*, VIII (1954), 312–22.

———— "A Proposal for the Northeastern Regional Library," *College and Research Libraries*, XI (1950), 238–44.

———— "University Libraries Face the Future," *Library Quarterly*, XXII (1952), 5–12.

Midwest Inter-Library Corporation and the Midwest Inter-Library Center. See Annual Reports (especially Fifth, 1954), and Newsletter, issued monthly.

Morsch, Lucile M. "Cooperation and Centralization," *Library Trends*, II (1953), 342–55.

Pafford, J. H. P. Library Co-operation in Europe. London, Library Association, 1935.

Peiss, Reuben. "Report from Europe," *College and Research Libraries*, XIII (1947), 113–19.

Philadelphia Bibliographical Center and Union Library Catalogue. Committee on Microphotography. Union List of Microfilms. Rev., enl. and cumulated ed. Philadelphia, 1951.

Richardson, E. C. "The National Library Problem To-Day," *Library Journal*, XXX (1905), Portland Conference issue, 3–9.

Rider, Fremont. "Library Cost Accounting," *Library Quarterly*, VI (1936), 331–81.

Schlundt, Esther M. "Services Available from Large Libraries," *Special Libraries*, XLV (1954), 375–83.

Shaw, Ralph R. "Machines and the Bibliographical Problems of the Twentieth Century," in L. N. Ridenour, *et al.*, Bibliography in an Age of Science. Urbana, University of Illinois Press, 1951, pp. 37–71.

———— "Mechanical and Electronic Aids for Bibliography," *Library Trends*, II (1954), 522–31.

Shera, Jesse H., and Margaret Egan (eds.). Bibliographic Organization: Papers Presented before the Fifteenth Annual Conference of the Graduate Library School, July 24–29, 1950. Chicago, University of Chicago Press, 1951.

Shera, Jesse H., and Margaret H. Egan. "Introduction," in S. C. Bradford, *Documentation*. 2d ed. London, Crosby Lockwood, 1953.

Sherwood, Janice W., and Eleanor E. Campion. "Union Library Catalogue: Services, 1950. Quo Vadis?" *College and Research Libraries*, XIII (1952), 101–6.

Shores, Louis. "Library Co-operation in the Southeast," *Library Quarterly*, XXII (1952), 335–41.

Tauber, Maurice F., and Associates. Technical Services in Libraries. New York, Columbia University Press, 1954.

Tyler, A. W., W. L. Myers, and V. W. Kuipers. "The Application of the Minicard System to Problems of Documentation," *American Documentation*, VI (1955), 18–30.

UNESCO. Enquête de l'Unesco sur l'emploi du microfilm, 1951: Unesco Survey of Microfilm Use, 1951. Reprint from *UNESCO*

Bulletin for Libraries, VI (February–March, 1952), Nos. 2–3, and May–June, Nos. 5–6. Paris, 1952.

U.S. Library of Congress. Annual Report of the Librarian of Congress for the Fiscal Year Ending June 30, 1953. Washington, D.C., 1954.

Walter, Alpheus L. "Fifty Years Young: Library of Congress Cards," *College and Research Libraries,* XIII (1952), 305–8.

White, Carl M. "A New Mechanism in the Organization of Library Service in the Northeast," *College and Research Libraries,* XI (1950), 228–37.

—— "Services to Scholars," *Library Trends,* III (1954), 151.

—— "A Turn in the Course of the University Library," *College and Research Libraries,* XII (1951), 314–20.

Williams, Edwin E. "Exchanges: National and International," *Library Trends,* II (1954), 562–72. Contains extensive bibliography.

—— Farmington Plan Handbook. Bloomington, Ind., Association of Research Libraries, 1953.

Wilson, Louis R., and Jack Dalton. "Restriction on the Use of Research Materials," *Library Trends,* II (1954), 545–53.

Wilson, Louis R., and Marion Milczewski. Libraries of the Southeast: A Report of the Southeastern Library Survey, 1946–1947. Chapel Hill, Published for the Southeastern Library Association by the University of North Carolina Press, 1949.

Winchell, Constance M. Guide to Reference Books. 7th ed. Chicago, American Library Association, 1951. Supplement, 1950–1952, Chicago, 1954.

Wright, Walter M. "Interlibrary Loan—Smothered in Tradition," *College and Research Libraries,* XIII (1952), 332–36.

XIV

BUILDINGS AND EQUIPMENT

The building in which the Main Library is housed was completed in 1919 and has been in constant use since. It is of the monumental type, with impressive central stairway and heavy, fixed walls, and is not so flexible or susceptible to easy modification or expansion as buildings planned in the 1920's and later. When it was first completed, it easily housed most of the collections of the University and provided for a high degree of centralization of library materials. With the rapid increase in the collections, however, space has become limited, and a rather large number of departmental and special libraries have been established on the campus. At present several of these have become so crowded or so unsuited to the uses to which they are put that consideration of the modification of the Main Library building and the coordination or consolidation of some of the departmental libraries is essential.[1]

THIS introductory comment to a discussion of the library building of Stanford University is typical of many that have been made in recent years regarding the physical condition of university libraries erected in the late nineteenth century and the early part of the twentieth century. As Reynolds [2] has observed, the university library building has become more complex as the services have increased in complexity. Educational methods, financial factors, professional library opinion, architectural developments, and previous buildings have influenced the kinds of library buildings erected by universities.

On many American university campuses, the library is one of

[1] Wilson and Swank, *Report of a Survey of the Library of Stanford University*, p. 148.
[2] "University Library Buildings in the United States, 1890–1939," *College and Research Libraries*, XIV (1953), 149–57+.

the most prominent buildings. This chapter is devoted to a consideration of this important unit of the physical plant of the university. Its major purposes are to describe the requirements for a satisfactory library building for a university, to discuss the various aspects of a building that will meet those requirements, and to consider the essential apparatus and equipment necessary for effective service. The material presented here is, in large measure, a synthesis of information on the subject, reflecting what appears to be best practice or currently accepted opinion. Consequently, the treatment lacks the detail which may be desired, since extended discussion would be required to present adequately all the matters involved.[3] Moreover, there is reason to believe that the future university library building may follow a pattern which is quite different from that of present structures, even those of the past decade. The effects of World War II upon educational programs and methods, the growth of storage libraries and interlibrary centers, the extension of cooperative enterprises in documentation and bibliography, the increased use of plastics and new building materials, the innovations in photography and microreproductions of various kinds, the publication of books in new forms, and developments in technology and building design will probably influence the nature of new library buildings. The policy of erecting buildings with permanent interiors, planned for a century or more, is being reappraised with the current emphasis placed on modular construction.

Although there is no scientific basis for stating what the requirements of an adequate library building are, various standards or principles have evolved from experience. While there has been some progress in the formulation of criteria for constructing college library buildings, particularly when enrollments, educational programs, and size of collections are fairly well established, these standards are not usually applicable to larger institutions. Among the factors which have a significant bearing on the character of the

[3] Two volumes which have provided useful information for this discussion are Burchard, David, and Boyd (eds.), *Planning the University Library Building*, and Fussler (ed.), *Library Buildings for Library Service*.

university library as distinguished from the college library are: (1) large enrollment, (2) extensive and varied curriculums, (3) relatively large numbers of graduate students, (4) emphasis on research, (5) existence of departmental organization, and (6) responsibility for continued preservation of materials, with minimal withdrawals. Not only do these factors affect the library, but they influence the quantity and quality of the demands made upon its physical facilities.[4]

Difficulties obviously arise in any attempt to set up detailed building requirements which will apply uniformly to all university libraries. No less than the book collection or the staff, the physical plant should be adapted to the needs of the particular institution. A so-called "adequate" library building for one institution will not necessarily serve effectively the purposes of another. There are many institutions—and some of high standing in the academic world—which house libraries in buildings which would be considered unsatisfactory by almost any set of standards. This does not imply that the provision of adequate library buildings would not improve the service in those institutions. While the physical plant may not rank in importance with the book collection and with the staff, there seems to be little question that the building carefully planned and adapted to the functions which the library is expected to perform will increase the effectiveness of the library program of any institution. This has been demonstrated repeatedly by the demands which are made upon new libraries as they are opened on university campuses throughout the country.

The importance of the physical plant, as well as the inadequacy

[4] Reynolds, "University Library Buildings in the United States"; Merritt, "Library Planning: A Bibliographical Essay," in Burchard, et al., Planning the University Library Building, pp. 128–41; and Reece, "Library Building Programs: How to Draft Them," College and Research Libraries, XIII (1952), 198–211. The Proceedings of the institutes on library building plans conducted by the Association of College and Reference Libraries Buildings Committee contain discussions which clearly show the relationship of the various factors in a particular institution which are directly involved in the type of library building selected. In the Proceedings of the Third Institute, held in Madison, Wisconsin, Edna Hanley Byers has contributed a bibliographical résumé of discussions on specific library buildings, 1953–54, and 1939–45 (Chicago, Association of College and Reference Libraries, 1954), pp. 94–108. The 1953 Proceedings includes a bibliography for 1945–53.

of a number of existing structures, has been impressed upon many librarians and other university administrators by recent changes in higher education. In many ways these changes have had far-reaching implications for libraries. Among the more important of these changes are: (1) the rapid growth in enrollments;[5] (2) the expansion of the curricula, involving the addition of new specialized courses, teaching departments, institutes, and professional schools; (3) the introduction of new methods of teaching—involving more initiative on the part of students—which have placed new responsibilities upon the library; and (4) the increased emphasis upon research. As a result of these developments, university libraries have been called upon to provide housing for more extensive book collections, reading rooms or separate libraries for increased numbers of undergraduates, individual study and research facilities for more graduate students and faculty members, special apparatus and equipment for careful preservation and reproduction of materials, and additional work space and other accommodations for larger library staffs. The magnitude of these changes can be illustrated by referring to the developments at Harvard University. Its collections now total over 5,000,000 volumes, and it has found it necessary to set up a complicated system of departmental and professional school libraries. Rare and specialized materials are now housed in the magnificent Houghton Library, and undergraduates have been provided special quarters in the pioneering Lamont Library. Little used materials have been shelved in the New England Deposit Library.

In the face of new demands, it is not surprising that many university library buildings have proved inadequate. Among the more serious shortcomings of these buildings have been the lack of sufficient space for books, readers, and staff; unsatisfactory location; inadequate ventilation, heating, and lighting; the absence of easy traffic channels; inadequacy in size to carry on all functions; inappropriate relations of space for related functions; the lack of

[5] It has been estimated by the American Council on Education that by 1965 the enrollments of institutions of higher education in the United States will be doubled.

flexibility; the use of space for vested, nonlibrary activities; and the lack of provision for expansion. Failure to foresee the rapid growth of universities, insufficient preliminary planning, lack of funds, the inexperience of librarians and faculty members, or the desire of an architect or donor to create a monument rather than a functionally useful building have been the principal causes of these inadequacies. Whatever the cause, many institutions have been faced with the problem of correcting deficiencies in their library plants.

How far the university should go in its building program depends on the nature of the collections and the kinds of services it wishes to provide. As Swank cogently noted:

Presidents, faculties, and libraries do need . . . to reconsider jointly the library program, to agree if they can upon what is wanted that is worth the cost. The library, in all its ramifications of service, is in fact capable of great expansion or contraction. But what expansion or what contraction must be defined in terms of the educational and research values that the university expects from the library. Given a clear understanding of these values, it is very likely that the university library will in the future, as in the past, do and cost whatever the university needs and desires.[6]

PLANNING
THE BUILDING

The most important requisite of a satisfactory library plant is careful planning. The necessity of detailed preliminary planning can scarcely be overestimated.[7] The university library building is a complex, highly specialized structure. It is intended for particular purposes, and its success in meeting the requirements of the institu-

---

[6] "The Cost of Keeping Books." (Paper presented at the Monticello [Ill.] Conference, October 30, 1954), p. 16. The full report is in Williams (ed.), *Problems and Prospects of the Research Library.*

[7] Burchard, *et al., Planning the University Library Building;* Beals, Henne, and Martin, "The Plan of Service as It Affects the Library Building," in Fussler, *Library Buildings for Library Service,* pp. 12–24; a good example of how plans can change drastically over a period of years is presented by J. P. Boyd in "Outline of a Building Program for the Princeton University Library." Dr. Boyd later became chairman of a Cooperative Committee on Planning New College and University Libraries. The work of this Committee is discussed in the "Foreword" to Burchard, *et al., op. cit.* The Buildings Committee of the Association of College and Research Libraries has been carrying forward in its discussions of projected buildings the work of the earlier committee.

tion depends to a great extent upon how well it is adapted to the functions which it is expected to perform. As has been emphasized earlier, those functions are determined by the educational objectives of the institution and by the methods used to achieve them. A clear understanding of the place of the library in the educational pattern of the institution is fundamental to the success of any building program. To arrive at such an understanding is the first step in planning. An intelligent plan will insure that the library building is adapted to local needs and conditions.

The importance of careful planning has received increasing attention in recent years by university officials, librarians, and architects. Functional design has been particularly emphasized. Prior to 1920 considerable weight was given to architectural effect in library construction and minor attention to functional requirements.[8] Monumental buildings were constructed which were architecturally impressive, even if they were not well suited to their purposes as libraries. One may easily observe sharp differences in two older ideas of library design by comparing the Low Memorial Library with the Butler Library on the Columbia University campus. The former, with octagonal interior, is an architect's monument to symmetry and balance; the latter, rectangular in shape, suggests an effort to meet the functional needs of a large urban university. Undoubtedly, if the Butler Library were being built today there would be many changes in the interior arrangements and equipment, since it has been found wanting in many respects.

A number of factors have been responsible for the change in attitude in regard to monumental buildings. Perhaps the most important have been the need for economy both in construction and in administration and the growing realization of the importance of flexibility and compactness in interior arrangement. From an architectural or aesthetic viewpoint, it is considered desirable that the library should be attractive and that it should harmonize within reasonable limits with the prevailing type of architecture on the

[8] Randall, "Some Principles for Library Planning," *College and Research Libraries,* VII (1946), 319–25; Ellsworth, "Educational Implications of the New Ideas in Library Construction," *College and Research Libraries,* VII (1946), 326–29.

campus. Beyond that, however, architectural manifestations should be subordinated to the demands of functional utility.

PARTICIPANTS IN PLANNING PROGRAM. The planning of a university library building should be a cooperative enterprise. The faculty and other representatives of the institution, as well as the architect and the librarian, should participate. If a building committee is appointed, the librarian, the library committee, a representative of the trustees, the treasurer, and the superintendent of buildings and grounds would constitute a suitable personnel. In a number of instances a faculty committee has been given the responsibility for preliminary planning. Consultants, usually librarians who have had considerable experience in building problems, are being used with greater frequency.

The function of the building committee is to make a thorough study of the library needs of the institution and to accumulate the data necessary for planning a suitable structure. With the objectives of the library clearly defined, the committee should determine the local needs systematically by consulting the representatives of all departments as to their needs and desires. The future educational plans of the university, so far as they can be ascertained, should be incorporated into the plan. The committee should draw upon the experiences of other libraries by studying plans of existing buildings, by consulting with librarians and building committees of other institutions, by visiting recently constructed libraries, and by making detailed studies of the needs of different units of the library in performing essential services. These preliminary studies or memoranda should show the capacity of the building, the types of facilities needed, the allocation of space to meet their detailed requirements, and other items which should enable the architect to prepare his plans.

The librarian has an important role in this preliminary planning. He should work closely with the building committee in preparing specifications and should pay particular attention to such matters as the functions of the various rooms, the relationships among them, the probable use of the building and its supervision, the flexibility of its interior, provisions for future expansion, and probable costs of operation. He should be prepared to plan each room in detail, determining the desired layout and the appropriate equipment. With this information at hand the architect may design a structure which will meet the needs of the local institution and at the same time be aesthetically appealing in harmony with the other buildings on the campus.

The role of the architect, especially if he has had experience with library buildings, begins after the librarian and university officials have outlined the basic service needs of the structure. The architect, however, is not merely a draftsman; he will have fundamental contributions to make in regard to arrangement of the several units. The architects who have participated in the discussions of the institutes of the Association of College and Reference Libraries have shown a firm grasp of the problems which beset librarians in their efforts to plan serviceable and economical buildings.

A carefully planned building will not only fit the needs of the university for the present but should permit alterations and additions to meet the demands of growth and changes in the future. Even though institutions may lack the funds necessary to construct buildings which meet all their requirements, their plans should be based on careful analysis of conditions. If funds are insufficient, a unit plan of construction, with temporary walls and partitions, is feasible. Such a plan, although generally more expensive ultimately, enables an institution to provide an adequate building over a period of years. The University of Illinois Library is an example of a large structure which is being erected on a unit plan. Similarly, the recent addition to the University of North Carolina Library was possible because of the recognition that future growth of the building would be necessary.

The plans for the new building at Pennsylvania [9] take many matters into consideration which were not given much attention in

<hr>

[9] Association of College and Reference Libraries, Buildings Committee, *The Third Library Buildings Plans Institute . . . Proceedings . . . January 30–31, 1954*, pp. 6–22.

the past, and the importance of the uses to which the library should be put in helping implement the teaching and research program are further emphasized. In the Colorado, Georgia, Iowa, Massachusetts Institute of Technology, Nebraska, and Princeton libraries, among other recent buildings, definite efforts were made to bring users and materials together in agreeable surroundings and under conditions conducive to a maximum of results.[10] The Princeton Library particularly reflects current concerns for flexibility in internal arrangements, coordination of research with the library, and special quarters for undergraduate work.

THE BUILDING SITE

Where to locate the new building is an important question which must be decided early in the planning of a new physical plant. Many institutions have worked out general developmental plans in which they have determined the location of future buildings on the campus and have allocated an appropriate site for the library. Universities which lack such plans or which have progressed to such an extent that building locations are permanently established must choose the most desirable site which happens to be unoccupied.

Several factors should be considered in selecting a site. It should be large enough to accommodate the present building and permit future expansion. Expansion may be either horizontal or vertical, or both. Vertical expansion may be the only possible method where ground space is limited. The amount of such expansion possible, however, is limited by structural conditions. It is therefore essential that the original building plans indicate clearly the possibilities of future expansion and that no other buildings be placed in the space for the future expansion of the library. The University of Illinois is an example of an institution which has carefully retained open space for future units of the library.

A second factor in choosing a site is the relation of the library

[10] Ellsworth, "The Library Building and the Reader," in Fussler (ed.), *Library Buildings for Library Service*, pp. 24–36.

to other buildings on the campus. If possible, it should be close to the geographical center of the campus or to the buildings which house heavy book-using departments and classrooms. Such accessibility is necessary for efficient library service. Frequently this is not possible. Even when such location is originally planned, expansion of the university campus and the construction of new units at a distance from the old center may alter it. A careful survey of the flow of traffic should aid in determining a suitable location for a new building.

A central location is frequently sought from an architectural, as well as from a functional, point of view. The library is usually a building of monumental character and of considerable size. Consequently, it may well occupy a central position. While placing the library in a central position may be strategic, it should not be surrounded on all sides by other buildings so that extension becomes impossible.

Other factors which should be taken into account are the surroundings and the physical orientation of the building. The surroundings should be quiet, in order to secure good working conditions in the building. Usually it is recommended that the building should face in such a way that the main reading rooms may have a northern or an eastern exposure. Since these rooms are often placed in the front, this means that the building should face north or east. In recent years, with a trend away from large reading rooms, some flexibility in physical orientation of the building is possible. The libraries of the universities of Michigan and North Carolina, with traditional large reading rooms, have northern exposures, making it possible to take advantage of light which is relatively even throughout the year and which does not expose the readers to the direct rays of the sun.

In addition to the approach to small reading rooms, other developments in library architecture which should be taken into consideration when determining the size and location of buildings are the extensive use of air conditioning, improvements in noise control, compact book storage, the development of storage libraries and interlibrary centers, and the utilization of microreproductions.[11] The last two developments are discussed in chapter xiii.

CENTRALIZATION
OF SERVICES

In chapter iv the question of centralization versus decentralization of library resources was considered. The solution of this problem must be decided before final plans can be drawn. In a particular institution it depends ultimately upon such variables as the size of the library, the amount of emphasis upon research, the funds available for library services and materials, the distance of the departmental buildings from the central library, and the philosophy of library service of the institution. Local traditions are also likely to influence the solution. A combination of the two plans—general centralization with limited decentralization—has worked to advantage in a number of institutions. Concentration of related fields under one roof, however, has received increasing attention on some campuses. This plan provides, in addition to the central library, several divisional libraries or branch libraries, with large book collections and competent staffs. These libraries, while providing more efficient service than the usual small departmental libraries devoted to single subject fields, would be more economical to administer and more easily coordinated with the central administrative organization. In addition to these libraries, small laboratory collections of duplicates could be maintained by departments requiring such materials. Such a plan seems suitable for a large university library which emphasizes research.

FUTURE
EXPANSION

The importance of providing in the original plans for future expansion was stressed earlier in the discussion of the site. The congested condition of the storage facilities, reading space, and working quarters of many university libraries within one or two decades after their erection suggests that planning committees must give more attention to future needs, owing to the steady growth of

[11] Burchard, *et al.*, *Planning the Library Building*, pp. 96–112.

university library collections. Just how much space should be allowed for expansion cannot be precisely known. As Metcalf [12] has pointed out, the rate of increase in collections of large libraries as observed by Rider [13] has dropped from 4 percent to well below 3 percent per annum. Rider had indicated that until 1938 the average college or university library had doubled its collections every sixteen years. Metcalf noted various reasons for the reduction in the rate of growth of libraries: (1) a 4 percent increase could not continue "indefinitely in a world that is increasing only one percent a year in population"; (2) increased rapidity in the deterioration of paper on which printed matter is published; (3) difficulty in providing the additional finances for library services as size of collections grow; and (4) the probable growth in the use of microreproductions and other mechanical devices.[14] On the basis of his observations at Harvard, which has the largest collections among American university libraries, Metcalf suggested that when a library reaches its maturity in collecting (strong in background materials), a 2½ percent annual growth in book collections indicates more rapid growth than is desirable. Despite his cautions against excessive growth in plant and in proportion of the institution's educational budget, Metcalf stated that "it would take time to reverse the present trend in university libraries. An institution planning a new building today should provide space for books sufficient to care for an increase in the book collections for twenty-five years at the present rate, and seating capacity for the anticipated increase in the study body during a similar period. But it is not too early to be thinking about 1980." [15]

With consideration for such factors as may affect an institution's library, the past growth of a library should aid in estimating probable future requirements. Since experience has demonstrated that a new building usually increases the use of the collections and services

[12] "Spatial Problems in University Libraries," *Library Trends*, II (1954), 554–61, esp. p. 558.
[13] *The Scholar and the Future of the Research Library.*
[14] *Op. cit.*, pp. 558–59.
[15] *Ibid.*, p. 559.

and frequently attracts gifts from a large circle of donors and friends, too much weight should not be given to statistics of use in the old building when estimating future needs.

ADAPTABILITY   Provision for flexibility to permit adaptation to changing conditions is likewise of great importance. The specific parts of the university library should be capable of elasticity of use and ease of modification to meet changes in university procedures and policies. Analysis of the demands made upon university libraries in recent years reveals that they not only have increased in volume but have also changed in character and emphasis. In many of the older plans of library organization, considered to some extent in chapter iv, great emphasis was placed on the division of materials on the basis of form, with separate departments for periodicals, documents, manuscripts, pamphlets, microreproductions, maps, and other materials. "The serious subject-approach to knowledge has been hampered by the growth of these departments, however desirable they may have seemed, and the scholar has been compelled to go to many places and to many catalogues in order to consult the library's resources in his field." [16] The planning of a new building should contain a reexamination of such departments, as special architectural and constructional provisions are necessary for them. They undoubtedly restrict the adaptability of the building if they represent permanent installations based on a concept of organization. This does not necessarily mean that there should not be *any* separation of materials, such as special collections, from the general stack.

MODULAR CONSTRUCTION. Burchard and his associates pointed out the need of careful examination of building programs from the point of view of adaptability. They wrote as follows:

Few contemporary librarians are willing to accept a building which imposes on the future the past or present pattern of book use and management. Almost every building now being planned seeks flexibility in some way. As a building concept, flexibility is not new. Office

[16] Burchard, *et al., Planning the University Library Building,* p. 27.

and warehouse buildings have, for example, long been constructed so that interior space can be rearranged more or less at will. Such possibilities are implicit in almost any modern frame building and seem well adapted to the indubitable need of flexibility in libraries.[17]

The modular system of construction has been introduced in library building to provide for flexibility. A module refers to the fairly specific column centering which tends to be uniform in a building. The module may be of any size, and actually has differed in libraries which have used it as a basis of interior construction. The module at Princeton University Library is 18′ x 25′. The assumption has been made that modular construction allows complete flexibility, since modules can be adjusted for any purpose which may arise. However, objections to modular construction include the facts that no module is perfect for all types of use, that a compromise is attained rather than a first-class building, and that the idea of flexibility is so strong that architect and librarian are likely to plan insufficiently for the future.[18]

Librarians who are interested in modular construction would do well to consider the various factors outlined by Ellsworth.[19] These evaluative factors involve the relation of the modular idea to the plan of library organization, expense of operation, aesthetic considerations, cost of construction, ventilation problems, ceiling heights, size of modules, kinds of movable partitions, lighting, attractiveness of interiors, effects on users, and general applicability to libraries. Ellsworth concludes his discussion of modular construction with the following statement:

In libraries where there is no need for flexibility, where codes do not permit, or where the predominant style of architecture clashes, and where there is no need for economy, other methods are more suitable. Artificial circulation and treatment of air are essential in most climates in a modular building and this costs money.[20]

[17] Ibid., p. 61.

[18] Metcalf, "Spatial Problems in University Libraries," p. 555.

[19] "Determining Factors in the Evaluation of the Modular Plan for Libraries," College and Research Libraries, XIV (1953), 125–128+. See also Bean and Ellsworth, Modular Planning for College and Small University Libraries.

[20] Ibid., p. 142.

ESSENTIAL   The facilities required for effective univer-
FACILITIES   sity library service will depend upon the
                             functions which the library must perform
in the particular institution. It is the responsibility of the planning
committee to determine what facilities will be needed and to see
that they are provided for in the building plans. Broadly speaking,
it may be said that a building should be designed to supply adequate
and efficient accommodations for materials, readers, and staff. It
should provide for the preservation, shelving, and storing of books
and other library materials; for the convenient use of those materials
by undergraduate and graduate students, research workers, and
faculty members; and for the work of the library personnel involved in acquiring and preparing books for use and in making
them easily available to readers. A detailed study of the needs of a
particular institution is fundamental to the provision of facilities
that will be adequate for effective service.

ACCOMMODATIONS FOR MATERIALS   "Readers and librarians are
much more compressible than books, and more libraries have become overcrowded and impossible to administer because of inadequate bookstacks than because of inadequate reading or administrative space. Or so it has seemed," noted Merritt [21] in his review of
problems of storage. Housing the enormous resources of the modern
university library presents a difficult problem to the library administrator. The bookstacks, which constitute the great reservoir of
the library, must be large enough to accommodate the present resources and future acquisitions. They should be so designed and
equipped as not only to house the collections but also to facilitate
their use. Their location, layout, construction, and equipment must
be carefully planned to meet current and future requirements for
housing and efficient service.

LOCATION OF STACKS. From the standpoint of both convenience
and future expansion, the location of the stacks is an important

[21] "The Book Stock," in Fussler (ed.), *Library Buildings for Library Service*,
p. 56.

element in the library building. The architectural style of the building will affect the position of the stacks to some extent, but modern planning strives to place the books as closely as possible to the readers. The stacks should be constructed in such a way that rearrangement or extension, vertical or horizontal, can be accomplished without major structural changes.

Vertical extension of the stack is part of the planning of the libraries at Rochester and Yale. With or without a tower arrangement, this type of extension requires that strong foundations be laid at the outset to carry the extra weight of additional stack floors. Provisions for future stack expansion should be clearly shown in the original building plans. Coney, commenting on the previously planned multi-tier expansion at Texas, observed that filling in the light wells would be preferable to constructing stacks on the upper floors of the tower.[22]

Horizontal expansion is more commonly found in university libraries. It is usually practical when the stack is erected at the rear of the building. Experience has shown that it is sometimes difficult, however, to expand both stacks and space for readers in effective relationships.

Location of stacks in the center of the building, as at Columbia, has the advantage of permitting use of all outside space for administrative and reading purposes. Space for expansion, however, can be found only within the area available as stack room. When such space is exhausted, even with rearrangement of shelving, only vertical growth is possible. Travel between the various reading rooms and administrative offices is also likely to be a handicap to readers and staff members.

In some of the older buildings, such as Widener at Harvard, and in new buildings, as at Princeton, underground stacks have played a prominent part in the storage of books. This space is sometimes

[22] "The University Libraries: Plans for the Next Twenty Years" (mimeographed; n.d.), p. 2. See also Merritt, "The Book Stock," for discussion of types of expansion and stack location and Burchard, et al., Planning the University Library Building, chap. iv, "Stack Arrangement and Construction."

allocated in relation to the specific needs of the service departments above the stacks.

Shelving of books is also found around the reading rooms. This is not a common construction in the United States, and is represented by the abandoned Low Memorial Library at Columbia University. The library of the University of Leeds has thirteen alcoves around a large circular reading room. Although access to the collections is immediate, expansion of both stack and reading space is not possible.

Most libraries have always provided some shelving in reading rooms, usually along the walls but sometimes on the open floors. In the libraries which are organized on the subject-divisional basis, housing of book collections in the reading rooms is a predominant practice. Colorado and Nebraska are examples of libraries which contain relatively large collections in the divisional reading rooms. Less active collections are stored in stacks at the rears of the buildings.

In modular constructions, the stacks and the reading spaces are intermingled to a greater extent than in other types of buildings. Moreover, as it has been pointed out, the space of the building as a whole is subject to easier changes as the needs occur. Iowa and Princeton provide examples of dispersion of various types of reading space among the stack floors.

DIMENSIONS OF THE STACK ROOM. Once the location of the stacks is determined, it is necessary to decide their dimensions and the number of volumes they are to house. In his paper on the spatial requirements in university libraries, Metcalf suggested stack space to care for an increase in book collections for twenty-five years.[23] Various writers on library building problems have tried to devise formulas for estimating capacities of shelving. Henderson,[24] who examined questions relating to book sizes and storage space, developed the "cubook," a unit of stack capacity. This unit is defined

[23] "Spatial Problems in University Libraries," p. 559.
[24] "The Cubook: A Suggested Unit for Bookstack Measurement," *Library Journal*, LIX (1934), 865–68; "Note of Correction," *ibid.*, p. 976; "Bookstack Planning with the Cubook," *Library Journal*, LXI (1936), 52–54.

as the "volume of space required to shelve the average book in a typical library." Allowances are made for shelf space left vacant. According to this formula, a single-faced section of stack, 3 feet long and 7½ feet high, has the following capacities: 100 cubooks (85 percent octavos, 13 percent quartos, and 2 percent folios) may consist of 117 volumes (87 percent octavos and 13 percent quartos), or 132 volumes (octavos only), or 67 volumes (quartos only), or 12 volumes (folios only). A million cubooks would occupy 676,363 cubic feet, or 90,181 square feet. It has been estimated that 15 cubooks per square foot of floor area may be used for approximating the size of the stack.[25] The dimensions of the aisles, tiers, ranges, shelves, carrels, and other elements of the stack have been fairly well standardized. Equipment houses have worked closely with librarians in developing these standards.

Much attention has been given recently to the installation of compact storage in libraries.[26] Although explored since the days of Melvil Dewey, compact book shelving has only since 1950 been widely publicized and used. Among the factors that Muller enumerates which should be studied by the librarian who is contemplating compact book storage are the following: (1) cost of shelving per linear foot; (2) mechanical functioning of the equipment; (3) relative accessibility and visibility of books; (4) efficiency in shelving, collecting, and shifting books; (5) ease of shelf labeling; (6) adaptability of the equipment to the floor area dimensions under consideration; (7) adjustability of shelves and drawers; (8) hazards and safety features; (9) relative quietness and noisiness in operation; (10) appearance; (11) adaptability to nonbook uses; and (12) reconvertibility to non-compact storage.[27] Study of

[25] *Ibid.*, p. 53. An allowance of 1.47 cubooks per cubic foot of stack may be made. For space requirements for various classifications of books when shelves are filled solidly with no open space, see Wheeler and Githens, *The American Public Library Building*, p. 415.

[26] Rider, *Compact Book Storage*; Muller, "Evaluation of Compact Book Storage Systems," in *The Third Library Buildings Plans Institute, Proceedings*, pp. 77–93, and "Compact Storage Equipment," *College and Research Libraries*, XV (1954), 300–8. Muller discusses the products of various commercial firms, and provides illustrations of different kinds of shelving which are available.

[27] *Ibid.*, p. 305.

compact storage continues, and librarians should have careful cost analyses made of possible savings before deciding on installations.

CONSTRUCTION AND EQUIPMENT. Planning the bookstack and its equipment is a difficult engineering problem, and requires the aid of experts in the field to work with the architect. This is particularly true at present with such developments as modular construction and compact storage.

The modern block type of stack now in general use is a self-supporting metal framework extending from basement to roof. This concentration of stacks within a stack chamber needs to be considered in relation to the distribution of stacks throughout the building, although buildings with basic stack areas utilize both approaches. In addition to the planning of the framework and the shelving, it is necessary to consider carefully such elements of the stack as deck floors; stairways, elevators; carrels; mechanical book conveyors; pneumatic tubes or other communication systems between the stacks and the delivery desk; shelving for special types of materials, such as newspapers, microreproductions, and oversize books; and lighting, heating, air conditioning, and other ventilation systems.[28] Fireproof construction is essential.

CARRELS. Free access to the stacks is highly recommended from an educational standpoint and is suggested for college library buildings by almost all authorities. Many university libraries have also introduced free access in their new buildings. In large metropolitan universities, however, the practical difficulties in the way of granting direct access to everyone are almost overwhelming. These difficulties have forced some of the larger libraries to keep their bookstacks closed to undergraduates. But while the general student body may have to be excluded from the stacks, graduate students, research workers, and faculty members require facilities for study and work which are in close proximity to their materials. The university library building should be liberally supplied with carrels or study cubicles. These may be placed along the window walls of

[28] Consideration of these problems is given in Burchard, *et al.*, *Planning the University Library Building*, and Fussler (ed.), *Library Buildings for Library Service*.

the various stack levels, being open or partly closed off from the stack, as in earlier buildings, or separated from the stack with entirely closed partitions and corridors. Recent practice has tended to place carrels in the interior of the stack.[29] Carrels have varied in size from 12 square feet to 30 square feet or more. Installations in which the completely inclosed type is used are usually air conditioned, the stack being lighted entirely by artificial illumination. As a result of separation and air conditioning, temperature and humidity conditions can be adjusted to meet the differing requirements of book storage and student use. The interior carrels at Princeton, which are adjustable in the bays in the stack areas, are equipped with individual ceiling light, reading lamp, desk shelf, bookshelves, typewriter stand, and sliding door with lock. Permanently installed carrels may need acoustical treatment for those who require typewriters.

ACCOMMODATIONS FOR READERS   Reading rooms should be planned to suit the needs of different types of users. They include rooms for assigned readings in "reserved" books; for general reading, supplemented by the use of reference books; for casual reading or browsing; for reading periodicals and newspapers; for consulting maps; for using microreproductions; for individual research; for seminars; and for divisional, professional, and graduate study. A small library may combine several of these different types of use in one large reading room, but in the university library they are generally separated because large rooms are required to house single activities or types of services. Moreover, as pointed out earlier, the monumental reading room, with its multiple-purpose approach, is disappearing, even though smaller rooms lose something in the way of architectural aesthetics and impressiveness.

The amount of reading space which should be provided for reading rooms will vary from one library to another. How much space is allotted to reading purposes will depend on such factors as (1) the present and future enrollment; (2) the types of readers to be served;

[29] Burchard, *et al.*, *op. cit.*, pp. 46–48.

(3) the character of the curriculum and the teaching methods, and the amount of reading they require; (4) the number of students who live off campus and commute daily; and (5) the presence on the campus of other facilities for study, such as departmental or dormitory libraries. The trend in library buildings has definitely been in the direction of providing reading room facilities for an increasingly larger proportion of the student body. In any estimate of the number of seats to be provided in a library system, attention should be given to the relation of the central library to other units of service. Burchard and his associates write on this point: "Space need be provided only for the students who are enrolled in departments whose library materials are located in the central library. If figured on this basis, which is more accurate and realistic than using the total enrollment, the conventional figure of providing seats for 25 percent of the total student body might well be changed to 50 percent of the students in the departments served. Students seated at tables require about 25 square feet of space. With more comfortable and informal furniture, this figure might well go up to 40 square feet or more." [30]

The number of reading rooms and the size of each can be ascertained only after a careful consideration of the various kinds of use for which provision must be made. The total seating capacity should be divided among different types of reading rooms as local conditions and the educational program of the institution require. Large reading rooms have been advocated in the past for their architectural effect as well as for economical supervision of large numbers of students. Small reading rooms, on the other hand, offer more congenial study conditions, with the possibility of closer supervision and improved service. The divisional reading rooms of some university libraries combine the advantages of providing a sufficiently large number of seats and yet attain a certain degree of distinctive service in related subject fields. Greater freedom in the use of books is also supported by providing subject specialists to aid the students in their work.

[30] *Op. cit.*, p. 32.

In many of the older buildings, the reading rooms generally provided are a main reading room and reference room, a reserved book or undergraduate reading room, a periodical and newspaper room, a documents room, seminar and consultation rooms, and individual research facilities such as faculty studies and carrels. Some library buildings, particularly in the larger universities, provide other quarters, such as graduate or divisional reading rooms, film rooms, music rooms, archives, and rare book rooms, and rooms for special collections.

GENERAL READING ROOM. The main reading room and the reserved book room are usually the largest reading rooms in the building. The purpose of the former is to provide space for general reading and study—both of library materials and of the students' own books—and for consultation of open-shelf reference works. When a general reading room is provided, it is located near the main catalog and the central circulation desk, so that books may be easily obtained from the stack and conveniently read. Such rooms are often on the second floor, across the front of the building. Today, efforts are made to locate extensively used reading quarters on the first floor. In regard to the height of the reading room ceiling, Ellsworth comments: "I suppose the planners of the Harper Memorial Library had in mind that readers in the main reading-room would be influenced by the atmosphere of the room. That may be so, but it is my impression that the University of Chicago students are no holier than students in other universities that do not possess such a reading room." [31] Undoubtedly, the planners were merely following an architectural style that only recently has been given severe scrutiny.

RESERVE BOOK ROOM. The traditional reserve book room of university libraries has also been severely criticized. Yet libraries as a group make provision for them. So long as the instructional staff depend on the library to furnish large groups of students with assigned readings, the reserve room will continue to flourish as one of the busiest library spots on the campus. Some of the university

[31] "The Library Building and the Reader," in Fussler (ed.), *Library Buildings for Library Service*, p. 32.

libraries provide more seats in the reserve book room than in the general reading room. Unless the functions of the reserve book room are taken care of by divisional rooms or by provisions of an undergraduate building such as the Lamont Library, separate space should be provided. Usually, the reserve reading room is placed on the ground floor with a separate entrance, so that the heavy traffic will interfere least with the other uses of the library.

PERIODICAL AND NEWSPAPER ROOMS. A separate reading room for periodicals and newspapers is sometimes a part of the university library building. The location of this room may be determined by several factors. If bound as well as current materials are available in the room, it will need to be placed near the stack. Since the periodical and newspaper collection is frequently used in reference work and since the reference department is sometimes responsible for administering the periodical room, this room may be placed adjacent to the main reading room. In a divisionally organized library, a general periodical room may not be necessary, as specialized periodicals will be housed in the divisional reading rooms. General periodicals may then be shelved in a small section of the general reference department.[32]

In a few institutions it has been desirable to install a separate newspaper room. This is more of a public library feature for the primary purpose of attracting transients away from the other rooms of the library. It may be useful, however, to have reading quarters of some kind close to the newspaper stacks. Newspaper volumes are heavy, and reduced handling should help to preserve them.

DOCUMENTS ROOM. A few libraries have installed documents rooms. If documents are segregated from other materials, special quarters are usually necessary for effective service. Colorado and Stanford have large documents rooms. In divisionally organized libraries, documents are included along with other materials on the subjects covered by the various units.

SUBJECT DIVISION AND SUBJECT ROOMS. One of the most important

[32] At Illinois, the south end of the general reading room has been converted into a periodical reading room. There are about 270 titles of the more popular current periodicals and about 3,000 bound volumes which are frequently needed for reference with periodical indexes. University of Illinois Library *Staff Manual*, p. 66.

developments in physical organization of the library is the concept of divisional reading rooms.[33] This development has been discussed earlier in chapter iv. It may be noted here that usually in this type of organization, there is a lower-division reading room, and separate rooms are provided for the sciences, the social sciences, and the humanities. These rooms are usually, but not necessarily, similar in construction, containing reading space, open shelves, and offices for the subject-specialist librarians. It is proper to observe that similar provision has been made in older buildings, such as the divisional reading rooms at Brown University and in the modern-language reading room at the University of Chicago.

Some of the older libraries also provide special reading rooms in certain subjects, such as education, business, law, medicine, or philosophy. Architectural requirements for these rooms do not differ noticeably from those necessary for other types of reading rooms. Varying local conditions of curricular emphasis and methods of teaching are the primary determinants as to the need of such facilities. The librarian is faced with the responsibility of reducing administrative costs to a minimum; and, although it may be possible to offer a higher level of service in such specialized quarters, the university may not be able to support them. Educational efficiency may suffer in favor of minimal administrative cost. In many of the larger universities, separate buildings or quarters are provided for major professional schools and departments.

ROOMS FOR LEISURELY READING. Recreational reading or browsing rooms, designed to encourage cultural reading, have come to be considered a common unit in the modern college or university library. The provision of a well-appointed browsing room can do much to increase the use of scholarly publications by the university clientele. Usually, such rooms are provided with carefully selected books, comfortable chairs, and attractive surroundings. Smoking is frequently permitted in them. For complete utility, they should be placed near the main traffic of the building, and might well be on

[33] A résumé of the divisional development appears in Wilson and Lundy, *Report of a Survey of the Library of the University of Notre Dame*, chap. vi.

the first floor. The University of Illinois Library maintains a browsing room in the central building and one in the Illini Union.

Contemporary library buildings have also included lounges, where conversation and smoking are permitted. Lounges can be either drab or attractive, but alert librarians have tried to make them comfortable for the users. While such rooms are not common in present libraries, they are likely to be included in new buildings. The Lamont Library at Harvard has included lounge space with collections of books available for the leisure reading of students. Lounge rooms may also be used for music listening, and for the display of exhibits of various kinds.

OUTDOOR READING COURTS. In several of the university libraries, outdoor reading courts have been provided. This corresponds somewhat to the roof reading rooms in some public libraries. Generally, such courts should be so constructed that supervision is kept at a minimum.

GRADUATE FACILITIES. Most of the rooms described above are used largely by undergraduate students, although divisional reading rooms attract graduate students in large numbers. In the university library, provisions are required for the advanced students, research workers, and faculty members in the form of graduate reading rooms, seminar and conference rooms, faculty studies, and carrels. Special reading rooms for graduate students are found in many university libraries. These rooms, each of which is devoted to one of a number of related fields of knowledge, are usually on the upper floors of the building. More common are seminar and conference rooms for the use of small groups engaged in research and discussion. The number of these rooms needed will depend on the extent to which seminar and conference methods of instruction are used. Such rooms should be included for specific purposes, rather than in the hope that some use will be made of them.

Small rooms are frequently provided for the use of faculty members engaged in research. These rooms, as well as the rooms for advanced students, should be located close to the stacks. Usually they are placed on the upper floors of the building so that the reading rooms for undergraduate students may be concentrated on the lower levels.

The facilities just described, as well as the stack carrels considered earlier, are designed specifically to meet the needs of those engaged in advanced study and research. In addition to these facilities, other quarters of the library are also used primarily by graduate students and faculty members. These are the map room, film reading room, rare book room, and other special collections rooms. Some libraries have also established music rooms for the use of those majoring in music as well as the general university clientele.

MAP ROOM. As was indicated in chapter xi, map collections in university libraries represent a type of material that has become increasingly important in research since World War II. Many university libraries which did not have map rooms have rearranged their facilities so as to provide special rooms for map storage and use. In a number of institutions, map storage and facilities for use are provided in conjunction with the geography departments.

RARE BOOK ROOM. Practically every new building erected in recent years has made provisions for the special care and use of rare books. The rare-book facilities range from fireproof vaults to extensive treasure rooms. In other institutions, sections of the stack have been partitioned off by grilles for the protection of rare books.

Outstanding among the rare book or treasure rooms are those of Duke, North Carolina, Texas, Virginia, and Yale. The Treasure Room of the Joint University Libraries in Nashville is a combined archive room, book arts room, and rare book room. The plans for the new University of Pennsylvania Library include spacious quarters for rare book collections, reading, and exhibitions.

In the past, librarians have not always taken proper care of rare items.[34] It was generally thought that a safe or vault provided sufficient protection of such items; but experience has demonstrated that usually the dangers of mildew, insufficient ventilation, and improper lighting under such conditions of housing are great.

[34] Butler, "The Rare Book Collection and the Bibliographical Museum," in Fussler (ed.), *Library Buildings for Library Service*, pp. 76–78.

Whether rare books are placed in a room within the central library building or in a separate building, as in the Clements Library at Michigan and the Houghton Library at Harvard, they require special care. This may involve special architectural treatment of the building. Theft of materials must be guarded against by means of control of entrances. Butler cautions against placing such a room "on the ground floor or close to any easy means of egress from the building." [35] Special precautions must be taken in the construction of the windows. In the Clements Library at the University of Michigan reinforced concrete walls, ceiling, and floor have been installed. In the second place, special attention should be given to ventilation of the rare book room. Protection against mildew is particularly necessary if the library is located in a damp climate. Temperatures should be maintained at approximately 70° F. and humidity at 50 percent. Air conditioning is a proper installation for the protection of rarities. It is particularly important that water and steam pipes be so installed that no possibility of flooding exists. In the third place, it is important that special provisions be made for lighting. Outlets for special lamps and wiring to handle complex electric machines may be necessary. Such apparatus should be closely connected with small workrooms attached to the rare book room. The installation of suitable bookshelves is also necessary. Shelves should be deep enough to take care of extra-sized volumes. The shelves may be made of wood or steel, as the occasion requires. The amount of dust, smoke, or chemicals in the air will determine whether or not the shelves should be inclosed in glass. Workrooms for preparation and repair and consultation rooms adjoining the rare book room proper should be so located as to have good natural lighting, satisfactory artificial lighting, and proper ventilation. A soundproof typing room near by is also a useful adjunct to the rare book room.

The features described above suggest that the rare book room should be a self-contained unit. Keys to the locks of doors and cabinets in the room should not be interchangeable with those used

[35] *Ibid.*, p. 76.

elsewhere in the building. It should also have its own clothing lockers and toilet facilities.

Since the rare book room is one of the chief attractions of the university library, it is important that special consideration be given to the elements of beauty, dignity, and elegance in its design and decoration. The rich contents of a well-planned and well-organized rare book room warrant such treatment, and represent a valid investment on the part of the institution.

EXTENSION ROOM. In several university libraries space is required for library extension service. At Michigan, North Carolina, and Virginia the rooms devoted to this service are of considerable size because they house extensive collections and a number of staff members. Since work of this kind is carried on with a fairly large collection of materials, sufficient shelving should be provided.

ARCHIVES, ETC. Other rooms for archives, local collections, collections of special materials, exhibits, museum objects, and other purposes are also sometimes included in the university library. Factors which determine whether special space for them is provided are: rarity and cost of material; size of the collections; type of equipment required for effective use; and whether provision for them involves special problems of construction, lighting, heating, ventilation, or other special conditions. The location of such rooms is determined largely by their nature and their relation to other collections.

MUSIC ROOM. Separate facilities for the preservation and use of music are sometimes provided in university libraries having large collections of recordings. Colorado contains a large room for the exclusive use of students and faculty members who wish to listen to phonograph recordings. The University of Pennsylvania plans to have audition rooms, a music reading room, and stack area for the Music Library to be located on the ground floor. Special shelving is necessary for the storage of music and recordings.

FILM READING ROOM. With the development of film collections in libraries, librarians have given special attention to the provision of quarters for their storage and use in new buildings. This is apart from the photographic laboratory, which is discussed later in this chapter. Films now collected by libraries include for the most part microfilms, although a number of institutions have considerable collections of motion pictures and slides. In many libraries, because of the inability to find suitable space, facilities for reading film have not been separated from the various reading rooms. New buildings, however, include separate film reading rooms, equipped with projectors, and plans for proposed buildings show such areas. Films should be housed in a room where ventilation and illumination can be controlled. Librarians have also found it convenient to locate the film reading room adjacent to the area designated for storage of films.

SPACE FOR EXHIBITS. The modern library building usually contains adequate space for displaying books and exhibiting materials. Displays are designed to call attention to new publications and to stimulate new interest in books. Exhibits usually are concerned with the presentation of materials of general cultural interest. In order that both displays and exhibits can be developed systematically, movable and fixed cork bulletin boards, recessed exhibit cases, and floor cases should be provided. Space in reading rooms and corridors should be utilized wherever possible. Special exhibit rooms, even though they are fitting for a library, should be carefully considered before including them in the building, particularly if an exhibition gallery is available on the campus. Considerable space may be used for exhibits if careful planning is followed. It is important to have such space near traffic lanes in the library, if the exhibits are to attract students and faculty members. All such space should be adequately lighted.

ACCOMMODATIONS FOR ADMINISTRATIVE PURPOSES Facilities for carrying on the work of the library constitute an essential element of the university library building. These include a number of different rooms for administrative purposes, among them: a delivery hall for borrowing and returning books; workrooms for the acquisition, recording, and preparation of books for use; offices for the librarian and his staff, departmental librarians, and other officials; a receiving and shipping room; staff room and kitchenette; storage rooms; a bindery and repair room; a photography room; and a printing room.

DELIVERY HALL. The delivery hall is often referred to as the "functional center" of the library. Here are generally located the public card catalog and the central charging or loan desk. Here, too, is the departure point for reading rooms, workrooms, and stacks. The size of the area is an important consideration. Not only should it be planned to accommodate the loan desk and the card catalog, but it should also be arranged to handle without confusion the large amount of traffic which passes through it to the various parts of the building. More than this, it should be large enough to care for the possible expansion of the card catalog and the loan desk. Unless unusual precautions are taken, the delivery hall cannot be enlarged without major structural changes if it is in the center of the building. Planning at the outset for future expansion of this area is imperative. The central location of the delivery hall is also attended with problems of lighting and ventilation which have sometimes led to the construction of skylights over the loan desks or the introduction of fixed light wells. The skylight rarely proves a satisfactory source of light; it frequently adds to the heat of the delivery area in summer, and it often is difficult to control in periods of rain or snow. The disadvantages of this arrangement are so marked and the improvement of systems of artificial lighting have been so great that this type of construction is generally regarded as uneconomical and undesirable. A workroom for the loan-desk staff is also desirable in this area.

The delivery hall just described has been of the traditional type usually found in university libraries. In the divisionally organized libraries, such as those at Colorado and Nebraska, the importance of the delivery hall as the principal place for the loan of books has been greatly reduced by the provision of loan desks in the divisional reading rooms.

The location of the public card catalog adds to the complication of the delivery hall. It should not be far from the main entrance, and it should also be near the circulation desk, the acquisition and catalog departments, and the bibliographical and reference services. Since its growth is inescapably related to the expansion of the book collection, ample space for additions and use should be provided.[36] A number of libraries, such as the University of Michigan, have been cramped for space for the public catalog because of the lack of room into which to expand.

In some libraries, an effort is made to relate the card catalog to the bibliographical sources of the collections. At Illinois, Princeton, and other institutions, a bibliography room or area adjacent to the public catalog and other card catalogs is provided. While these materials are used constantly by the members of the reference and processing staffs of the library, they are also readily available to the public. The organization of the library will have some effect on the size of the collection for the bibliography room, since divisional reading rooms will shelve the works in special fields. Tables, chairs, projectors for the use of microreproductions, and office and typing space for the librarians are normally needed in the bibliography room.

ACQUISITION AND CATALOG ROOMS. The most important staff workrooms are those which house the technical departments of the library.[37] Here books are ordered, received, accessioned, classified and cataloged, and otherwise prepared for use. The important factor to consider in planning these rooms is that the various processes involved are interrelated and that the flow of work from the ordering of books to placing them on the shelves should be orderly, systematic, and efficient. Separation on different floors of the acquisition department from the catalog department, for example, splits operations which should be closely correlated. Duplicate,

[36] Burchard, et al., Planning the University Library Building, pp. 38–40. It is pointed out that it is difficult to estimate size of catalogs unless there is some idea of titles held. The authors suggest that "2,500 trays should be provided to accommodate a catalogue of two million cards, for a collection of a half million titles." Such a catalog would require from 1,380 to 1,840 square feet of space.

[37] Tauber and Associates, Technical Services in Libraries, especially chapters iii and xiv. See also Miller, "The Technical and Administrative Functions of the Library," in Fussler (ed.), Library Buildings for Library Service, pp. 37–55.

expensive records may be necessary to save the time of staff workers who work between departments. Breaking the catalog department into several rooms limits efficiency and interferes with supervision of operations.

Sufficient space should be allotted for desks, office equipment, catalogs, book shelves, aisles, and offices for the heads of the technical units. It has been recommended that at least 100 square feet be provided for each staff member, with additional space for expansion. This extra space should be allowed within the general area set aside for the workrooms rather than in another part of the building, since separation of processes generally entails loss in efficiency.

The staff workrooms should be located near the public catalog and have direct access to the stacks. The number and arrangement of rooms vary from one library to another. In some buildings the technical services are grouped in one large room with double-faced shelving for partitions. This arrangement often saves space, provides flexibility, and makes supervision relatively simple. In other buildings the acquisition and catalog departments are in separate rooms, with a smaller bibliography room between them. If the acquisition department is on a floor below the catalog department, easy communication by stair and elevator should be provided.

OFFICES FOR ADMINISTRATORS. Offices for the librarian, the assistant librarians, and the heads of departments constitute another important type of staff accommodation which must be provided. The location of the librarian's office may be determined on the basis of two factors; proximity to the staff rooms and accessibility to the library's clientele. The latter may be of more importance than the former. The office should be so situated, however, that it may be reached without passing through other offices, workrooms, or reading rooms. Anterooms for the librarian's secretary, financial clerk, personnel officer, and other executive assistants should be provided. The offices of the assistant librarians and the departmental heads should be located near the work for which these officers are responsible.

RECEIVING AND SHIPPING ROOM. In order to handle efficiently the large amount of materials coming into a library, a receiving room is generally provided on the ground floor. This room should have easy access to the street and be provided with an unloading platform. If possible, ramps should be avoided. Space should be sufficient to permit unpacking and sorting of materials. Work tables, shelving, and shipping equipment should be provided. If the room is not on the same floor as the acquisition unit, communication with the processing rooms should be made possible by means of an elevator.

STORAGE AND SUPPLY ROOMS. In any library of considerable size, storage rooms for materials awaiting processing are required. They may be placed in the basement or in out-of-the-way rooms that can be secured. Shelving should be furnished in order to facilitate the listing of duplicates or other types of material. A part of the stack may also be used for unprocessed books.

Official supplies are frequently kept in a stock and supply room, located either as part of the administrative offices or in separate quarters in the basement. In some libraries the supply room is adjacent to the receiving and shipping room, which is a desirable location. Shelves, bins, and cupboards are necessary equipment.

BINDERY AND REPAIR ROOM. Few university libraries have binderies of their own.[38] In those libraries which have such units the great bulk, if not all, of the repairing, binding, and rebinding of books, serials, and pamphlets of the university libraries is done there. Unless a library has a large amount of binding to do annually, it may be advisable to follow the procedure of most libraries in sending materials to commercial binders.

If a bindery is desirable, it is probably best located in the basement, since heavy machinery is part of its equipment. Moreover, it is generally a noisy room and should be separated from space requiring quiet. Direct access should be provided to the technical departments.

PHOTOGRAPHY DEPARTMENT. Most new university libraries of any

[38] Tauber and Associates, *Technical Services in Libraries*, chap. xvii.

size contain quarters for the reproduction of library materials. Some small units are equipped with the basic apparatus necessary for producing negative and positive films and enlargement prints and perhaps photostats of ordinary books and manuscripts. Larger installations, such as those at the University of Chicago, Massachusetts Institute of Technology, and Princeton, are designed to work extensively in newspaper and periodical filming, to produce duplicate copies of films, and to undertake major filming projects, in addition to executing individual requests. It presupposes complete equipment and photographic apparatus, adequate physical facilities, and a highly trained personnel.[39] In the photographic laboratory, space is required for an office for records and administration, a camera room, an enlarging room, and a darkroom.

ROOMS FOR THE PUBLIC AND THE STAFF   The rooms mentioned above do not exhaust the list of quarters to be provided in a university library building. Public toilets, conveniently located coat rooms, janitors' quarters, and such facilities for staff comfort as rest rooms, lunch room, kitchenette, locker rooms, and lavatories must also be provided.

Quarters for the use of the staff deserve the careful consideration of the architect and the librarian. Not only is a staff room of importance for staff welfare, but it provides a suitable place for meeting friends and visitors and for group affairs. A staff room may be located in any of various places in the building, but it should be placed in an area that is conveniently reached. Lounge furniture, attractively arranged, and tasteful decoration will make the staff room a place of refreshment and relaxation.

EQUIPMENT   Once the general layout and the different types of accommodations for books, readers, and staff have been decided, the question of equipment should receive consideration. In a building as specialized as a university library, adequate equipment is especially important; and the task

[39] Fussler, *Photographic Reproduction for Libraries*, chap. v.

of planning is one that calls for expert judgment. Separate consideration must be given to each room in order that its equipment may be suited to its particular function. The advice of the librarian should be helpful in determining the various types of equipment needed, but the services of engineers and experts should be employed from the beginning. Among the most important items which must be provided are systems of lighting, air conditioning, heating and ventilating, acoustical treatment, floor coverings, furniture, and mechanical devices.

LIGHTING   "The lighting of the library ranks in importance, as a problem of social welfare, with the lighting of all work surfaces where difficult tasks of prolonged duration are being performed." [40] Librarians have always been concerned about proper lighting, but as Burchard and his associates point out, "proper and satisfactory lighting has been achieved less frequently than almost any other feature of the library erected in the twentieth century." [41]

Librarians have sought the advice of illumination experts in their lighting problems, and experimentation still continues. Unless lighting problems are considered at the outset in a building plan, it will be expensive and difficult to make changes later.

How much lighting is necessary has been a controversial matter, even among illumination experts. A uniformly illuminated field of view is the goal of good lighting. While some experts suggest that library lighting might be 30 foot-candles, others have recommended 40 to 50 foot-candles for library reading. Kraehenbuehl [42] has worked out a table of recommended foot-candles for various parts of the library building, ranging from 5 foot-candles for hallways and corridors to 25 foot-candles for all reading spaces.

Although it is desirable to take every advantage of natural lighting, it is important to make concessions to artificial illumination on an economic basis. Studies in brightness contrasts reveal that not

[40] Kraehenbuehl, "Modern Library Illumination," in Fussler (ed.), *Library Buildings for Library Service*, p. 141.
[41] *Planning the University Library Building*, p. 84.
[42] *Op. cit.*, p. 147.

only the lighting system but illumination and reflection from the surfaces of tables, windows, walls, ceilings, and books require careful consideration. Even natural lighting can be too extreme, and proper shades and blinds are necessary to shut off the glare from windows. Proper placement of chairs and tables is also necessary.

Problems faced by the librarian in deciding on a lighting system include the effects of ceiling heights, the relative advantages and costs of incandescent and fluorescent lighting, the nature of the fixtures, and the kind of lighting needed for specific areas in the building. These factors are involved in the economics of an illumination system, an important consideration for the university administration. Since they are discussed in detail by Kraehenbuehl and in the Burchard volume, they do not need elaboration here. It is only necessary to emphasize the importance of lighting in the library, and the librarian must make every effort to obtain the best illumination possible for his building.

AIR CONDITIONING   After a discussion of the problems which arise in air conditioning of a library, Burchard and his associates make the following statement:

The Committee finds itself unable to make categorical recommendations for the air-conditioning of all future libraries. It can categorically state that the original thinking about a library should not exclude air-conditioning, because it is so important a component of a truly modern building; it can urge that the decision as to how much air-conditioning can be afforded should be taken early in the writing of the program and with specific rather than general advice from experts; it can honestly suggest that some other elements of a library can appropriately be sacrificed to air-conditioning if the budget requires.[43]

The authors further note that a decision on air conditioning depends on "very concrete local considerations." They also stress the general desirability of air conditioning in the library.

Air conditioning is something more than keeping a library cool during the heat waves of summer. The American Society of Heating and Ventilating Engineers defines "air conditioning" as "the

[43] *Planning the University Library Building*, p. 83.

simultaneous control of all or at least the first three of those factors affecting both the physical and chemical conditions of the atmosphere within any structure. These factors include: temperature, humidity, motion, distribution, dust, bacteria, odors, toxic gases, and ionization, most of which affect in greater or lesser degree human health and comfort." The engineer also distinguishes among air conditioning installations for winter, summer, and year-round. The important advantages which a library may derive from air conditioning are: (1) aid in the preservation of materials and equipment; (2) ideal working conditions for the staff and readers; (3) reduction of dust; (4) the elimination of the cost and noise of electric fans; and (5) the provision of humidity control.

Librarians have been particularly concerned about the preservation of materials, the comfort of staff and readers, and the elimination or reduction of dust. Tests have shown that sunlight, extreme heat, dryness, dampness, and gases in the air are injurious to paper and leather; therefore, libraries must provide atmospheric conditions which will keep these factors under control. Changes in paper are nearly zero at a temperature of 65° F. and a relative humidity of 60 percent. For human comfort the temperature range in winter should be about 70° F.; in summer, from 72° to 82° F. Relative humidity for libraries would be about 40 to 50 percent for winter and summer.[44] For protection against dust the air should be filtered, washed, and treated with chemicals so that any acidic fumes arising from fuel or other sources may be eliminated.

NOISE PREVENTION   The prevention of excessive noise in libraries is of importance as an aid to effective use by students and as an essential to the comfort and conservation of the energy of staff members. This does not mean that no sounds should be made in the

[44] Detailed consideration of the factors of air conditioning is given by Burchard, et al., *Planning the University Library Building*, pp. 65–83, and by R. H. Gates, "Modern Air Treatment," in Fussler (ed.), *Library Buildings for Library Service*, pp. 114–40. Gates discusses such questions as heating, humidification, cooling, dehumidification, cleaning, circulation and distribution, refrigeration, control, adaptability of modular construction, costs, the T.E.G. (triethylene glycol) system, and purification and sterilization benefits.

library. "It is possible that libraries have been too quiet. This is not necessarily bad in itself, but it creates a psychological effect of entering on tiptoe." [45]

Librarians on the whole have recognized the need for places where students and faculty members can converse or listen to music. But they have also recognized a need—although ideal conditions are difficult to describe—for quiet for concentrated study or research, despite the fact that an occasional student may fall asleep in such surroundings.

Outside, or background, noises generally cannot be controlled except by double-glazing which involves air conditioning; [46] but noise within the building, owing to conversation, electric fans and ventilators, walking, and the use of telephones, typewriters, and other types of equipment, may be minimized. This is true even though the noise is due to corridors or stairways which concentrate traffic near entrances to reading rooms or to the use of building materials and equipment which reflect sound. Procedures include the use of acoustical materials for walls and ceilings in corridors, reading rooms, and workrooms; of soundproofing materials for the walls of the bindery or other rooms in which heavy machinery is in operation; of padding which contains insulating material for doors; and of carefully selected floor coverings.[47] Architectural advice on all of these matters is essential if the librarian is to secure the most satisfactory solution to the noise problem in his local situation.

MECHANICAL EQUIPMENT   To increase efficiency, to reduce errors, and to release the professional personnel from routine duties, librarians have installed a number of machines and special types of equipment which have been used successfully in business and in-

[45] Burchard, et al., op. cit., p. 106.

[46] McDiarmid and Tatum, "Library Noise," Library Quarterly, VIII (1938), 200–9.

[47] Floor coverings are selected on the basis of initial cost, maintenance cost, appearance, durability, and noiselessness. The U.S. National Bureau of Standards has issued a number of reports which describe analyses which have been made of various types of floor coverings.

dustry. Among these are communication systems, such as telautographs, teletypewriters, and pneumatic tubes; stenographic equipment, including typewriters, and various kinds of dictating and transcribing machines; and machines for handling departmental accounts, payrolls, fines, circulation statistics, and other library records. These include various types of calculating machines, punched-card machines, duplicating machines, and other devices employed in usual library operations.[48] The application of photographic devices, such as the "Photoclerk," developed by Ralph R. Shaw [49] at the United States Department of Agriculture Library, to various library operations, has made notable progress. Similarly, the use of punched-card systems, including those of the International Business Machines Corporation, has received added attention in the last decade.[50]

APPARATUS FOR SPECIAL USES   Special apparatus is frequently employed for purposes not common to all libraries.

BINDING DEPARTMENT. Since binding must be either done or directed by skilled artisans, only the more important items are listed. These are electric glue pots, electric paper-cutters, board-cutters, book sewing machines, backers, book presses and vises, eyelet machines, perforators, and electric punch and drill machines.

FUMIGATION. In some libraries, particularly those in warm climates where insects breed rapidly, fumigating equipment has been required. The University of Virginia Library, for example, has a vacuum fumigator which handles manuscript, archival, and other incoming materials which are likely to be infested with pests.

PHOTOGRAPHY DEPARTMENT. The kind of equipment necessary for the photographic laboratory depends on the nature of its work.

[48] Tauber and Associates, *Technical Services in Libraries*, chap. xxii. Annual lists (for last few years) of available equipment and suppliers have been included in issues of the *PNLA Quarterly, ALA Bulletin,* and *Library Journal.*

[49] Shaw, *The Use of Photography in Clerical Routines.*

[50] Blasingame, "The Applications of International Business Machines in Libraries"; Casey and Perry, *Punched Cards: Their Application in Science and Industry;* and Parker, *Library Applications of Punched Cards: A Description of Mechanical Systems.*

Among the major pieces of equipment needed in the medium-sized laboratory are cameras, book cradles, enlargers, checking and splicing equipment, trimming and printing equipment, a sink, a cabinet for chemicals, a mixing table, a paper-dryer, a film-dryer, and a film-washer.

PUBLIC SERVICE DEPARTMENT. Mention has already been made of pneumatic tubes used by the circulation department. Book lifts, book conveyors, special bins with movable bottoms that depress gradually as books accumulate on them, annuciator systems, electric or photographic charging machines, fine computers, visible and rotary card files, and time stamps are among other equipment used by the service departments.

REARRANGING, Instead of erecting a new structure, the li-
ALTERING, AND brarian sometimes is faced with the neces-
ENLARGING sity of rearranging, altering, and enlarging
LIBRARY BUILDINGS the existing building in order to provide
adequate space for readers, staff members, and book storage. The effect of lack of space for book storage is just as serious as is inadequate space for service areas, since it is not possible to give quick and efficient service when parts of the book collection have to be stored in some out-of-the-way space in boxes or when books are piled one upon another on the shelves.

Primary among the factors which tend to make a university library building inadequate are: (1) growth in the number of faculty members and students; (2) changes in methods of teaching; (3) rapid increase in materials; and (4) original faulty planning.[51] One or more of these factors may be involved in altering a building.

A decision to remodel a university library building should be made only after careful consideration. Frequently the decision to alter the present building is based on costs, assuming that the cost of remodeling will be considerably less than that of a new building. Wheeler and Githens warn that "remodelling requires greater in-

[51] For example, see discussion of the building in Tauber and Wilson, *Report of a Survey of the Library of Montana State University*, pp. 129–33.

genuity than building afresh," and they recommend the comparison of the plans and estimates for alterations with the corresponding items for a new building. When this is done, it may be discovered that the costs of remodeling so nearly approach those of a new structure that waiting until more funds are available for a new building will be justified.[52] Wheeler and Githens give three rules for alterations and additions:

1. List the spaces needed for an efficient library as though starting anew, then alter and add to the old building to accommodate these needs.

2. Alter as little as possible, add as much as possible, for addition is cheaper than alteration.

3. Tear down and start afresh if alteration will cost nearly as much as a new building; for remodeling is a compromise, and repair and maintenance costs are higher than for a new building.[53]

Alteration of the building requires remodeling of the interior of the building. It involves partitioning large vestibules and corridors; installations of mezzanines in two-story rooms; removal of partitions that cut the building into small rooms; and, as a part of the reorganization accompanying alteration, the utilization of waste spaces, such as portions of the basement and corridors.

STORAGE
LIBRARIES

One way of avoiding the construction of an entirely new building is to erect a storage library. In 1871 President Charles W. Eliot of Harvard University called attention to the problem of an addition to Gore Hall, and of the possibility of problems in storing materials. It was not until his report of 1898–99, however, that an outline of a storage plan was presented for consideration. Librarian William C. Lane of Harvard in his 1899–1900 report admitted that there was "dead wood" in the library collections which might be stored outside of the general collections. In his report of 1900–1901, President Eliot again returned to the project, and proposed that periodic consideration be given to the materials that were

[52] *The American Public Library Building*, p. 355.   [53] *Ibid.*

not used and which could be stored in a compact manner. Elkins [54] has traced the story of Eliot's efforts to push the idea of a storage library at Harvard, but it was not until 1942 that the New England Storage Library was established.[55]

At the present time the University of Michigan is planning a storage library. Iowa State College,[56] like Harvard, regards the storage building as one solution to the problem of pressure on the main building for storage space for new acquisitions. Harvard has additional storage space in Houghton and Lamont, but other libraries may study the storage library, either on an individual or on a cooperative basis, as a possible alternative to a new library.

BIBLIOGRAPHY

Association of College and Reference Libraries. Buildings Plan Committee. Proceedings . . . of the Institute, 1952–54. Chicago, 1952–54.

Beals, Ralph A., Frances Henne, and Lowell Martin. "The Plan of Service as It Affects the Library Building," in Fussler (ed.), *Library Buildings for Library Service*, pp. 12–24.

Bean, Donald E., and Ralph E. Ellsworth. Modular Planning for College and Small University Libraries. [Iowa City, Iowa] Privately Printed by the Authors, 1948.

Bibliographical Planning Committee of Philadelphia. Philadelphia Libraries: A Survey of Facilities, Needs, and Opportunities. Philadelphia, University of Pennsylvania Press, 1942.

Blasingame, Ralph U., Jr. "The Applications of International Business Machines in Libraries" (unpublished Master's thesis, Columbia University, 1950).

Boyd, Julian P. Outline of A Building Program for the Princeton

---

[54] "President Eliot and the Storage of 'Dead' Books," *Harvard Library Bulletin*, VIII (1954), 299–312.

[55] Metcalf, "The New England Deposit Library," *Library Quarterly*, XII (1942), 622–28; Osborn, "Books for the Deposit Library," *Harvard University Library Notes*, IV (1942), 80–83; Osborn, "The New England Deposit Library," *College and Research Libraries*, V (1943–44), 21–28; Doherty, "The New England Deposit Library," *Library Quarterly*, XVII (1948), 245–54, and XIX (1949), 1–18; Metcalf, "The New England Deposit Library after Thirteen Years," *Harvard Library Bulletin*, VIII (1954), 313–22; Walsh, "An Experiment in the Selection of Books for Storage," *Harvard Library Bulletin*, VIII (1954), 378–81.

[56] Friley and Orr, "A Decade of Book Storage at Iowa State College," *College and Research Libraries*, XII (1951), 7–10+.

University Library: Report from the Librarian to the Committee on the Library of the Board of Trustees, May, 1943. Princeton, N.J., 1943 (mimeographed).

Burchard, John E. "Postwar Library Buildings," *College and Research Libraries*, VII (1946), 118–26.

Burchard, John E., Charles W. David, and Julian P. Boyd (eds.). Planning the University Library Building. Princeton, Princeton University Press, 1949. See especially for further citations, chapter ix, "Library Planning: A Bibliographical Essay," prepared by LeRoy C. Merritt.

Butler, Pierce. "The Rare Book Collection and the Bibliographical Museum," in Fussler (ed.), *Library Buildings for Library Service*, pp. 76–78.

Casey, R. S., and J. W. Perry. Punched Cards: Their Application in Science and Industry. New York, Reinhold, 1951.

Coney, Donald. The University Libraries: Plans for the Next Twenty Years (mimeographed, n.d.).

Cooperative Committee on Library Building Plans. Meeting[s], 1945–49. Held at various places.

Doherty, Francis X. "The New England Deposit Library," *Library Quarterly*, XVIII (1948), 245–54; XIX (1949), 1–18.

Elkins, Kimball C. "President Eliot and the Storage of 'Dead' Books," *Harvard Library Bulletin*, XIII (1954), 299–312.

Ellsworth, Ralph E. "Determining Factors in the Evaluation of the Modular Plan for Libraries," *College and Research Libraries*, XIV (1953), 125–28.

—— "Educational Implications of the New Ideas in Library Construction," *College and Research Libraries*, XII (1946), 326–29.

—— "The Library Building and the Reader," in Fussler (ed.), *Library Buildings for Library Service*, pp. 24–36.

Friley, Charles E., and R. W. Orr, "A Decade of Book Storage at Iowa State College," *College and Research Libraries*, XII (1951), 7–10.

Fussler, Herman H. Photographic Reproduction for Libraries. Chicago, University of Chicago Press, 1942.

Fussler, Herman H. (ed.). Library Buildings for Library Service: Papers Presented before the Library Institute at the University of Chicago, August 5–10, 1946. Chicago, American Library Association, 1947.

Hanley, Edna R. College and University Library Buildings. Chicago, American Library Association, 1939.

Harvard University Library. The Houghton Library. Cambridge, Harvard College, 1942.

Henderson, Robert W. "Bookstack Planning with the Cubook," *Library Journal*, LXI (1936), 52–54.

———— "The Cubook: A Suggested Unit for Bookstack Measurement," *Library Journal*, LIX (1934), 865–68.

Illinois, University of, Library. Staff Manual. 2d ed. Urbana, Ill., 1948.

Kraehenbuehl, John O. "Modern Library Illumination," in Fussler (ed.), *Library Buildings for Library Service*, pp. 141–67.

Lyle, Guy R. The Administration of the College Library. 2d ed., rev. New York, H. W. Wilson, 1949.

McDiarmid, E. W., and G. R. Tatum. "Library Noise," *Library Quarterly*, XIII (1938), 200–9.

MacDonald, Angus A. "Building Design for Library Management," *Library Trends*, II (1954), 463–69.

Merritt, LeRoy C. "The Book Stock," in Fussler (ed.), *Library Buildings for Library Service*, pp. 56–70.

Metcalf, Keyes D. "The New England Deposit Library after Thirteen Years," *Harvard Library Bulletin*, XIII (1954), 312–22.

———— "Spatial Problems in University Libraries," *Library Trends*, II (1954), 554–61.

Miller, R. A. "The Technical and Administrative Functions of the Library," in Fussler (ed.), *Library Buildings for Library Service*, pp. 37–55.

Muller, Robert H. "Compact Storage Equipment: Where to Use It and Where Not," *College and Research Libraries*, XV (1954), 300–308.

———— "Evaluation of Compact Book Storage," in Association of College and Reference Libraries. Buildings Committee. *Third Library Building Plans Institute*. Chicago (1954), pp. 77–93.

Osborn, Andrew D. "Books for the Deposit Library," *Harvard University Library Notes*, IV (1942), 80–83.

———— "The New England Deposit Library," *College and Research Libraries*, V (1943–44), 21–28.

Parker, Ralph W. Library Applications of Punched Cards: A Description of Mechanical Systems. Chicago, American Library Association, 1952.

Randall, William M. "Some Principles for Library Planning," *College and Research Libraries*, VII (1946), 319–25.

Reece, Ernest J. "Building Planning and Equipment," *Library Trends*, I (1952), 136–55.

———— "Library Building Plans: How to Draft Them," *College and Research Libraries*, XIII (1952), 198–211.

Reynolds, Helen M. "University Library Buildings in the United States, 1890–1939," *College and Research Libraries*, XIV (1953), 149–57+.

Rider, Fremont. Compact Book Storage. New York, Hadham Press, 1949.

—— The Scholar and the Future of the Research Library. New York, Hadham Press, 1944.

Runge, Gretchen E., and Helen M. Pyle. Library Planning: Check List and Reading List. Prepared for distribution at the Special Libraries Convention, Cincinnati, O., May 15, 1954. Philadelphia, Pa., 1954 (mimeographed).

Shaw, Ralph R. The Use of Photography in Clerical Routines: A Report to the American Council of Learned Societies. Washington, D.C., American Council of Learned Societies, 1953.

Swank, Raynard C. "The Cost of Keeping Books" (paper presented at the Monticello [Ill.] Conference, October 30, 1954) (mimeographed).

Tauber, Maurice F., and Associates. Technical Services in Libraries. New York, Columbia University Press, 1954.

Tauber, Maurice F., and Eugene H. Wilson. Report of a Survey of the Library of Montana State University for Montana State University, January–May, 1951. Chicago, American Library Association, 1951.

Walsh, James E. "An Experiment in the Selection of Books for Storage," *Harvard Library Bulletin*, XIII (1954), 378–81.

Wheeler, Joseph L., and A. M. Githens. The American Public Library Building: Its Planning and Design with Special Reference to Its Administration and Service. New York, C. Scribner's Sons, 1941.

Williams, Edwin E. (ed.). Problems and Prospects of the Research Library. New Brunswick, N.J., Published by the Scarecrow Press for the Association of Research Libraries, 1955.

Wilson, Louis R., and Frank A. Lundy. Report of a Survey of the Library of the University of Notre Dame for the University of Notre Dame, November 1950—March 1952. Chicago, American Library Association, 1952.

Wilson, Louis R., and Raynard C. Swank. Report of a Survey of the Library of Stanford University for Stanford University, November 1946—March 1947. Chicago, American Library Association, 1947.

See also sections on library buildings of surveys listed in Bibliography of chapter xvi.

XV

OFF-CAMPUS RELATIONS
OF THE LIBRARIAN

IN chapter ii the relations of the university librarian to other officers and members of the university community were discussed. They were shown to constitute an important part of his professional activities, but they were only one part. In chapter xiii, which deals with the integration of resources for research, another aspect of the professional work of the librarian is revealed. His participation in the work of organizations not specifically related to the university community is shown, as well as the nature of the major undertakings in which he and representatives of the organizations engage. These activities, even though they may not always be understood by other members of the university, are important. In fact, they add greatly to the effectiveness of the librarian's work, and through participation in such activities the librarian is enabled to contribute directly and significantly to the advancement of librarianship and scholarship.

In the present chapter further and more specific consideration will be given to these off-campus relationships. Some of the organizations with which the librarian usually works will be listed; the nature of some of the enterprises in which he has engaged will be indicated; and by means of a limited group of case histories it will be shown how several university librarians of the past have actually worked with various organizations or combinations of organizations in carrying out specific undertakings.

ASSOCIATIONS AND ORGANIZATIONS   It is not possible to list every association and organization with which the university librarian, at one time or another, has worked. There are five groups of organizations, however, with one or more of which it has usually been customary for him to collaborate in special undertakings. These are: (1) library associations (local, state, regional, national, and international); (2) educational associations (in the same categories); (3) governmental offices and departments; (4) educational foundations; and (5) learned societies. These by no means exhaust the list, but they may well serve as illustrations.

Each of these groups, in turn, will be found to contain from half a dozen to a score or more associations or organizations which the librarian or the prospective university librarian can overlook only at the peril of himself and his library. Some of the most important in each category are the following:

LIBRARY ASSOCIATIONS. American Association of Law Libraries; American Library Association (especially its Boards on Acquisition of Library Materials, Education for Librarianship, International Relations, Personnel Administration, and Resources of American Libraries; its Committees on Archives and Libraries, Bibliography, Bookbinding, Buildings, Federal Relations, Friends of Libraries, Insurance for Libraries, Intellectual Freedom, Library Legislation, Photoduplication and Multiple Copying Methods, Public Documents, Public Relations, Relations with Publishers, Relations with Subscription Book Publishers, Statistics, and Subscription Books; and its Round Tables for Audio-Visual materials, Exhibits, Serials, and Staff Organizations; the Division of Cataloging and Classification and its committees); American Theological Library Association; Association of American Library Schools; Association of College and Reference Libraries; Association of Research Libraries; Canadian Library Association; Catholic Library Association; Cuban Library Association; Inter-American Bibliographical and Library Association; International Federation of Library Associations; Medical Library Association; Music Library Association; National Association of State Libraries; Pacific Northwest, Southeastern, and Southwestern Library Associations; Special Libraries Association, especially units engaged in work related to special and departmental libraries of universities; and Theater Library Association. Closely related to these are: the American Documentation Institute, Bibliographical Society of America, Bibliographical Society of the University of Virginia, Council of National Library Associations, Educational Film Library Association, International Federation for Documentation, and Society of American Archivists.

EDUCATIONAL ASSOCIATIONS. Adult Education Association, American Association of University Professors, American Association of University Women, Association of American Universities, Association of Land-Grant Colleges and Universities, Institute of International Education, National Association of State Universities, National Catholic Educational Association, National Education Association, and the North Central, Middle States, and Southern Associations of Colleges and Secondary Schools.

GOVERNMENT OFFICES AND AGENCIES. Armed Forces Medical Library, Library of Congress, National Science Foundation, Office of the Superintendent of Documents, Smithsonian Institution, U.S. Department of Agriculture, U.S. Office of Education, and United Nations and its affiliated agencies.

LEARNED SOCIETIES. American Council on Education; American Council of Learned Societies (including twenty-five organizations, such as the American Association for the Advancement of Science, American Antiquarian Society, American Philosophical Association, and Modern Language Association); American Standards Association; National Academy of Science; National Microfilm Association; National Research Council; and Social Science Research Council (including seven organizations, such as the American Historical Association, American Political Science Association, and American Sociological Association).

EDUCATIONAL FOUNDATIONS. Carnegie Corporation of New York, Carnegie Endowment for International Peace, Carnegie Foundation for the Advancement of Teaching, Carnegie Institution of Washington, Ford Foundation, General Education Board, Old Dominion Foundation, and Rockefeller Foundation.

These organizations have varied interests, many of which coincide with those of university librarians; their personnel and resources are extensive; and the opportunities which they present the librarian for effective cooperation in significant enterprises are many and challenging.

NATURE OF The type of activity in which these organ-
ACTIVITIES izations engage is indicated in part by their titles. Those enterprises in which they have participated and which have most appealed to the university librarian include: (1) the development of international cultural relations; (2) the compilation and publication of major catalogs and union lists; (3) the establishment of regional union catalogs and bibliographical centers; (4) the description of the holdings of individual libraries and groups of libraries; (5) the improvement of college and university book collections; (6) the improvement and support of education for librarianship; (7) the development of laboratories for the photographic reproduction of materials; (8) the reduction of costs of library technical operations; (9) the reclassification and recataloging of library collections; (10) the study of scientific aids to learning; and (11) the accomplishment of other undertakings—all of which are intended to contribute to the promotion of research and the advancement of scholarship and librarianship.

The annual reports and proceedings of these organizations describe in detail the character and extent of many activities which the organizations carry on and constitute one of the most important parts of the university librarian's professional literature. They furnish, probably better than many of the publications devoted exclusively to the consideration of library problems, background and perspective essential to an understanding of the educational objectives which universities, educational foundations, learned societies, and related organizations are attempting to achieve.

ACTIVITIES OF   The principal emphasis of the present chap-
UNIVERSITY   ter, however, will be devoted to presenting
LIBRARIANS   case histories of a few former university
                             librarians, which may illustrate how librar-
ians and representatives of other organizations work together and
thereby contribute to the advancement of scholarship and research.
The examples cited are not, in any sense, intended to be exhaustive
or to describe all the interests or activities of the individuals concerned but are illustrative of specific fields of interest or activity.
The statements are restricted to librarians who are either deceased
or have retired from active service. There are numerous examples
of currently active university librarians who are engaged in local,
state, regional, national, and international relations and projects.

JUSTIN WINSOR AND MELVIL DEWEY. For the purposes of this section the careers of Justin Winsor and Melvil Dewey, among the
founders of the American Library Association, may be bracketed.
Winsor's interest in the services and facilities of libraries began to
manifest itself early, when, as a freshman at Harvard in 1849, he
finished his *A History of the Town of Duxbury*. He did not complete his undergraduate work but went to Europe in his senior
year and spent two years studying literatures and languages and
preparing for the role of a man of letters. Fifteen years later, however, he was awarded his degree as of the class of 1853. In 1866,
at the age of thirty-five, he became a member of the board of
trustees of the Boston Public Library and wrote a noteworthy report on its activities in 1867. The next year he was elected superintendent or librarian of that library, and in 1877 he became
librarian of Harvard University. His interest in librarianship expressed itself in many ways during his first presidency of the American Library Association (1876–85). He was one of the founders
of the *Library Journal* (1876), and he participated in various activities of the association and related organizations. As president of the
American Library Association, he attended the organization meeting of the British Library Association in 1877; and he was re-
elected president of the American Library Association in 1897, to

represent it at an international conference of librarians in England and to extend the relations of American libraries with the libraries of Europe. He was a member of the American Antiquarian Society and the New England Historic Genealogical Society and was chairman of the organization meeting of the American Historical Association when it was founded in 1884. He was the third president of the last named association in 1887 and in that year delivered a notable presidential address entitled "Manuscript Sources of American History—the Conspicuous Collections Extant." In the publication of his *Memorial History of Boston* and his *Narrative and Critical History* he associated himself with a great many contributors who were members of these and other associations. In these and later publications he emphasized the importance of bibliography and cartography to a greater degree than previous historians had done—an importance which has been increasingly recognized in the field of historical writing. Through his knowledge of these subjects, gained in part through his work as a librarian, he contributed to a significant aspect of American scholarship.

Melvil Dewey, librarian at Amherst when he developed his decimal classification in 1876 and librarian at Columbia University when he became the head of the first library school in the United States in 1887 (moved to the New York State Library, 1889), was the most active of the founding fathers of the American Library Association; as secretary of the association (1876–90) and president (1890–91 and 1892–93), and as librarian of Columbia University and of the State Library of New York, he participated in the establishment and direction of an amazingly large number of library and related organizations. He became the first editor of the *Library Journal* and organized and directed the first establishment to concern itself with the provision of library furniture and supplies, later the Library Bureau. He assisted in the organization of the British Library Association and was the projector of the organization of the American Library Institute and the National Association of State Libraries; and, as secretary of the board of regents of the University of the State of New York and state librarian of New York, he or-

ganized the extension service of the latter institution. The founding
and direction of the Lake Placid Club and the Lake Placid Club
Education Foundation extended further his range of interests and
relations in the United States, as did the development of the Classification décimale universelle at Brussels.

Both Winsor and Dewey had the rare opportunity of helping
establish new organizations and exploring new fields. That they
succeeded in doing so, however, was due in large measure to their
ability to win the cooperation of others engaged in related activities
and thereby contribute to the development of librarianship and
through it to the development of scholarship as well.

ERNEST CUSHING RICHARDSON. E. C. Richardson, librarian and
associate professor of bibliology of Hartford Theological Seminary,
1880–90; librarian of Princeton University, 1890–1920; director of
the library, 1920–23; honorary director and research professor of
bibliography, 1923–25; and honorary consultant in bibliography at
the Library of Congress from 1925 until his death in 1939, represented a somewhat later period of library development than did
Winsor and Dewey. Yet he lived in advance of his day. Basic organization was not so much the order of Richardson's day as interest in the broader problems of bibliographical apparatus, the
building up of resources for research, and the extension of library
cooperation through cooperative purchase. A frequent visitor to
Europe, he extended his knowledge of library cooperation abroad
and participated in many of the conferences which centered his
attention upon bibliographical problems. His membership in organizations, such as the Preussische Akademie, the Società ligure
di Storia Patria, the Bibliographical Society of America, the American Historical Association, and the American Society of Church
History reflect his varied interests. He served as president of the
American Library Association in 1904–5 and of the American Library Institute from 1916 to 1919. As chairman of the American
Library Association Committee on Bibliography and as president of
the American Library Institute, he urged the establishment of the
Union Catalog of the Library of Congress and later had the great

satisfaction of directing the project. As consultant at the Library of Congress, while participating directly in the significant expansion of the resources of that institution and directing the formation of the Union Catalog, he established contacts with libraries in all parts of the country which possessed special collections, and he provided for the inclusion of their holdings in the Union Catalog.

C. C. Jewett, assistant secretary and librarian of the Smithsonian Institution in 1853, had proposed at the conference of librarians in New York in that year the establishment of a union catalog, a plan for cooperative cataloging, and the building up of the library of the Smithsonian Institution as the national library of the United States. The recommendations were not favorably received by his superior, and Jewett went to Boston and later became librarian of the Boston Public Library. The printing of cards for its own collections was begun in 1898 by the Library of Congress, and the sale of its cards to other libraries was provided for in 1901. It remained for Richardson, in his capacity as consultant, under the general direction of Putnam, to carry the first of the Jewett proposals into effect. In the discussions of European librarians and bibliographers the proposal to organize a world union catalog had frequently been made. Richardson thought of the Union Catalog of the Library of Congress as America's contribution to that undertaking; and, although the idea of the world catalog was never carried out, this important section of what might have become a world catalog was carried forward under Richardson's direction to a degree of coverage which made its continuance possible.

The record of Richardson's work as consultant in building up the resources of the Library of Congress was also important. On visits to Europe in behalf of the Library he was constantly on the lookout for manuscripts and books essential to American scholarship which were not to be found in American libraries. He was well aware that there were several million such volumes which should ultimately find their way into American libraries, and he perfected an arrangement with several of the eastern university libraries by which any important book in this category secured by him would be taken by one of the cooperating institutions. In a sense, it was an informal one-man Farmington Plan. Many of the procedures employed in cooperative purchase and in the development of union catalogs as they are known and practiced by American libraries today were initiated by him, and the work begun by him is increasing in significance constantly. In addition to his work in library associations, he served for a number of years as chairman of the Committee on Bibliography of the American Historical Association; and in 1902, with A. E. Morse, he edited the first volume of the publications issued by that association, under the title *Writings on American History*.

FRANK KELLER WALTER. Librarian of the University of Minnesota, 1921–43, and director of the division of library instruction at the University, 1928–43, Frank Keller Walter was a contemporary of many university librarians still active. After a period of teaching in public and private schools and as an instructor at Haverford College, Walter enrolled at the New York State Library School where he earned his bachelor's, and later, his master's degree. He had developed a strong background in bibliography and languages, which was later to help him build the collections at Minnesota. As a library assistant in the Brooklyn Public Library, as assistant to the director of the New York State Library School, as vice-director of the School, and as librarian of the General Motors Corporation in Detroit, Walter strengthened his knowledge of library materials, techniques, and the problems of the researchers. It was therefore not surprising that when James T. Gerould left Minnesota to go to Princeton, Walter was asked to take over the librarianship at the Minneapolis institution.

Like so many of his contemporaries, Walter was an extremely active person outside of his immediate responsibilities for developing a university library and a library school. He was concerned with the development of librarianship on a national basis. He was elected to the Council and Executive Board of the American Library Association, and served on the Editorial Committee. During his period in New York he had been president of the New York Library

Association and the American Association of Library Schools. He later served as president of the Minnesota Library Association and the Association of College and Reference Libraries. He was an active member of the Bibliographical Society of America, Gutenberg Gesellschaft, Medieval Society of America, American Library Institute, and the American Institute of Graphic Arts.

He lectured frequently in other library schools, and wrote extensively of problems in all types of libraries. Probably his most important contribution to the literature of librarianship and scholarship generally was his collaboration with Henry Bartlett Van Hoesen, another distinguished university librarian, in the preparation of *Bibliography: Practical, Enumerative, Historical,* an extensively used textbook for upperclassmen and graduate students. His other longer works were concerned with technical terminology in bibliography, periodicals for the small library, and printing by the library. Graduates from the Minnesota library school, trained under Walter and his staff, were well versed in the needs of scholars and research workers.

JAMES T. GEROULD. Aid to scholars by James T. Gerould, who served in the libraries of Columbia University (1897–1900), the University of Missouri (1900–06), the University of Minnesota (1906–20), and Princeton University (1920–38), was rendered primarily through the provision of union lists, which expedited the consultation and use of important collections of journals, transactions of learned societies, manuscripts, newspapers, and documents. The first of these notable indexes was the *Union List of Serials in the Libraries of the United States and Canada,* edited by Winifred Gregory, and published by the H. W. Wilson Company in 1927. The preparation of this monumental index involved the cooperation of forty libraries, which checked their holdings for inclusion and aided in underwriting the costs of the publication. A subsidy was received from the Laura Spelman Rockefeller Memorial to be used in listing the holdings of federal libraries in Washington. The work was undertaken by a committee of the American Library Association of which H. M. Lydenberg, C. W.

Andrews, Willard Austen, A. E. Bostwick, J. T. Gerould, and
Nathan Van Patten were members. Lydenberg was chairman of
the committee; but some time before the work was completed much
of the task of directing and carrying out the undertaking was
turned over to Gerould. The publication of supplements, issued
later and involving additional libraries, was also under the direction
of the committee, with Lydenberg as chairman and Gabrielle E.
Malikoff as editor. Two other lists followed in rapid succession.
The *List of Serial Publications of Foreign Governments, 1815–
1931*, appeared in 1933, with Miss Gregory as editor, Gerould as
chairman of the American Library Association committee, and the
H. W. Wilson Company as publisher. The American Library Association, the American Council of Learned Societies, and the National Research Council sponsored the undertaking; and assistance
in carrying it out was given by the Laura Spelman Rockefeller
Memorial and the Rockefeller Foundation. In 1937 *American
Newspapers, 1821–1936*, was issued, the project having been sponsored by the Bibliographical Society of America. Gerould was
chairman of the committee, with Lydenberg and Henry Spaulding
Parsons as members. The *Census of Medieval and Renaissance
Manuscripts in the United States and Canada*, edited by Seymour
De Ricci, with the assistance of W. J. Wilson, was issued through
the H. W. Wilson Company in 1935–37. The American Council
of Learned Societies had proposed this publication in 1925 through
a committee of which Professor Karl Young of Yale was chairman.
He was succeeded by Gerould, and a grant was made in 1929 by
the General Education Board to the Library of Congress, the proposal to be carried out through its Division of Manuscripts.

The importance of these indexes to scholars cannot be over-
emphasized. Their preparation involved the cooperation of hundreds of libraries, the assistance of numerous professional and
learned societies, and the wise support of a number of educational
foundations. Through his nearness to New York, his contacts with
individuals and organizations engaged in research and publication,
and his practical knowledge of publishing, Gerould greatly in-

creased the usefulness of these categories of resources for research to American scholars.

Gerould was also mainly responsible for the organization of the Association of Research Libraries in 1932. He was impressed with the importance of providing a medium through which the problems of research libraries could be considered effectively without involving a large, heterogeneous membership. As a result of the organization of the association, the members have been able to give sustained consideration to many proposals, some of which, such as *American Newspapers, 1821–1936,* and the book catalog of Library of Congress printed cards, have been carried through successfully.

ANDREW KEOGH. Born in England, Andrew Keogh, librarian of Yale (1916–38), is an example of a librarian who, although instrumental in developing a great library, saw the need of keeping active in national, regional, and local organizations. After only two years as college student, young Keogh accepted a position in the Newcastle-on-Tyne Public Library. Gradually, he worked himself into the position of reference librarian. At an international librarians' conference in England in 1897, he became acquainted with the visiting librarians from the United States. In 1899, he took a position with a bookstore, Hayes Cooke and Company, in Chicago. Later in the same year at the ALA Conference in Atlanta he again met James Lyman Whitney, of the Boston Public Library, who had been at the conference in England. Whitney proceeded to introduce him to other librarians. Before the meeting was over, Keogh was offered the assistant librarianship of the Cleveland Public Library. There were also other offers, but Keogh was determined to get a place in a scholarly library.

He waited patiently until an offer came from Yale. He became librarian of the Linonia and Brothers Library (1899–1900), reference librarian (1900–1916), and then librarian. In 1904, he acquired a Master's degree from Yale, and honorary doctorates were bestowed on him by Michigan (1928), Trinity College at Hartford (1930), and Middlebury College (1937). One of President Hadley's doubts in appointing him librarian of Yale concerned Keogh's qualifications in public relations, in the profession-at-large and among the Yale alumni. But Keogh rivaled his contemporaries in his activity in associational work. He was one of the founders and president of the Bibliographical Society of America, executive secretary of the American Library Institute, director of the New Haven Colony Historical Society, president of the Acorn Club of Connecticut, and president of the American Library Association (1929–30). He was a member of the Bibliographical Society (London), Oxford Bibliographical Society, American Antiquarian Society, New York Historical Society, Connnecticut Academy of Arts and Sciences, and the Connecticut Historical Society. He contributed extensively to professional literature, and edited several volumes. He developed alumni relations so effectively that during his period as librarian Yale was the recipient of numerous important gifts. Among his greatest contributions was the planning of the Sterling Memorial Library.

WILLIAM WARNER BISHOP. The foundations for the work of W. W. Bishop and for his services in the field of international library relations were laid during his stay in Rome in 1898–99 as a fellow in the American School of Classical Studies and during his membership on the staffs of the library of Princeton University, 1902–7, and the Library of Congress, 1907–15. In Rome he learned the importance of the mastery of foreign languages in international communication; and at Princeton, under Richardson, and in Washington, under Putnam, he came to a fine appreciation of the international character of the materials of scholarship. Rome was the meeting place of both ancient and modern civilizations and was rich in the monuments and arts of each. Washington, in the early days of World War I, was quickening its tempo of world leadership. Both capitals, consequently, gave him an excellent opportunity of sensing the importance of international contacts and understandings.

The off-campus service for which Bishop is probably best known in the United States is that which he rendered the Carnegie Corporation of New York in more than a decade as chairman of the various advisory committees appointed by the corporation to improve the book collections of American, Canadian, and Near Eastern colleges. Under his direction, approximately $1,900,000 was made available to colleges and institutions of different kinds. However, the activities of Bishop which were of greatest importance in their international aspects were: (1) participation in the organization and administration of the International Federation of Library Associations, (2) direction of the reorganization of the Vatican Library, and (3) assistance to Oxford and Cambridge universities and the League of Nations in projecting plans for library buildings.

The groundwork for the organization of the International Federation of Library Associations was laid by Bishop in 1924, when he was sent by the American Library Association and the Carnegie Endowment for International Peace to extend invitations to European librarians to attend the fiftieth anniversary meeting of the American Library Association. To his efforts was due in large measure the attendance of thirty-three representatives from foreign countries at the meetings at Atlantic City and Philadelphia in 1926 and the postconference visit of many of the delegates to libraries in other cities. As chairman of the Association's Committee on International Relations, he presided at the meeting at which the formation of an international committee was proposed; and he represented the association at the organization meeting of the International Committee in England on the fiftieth anniversary of the British Library Association in 1927. He was elected a member of the committee and in that capacity attended its meeting in Rome in 1928 to prepare for the first meeting, held in 1929 at Rome-Venice, of the World Congress of Libraries and Bibliography, now the International Federation of Library Associations. In 1931, at the meeting of the International Committee at Cheltenham, England, he was elected president of the federation and in that capacity served for a period of five years. Upon his retirement in 1936 he was elected an honorary president.

During his presidency the second conference of the International Federation of Library Associations was held in 1935 at Madrid-

Seville-Barcelona. In close touch with all the activities of the committee and the federation, Bishop was particularly concerned with the formulation of agreements concerning interlibrary loans and the exchange of librarians. He also helped arrange for the attendance of foreign librarians at the American Library Association meeting in Chicago in 1933.

The mission which took Bishop to Rome in 1927, to consider the reorganization of the Vatican Library, was assigned to him by the Carnegie Endowment for International Peace through its president, Nicholas Murray Butler, of Columbia University. After a visit to Rome in the spring of 1927, Bishop submitted recommendations and set in train a series of operations which resulted, in the course of a few years, in the adoption of a classification system and catalog code for the handling of the manuscripts and books of the library; the training of a number of Europeans in American library schools to carry on the work after the reorganization had been successfully begun; the presentation, by the Library of Congress, through the cooperation of Putnam, of a depository set of cards; the installation of a new steel stack of American manufacture; and the beginning of the publication and distribution of cards by the Vatican Library.

The relations maintained by Bishop with the older English universities and the League of Nations concerned the erection of suitable library buildings. The foundation involved in this assistance was the Rockefeller Foundation, which made large grants to all three institutions. Bishop met with the committees charged with the planning, and in the case of the commission of Oxford University he arranged for the inspection tour which it made of American and Canadian libraries. He also recommended that a similar tour be made to important European libraries. Through frequent visits to Europe, Bishop maintained direct contact with the commission charged with the erection of the League of Nations Library. He also served as a member of the committee on library experts who advised the International Institute of Intellectual Cooperation of the League—a body which, in addition to advising on library matters in general, issued important publications on the training of librarians in various countries and on popular libraries for workers. In 1937 Bishop accepted an invitation from the Chinese Library Association to visit libraries of China, but the mission could not be undertaken on account of the beginning of the war with Japan.

Apart from his official connections with these undertakings, Bishop assisted in the training of many foreign librarians enrolled in the library department at the University of Michigan and conferred informally with hundreds of visitors from foreign countries concerning many aspects of library development. His contacts with directors of various foundations and learned societies also afforded opportunity for the informal consideration of problems of significance to the advancement of libraries and scholarship.

Busy though he was with national and international library ventures, Bishop administered effectively the Library of the University of Michigan from 1915 to 1941. This was a period of significant development in the collections, services, and facilities of the Library.

From the ranks of retired librarians, three may be cited whose off-campus activities have centered, for the purpose of this discussion, the dramatization of the role of microphotography in libraries, the professional training of librarians, and the development of scientific collections. Brief consideration is given to the work of two nonuniversity librarians.

M. L. RANEY. The focusing of attention upon microphotography through libraries as an aid to scholars, the development of appropriate apparatus designed to meet the requirements of libraries, and the installation of special laboratories to facilitate the production and use of microfilm have engaged the attention of a large number of librarians, manufacturers, and workers in related fields. Science Service, the National Archives, the Library of Congress, the New York Public Library, and the libraries of Harvard, Yale, and the University of Chicago, as well as several of the manufacturers of photographic equipment, were among the first organizations to participate in experimentation and development of the field. The

dramatization of library interest in the development of microphotography, however, was directed largely by M. Llewellyn
Raney (Johns Hopkins, 1903–27, and Chicago, 1927–42).

Raney became impressed with the importance of this means of
increasing resources for research on a trip to eastern libraries in
the autumn of 1935. Upon his return to Chicago he began the
preparation of an exhibit of apparatus for the approaching mid-
winter meeting of the American Library Association. This exhibit
was followed by an all-day symposium on the subject by the leaders
in the field and a major exhibit of apparatus at the Richmond conference of the association in 1936. The papers presented at the
symposium were published, with Raney as editor, by the association in 1936 under the title *Microphotography in Libraries*. During
the same conference the Committee on Resources of American
Libraries was changed to a board by the American Library Association Council; and the Committee on Photographic Reproduction
of Library Materials, with Raney as chairman, was established by
the executive board. During the autumn of the same year the
Rockefeller Foundation made a grant to the University of Chicago
to equip a laboratory adequate to produce materials of a high
quality and to demonstrate the value of such materials when published in quantity for more than one library. Herman H. Fussler,
now director of the University of Chicago Library, was placed in
charge of the department and began the installation of apparatus.

While the plans for the laboratory were being carried into effect,
the American Committee on Intellectual Cooperation received an
invitation to participate in the Paris International Exposition in
1937. The committee, of which James T. Shotwell of Columbia
University was chairman, decided to demonstrate the possibilities of
microphotography as a means of promoting international intellectual cooperation. The American Library Association and the University of Chicago were asked to serve as joint sponsors of the
exhibit, under the direction of Raney. A grant was made by the
Rockefeller Foundation for the demonstration, and Raney and
Fussler carried out the program in the spring of 1937. The demon-

stration was unusual in that it was not merely an exhibit of equipment; in addition, the considerable parts of thirty files of journals of the period of the French Revolution which were not available in American libraries were filmed, the original files being in the Bibliothèque nationale.

As chairman of the American Library Association committee, Raney arranged a second symposium and exhibit of equipment for the New York Conference of the American Library Association in 1937. The proceedings of this meeting, with supplements, were edited by him and published under the title *Microphotography for Libraries* (1937). Another exhibit was arranged by him at the San Francisco conference in 1939. The *Journal of Documentary Reproduction*, projected under the editorial management of Charles E. Rush, chairman of the committee in 1937–38, was the logical successor to the two earlier publications. Raney was also responsible for arranging an exhibit of microphotographic materials for the Tenth International Conference of Chemistry in Rome in 1938 and for the provision of American papers for the sessions of the International Federation for Documentation at Oxford (1938) and at Zurich (1939). He also extended the range of his interests in the subject through an exhibit and a paper before the Inter-American Bibliographical and Library Association at its meeting in Washington in 1940 and through numerous articles in professional journals. One of the most distinctive outgrowths of this interest was the development of the laboratory at the University of Chicago through Fussler and the publication of his *Photographic Reproduction for Libraries; A Study of Administrative Problems* (1942).

CHARLES C. WILLIAMSON. C. C. Williamson, dean of the School of Library Service of Columbia University and director of libraries of Columbia from 1926 to 1943, spent the earlier part of his library career in activities that were somewhat removed from the special field of education for librarianship for which he is possibly best known by members of the library profession. He served as chief of the division of economics of the New York Public Library during 1911–14, and 1919–21; as librarian of the New York Muni-

cipal Reference Branch during 1914–18; as statistician of the Americanization studies of the Carnegie Corporation of New York during
1918–19; and as director of the Information Service of the Rockefeller Foundation during 1921–26. While librarian of the Municipal
Reference Branch, he served as a member of the advisory board
responsible for the publication of the *Bulletin of the Public Affairs
Information Service;* and, as chief of the advisory board in 1918, he
effected certain changes which have remained as permanent features of the service. The usefulness to scholars of this service, dealing with pamphlets, documents, and other ephemeral materials, has
long been recognized as being of the highest order.

Another publication of somewhat similar nature for which Williamson was responsible was *The Minutes of the Common Council
of the City of New York, 1784–1831.* Williamson had noticed that
scholars and city officials were constantly going through the bulky
and more or less illegible volumes housed in the city clerk's office.
He secured appropriations for editing the records, which were
issued in 1917 in nineteen volumes, and for a two-volume index,
issued in 1930.

In the Americanization studies, published under the direction of
Allen T. Burns (by Harper, in ten volumes), Williamson recruited
a small staff of trained librarians to assist the research workers
engaged in carrying out the studies. Although his work was anony-
mous, he participated in the preparation of the entire work and
compiled the greater part of the material for the volume *Americans
by Choice,* by John Palmer Gavit. During his connection with the
Municipal Reference Library, Williamson had also been associate
editor of the *American Political Science Review.* From 1921 to
1926 he occupied the newly created post of director of Information
Service at the Rockefeller Foundation. The extensive library of the
Foundation was placed in his department, and he was charged with
the foundation's publicity and the compilation, editing, and publication of its reports.

The relationship of these activities to the later service of Williamson, both as librarian and as dean, are apparent. He fully under-

stood the needs of the scholars of a great university and the importance of training and investigation in librarianship if American librarians were to meet the exacting demands made upon them in teaching, research, and industry.

The study of library schools begun by Williamson in 1919 for the Carnegie Corporation of New York and published in 1923 requires little comment, since its significance was widely discussed at the time the report was issued and many of the principles set forth in it have been generally applied to education for librarianship. It should be noted, however, that the paper read by Williamson at the Asbury Park conference of the American Library Association in July, 1919, which preceded the investigation and report, contained the suggestion that probably brought into being the Board of Education for Librarianship. In the later full-length report he urged that library schools be connected with universities; that their staffs contain a high percentage of full-time instructors chosen for distinction in training and ability; that the first year of study be general and basic; that specialization be reserved for the second and third years; and that a national examining board be created to formulate requirements concerning library training in general and to pass upon the credentials of library school graduates. The recommendation in the Asbury Park paper, providing for the establishment of a national examining board (similar to that of the British Library Association), charged with the setting-up of minimum standards, the organization of a plan of study, the holding of examinations, and the issuing of credentials, was not carried out in the form contemplated; but the Board on Education for Librarianship, established in 1924, has performed many of the functions suggested in Williamson's recommendations. It dealt with standards and curriculums and became the accrediting body of schools rather than of individuals; and it continues to concern itself with the changing conditions of library service broadly conceived.

The merging of the library schools of the New York State Library and the New York Public Library in 1926 under Williamson's direction, the reorganization of the curriculum of the School of

Library Service, the publication of syllabi for the various courses offered by the school, the development of extensive apparatus and procedures for examinations, experimentation in the development of tests applicable to prospective librarians, the establishment of a series of "Studies in Library Service," the development of a plan of part-time employment of students of the schools of New York and other libraries, and the securing of the endowment for the Melvil Dewey Professorship by the Carnegie Corporation represent other aspects of Williamson's interest in education for librarianship.

Two other activities of Williamson merit comment. Soon after he went to Columbia he found that the publication of the highly important catalog of the Bibliothèque nationale was dragging on interminably. He went to Paris to discuss the matter with the director, Roland Marcel, and secured a grant from the Rockefeller Foundation for Marcel to come to America to consider the matter further. An agreement was worked out with American subscribers to speed up the rate of publication, and a grant was received from the Rockefeller Foundation to supplement library support. As a result of this activity the French government agreed to increase its appropriation for the catalog. In recognition of his interest and the aid secured for the undertaking through him, Williamson was made a Chevalier de la Légion d'Honneur in 1929.

The publication of *Who's Who in Library Service* in 1933 and of the revised edition in 1943, edited by Williamson and Alice L. Jewett, has been of particular significance to librarians. Through the two editions librarians have been able to secure information concerning members of the profession about whom data would otherwise not be so easily available. A third edition of this work appeared in 1955.

CHARLES HARVEY BROWN. After taking his bachelor's and master's degrees from Wesleyan University, Charles Harvey Brown completed his course for the bachelor of library service degree at the New York State Library School in 1901. Then followed a sequence of experiences in a number of important libraries: assistant, Library of Congress (1901–3); classifier, John Crerar Library,

1903–4, reference librarian, 1904–9; assistant librarian, Brooklyn Public Library, 1909–19; and librarian, Iowa State College, 1922–46. During the period 1919–22, he served with the United States Navy, and for three years, 1916–19, he was active in the American Library Association War Service. As president of the Iowa Library Association, the American Library Association, and the Association of College and Reference Libraries, Brown was a constant contributor to the development of the profession. He has been chairman of many committees of the ALA and other groups. He has contributed voluminously to the literature, and is co-author of a treatise on *Circulation Work in College and University Libraries*.

But Brown's singular contribution to librarianship has been his work in the development of scientific and technical collections in American research libraries. As chairman of an ALA subcommittee on German periodicals, Brown was instrumental in clarifying a difficult situation in the importation and pricing of journals emanating from Germany. To this day he has been active in the Association of Research Libraries in analyzing the problem of German serials. Brown has been particularly successful in his dealings with foreign publishers, and this has been attributed to his energy, diplomacy, and tact in handling the situation.

Another of Brown's special interests has been the development of land-grant college libraries. He was the author of the section dealing with the library in the *Survey of Land-Grant Colleges and Universities*, issued by the U.S. Office of Education in 1930. He has worked actively with individual libraries, in addition to his splendid development of the collections at Iowa State, in improving their programs of acquisitions of scientific periodicals. He has served, since his retirement, as bibliographer at Louisiana State University, the University of Florida, and Florida State University. In 1944 he visited China for the purpose of assisting Chinese academic libraries.

H. M. LYDENBERG and HERBERT PUTNAM. Lydenberg and Putnam were not university librarians. They were, however, the librarians of the nation's largest public library (the New York Public Library) and of the Library of Congress, which, under Putnam, became the national library of the United States. Working in cities in which many learned societies, educational foundations, and governmental agencies had their official headquarters, both men were constantly in consultation with librarians and members of these organizations and with individuals and associations in America and abroad interested in aiding scholars through libraries. Lydenberg, in New York, was always at hand to aid in the formulation of such plans as the completion of Sabin's *Dictionary of Books Relating to America*, the publication of the various union lists previously mentioned, and the study of union catalogs, the durability of papers and films, microphotography, foreign importations in times of war, and many other subjects. As consultant and sponsor, his interest ranged over many fields and involved many organizations and agencies. Through the administrative organization of the library under his direction and the experts he utilized in staffing his services, he illustrated the best in administrative planning and practice in American libraries. His service as librarian of the Benjamin Franklin Library in Mexico City, after his retirement in New York, represented still another aspect of his interests. Through this library, established by the American Library Association and the Rockefeller Foundation, he interpreted cultural institutions in the United States to the people of Mexico; and during his term of appointment as director of the International Office of the Board on International Relations of the American Library Association, he extended his services to all parts of the world.

The work of Putnam at the Library of Congress has been fully described in the *Festschrift* published in his honor in 1929 and in the *Fortress of Freedom: The Story of the Library of Congress* (1942). His direction of the war service of the American Library Association in 1917–19 and his assistance to other libraries—through the printing of catalog cards and the publication of classification schedules, the provisions of depository catalogs, the development of the Union Catalog, the provision of consultant and bibliographical service for scholars, and his participation in the conferences of a national and international nature—were characteristic of his entire administration. The availability, for conference and consultation, of both Lydenberg and Putnam to all interested inquirers and the concern which they evidenced in all problems in which library service to scholars was involved splendidly illustrated the variety and scope of interest which it is the privilege of American university librarians to manifest, both within and without the university, in the advancement of teaching and research.

These case histories of the activities of individual librarians might well be supplemented by those of librarians and representatives of other organizations working in groups. The work of the staffs responsible for union catalogs in various parts of the country; of the bibliographical centers at Denver, Philadelphia, and Seattle; of the staff of the Library of Congress; and of the Association of Research Libraries, to mention only a few groups, would, if described in a similar manner, evidence a concern in all these aspects of librarianship and would emphasize a like concern in the solution of problems of cooperation, specialization, bibliography, and documentation which confront librarianship universally. The elimination of wasteful duplication and effort in building up greater resources for research workers, the discovery of means of processing various types of materials more speedily and in a less costly manner, and the extension of this cooperation and understanding to librarians everywhere are still major goals of the university librarian.

A significant development in the relations of university librarians is worthy of a final note. Although there has not been such collaboration of librarians with the presidents and graduate deans of the Association of American Universities as would have been productive of good results, the conference of librarians, presidents, and faculty members at Monticello, Illinois, in October, 1954, marks an important step in the right direction. This is a further extension of the collaboration that was present in the development of the Midwest Inter-Library Center. Some institutions have profited signally by having the librarian in the president's cabinet or on the administrative board of the graduate school. It is to be expected that the future will bring an intensification of this interest in the library on the part of the university administration.

BIBLIOGRAPHY

American Library Association. "ALA Handbook," *ALA Bulletin* (November issue).

Babb, James T. "Andrew Keogh: His Contributions to Yale," *Yale University Library Gazette*, XXIX (1954), 47–60.

Bay, J. Christian. "Frank K. Walter in Retrospect," *College and Research Libraries*, IV (1943), 309–11.

Bishop, William W., and Andrew Keogh (eds.). Essays Offered to Herbert Putnam by His Colleagues and Friends on His Thirtieth Anniversary as Librarian of Congress, 5 April 1929. New Haven, Yale University Press, 1929.

Branscomb, Lewis C. "Bio-bibliographical Study of Ernest Cushing Richardson" (unpublished Ph.D. thesis, University of Chicago, 1954).

Carnovsky, Leon (ed.). International Aspects of Librarianship: Papers Presented before the Eighteenth Annual Conference of the Graduate Library School of the University of Chicago. Chicago, University of Chicago Press, 1943. Also issued as April, 1954, issue of *Library Quarterly*.

Danton, Emily M. (ed.). Pioneering Leaders in Librarianship. First series. Chicago, American Library Association, 1953.

Dawe, George Grosvenor. Melvil Dewey, Seer, Inspirer, Doer, 1851–1931. Lake Placid, N.Y., Lake Placid Club, Melvil Dewey Biografy, 1932.

"Essays in Honor of Charles Harvey Brown," *College and Research Libraries*, VIII (1947), No. 3, Pt. 2.

Foster, William E. "Five Men of '76," *Bulletin of the American Library Association*, XX (1926), 312–23.

Godet, Marcel. "Libraries and Documentation," *Library Quarterly*, IX (1939), 185–92.

Goodrich, Francis L. D. "Theodore Wesley Koch, 1871–1941," *College and Research Libraries*, III (1941), 67–70.

Kilgour, Frederick G. "Justin Winsor," *College and Research Libraries*, III (1941), 64–66.

Lydenberg, Harry M., and Andrew Keogh (eds.). William Warner Bishop: A Tribute, 1941. New Haven, Yale University Press, 1941.

New York Public Library. Bookman's Holiday: Notes and Studies Written and Gathered in Tribute to Harry Miller Lydenberg. New York, New York Public Library, 1943.

[Papers in Honor of Pierce Butler] *Library Quarterly*, Vol. XXII (1952), No. 3.

[Papers in Honor of J. C. M. Hanson] *Library Quarterly*, Vol. IV (1934), No. 2.

[Papers in Honor of Louis R. Wilson] *Library Quarterly*, Vol. XII (1942), No. 3.

Salamanca, Lucy. Fortress of Freedom: The Story of the Library of Congress. Philadelphia, J. B. Lippincott Co., 1942.

"Tenth Anniversary Issue," *College and Research Libraries*, X (1949), No. 4. Includes papers relating to international aspects of library services.

White, Carl M. "The Place of the University in the Modern World," *ALA Bulletin*, XXXIV (1940), 305–18.

Williamson, Charles C., and A. L. Jewett, (eds.). *Who's Who in Library Service*. 2d ed. New York, H. W. Wilson, 1943.

Yale University, Library Staff. Papers in Honor of Andrew Keogh, Librarian of Yale University . . . New Haven. Privately Printed, 1938.

Proceedings, reports, and other papers of the various associations and organizations noted in this chapter. A general source of information on directories of societies and other groups is Winchell, Constance M., *Guide to Reference Books*, 7th ed., Chicago, American Library Association, 1951, pp. 71–73; and *Supplement, 1950–1952* (1954), p. 13. Projects of an international nature are frequently discussed in *American Documentation*, the *Journal of Documentation* (London), the UNESCO *Bulletin for Libraries*, *Libri*, and the Library of Congress *Information Bulletin*.

XVI

PUBLIC RELATIONS: EVALUATION THROUGH RECORDS, REPORTS, AND SURVEYS

AS was pointed out in chapter iii, in which finances are discussed, a number of questions have been raised regarding the activities and costs of university libraries.[1] In his paper at the Monticello Conference, sponsored by the Association of Research Libraries, and attended by librarians representing A.R.L. institutions, presidents of universities belonging to the Association of American Universities, and faculty members, Swank made the following observation:

There never was a great library that was not built by both scholars and librarians, working together—or let us say by people with both interests at heart; indeed, they are a single interest. Yet increasingly the faculty seem unable to diagnose the ailments of the library and librarians to interpret the needs of the faculty. More than ever before, the closest possible rapport is needed. Librarians cannot attain goals that they do not comprehend or about which the university has failed to advise them.[2]

Many librarians have been conscious of this need for effective public relations, even though some of them have been faulty in their approach. Experience has demonstrated that the librarian should maintain a regular evaluation of objectives, finances, book stock,

---

[1] Metcalf, "Why We Need to Be Investigated," *College and Research Libraries*, XV (1954), 383–87.

[2] Swank, "The Cost of Keeping Books" (Paper presented at the Monticello [Ill.] Conference, October 30, 1954), p. 1. The complete report of the conference may be found in Williams (ed.), *Problems and Prospects of the Research Library*.

services, personnel, and building and equipment; that he should utilize friends-of-the-library and other groups in promoting the interests of the library; that he should study ways and means of presenting budget requests effectively to the administration and through it to the boards and legislatures; that he should publish bulletins and other publications which deal with significant collections and related matters; and that he should seek the assistance of the library committee or board in discussing with other university interests subjects of importance to them. It is the purpose of this chapter to examine the program of evaluation followed by university libraries.

RECORDS AND REPORTS   Whether in business, industry, educational institution, governmental unit, or university library, records are kept and reports are made for the purpose of describing situations. University librarians, like administrative officers in other enterprises, are required to submit reports of their work at regular intervals. In addition to annual, semiannual, or monthly reports, the librarian is sometimes called upon to prepare special reports on projects or other activities of the library. The preparation of these reports is an important administrative duty, and involves a careful review and an analysis of the activities of a particular period or of a special project.

RECORDS. In order to describe the performance and measure the success of his organization, it is necessary for the librarian to have available significant and complete records of resources and services. Such records may help to show the accomplishments of the library, costs of its services, and the shortcomings in its organization.[3]

The various records kept by the university library may be conveniently grouped under three categories: (1) service records, (2) cost records, and (3) records of resources. The types of service records which libraries have kept may be summarized as follows:

[3] The question of statistics has been discussed in a challenging way by Rogers, "Measurement and Evaluation," *Library Trends*, III (1954), 177–87. This is a significant article in that the author makes the important point that there should be a direct connection between the use of statistics and effective public relations.

(a) circulation records, which may be gross or classified; (b) records of use of periodicals; (c) records of reference work; (d) records of interlibrary loans and use by non-university clientele; (e) records of the use of bibliographical tools; and (f) records of other or special types of use.

Gross circulation records indicate in a general way the extent of use by faculty, students, and others. Some libraries further break down circulation figures by types of users or of use, to show how the service is distributed, and how it changes from year to year. Some indication of the work done in a library by its clientele may be gathered from data concerning (1) circulation of books from the general library, departmental libraries, and special collections; (2) reserve-book circulation; (3) use of reference and open-shelf collections; (4) use of periodicals, newspapers, microreproductions, maps, and other nonbook materials; (5) use of extension materials; (6) use of books through interlibrary loan; (7) use of bibliographical tools; and (8) use of stacks by readers. Despite the contempt that some writers have leveled at circulation figures, apparently they serve a purpose of providing the librarian with some basis for estimating loads and pressures on personnel and resources.

The importance of keeping records of periodical use was indicated in chapter x. Funds for periodicals and serials comprise a large portion of the annual budget; and, unless some attention is given to the use of these materials, evaluation becomes difficult. This is particularly true of libraries having storage libraries, or participating in interlibrary centers. Decisions to transfer materials are usually based on quantity of use.

Difficulties in keeping an accurate check of reference service have been discussed frequently in library literature. Quantitative data concerning reference service give little information bearing on the quality of service. Rogers [4] has summarized the problems in using statistics of reference service. These are the difficulty in recording all use, the unattainability of qualitative analysis, and the invalidity

[4] *Ibid.*, pp. 180–83.

of appraisal on the basis of "search" and "research," or levels of difficulty in inquiries. A record of questions and sources for answering them, however, provides the reference librarian with a basis for estimating the abilities of personnel, for studying weaknesses in the reference and stack collections, for noting weaknesses in the card catalogs, and for improving the techniques of reference work.[5]

Library expenditures for catalogs and other bibliographical apparatus represent large annual outlays. Few libraries, however, have attempted to keep careful records of the use of such tools. Unless some knowledge is available of the ways staff, students, and faculty members use departmental library catalogs, for example, unnecessary and even misleading practices may be instituted and perpetuated.

Records of the use of materials by the general public, alumni, and other special groups are kept to show the extent of extension service. It is useful to the librarian to know, for instance, whether services to nonstudent and nonfaculty groups require more time than should be spared from the more essential functions of the library.

Two types of cost records are usually kept by the librarian. The first type—gross costs—includes total costs of the library's operation, staff salaries, and cost of supplies and equipment. This type of record provides both the librarian and the university administration with a means of determining the relative emphasis placed upon the library and other units of the institution.

In recent years more attention has been given to the second type of cost records—unit-cost records. Such records reveal the expenditures for specific library operations, such as cataloging, binding, circulation work, or reference service. These data enable the librarian to prepare his budget more intelligently. Without such information the administrator's pleas for funds are based on guesses rather than on specific knowledge of the cost of operations.[6]

[5] Christ, "Recording Reference Service," *College and Research Libraries,* VIII (1947), 23–27.

[6] A series of papers on "Scientific Management in Libraries" appears in the January, 1954, issue of *Library Trends.* The topics concern the scientific method and

Records of the book and other collections are kept by most librarians, although some librarians have no idea of their nonbook holdings. Records of materials needed are accumulated through suggestions made by students, faculty members, and library personnel. With the increase in the availability of microreproductions, the university librarian is in a better position to obtain cheaply copies of materials which would otherwise be unavailable.

Shortcomings of the library may be discovered by careful analyses of its equipment and services. Records of such studies should be available if the opportunity arises for instituting new services or for purchasing additional equipment. A complete inventory of equipment and supplies is essential to avoid unnecessary purchasing and to make it possible to locate apparatus and materials quickly.

REPORTS. As an official stocktaking device, the annual report is the record which the responsible administrator submits to his superior officer. It is the tangible review of the manner in which the library has operated. It serves the librarian and the staff as an instrument of evaluation by giving them the opportunity to examine the achievements of the year, and to learn wherein the library is falling short. It is an important instrument in library public relations.

Reports are parts of the permanent record of the library. Experiments, changes in personnel, and adjustments in organization and methods should be recorded. Events which seem of small importance at one time may later prove significant, if only to save the librarian from repeating errors.

Information concerning the work done should be included in the report, to clarify and reinforce the library's request for support.

---

its place in library administration, as well as practical aspects of management. In the "Introduction," Ralph R. Shaw observes: "Stated in its most fundamental terms, scientific management is really little more than organized common sense. As is true of the scientific method itself, it follows the dictum that man's judgment cannot be better than the information upon which that judgment is based." See also "Management Improvements in Libraries," *College and Research Libraries*, XV (1954), 188–204, and Tauber and Associates, *Technical Services in Libraries*, chap. xxii.

Librarians should not assume that university administrative officials are so familiar with operations and services that they can accept without question requests for increases in the budget; a precise statement of conditions and needs, with justification for any additions, is necessary.

Each university librarian's report also becomes a part of the source material of university librarianship. Together with staff manuals, carefully prepared reports generally provide a fruitful source of information to practicing librarians and students of library problems. Such materials, if available for several years, should make it unnecessary for librarians and students to write for data on current operations and practices.

The librarian is always in competition with other units of the institution for support. The annual report can be one of the most effective methods of educating the trustees, the administration, the legislature (in case of state institutions), the faculty, the alumni, the press, and a number of prominent citizens and patrons generally as to the work and needs of the library. A well-prepared and published report, intelligently distributed to an important group of individuals, will enlist support for library development and encourage gifts.

The following aspects of the library are usually included in an effective report: (1) state of the collections, and a record of important acquisitions; (2) use of the library; (3) statistics of the preparation units; (4) personnel matters, including activities of the staff members; (5) information regarding income and expenditures; (6) descriptions of improvements made in the building or of equipment added; (7) special problems of administration and organization; (8) description of efforts to improve the services of the library; (9) notes of special progress; (10) work of the separate departments or divisions, and (11) recommendations for the future.[7]

[7] See, for example, the recent reports of the Libraries of the University of California (combined report), Cornell, Oklahoma, Stanford, Temple, and Yale Universities.

SURVEYS   Facts reported in regular reports and casual
                                  surveys do not present comprehensively all
that may be desired unless they are related to a program of orientation, action, and systematic planning. The university library, although it differs from a business enterprise in that it is not required
to show a profit, requires periodic checks of its facilities and services for the purpose of measuring efficiency. The annual report,
while useful as a check on the operations and services, may lack the
perspective and breadth of view that are frequently found in a
thorough review or survey of conditions by expert, impartial observers.

The authorization for a survey generally comes from an individual or group within the institution—from the librarian, the faculty
library committee or board, the president, or the board of trustees.
Less frequently, it may come from outside the institution—from an
interested supporting constituency of the university, an educational
or philanthropic foundation, or an accrediting association. A few
libraries have found periodic surveys, for a particular time interval,
useful for planning purposes. Surveys of this type are frequently the
self-survey type.

PURPOSES OF THE SURVEY   While the specific purposes may differ
from survey to survey,[8] common motives have been found and may
be considered from national, regional, university, and local points
of view. These motives may be summarized as follows:

A. National level
   1. To discover how well the library meets the standards of national
      accrediting associations
   2. To determine specifically how the library may cooperate in a
      national plan of integrating library resources through participat-
      ing in bibliographical centers, interlibrary centers, etc.
B. Regional level
   1. To help bring about a greater degree of coordination and co-
      operation among libraries within a particular area

[8] Wilson, "The University Library Survey: Its Results," *College and Research
Libraries*, VIII (1947), 368–75.

2. To minimize the expenditures of individual libraries by concentrating book resources and special services
3. To estimate how effectively the library fits into a pattern of regional service; for a state institution, to estimate its service to other institutional libraries of a state
4. To discover how closely the library meets the standards of state or regional accrediting agencies

C. University level
  1. To determine how effectively the library can support the program of instruction and research
  2. To coordinate the library services on a campus
  3. To serve as a basis for action by the university, the state legislature, or other bodies

D. Library level
  1. To determine the status of the library in its academic setting
  2. To consider factors that limit or contribute to the efficiency of the university library in performing its services
  3. To help the library clarify its aims and functions
  4. To assist the library staff in solving unusual problems of immediate importance
  5. To aid the library in formulating a long-range policy in acquisition and service
  6. To suggest means for improving book and periodical collections, personnel, administrative organization, financial support, facilities and equipment, and use of materials.

In the Chicago and Pennsylvania surveys [9] the primary purposes were to discover facts concerning the collections. A series of specific questions concerning objectives, organization, finance, building, and other matters was presented to the surveyors at Columbia in 1944. The problem at Louisiana State University involved relationships between the growing department of archives of the university and the special collection of materials in the library relating to Louisiana and Louisiana history. At Dartmouth, a program for the future development of the technical services was the major question of the survey. At Cornell, Montana, and other institutions, general surveys were conducted for the purpose of charting a complete blueprint for long-range development of the libraries.

[9] See Bibliography at end of chapter for complete citations to surveys referred to in the following discussion.

TYPES OF SURVEYS   A library survey may be undertaken by the librarian, the faculty, the administration, or all of them in combination. Self-surveys are valuable, and have an important role in library administration. For certain reasons, however, it may be desirable to have surveys made by outside consultants.

SELF-SURVEYS. Any effective librarian is always trying to analyze and evaluate his own library situation. Although sometimes the impetus for a self-survey may come from faculty or administrative pressure, successful librarians operate on the basis of continuous study of organization, facilities, services, and routines. Self-surveys may be directed at clarifying the aims and functions of the library, determining the status of the library, isolating factors which limit or contribute to the efficiency of service, or at specific matters of immediate importance, such as changing the organization, establishing a new departmental library, evaluating book or other collections, examining the acquisition policy, setting up a personnel classification, reviewing the financial support, outlining a building program, or studying operations in the cataloging, binding, reference, or circulation departments.

One may sense this effort of librarians to study their problems by examining annual reports. For example, in his 1952–53 report, the librarian of Yale wrote:

Several years ago we started slowly in a valiant effort to simplify our cataloguing procedures and thus reduce the annual costs per book. Our success is graphically illustrated by the increase in production in the Catalogue Department as shown by the statistics at the end of this report and that of last year. We set up committees to cull our deferred cataloguing section, to survey our serial record files for exchanges, gifts, and purchases as well as the thousands of gift books which come in annually, with the result that we have canceled subscriptions to many serials of doubtful value and are much more critical of the monographs to be retained. We will currently and in the future buy more books and serials in microtext form, primarily to save space on our shelves for more important and more frequently used books.[10]

The Yale librarian further describes the method of handling materials which are classified as "little used." The new program of

[10] Yale University. *Report of the Librarian, 1952–1953*, pp. 6–7.

selective acquisitions and storage by size will allow, according to the librarian, space for books to be added for fifteen years.

Similar examples may be cited from other reports of attempts by librarians to solve not only building problems as related to book collections, but many other problems of operation and service. Such self-examination is designed to provide a basis for future action. In the report of the librarian of the University of Oklahoma for 1953–54, the following statement is made: "One of the major problem areas on which action still must be taken is the formulation of a long-range program of acquisitions for the sound guidance of our future development. The task is not simple and the help of everyone will be needed—the library staff, the Committee on University Libraries, the faculty, and the administration. One of the essential preliminary steps to the statement of acquisition policies is the acquiring of information about the adequacy of our present collections and program to provide a sound basis for the decisions which must be made." [11]

More and more libraries are facing the obligation to support a program of continuous study of problems. Whether these studies are conducted on a general basis or for a specific area of service, the stimulus is the recognition of the fact that the inherited problems of the past must be solved today.

SURVEYS BY OUTSIDERS. Outside surveyors are sometimes called in to serve an institution because detailed analysis of operations and problems has been lacking. This does not mean that the librarian is necessarily unaware of deficiencies. Indeed, many surveys have been initiated by librarians who, through experience and observation, have been able to single out the problem areas. They may have already assembled relevant data on the problems for the use of the surveyors. Although self-surveys are important and should be encouraged, a fresh outside viewpoint is sometimes helpful. In some cases, the exhaustive study of problems by outsiders will confirm conclusions tentatively reached by the librarian and his staff. This confirmation may have beneficial results for the library's program.

[11] University of Oklahoma Libraries, "Annual Report, 1953-54," pp. 2-3.

Frequently, as in the case of a new librarian, it is not possible for the library administrator and members of the staff, with their daily, pressing responsibilities, to engage in a systematic review of problems. Outside consultants with a knowledge of successful practice elsewhere may suggest innovations or solutions which have been applied satisfactorily to problems in other libraries.

Less frequently library surveys are instituted by the university administration or the board of trustees for the purpose of evaluating the services of the incumbent librarian. Such surveys may create delicate situations in the course of the investigations, but they are sometimes necessary for an objective clarification of conditions and relationships.

The selection of surveyors may be made directly by the institution involved, by an interested foundation, or by a library association acting as intermediary. In the case of surveys by accrediting agencies, the selection is made by the agencies.

In recent years, libraries have also been examined by management engineers, either working independently or jointly with library consultants. The Los Angeles Public Library survey was carried out under the supervision of the Los Angeles Bureau of Budget and Efficiency in cooperation with a group of library consultants. The New York Public Library survey represents an example of close cooperation and collaboration with management engineers.[12] The administration of the New York Public Library, however, has consulted with other librarians whenever it has found it desirable to do so. Management specialists, equipment manufacturers, building experts, and office-record consultants have been used by librarians for supplying data which are generally not available in either the professional literature or the experience records of libraries.

[12] Morris, "Techniques of Appraising the Administrative Strength of an Organization," *College and Research Libraries*, XIII (1952), 111-16, and "The Management Consultant in the Library," *College and Research Libraries*, XV (1954), 196-201; Kingery, "A Management Engineering Look at Cataloging," *College and Research Libraries*, XIV (1953), 52-56, and "What Happens When the Management Engineers Leave?" *College and Research Libraries*, XV (1954), 202-4.

A few university libraries have added to their staffs research assistants to work on specific problems. These individuals are usually under the general direction of the librarian, but have considerable latitude for the exercise of initiative and resourcefulness in the investigation of library problems. In most cases, they have not had training or experience in industrial and management engineering.

PROBLEM AREAS   The nature of the problems met by surveyors, of course, differ from library to library. When a total library situation is studied, a typical pattern of problems has generally been considered. This pattern differs only slightly from that found in nonlibrary enterprise. The history of the institution, the governmental relationships, educational objectives, finances, organization, personnel, controls, methods, facilities and equipment, and physical factors are consistently parts of the library survey approach. Integration of the library within the university, the state, the region, and the country, and education for librarianship (in those institutions having or planning training schools) are other factors which are sometimes examined.

HISTORY AND BACKGROUND. Most general surveys include a section on the history and background of the library. This is developed from various institutional and library reports, library committee reports, published materials relating to the university, and other records which are available to the surveyors. The history is important in assessing current problems since it usually provides the basis for the present status and operational problems of the library. Consideration is generally given to the educational and research development of the university in terms of curriculums and faculty, and to the relations of these to the various factors which are involved in an efficient library service.

GOVERNMENTAL RELATIONSHIPS. In some library surveys, it has been found that library service and support have suffered because specific legislation regarding the place and responsibility of the library has been lacking. Surveys have clearly pointed out how

particular library systems might be strengthened by such procedures as codifying regulations, improving the position of the
librarian with respect to knowledge of developments affecting the
library, activating library committees so that they help in library
planning and programs, emphasizing the need of centralization of
administrative direction, pointing out deficiencies in personnel
policy of the university, and indicating ways by which the librarian
can work with the administration and the faculty members. It has
been useful in surveys to refer to successful situations where governmental relationships are concisely stated. These have been discussed in detail in chapter ii.

EDUCATIONAL OBJECTIVES. The library is not merely a passive
organization, responding to the demands made upon it by the university. It is active not only in such response to demands, but it
anticipates the needs for certain kinds of service. The surveyors
generally examine the degree of participation of the library in the
formulation of the educational program of the university, and how
it functions on an active teaching and research level.

FINANCIAL ADMINISTRATION. Funds are essential for carrying on
the library program. It is therefore important to show how well
the library has been financed and how well the funds have been
spent. In both the Cornell and the Stanford surveys, for example, it
was found that the library systems were actually spending more for
library purposes than was usually indicated in their statistical reports. A detailed examination of budgetary procedures will sometimes reveal hidden expenditures which are actually devoted to
library purposes. The study of financial administration will also
suggest improved methods of bookkeeping and accounting, records,
and reporting. Surveys of some state institutions have been instrumental in eliminating roadblocks which occur in the purchasing
of books through state purchasing agents.

ORGANIZATION AND ADMINISTRATION. One of the usual trouble
spots in university library service is faulty organization and administration. At Stanford, the central administration was "found
to be too weak to serve adequately the interests of all instructional

and research departments." In other institutions it has been found that library units have developed without relation to central services. Moreover, surveys have been concerned with the nature of the organizational pattern as a whole—a clear delineation of the objectives of the library, the type of administrative officers necessary and their specific responsibilities, the character and number of positions needed to do the work of the library, and the distribution of the positions. A clear statement of the functions of each person who is placed on the staff is essential.

TECHNICAL SERVICES. In acquisitions, cataloging and classification, binding, and photographic service, operations assume special importance in library administration. Even in small library operations, considerable waste can occur in the use of professional assistants for clerical work. In large operations, which may involve the acquisition, recording, organizing and servicing of materials in all forms on all subjects in many languages, the use of personnel well trained in subject fields and with linguistic ability has been found to be essential. The technical services in an effectively operated library will provide prompt flow of work, economical routines, simple but adequate forms, and proper use of mechanical equipment. Poor technical facilities and operations have frequently been the primary reason for a library's failure to provide effective service. Surveys have revealed that there is a high correlation between failure in technical operations and the ability of the library personnel to provide adequate readers' services.

READERS' SERVICES. The study of readers' services is concerned usually with the calibre of the reference service, the nature and effectiveness of the circulation system and interlibrary loans, and the character and problems of the departmental and branch libraries and special collections. Questions of organization, controls, facilities, collections, and operations are involved here as elsewhere.

PERSONNEL. In the Stanford survey, the portion of the summary concerning personnel began with the statement: "The problems relating to library personnel are among the most urgent confronting the Administration in its effort to improve the library program."

Then followed specific recommendations calling for a reclassification of positions, a listing of needed positions, recruitment of individuals with proper educational background and experience, particular need for personnel with subject specializations, and the inclusion of professional librarians in the membership of the university staff. In most other surveys, considerable attention is given to organization, size and training of the staff, division of professional from clerical activities, working conditions, salary scale, physical quarters, and morale.

COLLECTIONS. Examination of a library's holdings becomes an involved task since acquisition and collections need to be considered in conjunction with a study of the instructional and research plans of the institution. These vary considerably from institution to institution in various time periods, and the considerations of support, distribution of the book funds, and character of the collections call for tailored measurements. The use of various book, periodical, and other lists for checking against a library's collections has been extensive. Such evaluations, however, have been subject to some criticism. It is important to point out the richness of holdings as well as the gaps.

USE OF LIBRARIES. The true evaluation of a library should be arrived at by a study of the extent to which its clientele accomplishes its purposes. Company and other special libraries are compelled constantly to justify their existence—they are either integral parts of the organizations supporting them or they are short-lived. There is no reason why other types of libraries should not justify their expenditures in terms of the achievements of their patrons. For this reason, those engaged in general surveys are keenly conscious of the need to examine user satisfaction and difficulties.

BUILDINGS AND EQUIPMENT. Lack of adequate building space for readers, books, and staff may be a primary reason for a library's troubles in service. In most general surveys, building problems are of a pressing nature. The surveyors are frequently faced with the need to examine plans for new structures, or with the development of plans for renovations or expansions. Unless it is stipulated, surveyors do not draw up plans for a new building. Indications of the essentials of a new structure may be included. Moreover, recommendations may involve working out plans for a better utilization of floor space, the purchase of efficient furniture and other equipment, the installation of modern lighting and ventilating systems, the painting of walls, and so on. Some surveys have included alternative steps for the library in its building program.

COOPERATION. Another general area studied in some of the university library surveys has been state and regional cooperation. In state universities, the problem of support may involve the usual availability of limited funds for all state-aided educational and library facilities. The surveyors are sometimes called upon to outline a program of cooperation which will be designed to make the greatest use of the funds which are available. Specialization in material collecting, exchange programs, coordinated use of standard forms, and other proposals have been developed.

EDUCATION FOR LIBRARIANSHIP. In several of the surveys of university libraries, the development of departments of library science, particularly for the training of school librarians, was also included as a specific objective. Consideration must be given to the general problem of library training in the state and region, and an evaluation must be made of the faculty, curriculums, facilities, and other factors which are essential in an effective library school program.

METHODOLOGY OF SURVEYS   In an observation on the methodology of surveys, Devereux C. Josephs, president of the Carnegie Corporation of New York, remarked that there was some reason to be critical of detailed, statistical analyses. Instead of intensive investigations, replete with questionnaires, interviews, statistical tabulations, charts, and other manipulations, he suggested that serious attention be given to "the perception of a single person." [13] This is the expert, the person with an extensive background in the field, who can size up a situation without unearthing its entire background. Undoubtedly, there are certain cases where the doctor can

[13] Carnegie Corporation of New York, *Annual Report*, 1946, p. 29.

quickly diagnose an ailment, perhaps without even removing his coat. There are many others, however, which require intensive study and research. Similarly, there is a wide range in the methodology of library surveys. Some problems are relatively simple, and require only the expert advice of a specialist in the field. A binding expert can quickly tell whether or not bindings on periodicals are satisfactory; an experienced cataloger can evaluate the cataloging procedures of a library in a relatively short period of time. An experienced librarian, within certain limits, can apply personal judgment to a general library situation, and possibly his conclusions would not be very different from those which had been developed out of a lengthy and detailed survey.

It is not likely, however. A full-scale survey of a library or of some other enterprise has usually come into being because of the difficulties encountered in attempting an evaluation. For example, a detailed analysis may be necessary to change the searching operations in a complex university library system. When all the aspects of a university library are set down, one quickly realizes that only by constant attention to details do the larger elements of service take care of themselves.

Subjective evaluations are part of a survey. Together with objective evidence, obtained through study of documentary materials, testing, assembling of information through questionnaire, interview and visit, checking of lists, and other procedures—the experience of the surveyor is brought to bear on the specific questions involved in the survey. It may be worth while to examine in somewhat more detail the procedures which have been used in surveys of libraries.

DOCUMENTARY MATERIALS. The use of documentary materials— minutes of committees, reports, manuals, correspondence, catalogs, records of various kinds—is a general practice in developing the history and background of the library. Such materials are also useful for other parts of the survey, such as governmental relationships and administrative and departmental practices.

STATISTICAL COMPILATIONS. An examination of past surveys reveals that a principal method of evaluating libraries has been by comparison. This method has taken various forms: (1) the present condition of the library is compared with its condition in preceding years; (2) the library is compared with other aspects of the university; (3) it is compared with libraries of similar institutions; and (4) it is compared with external standards, which are frequently statistical in form.

The procedure of reviewing the library's progress is helpful in revealing long-term trends. Such elements as the book collections, the budget, book use, cataloging production, and professional qualifications and salaries of staff members are analyzed for variations from year to year.

Certain aspects of the library may be examined in relation to comparable aspects of the university as a whole. For example, the variation of library expenditures from year to year may be compared with annual institutional expenditures. This type of comparison is significant only as a real relationship between them can be shown. The growth of enrollment, faculty, curriculums, and special programs needs to be related to library costs.

The method of comparing the surveyed library with similar libraries has been used in many recent surveys. Such factors as book collections and expenditures are compared. This procedure has been facilitated since Works's survey [14] of 1927, in which it was extensively applied and the data made readily available. Since that time, comparable data from an increasing number of university libraries have been recorded. Nevertheless, inter-institutional comparisons are difficult because a number of university libraries do not furnish data concerning their activities; or, if they do, they report so infrequently as to make accurate comparisons all but impossible. When comparisons between institutions are made, one should be certain that data are actually comparable. Thus, a record of expenditures which includes janitorial or student assistance should not be compared directly with one which does not. This requires precise definitions and consistent methods of collecting data.

[14] Works, *College and University Library Problems.*

Probably the most effective way of measuring the work of a library is to examine it in relation to a set of standards. Donker Duyvis [15] has recently discussed the application of standardization to librarianship and bibliography. As he observed, standardization attempts "to bring production to a higher level, to guide and plan judiciously the necessary diversity in order to promote harmony in variety, and to assure that human labor will be used in a worthy way. By eliminating waste of energy and by expelling gradually the inferior varieties in production, standardization should make its contribution to progress." [16] The major and direct aims of standardization are interchangeability, facilitated inspection and control, and facilitated training. While standards in this sense may be applied to librarianship in some areas, such as bibliographic form, periodical format and binding and photographic equipment, the products and materials on the whole are intellectual, and are not easily definable in mathematical and quantitative ways.

The major problem in developing a set of standards in many aspects of librarianship is that institutions vary in their objectives. Consequently, the university which tries to adjust its services to the specific needs of the institution for which it exists differs somewhat from all other university libraries. The quantitative results which national agencies such as the American Library Association, accrediting bodies, and the U.S. Office of Education have arrived at are sometimes reduced to averages and referred to as standards. Actually, they are reports of current practice. However, some aspects of the university library may be evaluated in relation to standards in a broad sense. For example, the plan of government and the administrative organization of the library may be appraised in the light of standards evolved in such fields as business or government. Some effort has been made to arrive at standards through the study of unit costs of certain library activities, such as cataloging. Recent summaries [17] of such studies emphasize the limitations

15 "Standardization as a Tool of Scientific Management," *Library Trends*, II (1954), 410–27.
16 *Ibid.*, p. 410.
17 Reichmann, "Costs of Cataloging," *Library Trends*, II (1953), 290–317; Morsch, "Scientific Management in Cataloging," *Library Trends*, II (1954), 470–83.

for general application. The many variables which are present in cataloging programs make it inadvisable to use such figures to measure production, unless there is a careful definition of the situation. Even then, the figures may be suggestive rather than regarded as standards.

CHECKING HOLDINGS. In addition to comparisons which may be made in regard to size of collections, surveyors frequently have used the device of checking holdings against listings in various bibliographies of books, periodicals, and other materials. Obviously, this is a complex problem, since collections are built on the basis of functions of the university, methods of instruction, and the general past history of purchases, gifts, and exchanges. The use of lists provides some basis for the evaluation of the holdings, particularly if the results are later employed for filling in gaps. In the Chicago survey, 200 members of the staff of the university checked titles appearing in the *Union List of Serials in Libraries in the United States and Canada* for desiderata and in standard subject bibliographies for books. In the Stanford survey, special listings of subject fields included in the *Union List,* certain subjects listed in Hawkins' *Scientific, Medical, and Technical Books Published in the United States of America, 1930–1944,* and periodicals and serials on the English language in *A Bibliography of Writings on the English Language from the Beginning of Printing to the End of 1922* were checked for the library's holdings. At Montana, special lists in business, education, forestry and journalism were checked. The possibilities are endless, and the results are only as valid as are the listings included in the bibliographies.

In most surveys an effort is made to determine serious gaps in the collections. Faculty members are helpful in providing such information. Usually they are requested to furnish reports in their special fields.[18] In the Pennsylvania [19] survey, a pilot study was

[18] Tauber and Wilson, *Report of a Survey of the Library of Montana State University for Montana State University, January–May, 1951.* Appendix C, pp. 151–63, contains a description of the "Estimates and Needs" of the Department of History and Political Science.

[19] David, "On the Survey of a Research Library by Scholars," *College and Research Libraries,* XV (1954), 290–91+.

made to guide the faculty members in their evaluation of the collections. It was designed "to be definite and factual and reveal weaknesses as well as strength."

JOB ANALYSES. Most general surveys include sections dealing with personnel. In fact, it has become abundantly clear that personnel is the key to good library administration. Scientific management has very little value unless related to the people who are managing and are being managed. Detailed descriptions and analyses of all jobs that are present in a library system are essential for any evaluation of the personnel. These analyses are supported by data obtained by questionnaires, interviews, observation, examination of the flow of work, and time and motion tests. Surveyors have to gain the full cooperation of the staff members if the necessary data are to be assembled easily.

OTHER DEVICES. The examination of the various surveys which have been made of university libraries will reveal other measures which have been used by the consultants. Tables 14–16 summarize methods and devices used in appraising personnel, financial support, and resources, respectively. It is possible to discuss at length the advantages and limitations of any of these methods and devices, but it is unlikely that such discussion would add much to the solution of the general problem of measurement. The various methods and devices represent a definite effort on the part of experienced librarians to evaluate the results of their work. Local conditions should determine which of the methods should be employed for a particular library.

RESULTS OF SURVEYS   Seven results may be said to be common to the general surveys, and, to a less extent, to the limited surveys also.[20] In both instances it may not be correct to attribute the results entirely to the effect of the survey since libraries, like other human institutions, are subject to many influences. The surveys, however, have been characterized as probably having exerted the greatest single influence in effecting the results.

[20] These results are discussed in detail in Wilson, "The University Library Survey: Its Results," *College and Research Libraries*, VIII (1947), 368–75; see also Tauber, "Surveys by Librarians," *College and Research Libraries*, XV (1954), 188–96.

TABLE 14: METHODS AND DEVICES USED IN SURVEYING THE PERSONNEL OF UNIVERSITY LIBRARIES

	Cor-nell	Den-ver	Fla.	Ga.	Ind.	Miss.	Mont.	N.H.	N.C.	Notre Dame	S.C.	Stan-ford
FINANCIAL SUPPORT AND SALARIES												
Total expenditures	+×	+	×	×	×	×	+×		+	+	×	×
Comparison of library and faculty salary budget				+	+				+			
Comparison of library salaries with "equivalent" faculty positions				+	+							
Salary range	+				×	+				+×		×
Comparison with standards: ALA				∞	∞							
Average salary				+	+					+		
Average appointing salary			+		+							
SIZE OF THE STAFF												
Number	+×	+	+	+	×	×	+×	+	+	+	×	+
Growth	+		×	×		×						
Number of professional staff in major departments	+				×					+		
Ratio of staff to students			+	+	+				+			+
Ratio of staff to faculty					+				+			
Staff, enrollment and volumes accessioned and cataloged			×								×	
Overtime as a test of adequacy of the size of staff			+		+							
MISCELLANEOUS												
Age	+			+	+	+				+	+	+
Education	+		+	+	+	+	+			+	+	+
Experience	+		+	+	+	+	+			+	+	+
Language abilities	+									+	+	+
Period of service	+						+					+
Professional activities	+			+	+	+	+			+		+
Sex										+		
Status in comparison with faculty	+			+	+		+	+		+	+	+

KEY: + = The Library itself; information and/or statistics for a single year, or comparison with self either at separate dates or over varying periods of time.

× = Comparison with other institutions; information and/or statistics for a single year, or comparison either at separate dates or over varying periods of time.

∞ = Comparison with standards or bibliographies as indicated.

1. First of all, during the course of a survey the attention of the administrative officers and many members of the faculties is centered upon various aspects of library administration and service. Informed thinking about the library generally results in opening the channels of communication for the transmission of ideas about the library among administration, library, and faculty that surveyors frequently find all but closed.

2. The second result is the education of the administration concerning the role of the library in the teaching and research programs of the university. The saying has long been current that it takes a university president at least five years to gain this understanding. If he has not already gained it, the final conference with the surveyors, supported later by the typed, mimeographed, or printed report, gives impetus to the process.

3. A third result sometimes takes the form of the codification of a library policy for the university.

4. Not only is a policy for the library set forth but a program of action for the library is developed.

5. To underwrite the library programs growing out of the surveys, greater financial support has been obtained. This has come principally from two sources: the state legislatures and educational foundations. Increased appropriations have been secured for personnel and books. The funds secured from educational foundations have been used for the purchase of special collections, for the employment of personnel for the inauguration of programs of training, and for the development of bibliographical apparatus.

6. The survey may result in the solution of specific problems in any of the areas which keep the library from maintaining its services on a high level.

7. A final by-product of the surveys is the stimulation of the library staff. Not only is attention focused on the objectives of the university, but it emphasizes the part that individual staff members may play in achieving the aims of the institution. The effect is tonic and leads to more efficient library service. Furthermore, the effect may extend beyond the boundaries of the campus. The

TABLE 15: METHODS AND DEVICES USED IN SURVEYING THE FINANCIAL SUPPORT OF UNIVERSITY LIBRARIES

	Cor-nell	Den-ver	Fla.	Ga.	Ind.	Miss.	Mont.	N.H.	N.C.	Notre Dame	S.C.	Stan-ford
RELATION OF LIBRARY TO PARENT INSTITUTION Comparison of the library budget with the budget of the institution as a whole	+	+	+·	+	+	+	+×	+	+	+	+	+
Percentage of the library budget to the total budget of the institution	+×	+	+∞	+∞	×∞	+∞	+ ×∞	+	+	+	+	
Relation of library expenditure to other educational expenditure in the institution	+×						+×					+
RELATION OF LIBRARY TO OTHER PARTS OF INSTITUTION Departmental instruction and research	+											+
Two departments			+									
English department				+								
Chemistry department				+								
Law school library			+		+							
Medical school library					+							
THE LIBRARY ITSELF Total budget (see also Total income)	+	+								+		×
Total expenditures	+×	+∞	×	×	×	×	+×	+	+	+	+×	+
By class of expenditure (see also tables on Personnel and Resources)	+						+×		+	+'	+	+
Total income (see also Total budget)										+'		
By source							+			+	+	
Expenditures per student	+	+	×	×	×	×	+	+		+	+	+
Comparison with standards: ALA		∞	∞	∞	∞	∞	∞			∞	∞	
Lewis				∞								
Patton				∞								
Randall and Goodrich			∞	∞								
Wilson				∞								
For materials					+					×		
Comparison with standards: ALA					∞							
For services			+		+	+				×		
Expenditures per faculty member			×	×	×	×	+			+	+·	
Comparison with standards: ALA					∞							
Lewis				∞								
Patton				∞								
Distribution of library budget (see also Total expenditures, By class of expenditure)			+	+	+	+	+				+	+
Distribution of periodicals and serials budget by subject fields							+					

KEY: + = The Library itself; information and/or statistics for a single year, or comparison with self either at separate dates or over varying periods of time.

× = Comparison with other institutions; information and/or statistics for a single year, or comparison either at separate dates or over varying periods of time.

∞ = Comparison with standards or bibliographies as indicated.

TABLE 16: METHODS AND DEVICES USED IN SURVEYING THE RESOURCES OF UNIVERSITY LIBRARIES

	Chicago	Cornell	Denver	Fla.	Ga.	Ida.	Ind.	La.	Miss.	Mont.	N.H.	N.C.	Notre Dame	Pa.	S.C.	Stanford
FINANCIAL SUPPORT																
Library as a whole		×	+						×				+×		×	+×
Average annual expenditures			×				×						+		×	
Percentage of university expenditures for books													+			
Per student expenditures for books (see also Table 15)													+			
Departmental libraries		+		+					+				+	+		
Percentage of budget allotted to each							+									
Expenditure per credit hour for each							+									
Departmental estimates of funds needed to bring collections up to satisfactory strength		+							+				+		+	+
Expenditures per subject (see also Departmental libraries)		+					+	+								
SIZE OF THE COLLECTION																
Total volumes	+×	+×	×	×			×	+×	×	+×	+	+×	+×		×	×
By subject, class, or department	+										+	+	+			
Rate of growth	+×	×	×	×			×	+×	×	+×			+×		×	×
CONTENT OF THE COLLECTION																
Faculty evaluation of resources (see also Periodicals and Departmental estimates of funds)							+		+		+		+		+	+
Student reports of failure to obtain materials							+									
Survey of library materials by subject (see also below)	+	+												+		
Checking against bibliographies: "American Book Production 1948," *Publishers' Weekly*, 155:279, Jan. 22, 1949										∞						
Books for Catholic Colleges													∞			
Mohrhardt, *List of Books for Junior College Libraries*									∞							
Number of foreign titles acquired, *Library Quarterly*, 15:313-23, 1945		∞														
Shaw, *List of Books for College Libraries* (* = checked 1931-38 supplement also)				∞			∞		∞	∞*					∞*	
Selected subject bibliographies (see also below)	∞															
Collateral reading material Duplication of materials							+									
Checking against bibliographies: National Council of Teachers of English, *Good Reading*					∞		∞									
North Central Association, *Checklist*							∞									

KEY: + = The Library itself; information and/or statistics for a single year, or comparison with self either at separate dates or over varying periods of time.

× = Comparison with other institutions; information and/or statistics for a single year, or comparison either at separate dates or over varying periods of time.

∞ = Comparison with standards or bibliographies as indicated.

	Chicago	Cornell	Denver	Fla.	Ga.	Ida.	Ind.	La.	Miss.	Mont.	N.H.	N.C.	Notre Dame	Pa.	S.C.	Stanford
Periodicals																
Number of titles		+	+							+ ×				+		+
Comparison of titles received					×							+				
Comparison of volumes accessioned and cataloged												+				
Faculty evaluation of number and quality of titles							+									
Checking against bibliographies:																
Allerding, *List of Engineering Periodicals*						∞										
Art Index				∞												
ARL–Brown, Most-cited scientific periodicals		∞					∞			∞			∞			∞
Chemical periodicals listed in *Science*, 66:385-89, 1929					∞											
"A Classified List of Educational Publications: Periodicals in the United States," *Phi Delta Kappan*, 32:72-93, 1950										∞						
Education Index							∞									
Engineering Index						∞										
Hanford Technical Library Periodical List						∞										
·Litchfield, *Classified List of 4800 Serials Currently Received in the libraries of the University of Pennsylvania and of Bryn Mawr, Haverford and Swarthmore Colleges.*														∞		
Lyle-Trumper, *Periodicals for the College Library* (various eds.)			∞	∞	∞	∞			∞					∞		
Master list made from *Union List of Serials* and supplementary sources	∞															
North Central Association, *Checklist of Periodicals*							∞							∞		
Public Affairs Information Service							∞									
"A Selected List of Modern Scientific Journals," *American Journal of Pharmaceutical Education*, 14:614-24, 1950										∞						
Southern Association of Colleges and Secondary Schools, *Checklist of Periodicals*					∞										∞	
Ulrich's Periodicals Directory, 5th and/or 6th ed.						∞				∞						
"Union List of Biological Periodicals in the Libraries of Duke University, North Carolina State College, University of North Carolina, and the Woman's College"					∞											

KEY: + = The Library itself; information and/or statistics for a single year, or comparison with self either at separate dates or over varying periods of time.

× = Comparison with other institutions; information and/or statistics for a single year, or comparison either at separate dates or over varying periods of time.

∞ = Comparison with standards or bibliographies as indicated.

	Chicago	Cornell	Denver	Fla.	Ga.	Ida.	Ind.	La.	Miss.	Mont.	N.H.	N.C.	Notre Dame	Pa.	S.C.	Stanford
CONTENT OF THE COLLECTION (Continued)																
Reference books																
Checking against bibliographies:																
Mudge-Winchell, *Guide to Reference Books*, 6th ed. and suppls.; 7th ed.	∞						∞			∞			∞		∞	∞
Shores, *Basic Reference Books*, "Core Collection"		∞					∞		∞						∞	
Southern Association of Colleges and Secondary Schools, *Preliminary List of Reference Books*				∞	∞				∞						∞	
Special collections																
Number of volumes and description of collections		+											+			+
Subject fields or collections																
Checking against bibliographies:	∞															
Librarianship:																
ALA books and pamphlets							∞									
H. W. Wilson Co. catalog							∞									
University of Chicago Press catalog, "Library Science"							∞									
Humanities:																
"Bibliographies: Individual Authors," *Literary History of the United States*, v. 3													∞			
Important periodicals and books on English literature listed in *PMLA*, 55:1215-77, 1940		∞.														
The Journalist's Bookshelf and suppls.										∞						
Kennedy, *A Bibliography of Writings on the English Language from the Beginning to the End of 1922*													∞			∞
National Association of Schools of Music, *List of Books on Music* and suppls.										∞						
"Section F: History of Christianity," *A Guide to Historical Literature*													∞			
Thomson, "A Cross-Section of Medieval and Renaissance Holdings in American Libraries," *Progress of Medieval and Renaissance Studies in the United States and Canada*, Bulletin, 16:50-51, 1941													∞			
Thomson, "Monographic Holdings of American Libraries in the Medieval and Renaissance Fields," *Progress of Medieval and Renaissance Studies in the United States and Canada*, Bulletin, 18:28-52, 1944													∞			

KEY: + = The Library itself; information and/or statistics for a single year, or comparison with
self either at separate dates or over varying periods of time.

× = Comparison with other institutions; information and/or statistics for a single year,
or comparison either at separate dates or over varying periods of time.

∞ = Comparison with standards or bibliographies as indicated.

	Chi-cago	Cor-nell	Den-ver	Fla.	Ga.	Ida.	Ind.	La.	Miss.	Mont.	N.H.	N.C.	Notre Dame	Pa.	S.C.	Stan-ford
Science and Technology: *Bibliography and Index of Geology Exclusive of North America,* v. 14						∞										
Hawkins, *Scientific, Medical, and Technical Books Published in the United States of America, 1930-44* and suppls.		∞				∞				∞			∞			∞
Krueger, *Check List of Forestry Items in a Working Library*										∞						
Social Sciences: Bogardus, *Sociology,* 3d ed.						∞										
Bradford, *Marketing Research,* 1st ed.						∞										
Coman, *Sources of Business Information*						∞				∞						
Educational Books of 1946-1949, *Phi Delta Kappan*										∞						
Encyclopedia of the Social Sciences, v. 7, pp. 389-91						∞										
Hicks, *The Federal Union*						∞										
Lerner & Lasswell, *The Policy Sciences*						∞										
A London Bibliography of the Social Sciences		∞														
Sixty Educational Books (1937-39)							∞									
Wilgus, *Development of Hispanic America*																∞
Departmental and school libraries Number of volumes and descriptions in house and/or departmental libraries		+														+.
Comparative growth of libraries in law, medical, and dental schools							+									
Comparison of size of the law library with size of the libraries in the member-institutions of the American Association of Law Schools							×	×								
Comparison of size of the law library with the libraries of the institutions of the American Bar Association survey of approved schools				×			×									

KEY: + = The Library itself; information and/or statistics for a single year, or comparison with self either at separate dates or over varying periods of time.

× = Comparison with other institutions; information and/or statistics for a single year, or comparison either at separate dates or over varying periods of time.

∞ = Comparison with standards or bibliographies as indicated.

survey is read by other librarians in the state, region, and nation. It becomes a part of the professional literature that sets standards and holds up ideals for librarianship generally.

The criticism has been made that university library surveys are very much alike in form and scope, that they are elementary, and that when one is read there is little need to read the others. Such criticism is easy to make but is wide of the mark. They have been somewhat alike because they represent prescriptions for libraries—for different libraries, however—and they are directed at specific as well as general ends. They are elementary because they have been intended for administrative officers and faculty members who are not experts in library administration but whose sympathetic understanding and cooperation are essential to the carrying out of an effective, significant library program. Potentially, they have great strength as instruments for the development of sound public relations.

BIBLIOGRAPHY

American Library Association. A Survey of Libraries in the United States, 4 vols. Chicago, American Library Association, 1926–27.

American Library Association. Board on Salaries, Staff, and Tenure. Classification and Pay Plans for Libraries of Institutions of Higher Education. 2d ed. Vol. III—Universities. Chicago, American Library Association, 1947.

Bibliographical Planning Committee of Philadelphia. A Faculty Survey of the University of Pennsylvania Libraries. Philadelphia, University of Pennsylvania Press, 1940.

—— Philadelphia Libraries; a Survey of Facilities, Needs and Opportunities, a Report to the Carnegie Corporation of New York by the Bibliographical Planning Committee of Philadelphia. Philadelphia, University of Pennsylvania Press, 1942.

—— Philadelphia Libraries and Their Holdings; Data Compiled as Part of a Report on Philadelphia Libraries to the Carnegie Corporation of New York by the Bibliographical Planning Committee of Philadelphia. Philadelphia, University of Pennsylvania Press, 1941.

Blegen, Theodore C., and Keyes D. Metcalf. A Survey of the Libraries of the State Historical Society of Wisconsin and the University of Wisconsin. [Madison?] 1943.

Brown, Charles H. Library Resources in Selected Scientific Subjects at Louisiana State University. [Baton Rouge] Louisiana University Library, 1950.

Burgess, Robert S. "The Sources of Library Statistics" (unpublished Master's thesis, Graduate Library School, University of Chicago, 1942).

Burns, Norman. "Accrediting Procedures with Special Reference to Libraries," *College and Research Libraries*, X (1949), 155–58.

Carlson, William H. The Development and Financial Support of Seven Western and Northwestern State University Libraries. Berkeley, University of California Press, 1938.

Carnegie Corporation of New York. Annual Report. New York, 1946.

Carnovsky, Leon. "Measurements in Library Service," in C. B. Joeckel (ed.), *Current Issues in Library Administration* . . . Chicago, University of Chicago Press, 1939, pp. 240–63.

———— "Self-Evaluation, Or, How Good Is My Library?" *College and Research Libraries*, XV (1954), 290–91.

Christ, Robert W. "Recording Reference Service," *College and Research Libraries*, VIII (1947), 23–27.

"College and University Library Statistics," published annually in February issue of *Bulletin of the American Library Association* (since 1943 in *College and Research Libraries*, most recently in the January issues).

Columbia University Libraries. Reader Survey, Spring, 1953; Analysis of Findings. [New York] 1954.

Coney, Donald, H. H. Henkle, and G. F. Purdy. Report of a Survey of the Indiana University Library for the Indiana University, February—July 1940. Chicago, American Library Association, 1940.

Cresap, McCormick, and Paget. The New York Public Library: Survey of Acquisitions. New York, 1951. Available only on loan.

———— The New York Public Library: Survey of Preparations, Reference Department. New York, 1951. Available only on loan.

David, Charles W. "On the Survey of a Research Library by Scholars," *College and Research Libraries*, XV (1954), 290–91.

Downs, Robert B. The Library Building Situation at Louisiana State University; a Survey Report, with Recommendations. [Baton Rouge? 1947.]

———— Opportunities for Library Cooperation and Coordination in the Richmond Area; Report on a Survey, with Recommendations. [Urbana, Ill. 1947.]

Donker Duyvis, Fritz. "Standardization as a Tool of Scientific Management," *Library Trends*, II (1954), 410–27.

Fayol, Henri. General and Industrial Management. Trans. by Constance Storrs. London, Pitman, 1949.

Hand, Elinor. "A Cost Survey in a University Library," *Library Journal*, LV (1930), 763–66.

Howard, Paul. "Library Staff Manuals and a Theory of Library Management" (unpublished Master's paper, Graduate Library School, University of Chicago, 1939).

Idaho University. Library. "Survey of University Library Holdings," *Bookmark* (University of Idaho), V (Sept., 1952), 1–78.

Iowa State College of Agriculture and Mechanic Arts. Library. Report of Iowa State College Library, 1935–37. Ames, Iowa State College Library, 1938.

Kaiser, John B. "Personnel: The Key to Administration," in C. B. Joeckel (ed.), *Current Issues in Library Administration* . . . Chicago, University of Chicago Press, 1939, pp. 279–300.

Kingery, Robert E. "A Management Engineering Look at Cataloging," *College and Research Libraries*, XIV (1953), 52–56.

———"What Happens When the Management Engineers Leave?" *College and Research Libraries*, XV (1954), 202–4.

Kuhlman, A. F., and Icko Iben. Report of a Survey on the University of Mississippi Library for the University of Mississippi. University, Miss., 1940.

Leupp, Harold L. "The Cost Survey of the University of California Library," in American Library Association, *College and Reference Section Yearbook*, III (1931), 85–93.

Lyle, Guy R. The Administration of the College Library. 2d ed. New York, H. W. Wilson, 1949, chap. xvi.

McCarthy, Stephen A. Report of Survey of the Library of the University of New Hampshire, January—February 1949. [Ithaca, N.Y., 1949.]

McDiarmid, Errett W. The Library Survey: Problems and Methods. Chicago, American Library Association, 1940.

Metcalf, Keyes D. Report on the Harvard University Library: A Study of Present and Prospective Problems. Cambridge, Harvard University Library, 1955.

——— "Why We Need to Be Investigated," *College and Research Libraries*, XV (1954), 383–87+.

Metcalf, Keyes D., and D. H. Clift. Report of a Survey of the University of Minnesota Library, for the University of Minnesota. Chicago, American Library Association, 1949.

Miles, Arnold, and Lowell Martin. Public Administration and the Library. Chicago, University of Chicago Press, 1941.

Miller, Robert A. "Cost Accounting for Libraries: A Technique for Determining the Labor Costs of Acquisition and Cataloging Work" (unpublished Ph.D. thesis, Graduate Library School, University of Chicago, 1936).

Minnesota, University of, Library. "Report of the University Library,

July 1, 1940—June 30, 1941." Presented as manuscript, 1941. This report has a twenty-year summary.

Morris, T. D. "Techniques of Appraising the Administrative Strength of an Organization," *College and Research Libraries*, XIII (1952), 111–16.

—— "The Management Engineer in the Library," *College and Research Libraries*, XV (1954), 196–201.

Morsch, Lucile M. "Scientific Management in Cataloging," *Library Trends*, II (1954), 470–83.

Oklahoma, University of, Libraries. Annual Report, 1953–54. [Norman, 1954.]

Orr, Robert W., and W. H. Carlson. Report of a Survey of the Library of the Texas A. and M. College, October, 1949 to February, 1950. College Station, Tex., Texas A. and M. College, 1950.

Osteen, Phyllis. "In-Service Training of Executives" (unpublished Master's thesis, Columbia University, 1947).

[Potter, A. C.] The Library of Harvard University: Descriptive and Historical Notes. 4th ed. Cambridge, Harvard University Press, 1934.

Randall, William M., and F. L. D. Goodrich. Principles of College Library Administration. 2d ed. Chicago, American Library Association, 1941.

Raney, M. L. University of Chicago Survey, Vol. VII: The University Libraries. Chicago, University of Chicago Press, 1933.

Reeves, Floyd W. "Some General Principles of Administrative Organizations," in C. B. Joeckel (ed.), *Current Issues in Library Administration* . . . Chicago, University of Chicago Press, 1939, pp. 1–21.

Reichmann, Felix. "Costs of Cataloging," *Library Trends*, II (1953), 290–317.

Rogers, Rutherford D. "Measurement and Evaluation," *Library Trends*, III (1954), 177–87.

"Scientific Management in Libraries," *Library Trends*, II (1954), 359–483.

"Statistics for College and University Libraries," issued annually since 1912–13. Now collected by the Princeton University Library.

"Statistics of Southern College and University Libraries," issued annually at the Louisiana State University Library.

Swank, Raynard C. "The Cost of Keeping Books" (paper presented at the Monticello [Ill.] conference, October 30, 1954).

—— Report on Selected Problems of the Technical Departments of the University of Illinois Library. (University of Illinois Library School Occasional Papers, No. 42) Urbana, 1955.

Tauber, Maurice F. "Surveys by Librarians," *College and Research Libraries*, XV (1954), 188–96.

———— A Report on the Technical Services in the Dartmouth College Library, March—May 1952. Hanover, N.H., 1952.

Tauber, Maurice F., and Associates. Technical Services in Libraries. New York, Columbia University Press, 1954.

Tauber, Maurice F., and W. H. Jesse. Report of a Survey of the Libraries of the Virginia Polytechnic Institute for the Virginia Polytechnic Institute, January—May 1949. Blacksburg, Virginia Polytechnic Institute, 1949.

Tauber, Maurice F., and L. Quincy Mumford. Report of a Survey of the Technical Services of the Columbia University Libraries, December 28, 1943—January 8, 1944. New York, Columbia University Libraries, 1947.

Tauber, Maurice F., and E. H. Wilson. Report of a Survey of the Library of Montana State University for Montana State University, January—May 1951. Chicago, American Library Association, 1951.

Thompson, L. S. "Suggestions for Statistical Records," *College and Research Libraries*, VI (1945), 210–18; 322–31.

U.S. Office of Education. "Library Statistics of Colleges and Universities with Enrollments of 5,000 Students or More." Issued annually.

Waples, Douglas, *et al.* The Evaluation of Higher Institutions, Vol. IV: *The Library*. Chicago, University of Chicago Press, 1936.

Wight, Edward A. "Methods and Techniques in Library Surveys," in L. R. Wilson (ed.), *Library Trends* . . . Chicago, University of Chicago Press, 1937, pp. 344–60.

Williams, Edwin E. (ed.). Problems and Prospects of the Research Library. New Brunswick, N.J., Published by the Scarecrow Press for the Association of Research Libraries, 1955.

Wilson, Louis R. A Report on the Mary Reed Library. [Denver] University of Denver, 1947.

———— "The University Library Survey: Its Results," *College and Research Libraries*, VIII (1947), 368–75.

Wilson, Louis R., H. Branscomb, R. M. Dunbar, and G. R. Lyle. Report of a Survey of the University of Georgia Library for the University of Georgia, September—December 1938. Chicago, American Library Association, 1939.

Wilson, Louis R., R. B. Downs, and M. F. Tauber. Report of a Survey of the Libraries of Cornell University for the Library Board of Cornell University, October 1947—February 1948. Ithaca, Cornell University, 1948.

Wilson, Louis R., A. F. Kuhlman, and G. R. Lyle. Report of a Survey of the University of Florida Library for the University of Florida, February—May 1940. Chicago, American Library Association, 1940.

Wilson, Louis R., and F. A. Lundy. Report of a Survey of the Library of the University of Notre Dame for the University of Notre Dame,

November 1950—March 1952. Chicago, American Library Association, 1952.

Wilson, Louis R., K. D. Metcalf, and Donald Coney. A Report on Certain Problems of the Libraries and School of Library Service of Columbia University, 1944. New York, Columbia University Libraries, 1947.

Wilson, Louis R., and M. A. Milczewski (eds.). Libraries of the Southeast, a Report of the Southeastern States Cooperative Library Survey, 1946–47. Chapel Hill, Published for the Southeastern Library Association by the University of North Carolina Press, 1949.

Wilson, Louis R., and Robert W. Orr. Report of a Survey of the Libraries of the Alabama Polytechnic Institute, November 1948—March 1949. Auburn, Alabama Polytechnic Institute, 1949.

Wilson, Louis R., and R. C. Swank. Report of a Survey of the Library of Stanford University for Stanford University, November 1946—March 1947. Chicago, American Library Association, 1947.

Wilson, Louis R., and M. F. Tauber. Report of a Survey of the University of South Carolina Library for the University of South Carolina, February—May 1946. Columbia, University of South Carolina, 1946.

Works, George A. College and University Library Problems: A Study of a Selected Group of Institutions . . . Chicago, American Library Association, 1927.

Yale University. Report of the Librarian, 1952–53. New Haven, 1953.

XVII

PROBLEMS IN

UNIVERSITY LIBRARY DEVELOPMENT

PROBABLY some of the most penetrating discussions, frequently accompanied by detailed reports, of contemporary university library problems have occurred at the conferences of the Association of Research Libraries, which has been meeting regularly since 1932. Briefs of the "Minutes" of this association have been published in *College and Research Libraries* for a number of years. In 1954, it was decided that the full "Minutes" would be available to all librarians who wished to acquire them.

An examination of the "Minutes" of the Association of Research Libraries provides a partial basis for an enumeration and discussion of problems which beset university librarians today. That there is a great need for a systematic program of research into these problems will be evident. Such a program requires the coordinated efforts of the various library associations, university librarians, directors of library schools, teachers, and advanced students. Particularly necessary is the development of methods and procedures, the use of studies which have already been made as bases for other studies, and the assembling of fundamental data which are basic for future studies. Perhaps the contemplated comprehensive investigation of university libraries,[1] under the sponsorship of the Association of American Universities, will provide answers to many questions which are as yet unanswered.

[1] Dix, "Financial Problems of University Libraries"; Metcalf, "Why We Need to Be Investigated," *College and Research Libraries*, XV (1954), 383–87+; Williams (ed.), *Problems and Prospects of the Research Library*.

In addition, some attention was given in the preceding chapters to problems in the field of university librarianship which merited systematic study. It is the purpose of this chapter to bring some of these problems together with those suggested by the A.R.L., the Association of College and Reference Libraries, writers in *Library Trends,* and other groups and individuals, and to relate them to available data. These problems may be conveniently grouped under the following headings: (1) history of university libraries, (2) organization and administration, (3) finance, (4) personnel, (5) technical services, (6) services to readers, (7) bibliography and documentation, (8) book and other collections, (9) cooperation and specialization, and (10) buildings and equipment.

Prior to a discussion of these problems, however, it should be emphasized that because of changes in the Master's program in many library schools, particularly in those which do not require a course in the methodology of research and a thesis, fewer individuals are being trained in research than were before the new programs were established. Although some schools require a project or a thesis, these studies are not of the same calibre as those which were prepared on the advanced level in the former two-year library school programs. With doctoral programs now available at five library schools, there are more persons studying for the doctorate, but the total number is small. Production of doctoral studies in the library schools has been distressingly low.

Allied to this condition is the question of the meager support of research into library problems. In connection with the funds available for 1948–49, Leigh makes the following comment:

In fact, only $4,320 was available in all eight library schools of the sample, compared with more than $1,000,000 for engineering, much more than the $100,000 each for business and for education, about $15,000 each for architecture and law, $8,600 for journalism, and $6,500 for nursing. Only social work received less for this purpose.[2]

[2] Leigh, *The Public Library in the United States,* pp. 212–13; see also Dane, "The Need for a Research Program in Library Problems," *College and Research Libraries.* XVI (1955), 20–23.

Obviously, more financial support of projects, whether by universities, associations, industry, or the government will be necessary if progress is to be made.

HISTORY OF   No comprehensive study of the history of
UNIVERSITY   university libraries in the United States is
LIBRARIES   available at the present time. The study of
Colonial college libraries by Shores covers the period 1638–1800 for nine libraries.[3] Here are discussed the rise, growth, and administration of the college library during the Colonial or pre-Revolutionary period. Its contribution to Colonial higher education is analyzed, and the indebtedness of the modern college library to its predecessor in matters of organization, administration, and use is indicated. Although it does not discuss fully the problem of the content and nature of the book collections and how they were used in the early libraries, the volume is significant in that the author attempts to describe the part which the library played in the beginnings of higher education in America. He has brought together in convenient form a body of material which can be used for further study. In addition to consulting obvious sources —Colonial general histories—the author made personal visits and examined such sources as trustee and faculty minutes, various administrative records, presidents' correspondence, library catalogs, old charging books, speeches and addresses, biographical sketches, and miscellaneous material in order to obtain an accurate description of the origin and growth of these early libraries—Harvard, William and Mary, Yale, Princeton, Columbia, Pennsylvania, Brown, Rutgers, and Dartmouth.

Brough's *Scholar's Workshop* [4] represents an effort to trace the conceptions of library service that developed from the work of Winsor, Dewey, and others in four universities—Chicago, Columbia, Harvard, and Yale. Such questions as the place of the library in the university, the functions of the library, the differentiation of

[3] Shores, *Origins of the American College Library, 1638–1800.*
[4] *Scholar's Workshop: Evolving Conceptions of Library Service.*

services, the nature and extent of collections, the accessibility of books, the kind and amount of aid to be given readers, and the role of the librarian are considered. Despite certain limitations, the volume is well documented and should serve as a source of information to students of university library history. It is by no means a full picture of the historical background of university libraries in America.

Historical aspects of several institutions have been recorded by a number of Master's students.[5] Thus, there are available such studies as those of R. B. Duncan, "History of the George Peabody College Library, 1785–1910," (1940); L. E. Wilcox, "History of the University of Illinois Library, 1868–1897," (1931); T. E. Ratcliffe, "Development of the Building, Policy, and Collections of the University of Illinois Library in Urbana, 1897–1940," (1949); Eliza Atkins, "A History of Fisk University Library and Its Standing in Relation to Libraries of Other Comparable Institutions," (1936); Dora Smith, "History of the University of California Library to 1900," (1936); Joyce F. Bruner, "History of the University of Louisville Libraries to 1953," (1953); and G. S. Bobinski, "Brief History of the Libraries of Western Reserve University to 1952," (1952). Recent doctoral studies on university libraries include those of R. E. Bidlack, "University of Michigan General Library: The History of Its Beginnings, 1837–1852," (1954); C. H. McMullen, "Administration of the University of Chicago Libraries, 1892–1928," (1949), and B. E. Powell, "Development of Libraries in Southern State Universities to 1920," (1946). These last three studies are fairly comprehensive, and should provide bases for further investigations. "Libraries of South Carolina: Their Origins and Early History, 1700–1830" (1944) by Frances L. Spain, also contains materials dealing with academic libraries.

Clemons's study of the University of Virginia Library [6] not only reveals the story of the library at Charlottesville, but it is also a commentary on the history of the university itself. Librarian at

[5] Full citations of these studies may be found in *Library Literature*, under the heading "Library Schools—Theses."
[6] *The University of Virginia Library, 1825–1950.*

Virginia from 1927 to 1950, Clemons approached his subject with a deep understanding of its background and problems. Although there have been several extensive histories of public libraries written by former librarians, this is a pioneer effort in the university library field. Among the features of the volume are the sketches of the first nine librarians, covering the period from 1825 to 1927. Dumas Malone includes a sketch of Clemons in a "Foreword" prepared for the volume.

A number of studies have been made of special departments or practices of libraries. Examples include those made of Illinois in 1936 by Edna R. Ralston on the order department, Evelyn M. Hensel on the catalog department, Kathleen M. Ruckman on gifts and exchanges, and R. W. McComb on the browsing room; of early cataloging practices at Harvard and Yale, by M. Beverley Ruffin in 1935; and of early cataloging practices at Princeton, Columbia, and Pennsylvania, by Ruth Schley in 1946. Mildred Straka in 1951 prepared "An Historical Review of the Cataloging Department of the Columbia University Libraries, 1883–1950." Various historical aspects of university libraries have appeared in the form of articles in journals. K. D. Metcalf and others, for example, have written a series of papers in the *Harvard Library Bulletin* on early Harvard library history, as well as on departments and practices. Contributions to library history have also been prepared for several *Festschriften*, such as F. K. Walter's "Notes on the Beginning of a Mid-West University Library" (Minnesota), which appeared in *Essays Offered to Herbert Putnam* . . . (1929), and Anna M. Monrad's "Historical Notes on the Catalogues and Classifications of the Yale University Library" in *Papers in Honor of Andrew Keogh* . . . (1938).

Rothstein's "The Development of Reference Services" is primarily an evaluative study of one of the major functions of the research library. The author shows that reference service in the modern research library is a development of the interweaving of academic traditions, public library practice, and special librarianship. Such studies should help to clarify the issues in the various areas of librarianship and to guide students in further intensive investigations.

Finally, attention should be called to the chapters on historical backgrounds which appear in the general library surveys. Although these sections are primarily directed at problems of history which relate to the specific survey, they contain materials which should be helpful to the student of library history.

Only through a series of histories of individual libraries will it be possible to write a comprehensive chronicle of university libraries and their role in higher education. Careful historical studies, based upon sound scholarship and keen insight, should go a long way in producing a body of data needed to prepare a definitive study of the American university library. Critically and forcefully, Shera [7] has outlined the nature and defined the purposes and value of library history. A firm believer in the necessity for librarians to have a "clear historical consciousness," he wrote:

Without such a "clear historical consciousness," is the librarian likely "at times to serve his community badly"? Indeed, without such an understanding, he is in constant danger of not serving his community at all. The degree of his success will be largely determined by the extent to which practical considerations are founded upon historical truth. To paraphrase the words of a German writer on archeology, library history is not an esoteric or special branch of knowledge but a synthesis of life itself. When we busy ourselves with library history, librarianship as a whole becomes our subject. History is not an occasional or partial affair, "but a constant balancing on the point of intersection where past and future meet." [8]

ORGANIZATION AND ADMINISTRATION

The controversies which center about certain types of administrative organization will not be settled until systematic studies are made of the efficiency of existing patterns. For example, subjective pressures, rather than objective data supplied by precise studies, have been largely responsible for the building up of departmental

[7] "The Literature of American Library History," *Library Quarterly*, XV (1945), 1–24; and "On the Value of Library History," *Library Quarterly*, XXII (1952), 240–51.

[8] *Ibid.*, p. 251. The quotation at the beginning is from Butler, *An Introduction to Library Science;* the quotation at the end of the passage is from C. W. Ceram [pseud.], *Gods, Graves, and Scholars* (New York, Knopf, 1952), p. 20.

library systems on many campuses. As Swank observed: "It seems to me that any basic consideration of the library problem must begin with the function of the university and the kinds of library service that each requires. It should include the compatibility of these functions in the library, and the economics of their fusion or separation." [9] Undoubtedly, the growth of the departmental system has been linked with the specialization in subject interests which have developed in universities in the last quarter century. Has it been overdone, however? Studies of departmental and branch library systems appear to be essential. Evidence is needed on the question of the relation of reading and research use to the location of books on a campus. If reading and research are not impeded by location, then administrative convenience and economy should prevail. If one system directly increases or measurably facilitates use, then this system should be weighed against administrative questions.

DIVISIONAL ORGANIZATION. "Are subject-divisional types of library organization more expensive to administer than traditional forms?" [10] Objective data are lacking in regard to the general administrative structure of the university library. As was pointed out in chapter iv, proponents of the divisional organization regard it as a progressive step in increasing the use of the library. [11] However, more objective guidance is needed by librarians and university officials who are interested in this development. What kinds of libraries should have divisional organization? How expensive are they to operate?

UNDERGRADUATE LIBRARY. "What are the educational advantages of separate undergraduate or lower-divisional libraries in universities?" [12] The development of the Lamont Library at Harvard, the

[9] "The Cost of Keeping Books" (Paper presented at the Monticello [Ill.] Conference, October 30, 1954), p. 3. The full report is in Williams (ed.), *Problems and Prospects of the Research Library.*

[10] Downs, "Introduction," in "Current Trends in College and University Libraries," *Library Trends,* I (1952), 4. Downs has raised a number of questions which can be answered only through research.

[11] Wilson and Lundy, *Report of a Survey of the Library of the University of Notre Dame,* chaps. iv and vi. The discussion considers many of the questions involved in divisional organization.

[12] Downs, *loc. cit.*

freshman-sophomore library at Minnesota, and the planned undergraduate library at Michigan raise questions which librarians will
need to answer with evidence beyond surmise. Many other universities have undergraduate libraries. Do they serve the purpose for
which they are intended? What are the problems of the undergraduate library in the university?

COMBINING OPERATIONS. What have been the effects of the organization of libraries on the basis of "technical services" and "readers'
services"? [13] This type of organization is likely to be expensive
from the point of view of administrative costs, and librarians are
obligated to show wherein economy or greater production and
improved service are derived from the consolidation of units. No
special study has been made of the consolidations of other units of
the library.

SPECIAL MATERIALS. The organization of special materials in university libraries has always posed a problem of costs and service.
What kinds of segregation are desirable? What are the purposes
and services of special collections departments? What are the
criteria for establishing such departments? To what extent should
there be division of materials on the basis of form—documents,
pamphlets, maps, microreproductions, and manuscripts? While librarians have made considerable headway in organizing special
materials, studies might well be made of the present systems of
handling them.

FINANCE   In many of the basic problems of university
                           librarianship, the problem of finance raises
its evil head. If libraries had sufficient funds, there would be no
reason why they should be investigated in the sense that has been
implied by some critics of libraries. Studies for the purpose of
providing information for changing operations in the interests of

---

[13] A discussion of some of the problems involved is included in Tauber and Associates, *Technical Services in Libraries*, chap. ii. A recent report by the ALA
Division of Cataloging and Classification, Committee on Administration, entitled
"Technical Services: Policy, Organization, and Coordination" (1954) contains data
of a survey made of libraries organized on a "technical services" basis.

economy, or to improve service, are essential. In the chapter dealing with cooperative enterprises, it was pointed out that the idea
of specialization in collecting contained the implication of the
availability of materials to anyone needing them. How true can
this be from a financial point of view? How can individual libraries
afford to set themselves up as reservoirs for materials to be used by
scholars anywhere? Some movement to adjust this is already visible.
A few university libraries have introduced fees for non-university
users, including alumni. Some public libraries have established research information services for industry on a fee basis.[14] Growth of
such agencies as Documentation, Inc., in Washington, D.C., and
the Battelle Memorial Institute, in Columbus, suggests the increased
activity of private agencies in projects that are within the
sphere of responsibility of the research library. Fees appear to be
inevitable unless universities, industry, or the government are willing to alleviate a growing financial burden. It would seem proper
to examine this situation thoroughly. Instead of individual libraries'
setting up institutional fee systems, is there any basis for a national
fee system similar to that used by banking enterprises in their
check charges? The Association of Research Libraries has raised
the question of a clearing house which might possibly be an answer
to the national problem of the use of regional reservoirs of books
and other materials.

Finance is important in other areas as well. As Barnes points out:
"The order department might easily spend the entire income of the
university library. In fact, all money spent on service—on all other
phases of the library machinery—must represent a reduction in
the resources available in the collection. As a result the university
library must choose between services and resources." [15] The implication of this observation is that every new service needs to be
scrutinized carefully for its financial obligations.

A number of the financial problems of university libraries are

[14] John Crerar Library. *Dissemination of Information for Scientific Research and Development.*
[15] The University Library—Services or Resources?" *Library Quarterly,* XXII
(1952), 178.

discussed in a recent issue of *Library Trends*.[16] Essentially the interest of the Dix report [17] was the financial questions involved in library administration. It is apparent that the financial support of a university library is so bound up with the individual institution's program that it is difficult to arrive at generally applicable formulae.[18]

PERSONNEL Some of the problems of personnel were suggested in chapters vii and viii. There remain many unsolved problems to which university librarians and students of personnel should give their attention. For example, what kinds of preparation make for success in university librarianship? What new methods may be devised for the selection, orientation, and development of the library's professional staff? What evaluation may be made of the products of the new programs of library schools? What is the desirable ratio between professional and clerical staff? How far can the university library administration go in using committees of the staff to accomplish basic objectives? How can the placement problem be improved? [19]

Related to the general problem of personnel, of course, is the place of scientific management in the library. In his summary of the papers included in the special issue of *Library Trends* on scientific management, Shaw observed: "In some papers they show conclusively that the 'priceless ingredient' in scientific management is man." [20]

Substantial studies are needed of such areas as supervision and morale, job analysis, the personnel officer in the university library, position classification and pay plans, mobility of staff, and civil service in university libraries. Public relations and the university library staff is another subject that needs extensive exploration.

[16] "Current Acquisitions Trends in American Libraries," *Library Trends*, III (1955), 333–470.
[17] *Op. cit.*
[18] Lundy and Renfro, "Problems Confronting University Libraries," *College and Research Libraries*, XII (1951), 237–40+.
[19] "Current Trends in Personnel Administration," *Library Trends*, III (1954), 3–94.
[20] "Introduction," in "Scientific Management in Libraries," *Library Trends*, II (1954), 360.

University librarians are still confronted with the problem of the appointment of nonlibrarians to important research library posts. Most university administrators are aware that their institutions are likely to be best served when their libraries are entrusted to librarians who are skilled in acquiring, processing, and servicing library materials, in building up a competent staff and maintaining high morale within it, and in furthering teaching and research by means of a nice adjustment of the library to institutional ends. In several instances in the last decade librarians recruited from the ranks of professors and laymen have been replaced by professional librarians. More biographical studies are needed to show the contributions of the professional librarian to the development of library service. It is easy to criticize librarians for shortcomings; it is just as easy to point out the defects, sometimes reaching the point of disaster, of the administrations of some nonlibrarians. The problem requires objective study.

Related to the problem of appointment of nonlibrarians is the basic matter of recruitment into the profession. Not only is this a problem of chief librarians; it is also a problem of departmental librarians, particularly in the sciences and technical fields.[21] Recruitment is still the number one problem of the profession.

A final personnel problem of the university librarian is the question of status. This is a controversial issue, with prominent librarians having opposing views. The controversy, however, is due in part to the confusion which exists as to the nature of the benefits status will confer. Should it confer academic title with equivalents in professorial rank, remuneration, and other benefits? Or should it be concerned primarily with recognition of professional training and experience in terms of service on academic committees, in salary, vacation, insurance, retirement, and other benefits, without reference to academic titles? Point is added to the controversy since in some institutions nonfaculty personnel are largely excluded from institutional benefits, whereas in others, if the profes-

---

[21] Brown, "Librarianship and the Sciences," in Shores (ed.), *Challenges to Librarianship*, pp. 69–91.

sional librarians are not given faculty status, they are automatically classed with the clerical personnel.[22] What are the real advantages to a university in having its professional members of the library staff as part of the faculty? On the basis of the different points of view that persist, apparently the question requires the continuing examination on the part of administrators, librarians, and faculty members.

TECHNICAL SERVICES Mention has been made of the practice of consolidating the technical units—usually acquisitions, cataloging and classification, and binding, and sometimes including photographic reproduction. The report of the Committee on Administration of the ALA Division of Cataloging and Classification has been cited earlier. The study by Reichmann [23] of the relations of the acquisition department to other services of the library throws further light upon this problem of administration. Technical services divisions should be constantly scrutinized from the point of view of economy and efficiency in the library organization.

ACQUISITIONS. Questions relating to the operation of the acquisitions department which require study include such matters as the definition of an acquisition policy, book selection practices, and internal procedures. It has been difficult to generalize about acquisition programs, except on a broad basis, because of the local variations which are involved. For example, what effect has an exchange program on the building up of collections? Should the practice of establishing blanket orders with certain publishers be extended? What improvements can be made in the financial and accounting systems of the acquisitions department? How have the rising costs of books and other materials (such as foreign periodicals) affected the budgets of acquisitions departments? What ef-

[22] Lundy, "Faculty Rank for Professional Librarians," *College and Research Libraries*, XII (1951), 11–19; 109–22; and Carlson, "The Trend toward Academic Recognition of College Librarians," *College and Research Libraries*, XVI (1955), 24–29.
[23] "Management and Operation," *Library Trends*, III (1955), 462–70.

fects have microreproductions had on the procedures of the acquisitions department?

CATALOGING AND CLASSIFICATION. A review of cataloging problems reveals the existence of many basic issues. Primary among these are the revision of the rules of entry for cataloging, control over the growing size of catalogs, maintenance of catalogs, the efficient handling of special materials, improvements in subject cataloging,[24] expansion of cooperative and centralized cataloging,[25] and how to make the catalog a more effective research tool. Such matters as catalog production, transliteration, and levels of cataloging for different types of material have been discussed by members of the Association of Research Libraries in terms of their special needs. Research is needed on the use of catalogs, particularly in connection with divided and classified catalogs.[26]

A recent proposal made by Felix Reichmann of Cornell University suggested the elimination or curtailment of the subject approach in university card catalogs and substitution of an enlarged *Library of Congress Catalog; Books: Subjects* and bibliographies. The recommendation of an A.R.L. Committee which examined this proposal indicated lack of data on which a decision could be made. However, it is an important question which requires the attention of librarians generally.

Suggestions to eliminate systematic classification have also been made. Although some university libraries have organized certain collections by schemes other than systematic classification, most collections are arranged either by the Library of Congress or the Dewey system. Solution of classification problems appear to be an individual library's responsibility, rather than one of general appli-

[24] Lilley, "Evaluation of the Subject Catalog," *American Documentation*, V (1954), 41–60, contains a selected bibliography of studies of the subject catalogs, particularly of those made at the University of California (Berkeley), by W. H. Brett, A. E. Markley, and L. C. Merritt. See also "Standards for Subject Headings: Papers Presented at the DCC Program Meeting, June 24, 1954," by Wyllis E. Wright, Carlyle J. Frarey, and Richard S. Angell, *Journal of Cataloging and Classification*, X (1954), 175–97.

[25] Morsch, "Cooperation and Centralization," *Library Trends*, II (1953), 342–55; contains a lengthy bibliography.

[26] Frarey, "Studies of the Use of the Catalog: Summary and Evaluation," in Tauber (ed.), *The Subject Analysis of Library Materials*.

cation. Undoubtedly, the classified catalog should be given further consideration. Shelving by size and accession number has been followed by some libraries which have set up collections of little-used materials.

Coordinate indexing,[27] which is in use in a number of special libraries, has also been suggested as a possible device for retrieval of information in the university library. It has been applied primarily to the organization of scientific and technical reports. Some limited studies have been made of this system, but there has been no general installation in a university library.

CONSERVATION AND BINDING. Among the problems on the agenda of the Association of Research Libraries in recent years has been the preservation of library materials. Despite the availability of a number of excellent manuals on bookbinding and care of library materials generally, great concern has been expressed regarding the deterioration of books and other publications issued since about 1870 on wood pulp stock.[28] Among the objectives in an acceptable process of preservation listed by Kremer are legibility, permanency, durability, absence of discoloration, special resistances, utilization (usable format), rapidity of execution, and economy. Solutions which have been proposed include sizing, silking, tissuing, transparent coating, laminating with cellulose acetate sheeting, and print transfer. Progress in lamination and restoration has been made through the work and experimentation of Barrow.[29]

The attention of the A.R.L. to matters of preservation represents a step in the right direction. Nevertheless, there have been few studies of problems in the general field of conservation and binding that have been of particular value to the library administrator.[30]

---

[27] Taube and Associates, *Studies in Coordinate Indexing.*

[28] Kremer, "Preservation of Wood Pulp Publications," *College and Research Libraries,* XV (1954), 205–9.

[29] Kremer, *op. cit.;* Barrow, *Procedures and Equipment Used in the Barrow Method of Restoring Manuscripts and Documents,* and "An Evaluation of Document Restoration Processes," *American Documentation,* IV (1953), 50–54.

[30] Stratton, "Library Binding Practices in College and University Libraries." See also bibliographical "Notes" in Tauber and Associates, *Technical Services in Libraries,* pp. 449–54. The January, 1956, issue of *Library Trends* will be concerned with "Conservation of Library Materials."

Charles H. Brown, as chairman of the Serials Committee of the A.R.L., made a number of analyses of the rising costs in binding serials. Another study which might be of value to the librarian involves unit expenditures for binding, repairing, and other conservation practices.[31] No extensive study has been made of the problems and procedures in operating a university library bindery; nor has there been any systematic investigation of university library binding, whether done by outside commercial binders or within the library. Particularly needed are detailed studies of the preservation of fugitive materials, and analyses of such practices as the application of "budget bindings" and plastic adhesives.

Related to the problem of preservation is the policy of discarding materials. With the growth in the size of university libraries, and the increase in deterioration, more attention is being given to the practice of discarding.[32] This represents a basic change in the philosophy of university librarians to retain all materials. It also represents an area in which considerable guidance is needed by librarians generally.

SERVICES
TO READERS

In their survey of problems confronting the university library, Lundy and Renfro[33] found an overwhelming interest expressed by librarians in the organization of books for more effective use. In the section above devoted to "Organization and Administration" attention was given to such matters as divisional organization and the undergraduate library. Additional areas in which investigations are needed are courses of instruction in library use for undergraduate and graduate students, faculty and student use of the library, teaching and counseling services, the use of research specialists on the staff, and extension services. There have been many

[31] For example, Rider, "Does Our Bindery Pay?" Wesleyan University Library, *About Books*, XVIII (1948), 4–5.

[32] Barnes, "The Discard Program of the University of Oregon Library," *The Call Number*, XVI (1954), 6–8; Yale University, *Report of the Librarian, 1952–1953*, pp. 7–8.

[33] "Problems Confronting University Libraries."

articles on some of these problems, and Wilson and his associates [34] have prepared a guide for the college level.

Much experimentation is going on in circulation services. Evaluation of new charging systems is highly desirable.[35] The Princeton plan of opening the collections to all readers and the introduction of "reading oases" also represent steps which require appraisal. Reevaluations are needed of the closed stack policy, carrel use, smoking rooms, reserve book policies, loan periods, systems of fines, and borrowing privileges for outsiders.[36]

BIBLIOGRAPHY AND DOCUMENTATION — University librarians have always been concerned with the development of bibliographical control of the literature in all fields. The conference on bibliographic organization [37] in 1950 explored such areas as "(1) what materials are characteristically most used in each field, (2) what services are available for the location of such materials, (3) what agencies are responsible for the preservation and organization of the materials, and (4) what techniques may be employed to expedite the whole process." The papers in the volume edited by Shera and Egan reveal the looseness of the field, and the need for further studies and concerted attack if the foundations for the solution of bibliographic problems can be adequately laid. In practically every paper there are observations concerning the gaps in the knowledge of librarians and the need of thorough studies in bibliographic management [38] involving the tools, the users, the producing agencies, and "the distribution of the ultimate benefits of effective bibliographic organization and the judicious location of responsibility for support."

[34] Wilson, Lowell, and Reed, *The Library in College Instruction.*

[35] Forrest, "An Experiment in Charging in the Circulation Department, Columbia University Library"; also Stubblefield and Forrest, "Columbia's New Charging System," *College and Research Libraries*, XIV (1953), 381–86.

[36] Interesting questions on all these topics are raised by Hamlin, "Service Report from Pennsylvania," *College and Research Libraries*, XI (1950), 63–68.

[37] Shera and Egan (eds.), *Bibliographic Organization;* Egan (ed.), "The Communication of Specialized Information," *American Documentation*, IV (1953), Nos. 3 and 4.

[38] *Ibid.*, see "Synthesis and Summary," by Egan, esp. p. 263.

Prominent among the topics discussed by the A.R.L. have been those in the area of bibliography and bibliographical control: abstracting, indexing, translating, book catalogs, union lists, preparation of bibliographies (United Nations documents, masters' essays, newspapers on microfilm, drama, Slavic materials, foreign documents, and national congresses are examples), copyright, publishing, and transliteration.

The American Documentation Institute, the organization in the United States that has directed its attention to specific projects in many of the areas of interest to research librarians, has been emphasizing (1) technical developments (printing, and other forms of reproduction, selecting and sorting devices), (2) publication of research materials—both the raw materials and the product, (3) bibliographic improvement in all disciplines, and (4) the study of copyright. The organization has done much to clarify the problems which exist in the preparation, production, dissemination, and recording of technical reports. In this area, it has worked closely with the Special Libraries Association and various scientific and technical groups. University librarians have much to gain by keeping close contact with the studies which are reported in *American Documentation* and the *Journal of Documentation* (London).

BOOK AND OTHER   Problems relating to the book and other
COLLECTIONS   collections of the university library were
discussed in chapters ix–xi. Prominent among these is the growing size of the library. As Vosper noted: "One pressing consequence of the continually speeding race to keep abreast of published materials has been that major research libraries have grown so large as to create a difficult and expensive social problem." [39] The various means that librarians have taken to absorb the large collections and make them easily available to research workers are still in a state of flux. Despite the development

[39] "Resources of University Libraries," *Library Trends*, I (1952), 58–72, esp. p. 67ff. Contains an extensive bibliography on book collections and the problems they bring to libraries.

of photographic reproduction, books apparently are here to stay—at least for a while.[40]

But the questions of how many and what books a university library should collect are not settled matters. One problem that needs further examination is the gift and exchange policies of libraries. On this point, Swank observed: "The librarian's share of guilt in the accumulation of dead wood is greatest in acquisition by gift and exchange. About half of all books added to some libraries are not selected for purchase at all. Some are solicited, some just appear. A great many should be added, but along with the good and relevant material there always arrive tons of stuff that should not." [41] Selection and rejection remain basic questions for which the university librarian must seek suitable answers.

Acquisitional policies in regard to all types of materials that the library collects are also subject to constant reexamination. What should the library collect in the way of archives—institutional, industrial, or governmental? How may the university librarian cooperate with the Society of American Archivists, which has been studying this question? What kinds of maps, manuscripts, and microreproductions should be collected? The possibilities are endless. How are the collections related to the instructional and research programs? What parts do rental collections and paperback books play in the present program of student reading? What are library policies in replacing materials and obtaining out-of-print books? What should be the role of the library in collecting rarities and building up special collections? What sort of an evaluation may be made of exhibit programs of libraries? What kind of insurance of collections is necessary? [42]

Collections in university libraries and in other research libraries have been developed on the basis that they should present all points of view. Although there has been no general attack on the theory

[40] Downs, "Are Books Obsolete?" *Library Journal*, LXXIX (1954), 2269–73.
[41] "The Cost of Keeping Books," p. 9.
[42] Mixer, "New Insurance for Library Collections," *Library Journal*, LXXIX (1954), 1539–43.

that a university library should have in its collections volumes dealing with questionable ideas, there have been instances of pressure, particularly in regard to "labeling." [43] Undoubtedly, this is a current problem which requires the close attention of all librarians.

Problems in building the university book collections concern both the library staff and the faculty. Careful studies are essential if the solutions are not to be arbitrary and short-sighted.

COOPERATION AND   Obviously, one of the goals of cooperative
SPECIALIZATION   enterprises and projects in specialization in
                         collecting is to help solve some of the problems of growth and expanding costs. But how do these cooperative programs function? What have been their real accomplishments? How do they appear when they are subjected to objective evaluation? Mention was made of shortcomings in chapter xiii. All university librarians are interested in estimating the worth of union catalogs, bibliographical centers, interlibrary centers, and programs in specialized acquisitions. Qualitative as well as quantitative studies are necessary if librarians are to be able to introduce definite programs of action. Moreover, such information is essential if existing projects are to receive the support they require, or if new projects are to be started.

Further progress in the area of library cooperation and specialization should include careful self-surveys of many libraries. These are necessary for any aggressive plan of cooperative action. Such studies should aid in formulating definite policies of acquisition so as to eliminate or reduce wasteful competition and duplicate purchasing. Attention is necessary to such problems as the allocation of responsibility for collecting in special fields by groups of libraries, cooperation in use of materials, cooperation in compilation of bibliographies and projects in documentation, cooperative and centralized cataloging and classification, cooperative storage of books and

[43] Clapp, "The Large Research Library," in Dix and Bixler (eds.), *Freedom of Communication*, pp. 38–43; Dix, "Intellectual Freedom," *Library Trends*, III (1955), 299–307.

little-used materials, cooperative filming programs, and cooperation of libraries with learned societies and other organizations interested in research.

BUILDINGS AND   In the "Introduction" to *Library Buildings*
EQUIPMENT   *for Library Service* [44] Fussler makes the fol-
                     lowing comment:

Not only is the ideal library yet to be designed and erected, but the existing approaches to it leave much to be desired. Anyone at all familiar with library buildings will recognize that there are very few libraries— even among the recent ones—that are wholly convenient, pleasant, and efficient places in which to read, study, or work.

Is it, as Fussler further speculates, because librarians do not have a perfect knowledge of what goes on within libraries? Actually, the volume edited by Fussler and the Burchard volume [45] as well as the *Proceedings* of Library Building Plans Institutes conducted by the Association of College and Reference Libraries Building Commit- tee, contain many suggestions that librarians are beginning to erect structures on the basis of functional needs. The university librarian who is planning a new building or a remodeling has much more data to guide him than he did in the 1940's. Some of the innovations in library buildings were discussed in chapter xiv. But there are many questions which still are raised by librarians. What scientific bases can be devised for evaluating and planning library buildings? Are sufficient data available to guide librarians in making decisions on modular construction, compact storage, reading space, illumina- tion, ventilation, flooring and the many other aspects of library buildings? What will be the library building of the future in re- lation to the various cooperative undertakings that have been es- tablished or have been proposed?

Librarians, with access to the latest information in books and

[44] *Library Buildings for Library Service*, p. vi.
[45] Burchard, David, and Boyd, *Planning the University Library Building: A Sum- mary of Discussions by Librarians, Architects and Engineers.* Chap. ix, "Library Planning: A Bibliographical Essay," prepared by LeRoy C. Merritt, is a useful guide to source material on buildings.

journals, have been aware of developments in technology and management. The recent literature of librarianship [46] reveals constant attention to possible applications. As Swank observed, "librarians have tried every useful gadget—from IBM to teletype—that has come to their attention." [47] They have not only tried these new pieces of equipment, but some librarians, such as Ralph R. Shaw and Fremont Rider, have contributed inventions of their own. As a group, however, librarians have not been efficiency experts or mechanically-minded. This may be the penalty which librarianship pays for having recruited its membership largely from those whose basic training has been in language, literature, history, and philosophy rather than in social science, science, and engineering. The profession as a whole is in need of careful evaluation of new equipment and techniques which come upon the market. The pattern set by Shaw in his experiment with the "Photoclerk" is suggestive of the type of testing and appraisal that might well be made with other apparatus designed for library use.

SUMMARY   Only a relatively small number of university library problems which require investigation have been raised in the preceding pages. They should indicate, however, that the field is wide open for study. Librarians have become more introspective and have not been as willing as they have been in the past to accept the status quo or the opinions of the leaders in the profession. It is true, of course, that university librarians are busy people, as their many functions as outlined in this volume amply demonstrate. They have had practical problems to solve in order to meet the diverse demands of an increasing number of users, and in a considerable number of instances they have been eminently successful in doing this. Yet, after a period of rapid progress in handling geometrically increasing book collections, in building new libraries, and in developing larger and more varied staffs, librarians have reached the point where they must reconsider

---

[46] Wilson, "The Challenge of Library Literature to Education for Librarianship, 1923–1953," in Shores (ed.), *Challenges to Librarianship*, 125–40.
[47] "The Cost of Keeping Books," p. 14.

and appraise their activities. Traditional assumptions are being questioned. Librarians must accept these criticisms and carefully examine the foundations of their activity. There is every reason to believe that library service to the university community will in the end be benefitted by such investigation.

BIBLIOGRAPHY

Association of College and Reference Libraries. "Brief of Minutes of Meetings," appearing in various issues of *College and Research Libraries*.

Association of Research Libraries. "Minutes," 1952–55 (mimeographed).

Barnes, E. B. "The University Library—Service or Resources?" *Library Quarterly*, XXII (1952), 177–79.

—— "The Discard Program of the University of Oregon Library," *The Call Number* (University of Oregon Staff Association), XVI (1954), 6–8.

Barrow, W. J. "An Evaluation of Document Restoration Processes," *American Documentation*, IV (1953), 50–54.

—— Procedures and Equipment Used in the Barrow Method of Restoring Manuscripts and Documents. Richmond, Va., 1952.

Berelson, Bernard. "Advanced Study and Research in Librarianship," in his *Education for Librarianship: Papers Presented at the Library Conference of the University of Chicago, August 12–21, 1948.* Chicago, University of Chicago Press, 1949, pp. 207–25.

Brough, Kenneth J. Scholar's Workshop: Evolving Conceptions of Library Service. Urbana, University of Illinois Press, 1953.

Brown, Charles H. "Librarianship and the Sciences," in Shores (ed.), *Challenges to Librarianship*, pp. 69–91.

Burchard, John E., Charles W. David, and Julian P. Boyd. Planning the University Library Building: A Summary of Discussions by Librarians, Architects, and Engineers. Princeton, Princeton University Press, 1949.

Butler, Pierce. An Introduction to Library Science. Chicago, University of Chicago Press, 1933.

Carlson, W. H. "The Trend toward Academic Recognition of College Librarians," *College and Research Libraries*, XVI (1955), 24–29.

Carnovsky, Leon. "Why Graduate Study in Librarianship?" *Library Quarterly*, VII (1937), 246–61.

Clapp, Verner. "The Large Research Library," in Dix and Bixler (eds.), *Freedom of Communication*, 38–43.

Clemons, Harry. The University of Virginia Library, 1825–1950: Story of a Jeffersonian Foundation. Charlottesville, University of Virginia Library, 1954.

"Current Acquisitions Trends in American Libraries," *Library Trends,* III (1955), 333–470.

Dane, Chase. "The Need for a Research Program in Library Problems," *College and Research Libraries,* XVI (1955), 20–23.

Dix, William S. Financial Problems of University Libraries: A Summary. Prepared for the Association of American Universities, March, 1954. Princeton, N.J., 1954 (mimeographed).

——— "Intellectural Freedom," *Library Trends,* III (1955), 299–307.

Dix, William S., and Paul Bixler (eds.). Freedom of Communication: Proceedings of the First Conference on Intellectural Freedom, New York City, June 28–29, 1952. Chicago, American Library Association, 1954.

Downs, Robert B. "Are Books Obsolete?" *Library Journal,* LXXIX (1954), 2269–73.

——— "Introduction," in "Current Trends in College and University Libraries," *Library Trends,* I (1952), 3–7.

Egan, Margaret E. (ed.). The Communication of Specialized Information: Papers presented before the Seventeenth Annual Conference of the Graduate Library School of the University of Chicago, August 11–15, 1952. Chicago [University of Chicago] 1954. Also appeared in *American Documentation,* IV (1953), Nos. 3–4.

Forrest, Fred H. "An Experiment in Charging in the Circulation Department, Columbia University Library" (unpublished Master's essay, Columbia University, 1952).

Frarey, Carlyle J. "Studies of the Use of the Catalog: Summary and Evaluation," in Tauber (ed.), *The Subject Analysis of Library Materials.*

Fussler, Herman H. (ed.). The Function of the Library in the Modern College: Papers Presented before the Nineteenth Annual Conference of the University of Chicago, June 14–18, 1954. Chicago, University of Chicago, Graduate Library School, 1954. Also published in *Library Quarterly,* October, 1954.

——— Library Buildings for Library Service: Papers Presented before the Library Institute at the University of Chicago, August 5–10, 1946. Chicago, American Library Association, 1947.

Hamlin, Arthur T. "Service Report from Pennsylvania," *College and Research Libraries,* XI (1950), 63–68.

John Crerar Library. Dissemination of Information for Scientific Research and Development, with Special Reference to the Work of the Research Information Service. Chicago, 1954.

Kremer, Alvin W. "Preservation of Wood Pulp Publications," *College and Research Libraries,* XV (1954), 205–9.

Leigh, Robert D. The Public Library in the United States. New York, Columbia University Press, 1950.

Library Literature. New York, H. W. Wilson, 1946–54.

Library Trends. Urbana, University of Illinois Library School. See especially issues of July, 1952; July and October, 1954; April, July, and October, 1955.

Lilley, Oliver L. "Evaluation of the Subject Catalog," *American Documentation*, V (1954), 41–60.

Lundy, Frank A. "Faculty Rank for Professional Librarians," *College and Research Libraries*, XII (1951), 11–19, 109–22.

Lundy, Frank A., and Kathryn R. Renfro. "Problems Confronting University Libraries," *College and Research Libraries*, XII (1951), 237–40.

Metcalf, Keyes D. "Financial Problems of University Libraries: A Proposal for a Conference," *Harvard Library Bulletin*, VIII (1954), 5–13.

——— "University Libraries Face the Future," *Library Quarterly*, XXII (1952), 5–12.

——— "Why We Need to Be Investigated," *College and Research Libraries*, XV (1954), 383–87.

Mixer, Charles W. "New Insurance for Library Collections," *Library Journal*, LXXXIX (1954), 1539–43.

Morsch, Lucile M. "Cooperation and Centralization," *Library Trends*, II (1953), 342–55.

Reichmann, Felix. "Management and Operation," *Library Trends*, III (1955), 462–70.

Rider, Fremont. "Does Our Bindery Pay?" Wesleyan University Library, *About Books*, XVIII (1948), 4–5.

Shaw, Ralph R. "Introduction," in "Scientific Management in Libraries," *Library Trends*, II (1954), 359–60.

——— The Use of Photography for Clerical Routines: A Report to the American Council of Learned Societies. Washington, American Council of Learned Societies, 1953.

Shera, Jesse H. "The Literature of American Library History," *Library Quarterly*, XV (1945), 1–24.

——— "On the Value of Library History," *Library Quarterly*, XXII (1952), 240–51.

Shera, Jesse H., and Margaret E. Egan (eds.). Bibliographic Organization: Papers Presented before the Fifteenth Annual Conference of the Graduate Library School, July 24–29, 1950. Chicago, University of Chicago Press, 1951.

Shores, Louis. Origins of the American College Library, 1638–1800. Nashville, Tenn., George Peabody College, 1934.

Shores, Louis (ed.). Challenges to Librarianship. (Florida State University Studies, No. 12.) Tallahassee, Florida State University, 1953.

"Standards for Subject Headings: Papers Presented at the DCC Program Meeting, June 24, 1954," by Wyllis E. Wright, Carlyle J. Frarey, and Richard S. Angell, *Journal of Cataloging and Classification*, X (1954), 175–78.

Staveley, Ronald. Notes on Modern Bibliography. London, The Library Association, 1954.

Stratton, John B. "Library Binding Practices in College and University Libraries" (unpublished Master's essay, Columbia University, 1952).

Stubblefield, Louise, and Fred H. Forrest. "Columbia's New Charging System," *College and Research Libraries*, XIV (1953), 381–86.

Swank, Raynard C. "The Cost of Keeping Books" (Paper presented at the Monticello [Ill.] Conference, October 30, 1954) (mimeographed).

Taube, Mortimer and Associates. Studies in Coordinate Indexing. Washington, D.C., Documentation, Inc., 1953–54.

Tauber, Maurice F. (ed.). The Subject Analysis of Library Materials. New York, School of Library Service, Columbia University, 1953.

Tauber, Maurice F. and Associates. Technical Services in Libraries. New York, Columbia University Press, 1954. Chaps. xxi and xxii.

Vosper, Robert. "Resources of University Libraries," *Library Trends*, I (1952), 58–72.

Williams, Edwin E. (ed.). Problems and Prospects of the Research Library. New Brunswick, N.J., Published by the Scarecrow Press for the Association of Research Libraries, 1955.

Wilson, Louis R. "The Challenge of Library Literature to Education for Librarianship, 1923–1953," in Louis Shores (ed.), *Challenges to Librarianship*. (Florida State University Studies, No. 12), Tallahassee, Florida State University, 1953, pp. 125–40.

Wilson, Louis R., Mildred H. Lowell, and Sarah R. Reed. The Library in College Instruction. New York, H. W. Wilson, 1951.

Wilson, Louis R., and Frank A. Lundy. Report of a Survey of the Library of the University of Notre Dame for the University of Notre Dame, November 1950—March 1952. Chicago, American Library Association, 1952.

Yale University. Report of the Librarian, 1952–1953. New Haven, 1953.

See also annual reports and surveys of individual libraries.

INDEX

Abstracts of dissertations, 396
Academic status: assistant librarian, 321; librarian, 22-23, 37, 53, 321; library staff, 37, 61, 287, 298, 320-22, 596-97
Accessioning: trend away from, 189
Accessions: mimeographed list of, 351
Accounting and financial reporting, 101-9
Accounting methods, 103-5
Acquisition department, 161-74; duties of administrative officer, 162-63; information as to free balance of funds, 106; organization, 165-66; personnel, 166; physical quarters, 511-12; principal object, 209; problems of, 597-98; training of assistants, 277; work week, 306
Acquisition of materials: aid of Library of Congress, 23; allocation of funds for, 45; cooperation between faculty and librarian, 46; purchasing procedures, 60; unusual sets or collections, 48
Acquisition policy, 603; elements of program, 348-55; governed by university program, 19-20; long-term project, 358, 561; responsibility for, 349-52
Administration: theory of, 115-22; applied to libraries, 122-41; see also University library administration
Administrative assistant, see Assistant to the librarian
Administrative board, university: functions, 41-42
Administrative office assistant: salary, 302
Administrative officers of university library, 125-27; titles, 126
Adult Education Association: participation of university librarians in, 528
Agricultural extension: relation to librarian, 50-51

Air conditioning: in library building, 490, 516-17; of carrels, 500; use in preservation of materials, 517
Air University: library, 28
Alabama, University of: ratio of library expenditures to faculty, 98
Alabama Polytechnic Institute: library survey, 10
Alumni: library service to, 66, 245-46
American Archivist, 401; publication program, 8
American Association of Law Libraries: aid in exchange of duplicate materials, 170; participation of university librarians in, 527
American Association of University Professors: membership of librarians in, 336, 528; University of Kentucky chapter, 321
American Association of University Women: participation of university librarians in, 528
American Committee on Intellectual Cooperation: demonstration of microphotography, 542
American Council of Learned Societies: aid in research projects, 6; participation of university librarians in, 528; sponsor of *Census of Medieval and Renaissance Manuscripts,* 536; sponsor of *List of Serial Publications of Foreign Governments,* 536
American Council on Education: participation of university librarians in, 528
American Documentation: publication program, 8; reports on experiments in photographic applications to librarianship, 201
American Documentation Institute, 602; microfilm projects, 475; participation of university librarians in, 528
American Historical Association: Com-

American Historical Association (*Cont.*)
mittee on Bibliography, 534; concern
with archival collections, 401; policy
on handling of manuscripts, 398-400
American Imprints Inventory, 460
Americanization studies (A. T. Burns):
Williamson's connection with, 544
American Library Association: aban-
donment of placement service, 285;
advice as to selection of chief librarian, 283; Board of Education for
Librarianship, 264, 268; Personnel Administration, 291; Board on Resources
of American Libraries, 473; cataloging
rules, 188; Committee on Annuities,
Pensions, and Life Insurance, 324;
Committee on Cooperative Microfilm
Projects, 388; concern with problem
of newspapers in libraries, 388; concern with technical standards in microfilming, 473; Cooperative Cataloging Committee, 457; Division of Cataloging and Classification, 180, 192, 527,
597; efforts toward international library cooperation, 475; founders, 530,
531; organization, 457; participation
of university librarians in, 527; personnel classification and pay plans, 96;
Public Documents Committee, 380;
relations with Library Binding Institute, 197; Retirement Plan, 326; salary
recommendations for junior professional librarians, 303; sponsor of *List
of Serial Publications of Foreign
Governments*, 536; Staff Organizations Round Table, 336; statistical
compilations, 11; study of use of university libraries by graduate students,
218; support of bibliographic projects,
459; *Survey*, 9
American Library Institute, 531
American Newspapers, 1821–1936
(Gregory), 460, 537; Gerould's part
in, 536
American Philosophical Society: American history sources in, 217
American Society of Heating and
Ventilating Engineers: definition of
air conditioning, 516
American Standards Association: participation of university librarians in,
528
American Teachers Union, 335
American Theological Library Associa-

tion: participation of university librarians in, 527
*American Universities and Colleges:
1952*, 90
Amherst College: Dewey's librarianship
of, 531
Andrews, C. W.: committee member
on *Union List of Serials*, 536
Annuities: handled by business office,
61; *see also* Retirement plans
Applications file, 285
Architect: role in planning building,
488
Architectural effect: in library construction, 486
Archival materials: acquisition by university library, 398, 400-403, 603; collection at Virginia, 7; handling, 235-
36, 402; research material, 368; rooms
for collections of, 508
Arizona: legislation affecting libraries
of state institutions, 29
Armed Forces Medical Library: participation of university librarians in,
528
Army Map Service, 237, 405
Assembly of Librarians of the Americas, 476
Assistant librarian: academic status, 321;
as head of general readers' department, 213-14; duties, 128-29; office,
512; promotion of other staff member
to position, 314-15; promotion to
chief librarianship, 313-14; relation to
departmental heads, 140; relation to
librarian, 132, 134; salary, 300-301
(*tab.*), 301-2; training, 273-74
Assistant to the librarian: duties, 140-41
Associate librarian: salary, 301-2; training, 273-74
Associates of the library, *see* Friends
of the library
Association of American Library
Schools: participation of university
librarians in, 527
Association of American Universities,
549; participation of university librarians in, 528; sponsor of investigation of university libraries, 586
Association of American University
Presses, 17, 63
Association of College and Reference
Libraries, 91, 587; aid in exchange of
duplicate materials, 170; aid in place-

ment, 285; Building Committee, 605; building discussions, 488; efforts to compile salary statistics, 296; establishment, 8; microfilm projects, 475; participation of university librarians in, 527; statistical compilations, 11, 101; support of bibliographic projects, 459
Association of Land-Grant Colleges and Universities: participation of university librarians in, 528
Association of Research Libraries, 82, 91, 109, 460; C. H. Brown's activity in, 547; Committee on the Use of Manuscripts by Visiting Scholars, 204; concern with problem of newspapers in libraries, 386, 388; discussions of contemporary university library problems, 586; interest in cooperative cataloging practices, 459; interest in preservation of different types of material, 198, 599; microfilm projects, 473, 475; organization of, 8, 537; participation of university librarians in, 527; policy on handling of manuscripts, 398-400; proposal for use of regional reservoirs of library materials, 594; sponsorship of Monticello Conference, 552; standardization of subject headings, 180; support of bibliographic projects, 459
Atlanta: union catalog, 54, 463
Atlases: sources for selection, 405-6
Atomic Energy Commission: distribution of publications, 378; science fellowships, 6
Auditory materials: collections in university libraries, 418
Austen, Willard: committee member on Union List of Serials, 536
Austin, Texas: union catalog, 463
Australian Commonwealth National Library: Annual Catalog of Australian Publications, 384
Austria: dissertations prepared in, 396
Author entries: simplification, 192
Authority file: sometimes combined with official catalog, 181
Authority in library administration, 118
Authors' readings: promotion of reading habit through, 56

Bachelor's degree, for library training, 264

Baltimore Public Library, see Enoch Pratt Free Library
Bancroft fund: allocation to purchase of materials in American history, 82
Barnes, E. B.: quoted on distribution of library income, 594
Barr, Pelham: criticism of library binding practices, 193-94
Barrow, W. J.: cited on preservation of materials, 599
Basic books: in library collections, 356
Battelle Memorial Institute, 594
Belgium: dissertations prepared in, 396; library training in, 269
Belgium. Bibliothèque Royale: Bibliographie de Belgique, 384
Benjamin Franklin Library in Mexico City: Lydenberg's librarianship of, 548
Bennett, Fleming: cited on acquisition of current books, 367
Berelson, Bernard: Education for Librarianship, 9; quoted on advanced training in librarianship, 265
Berlin, University of: courses in librarianship, 268
Bibliographers: service to library users, 442; training, 277
Bibliographical apparatus: aid to scholarly use of library, 443-44
Bibliographical Center for Research, Denver, 463
Bibliographical centers, 24, 54, 462-65; aid in exchange of duplicate materials, 170; aid to scholarly use of library, 443-44; cooperative purchasing programs, 78; interest of university librarians in, 529
"Bibliographical Organization, Basic Study of," 444
Bibliographical services: information to faculty, 46
Bibliographical Society of America, 536; founders, 538; participation of university librarians in, 528
Bibliographical Society of the University of Virginia: participation of university librarians in, 528
Bibliographical works: efforts to relate to card catalog, 511; for cataloging department, 187-88
Bibliographie de la France, Supplément F, 384

Bibliographies: checking for book selection, 357-58; cooperative enterprises, 8, 459-62; provision for research institutes, 50

Bibliographie sélective des publications officielles françaises, 384

Bibliography: courses in, 46, 56; problems in, 601-2

Bibliography: Practical, Enumerative, Historical, 535

Bibliography of Research Studies in Education, 460

Bibliography of Writings on the English Language, 571

Bibliothèque nationale: catalog, 546; individual storage library, 469

Billings, John Shaw: contributions to scholarship, 272

Bills, duplicate, *see* Dealer's file

Binderies, commercial, 196-97

Binderies, library, 195-96, 600

Binding, 599-60; centralization of funds for, 99; costs, 196, 600; funds, 193; repair work, 197; special materials, 197-98

Binding department, 193-98; apparatus, 519; organization, 194-95; physical quarters, 513

Binding librarian: responsibilities, 194-95

Binney, Horace: establishment of Stephen Girard Trust, 368

Bishop, William Warner: professional career, 538-41

Bitting, Barbara, 324

Boggs, S. W., and Dorothy C. Lewis: quoted on map organization, 406-7

Bookbinding, *see* Binding

Book club members, *see* Friends of the Library

Book collecting: technical procedures, 355-61

Book collections, 367; problems, 602-4; purchase *en bloc,* 360-61; records, 556; *see also* Acquisition policy

Book dealers: single dealer for current American titles, 168

Book fund: allocation, 100, 351; definition, 99; distribution, 99-101; relation to acquisitions department load, 162; status, 350

Book jackets: display, 430

Bookkeeping, 73; centralization, 105-6; records, 106-7

Book lists, annotated: for students, 430

Bookplates: for gift materials, 174

Books: in university library collection, 366-72; purchasing, 75; storage space in library building, 490

Book selection: decentralization, 119; originating with faculty members, 163

Book selector (*term*), 355-56

Bookstacks, 228; construction and equipment, 499; dimensions of room, 497-99; free access to, 499; horizontal expansion, 496; location, 495-99; underground, 496-97; vertical extension, 496

Bookstore, university: relations of library with, 64, 437; stimulation of reading habit, 56, 435-38

Born, L. K.: cited on cooperative microfilming, 473, 474

Borrowing privileges: uniformity, 221

Boston: library collecting agreements in, 467

Boston Public Library: additions to national Union Catalog, 462; Winsor's report on activities, 530

Boston University Library: American history sources in, 217; classified catalog, 177

Bostwick, Arthur E.: committee member on *Union List of Serials,* 536

Branch libraries, 592

Branscomb, Lewis C.: study of gift policies of university libraries, 173

Briet, Suzanne: cited on library training in Europe, 267

British government documents: acquisition by university library, 383-85

British Library Association, 531; control of education for librarianship, 268

British Museum: catalog, 461; individual storage library, 469

Broadsides: collections of, in university libraries, 410

Broberg, J. W., and R. E. Dunbar: questionnaire on chemistry department libraries, 211-12

Brochures: collections in university libraries, 410; for gift materials, 174

Brooklyn Public Library: scientific management in, 124

Brough, Kenneth J.: quoted on instruction in use of library, 439; *Scholar's Workshop,* 10, 588

Brown, Charles Harvey: analyses of

rising costs in binding serials, 600; cited on cost of interlibrary loans, 454; cited on special librarianship, 277; professional career, 546-47

Brown, Charles Harvey, and H. G. Bousfield: *Circulation Work in College and University Libraries*, 9

Brown, Lloyd A.: cited on handling of maps, 407

Brown University: library committee, 39; name, 13

Brown University Library: American history sources in, 217; broadsides collection, 410; divisional reading rooms, 504; Friends of the Library, 354; history, 588; incunabula collection, 403; musical recordings, 408, 418; subject arrangement, 146

Browsing rooms, 28-30, 504-5; control by circulation department, 222; effectiveness, 229; promotion of reading habit through, 56, 433-34

Bryan, Alice I.: cited on civil service in libraries, 288

Bryn Mawr College: name, 14

Budget, 94-101; formula, 20; comparison with other years, 95; periodical subscriptions, 373; procedures, 58-59, 93-101

Budgeting: as element of administration, 117

Buildings and grounds office: relations with librarian, 62

Burchard, John E. and others; cited on library buildings, 605; *Planning the University Library Building*, 9; quoted on air conditioning, 516; quoted on flexibility in library building, 493-94; quoted on lighting, 515, 516

Business manager, university: functions, 72

Business office, university: accounting responsibility for book orders, 104; relation to librarian, 57-62

Butler, Pierce, *Librarians, Scholars, and Booksellers at Mid-Century*, 10

Butts, R. Freeman: discussion of function of university, 14-15

Cabeen, Violet A.: quoted on foreign documents, 383

Calculating machines: use in library, 519

California: depositories of state documents in other states, 380

California, University of: doctorate in library work, 265-66; enrollment (1954), 4; ratio of library expenditures to faculty, 98; report of Library Committee, Academic Senate, Northern Section, 83-90

California, University of, Library: aid to smaller libraries, 452; assistant librarians, 134; catalog department, 178-79 (*charts*), 183, 185; general organization, 139 (*chart*) gift policy, 170, 173; gifts and exchange department, 171 (*chart*); guide to manuscript collection, 398; history, 589; hours of student assistance, 261; inactivity in publishing bibliographical guides, 461; loan department, 219, 220 (*chart*), 222; map collection, 405; microfilm collection, 416; musical recordings, 408, 418; newspaper acquisition, 388; nonmusical recordings, 418; order department, 167 (*chart*); periodical collection, 372; photographic service, 198, 199 (*chart*); ranking system of staff, 256; serial department, 234 (*chart*); *Staff Manual*, 329-30; use of punched-card systems, 107; Western history collection, 7

California, University of (Los Angeles): ratio of library expenditures to total institutional expenditures, 97

California, University of (Los Angeles), Library: "Branch Library Code," 152; interlibrary loans, 451; microfilm collection, 416

California State Library: newspaper acquisition, 388; union catalog, 463

Canada: dissertations prepared in, 396; official bibliographies of government documents, 384

Canadian Library Association: participation of university librarians in, 527

Card catalog, see Catalog

Carlson, W. H. (ed.): *College and University Libraries and Librarianship*, 9

Carnegie Corporation of New York: aid in research projects, 6; participation of university librarians in, 528; study of library schools, 545; W. W. Bishop's service to, 538-39

Carnegie Endowment for International Peace: participation of university librarians in, 528

Carnegie Foundation for the Advancement of Teaching: participation of university librarians in, 528

Carnegie Institution of Washington: participation of university librarians in, 528

Carnovsky, Leon: quoted on education for librarianship in Europe, 269

Carrels, 499-500, 505

Case histories: former university librarians, 530-49

Catalog, 177, 180; adequacy, 21; assistance by catalogers in use of, 190; development, 175-76; insurance on, 80; interest of university librarians in, 529; location, 510-11; maintenance, 191; microfilm copy, 80; provisions for special libraries, 48-49; publication, 7; records of expenditures for, 555; utility, 192-93; see also Classified catalog; Dictionary catalog; Divided catalog

Catalog department, 175-93; administrative standards, 188; duties of chief, 186-87; location, 181; measurement of efficiency, 188-89; organization and administration, 182-87; personnel, 186; physical quarters, 511-12; reference and bibliographical apparatus, 187-88; scope of work, 176-77; simplification of precedures at Yale, 560; span of control in, 120; University of California library, 178-79 (charts), 183, 185; work week, 306

Catalog of Books Represented by Library of Congress Printed Cards, 460

Catalogers: assistance in use of catalog, 190; subject backgrounds for, 267; training, 277

Cataloging: arrears, 188-89; centralized versus decentralized, 185-86; costs, 192; efforts to simplify operations, 175; problems, 598-99; promptness, 168, 187; supervised by head cataloger, 183; see also Recataloging

Cataloging manuals and codes, 188

Catholic Library Association: participation of university librarians in, 527

Census of Medieval and Renaissance Manuscripts in the United States and Canada (De Ricci), 460, 536

Centralization: administration, 47, 119, 142; cataloging, 185-86, 457-59; circulation department, 219, 221; effect on building planning, 491; principles for future policy, 152-53; reference service, 210, 211

Centralized cataloging service in Library of Congress: proposed by Ellsworth, 458

Chafee, Zechariah, Jr.: quoted on research materials, 368

Chambers of commerce: source for pictorial materials, 415

Chapel Hill—Durham, N.C.: union catalog at, 463

Charleston Society Library: American history sources in, 217

Charles University, Prague: program to provide personnel for scholarly libraries, 269

Charts: collections of, in university libraries, 410

Chattanooga, University of, Library: shares building with public library, 65

Chemistry: departmental libraries for, 211-12

Chicago: library collecting agreements in, 467; municipal reference library, 382

Chicago, University of: doctorate in library work, 265-66; former general administrative board, 41; Harper Memorial Library, 502; Industrial Relations Center Library, 409; library survey, 10; observatories, 4

Chicago, University of, Commission on the Future Policy of the University Libraries, 150, 270

Chicago, University of, Libraries: aid to smaller libraries, 452; assistant librarians, 134; Atlases in Chicago, 461; conceptions of library service, 588; cooperation in Midwest Inter-Library Center, 55; gift policy, 173; guide to manuscript collection, 398; history, 589; inactivity in publishing, 461; incunabula collection, 403; language reading room, 504; map collection, 403, 404; microfilm collection, 416; Near East material, 7; Newspapers in Libraries of Chicago, 461; organization (1955), 136 (chart); organization on basis of subject divisions, 146; photograph department, 514; Publications of *Cook County, Illinois,* 461; service for undergraduates, 156; survey, 559; 571

Chinese collection: Harvard, 7

Cincinnati, University of, Library: service for undergraduates, 156

Circulation assistants: training, 277

Circulation department, 219-30; administrative organization, 219, 221; division of work, 223; functions, 221-22; personnel, 222-23; reduction of work by subject arrangement, 147; regulations, 224; relation to photographic department, 201

Circulation librarian: qualifications, 223

Circulation records, 554

Circulation Work in College and University Libraries, 547

Civil service, *see* Library staff—civil service; Universities with civil service

Classical education: trend away from, 15

Classification: definition, 176; government documents, 379; problems, 598-99; similarity to subject cataloging, 185; supervised by head cataloger, 183; *see also* Reclassification

Classification décimale universelle, 532

Classified catalog, 599; shelf list as, 182; use in some university libraries, 177

Classified List of United States Government Publications, 377

Clements Library, *see* Michigan, University of, Library—Clements Library

Clemons, Harry: history of the University of Virginia Library, 589-90

Clerical assistants: duties, 279-80; morale, 280; salaries, 304; selection, 284; training, 278-80

Cleveland: union catalog, 54

Cleveland Public Library: individual storage library, 469; organization on basis of subject divisions, 146

Clipping files: in university libraries, 410-11

Coat rooms, 514

Cohen, Joseph L.: study of technical services, 183

College and Research Libraries, 586; publication program, 8; reports on experiments in photographic applications to librarianship, 201

College libraries: in university libraries,

155; statistics (1940–41), 84-85 *(tab.)*; (1953–54), 86-87 *(tab.)*

College libraries, southern: statistics (1940–41), 88 *(tab.)*

Colonial Williamsburg Research Library: American history sources in, 217

Colorado, University of, Library: building, 489; collections on divisional reading rooms, 497; delivery hall, 510; introduction of subject arrangement, 146; musical recordings, 418; music room, 408, 508

Colorado School of Mines: name, 14

Columbia University: administrative boards, 42; Dewey's librarianship of, 531; doctorate in library work, 265-66; enrollment (1954), 4; name, 14

Columbia University Libraries: aid to smaller libraries, 452; assistant librarians, 134; Avery Architectural Library, 149; Bancroft fund, 82; branch of public library in, 65; Butler Library, 486; college library, 156; College of Physicians and Surgeons of Library, 149; conceptions of library service, 588; departmental libraries, 149; divisional organization, 134; documents catalogers, 185; fees for non-university users, 91; funds from endowments, 81; guide to manuscript collection, 398; historical review of Cataloging Department, 590; history, 588; inactivity in publishing, 461; incunabula collection, 403; insurance of collections, 80; interlibrary loans, 451; Low Memorial Library, 486, 497; microfilm collection, 416; motion picture films, 417; musical recordings, 408, 418; Nicholas Murray Butler Librarian, 144; organization (1944–48), 137 *(chart)*; organization (1955), 138 *(chart)*; protection of rare books, 507; ranking system of staff, 256; separate cataloging units, 186; stacks in center of building, 496; study of early cataloging practices, 590; survey, 10, 559; use of punched-card systems, 107; Williamson's directorship of, 543

Columbia University School of Library Service, 52; Williamson as dean of, 543, 545-46

Colwell, Ernest C.: quoted on cooperation between universities, 449

Comité de Coordination pour la Documentation des Sciences Sociales, 384
Command, unity of: in library administration, 118
Commission Interministerielle de Documentation et Diffusion, 384
Commission on Financing Higher Education, 10
Committees of the faculty: relation to librarian, 44-46
Committees of the library staff, 44
Common Council of the City of New York, Minutes of: Williamson's connection with, 544
Compact storage, 498-99
Coney, Donald: cited on need for specialization in cataloging, 185; cited on planning for stack extension, 496; quoted, 125; on cost control, 109; on gifts, 170, 172; on Lamont Library, 156; on specialization in collecting, 467
Conference of Medical Librarians, London (1953), 476
Conference rooms for graduate students, 505
Connecticut Historical Society: American history sources in, 217
Connecticut State Library: American history sources in, 217
Conservation of knowledge and ideas: function of the university, 16
Contingent fund: for purchase of books, 75
Continuations: definition, 374
Cooperation, international, 475-76
Cooperation, library, 449-76, 604-5; acquisition, 7, 23-24; surveys, 567; use of resources, 53-54
Cooperation in university library administration, 9
Cooperative buying, 78; Richardson's initiation of, 534
Cooperative cataloging, 457-59
Cooperative Committee on Library Building Plans proceedings, 9
Coordinate indexing, 599
Coordinating as element of administration, 116
Copyright: application to microfilms, 203-4
Cornell University: library survey, 10; ratio of library expenditures to faculty, 98

Cornell University Library: aid to smaller libraries, 452; American history sources in, 217; departmental libraries, 152; gift policy, 173; guide to manuscript collection, 398; impossibility of complete centralization, 142; incunabula collection, 403; interlibrary loans, 451; separate cataloging units, 186; survey, 559, 564
Correlated-order forms, see Multiple-form order slips
Correspondence courses, see Home study
Cost control, 108-9
Cost records, 102, 555
Council of National Library Associations: participation of university librarians in, 528
Counseling office: relation to librarian, 57
Counseling of students: library participation in, 428, 431
County documents: acquisition by university library, 381-82
Cuban Library Association: participation of university librarians in, 527
Cubook (unit of stack capacity), 497-98
Current books: acquisition, 367-69
Current materials: acquisition, 359-60
Cyrillic alphabet material: University of California Library, 233
Czechoslovakia: library training, 269

Dartmouth College: importance of library, 14
Dartmouth College case, 30
Dartmouth College Library: funds from endowments, 81; history, 588; survey, 559
Daugherty, Donald H., and Lloyd E. Blauch: definition of "university," 14
David, Charles W.: cited on cost of interlibrary loans, 455
Deans: relation to librarian, 44-46
Debating groups: relation of library to, 431
Debating materials: library extension service, 245
Decentralization: of cataloging, 185-86
Delivery hall, 510-11
Demotion in university library service, 316
Denmark: dissertations prepared in, 396

Denver, University of: library survey, 10

Departmental assistants: training, 277

Departmental committees: part in acquisition policy, 350

Departmental librarians: duties, 129, 132; department offices, 512; promotion of other staff member to position, 314-15; relation to librarian, 44-46; salaries, 302-3; subject backgrounds for, 267; supervision over departments, 140; training, 273-77

Departmental libraries, 157, 592; administration, 46; administrative and educational aspects, 150-52; allocation of book funds to, 99-100; cataloging, 191; definition, 149; hours of service, 305; reference service, 210-11; relation to central library, 149-50; relation to librarian, 47-49; systems of organization, 148-56; titles of supervisors, 126

Departmental organization, 161-204; duplication of reference books, 366

Departmentation: in library administration, 120-21

Depository catalogs, 181; aid to scholarly use of library, 443-44

Depository libraries: for U.N. publications, 386

Depository system, 377

Deposits for non-academic users, 79

Deposit system for fines, 78

De Ricci, Seymour: editor of Census of Medieval and Renaissance Manuscripts, 536

Descriptive cataloging: definition, 176; organization of work in cataloging department, 185

Desiderata lists, 359

Detroit Public Library: programs of service for industry on basis of fee payments, 92

Dewey, Melvil, 498; professional career, 531-32

Dictating and transcribing machines, 519

Dictionary catalog: size, 193; usual in university libraries, 177

Directing: as element of administration, 116

Director of university library, see University librarian

Discarding, 600

Discipline: in library administration, 118

Discounts: for prompt payment, 77; on books, 77-78

Dismissal in university library service, 317-18

Divided catalog, 177, 180

Divisional librarian, 144; graduate degree in subject, 147; promotion of other staff member to position, 314-15

Divisional libraries: serials, 235

Divisional organization, 592, 600; effect upon reference service, 212

Divisional reading rooms, 503-4

Division of labor in library administration, 117-18

Doctoral dissertations, 17; acquisition by university library, 394-99; administration and organization, 396; for exchange purposes, 169; on history of university libraries, 589; photographic reproduction, 396; printed abstracts, 396; publication requirement, 395

Doctoral Dissertations Accepted by American Universities, 460

Doctorate: as requisite for chief librarianship, 282; at library schools, 587; increase, 5; increased demand for in librarianship, 262; in library work, 265-66; required in Germany for university librarians, 268; see also Ph.D. degree

Doctor of Library Science degree, 266; Columbia University School of Library Service, 266; University of California, 266

Documentation: problems in, 601-2

Documentation, Inc., 594

Document centers, regional, 380

Documents department, 230-31; physical quarters, 503

Documents Expediting Project, 78

Dodgers: collections of, in university libraries, 410

Doherty, Francis X.: discussion of New England Deposit Library, 54

Dormitory libraries, see House libraries

Downs, Robert B.: cited on Midwest Inter-Library Center, 471-72; cited on union lists, 461; questionnaire on university libraries, 11; quoted on civil service in libraries, 286-87; on failure of libraries to publish, 461; on specialization, 465-66

Drama materials: library extension service, 244

Dramatic associations: relation of library to, 431

Duke University: library committee, 39

Duke University Library: aid to smaller libraries, 452; cooperation in collecting Latin American documents, 385; gift policy, 173; microfilm collection, 416; newspaper acquisition, 388; rare book room, 198, 506

Dunbar, Ralph W.: quoted on civil service in libraries, 287

Dunlap, Leslie W.: cited on aid to scholars of reference librarian, 216, 218

Duplicates: sale as source of income, 92; use for exchange, 170

Duplicating machines, 519

Educational associations: participation of university librarians in, 528

Educational Film Library Association: participation of university librarians in, 528

Educational foundations: participation of university librarians in, 528

Educational institutions: source for pictorial materials, 415

Educational program, see University courses

Education for librarianship, 262; advanced training, 265; basic training, 263; first-year professional training, 263-65; interest of university librarians in, 529; specialization in training university librarians at Illinois and Michigan, 267; surveys, 567; Williamson's interest in, 546

Efficiency: measurement in cataloging, 188

Egan, Margaret E., and Keck, Lucile L.: cited on fugitive materials, 409

Egypt: official bibliographies of government documents, 384

Eliot, Charles W.: cited on storing materials, 521-22

Ellsworth, Ralph E.: proposal for centralized cataloging service, 458; quoted on Harper Memorial Library, 502; on modular construction, 494

Emergency purchases and services, 45

Endowment: financial administration, 59; library income from, 81-82

England: education for librarianship in, 268-69

Enoch Pratt Free Library, Baltimore: organization on basis of subject divisions, 146

Equipment, 514-18, 605-6; inventory, 556; responsibility of librarian, 21-22; surveys, 566-67

Equipment firms: librarian's contacts with, 61-62

Equity in library administration, 121

Esprit de corps in library administration, 122

Essex Institute (Salem, Mass.): American history sources in, 217

Esterquest, Ralph T.: cited on Midwest Inter-Library Center, 397

Estes, Rice: cited on rental collections, 434

Estimated totals of departmental commitments, 103

Ethics of librarians, see Library staff—ethics

Europe: Library training in, 267-69

European libraries: staff classification, 255

Examinations: for staff promotion, 290

Exchange, 359; accumulation of dead wood, 603; acquisition procedures, 168-74; materials suitable for, 169; relation between library and university press, 63; use of doctoral dissertations, 395; use of reprints, 413

Exhibits, 430; gift materials, 174; rooms for collections of, 508; space for, 509; to stimulate student interest in library, 56

Expensive materials: methods of saving purchase of, 358

Extension department, 237-38, 240-47; physical quarters, 508

Extension service: administration by university library, 51; coordination of services, 246-47; distribution of musical recordings by, 418; facilities and resources, 240, 242; operating expenses, 238; organization, 240; records of, 555; University of Michigan, 239 (chart), 240, 241 (chart), 242; see also University extension

Facsimile transmission: use in interlibrary cooperation, 456

Faculty members: borrowing privileges, 224; committee on the library, 43-44; functions, 40-41; part in acquisition policy, 350, 351-52; part in book selection, 163; pressure for departmental libraries, 211; relations of library with, 430; relation to librarian, 46-47; salaries compared with those of library staff, 321

Faculty status, see Academic status

Families of faculty members and administrative officers use of university library, 66

Farmington Plan, 78, 368, 468-69; effect on interlibrary lending, 452; inception, 23

Favoritism: avoidance of, 332

Fayol, Henri: cited on administration, 117; *Industrial and General Administration*, 115

Fearing collection, 400

Federal agencies: distribution of publications to libraries, 378

Federal documents: acquisition by university library, 377-79; organization for use, 379; technical reports, 378-79

Federal government: relation to universities, 15; relation to university libraries, 28; revised classification of library positions, 299

Fees: for non-university users, 90-92, 594; trend away from, 90-92

Fellow of the Library Association (England): degree of, 269

Fellowships: for library staff, 323-24; funds for, 5-6

Film reading rooms, 508-9

Finance of Higher Education (Russell), 10

Financial administration, 71-113

Financial statistics, 101-2; difficulty of obtaining, 11

Financing Higher Education in the United States (Millett), 10, 71, 94, 108-9

Fines, 225; collection, 74, 78-79; uniformity, 221; value of, 79

Fireproof construction of bookstacks, 499

First editions: collection by university libraries, 369-70

Fisk University Library: history, 589

Fixed charges: in library budget, 96

Flexner, Abraham: attitude toward librarianship, 270; cited, 14

Florida: library collecting agreements in, 467

Florida, University of, Library: administration of extension service, 51; slide collection, 417; survey, 10; use of punched-card systems, 107

Foerster, Norman: cited, 14

Folders: collections in university libraries, 410

Ford Foundation: aid in research projects, 6; participation of university librarians in, 529

Foreign documents: acquisition by university library, 383-85

Foreign drafts, 102

Foreign exchanges: use of university press remainders, 170

Foreign languages: need by acquisitions department staff, 163; need in binding department, 194; organization of cataloging by, 185

Foreign publications: acquisition furthered by Farmington Plan, 468; L.C. aid in acquisition, 468; order routine, 166; small quantity buying, 77

Fortress of Freedom: the Story of the Library of Congress, 548

France: dissertations prepared in, 396; library training in, 267-68

Fraternity house libraries, see House libraries

Freight charges, 77

French government documents: acquisition by university library, 384

Friends of the library, 7, 66, 553; aid in acquisition of materials in special fields, 48; alumni among, 246; donations to library through, 353-54

Fry, Bernard M.: quoted on technical reports, 379

Fugitive materials: collection by university library, 409-18

Fulbright scholarship: to librarians, 322

Fumigation: equipment for, 519

Functional arrangement, 142, 144, 146; criticisms, 144

Functional requirements in library construction, 486

Furness Memorial Library of Shakespeariana, 361

Fussler, Herman H.: cited on applications of copyright law to films, 203-4;

Fussler, Herman H. (*Continued*) on microphotography, 201-2, 474; description of department of photography, 200; director of University of Chicago Library, 542; *Function of the Library in the Modern College,* 10; *Library Buildings for Library Service,* 9; quoted on acquisition policies, 348-49; on library buildings, 605; on microfilms, 416, 475

General Education Board: aid in research projects, 6; participation of university librarians in, 529; sponsor of *Census of Medieval and Renaissance Manuscripts,* 536; subsidies to ALA Cooperative Cataloging Committee, 457

General Interlibrary Code of 1952, 454, 455

General public: use of university library, 65-66

George Peabody College Library: history, 589

Georgia: legislation affecting libraries of state institutions, 29

Georgia, University of: library survey, 10

Georgia, University of, Library: building, 489; photographic installations, 198

Germany: dissertations prepared in, 395, 396; library training in, 267-68

Gerould, James T.: bibliographical work, 459; professional career, 535-37

Gerritsen, A. H.: *La Femme et le féminisme,* 361

Gifts, 359; accumulation of dead wood, 603; acknowledgment of, 173; acquisition procedures, 168-9, 170-74; financial administration, 59; stipulations by donors, 173

Governmental offices and agencies: activities of university librarians in, 528

Governmental research contracts: library implications, 93

Government bureaus: source for pictorial materials, 415

Government documents: acquisition by university library, 376-86; availability to public, 66; cooperative acquisition, 385; library of University of Minnesota required to collect, 32; research

material, 368; subject placement, 231; *see also* County documents; Documents department; Federal documents; Municipal documents; State documents

Graduate students: aid in developing library collections, 355; reading rooms for, 505-6; use of university libraries, 218

Graduate study: development, 4; introductory courses in, 56

Graphic materials: collections in university libraries, 413-14

Graphic rating scale, 291

Great Britain: dissertations prepared in, 396

Green, S. S.: early advocate of interlibrary loans, 450

Grievances: provision for discussion, 332

Gross, P. L. K., and E. M. Gross: evaluation of periodicals, 373-74

Guides to the library, 429

Gulick, Luther H., and L. Urwick: cited on administration theory, 115

Hamlin, Arthur T.: quoted on endowment funds, 82

Hampshire Inter-Library Center, South Hadley, 472

Hand, Elinor: cited on cost of interlibrary loans, 454

Hardin, Ruth: table of "Checklists of State Publications Currently Issued," 380

Harrington, Roseanne H., and Guy R. Lyle: cited on merit rating form, 291

Hartford Theological Seminary Library: Richardson's librarianship of, 532

Harvard College Library: catalog department, 183, 184 (*chart*), 185; funds, 59; organization of manuscripts, 400

Harvard Library Bulletin, 156, 590; publication program, 8

Harvard University: enrollment (1900), 3; increase in endowment, 4-6; name, 13; operation of New England Deposit Library, 469; *Place of the Library in a University,* 10; responsibility of librarian to president, 132

Harvard University Library: additions to national Union Catalog, 462; aid to smaller libraries, 452; American history sources in, 217; broadsides collection, 410; buildings, 484; catalog, 191; Chinese collections, 7; classification of archival collections, 402; conceptions of library service, 588; departmental libraries, 148, 151-52; divisional organization, 134; fees for non-university users, 91; funds from endowments, 81; gift policy, 173; guide to manuscript collection, 398; history, 588; Houghton Library, 198, 217, 507; hours of student assistance, 261; housing of rare book collection, 372; incunabula collection, 403; initiation of New England Deposit Library, 55; Lamont Library, 156, 503, 505, 592; music collection, 407; music recordings, 408; organization (1953), 130-31 (*chart*); separate cataloging units, 186; service for undergraduates, 156; size, 6, 346, 492; storage of little used materials, 521; study of early cataloging practices, 590; underground stacks, 496; use of commercial photographic firms, 198; Widener Collection, 371, 400; Winsor's librarianship of, 530

Hawkins, R. R.: *Scientific, Medical, and Technical Books Published in the United States of America, 1930–1944,* 571

Henderson, Robert W.: cited on stack space, 497

Hierarchy: in library administration, 119-20

Hirsch, Rudolf: *Changing Patterns of Scholarship and the Future of Research Libraries,* 10

Hispanic-American materials: Tulane University, 7

Historical Records Survey, 460

Historical Society of Pennsylvania: American history sources, 217

H. M. Stationery Office: lists of British documents, 383

Hoage, Annette: cited on turnover of staff, 316

Hodgson, James G.: cited on interlibrary loans, 454

Hofstadter, Richard, and C. DeWitt Hardy: cited, 14

Holiday hours of library service, 307

Hollis, E. V.: cited, 14

Home study: relation to librarian, 51-52

Hook, Sidney: cited, 14

Hoover Library of War, Revolution, and Peace, 154; war-poster collection, 412

Houghton Library, *see* Harvard University Library—Houghton Library

Hours of opening: flexibility, 221

Hours of service, 305-7

House libraries, 28-30; promotion of reading habit through, 56, 434-35

Huntington Library: American history sources in, 217; manuscript collection, 398; studies of preservation of materials, 198

Hutchins, Margaret: cited on duties of reference librarian, 214

Hutchins, Robert M.: cited, 14

IBM equipment, see Punched-card systems

Idaho, University of: library survey, 10

Illinois, University of: doctorate in library work, 265-66; faculty rank for librarians, 322; statutes relating to library, 35

Illinois, University of, Library: additions to national Union Catalog, 462; bibliography room, 511; browsing room, 505; centralization, 142; Chicago Undergraduate Division, 428; departmental libraries, 148, 149; divisional organization, 134; gift policy, 173; history, 589; inactivity in publishing, 461; incunabula collection, 403; loan department, 219, 222; map collection, 237, 404; microfilm collection, 416; musical recordings, 408, 418; newspapers in, 386; organization, 135 (*chart*); size, 6; slide collection, 417; space for future units, 489; staff classification, 299; studies of different departments, 590; unit plan of building, 488

Income of university libraries: recording, 73-74; sources of, 80-93

Incunabula: acquisition by university library, 369-70, 403

India: official bibliographies of government documents, 384

Indiana, University of: library survey, 10

Indiana, University of, Library: gift policy, 173; inactivity in publishing, 461; ratio of library expenditures to total institutional expenditures, 97

Individual interests of staff: subordination to common good, 119

Industrial and business organizations: source for pictorial materials, 415

Information service: library extension, 245

Initiative in library administration, 122

In-service training, 309

Institute of International Education: aid in research projects, 6; participation of university librarians in, 528

Instruction in use of library, 428-31; by loan desk staff, 222; for beginning students, 426, 427; graduate level, 439-41; professional level, 441; undergraduate, 438-39; see also Orientation of students

Insurance: handled by business office, 61; for library staff, 326

Insurance of library collections: evaluating for, 79-80, 603

Inter-American Bibliographical and Library Association: participation of university librarians in, 527

Inter-American Library Conference (1946), 476

Interdepartmental relations, 338

Interlibrary centers, 55, 368, 470-73; aid in exchange of duplicate materials, 170

Interlibrary loan request form, 453

Interlibrary loans, 24, 450-57; aid to scholarly use of library, 443-44; clientele, 453-54; control by circulation department, 222; costs, 454; fees, 455; organization, 454, 455-56; relation to photographic department, 201-2; responsibility for, 221; types of materials loaned, 452-53; use by special libraries, 49; use to save expensive purchases, 358

International Business Machines Corporation, 519

International Conference on Science Abstracting (Paris, 1949), 476

International conferences of librarians, see Library conferences, international

International Congresses and Conferences, 1840–1937, 460

International cultural relations: interest of university librarians in developing, 529

International Federation for Documentation: participation of university librarians in, 528

International Federation of Library Associations: Bishop's part in organizing, 539, 540; participation of university librarians in, 527

Internship systems: for special libraries, 276-77

Interpretation of new knowledge: function of university, 18

Interviews for appointment candidates, 286

Inventory: relation to catalog department, 190

Invoices, 76

Iowa: library collecting agreements in, 467

Iowa, State University of: ratio of library expenditures to faculty, 98

Iowa, State University of, Library: building, 489; dispersion of various types of reading space among stack floors, 497; gift policy, 173; microfilm collection, 416

Iowa State College: name, 14; plan for storage library, 522

Iowa State College Library: librarianship of Charles H. Brown, 547

Ireland: official bibliographies of government documents, 384

Irish court decisions: as source material, 368

Italy: library training in, 269

Jackson, W. A.: quoted on rare book collections, 369, 370, 371-72

Jackson, William V.: cited on formal library course on advanced level, 449

Janitorial service, 62

Janitors' quarters, 514

Japan: library training in, 269

Jewett, Charles C.: cooperative cataloging proposal, 457; proposes Smithsonian Institution as national library of U.S., 533

Job analyses: in university library surveys, 572

John Crerar Library: additions to national Union Catalog, 462; disposal of out-of-scope books, 361; programs of service for industry on basis of fee payments, 92

John Rylands Library: catalog, 461

Johns Hopkins University: increase in endowment, 4-6; precursor of American universities, 3

Johns Hopkins University Library: organization on basis of subject divisions, 146

John Simon Guggenheim Memorial Foundation: aid in research projects, 6

Joint University Libraries, Nashville: motion picture films, 417; Treasure Room, 506

Josephs, Devereux C.: cited on methodology of surveys, 567

Journal of Cataloging and Classification: publication program, 8

Journal of Documentary Reproduction: founding, 543

Journal of Documentation: publication program, 8; reports on experiments in photographic applications to librarianship, 201

Kaiser, John B.: quoted on civil service in libraries, 287

Kansas, University of, Library: acquisition of out-of-scope books from John Crerar Library, 361

Kelly, Fred J., and J. H. McNeely: study of purchasing procedures, 60

Kentucky, University of, Library: microfilm collection, 416; postal card collection, 415

Keogh, Andrew: professional career, 537-38

Kerr, Chester: cited on university presses, 63

Kidder, Robert W.: cited on interlibrary loans, 454

Korean War: participation of university personnel in, 18

Kraebenbuehl, John O.: table of recommended foot-candles, 515, 516

Kremer, Alvin W.: cited on preservation of materials, 599

Laboratory collections, 154

Lacy, Dan: cited on cooperative microfilming, 473

Lake Placid Club: organized by Melvil Dewey, 532

Lake Placid Club Education Foundation: organized by Melvil Dewey, 532

Lamont Library, *see* Harvard University Library—Lamont Library

Land-grant colleges: agricultural extension, 50; inadequate support for granting Ph.D. degree, 99

Land-grant college libraries: C. H. Brown's interest in development of, 547

Lane, William C.: cited on storing materials, 521

Language, *see* Foreign languages

Language clubs: relation of library to, 431

Lantern slides: product of photographic department, 201

Latin America: government documents, 384; library training, 269

Laura Spelman Rockefeller Memorial: subsidy toward the *Union List of Serials*, 535-36

Law departmental libraries: hours of service, 305

Leaflets: collections in university libraries, 410

League of Nations: Bishop's service to, 539; publications of, 385-86

Learned, William S.: cited, 14

Learned societies: participation of university librarians in, 528

Leaves of absence for study or projects, 322

Lectures on library use, 430

Leeds, University of: shelving of books in reading room, 497

Legislative senate: functions, 40-41

Leigh, Robert D.: quoted on library administration, 123; on meagerness of funds for research into library problems, 587

Lending service, *see* Rental collections

Leyh, Georg: cited on education for librarianship in Europe, 268

Librarian: academic status, 22-23, 37, 53, 321; annual report, 557, 560-61; appointment, 39, 40; authority over all book collections, 142; cooperation with other institutions, 47; director of library school, 53; duties, 36, 127-28; encouragement of professional de-

Librarian (*Continued*)
velopment of staff, 307-8; gift program planning, 172; initiation of survey, 561; information as to university policy, 40, 95-96; justification for increased funds, 83; knowledge of legal basis of university necessary, 33; membership in senate or faculty, 41; membership on administrative board, 41; membership on faculty library committee, 44; need of broad outlook, 9; nonlibrarian appointees, 270, 596; off-campus relations, 526-51; office, 512; promotion of staff member to position, 313-14; public relations, 552-80; purchasing responsibilities, 75-76; relation to faculty, 37; relation to president and deans, 132, 549; relation to university administration, 34, 37-66; responsibilities, 298-99; responsibilities in acquisition policy, 349-50; responsibility for arrangement of space and installation of equipment, 22; role in planning of building, 487-88; sabbatical leave, 323; salary, 299, 301; salary, comparative table, 300-301 (*tab.*); selection, 262-73, 282-83; span of control, 120; training, 262-73; training in Europe, 267-69; vacation, 318

Librarianship, training for, *see* Education for librarianship

Libraries, small: dependence on large libraries, 452

Library administrators: offices for, 512

Library associations: participation of university librarians in, 527

Library Binding Institute, 193, 197

Library budget: size, 71; submission to president, 40

Library building, *see* University library building

Library Building Plans Institutes, 605

Library Bureau: organized by Melvil Dewey, 531

Library cards, printed: distribution, 7

Library collections: surveys, 566

Library committee: functions, 42-43; medium of communication between trustees and librarian, 39; provision for, 36

Library conferences, international, 8, 476

Library council: definition, 340

Library extension service, *see* Extension service

Library funds: influence of librarian's report on increase of, 557

Library government: policy, 24-25

Library guild, *see* Friends of the library

Library Journal: founders, 530, 531

Library materials: change in character, 7; methods used in surveying, 576-79 (*tab.*); organization for use, 21; preservation, 517, 599-600; records, 556

Library of Congress: aid in acquisition of materials, 23; aid in cataloging doctoral dissertations, 397; aid to smaller libraries, 452; American history sources in, 217; book catalog of, 181, 537; card printing and distribution, 7, 175, 457-58; cards for U.N. documents, 386; catalog, 461; cataloging rules, 188; *Catalog of Books Represented by Library of Congress Printed Cards,* 180, 181, 443, 537, 598; *Catalog of Copyright Entries,* 406; classification system, 177, 190, 191; concern with technical standards in microfilming, 473; Cooperative Cataloging Section, 458; distribution of duplicate foreign documents to university libraries, 385; facsimile transmission, 456; *Guide to the Official Publications of the Other American Republics,* 384; *Information Bulletin,* 8; manuscript collection, 398; map cataloging, 407; microfilms of early state records of American colonies, 474; *Monthly Checklist of State Publications,* 380; participation of university librarians in, 528; Putnam's librarianship, 547-48; scientific management in, 124; Union Catalog, 443, 462, 532-33; Union Catalog Division, 463; use of teletype, 456

Library of Congress Cooperative Acquisitions Project, 78, 468

Library of Congress depository card catalog, 177, 181

Library problems: lack of funds for research into, 587

Library profession: recruitment, 596

Library publications: for exchange purposes, 169; sale as source of income, 92

Library resources: control of librarian over, 36

Library school: courses directed at special problems of college and university libraries, 264; in university, 7; primary source of personnel, 285; printing of publications through university press, 63; relations with university library, 52-53; required attendance for promotion, 311; Williamson's study of, 545

Library space: increased demand for, 7; responsibility of librarian, 21-22

Library staff, 595-97; academic status, 37, 287, 298, 320-22, 596-97; adjustment to organizational system, 141; appointment, promotion, and dismissal, 40; attendance at library meetings, 311; civil service, 29; classifications, 61, 255-58, 298; competence an essential of university library program, 20-21; democracy in organization of, 342; demotions and dismissals, 40, 316-18; employment of, 60-61, 285; ethics, 327-33; health, 334-35; hours of work, 305-7; increased demand for, 7; induction and training of new members, 309-10; institutional privileges, 22-23; lack of central employment agency, 285; leaves of absence, 322-23; legal status in public institutions, 32; measurement of effectiveness, 289-92; methods and devices used in surveying, 573 (tab.); morale, 308, 331, 337; opportunities for advanced study, 313; part in acquisition policy, 350, 351-52; percentage of budget for, 20; professional development, 307-26; ratio of professional to nonprofessional members, 261; records of expenditures for, 102; recreation, 334; relations to society and governing authority, 328-30; release to serve on projects, 323; rest rooms, 514; salaries (see Salaries); selection, 282-89; size, 71, 258-61; special assignments, 45-46; stability, 122; stimulation as result of survey, 574; surveys, 565-66; training, 261-81; training for promotion, 310; training in subject fields, 21; training to increase efficiency, 310; transfer from one position to another, 315-16; types of workers, 254-58; see also Catalog department—Personnel; Line and staff; Staffing

Library surveyors: selection, 562

Library tours, 430

Library Trends, 11, 587; discussion of financial problems, 595; lighting of university library, 515-16; papers on scientific management, 595; publication program, 8

Line and staff in library administration, 121

Linguistic ability, see Foreign languages

List of Serial Publications of Foreign Governments, 1815-1931, 460, 536

Loan desk: activities, 222; speed of service, 221, 223-24; see also Delivery hall

Loan-desk staff: workroom for, 510

Loan periods, 224; flexibility, 221

Local collections: rooms for, 508

London, University of: School of Librarianship, 269

Los Angeles: municipal reference library, 382

Los Angeles Public Library: organization on basis of subject divisions, 146; survey, 562

Lost books: charges for, 79

Louisiana: depositories of state documents in other states, 380; library collecting agreements in, 467

Louisiana, University of: faculty rank for librarians, 322

Louisiana, University of, Library: merit rating form used, 291; microfilm collection, 416; musical recordings, 418; survey, 559

Louisville, University of, Libraries: history, 589

Lounges in university libraries, 505

Lower-level libraries, 435

Lowell, Mildred H.: cited on library collecting agreements, 468

Lucy, Mary L.: cited on interlibrary loans, 453, on cost of interlibrary loans, 455

Lundy, Frank A.: quoted on academic status, 321

Lundy, Frank A., and Kathryn R. Renfro: survey of problems of university library, 600

Luttrell, Narcissus: diary of, 368

Lydenberg, H. M.: committee member on American Newspapers, 536; committee member on Union List of

Lydenberg, H. M. (*Continued*)
Serials, 535; professional career, 547-48

Lyle, Guy G.: cited on library handbooks, 429; on merit rating form, 291

Lyle, Guy G. and others: *Administration of the College Library*, 9

McAnally, Arthur M.: quoted on library organization, 134

McCarthy, Stephen A.: cited, 97; cited on land-grant college library expenditure, 99; quoted on endowment funds, 82

McDiarmid, E. W.: quoted on dismissals, 317; quoted on training for clerical assistants, 279

McMillen, James A.: cited on academic status, 320

Malikoff, Gabrielle E.: editor of supplements to *Union List of Serials*, 536

Malone, Dumas, 590

Maloy, Miriam C.: cited on academic status, 320

Management, unity of: in library administration, 119

Management engineers: conduct of library surveys by, 562

Manuscripts: acquisition by university library, 398-400; handling of collections, 235-36; organization for use, 400; research material, 368

Map librarian: responsibilities, 237

Map rooms, 237, 506

Maps: acquisition by university library, 403-7; arrangement and records, 406-7; comparative size of collections in university libraries, 405 (*tab.*); sources for selection, 405-6; storage and equipment, 406; uses, 404

Maryland, University of: bookmobile, 242

Maryland Historical Society: American history sources in, 217

Maryland State Library: American history sources in, 217

Massachusetts Historical Society: American history sources in, 217

Massachusetts Institute of Technology: name, 14

Massachusetts Institute of Technology

Library: building, 489; photograph department, 514

Master's degree for library training, 264, 265, 267; changes in program for, 587; Columbia University School of Library Service, 266

Master's essays, 16; acquisition by university library, 396; on history of university libraries, 589

Mechanical equipment, 61, 518-20, 606

Medical Library Association: aid in exchange of duplicate materials, 170; internship system, 276; participation of university librarians in, 527

Medical school library: hours of service, 305; separation of budget, 100

Melinat, Carl H.: cited on interlibrary loans, 453

Merritt, LeRoy C.: quoted on storage problems, 495

Metcalf, Keyes D.: cited on increase in library collections, 492; on stack space, 497; on early Harvard library history, 590; cooperative cataloging suggestions, 459; quoted on departmental libraries, 151-52; report on the Harvard libraries, 10

Mexico: government documents, 385

Michigan, University of: doctorate in library work, 265-66

Michigan, University of, Library: Bishop's librarianship of, 541; Clements Library, 198, 507; departmental libraries, 152; extension room, 508; extension service, 239 (*chart*), 240, 241 (*chart*), 242; gift policy, 173; history, 589; housing of rare book collection, 372; inactivity in publishing, 461; incunabula collection, 403; microfilm collection, 416; musical recordings, 418; northern exposure of reading room, 490; package service, 241 (*chart*); plan for storage library, 522; planned undergraduate library, 593; public catalog space, 511; service for undergraduates, 156; use of commercial photographic firms, 198

Microcards: collections in university libraries, 415-16

Microfilm: application to potential needs of research workers, 474; cataloging, 202-3; collections in university libraries, 415-16; cooperative projects,

473; interlibrary loans, 453; lending practices, 202; research material, 368; storage, 203

Microfilming centers: international network needed, 474

Microfilming of dissertations, 395

Microfilming of newspapers, 388

Microlex, 416

Microphotographic laboratories: use by special libraries, 49

Microphotographic reproduction, 24, 55, 200-201, 443

Microphotography: groups of materials serviced for lending, 202; Raney's contribution to use by libraries, 541-43

Microphotography for Libraries (Raney), 543

Microprints: collections in university libraries, 415-16

Midwest Inter-Library Center, 55, 470-72, 549; acquisition program, 471; collection of French theses, 397; dedication, 449; foreign government gazettes and parliamentary papers, 385; inception, 23; use of teletype, 456

Miller, Robert A.: cost study of acquisitional work and cataloging, 164

Millett, John A.: *Financing Higher Education in the United States*, 10, 71, 94, 108-9

Milwaukee: municipal reference library, 382

Milwaukee Public Library: use of teletype, 456

Minicards, 475

Minnesota, University of: library survey, 10

Minnesota, University of, Library: freshman-sophomore library, 593; history, 590; hours of student assistance, 261; inactivity in publishing, 461; microfilm collection, 416; required to collect and preserve government documents, 32; state control over, 34; Walter's librarianship of, 534

Mississippi, University of: library survey, 10

Missouri, University of, Library: gift policy, 173; use of punched-card systems, 107

Modular construction: in library building, 493-94

Montana, University of: library survey, 10; responsibility of librarian to senior academic dean, 132

Montana, University of, Library: checking holdings against lists, 571; organization, 133 (*chart*); survey, 559

Monticello Conference, 549, 552

Mood, Fulmer, and Vernon Carstensen: cited on care of archives, 236

Morsch, Lucile M.: cited on cooperative and centralized cataloging, 457-59; study of cataloging costs, 192

Moscow Institute of Library Economy, 269

Motion pictures: collections in university libraries, 417

Motion picture studios: source for pictorial materials, 415

Muller, Robert H.: cited on book storage, 498; on library salaries, 321; study of work hours, 305, 306

Multiple-form order slips, 168

Municipal documents: acquisition by university library, 382-83

Municipal reference libraries: lists of municipal documents, 382

Municipal universities: budgetary procedures, 58-59; relation to city council, 31-32

Municipal university libraries: administration, 124

Munson, Frances L.: study of LC depository catalog at Columbia, 181

Museum objects: collections in university libraries, 418; rooms for collections, 508

Musical recordings: collections in university libraries, 408; control by music departments, 418

Music collections: housing, 408; in university libraries, 407-8

Music Library Association, 408; *Notes*, 408; participation of university librarians in, 527

Music rooms, 408, 508

Nashville, Tenn.: union catalogs, 54, 463

National Academy of Science: participation of university librarians in, 528

National Archives: concern with archival collections, 401; practice in organization manuscripts, 400; studies of preservation of materials, 198

National Association of State Libraries, 380, 531; participation of university librarians in, 527-28

National Association of State Universities: participation of university librarians in, 528

National Catholic Educational Association: participation of university librarians in, 528

National Education Association: participation of university librarians in, 528

National Institutes of Health Library: facsimile transmission, 456

National Microfilm Association: participation of university librarians in, 528

National Research Council: participation of university librarians in, 528; sponsor of *List of Serial Publications of Foreign Governments*, 536

National Research Foundation: aid in research projects, 6

National Science Foundation: fellowships, 6; participation of university librarians in, 528; study of use of university libraries by graduate students, 218

Near East: material on, at Chicago, 7

Nebraska, University of, Library: building, 489; collections in divisional reading rooms, 497; delivery hall, 510; departmental libraries, 152; divisional librarian in science and technology, 212; introduction of subject arrangement, 146

Nebraska State Library: union catalog, 463

Nepotism in university libraries, 329-30

Netherlands: dissertations prepared in, 396; official bibliographies of government documents, 384

Newark Public Library: individual storage library, 469

Newberry Library: manuscript collection, 398

New books: announcements of, 430

New England Deposit Library, 54, 469-70, 522

New Hampshire, University of: library survey, 10

New Hampshire State Library: union catalog, 463

Newspaper microfilm project: University of California Library, 233

Newspaper room, 503

Newspapers: acquisition by university library, 386-89; as research materials, 387-88; cooperative collecting, 388; preservation, 388

Newspapers, foreign, 387-88

Newspapers on Microfilm (Schwegmann), 461

Newsreels: collections in university libraries, 417

New York City: library collecting agreements in, 467

New York Municipal Reference Library, 382; Williamson's librarianship, 544

New York Public Library: additions to national Union Catalog, 462; aid to smaller libraries, 452; American history sources in, 217; book selection, 349; catalog, 461; Lydenberg's librarianship, 547-48; manuscript collection, 398; scientific management in, 124; studies of preservation of materials, 198; survey, 562

New York Public Library, Library School of, 52; merger, 545

New York Society Library: American history sources in, 217

New York state: library collecting agreements in, 467

New York State Library: Dewey's librarianship of, 531

New York State Library School, 52; Dewey's association with, 531; merger, 545

New York State Medical Society Library: aid in cataloging doctoral dissertations, 397

New York University: enrollment (1954), 4

New York University Library: classification of archival collections, 402; inactivity in publishing, 461

Noise control, 517-18; in library building, 490

Nonlibrarians: appointment to university libraries, 270-73, 596

Nonprinted materials: collections in university libraries, 413-18

Nonprofessional staff: attendance at library meetings, 312; status, 61; vacations, 318

North Carolina: legislation affecting libraries of state institutions, 29; statutes relating to university library staff, 328-29

North Carolina, University of, Library: administration of library extension service, 51; aid to smaller libraries, 452; Bull's Head Bookshop, 65, 437; cooperation in collecting Latin American documents, 385; extension room, 508; Friends of the Library, 354; incunabula collection, 403; microfilm collection, 416; microfilms of early state records of American colonies, 474; musical recordings, 418; newspaper acquisition, 388; northern exposure of reading room, 490; rare book room, 198, 506; size, 6; specified budgetary procedures, 32; unit plan of building, 488

North central area: library collecting agreements in, 467

North Dakota Agricultural College: decisions as to departmental libraries, 211

Northeastern states: proposed cooperative regional library, 472

Northwestern University Library: inactivity in publishing, 461; rare book rooms, 198

Norway: dissertations prepared in, 396; library training in, 269

Notre Dame University: library survey, 10

Nuclear Science Abstracts, 378

Off-campus courses: extension service, 242, 244

Official catalog, 180-81

Oklahoma, University of, Library: departmental libraries, 152; long-range program of acquisitions, 561

Ohio: library collecting agreements in, 467

Ohio, University of, Library: inactivity in publishing, 461; musical recordings, 418

Ohio State Library: union catalog, 463

Old Dominion Foundation: participation of university librarians in, 529

Older materials: acquisition, 355-59

Open-shelf reserves, 227

Open shelves: for stimulation of reading habit, 432

Order department: University of California, 167 (*chart*)

Order files, 103

Order forms, 102

Order in library administration, 121

Order librarian: training, 162

Order procedure, 163-68; centralization, 119; routines, 164-65; *see also* Acquisition of materials

Oregon: centralized system of libraries of state institutions, 142n; legislation affecting libraries of state institutions, 29; purchasing for system of educational institutions, 78; unification of state institution libraries, 29, 31

Oregon, University of, Library: Association of Patrons and Friends, 354; introduction of subject arrangement, 146

Organizational systems, 141-47

Organizations: aid in developing library collections, 354

Organizing: as element of administration, 116

Orientation of students: library participation in, 56, 428-31

Osborn, Andrew D., and Susan M. Haskins: cited on catalog maintenance, 191, 193; quoted on dictionary catalog, 193

Outdoor reading courts, 505

Out-of-print items: order routine, 168; small quantity buying, 77

Overdue books, 225

Pacific Northwest: library collecting agreements in, 467

Pacific Northwest Bibliographical Center, Seattle, 463

Package libraries, 242; University of Michigan Library, 241 (*chart*)

Pamphlets: collections in university libraries, 411-12

Parker, Ralph H.: cited on income of state university libraries, 82; cited on punched-card systems, 107, 108

Parsons, Henry Spalding: committee member on *American Newspapers*, 536

Payment of bills, 76

Pennsylvania, University of: Furness Memorial Library, 361; library survey, 10; name, 13

Pennsylvania, University of, Library: aid to smaller libraries, 452; building, 488; collection of primitive music and music of ancient civilizations, 408; guide to manuscript collection, 398; history, 588; incunabula collection, 403; musical recordings, 418; music room, 508; pilot study or holdings, 571; rare book room, 506; slide collection, 417; study of early cataloging practices, 590; survey, 559

Pennsylvania State College: ratio of library expenditures to total institutional expenditures, 97

Pensions, see Retirement plans, 324-26

Periodical room, 503

Periodicals: acquisition by university library, 372-74; evaluation, 373; indispensable source materials for research, 373; records of use, 554; selection, 359-60

Periodicals department, 231-32

Periodicals librarian: activities, 231

Periodic tests of staff efficiency, 290

Personnel administration, 253-93; see also Library staff

Petty cash: use in payment of freight charges, 77

Ph.D. degree: in library science, 266; ratio of library expenditures to, 98; University of California, 266

Phelps, Orme W.: quoted on organization of librarians, 335

Philadelphia Bibliographical Center: Union List of Microfilms, 475

Philanthropic foundations: aid in research projects, 6

"Photoclerk," 519, 606

Photograph collections: comparative size in 15 university libraries, 414 (tab.); in university libraries, 414-15

Photographic devices: use in library, 519

Photographic projects, cooperative, 473-75

Photographic Reproduction for Libraries (Fussler), 543

Photographic reproduction of materials: dissertations, 396; interest of university librarians in, 55, 529; see also Microphotographic reproduction

Photography department, 198-204, 513-14; charges for service, 92; equipment, 519-20; personnel, 201; relation to other departments, 201-4; University of California, 198, 199 (chart)

Photostats: product of photographic department, 201

Picture collections, 414-15

Planning as element of administration, 115

Plaques for donors, 174

Playbills and programs: collections in university libraries, 412

Pneumatic tubes: use in library, 519

Pope, Herman G.: cited on staff classification, 258

Pope, Mary F.: cited on attendance by non-proffessional staff at library meetings, 312

Postal card collections, 415

Posters: collections, 412; directing library users, 429

Posting machine: as device for keeping library accounts, 105

Predeek, Albert: cited on education for librarianship in Europe, 268

Preparations departments: principal object, 209; see also Catalog department

Preprints: collections in university libraries, 412-13

Preprofessional training for librarianship, 263

President, university: relation to librarian, 39-40

Princeton Conference on exchanges, 476

Princeton University: name, 13

Princeton University Library: aid to smaller libraries, 452; bibliography room, 511; building, 489, 494; carrels, 500; dispersion of various types of reading space among stack floors, 497; Friends of the Library, 354; funds from endowments, 81; gift policy, 173; guide to manuscript collection, 398; history, 588; hours of service, 305; incunabula collection, 403; librarianship of James T. Gerould, 535; microfilm collection, 416; photograph department, 514; Richardson's librarianship of, 532; study of early cataloging practices, 590; underground stacks, 496

Print collections, 414-15; comparative size in 15 university libraries, 414 (tab.)

Printed materials in unusual form: collections, 409-13

Prints: product of photographic department, 201

Probationary period in personnel administration, 288-89

Process: organization of cataloging by, 183

Production records: for staff members, 289-90

Professional associations: participation of staff members in, 308, 311-12, 332

Professional education: development, 4

Professional school libraries, 149; administration, 46; cataloging, 191; relation to central library, 149-50; relation to librarian, 47-49

Professional staff: academic status, 61; comparative size of, 260 (*tab*.); salaries, 303; selection, 284; training, 277-78; vacations, 318

Promotions, 313-15; training for, 310-11

Providence, R.I.: library collecting agreements in, 467

Providence Public Library: individual storage library, 469

Prussian State Library: courses in librarianship, 268

Public Affairs Information Service Bulletin, 381, 411; Williamson's connection with, 544

Publication of results of research: function of university, 17

Public catalog, *see* Card catalog; Catalog

Publicity for gift materials, 174

Public library: book selection, 349; branch in university library, 65; research information services for industry, 594

Public Library Inquiry, 123

Public-relations office: relations with library, 429

Public toilets, 514

Public universities: relation to government, 31-33

Publisher: direct ordering from, 168; source for pictorial materials, 415

Publishers' Weekly: list of pamphlet material, 411

Punched-card machines, 61, 104, 519; application to library financial administration, 107-8

Purchasing: routines involved in, 60, 74-76, 164-68; *see also* Acquisition department; Order department

Purchasing agents, 359

Putnam, Herbert: professional career, 547-49

Racine Public Library: use of teletype, 456

Radio: as medium for presenting information, 245

Randall, W. M., and F. L. D. Goodrich: *Principles of College Library Administration*, 9

Raney, M. Llewellyn: professional career, 541-43

Rare-book department: relation to photographic department, 201

Rare-book room, 506-8

Rare books: access to, 370; analysis of use, 371; care of, 198, 506-7; collection of, 369-72; housing, 372; influence on students, 370; interlibrary loans, 453; order routine, 168; relation to functions of the university, 371

Rating systems for library staff, 290-92

Readers' advisory service: in university library, 431, 442

Readers' services, 212-14, 600-601; consolidation, 593; separate division, 182; surveys, 565

Reading courses and lists: library extension service, 244

Reading habit: promotion of, 56, 352, 426, 432-38

Reading rooms, 500-508; amount of reading space, 500-501; north light, 490; shelving of books in, 497; total seating capacity, 501

Recataloging, 190-91

Receiving and shipping rooms, 513

Reclassification, 190-91

Recreational reading rooms, *see* Browsing rooms

Reference assistants: training, 277

Reference collection, 218-19, 366-67; duplication of items, 366; for cataloging department, 187-88

Reference librarian: activities, 209-10, 214-15; qualifications, 215; relation to students, 56; subject backgrounds for, 267

Reference service, 209-12, 214-16; administrative organization, 210-12; definition, 209; history of development, 590; informing faculty of, 46; interlibrary lending generally centralized

Reference service (*Continued*)
in, 454; library extension, 245; records of, 554-55; relation to photographic department, 201

Registrar: relation to librarian, 57

Reichmann, Felix: proposal for subject analysis, 598; study of cataloging costs, 192; study of relations of acquisition department to other services, 597

Relaxation periods for staff, 307

Remainders: use by library for foreign exchange, 170

Remuneration, *see* Salaries

Rental fees: collection by library, 74

Rental collection, 228; control by circulation department, 222; function in university library, 64; in university bookstore, 437-38; source of income, 93; stimulation of reading habit by, 434

Repair room, 513

Repair work, *see* Binding-repair work

Reporting: as element of administration, 116

Reprints: collections in university libraries, 412-13; of publications by university personnel, 413

Reproduction of materials, *see* Microcards; Microfilm; Microlex; Microphotographic reproduction; Minicards; Photographic reproduction of materials

Research: book collections for, 367; development, 4; expenditures for, 5; fees for, 594; function of library in supplying resources, 19-21; function of the university, 16-17; relation of reference librarian to, 216, 218; relation to book collections, 365-72; training in, essential to university librarian, 271

Research institutes: relation to librarian, 49-50

Research officer, *see* Assistant to the librarian

Reserve book room, 225-28, 502-3; control by circulation department, 222; hours of service, 305; personnel, 227

Residence hall libraries, *see* House libraries

Responsibility: in library administration, 118

Responsibility, lines of, 132

Retirement plans: distribution of librarians in 66 universities, 325 (*tab.*); *see also* Annuities

Reversion of unexpended funds, 103

Reynolds, Helen M.: cited on university library building, 481

Rhode Island, University of, Library: periodical collection, 372

Rice Institute Library: service for undergraduates, 156

Richardson, Ernest Cushing: bibliographical work, 459; early advocate of interlibrary loans, 450; professional career, 532-34

Rider, Fremont: cited on cost of interlibrary loans, 455; on increase in library collections, 492; inventions, 606

Rochester University: Sibley Music Library, 408

Rochester, University of, Library: bookstacks, 496; classification of archival collections, 402; musical recordings, 408, 418; music collection, 407

Rochester Public Library: organization on basis of subject divisions, 146

Rockefeller, John D., Jr.: grant to national Union Catalog, 460

Rockefeller Foundation: aid in research projects, 6; grant to Bibliothèque nationale to complete catalog, 546; grant to University of Chicago, 542; participation of university librarians in, 529; sponsor of *List of Serial Publications of Foreign Governments*, 536; Williamson's librarianship, 544

Rogers, Rutherford D.: cited on statistics of reference work, 554

Rossiter, Clinton L.: sources for *Seedtime of the Republic*, 217

Rothstein, Samuel: history of reference service, 590

Royal Society Scientific Information Conference (London, 1948), 476

Rush, Charles E.: editor of *Journal of Documentary Reproduction*, 543

Russia: library training in, 269

Rutgers University: name, 14

Rutgers University Library: borrowing privileges for all residents of state, 65; history, 588

Sabbatical leaves, 323

Salaries, 296-304, 321-22; fairness, 119

Salary statistics: difficulty in obtaining, 296

"Scalar principle," *see* Hierarchy

Scholarship: aid of reference librarian to, 216

Scholarships: funds for, 5-6

Science clubs: relation of library to, 431

Science librarianship, 274-76

Scientific and technical books: C. H. Brown's part in developing collections, 547; discounts, 78

Scientific management: an essential basis for proper budgeting, 117-22; in library administration, 122-24, 595

Seattle, Wash.: union catalog, 54

Security-classified publications: acquisition, 379

Seminar libraries, 149-50, 155

Seminar rooms: for graduate students, 505

Seminars: librarian participation in, 56; relation to librarian, 50; use of library resources for, 449

Serials: acquisition by university library, 374-76; binding costs, 600; budgetary charge, 233; centralization of funds for, 99; definition, 232, 374; funds for, 375; lending, 235; procedures for selecting, 375-76; research material, 368

Serial Slants: publication program, 8

Serials department, 232-33, 235; organization and administration, 376; reference service, 233, 235; University of California, 234 (*chart*)

Shakespeare: Van Antwerp copy of first folio, 371

Shaw, Ralph R.: cited on use of Ultrafax, 457; development of the "Photoclerk," 519, 606; quoted on scientific management, 122-23, 595

Shelf list, 182; as classified catalog, 182

Shelving, *see* Bookstacks

Shera, Jesse H.: quoted on subject specialization for departmental librarians, 275; on value of library history, 591

Shera, Jesse H., and Margaret E. Egan: *Bibliographic Organization,* 10; cited on bibliographies, 601

Sherwood, Janice W., and Eleanor E. Campion: report on five major union catalogs and bibliographical centers, 463, 464

Shipping rooms, *see* Receiving and shipping rooms

Shores, Louis: study of Colonial college libraries, 588

Shotwell, James T.: chairman of American Committee on Intellectual Cooperation, 542

Signs directing library users, 429

Slavic language materials: cataloging, 185

Slide collections, 416-17

Smith-Lever Act (1914), 51

Smithsonian Institution, 528; proposed as center for cooperative cataloging, 457-59; proposed as national library, 533

Social Sciences Research Council: aid in research projects, 6; participation of university librarians in, 528

Social security: handled by business office, 61

Societies: aid in developing library collections, 354

Society of American Archivists, 603; concern with archival collections, 401; participation of university librarians in, 528

Sorbonne: École des Chartes, 268

Sorority libraries, *see* House libraries

SORT, *see* American Library Association—Staff Organizations Round Table

Sound recordings, 55

Source materials: courses in, 46

South Africa: dissertations prepared in, 396

South Carolina: libraries of, 589

South Carolina, University of: library survey, 10

Southeast: library collecting agreements in, 467

Southeastern Library Association: microfilm projects, 475

Southern States: university libraries, 589

Spain, Frances L.: cited on library salaries, 321

Spain: dissertations prepared in, 396; library training in, 269

Span of control in library administration, 120

Special collections, 153-54; cataloging, 191; hours of service, 305; rooms for, 508

Special collections department: relation to photographic department, 201

Specialization in collecting, 459-65, 604-5; financial aspects, 594; obstacles, 466; programs, 467-69

Special librarians: training, 274-77

Special Libraries Association: aid in exchange of duplicate materials, 170; microfilm projects, 475; participation of university librarians in, 528; placement service, 285; support of bibliographical projects, 460

Special materials: organization by, 593

Special reading courses: for stimulation of reading habit, 432

Stackmaster, see Superintendent of the stacks

Stacks, see Bookstacks

Staff associations, 335; accomplishments, 338; professional activities, 337; social activity, 337

Staffing as element of administration, 116

Staff manuals, 342; use for student assistants, 281

Staff meetings, 339

Staff publications, 341-42

Staff rooms, 333-34

Stallmann, Esther L.: cited on library internship, 276

Standardization in evaluating university libraries, 570

Stanford University: courses with emphasis on library resources, 449

Stanford University Library: aid to smaller libraries, 452; building, 481; gift policy, 173; inactivity in publishing, 461; musical recordings, 418; need of map collection, 404; special collection, 154; survey, 10, 564, 565; survey of holdings, 571

State documents: acquisition by university library, 380-81; cataloging, 381; suggestions for improved distribution, 380

State governments: relation to libraries of state universities, 28-29

State historical groups: microfilm projects, 475

State laws: effect on university library staff, 328

State libraries: depositories for state publications, 380

State universities: budgetary procedures, 58-59; corporate status, 32; extension work, 18, 51; legislative enactments, 28; purchasing procedures, 60, 74; relation to legislature, 31; travel funds, 312; utilitarian slant, 15

State university libraries: administration, 124; income, 82-83; order forms, 103; relation with press, 170

Stenographic equipment: use in library, 519

Stephen Girard Trust Law: source materials, 368

Stieg, Lewis F.: cited on retirement plans, 324

Storage and supply rooms, 513

Storage libraries, 54-55, 469-70; avoidance of new construction by, 521-22

Storage space: in library building, 495-500

Strout, Donald E.: cited on library salaries, 303-4

Student assistants, 57, 261; rates of pay, 304; selection, 284; sources of university librarians, 263, 281; training, 280-81

Student organizations: relation of library to, 431

Student orientation, see Orientation of students

Students: aid in developing library collections, 355; relation to university librarian, 55-57

Study cubicles, see Carrels

Study habit: development of, 352

Study outlines: library extension service, 244

Subject: organization of cataloging by, 185

Subject arrangement: in university library, 146-47

Subject catalog: criticisms, 180, 192; elimination proposed, 598

Subject cataloging definition, 176; similarity to classifying, 185

Subject division rooms, see Divisional reading rooms

Subject evaluations: as part of a survey, 568

Subject fields: development of fundamental collection, 355; in training for librarianship, 21, 267; materials in related fields, 360; personnel, 210-11; standard treatises for reference use, 366

Subject headings: for clipping files, 411
Subject specialization: effect on university librarianship, 271; for special librarians, 275
Subprofessional assistants: salaries, 304; selection, 284; training, 278-80; *see also* Clerical assistants
Summer hours of library service, 307
Summer months: vacations in, 319
Summer school: library schedule, 319
Sunday hours, 306
Superintendent of the stacks: duties, 228
Supplies: purchase, 60
Supply room, *see* Storage and supply rooms
Survey of Land-Grant Colleges and Universities, 90
Survey of library collection, 54; as basis for selection, 356
Swank, Raynard C.: cited on subject catalog, 180; quoted on accumulation of dead wood, 603; on consideration of library problems, 592; on library program, 485; on relations between librarian and faculty, 552; on subject-divisional plan, 147; on use of gadgets, 606
Sweden: dissertations prepared in, 396; official bibliographies of government documents, 384
Switzerland: dissertations prepared in, 396; library training in, 269; official bibliographies of government documents, 384
Sypher, Wylie: quoted on fees for non-university users, 91

Tauber, Maurice F.: *The Subject Analysis of Library Materials,* 10
Tauber, Maurice F., and Associates: *Technical Services in Libraries,* 10
Tax exemption: private universities, 30, 33
Tax withholding: handled by business office, 61
Teachers College, Columbia University, Library: consultant service, 431
Teaching: activities of reference librarian, 215-16; function of library in supplying resources, 19-21; function of the university, 16; participation of library staff in, 319-20

Teaching and research level for university library, 425-27
Technical operations: costs, 529
Technical reports, 378-79, 409
Technical services: consolidation, 593, 597; surveys, 565; workrooms, 511-12
Technical services division: binding department unit of, 194; development, 165, 182; *see also* Preparations department
Telautographs, 519
Teletype: use in interlibrary cooperation, 456
Teletypewriters, 519
Television: as medium for presenting information, 245
Television, closed circuit: use in interlibrary cooperation, 456, 457
Temporary catalog slip: obviated by prompt cataloging, 168
Texas: library collecting agreements in, 467
Texas, University of: observatories, 4; ratio of library expenditures to faculty, 98
Texas, University of, Library: acquisition of Mexican documents, 385; aid to smaller libraries, 452; departmental libraries, 149; plan for multi-tier expansion, 496; rare book room, 506; use of punched-card systems, 107
Texas A. and M. College: library survey, 10
Theater Library Association: participation of university librarians in, 528
Thompson, L. S.: cited on attendance by nonprofessional staff at library meetings, 312; on seminar libraries, 150, 155; quoted on education for academic librarianship in Europe, 268; on library salaries, 321
Three-position plan of training for promotion, 311
Titles of administrative officers, 126-27
Toledo Public Library: organization on basis of subject divisions, 146
Tourist agencies: source for pictorial materials, 415
Tracing of unlocated items, 224
Trade unions: lack of interest of university librarians in, 335-36
Transfer of personnel, 315-16
Travel bureaus: source for pictorial materials, 415

Travel expenses, 312
Trustee committee on the library, 43
Trustees, university: relation to librarian, 39
Tucker, Harold W.: definition of inservice training, 309
Tulane University Library: cooperation in collecting Latin American documents, 385; Hispanic-American collections, 7
Turnover of staff, 316
TWX teletype system: use in interlibrary cooperation, 456
Type of material: organization of cataloging by, 185
Typewriters, 519

Ulrich, C. F.: *Periodicals Directory*, 359
Ultrafax: use in interlibrary cooperation, 456
Undergraduate library, 592, 600
Undergraduates: service for, 156
UNESCO: aid to document acquisition, 385; directory of world microfilm facilities, 474; efforts toward international library cooperation, 475; promotion of exchange relationships, 170
Union Catalog of the Western Reserve University Library, Cleveland, 463
Union catalogs, 7, 24, 181, 462-65; aid to scholarly use of library, 443-44; maintenance by catalog department, 177; participation of university libraries in development, 54; services, 463-64; sometimes combined with official catalog, 181
Union catalog, national: compared to regional union catalogs, 464
Union catalogs, regional: interest of university librarians in, 529
Union Library Catalogue of the Philadelphia Metropolitan Area, 463
Union List of Microfilms, 416, 461
Union List of Serials in Libraries of the United States and Canada (Gregory), 460, 571; Gerould's contribution to, 535-36
Union lists: cooperative enterprises, 459-62; interest of university librarians in, 529
Union lists of serials, 7; checking, 375
USSR, *see* Russia
Union Theological Seminary: name, 14

Unit-cost estimates: in library budget, 96
Unit-cost records, 555
Unit plan of construction, 488
United Nations: activities of university librarians in, 528; publications of, 385-86
United Nations Documents Index, 385
United Nations Educational, Scientific, and Cultural Organization, *see* UNESCO
U.S. Bureau of the Census: distribution of publications, 378; information relating to municipalities, 382
U.S. Department of Agriculture: activities of university librarians in, 528
U.S. Department of State: efforts toward international library cooperation, 475
U.S. Government Research Reports, 379
U.S. Office of Education, 460; increased ease in gathering financial statistics, 101; participation of university librarians in, 528; report on scholarships and fellowships, 5; statistical compilations, 11
U.S. Office of Technical Services, 379
U.S. Public Health Service: aid in research projects, 6; distribution of publications, 378
U.S. Superintendent of Documents: activities of university librarians, 528; classification system, 379; purchase of documents from, 378
United States Book Exchange, 170
Universities, private: freedom from state control, 29-31
Universities with civil service: selection of personnel, 286
Universities with library schools: selection of staff members for library, 283-84
Universities without library schools: selecting staff members for library, 284-85
University: cooperation with other universities, 449; development in U.S., 3-6; functions, 13-18; integration of library with policies, 22-23; librarian's knowledge of program changes, 95-96; library policy, 574; library resources, 35; relationship to state, 29-31; role in research, 5
University, state, *see* state universities

University administration: initiation of library survey by, 562; knowledge of library as result of survey, 574; *see also* Administrative board, university

University committees: for supervision of research and instructional work, 47

University council: functions, 42

University courses: curricular collections, 367; library support for, 357; reduced fees for library staff, 313

University extension, 17-18; function of library in supplying resources, 19-21; relation to librarian, 50-51

University libraries, southern statistics (1940–41), 88 (*tab.*); statistics (1952–53), 89 (*tab.*)

University library: accounting responsibility for book orders, 104; administration, 8, 114-60, 297-98, 564-65, 591-93; archival collections, 402; bibliographic work, 460; bindery, 195-96; book and periodical budgets, 77; book selection, 349-52; business functions, 72-73; changing character, 11; checking holdings against bibliographies, 571; committees, 339-41; comparative size of staff, 260 (*tab.*); cooperation with other libraries, 449-76; descriptions of holdings, 529; division into functional departments, 161-204; educational objectives, 564; essentials of program, 19-27; evaluation in relation to standards, 570-71; evaluation of use, 566; fees for non-university users, 91; finance, 24, 564, 593-95; functional organization, 441-42; gift policies, 173; governmental relationships, 563-64; growth, 347 (*tab.*), 492; growth in size of staff, 259 (*tab.*); growth in U.S., 6-7; history, 588-91; housing of union catalog and bibliographical center by, 464; improvement of book collections, 529; increasing effective use, 441-45; integration with administrative and educational policies of university, 22; integration with community, state, regional, national, and international library resources, 23; internal governmental policy, 34-37; lack of clarity in government, 34; legal bases of government, 33-34; legal bases of organization and administration, 29-33; legal relation to state or city, 32; loans to smaller libraries, 452; methods used in surveying financial support, 575 (*tab.*); methods used in surveying resources, 576-79 (*tab.*); organization 143 (*chart*), 145 (*chart*), 564-65, 591-93; organization by services, 593; organization on basis of form, 493; problems in development, 586-610; records, 553-56; reports, 556-57; service to alumni, 245-46; services to other libraries, 246; size, 346; sources of income, 80-93; staff bulletins, 429; statistics (1940–41), 84-85 (*tab.*), (1953–54), 86-87 (*tab.*); teaching function, 425-45;

University library building, 481-514, 605-6; accommodations for administrative purposes, 509-14; accommodations for materials, 495-509; adaptability, 493-94; architectural effect vs. functional requirements, 486; essential facilities, 495; factors affecting character of, 482-84; inadequacies of old structures, 484-85; participants in planning program, 487-89; physical orientation, 490; planning, 141, 485-89; planning for expansion, 489, 490, 491-93; rearranging, altering, and enlarging, 520-21; site, 489-91; surroundings, 490; surveys, 566-67

University library expenditures: ratio to total institutional expenditures, 96-99

University library surveys, 8, 558-80; comparative statistics, 568-69; documentary materials, 568; history and background of library, 563; methodology, 567-68; problem areas, 563-72; purposes, 558-59; results, 572, 574, 580; self-surveys, 560-61; surveys by outsiders, 561-63; types, 560

University Microfilms, 395; *Dissertation Abstracts,* 473

University placement office: used to obtain library staff members, 285

University press: bookstore as outlet for, 436; functions, 17; publications for exchange purposes, 169-70; relations with librarian, 62-64; relations with library, 169-70; role in publishing results of research, 5, 7

University publications: copy given to library, 63; for exchange purposes, 169

Vacations of library staff, 318-19
Van Hoesen, Henry Bartlett: co-author of *Bibliography*, 535
Van Horne, Bernard: quoted on personnel administration, 253
Van Patten, Nathan: committee member on *Union List of Serials*, 536
Vatican Library: Bishop's service to, 539; catalog, 461
Vatican School: program to provide personnel for scholarly libraries, 269
Vermont, University of, Library: hours of student assistance, 261
Vermont State Library: Union catalog, 463
Vertical File Service Catalog: list of pamphlet material, 411
Virginia: library collecting agreements in, 467
Virginia, University of, Library: collection of archives, 7; criteria for collecting archives, 401; extension rooms, 508; history, 589; incunabula collection, 403; motion picture films, 417; newspaper acquisition, 388; rare book room, 506; vacuum fumigator, 519
Virginia Polytechnic Institute: library survey, 10
Virginia State Library: American history sources in, 217; newspaper acquisition, 388
Visiting librarians and scholars: use of university library, 66
Vocational counseling: provision of materials by library, 431
Voigt, Melvin J.: study of ratio of professional to nonprofessional staff, 261
Vosper, Robert: quoted on size of collections, 602

Walter, Frank Keller: co-author of *Bibliography*, 535; professional career, 534-35
Washington University (St. Louis) Library: motion picture films, 417; musical recordings, 418
Weber, Dorothy: quoted on clerical assistants, 280
Western Reserve University, Libraries of: history, 589
Wheeler, Joseph L., and A. M. Githens: cited on cost of remodeling, 520-21
White, Carl M.: study of interlibrary loan services, 451

Whitmarsh, Agnes: cited on handling of maps, 406
Who's Who in Library Service, 546
William and Mary, College of, Library: American history sources in, 217; history, 588
Williams, Edwin E. (ed.): *Problems and Prospects of the Research Library*, 10
Williamson, Charles C.: professional career, 543-56; study of library schools, 545
Wilson, Louis R., and Marion A. Milczewski: cited on land-grant college library expenditure, 99
Wilson, Louis R., and others: *The Library in College Instruction*, 10, 601
Wilson, Louis R., and Raynard C. Swank: quoted on map policy, 404, on Stanford University library building, 481
Wilson, W. J.: co-editor of *Census of Medieval and Renaissance Manuscripts*, 536
Winchell, Constance M.: cited on union lists, 461; information on bibliographical listing of foreign dissertations, 396; quoted on use of newspapers, 387
Winsor, Justin: contributions to scholarship, 272; professional career, 530-31
Wisconsin: cooperation of state library agencies, 51; library collecting agreements in, 468
Wisconsin, University of, Library: hours of student assistance, 261; inactivity in publishing, 461; microfilm collection, 416; photographic installations, 198; state control over, 33
Wisconsin Historical Society: microfilm collection, 416
Wood pulp stock: deterioration, 599
Woods, Bill M.: cited on map collections, 237
Working conditions for library staff, 333-34
Works, George A.: *College and University Library Problems*, 9, 569
World catalog: proposed, 533
World War II: participation of university personnel in, 18
Wriston, Henry M.: attitude toward library personnel, 270

Writing clubs: relation of library to, 431

Wyer, James I.: cited on duties of reference librarian, 214

Yale University Library: aid to smaller libraries, 452; American history sources in, 217; Associates of the Library, 354; bookstacks, 496; conceptions of library service, 588; funds from endowments, 81; history, 588, 590; improvement of cataloging procedures, 560; incunabula collection, 403; Keogh's librarianship, 537; map collection, 237; musical recordings, 418; rare book room, 198, 506; size, 6; study of early cataloging practices, 590

Young, Karl: committee chairman on *Census of Medieval and Renaissance Manuscripts*, 536